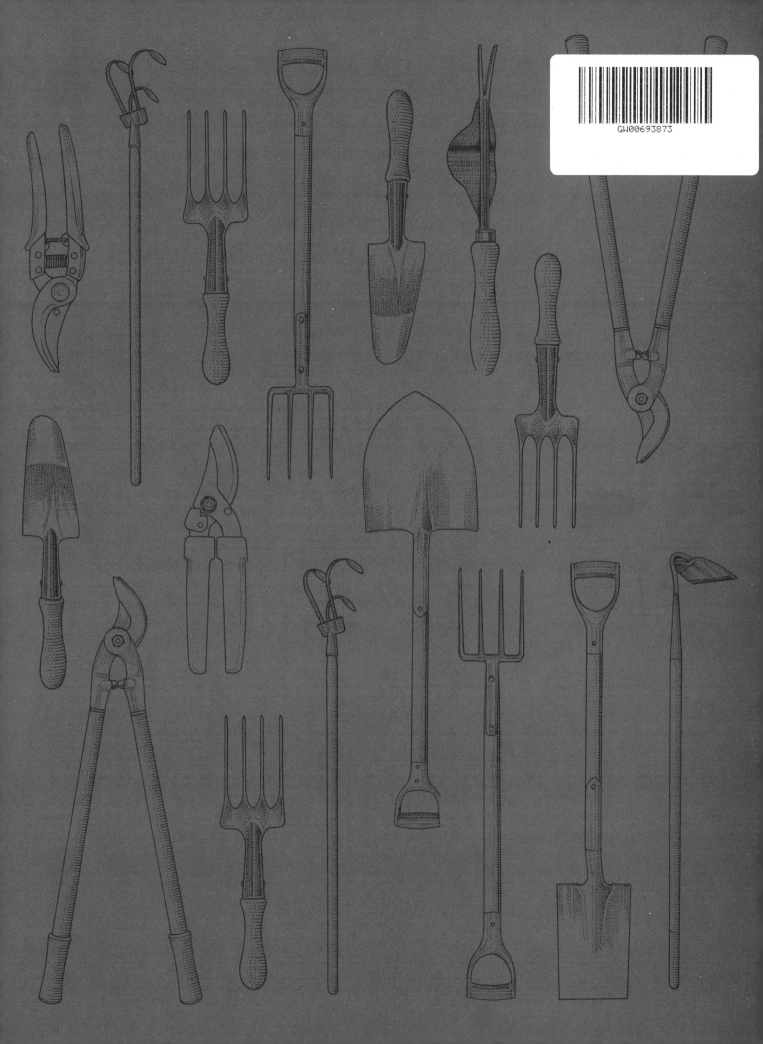

Secrets & Tips
from
Yesterday's Gardeners

Secrets & Tips from Yesterday's Gardeners

A practical guide for
Australian and New Zealand gardens

READER'S DIGEST

Secrets and tips from yesterday's gardeners

Being outdoors on a summer's evening, breathing in the heady aromas of the garden, watering our thriving plants and taking a quiet satisfaction in what we have conjured up from the earth: these are timeless moments, when the world stands still; moments when it is possible to imagine what it must have been like in our great-grandfather's garden, far removed from the noise and pollution, and the hustle-bustle of modern life; when it was easier to feel in tune with nature.

This is why more and more of today's gardeners are returning to the traditional practices of those simpler times, seeking alternatives to harsh chemicals and intrusive modern methods. In this book, we have gathered a vast store of old-fashioned gardening knowledge; down-to-earth tips learned through trial and error; secrets that have been passed down by word of mouth; wisdom born of a lifetime's patient observation. But because past generations were, above all, practical and forward-looking, we have not forgotten the latest scientific advances. We have therefore brought together the best of yesterday and today. Dip into any page and you're sure to discover many useful nuggets of information. Some are grounded in science, others in common sense, some may surprise you – but they all work.

In **Planning a traditional garden**, find out how romantic cottage-style planting works with nature to discourage pests or how you can create a haven for wildlife.

In **Flowerbeds and borders**, learn the secrets of using flower shapes and colours for the most pleasing effects then, at the end of the growing season, gather free seeds for next year's flowers. And see how something as simple as old newspaper can help to germinate and protect your seedlings. **Ornamental trees and shrubs** reintroduces you to some of the best of the old-fashioned roses, and rekindles our long-standing affection for climbers of all sorts as they scramble over fences and trellises. Be inspired to plant trees for future generations, and learn some of the tried-and-tested techniques that will help them to live a long and healthy life.

When it comes to growing fruit and vegetables, the experience of traditional gardeners really comes into its own. **The vegetable garden** and **Fruit from the garden** will tempt you to try the old-fashioned varieties whose superior flavours our grandparents would have savoured, plus some disease-resistant newcomers as well. If you've never grown your own peaches or figs, pumpkins or herbs, you'll find plenty within these pages that will inspire you to indulge in this very satisfying pastime.

Above all, yesterday's gardeners took pride in the sound cultural practices that freed them from reliance on toxic chemicals. **Garden basics** contains hundreds of practical tips, from combination planting and attracting birds and beneficial insects, to ensuring that plants are strong enough to ward off pests and diseases naturally. They make such good sense, you'll wonder how we ever lost sight of this timeless wisdom.

Finally, to help you appreciate the rhythm of the seasons and take advantage of every precious moment in your garden, there is **A gardener's calendar**, highlighting all those productive and enjoyable day-to-day tasks that send you to bed at night tired, but refreshed by your labours and satisfied by nature's bountiful harvest.

Contents

Planning a traditional garden

Designing your ideal garden

Although once only grand houses had gardens that were formally designed, yesterday's gardeners knew the value of maximising every centimetre of their space. To do the same today, familiarise yourself with your existing garden, then make a meticulous plan.

Making a plan

GETTING STARTED Before you begin, check with your local council to see whether your garden is covered by any planning regulations. Mature trees may be protected and, if your house happens to be a heritage listed building or there is one nearby, you may encounter council restrictions on layout and height in the garden. If you need to apply for permission to make changes, then it's a good idea to get started early.

WHAT IS YOUR GARDEN WISH LIST? Think about what you want your garden to do. It should reflect your lifestyle, the people who will be enjoying it and the time you plan to spend in it, whether it is relaxing, playing, swimming in the pool or tending the plants.
● If you have small children in the family and enjoy kicking a ball around with them, go for a lawn and edge it with borders of robust evergreen shrubs and grasses rather than delicate flowers.
● If you want to relax and entertain in your garden, lay a patio surrounded by fragrant low-maintenance borders.

TOP TIPS FOR GARDEN PLANNING It is best to plan your project on paper first. You can always refine your ideas by developing several versions, but date them so you know which one is current.
● **MAP OUT THE EXISTING GARDEN** Make sure you include everything. A plan made to a scale of 1 cm : 1 m (1:100) is the minimum. If you can, particularly if your garden is small, use a scale of 2 cm : 1 m (2:100).

● **IDENTIFY YOUR BOUNDARIES** Mark where there are fences, walls or hedging. Make a note of the hedging style (deciduous or evergreen, clipped or natural) and show the spread of the foliage.
● **MARK OUT THE HOUSE** Include all major structures and any areas of hard landscaping. Then draw in details such as paths, sheds, compost bins, pergolas and water features.
● **NOTE THE EXISTING BORDERS** Draw in flowerbeds, herb or vegetable gardens and other large areas of planting.
● **MARK THE ORIENTATION** Note down north and mark areas where shade is cast.
● **REMEMBER SERVICES** Detect and note in red all electricity and telephone cables, and gas and water pipes that already cross your land, as well as those you plan to put in. Keeping a record will save you from stumbling across them at a later date.

Have fun designing your garden with shapes cut to scale. Design kits are available, or you can make one up yourself.

Mark everything on your garden plan and use string lines to pinpoint features for an accurate result.

USING A PROFESSIONAL If you hire a professional to design your garden, insist on a written contract and ask for several references – and be sure to follow them up.
● Never let yourself be saddled with an idea you feel may be unsuitable. Choose a qualified professional who is willing to spend time in discussion with you at the planning stage and who will take into account your wishes and your needs. But remember, they are the expert, and listen to their good advice.

GET YOUR OWN QUALIFICATIONS You could also enrol in a garden design course to learn all the tips and tricks of the professionals yourself. Also, visiting local colleges, nurseries and gardens can help provide inspiration and show you how the elements of a garden work together.

A FULL-SIZED PLAN The best way to test your plan's suitability for the space you have available is actually to mark it out on the ground and live with it for a while.
● The simplest method is to use a hose, length of rope or fluorescent spray paint to mark out the shape of the flowerbeds, lawns, play spaces and other large areas. Use stakes and twine to represent the exact shape and height of the hedges.
● Outline the paths with stakes and heavy string that is clearly visible – coloured clothes line is ideal.
● To visualise a vegetable patch, lay down planks and use a rake to draw in the plant rows. Remember, you will need to be able to pull up a vegetable in the middle of the patch without having to tread on the bed.

MAKE A NOTE OF WHICH DIRECTION YOUR GARDEN FACES This way you will see what you can plant and where: some plants love full sun, others prefer semishade and still others like morning sun. Don't forget to take into account the shadows thrown by hedges and large trees when planting, as they can be just as solid as the shadows cast by buildings.

PLAN YOUR LIGHTING IN ADVANCE Start thinking about where to position any artificial lighting at the outset.
● A light at each entrance, and several positioned along pathways and on the patio, will aid visibility – and add life – at night

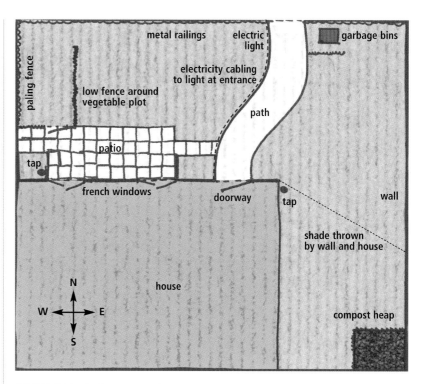

DRAW A PLAN OF THE EXISTING GARDEN STRUCTURE

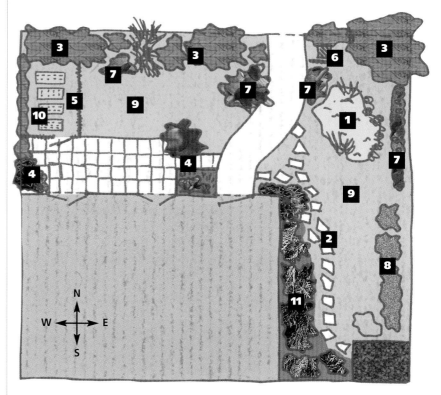

MARK IN PLANNED PLANTING AREAS AND NEW FEATURES
Draw in new features, such as the pond **1**, walkway **2**, front hedge **3** and the plants to surround the patio **4**. Mark out the boundaries of the vegetable garden **5** and the screen for the garbage area **6**, then the flowerbeds **7**. In autumn, plant fruiting shrubs such as blueberries and raspberries **8**, sow the lawn **9** and prepare the soil of the vegetable garden **10**. Note the areas of the garden that are in shade **11** and only use plants here that can tolerate this position.

Lights add direction, ensure safe access and highlight features. Plan them as you plan the garden.

and in the winter. It's a good idea to illuminate any steps, raised areas and all the doorways leading into the house.
● Plan to have a number of lighted areas, not just one. It is more effective to have several low-voltage small lights rather than a single floodlight: the lights will not dazzle and, at night, your garden will feel lively and warm. A bulb brighter than 100 watts will accentuate the 'black hole' of unlit space behind and may also annoy your neighbours.

MEASURE A SLOPE Use stakes and a spirit level to calculate your garden's change in height. This is useful when planning a terrace or steps. The incline of a slope is expressed as a percentage or a ratio. A slope with a gradient of 8 per cent increases by 8 cm for every 1 m in length, or by 8 m for every 100 m.

WHAT ABOUT THE VIEW? Don't forget to look beyond your garden to its immediate surroundings. There may be something you would like to hide from view or maybe you want to maximise a great outlook.

WORK OUT THE SIZE OF A TERRACE OR PATIO Calculate the size you think you need – and then add an extra 1.5 m to each side. Size is difficult to judge exactly, so be as generous as you can when planning.

PLANNING FOR A WATER FEATURE
Think carefully about the kind of water feature that is fitting for your style of garden.
● You may consider a raised or sunken pond, a waterfall or a self-contained fountain. The site itself will affect your choice: a running stream or waterfall is natural on a sloping site, whereas a pond needs a level area where the ground is easy

to excavate. If you have rock close to the surface or a high water table, then a sunken pond is not going to be practical.
● Remember to include electrical provision for a pump or lighting, if needed.
● Water deeper than 30 cm may require fencing under local council requirements.

SWIMMING POOLS If in the future you might like to put in a swimming pool, you will obviously need to leave appropriate space and consider your planting – don't plant deciduous trees that will drop their leaves into the swimming pool.

ALL MOD CONS If you want to keep a back gate locked, a bell might be useful, and a remote control system to open and close your gates can be practical and good for security. If you want either of these in your garden, plan and install them early on.
● Install sturdy, covered power points where you will most often use electrical equipment.
● Make sure you have several outside taps throughout the garden.

Make the most of your space

CREATE A WINDOW ON THE WORLD
A garden without a view can quickly become boring. If yours is enclosed by high walls, think about creating openings in them to give views onto the world outside. Inside the garden, establish some areas with low-growing plants to create a more open aspect.
● Openings also give an impression of space in a limited area. If your view is blocked, or is not a good one, consider painting a trompe l'oeil of an open gate, or of a window looking out onto a landscape.

BLURRING BOUNDARIES Make your garden look bigger by planting shrubs at the end. They will disguise the length of a short plot by obscuring the boundary and merging into the plants of the neighbouring garden.
● Other 'defects' can also be remedied. If you have a difficult corner, disguise it by planting a large, bushy evergreen there. Make a feature of a narrow spot by using foliage on both sides to create a leafy entry that opens out onto another part of the garden.

Changes of level add interest and make the garden usable.

Use an opening in a wall, fence or hedge to draw attention to an eye-catching view.

CHANGE THE PERSPECTIVE
To prevent a thin garden looking like a corridor, avoid features which focus the eye on the far end.

● Don't run a straight path down the length of the garden. Instead, use stepping stones in a curved line, or place a lattice at right angles to the side boundaries and add a fountain and decorative foliage plants.

● Interrupt a long straight view and create interest by using hedges, mixed beds with contrasting heights, small trees or a gazebo surrounded by shrubs.

● Try creating various levels, each higher than the last, or running a winding pathway from one side of the garden to the other, and softening parallel walls with climbing plants.

CONSIDER PLANTING A ROW OF TREES
In a large garden, an avenue of trees is a good way to line a path, highlight a view or direct the eye towards a specific point such as the house, a bench or a statue. You could plant a single row that runs along one or both sides of a path or, if you have an ample amount of space, a double row with the trees staggered.

● A line of trees is most effective if it is made with a single species. Before choosing which one, find out its height and spread when it is fully grown to avoid overcrowding, and having to prune too often. Named varieties are the best choices as they will be uniform in height and spread.

USE LEVELS TO CREATE SPACE
In a very small garden, different levels not only add some interest, they give you more space for planting. Don't let a lawn take up the centre of your garden – instead, create terraced levels, steps where you can cluster some pots, and rockeries against walls. Use containers of all kinds to increase your planting area.

PRACTICAL REMINDERS FOR SLOPING GARDENS
On sloping ground, plan to have winding paths and steps, which are both convenient and interesting. They will make your maintenance work easier and your garden will look more varied.

● Have hoses long enough to reach all parts of the garden or install extra taps to avoid having to carry water up or down a slope.

● If your house is at the top of a slope, don't isolate it further by surrounding it with a bare lawn. Plant shrubs and perennials on at least two sides to unite house and garden and to soften the harshness of the position.

HIDE AN AREA FROM VIEW
A concealed space provides parking or hides your bins without spoiling the beauty of your garden. Plant a hedge or erect a fence then smother it with climbing plants to screen any eyesores.

ENLARGE YOUR GARDEN WITH WATER
However small, a water feature makes a garden look larger by reflecting its surrounds. If you have a small garden, site the water feature in the foreground, make it long rather than wide, and angle it in the direction of the garden's length.

CREATING AN ILLUSION OF DEPTH
Install a mirror on a wall at the end of the garden, and frame it with dense foliage to mask its edges. Choose a shady spot so that the mirror doesn't reflect blinding sun.

● Stand a mirror on the bank of a pond, and the water will seem wider and deeper.

● Another way to create a feeling of depth is to make the pool narrower as it recedes from view. This makes it appear longer.

PATHS WITH PERSONALITY
A garden path is an important design feature in most gardens. Avoid a straight one if you can – a curved or zigzagged path creates interest and changes the shape of your garden. Avoid hard edges – instead, soften them with low-growing shrubs of varying shapes. Also avoid having the garden gate too close to the house – you may have to walk further but the effect will be much more attractive.

An overgrown garden with many types of plants makes a wildlife-friendly garden.

Creating a garden step by step

The balance between hard landscaping and planting has changed with fashion over the years, as have garden styles and materials. But it is always important to establish the basic structure of your garden before you start putting in any plants.

Starting points

WHAT COMES FIRST? Start with the paths and any structures, then the areas around the house, as all the other parts of the garden will revolve around these. Feel free to develop your initial plans as you go along.

COMMIT YOURSELF ONLY TO ESSENTIAL EXPENSES Initially, the essential jobs are levelling or shaping the site, adding drainage systems, digging compost into poor soil and making trench networks to carry drains and utilities. Plan these thoroughly, rather than launching straight into large projects that may turn out to be unsuitable. For example, it would be a big mistake to start building an elaborate pergola only to find that it obscures a large part of the garden, or casts shade over the area where you were planning to put in a pond.

PROTECT YOUR TREES Before doing any major jobs, protect the trees you intend to keep. Stand a wigwam of 1.5 m long planks around the tree trunk and tie them in place. Where less protection is needed, use canvas or plastic covers, or tie coloured tags to stems.

GET AN OVERVIEW First, remove any weeds from your site. Leave as many trees and shrubs as you can at this stage, unless they are dangerous or in the way. They may just need pruning rather than removing.
● Don't throw away stones, even small ones. You'll be glad of them later as a base for laying paths, for improving soil drainage or creating a rockery or terracing.

A traditional brick path overgrown with plants adds to the atmosphere of an old-fashioned cottage garden. The foliage spills over the path, softening the edges.

● Hold on to any topsoil if the site has to be stripped so you can put it back once the construction work is finished.

DO THE DIGGING JOBS FIRST Specific safety rules govern the required depth of trenches for pipes and cabling. To ensure all guidelines are adhered to, it's a good idea to use a professional. Get them in to dig the trench networks before you do any planting or lawn laying. Keep trenches well away from any planned or existing trees, or the pipes and cables may be damaged by roots.

COLD WEATHER WORK Autumn and winter are the best times of the year for large jobs. Professional landscaping firms are more available at this time of year, and the garden is clearer during this dormant period.

WATCH OUT

DON'T COVER UP MANHOLES
Make a note of all the manhole covers or inspection pits on your garden plan and keep the plan safe. Even if you don't know what's below them, they are there for a reason, and you may need to use them at some time in the future. You can conceal the covers by surrounding them with groundcover plants, shallow-rooting shrubs or screening walls, or use special manhole covers into which you can set paving. Or, sit an attractively planted container on top of the manhole cover.

- After major landscaping, let the soil settle for a week or two before continuing with any planned construction projects.
- Once all your structures are in place, dig in lots of manure to enrich your soil, adding gypsum to heavy clay.

PREVENT SLIPPING
Choose nonslip paving surfaces wherever possible – textured surfaces grip best. Smooth paving becomes slippery when wet so only use it for covered areas.
- Moss and lichen can help to make your paths look weathered, but if you want to remove them, try a high-pressure hose and a scrubbing brush before using chemicals.
- If you have to use chemicals, check that they are suitable for your stonework before purchase. Some treatments for moss, for example, will permanently stain a patio.

BRICK PATHS FOR OLD-WORLD CHARM
You can easily lay a simple garden path made from old weathered bricks.
- Level the ground, dig a narrow path to the depth of the bricks plus 15 cm, smooth in a 15 cm layer of coarse sand, then set in your bricks. Finally, brush in more sand to fill the joints. Experiment with classic patterns, such as blocks or diamonds, to suit your house.

SAFER SLOPES
On gentle slopes, why not try creating a 'donkey path' – shallow steps built with wooden logs. Drive wooden posts or steel reinforcement bars into the ground in front of each end of your logs to stop them rolling down the slope. Don't worry about banking up the soil or sand behind the logs; this will happen naturally over time.

RETAINING EARTH ON A STEEP SLOPE
For slopes with a gradient of over 8 per cent, build a series of low retaining walls using stones from the garden to create terraces that follow the contour of the slope. The steeper the slope, the higher the walls should be. Walls over 1 m usually need to be designed and approved by an engineer.
- Make sure that adequate drainage holes (known as weep holes) are included at the base of solid walls to allow for drainage and seepage. Water trapped behind walls can lead to the walls collapsing after rain.

STEPS THAT ARE EASY TO CLIMB
Always build steps starting from the bottom and working up. Spend time working out the height and width of your steps. Risers (the step up) should be a minimum of 10 cm and a maximum of 18 cm high and, as a general rule, the width of the tread (the step from front to back) plus double the height of the riser should total 65 cm. Therefore, to get a comfortable width for the tread of your steps, decide on the height of your riser, double it and then deduct this measurement from 65 cm. Make all steps in a flight the same width and height.

THE WIDTH OF PATHS
Make sure your garden paths are wide enough for everyday use. On main paths, a minimum width of 1.5 m (but preferably 1.7–2 m) will allow two people to walk comfortably side by side.
- Elsewhere, make sure that your paths are wide enough for a wheelbarrow, and construct turning circles at convenient points along the path so that you neither have to tread on your borders as you turn the barrow around, nor pull it backwards – which is bad for your back.

Look for nonslip pavers for steps, for safer access.

A path of log risers and gravel infill is low key and low cost.

LAYING AN INFORMAL PATH

A practical and relatively inexpensive way of providing a walkway, individual stepping stones also have an enduring cottage charm. To lay the path you will need a solid rubber mallet, a spade, a trowel and some sand to stop the stones sinking. You may also need help to lift stones or pavers.

1 Position the stones on the grass, cut around the edges of each one and carefully remove the turf.

2 Dig down 3–5 cm deeper than the thickness of the stones. Spread a 5–8 cm layer of sand in each hole and then level.

3 Replace each stone carefully in its hole.

4 Using the mallet, drive the stones into the sand, wedging them in so they are flush with the ground.

5 Fill in any gaps around the edges of the stones with a mixture of sand and soil, then pat down.

6 Sow grass seed or plant runners in any bare areas in the lawn. Water with a fine rose until the new grass is established.

Access paths around planted areas and between hedges and beds only need to be 50 cm wide. In the vegetable garden, just 20–30 cm between beds should be sufficient.

LAYING PATHS Any path that is likely to see heavy wear needs a good sub-base or foundation. Excavate the ground to firm subsoil, or until deep enough to take 10 cm of hardcore (such as crushed granite) and 5 cm of sand as well as the surface material. Tamp down soil and hardcore with a plate compactor, or use a roller, then rake the sand level before adding paving or gravel.

On paths that are used less frequently, a layer of sand should be enough to bed in paving stones. Dig to a depth equal to the depth of the paving stones, plus 5 cm, pour in the sand and lay the paving stones on top, making sure they are level. Fill in the gaps by brushing fine sand over the path.

To reduce the amount of weeding needed on bark or gravel paths, lay a semipermeable membrane under the hardcore.

EXPERIMENT WITH COLOURS The options afforded by colourful modern materials are endless and can be used to create mood or drama in the garden. Blue pergolas smothered with pastel flowers and grey foliage conjure up the sun-faded look of yesterday's gardens. Untreated wooden fences stained black contrast dramatically on a sunny day with evergreen plants and bright flowers. Subtly used, red or yellow bricks can create striking patterns in paths.

TREATED TIMBERS Much of our outdoor construction is carried out with treated pine (also called CCA treated timber). This timber comes in various grades depending on its use. For example, H4 is suitable for in-ground use and should be used anywhere the timber comes into contact with the soil. It is treated with wood preservatives including chromium, copper and arsenic, making it unlikely to rot and resistant to termite attack. Recently, concerns have been raised over the safety of these treated timbers, especially where used for the construction of play equipment and outdoor furniture, and to edge garden beds. This has led some gardeners to seek alternatives. In the days before treated timber was available, fences and garden beds were constructed using hardwoods or woods treated with sump oil

or creosote. Where timber will come in contact with the soil it needs to be protected against wood rots and termite attack.

One simple precaution against rots and termites is to attach upright posts for pergolas or climbing frames to metal stirrups, or sleeves, which are anchored in the ground. These metal stirrups raise the timber above contact with the ground. In some areas, it is necessary to use metal stirrups to meet with council requirements.

Whether using treated or untreated timber, remember to paint freshly cut surfaces with a wood preservative as protection against weather, fungal rots and insect attack.

Don't burn offcuts or inhale sawdust from CCA treated timber as it is dangerous.

ORDER IN NEW TOPSOIL If the earth in your garden has been 'stripped' by building work you will need enough topsoil or organic garden mix to provide a 30 cm deep layer for a lawn, 40 cm for perennial plants and 60 cm for shrubs and hedges. For trees that are planted individually, you will need 1–4 cubic metres of soil. Your builder or

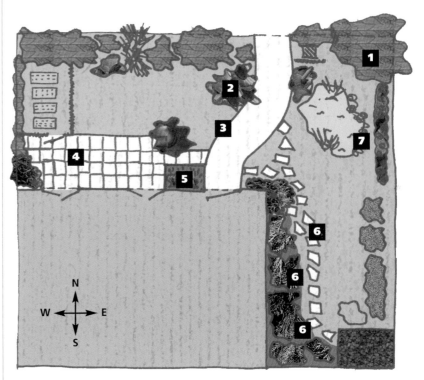

THE BEST SPOTS FOR LIGHTING

When installing lighting in your garden, think about aesthetics as well as practicalities. Here are some suggestions for good lighting. Under a feature shrub **1**. Between perennials and shrubs, to light up the display **2**. Level with the ground along the edge of a path **3**. Near the entrance to the vegetable garden **4**. In a patio corner **5**. Small lights to create atmosphere **6**. To highlight the pond **7**.

landscape supplier will help you to work out the quantities that you will require.

● Any soil that has been moved or added will subside by approximately 20 per cent once it has settled and been watered. So take this into account and order extra, especially if you are intending to create raised beds.

Now you're ready to plant

CHOOSE PLANTS THAT WILL FLOURISH
The secret of success is to match plants with the type of soil and different conditions – sun, shade, moist or dry ground – in your garden. Take a close look at other gardens nearby to see which plants are doing well before drawing up your own planting list.

TRY A 'DRY RUN' AT PLANTING
Once you have most of your plants and are ready for planting, check to see how they will look in position. Lay out the plants in their pots in the places where you intend to plant them, using tall stakes to simulate trees. Leave a space around the plants to represent the spread they will eventually achieve. Think about any shade they might cast, whether they will block any views and whether you're happy with the overall effect.

START PLANTING IN EARLY SPRING
By this time, any organic matter you added over the autumn and winter to improve the soil should be broken down. Give priority to the plants that will form the basic framework of your garden, such as large trees, hedges and border plants, and groundcover plants for rockeries and embankments.

SAVE YOURSELF TIME
Bygone gardeners had time to lavish on their gardens, but there are many low-maintenance grasses and shrubs that are just as appealing as herbaceous perennials and annuals. Plant your favourites near the house, so you can enjoy them and look after them whenever they need it.

ESTABLISH 'THE LOOK' QUICKLY
Plant fast-growing perennials, such as achillea, aster, daylily, geranium, larkspur, red valerian (*Centranthus ruber*), scabiosa and any of the salvias. Consider putting in some of the most

For an environmentally friendly garden, it's best to use hardwoods or timbers treated with a non-toxic product for the construction of pergolas, lattices and garden beds.

prolific old-fashioned groundcover plants, such as dead nettle, lamb's ear or snow-in-summer, which will speedily stop the ground looking bare.

● From the first year, sow fast-growing annuals such as cosmos, mirabilis, nasturtium and poppies to fill in gaps between young shrubs and perennials.

FOR HEDGES, CONSIDER COSTS AND PRIORITIES
For a trimmed and shaped hedge, choose very young plants, which you can buy cheaply and then shape as they grow. But if you want instant privacy, you need to buy plants that are 1.5–2 m high, although this is an expensive option.

● A cheaper alternative is to use smaller plants and temporarily screen the areas that you most want to conceal with a fence or a natural-looking bamboo or woven screen.

● Another interim solution is to plant a temporary hedge of quick-growing, tall annual plants, such as sunflowers, alongside your small, slower-growing hedge plants. They will create a short-term but decorative effect while you wait for the hedge to grow.

● Fast-growing shrubs such as abelia or dwarf bottlebrush make excellent hedges.

INSTALL THE LAWN LAST
Make laying or sowing a lawn the last job you do so you don't ruin the new surface by walking and barrowing over it as you develop other areas.

EDGING A BORDER WITH BOX
Box makes an attractive traditional edging plant for formal garden beds.

● First prepare the bed by digging the border well.

● Stretch a piece of string 15–20 cm from the edge and follow this line when you are planting.

● Position the individual plants 5–10 cm apart then give each plant a thorough soaking at the base to wet the roots.

● Box is a slow grower. To help your plants fill out and form a continuous hedge, clip lightly in mid-spring and late summer.

Flowers and colour all year round

A visually successful garden provides year-round colour and interest. To achieve this, plan a blend of evergreen and deciduous trees, flowering shrubs and climbers, bulbs, perennials and annuals.

Interest through the winter months

GETTING A GOOD BALANCE Winter is when you reap the rewards of your good planning. In climates with mild winters, cooler months can be a time for flower colour and fragrance. Even in cold areas, when growth is dormant, there are plants that bloom and fill the winter air with scent. For winter climate control, select evergreen plants for protection from cold winds but use deciduous plants around the house to let the wonderful winter sunshine stream in.

BEAUTIFUL CATKINS The award for the longest catkin goes to *Garrya elliptica* (right). Its slender silver catkins drape branches in mid to late winter and can reach 30 cm long.
● *Garrya* thrives in a cool to mild climate and can be trained against a wall.

● *Corylus avellana* 'Contorta', the corkscrew hazel tree, makes an eye-catching show with its twisted branches and yellow catkins.

CHOOSE COLOURFUL FAVOURITES FOR GREY DAYS The flowers of *Daphne mezereum* 'Grandiflora' are bright purple, appear from late winter to early spring and have a wonderful fragrance. Beware the scarlet berries, which are very poisonous.

WINTER CHEER The yellow flowers of winter-flowering plants, such as wattles, will gladden the eye on the dullest winter day. In cold climates, where winter flowers are scarce, consider *Jasminum nudiflorum*, which has no fragrance but is charming leaning against a low wall or wooden fence. Witch hazel (*Hamamelis*), has – in addition to its highly individual brightly coloured flowers – a delicate scent. Winter sweet (*Chimonanthus praecox*), which flowers in midwinter, is also sweet smelling.

The striking catkins of Garrya elliptica add interest to cold winter gardens.

FOR A VARIED WINTER DISPLAY
To brighten up winter, include plants with flowers or interesting evergreen foliage to offset the bare branches of deciduous trees. Golden flowers – like a pool of sunlight – are particularly welcome on a dull winter's day. Where it's too cold to spend much time outdoors, place plants with winter interest where they can be appreciated from indoors.

JUNE
FLOWERS Abutilon, aster, bergenia, camellia (sasanqua), chrysanthemum **1**, cyclamen, euryops, gordonia, *Iris stylosa*, pansy, poinsettia **2**, primula, reinwardtia, *Salvia leucantha*, strelitzia, witch hazel **3**.
FOLIAGE OR BARK Aucuba **4**, conifers, *Nandina domestica* 'Nana', ornamental kale.
FRUITS *Auranticarpa rhombifolia* (syn. *Pittosporum rhombifolium*), blueberry ash, citrus, crab-apple, hawthorn.

JULY
FLOWERS *Banksia* 'Giant Candles' **5**, *Camellia japonica* **6**, crowea, erythrina, Geraldton wax, grevillea, hardenbergia, japonica (*Chaenomeles* spp.), kalanchoe, magnolia, poppies.
FOLIAGE OR BARK Conifers, crepe myrtle, dogwood, 'Sango-kaku' maple.
FRUITS Callicarpa, *Cotoneaster horizontalis*, cumquat, holly, mahonia, *Melia azederach*, snowberry.

AUGUST
FLOWERS Azalea, *Camellia japonica* **6**, calendula, clivia, daisies, diosma, garrya, hellebore, hippeastrum, leucadendron, polyanthus, protea, *Prunus mume*, pyrostegia, snowflake, waratah, wattle.
FOLIAGE OR BARK Conifers, bromeliads, lamium, New Zealand flax, silver birch, variegated holly.
FRUITS Blue holly, elaeagnus, skimmia, snowberry.

COMBINE WARM, BRIGHT REDS AND YELLOWS For the run up to spring, set off the early-blooming yellow forsythia with orange-red japonica or deep rose-red *Ribes sanguineum* – their flowers go together beautifully and will last through the season to accompany your spring bulbs.

GRASSES ARE STRIKING IN THE WINTER LANDSCAPE Do not cut back wispy ornamental grasses such as pennisetum, miscanthus and carex – they look stunning touched by a morning frost. Leave some herbaceous perennials standing, as their dead stems protect the dormant plants beneath them from frost. The transparent pods of honesty and dried flower heads on hydrangeas and bergamot will also add texture and interest to the winter garden.

A succession of colour

THE LAST FROST Once this important date has passed you are safe to plant out any frost-sensitive plants and most annuals. As a rough guide, overnight temperatures generally remain above freezing from the end of August in northern and coastal climates but frosts may continue in southern, mountain, table-land and inland areas until late September or October. Don't rely on the calendar alone and keep an eye on temperatures and weather forecasts. Experienced gardeners in your area will be able to tell you about your specific local conditions and the likelihood of late frosts.

SMALL BULBS IN SPRING In cold climates smaller bulbs are first to bloom, enlivening bare earth with *Iris reticulata,* snowdrops, snowflakes and winter aconites.
● For long colour, combine spring bulbs with colourful annuals, such as pansy and primula, and perennials, such as *Helleborus orientalis*, heuchera and phlox.

FLOWERS TO LAST THE SUMMER For a new garden, you need species that provide a good season of colour and establish quickly.
● **PERENNIALS** At their best in early and midsummer are *Anthemis tinctoria* 'E. C. Buxton', the cranesbill geraniums (*Geranium*

psilostemon or *G. endressii*), gaura, nepeta, *Scabiosa* 'Butterfly Blue' and valerian.
● **SHRUBS** Early spring is a time of rapid growth. Roses burst into a mass of new growth while flower buds appear on bottle-brush. Prune abutilon, fuchsia and hibiscus in early spring to encourage strong new growth and plenty of flowers through summer.
● **ANNUALS** Plant old-fashioned favourites such as cleome, cosmos, nasturtium, nigella or other flashy annuals for instant colour and a denser planting in your garden.

REMEMBER AUTUMN COLOUR Flowers are bountiful in summer, but don't let late autumn be a low point. When planting, think about creating spots of autumn colour: asters, dahlias and windflowers will support the cooler tones of buddleias, late fuchsias, hebes and *Tamarix ramosissima*.
● **KEEP WATERING** Autumn leaf colour will be briefer if the summer has been dry. From late February, start watering the base of plants that are due to flower at the end of the season to make sure they don't dry out.
● **COLOURFUL LEAVES** Autumn leaf colour from shrubs and trees is a joy in a cold-climate garden. Where space is tight grow deciduous street trees and use climbers such as ornamental grapes for autumn colour.
● **EARLY-FLOWERING TREES AND SHRUBS** Extend the impact of spring in your garden by selecting trees and shrubs that bloom in winter (June, July or August). In warmer areas expect winter-flowering plants to bloom earlier in winter than they do in colder areas.
● **DECORATIVE BERRIES** Many traditional autumn berry plants such as cotoneaster, hawthorn, holly and pyracantha are weeds. For berries that don't pose a problem, consider callicarpa, clivia, crab-apple, lillypilly, persimmon, *Rosa rugosa* and viburnum.

At the height of summer, achilleas, delphiniums, nepetas and roses create a vibrant clash of colour.

Plant pansies with late winter- and spring-flowering bulbs for a colourful garden.

Phlox subulata adds a splash of colour to early spring cool-climate gardens.

A rock garden bursting with life

Rockeries go in and out of favour, but taking inspiration from elements of the natural landscape and re-creating them in your own garden can be very effective. Find or construct a rocky slope, and you can add a brilliant array of drought-hardy plants.

Create a colourful garden

MAKING THE MOST OF A DIFFICULT SPOT If you have an awkward slope, a dry embankment or a hot, dry spot in your garden that is quite difficult to access, a rock garden could provide a low-maintenance, high-impact design solution. Use rocks as a base to mound up or retain the soil on a slope and to create planting areas in a harsh environment. A pocket of good soil or potting mix behind each rock will give plants the opportunity to establish new growth.
● Mound gardens made with rubble are also ideal for planting Australian native plants. Arrange large rocks over the mound to help stabilise the rubble, add a decorative element and provide support for plants and protection for their roots.

CHOOSING THE RIGHT SPECIES Plants that thrive in rock gardens love well-drained soils and full sun. Many come from arid coastal areas where there is lots of sun, but little soil. Even the most drought-tolerant plants need regular watering to establish their root system – particularly in dry times.
● Good choices for a low-maintenance garden in full sun are: the shrubs aeonium, crassula, daisies, grevillea, New Zealand flax and osteospermum; the groundcovers arctotis, blue chalk sticks, gazania, grevillea (prostrate forms), ice plant, trailing lantana (*Lantana montevidensis*) and wattle (prostrate forms); the annuals alyssum, Californian poppy, marigold (dwarf forms) and portulaca.

START WITH A SLOPE If you can make use of an existing slope in your garden it will make creating your rockery much easier. If however, you do not have a natural slope, create a gentle mound in a corner of your garden. Always remember that a shallow slope looks far more natural than a sudden steep mound in an otherwise flat garden: as a general rule, for every 30 cm the bed is raised above ground level, it should be 1–1.5 m wide at the base.
● Do not be tempted to make a rock garden under an established tree. Not only will the falling leaves smother plants, the build-up of rocks and soil over the tree roots will eventually kill the tree.

PATIENCE BEFORE PLANTING If you are building a rockery from scratch, wait until the rocks and soil have stabilised in their new position before planting.

Sun-loving dianthus, primulas and stonecrops soften the craggy lines of a rockery.

Use an effective mix of garden plants to mimic the ones you might find growing on a rocky outcrop in the wild.

ALPINE PLANTS Although rock gardens are usually associated with plants from hot, dry areas, in cold or mountain climates they are the ideal areas for growing alpine plants. Create a patchwork of low-growing perennials with balloon flower, cranesbill, fairy foxglove, gentian, houseleek, maiden pink, mossy saxifrage, pasque flower, salmon primrose and stonecrop.

PROVIDE VOLUME Add high points and interest to a rockery with dwarf conifers, such as juniper, or small shrubs, such as daisies or hebe, which won't overshadow perennials. Lavender, rock rose, rosemary, thyme and other scrubland plants will tolerate rockeries that become very hot in summer. Ferns and hostas are good for shady banks.

TOP TIPS FOR CHOOSING ROCKS
Locally quarried stones will look more natural and cost less than rocks brought from other parts of the country. Use a variety of sizes, but do not go any smaller than the size of a 5-litre bag of potting mix and do not mix two different kinds of rock.
● **QUALITY NOT QUANTITY** A few large, flattish stones look more effective than many smaller ones, and they are also more stable.
● **AVOID BUSH ROCK** Rocks should not be collected from bushland areas (indeed in most areas it is illegal to remove bush rock). Although highly attractive to gardeners, bush rock provides important habitat for native plants and animals, and is particularly important during times of bushfire. Avoid rock sold as bush rock unless it has been taken from land earmarked for clearing and redevelopment. Use quarried rock instead.
● **USE SANDSTONE** Look for slabs of recovered sandstone. Their irregular shapes give them a natural look. You can also buy artificial sandstone, which is less expensive.
● **FOR SMALL PLANTS** Keep soft chalky volcanic rocks, such as scoria and tufa, for your more precious plants. The porous nature of volcanic rock means that it is extremely free draining and small plants can be grown in the cavities in its surface.
● **AVOID GRANITE AND FLINT** The size of the pieces, their shapes and resistance to erosion make them unsuitable for a rockery.

A NATURAL EFFECT Position rocks to mimic a natural rocky outcrop. Place them in steps, with the largest blocks lower down.

1 If your garden does not have a natural mound or sunny slope, build one up with broken brick, rubble and soil.

2 Prepare a mix of garden soil, potting mix and compost or buy in organic garden mix and spread over the surface.

3 Position the first rocks at the base of the rockery; let the natural lines in the stone flow in the same direction.

4 Place the next row using a stout stick or crowbar to move and raise the blocks.

5 Fill around each new row of rocks with soil mix, tamping it down thoroughly between the stones.

6 Tuck the plants into pockets of earth between the rocks. Cover bare earth around them with gravel.

● Keep the best pieces for the most visible rocky sections. Bury lower blocks so that they seem to emerge naturally from the earth.
● Lay the rocks in horizontal layers to imitate the natural strata of the landscape. Make sure the 'grain' of each rock follows the same direction, without being too regular.
● Start at the bottom of the slope and work upwards, laying the largest slabs on their flattest side first and inclining them slightly backwards for stability.

THE RIGHT SOIL The best planting mix for rockeries is freely draining, made up of equal parts of potting mix, good garden soil and compost. Mix the ingredients thoroughly and then spread it over the surface of the rockery to a depth of 20–30 cm.
● Water helps the soil to settle by carrying fine particles of earth with it into crevices between the rocks. Water the soil with a fine rose for 20 minutes daily. Bear in mind that digging up soil increases its volume, so allow for soil levels to drop over time.

WHEN TO WATER During their first year, protect your rock plants from drying out by keeping the soil just moist. Once they're established, you only need to water them

WATCH OUT

If you build your own rockery, be careful how you carry rocks. Raise them with a crowbar, always bend your knees and keep your back straight when lifting. Shift slabs zigzag fashion, pivoting them on their corners, and use a trolley or get help to carry larger rocks. Wear steel-capped boots and thick protective gloves.

properly in times of drought or when new plants are added. When it is hot and dry, hoe gently around the plants to break up the hard crust, then water slowly and carefully to avoid dislodging the plants. Otherwise, just leave them alone.

WELL-FED PLANTS To give plants a boost at the end of winter, surround rockery plants with compost enriched with blood and bone or add leaf mould or other organic mulch mixed with well-rotted manure or compost. Scatter some slow-release fertiliser over the garden and water it in well.

TOP UP GRAVEL Gravel that is spread between plants on a slope will gradually get washed away by rain and it will eventually expose the soil below. Make sure that you renew or replace this protective layer of gravel once a year in spring.

Ideal growing conditions

SURVIVAL OF THE FITTEST As your rock garden grows, some plants will thrive and others may fail to perform. Replace the slow performers with more of the species that are successful. Some pruning may be necessary to keep the very vigorous plants, especially groundcovers, in check so that they don't

Pretty gazanias, with their daisy-like flowers, naturalise in full sun and are perfect for growing in rock gardens.

smother their neighbouring plants or the rocks that you want to display.
● Gazanias (above) with their bold orange, yellow or brown tones adapt readily to hot dry spaces. Use them as a groundcover in dry spots where other plants have failed.

PLANTING SECRETS To give plants the best start, mix a dose of fertiliser with your planting mix and put a handful of potting mix under each plant's root ball.
● When you have filled the hole, remember to water the ground until it is saturated.
● After planting, spread a layer of gravel or coarse sand between the plants. This is not only attractive, it also stops weeds, reduces evaporation and surface compaction, and prevents standing water from rotting the base of the plants.

BEYOND THE WALL
There is usually at least one dry, neglected spot in a garden that needs sturdy plants. For instance, if a property has a brick wall to provide privacy and cut noise and pollution from the passing traffic, these walls can have planter boxes on the street side – and these boxes can be harsh spaces for plants. One old-fashioned plant that thrives in such neglected spots is the dietes, or wild iris. Its narrow, swordlike leaves provide year-round interest and peak flowering occurs in spring. Although dietes' flowers only last a day, new buds open each day for a succession of flowers and they spot flower throughout the year.
● Also try strelitzias and ornamental grasses in these growing situations.
● In a shady spot grow sasanqua camellias.

Gardener's Choice

PLANTS TO DECORATE A WALL OR PAVING
The crevices in dry-stone walls are suited to planting. There are many plants that grow naturally in rock crevices or that trail over boulders. The areas beside stone steps or between pavers are also ideal spaces to grow these species.

IN FULL SUN Alyssum, aubrieta, Californian poppy, catsfoot, crassula, dianthus, dwarf bellflower (*Campanula portenschlagiana*), *Gypsophila repens*, *G. tenuifolia*, linaria, nemophila, pennywort, sea campion (*Silene uniflora*), seaside daisy (*Erigeron karvinskianus*) **1**, sedum (*Sedum oreganum*) **2**, sempervivum, stonecress, thyme, wall rue and wallflower.

IN PARTIAL SHADE Australian native violet (*Viola hederacea*), ferns, phlox (*Phlox borealis*, *P. nivalis* and *P. subulata*), rock cress (*Arabis*) and saxifrage.

A succession of iris-like flowers on dietes means pretty flowers for many months.

A traditional cottage garden

Flowers and vegetables have been a feature of cottage gardens since medieval times. But it was the 19th-century cottage gardeners who, by necessity, became experts in combining flowers and vegetables attractively in their small plots. The practices they developed are just as relevant for gardeners today.

Creating the look

A RIOT OF COLOUR The classic cottage garden is a mass of romantic informality characterised by a glorious summer display of old-fashioned flowers. This style is suitable for any garden, large or small. It can be low on maintenance too, with plants left to self-seed and tumble over pathways and edges.

PLANT IN LAYERS To create the cottage garden style successfully, you need to think of your planting as a system of layers.
● Use trees and shrubs for structure, and hedges to create frameworks either around the whole garden or for individual borders.
● Plant climbers to scramble through hedges and clamber up arbours, arches and walls.
● Use old-fashioned flowers and herbaceous perennials for the bulk of your planting.

● Include some vegetables and herbs among or alongside your flowering plants.
● Fill gaps in beds and borders with annuals and bulbs for colour throughout the year.

FORMAL OR INFORMAL? The prime feature of a cottage garden is 'controlled informality', but your garden can be a regular or more relaxed system of flower-beds. Aim for an almost overcrowded effect in your garden beds and borders.
● Edge rectangular beds with box or lillypilly hedging, or create kidney-shaped beds and plant them right up to your lawn.
● Set out the plants in informal drifts and swathes, mixing species and colours to get a fantastic mass of flowers.
● Allow plants to grow and spread naturally, rambling over pathways and lawn edges.
● Repeat a number of key plants throughout the beds to link them and give them rhythm.

COMBINATION PLANTING Mix flowers, vegetables, fruit and herbs all together in the same beds. The original cottagers did this to provide food for the table and to experiment with a range of flowers for colour.
● Include flowers such as marigolds and nasturtiums to repel pests from your crops.
● Plant a citrus or stonefruit tree among ornamentals for their flowers as well as fruit.
● Grow beans and gourds up rustic arches with other climbers for added interest.

LOW MAINTENANCE A cottage garden isn't time consuming. Formal pruning is not needed, annuals self-seed and the plants cramming the beds will suffocate weeds.

Give cottage flowers daily care with dead-heading, watering and checking for pests.

OLD-FASHIONED VARIETIES Choose a selection of the following flowers to get the look of your cottage garden just right: achillea, aquilegia, bellflower, bleeding heart, delphinium, foxglove, hollyhock, larkspur, lupin, verbascum and wallflower.

FLOWERS FOR CUTTING AND SCENT
One of the joys of a cottage garden is having flowers to bring into the house. Grow a variety of annuals and biennials as well as perennials in your garden, including:
● **PLANTS FOR DRYING** Some of the most successful are calendula, rose and statice.
● **FLOWERS FOR VASES** Popular cut flowers include dahlia, gladiolus and lilies.
● **AROMATIC AND HONEY-PRODUCING PLANTS** Dianthus, lavender, nicotiana and sweet pea attract bees to the garden.

ANNUALS FOR SPRING AND SUMMER
Give instant colour to your garden and window boxes with annuals. Let them reseed to save yourself buying new plants next year.
● In shady areas use busy lizzies, evening primroses, mimulus, pansies and primulas if your site is moist, or foxgloves if it is drier.
● For windy, exposed sites use cornflowers, honesty, poppies, rudbeckia and wallflower.
● For containers try ivy geranium, lobelia, nasturtium, osteospermum, petunia or snapdragon for a trailing effect.

TRADITIONAL GARDEN STYLES Knot or parterre gardens are a formal planting style from 16th-century England and Renaissance France. Their evergreen hedging provides year-round structure.
● **TO CREATE A KNOT GARDEN** Use dwarf evergreen shrubs such as box to form low hedges planted in intricate patterns and geometric shapes. Fill the beds between the hedges with an informal selection of the flowering herbaceous plants you might use in a cottage garden or with herbs. Add height with topiary and keep the hedges trim.
● **FOR A PARTERRE** (a French word meaning 'on the ground') Use the same pattern of low evergreen hedging as the knot garden, but fill in with a low-growing or monochrome planting in the centre. Coloured or natural gravels alternated in the beds can also give a particularly striking effect. Plant columnar yew or cypress to complete the look.
● **VIEWING THE EFFECT** Both of these styles will look delightful at ground level, but they

really come into their own when they are viewed from above, at the top of a slope or from an upstairs window.

A SECRET GARDEN Arbours and secluded spaces planted with scented flowers have been a popular feature of gardens since the Dark Ages. Courtiers and wealthy families lived communal lives under the eyes of their family and retainers. Then, as now, the secret garden provided an intimate spot for quiet contemplation and privacy.
● **DEFINE A CORNER** Separate an area from the rest of your garden with trees and shrubs. Tall hedging is perfect as it means your secret garden can't be seen easily. You could also use large-leaved plants for the same effect.
● **A DRAMATIC APPROACH** Make an opening in the hedge, or wind a path beneath low-hanging trees so that visitors discover your secret spot almost by accident.
● **A FRAGRANT RETREAT** Introduce strongly scented plants to create a heady aroma in the enclosed space of your secret garden.

A MEDITERRANEAN GARDEN The long tradition of gardening in Mediterranean countries can provide inspiration for gardens with a similar climate. Areas with cool wet winters and hot dry summers are particularly suited to Mediterranean plants. In areas that are frosty in winter, some plants may need frost protection when young. Use plants such as artemisia, basil, lavender, rosemary, sage, thyme and clumps of agapanthus, foxtail lily (*Eremurus* hybrids) and red hot poker – and include climbers such as wisteria or a grapevine draped over a pergola to provide welcome summer shade.

Left: The Tudor knot garden was created with a complex pattern of rectangular, diagonal and circular hedges. Simpler designs can add structure and formality to a modern garden.

Create hidden spaces even in a small garden with a wall or a hedge that hides a part of the garden.

HERBS THAT HEAL
For hundreds of years, an important part of every cottage garden was the 'herbal pharmacy', filled with plants that provided the only medicines most people had. Today, these herbs are once again popular in natural remedies. You can make therapeutic teas from many herbs – use dill, fennel, marigold or mint to aid digestion, sage for a sore throat, rosemary for a headache, chamomile to aid sleep or calm an upset stomach, or feverfew to reduce a fever.

- Silver foliage plants are a feature of Mediterranean gardens. As well as lavender, include artemisia, carnation, globe artichoke, helichrysum, lamb's ear and rock rose.
- To provide volume, contrast and evergreen foliage, plant some pointed conifers such as cypress or juniper.
- Include the Mediterranean olive tree, in the ground, or in a large pot. Citrus, pears and almonds also make good feature trees.
- Oleanders are excellent in a Mediterranean-style garden. With their white, pink, red or apricot late-spring to summer flowers they can be used as screen plants or grown in large pots, or even pruned as standards. For year-round colour try variegated cultivars.
- Bay trees lend themselves to shaping as potted topiary specimens. They look superb in a gravel garden in large terracotta pots.

THE SECRETS OF COMPOSITION

Although beds in traditional gardens are informal, you will create a better effect if you follow a few basic design principles.
- Think about the height of the plants you plan to grow in your beds. Keep taller plants such as veronica and salvia towards the back and bring the height down towards the front. Here you can use low plants and groundcovers such as species geranium and scabiosa. Build up to tall plants at the centre of long beds to add interest and drama.
- To soften the edges of your beds, use spreading plants such as heuchera, erigeron, osteospermum and geum.
- Always plant individual species in odd numbers, in threes, fives or sevens. This is easier on the eye. Use a larger number of plants to create meandering drifts.
- Try to repeat species or colours in your beds for a sense of continuity and balance.

TOP TIPS FOR THE TOTAL LOOK

To complete your old-fashioned garden style, you must select the right materials and accessories. Any features must suit the style of your garden. Avoid modern or urban materials and go for rustic, traditional styles instead. Anything that is weathered, antique, reclaimed or recycled can be ideal.
- **WALLS** Build garden structures that are sympathetic with their surroundings. Echo the style of your house if you can, by using appropriate stone, slate or traditional brick.
- **SURFACING** Select materials that will complement the other features in your garden. Traditional choices include gravel, cobbles and setts, as well as brick paving. Steer clear of concrete slabs but, if you have no option, try crazy paving.
- **GROUNDCOVER** Interplant paving with alchemilla, saxifrage and sempervivum.
- **EDGING** Edge your flowerbeds with wooden boards, old bricks set into the ground at an angle, or decorative Victorian edging tiles with scrolled or scalloped tops.
- **FENCING** Use post-and-rail fencing or low hedges to create boundaries.
- **CONTAINERS** Use traditional unglazed terracotta for pots or recycle old baths, buckets or found objects.

Geraniums and pelargoniums grow easily from cuttings. Make a collection in your cottage or Mediterranean-style garden. From left: 'Rosemary', 'Occold Shield' and 'Lady Plymouth' (grown for its scented leaves).

Gardener's Choice

COTTAGE GARDEN FAVOURITES

DAHLIAS The dahlia is the queen of the flowerbed from summer until late autumn. Tubers can be planted in spring, but wait until early November in cold climates. Plant tubers 8 cm deep for dwarf varieties and 12 cm for more vigorous plants. Planting too deeply reduces the number of flowers.

HOLLYHOCKS Choose traditional varieties of hollyhocks with simple flowers rather than the modern double blooms. As hollyhocks are biennial, sow the seeds – which you have collected in the autumn – in a corner of your garden and move the plants to their permanent positions the following year.

PEONIES Peonies are beautiful choices for a cool climate but resent disturbance so plant with care, selecting a well-drained position with additional organic matter. Avoid digging around their roots and keep plants well watered.

FOXGLOVES Foxgloves are perfect self-seeding plants to use around beds. Allow the flower spikes to surprise you in late spring. Combine foxgloves with decorative alliums, larkspurs and lupins to add a little statuesque drama at the back of a garden bed.

Add soothing water to your garden

In times past, artificial ponds, lakes, fountains and water cascades were possible only in grand gardens. Now anyone can easily devise a water feature to suit their garden and their budget, and enjoy the enchantment, peace and serenity it brings.

A well-planned garden pond

THE BEST SITE FOR A POND Your pond or pool should be visible from the house, but not so near that wildlife will be scared away.

● If the ground slopes, choose a lower corner of the garden to site your pond: it will seem much more natural here, as water naturally collects at the lowest level.

● A pond should be situated at a distance from any fruit trees or plants that might be treated with chemicals.

● An open, sunny position provides the best conditions to grow most aquatic plants. In cold climates, make sure you don't site your pond in a frost pocket or in a spot that is exposed to the weather. This will restrict the plants you can successfully grow and it may mean that your pond will need protection over the winter months.

● Only add fish if your pond is at least 80 cm deep. Watch the water conditions in hot weather as the fish will suffer if the temperature goes above 25°C. In hot or windy weather, ponds will lose water due to evaporation. Regularly top up ponds during periods of hot weather.

A WATER FEATURE ON THE TERRACE
If you don't have space for a pond, take a tip from yesterday's gardeners and improvise. Use a large basin, stone trough or a half-barrel, or a decorative glazed pot.

● Plug drainage holes in pots with a silicone sealant and paint the inside of the pot with waterproofing paint.

● To prepare a wooden half-barrel for use as a pond, fill it several days before you plan to plant it up so that the wood swells and becomes completely watertight.

● Choose water plants that like warmth because such a small volume of water will heat up quickly. Try a miniature variety of water lily, which will flourish in less than 40 cm of water. Give the arrangement some height with a clump of plumed foliage, such as dwarf papyrus. Include an oxygenator, such as *Myriophyllum aquaticum*, or install a small fountain with a submersible pump to add oxygen to the water.

WATER PLANTS NEED SUNLIGHT Make sure that you site your pond where it will get at least 5 hours of light a day – if possible, the morning sun.

A pretty blend of herbaceous plants along the bank merges with flowering irises and floating water lilies to integrate this pond naturally into its environment.

WATCH OUT

BEWARE OF DROWNING
Water attracts children and it is important to remember that a child can drown in as little as 10 cm of water. In most areas ponds deeper than 1 m must be fenced. Check with your local council about restrictions in your area. Water depth can be reduced by adding large river pebbles to a pond.

● Cover small ponds (under 10 square metres) with wire netting – the vegetation will hide most of it. Surround larger features with a 1 m high fence and a locked gate.

● Avoid steep banks, which make it difficult to climb out of the water.

● Notify your insurer of your water feature.

● Prevent electrocution by placing electric cables in a sealed watertight casing.

• Position it away from overhanging trees, which cast shadows on the water. Also remember that overhanging trees will drop their leaves and twigs in the pond. Without regular cleaning these will affect water quality and appearance. Tree roots can also interfere with pond liners.

PROVIDE A POWER POINT Plan ahead in case you want to install a pump to circulate the water and prevent stagnation. You can also light your pond at night and make it a feature of any evening parties.

START IN WARM WEATHER Late spring to summer is the best time to create your pond. The water will warm up quickly and this will create the perfect environment for your first water plants.

CHOOSING THE SHAPE OF YOUR POND
If your pond is close to the house, it is best to choose a formal shape with simple lines. Further away from the house or in a large garden, your pond can be a more irregular, organic shape, which will blend into the surrounding natural landscape.

THINK BIG The bigger it is, the more natural your pond will look. A large area of water also has a more stable temperature, which is better for both wildlife and plants. But as a rule of thumb, a pond should take up no more than one third of the space in your entire garden.
• Aim for a minimum depth of 80 cm so that plants and fish can survive during the summer without stress. The impression of depth can be exaggerated by using a dark-coloured pond liner.

DIGGING A POND YOURSELF This is the most economical way to install a pond, and allows you to achieve the size and structure you want. A flexible butyl liner is the best material to use, as it is a hardy material which can last for decades.
• A 1 mm thick butyl liner is adequate for an average-sized pond. If the area is more than 100 square metres or if the ground is very stony, go for 1.5 mm. To estimate the size of liner you need, first measure both the maximum length and the maximum width of the hole you have dug. Then to each of these measurements add twice the maximum depth you have dug for your pond, plus

30 cm. This will give you the length and width of the liner you will need to buy, including enough left over to overlap the edges of the pond.

THINGS TO CONSIDER WHEN YOU'RE DIGGING Check the rim of your pond is level all around using a spirit level – any differences in height will be very noticeable once the pond is full of water.
• Make shelves around the edge of the inside of the pond at least 30 cm wide and at different depths. This will enable you to grow a whole range of water plants.
• Instead of carting them away, why not make a rockery with the earth and stones you've cleared when digging your pond?

PLANNING FOR OVERSPILLS There are two things you can do to combat flooding. The first is to make one side of the bank lower than the others so that any water overflows into an area of the garden filled with plants that can thrive in these boggy conditions, such as cannas. Another technique is to install an overflow pipe into your main drainage system. Fix a grille to the mouth of the pipe to prevent vegetation from causing a blockage.

In a small space, grow miniature water plants in a large pot or barrel. Fill in drainage holes and seal porous interiors.

INSTALLING A POND

1 Mark out the shape of the pond on the ground. Tap in stakes every 30 cm around the edge of the shape.

2 Excavate to the depth of your pond plus 15 cm. Gently slope the sides and remove 15 cm of turf all round.

3 Remove stones, spread a layer of fine sand, then cover with old carpet, strips of cardboard or newspaper.

4 Install the pond liner on a warm day so it will be flexible. Stretch the liner out from the centre and secure edges with rocks.

5 Don't worry about wrinkles in the liner as the weight of the water will remove them. Run in water slowly to fill the pond.

6 Allow the liner to settle for several days after filling it with water. Then trim the edges and conceal them with earth or stones.

FISH IN THE POND In addition to their visual appeal, fish such as goldfish are great little gardeners for aquatic plants. They clean and trim ceaselessly and control mosquitoes by devouring their eggs and larvae. However, fish soil the water with their excreta and stir up the mud at the bottom. If you do want to introduce them into your pond, take advice when you buy them on suitable numbers for your size of pond, and use a filter to keep the water clean and clear.

INTRODUCE FISH SLOWLY Wait at least 6 weeks after filling your pond before putting in fish, and check that the pH (this is the acid/alkali balance of the water) is neutral.
● When you bring your fish home, do not put them directly into the pond. There will probably be a temperature difference between the water in the bag they were brought home in and the water in the pond. Float the bag of fish in the pond, still closed, for at least 20 minutes to allow the water temperatures to equalise. You can then safely introduce the fish into their new habitat.

Goldfish or small native fish do a good job in keeping ponds free of mosquito larvae.

A pond teeming with life

HIDE THE EDGES OF YOUR POND WITH PLANTS The roots of the plants will stabilise the ground around the banks of the pond. Mix flowering plants with foliage plants and create added interest by varying the species. The following plants are adapted to damp soil and will tolerate temporary immersion in up to 10 cm of water:
● **FLOWERING PLANTS** Astilbe, daylily (*Hemerocallis*), Japanese primrose, ligularia, lysimachia, marsh marigold (*Caltha palustris*), mimulus, *Narcissus poeticus* 'Actaea', rose mallow with giant flowers (*Hibiscus moscheutos*) and Siberian iris.
● **PLANTS WITH DECORATIVE FOLIAGE** Carex, fern, hosta, miscanthus, papyrus, phalaris and rodgersia.
● **KEEPING PLANTS MOIST** During a dry summer, pack a layer of mulch around your plants to keep them moist. If you do have water available, make sure you top up your pond frequently.

STAR PERFORMERS Floating plants that actually take root in the water itself are useful as they are the most decorative and wide spreading. Of these plants, the water lilies (*Nymphaea* spp.) are the undisputed star performers. They will thrive in an unobstructed sunny site in still water.

DON'T OVERDO PLANTING Do not cover more than half the total surface area of the water with floating plants. Leaving plenty of

Floating plants weed warning

While floating plants can be great for ponds, they should never be released from home ponds or aquariums as they have become serious weeds in our natural water courses. Two popular plants, water hyacinth and water lettuce, should not be introduced into ponds. Also, a floating weed, ferny azolla, can quickly choke a pond. It can be accidentally introduced when buying other pond plants so always rinse new plants thoroughly.

PLANT	CHARACTERISTICS
Nardoo or water clover (*Marsilea drummondii*) (left)	Leaf resembles a four-leaf clover. A type of fern, anchored to the ground so it can be grown in pots. Its sporocarps (seedlike structures that bury themselves in the mud) are rich in starch and can be harvested as a wild food.
Water chestnut *Trapa natans*	Suitable for still, shallow pools. Helps to purify the water. Annual, but reseeds itself. (Not in Western Australia)

Water lilies need a sunny spot in order to flower well.

1 2
3 4

5 6

clear, reflective surface visible will make your pond seem bigger, which is especially important in a small garden where you are trying to create the feeling of space.

● Aquatic plants should never be packed too tightly together. Make sure you plant them out according to the information provided on the plant labels.

'POTTING' AQUATIC PLANTS The easiest way to grow aquatics is in special mesh baskets. Line with hessian, add 5 cm of garden soil, then insert the plant. Fill in with more soil, firm well, then top-dress with gravel or pebbles and trim the hessian.

CREATE A CALMING BACKGROUND

If your pond is small and if your garden conditions allow it, give the pond area an oriental feel by surrounding it with acid-loving shrubs and trees. Shrubs and trees such as azaleas, Japanese maple (*Acer japonicum*), juniper and rhododendron all look at home around water.

WAIT TO ADD THE PLANTS

If you have filled your pond with tap water, allow several weeks for the chlorine to evaporate before introducing the plants, or use a product that will neutralise the chlorine.

● Water plants do best in the warmer months of the year, so spring and summer are the best times to plant them.

● Before adding aquatic plants to the pond, rinse them carefully with tap water to wash off any weeds, pests and parasites.

CLEANSE THE WATER OF YOUR POND NATURALLY

Plants that develop under the surface are called submerged oxygenators. They are sometimes overlooked as they are thought to be less attractive than other aquatic plants, but they play a vital role in oxygenating the water. They also shade and nourish the animal life of the pond. However, they are often very fast growing so plant only four or five. Stop them becoming invasive by thinning out in late autumn.

● **ORNAMENTAL OXYGENATORS** Choose from *Houttuynia cordata*, a water violet; myriophyllum; and *Ranunculus aquatilis*, a water buttercup, which has clusters of small white flowers above underwater leaves. (Note: Some water plants are prohibited weeds in parts of Australia so may be unavailable in your area.)

You can keep papyrus under control in a container that is submerged in the pond.

MAKING A BALLAST If you need to plant something at a depth greater than 30 cm, there's no need to get wet! Dig up a small clump of grass, wrap it around the roots of the aquatic plant you wish to position and secure it with a rubber band or wire. Throw it gently into the water where you want it to settle. The weight of the turf will make the plant sink to the bottom where new roots will spring up and anchor it.

LOWER PLANTS GRADUALLY Do not plunge plants with floating foliage straight into deep water. Introduce them over time

Before adding new plants to the pond, wash their roots and foliage to remove unwanted weeds and pests.

Marginal plants

With only their roots actually in the water, these shallow-water plants can tolerate long periods of dryness when the water level falls. They conceal the edges of an artificial pond and attract a variety of wildlife, for which they provide a refuge. Restrict the spread of the most invasive of these plants by containing them in submerged baskets.

PLANT	CHARACTERISTICS
Acorus (sweet flag) **1**, papyrus, rushes and scirpus	Tall, decorative clumps to give height and structure to the pool.
Aquatic mint	Thrives in moving water. Very fragrant.
Marsh trefoil	Pretty, star-shaped flowers. For acid soil.
Pontederia **2**	Abundant spikes of blue flowers in summer. Hardy.
Reeds and typha	Place to the south of a big pool to protect other plants from wind. Grow in baskets to limit invasiveness. (Typha not WA.)
Sagittaria **3** (arrowhead)	Ideal in moving water. Foliage provides underwater oxygen. (Not in WA.)
Water iris **4**	Attracts dragonflies.

by placing them on brick supports, which can gradually be lowered as the plant settles, and finally removed altogether. This way, the plants will adapt to the conditions of your pool and the leaf stems will have time to grow to the required height.

● To place an aquatic plant out in the middle of the pond, you will need someone to help you. Take a length of rope each and loop it through a handle on opposite sides of the basket holding the plant, so that each of you is holding both ends of your piece of rope. Then, while standing on opposite sides of the pond from each other, lower the plant gently into place and retrieve the ropes back through the basket handles.

Maintaining your pond

TOP TIPS FOR COMBATING ALGAE

In high summer, when the pool is in full sunlight, algae can spread rapidly, turning the whole pond green.

● **AVOID ALGICIDES** They solve the problem only temporarily without tackling the cause.

● **USE NATURAL REMEDIES** Throw a handful of rye or barley straw into the water every 4 to 6 months. This is said to encourage the development of bacteria which prevent thread algae growing.

● **INTRODUCE FLOATING PLANTS** Frogbit (*Hydrochorus morsus-ranae*), water chestnut (*Trapa natans*) and water lilies will restore the biological balance and shade the pool, keeping the water at a constant temperature.

● **DON'T OVERFEED THE FISH** Too much fish food pollutes the water. There is actually no need to feed in summer, nor in winter when fish are dormant.

If your water lily buds become aphid-infested, immerse them for several days using chicken wire.

FLUSHING OUT APHIDS Water lily buds can become infested with aphids. It is easy to control these pests, and there is no need to spray – simply drown them by using chicken wire to immerse the afflicted plant in water for several days.

A BAD SMELL IN THE POND This indicates that organic matter is breaking down in the water, absorbing oxygen and causing poor development of plants and fish. It may even kill them.

● To prevent this terrible smell, remove and change one third of the water, and lower the pH by using proprietary pH granules. (In the past gardeners might have immersed a small cotton bag filled with peat.)

● If they are available in your area, introduce oxygenating plants such as *Ceratophyllum*, *Myriophyllum* and *Potamogeton*.

● You can also use surface-floating plants, which will shade the pool and keep the water temperature stable.

REMOVE LEAVES In summer, clear all the leaf debris from the pond. Then, at the beginning of autumn, lay poles over the pond and cover it with a net. This will keep dead leaves from falling in. Clear fallen leaves off the net periodically and then remove it from the pond in spring.

WATER YOUR POND IN SUMMER

To top up any water lost through natural evaporation without scaring the fish, disturbing the plants or stirring up mud, just gently dribble water in with a hose.

PROVIDE SHADE FOR YOUR POND

Plant a tree near your pond, but not overhanging, to give a few hours of daily shade in summer. This will help prevent overheating and slow the growth of the aquatic plants. Select trees such as paperbarks or bottlebrush, and choose varieties that are under 10 m tall. Avoid conifers, as any needles or resin that drop into the water will make it more acid.

REMOVING ALGAE Fix a piece of chicken wire over the tines of a garden fork to make an effective net for scooping up algae.

● Do not discard what you lift out. Instead, put it on your compost heap and use it to enrich the rest of your garden with its free and valuable nitrogen.

1 Divide plants after flowering. Begin by tidying up the plant and removing any old stems with secateurs.

2 Lift the clump from the water and take the plant out of its container. Leave it by the side of the pool to drain.

3 Divide the plant as you would any herbaceous perennial by inserting a spade through the cluster of shoots and severing it.

4 Pot each new plant in a basket of good garden soil and add a generous layer of gravel to keep the soil in place.

Indoor gardening and courtyards

Thanks to the Victorian plant collectors, a huge range of exotic indoor plants is available today. However, indoor plants can also be grown on sheltered patios or balconies, and in courtyards and light wells.

Keep your plants healthy

BUYING TIPS Try to buy plants in bud rather than in full flower, so you can enjoy them for longer. Avoid pots with waterlogged or dried soil. Examine the underside of the leaves carefully: this is where various common pests such as mealy bug, whitefly and scale insects gather. If there are roots coming out of the drainage holes, this means that the plant is compacted – don't buy it. For advice on buying plants, see pages 260–1.

SETTLING IN When you get a new plant home, don't put it with your other plants right away. Let it acclimatise in a draught-free spot out of direct sunlight. Keep an eye on it to make sure it has not brought any pests into the house, balcony or courtyard.
● Most plants sold commercially are grown in potting mixes which dry out quickly and don't hold nutrients. Repot new plants (see opposite page) when you get them home.

WATERING: DON'T BE TOO HEAVY-HANDED More plants die from too much water than from too little. Let your plants almost dry out before watering and try to water in the morning, wetting the potting mix thoroughly. Water at the base of the plant with a watering can with a long spout. Stand pots on feet for good drainage, or if a plant stands in a saucer, pour away any water still in the pot saucer an hour after watering.

LET TAP WATER STAND BEFORE WATERING Tap water contains chlorine, which can be harmful to plants. However, if

Gardener's Choice

A PLANT FOR EVERY SITUATION

TEMPORARY DISPLAY These plants can be enjoyed indoors but return them outdoors after 3–4 weeks: aeonium, azalea, bromeliads, chrysanthemum, cactus, cymbidium orchid, echeveria, poinsettia and strelitzia.

BRIGHT LIGHT Plants that can be placed at a north-facing window with a thin curtain, or at an east or west-facing window, are African violet **1**, anthurium, aphelandra, codiaeum, cyperus, dieffenbachia, exacum, hypoestes, palms, phalaenopsis and streptocarpus.

SEMISHADE Chain of hearts (*Ceropegia linearis* subsp. *woodii*), epiphyllum, primula, schefflera, scindapsus, spathiphyllum. Ferns such as nephrolepsis **2**, sparmannia and syngonium will thrive behind a south-facing window, or 2 m from a well-exposed window.

SHADE The following plants need to be situated in the middle of a bright room or around 1.5 m from a south-facing window: adiantum, aspidistra, cissus, philodendron and tolmiea **3**.

you let water stand in an open container for several hours, the chlorine will evaporate. The water will also rise to room temperature, which is better for roots.

PROVIDING HUMIDITY Group plants on a tray half-filled with gravel or pebbles. Pour water into the tray, and keep it topped up so that the gravel stays wet. This will create all the humidity most indoor plants need.
● Plants that require very high humidity can be mist-sprayed with soft water – use rainwater if your tap water is too hard. Spray

A colourful array of flowering indoor plants, such as cyclamen, primula and hyacinth, will enhance a sunny windowsill.

the water sparingly on plants with hairy leaves, and avoid direct sunlight as water droplets cause scorching.

PLANTS IN TERRACOTTA POTS

These need watering more frequently than plants in plastic pots, as water evaporates through the porous clay surface. For hanging baskets or pots that are difficult to reach, use plastic.
● Hanging baskets are difficult to water. The modern invention of water-retaining gel, which is mixed into the potting mix when you plant the basket, helps to reduce the frequency of watering.

TOP TIPS FOR FEEDING

Indoor plants like fertiliser rich in nitrogen as it encourages leaf growth. Fertilisers rich in phosphorus and potassium will stimulate flowering.
● **FEED WHEN ACTIVE** Feed indoor plants once a fortnight throughout their active growing period, which is between September and March. When the plant is dormant, feed it only once a month or not at all, depending on the plant. However, plants that flower during winter do not rest, so continue to feed them fortnightly.
● **NEVER APPLY FERTILISER TO DRY POTTING MIX** It won't soak through the soil evenly and can damage the roots.
● **PLAN AHEAD** When potting on, add slow-release fertiliser balls, which last for about 5 to 6 months, to the surface of the mix.

● **ENCOURAGE FLOWERING** Give a specially formulated flowering-plant fertiliser to winter-blooming plants, such as African violets, and you will have abundant flowers.

CLEAN AND HEALTHY

Your plants' leaves need regular dusting to stop their leaf pores clogging up. Wash wide-leaved plants with a sponge or soft cloth soaked in clean water (top right) and kept only for this job.
● Use leaf polish on broad-leaved plants only after you have dusted them. Be sparing as polish can block leaf pores.
● Dust cacti, succulents and downy-leaved plants using a dry, thin paint brush, a shaving brush (bottom right) or a soft toothbrush.
● Shower plants with thin leaves such as ferns and palms regularly by spraying them with lukewarm water in the shower or bath. Make sure you let them drain off before putting them back in their place.

PROVIDE THE CORRECT LEVEL OF LIGHTING

All so-called indoor plants are natives of tropical and subtropical areas. Few are happy with very weak light but they also cannot tolerate strong direct sunlight in summer. In their natural environment these plants are protected from scorching by the leaves of the natural tree canopy.

Large leaves become dusty so should be regularly cleaned with a damp cloth.

A shaving brush is an ideal tool to keep a cactus dust free.

REPOTTING AN INDOOR PLANT

1 Immerse pot in water so that the root ball is easy to remove, then gently ease it from the pot.

2 Cover drainage holes with mesh. Then partially fill the pot with a good-quality potting mix.

3 Place root ball so its top is level with rim base of the pot. Fill with potting mix, firming down well.

4 Water well allowing the pot to drain. Add more potting mix if necessary once surface has settled.

● **INDOOR LIGHT IS NOT IDEAL** Indoors and on balconies, light intensity diminishes quickly away from the window or railing, even if your eyes do not perceive this clearly. Too little light makes leaves pale and stunted and the stems thin and weak.

● **YELLOW LEAVES** If a plant doesn't get enough light, it produces less chlorophyll, causing it to yellow, wilt and lean towards the light. Change its position or give it daily bursts of artificial light. Any source is good, but the best are 'daylight effect' neon tubes or bulbs that can be used in ordinary sockets.

● **ROTATE YOUR POTS** Turn your plants by a quarter of a circle every week or so. This will encourage them to grow evenly and will prevent the stems from becoming straggly.

● **LIGHT BALANCE** Young seedlings, cuttings, variegated plants and plants with coloured leaves all need a lot of light, but very strong sunlight will damage the foliage.

● **WINTER SUN** Remember that in winter there is much less natural light than in summer and you may need to move some plants to a north or west-facing ledge to compensate for this.

PROPAGATING PLANTS FOR YOUR INDOOR GARDEN

1 To take leaf cuttings, cut a leaf stalk 5 cm from the leaf. Fill a seed tray with a suitable potting mix and firm it down. Insert the leaf stalk at an angle. Water and keep at about 20°C. Feed with liquid fertiliser as new plants emerge.

2 For begonias, in late summer cut a leaf 2 cm from the base. Cut across the large veins on the underside. Lay the leaf, cut-side down, in moist potting mix and secure it with pebbles. Keep covered at 20°C, until new plantlets sprout.

3 In spring, propagate perennials by cutting off 10 cm shoots from the base of the plant at crown level. Plant the cuttings singly in 8 cm pots in a greenhouse or cold frame. Keep them moist and frost free. Plant out in the garden in autumn.

SOAKING SHOWERS Take advantage of steady rain to take your indoor plants outside. The rain will wash the leaves and water them at the same time. Move them to drain off in a shady corner as the sun that follows the rain may burn them.

● Indoor plants will enjoy spending time outside, so put them in a shady corner out of the wind. For good health, rotate plants so they spend as much time outdoors as in.

● In cold areas, wait until nighttime temperatures no longer fall below 10°C before leaving plants outside.

● Give plants more water when outside, as the sun and wind have a drying effect.

● Remember to bring your plants back inside when the weather starts to cool.

REPOT IN SPRING For the majority of indoor plants, you can start repotting from the beginning of spring, when plants are just emerging from their winter rest period. However, never repot a dormant plant.

● If a plant is pot-bound choose a new pot one size bigger than the old one – plants do not like being moved from a pot that is too small to one that is far too big.

● To prevent the roots obstructing the drainage hole, put a piece of mesh or flywire over the hole before adding potting mix. Raise pots slightly on blocks or pot feet.

● Some plants, such as palms, don't like root disturbance and thrive with their roots confined. Don't repot them, just replace the old surface potting mix with fresh moist potting mix in spring.

● After repotting, wait a few weeks before feeding your plants.

THE RIGHT TIME TO STAKE PLANTS Climbing plants will collapse without support, and the stems of very heavy flowers such as amaryllis and lilies will bend or break. Repotting is the best time to think

DID YOU KNOW?

TOP TIPS FOR HEALTHY PLANTS

● Let air circulate between your plants by not placing them too close together.

● Air the room regularly but avoid creating draughts.

● Do not let water stagnate in pot saucers, as this encourages fungal diseases. Empty saucers after watering.

● Lightly rake the surface of the soil regularly to stop the roots from suffocating and the soil from compacting.

● You should regularly top up potting mixes.

Use foliage plants to provide interest in otherwise dull areas of the house.

An upturned bottle of water will slowly water an indoor plant if you have to be away from home for some time.

MAKING A GARDEN IN A BOTTLE

1 To make a miniature home for exotic plants, pour a bed of clay beads into a pot-bellied glass bottle – available from most garden centres.

2 Add a thin layer of powdered charcoal and spread over it a layer of good indoor plant potting mix.

3 Part-fill the bottle with the potting mix and put in the plants. Take care not to plant them too close together so they have room to grow.

4 Pour a little water down the sides of the bottle from time to time. This is one container display that will require very little watering.

about putting in stakes and mini-trellises, as you will not damage the roots or the bulbs. Drive the stakes deep into the soil so that the plant and its stake will not topple over.

GOING ON HOLIDAY? If you are going away for more than a fortnight in hot weather, prune at least a third of any hanging foliage from fast-growing plants and remove the flowers to reduce their need for water.
- To provide water while you are away, insert an upside-down plastic bottle filled with water into each plant pot or use small terracotta cones connected to a water tank. The water will be slowly drawn into the soil.
- Don't leave your plants in a sink full of water, as you are likely to drown them. Instead, put them on the draining board on capillary matting (available from nurseries) soaked in water, or a heavy cloth with one end soaking in the sink. The plants can then absorb the water slowly.

- Use self-watering planters with care. Unless your species need lots of water, use these planters only if you will be away for a long time. These systems keep the lower part of the potting mix constantly wet, which causes the roots to rot.

DON'T IGNORE WARNING SIGNS If the edges of leaves start to turn brown, the air in your room may be too dry. Mist affected plants regularly with water and put them on a tray covered with wet gravel or pebbles. If you cut off the brown ends of the leaves, make sure you always leave a thin strip of brown, as cutting the living leaf will scar it and dry it out even more.
- If a plant's leaves are rolling up over themselves, look as if they have been burnt in large patches or are slightly reddened, or if its flowers are fading quickly, your plant may be getting too much light. Move it to a shadier position or put a thin curtain on the window so it's not in direct sun.
- If leaves are yellowing and falling off, the plant may be getting too much water or not enough light. Reduce your watering then, if it doesn't improve, move the plant.

Conservatories, greenhouses, shadehouses and bushhouses

ADD A CONSERVATORY Once very popular in cool climates and in gardens of yesteryear, a conservatory is now rare in Australia and New Zealand. Sited on the cooler south or eastern sides of the house the conservatory can provide a sheltered but brightly lit area which increases your indoor space and provides a wonderful space to create a lush garden. In cold or frost-prone climates, a conservatory may be the ideal space to protect tender plants from the cold.
- Give a conservatory garden a tropical feel by filling it with large potted palms, such as rhapis palms, colourful foliage plants including bromeliads, and orchids, such as dendrobiums and cymbidiums.
- Conservatories tend to get very hot if they are exposed to full sun, so be sure to provide

YESTERDAY'S SECRETS

EASY CUTTINGS
Here is an easy and cheap way to propagate a large number of plants, such as cyperus.
- Cut off the ends of the leaves to within a few centimetres from the centre of the head (below top).
- Immerse the cutting upside-down with its head in water (below centre).
- Leave in a warm, light place and, in a few weeks, a mass of roots will have appeared (below bottom). You can then plant your rooted cuttings in moist compost and grow them into adult plants.

them with good ventilation and movable internal shade screens so you can control the temperature and air flow.

USE THE VERTICAL SPACE Even if your indoor garden is enclosed under a glass roof, make the most of the walls. Paint them a light, bright colour such as white or light blue, to reflect light into the space and provide increased light for plants.
● If space permits, attach parallel wires to the walls so you can train a climber or espalier a shrub up them.
● The walls can also be hung with half hanging baskets planted with cascading plants to make the most of vertical space.

WHY HAVE A GREENHOUSE? When gardens were large and much of what was grown in gardens was propagated from seeds or cuttings, some form of greenhouse was vital for the keen gardener. In a shadehouse or glasshouse in their backyard, gardeners grew plants for their gardens. With the ready availability of plants at nurseries and garden centres, less home propagation occurs. Today a greenhouse is more likely to be found in the home of a gardener who is passionate about propagation or who collects certain plants such as cacti or orchids or who has a passion for tropical plants but lives in a cool climate. If you want to develop your

gardening skills or start a plant collection, consider including a small greenhouse in your garden. This can be a simple DIY structure with a skin of UV-treated plastic or shadecloth. In warm climates, shadecloth keeps temperatures down in summer and is the preferred covering.

COLD FRAMES If space is at a premium but you are keen to propagate your own plants you need a cold frame. A cold frame consists of a framework of wood, metal, concrete or brick, covered by panes of glass called lights. A portable frame in wood or metal is the most convenient type as you can move it in or out of the sun. Use a frame instead of, or in addition to, a greenhouse to protect plants from the cold in winter.

YOUR PLANTS NEED AIR The amount of glass in your greenhouse that is given over to ventilators should equal at least a sixth of the floor space. Use hinged vents on the roof and sides and louvres in the sides below the staging.

TOO MUCH HEAT IS A BAD THING
During summer, you will need to shade your greenhouse, shadehouse or conservatory from the sun. The traditional method is to whitewash the outside of the glass with a weak mix of 1 part paint to 100 parts water. This is usually done in spring to last through the summer months. Roller or concertina blinds are a better-looking option and are flexible, allowing you to adjust light levels according to the changing weather.

A GOOD HEAT SOURCE Electric heaters are a good choice if you have a power supply. Choose a heater that is thermostatically controlled so you do not waste heat.

Courtyards

CREATE AN ATMOSPHERE WITH FURNISHINGS Turn your courtyard or balcony into a lush tropical paradise with foliage plants such as bromeliads and palms. Add to the feeling with woven furniture, which add to the tropical or resort feel.

MAKE THE MOST OF SPACE A small courtyard needn't restrict gardening. Walls, feature pots and a raised garden bed around

YESTERDAY'S SECRETS

GRANDMA'S BUSHHOUSE
In years gone by ferns, palms and orchids were favourite plants. They were used to decorate homes or verandas. These shade-loving plants were often grown in a home-made shadehouse called a bushhouse which was knocked together with rough timber. Shade was provided by a roof of narrow timber lathes sometimes augmented with the large fronds from tree ferns, palms, or banana leaves or with a climber such as quisqualis trained over the roof. The earliest bushhouses were shaded with the branches of the tea tree (*Melaleuca* spp.). Many of these buildings have long since disappeared, but if you want to grow ferns, small palms or orchids, and your garden doesn't have the shade you need, consider taking a leaf out of Grandma's book and building a good old-fashioned bush-house. Shadecloth can be substituted for timber lathes. Bushhouses are also a great place to rest indoor plants and propagate new plants for your garden.

the edge of the courtyard provide plenty of room to grow a wide range of plants.

● Cane begonias are ideal courtyard plants. They are narrow but can reach 1–2 m in height making them ideal to grow against a wall. They have decorative leaves and flower over many months. They also enjoy shade, but tolerate short periods of direct sun.

MAKE A THREE-DIMENSIONAL SCENE
A small garden, that's too tiny for sitting or eating in, shouldn't be ignored. Transform it into a living painting to be viewed through windows from inside. Arrange the garden so it looks good from indoors by planting around a focal point centred on the window. Add decorations such as wall plaques, a central fountain or deceive the eye with a trompe l'oeil painting. The fountain can be lit up at night as a stunning feature.

LAYERING Plants that cascade over the edges of pots or planter boxes add another dimension to a small garden. Australian native violets or a groundcover campanula are excellent shade choices. For a sunny spot select Spanish shawl (*Heterocentron elegans*), which is flat in its growth with masses of small magenta flowers through summer.

MICROCLIMATES A sheltered but sunny courtyard can be a warm microclimate suited to growing plants from warmer climates than your own. Experiment with lush combinations of cymbidium orchids, foliage plants such as crotons and clumping palms such as rhapis.

● As courtyards are surrounded by walls – sometimes the walls of the neighbouring houses – they can experience heavy shade for much of the day. Occasionally this dense shade is punctuated with short bursts of hot sun. In these situations concentrate on shade-loving plants. If foliage is burnt by the sun, increase watering and arrange taller plants so that sun-sensitive foliage plants are shaded.

LIVING SHADE An outdoor umbrella provides shade but try a living umbrella in the form of a tree, trained as a standard. Consider mop top robinia or lipstick maple.

CLIP AND SHAPE One of the most vital tools to own if you have a courtyard garden is a good pair of secateurs. Clip plants to provide more room and added interest.

Make the most of small spaces by clipping and shaping plants.

Shaping plants prevents them from overcrowding each other. By training shrubs into topiaries, such as a ball of growth on top of a tall stem, you open up the ground level for more plants. Plants that can be clipped include box, camellias, conifers, cumquats, durantas, lillypillies and murrayas.

A paved area adjacent to the house can be a suntrap that is ideal for heat-loving plants such as frangipani.

Gardener's Choice

COLLECTORS' PLANTS
You can use a bushhouse or shadehouse to grow and display your tropical plant collections.

ORCHIDS Cymbidium orchids **1** grow well in the dappled shade of a bushhouse but lush green leaves indicate too little light. Also try dendrobiums (including native species), phalaenopsis and the chocolate orchid (*Stanhopea*), which flowers from the base of the pot so grows best in a hanging basket.

CACTI The jungle or leaf cacti include zygocactus **2**, epiphyllum and rhipsalis. These epiphytes grow well in hanging baskets with free-draining potting mix.

BEGONIAS There are many begonias to collect. Rex begonias **3** with their coloured and patterned leaves are readily propagated by leaf cutting so it is easy to increase your collection. Tuberous begonias **4** are grown from tubers and produce decorative flowers in a wide range of colours and shapes.

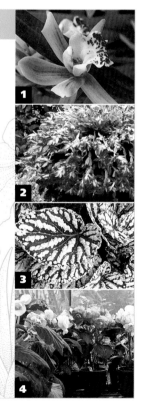

Planting around a swimming pool

A swimming pool is a wonderful asset for a family-friendly back garden. Pools come in all shapes and sizes and can be built just about anywhere – even on a rooftop. However, it is important to blend the swimming pool into the backyard with careful planting and siting so it becomes a feature in your garden.

Planning your swimming pool

FORWARD PLANNING A swimming pool is often on the wish list for the backyard but due to budgets may not be built for several years. If you are starting your garden from scratch, and you would like a swimming pool in your backyard in the future, make space for it as you lay out your garden. This doesn't mean that you need to leave a space empty, waiting for the pool. The area should be earmarked for temporary gardens or as a play area but don't plant trees or erect any structures that will be difficult or expensive to remove. Also plan ahead for access as pool builders will need to bring in digging equipment and also will need to be able to take out soil and rock during the excavation process. Access can be through the garage on narrow blocks provided a door is included on garden side of the garage.

LOCATING YOUR SWIMMING POOL
The ideal place for the pool is in an open, sunny spot, visible from the house. This allows you to monitor activity in the pool from indoors, which is important when kids are using the pool. Pools can be any size or shape you want from a narrow lap pool or a small plunge pool where space is limited.
● Make the most of the view of the pool by investing in glass fencing. While still meeting safety requirements, a glass fence turns the pool into a feature and also allows the view beyond the pool to be enjoyed.

BACKWASHING In these days of water conservation you can make use of the water that is discarded when the pool filters are cleaned in a process called backwashing. If you have a large lawn you can discharge salt water without causing much harm. However, in small areas where the water is likely to spread into neighbouring properties it is best to let the water discharge down the drain.

The lush planting transforms this swimming pool into a tropical water feature.

LEAF-PREVENTION IDEAS Leaves dropping into the pool from overhanging trees are a perennial problem for swimming pool owners. Often they are blown into the pool from neighbouring trees and can even lead to unfortunate disputes between neighbours. The best way to prevent leaves from falling into your swimming pool is to invest in a simple pool cover. The cover will also keep the water in the pool warmer and will therefore increase the swimming season.

● Although most pool owners want to minimise the number of trees around their pool, trees do provide welcome shade. Deciduous trees are a great choice for pool-side planting for shade. As they drop their leaves in autumn, the pool can simply be kept leaf-free by using a pool cover through the cooler months of the year.

● Shady sails can be an alternative to a pool-side tree. You can select from a large range of colours and sizes. Sails are available at homeware and chain stores or can be custom made for your site.

PLANTS TO AVOID Plants that drop small leaves or leaflets, which are thorny or spiky, or attract lots of bees are best avoided near swimming pools. Some problem plants near swimming pools include cacti and thorny succulents, jacarandas, many conifers, roses and silky oaks.

POOL FENCES must be kept free of plants that could assist a child to gain access to the pool. Don't try to hide pool fencing with

Integrate the house and the swimming pool with a shade structure, such as a pergola.

When planting around a swimming pool, select plants that will not drop leaves into the water.

shrubs, strongly branched climbers or trees. Instead use soft foliage such as dwarf New Zealand flax or agapanthus.

HIBISCUS BRIGHTEN THE POOL-SIDE
Hibiscus (*Hibiscus rosa-sinensis*) are very popular pool-side plants in frost-free, warm to tropical climates. With brightly coloured flowers from reds and oranges through yellows to pinks and whites, hibiscus plants may be small and compact in size at around 1 m high or can be quite tall, growing up to around 3 m in height.

● When selecting hibiscus make sure that you choose varieties that will grow to a height and width that suits the space you have available. If there isn't space to grow hibiscus in garden beds around the pool, grow dwarf varieties in pots such as 'Ritzy', which has small bright orange flowers over many months.

● Spring pruning will set hibiscus plants up for good strong growth and a long flowering season. Keep the plants in full flower through the summer swimming season with a 5–7 cm deep layer of mulch of organic matter under each plant and monthly feeding with hibiscus food. Remove spent flowers regularly to encourage blooms.

Container gardening

Gardeners have long used plants in containers to add an extra dimension to their gardens, whether formal or informal. They brighten a windowsill or a balcony, and a large garden can benefit too: you can plant and replant them easily and move them about at will.

A garden in a pot

MAKE THE MOST OF YOUR SPACE
Gardeners have always had to be creative to optimise their use of space, especially in smaller gardens. To maximise your planting area, arrange pots at different levels: on the ground, on a pedestal or on a wrought iron latticework shelf. You could also position pots at higher levels: hooked onto railings, fixed on a wall in metal potholders or hanging from a canopy.

PRESERVE YOUR PRIVACY If you have a balcony, use plants to frame the view and provide a screen from the world outside. Grow climbing plants and evergreen bushes in a trough and hang window boxes and baskets around the windows. For the best flowering plants, consider star jasmine, petunia, lobelia or ivy geranium. To decorate a stairway, create a cascade of flowers by placing pots every two or three steps.

YOU DON'T HAVE TO BE CONVENTIONAL For centuries, thrifty gardeners have used almost any unwanted type of container to hold plants. Instead of buying special plant pots, you too can recycle salvaged items for planters. Plants will grow in just about anything that can hold potting mix and that has drainage holes. Try using galvanised metal buckets, old milk churns, saucepans or cans with holes pierced in them, either painted or left as they are. Architectural salvage – such as old chimney pots, clay pipes and butler sinks – can also be transformed into miniature gardens with old-world charm.
● Wooden half-barrels, wicker baskets and old wash boilers from scrapyards or antique dealers can also make attractive planters.

● Provide drainage holes in the base of all containers. Cover the holes with mesh so that the potting mix doesn't fall out.

WHAT KIND OF POTTING MIX? Don't use garden soil in containers, but use a potting mix specially formulated for the plants you grow. Look for potting mixes that are high-quality and meet the Australian Standard in either regular or premium. There are special potting mixes for terracotta pots, hanging baskets, orchids, roses, African violets, acid-loving plants, Australian native plants, bulbs and many other types of plants.
● Potting mixes are made from composted pine bark with added fertilisers and soil-wetting agents. Some also contain bark, gravel and other products for improved drainage and aeration.
● In large containers (larger than 30 cm) where plants may grow undisturbed for several years, it is possible to add bagged soil or compost to the potting mix. The larger the container and the plant, the higher the

For maximum effect, group pots together to show off contrasting textures and colours.

Many succulents have very decorative fleshy leaves. Complement them with a simple container.

percentage of soil needs to be – you can include a ratio of up to 50:50 potting mix to soil. The addition of soil reduces slumping in the pot which will be noticed when soil levels appear to drop. Soil added to the potting mix will also make pots heavier and less prone to blowing over in windy or exposed situations.

● One traditional gardening tip that you don't need to follow when using modern potting mixes is adding drainage materials to the base of pots. This is no longer necessary and indeed can adversely affect drainage in the pot and may also provide homes for unwanted pests such as snails and ants.

● To avoid potting mix washing through the drainage holes in the base of pots, cover the holes with a layer of mesh or shadecloth.

MAKE THE MOST OF EACH POT
To get the most impact from a container, consider growing a shaped or standard plant and then underplanting it with low-growing or cascading plants such as as convolvulus, mini mondo grass or trailing lobelia. You can maintain the standardised shape of the main plant with regular clipping.

KEEP SAUCERS EMPTY
You should regularly empty saucers or drip trays after watering your plants (and also after rain if the plant is outdoors) so as not to impede the natural drainage from the container. Many potted plants suffer root death because they've been allowed to stand in waterlogged containers.

● Water in saucers under pots may also provide a breeding area for mosquitoes.

● To improve container drainage, raise your pots slightly off the ground on pot feet, small blocks or bricks.

ROUGH UP THE SURFACE
Every couple of weeks, break up the crust of soil on the surface of the pots with a fork. This allows water to saturate the potting mix – your plants can die of thirst, even if watered, if the soil is impenetrable.

FEED YOUR PLANTS
If you have not included a slow-release fertiliser in your potting mix, make sure that 6 weeks after planting you start feeding your container plant with a high-potash feed. For a natural tonic, try seaweed extract as a foliar feed. Every spring remove the top 2 cm of potting

mix from containers that are permanently planted and replace it with fresh potting mix combined with a little fertiliser.

TOP TIPS FOR WATERING
Plants in pots are more dependent on you for water than those growing in the ground. Remember that hot or windy weather will dry out pots quickly, so keep a watchful eye on them in these conditions and be prepared to water them several times a day if needed.

● **LET IN THE RAIN** Check that there is nothing sheltering containers and window boxes from rainfall, and that the rain can penetrate the soil and will not simply run off the plants' foliage.

● **MULCH TO PREVENT DEHYDRATION** Protect large plants in pots from drying out by adding a layer of pebbles or glass beads on top of the potting mix.

● **USE GROUNDCOVER** Grow groundcover plants as an indicator of soil conditions at the surface of the pot. When they look limp you know that the top few centimetres have dried out, so the pot needs watering.

● **WATCH FOR SOIL SHRINKAGE** If the soil shrinks so much that it starts to come away from the side of the container, immediately plunge the pot into water. Allow the plants to drink for up to an hour.

To create an eye-catching focal point, choose an attractive pot and fill it with plants that trail and overflow.

Gardener's Choice

THE BEST PLANTS FOR CONTAINERS

FOR A PARTLY SHADED CORNER Enliven dark corners with bright colours and foliage. Plants that prefer or tolerate partial shade are begonia, bromeliads, ferns, fuchsia **1**, hellebore, hosta, hyacinth, hydrangea and impatiens.

ON A BALCONY IN FULL SUN Choose alyssum, brachyscome, cumquat, daisies **2**, gardenia, geranium and pelargonium (particularly trailing ivy geranium), Indian hawthorn, petunia (summer colour), succulents like kalanchoe 'Flapjacks' **3** and verbena.

IN AUTUMN OR WINTER Bowls of annuals and bulbs will cheer up a dull corner. Plant aster, calendula, marigold, pansy, primula and polyanthus. For small bulbs try crocus, daffodil (miniature varieties), snowflake and star flower (*Ipheion uniflorum*). Forced tulips, cymbidium orchids and hyacinths in flower are available at nurseries for instant colour.

A soft and springy carpet of green

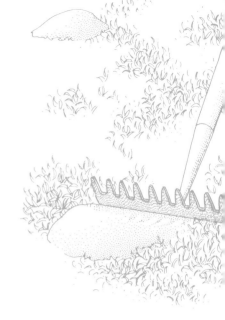

Whether it is a stretch of hard-wearing grass used by the family at weekends or an impeccable striped green sward, lawn provides an open space to give pace to your garden – it unifies the different sections and provides a foil for the colourful plants.

Establishing a new lawn

KEEP IT SIMPLE Sharp corners and complicated edges will deteriorate quickly, so the more straightforward the shape of your lawn, the longer it will last.

EASY CARE You can slope a lawn so that the rain penetrates the surface rather than running off onto patios or footpaths, but don't sow grass on a slope of more than 25 degrees. Consider laying a path from wherever your lawnmower is kept to the lawn.

GIVE IT AN EDGE Put in edging to avoid mowing your border flowers. Edging a lawn also helps define paths and flowerbeds and keeps the garden neat and easy to maintain. Traditionally, edges were made of terracotta ropework tiles or bricks, but any suitable materials can be used, from reclaimed building timber to logs.

TO TURF OR SOW? Sowing grass seeds is the simpler and cheaper option when laying a lawn, but for quick results lay turf. This can be done at any time of year, but avoid very wet, dry or cold spells. Many warm-season grasses are only available as turf.

MIX YOUR SEEDS Many grass seeds are used for lawns and each species or variety has its own particular properties. Some may be quick to establish; others wear well or provide different colours and textures. You need a mixture of different seeds to get an even lawn. Seeds are usually sold ready-mixed, but make sure you shake it well before sowing to ensure it is evenly spread.

WHEN TO SOW A LAWN The best time to sow grass seeds is in autumn, when they are without competition from weeds. In mild regions, sow until the middle of May. Germination is slower in spring, but you can sow in September if the soil is moist and warm enough, and the air temperature has reached 10°C. If you wait until summer, from November to February, the seeds won't be able to cope with the hot weather unless you water them with a fine rose once or twice a day.
● Check the packet to see how much you should sow. Mix the seeds with sand for even coverage and use more around the edges of the lawn, where the grass should be denser to cope with extra wear.

PREPARING THE SITE When the soil is dry, firm by treading the soil down evenly with your heels. Make sure there are no hollows that would make your mower scalp the turf. Do not do this when the soil is wet. Rake the soil to a fine tilth and leave it for a couple of weeks to allow weed seedlings to germinate. Then rake these away and level the soil again. A few days before you sow your lawn seeds, rake in some fertiliser containing nitrogen, phosphorus and potassium.
● You can sow seeds with a machine, with a grass seed hopper or by hand. Either way, scatter the seeds evenly, half in one direction and the other half at right angles to this.
● If sowing by hand, mark out your site into equal areas and weigh out how much you need per section.

● After sowing, rake the surface lightly. If the weather is particularly dry, water the seeds regularly to help them to germinate.
● Once the newly sown grass has reached a height of approximately 5 cm, cut it with a rotary mower with the the blade set to around 2 cm. This will encourage sprouting and thicken the grass.

Maintaining a lawn

LAWNS NEED AIR To keep a lawn really healthy, at the start of spring and in the autumn, get rid of any surface debris, then aerate and loosen the soil with a scarifier or spring-tined rake.
● The traditional way to aerate the soil is to use a garden fork. Drive it in using your foot, straight down and as deep as possible, moving it from side to side to enlarge the

Gardener's Choice

SEEDS FOR SUCCESSFUL LAWNS IN A COLD CLIMATE

A FINE FINISH Grasses such as bents and creeping red fescue are remarkable for their fine foliage, and they form an attractive dense lawn in a cold climate. They can be mown frequently to the shortest setting on your mower.

A GRASSY PATH OR PLAY AREA Kentucky bluegrass, ryegrass, tall fescue and yellow oatgrass are reasonably disease- and pest-resistant and hard wearing. Perennial ryegrass grows quickly and stays green in winter.

GRASS ON DRY GROUND Use Chewing's fescue (*Festuca rubra* 'Commutata'), creeping red fescue (*F. rubra* 'Rubra') or hard sheep fescue (*F. ovina*). In summer, creeping red fescue remains green the longest.

GRASS IN PARTIAL SHADE Ryegrass, creeping red fescue or rough-stalked meadow grass (*Poa trivialis*) can cope with some shade, although no grass will grow in complete shadow.

holes. Then water the ground, or wait for rain, and scatter some fertiliser. A good top-dressing is 4 parts silver sand, 2 parts loam and 2 parts compost.
● A less labour-intensive, modern method is to walk the ground using spiked shoes, or you can use a spiked roller.

RIGOROUS CHECKING It is important to give the lawn a quick check-over before mowing. Examine the grass, removing any lumps of earth and picking up stones, branches, windfalls or anything else that might damage the blades of your mower or spin off and break a window.

ALL ABOUT MOWING Only mow your lawn when it is actively growing. This can be weekly in summer but may only be fort-nightly or monthly at other times of the year. In times of drought most lawns do not need to be mowed unless they are receiving irrigation. To keep the lawn in good shape here is some good old-fashioned advice:
● Never cut off more than the top third of the grass. Mowing too closely can stress the lawn and expose the earth, which in turn encourages weed growth.
● The more a lawn is used, the longer the grass should be.
● Leave the clippings on the lawn as often as possible – they will break down quickly and feed the grass.
● After mowing, wait between 2 and 4 days and water well before applying fertiliser or herbicide (weedkiller).
● Never mow wet grass – wait for the grass to dry out after it has rained.

WATER WHEN THE TEMPERATURE IS COOLER Most established lawns should be able to recover from periods of drought, but in order to maintain a high-quality lawn you need to water often enough to keep up a healthy even green growth. On sunny days, droplets of water will form tiny lenses that can burn foliage. Therefore, the best time to water a lawn is either in the morning or in the early evening, to prevent scorching and reduce evaporation. Make sure you water thoroughly enough to moisten the soil to a depth of about 15 cm. To check that the ground is wet enough, you can use a bulb planter to remove a small cylinder of earth from a little-used corner of the lawn, replacing it carefully afterwards.

1 Dig out your future lawn with a garden fork. Rake the site then tread down the soil both firmly and evenly.

2 To give an even surface, you can also use a roller, particularly if your site is very uneven to begin with.

3 Mark out the site into areas and scatter seeds evenly, half in one direction, half at right angles to this.

4 Cover the seeds by raking lightly. Net the area to deter birds and, if the weather is dry, water regularly.

FEEDING THE LAWN Twice a year, in spring and autumn, 2 to 4 days after cutting the grass, apply an NPK (nitrogen-phosphorus-potassium) fertiliser to your lawn. Look for fertilisers formulated for lawns. Water the grass thoroughly to ensure that the nutrients dissolve into the soil without burning the grass roots.

● To revive a tired lawn, use a booster fertiliser, otherwise use a slow-release type or seaweed extract at the correct dilution.

Gardener's Choice

GRASSES FOR HEAT AND DROUGHT TOLERANCE

FINE LAWNS Couch lawns will give the fine foliage associated with closely mown lawns. They are high maintenance but rewarding. 'Santa Ana' and 'Tifdwarf' are among the best varieties to select for a fine lawn. Queensland blue couch will perform well in subtropical and coastal areas.

FAMILY NEEDS Most families want a lawn that looks good but is great for kids too. Some couch varieties such as 'Wintergreen' and 'Greenlees Park' strike a balance between fine blade and durability. These lawns turn straw brown in cold or frosty winters. Increasingly popular, especially in coastal areas, are the new generation soft-leaved buffalos. Bred for their drought hardiness there are many varieties coming on the market but look for 'Palmetto' and 'Sir Walter'.

ROUGH AND TUMBLE Where the lawn is really going to take a battering and you are wanting a lawn grass that's equal to it, select kikuyu. It is drought-hardy but will brown in frosty winters. One shower of rain will have it green and lush once temperatures warm. Its main drawback is its vigour. In summer it will need weekly mowing to keep it under control and it is wise to have a root barrier between kikuyu lawns and garden beds.

SHADE ZONES Although no grass will thrive in deep shade, several do well in filtered lights. In warm climates try Durban grass (also called sweet smother) under trees and in shaded areas. It has a coarse leaf blade and should be mown high.

● Do not apply nitrogen-rich fertiliser in the autumn, as too much lush growth late in the season can encourage diseases.

TOP TIPS FOR BEATING WEEDS Mow regularly to protect your grass from invasion by certain weeds by preventing them from running to seed in the first place. If it is already too late, or if your lawn is infested with low-growing weeds that are unaffected by mowing, remove them by hand. Although this can be hard work, particularly if your lawn is large or rather neglected, this traditional method is the least damaging to the environment. Alternatively you can invest in a selective herbicide that's safe to use on your particular lawn variety.

● **MANUAL REMOVAL** Dig out any long-rooted weeds such as daisies and dandelions with a long, narrow trowel, weeding tool or old blunt knife. You will find the task easier if the ground is soaked first. Afterwards, tamp the soil down and sow grass seeds or use a piece of runner to repair any bare areas, making sure it is protected from birds.

● **EXPOSE HIDDEN INVADERS** If your lawn contains many weeds, rake it before mowing. This exposes the stems of creeping weeds that would otherwise lie flat and therefore avoid the mower.

YESTERDAY'S SECRETS

VINEGAR, SALT, WATER AND ELBOW GREASE

Brown vinegar diluted with equal amounts of water is an effective weedkiller. Also try salt – it will burn weeds. Boiling water poured over weeds is a good way to remove them along the edges of paths or between cracks in paving. Raking removes moss and leaves from lawns. Sweeping with a stiff broom cleans up hard surfaces without the need for noisy leaf-blowers.

LAYING TURF IN ROLLS OR SQUARES

1 Dig over your site and incorporate some slow-release fertiliser.

2 If your site is hard to dig, use a mechanical rotavator, then level and firm the soil.

3 Rake the surface carefully: it should be perfectly flat. Lumps will cause bare patches when you mow.

4 Wet the soil with a fine spray to help the turf to bed in quickly. Make sure the ground is evenly moistened.

5 Unroll the turf or position the squares, following a straight line nearby, such as the edge of a border.

6 Butt the joins firmly to avoid creating holes, and stagger the joints. Finish with another generous soaking.

● **USE DYED HERBICIDE** If you have to resort to chemicals to tackle particularly persistent weeds, add some biodegradable dye to diluted herbicide in your watering can to enable you to see where you've sprayed and avoid going over the same place twice. Work in calm, mild weather (14–25°C) and use a less concentrated solution on a young lawn.

REPAIRING A BARE PATCH The easiest way to repair a bare patch in a prominent place in your lawn is to cut out the damaged area, including a little of the good turf immediately around it, and replace it with a piece the same size from a less obvious part of the lawn. Then fill in the place you took the turf from with some garden soil and a top layer of sandy soil, level the area, reseed or replant it and water it thoroughly.

FILLING A DIP Using an edging iron, cut a cross in the middle of the sunken area, then fold back the turf. Loosen the soil to aerate it, fill the hole with garden soil, replace the turf over it and put some sandy soil on top. Firm the area gently then sow seeds to fill in any gaps, and water.

MOSS IN YOUR LAWN? Prevention is better than cure and moss is normally an indication that your site is too shady, compacted, too wet or that you have mown the grass too severely.
● If regular raking, scarifying and aerating fails to get rid of moss, apply anti-moss fertiliser or chemical moss killer and remove blackened moss with a spring-tined rake. Don't throw the moss on the compost heap.

BUMPS, LUMPS AND HOLES There are a number of critters that like to feed in your lawn at night leaving mounds of dirt or holes in the lawn. Likely culprits include bandicoots and rabbits. Insects also make small earth mounds in lawns.
● Although bandicoot mounds look unsightly, they are doing you a favour by eating beetles and their larvae, which may be damaging the lawn. Fill in the holes regularly. If the damage is getting out of hand, wire the area with mesh to prevent access. A pile of mulch or compost may provide an alternative place for digging.
● Rabbits are probably feeding on tree or grass roots – wire mesh fencing around the perimeter is the only way to keep them away.

A wildflower meadow

STRIP THAT TURF! In an existing lawn with vigorous grasses, you may need to take up the turf to give your wildflowers a chance. Make sure you don't strip the topsoil with the turf. Because the meadow will not be mown as frequently as a lawn, eradicating weeds before you seed is also important.

REDUCE SOIL FERTILITY Remember not to apply fertiliser or remove any grass clippings for at least 1 year before you begin sowing your wildflower meadow. This actually prepares the soil for sowing by returning it to a more natural state.

GET A HEAD START Plant pot-grown wildflowers in the spring or autumn. These will give the meadow some cover while your seeds grow. Bulbs planted in autumn, such as ixias and freesias, will naturalise in a lawn.

SOWING THE MEADOW Use clumping grass such as tall fescue or ornamental grasses that won't compete with flowers. Scatter your wildflower mix in the early autumn or, if you live in a cold area, wait until spring.

LET THE SITE DECIDE Choosing which flowers to grow depends on whether your meadow is in shade or sun or has damp soil. In an open sunny site, use bellflowers, cornflowers, ox-eye daisies, paper daisies, poppies and scabiosas. In a damp site, plant ragged robin and meadowsweet.

MAINTAINING YOUR MEADOW It is best to cut a spring-flowering meadow from midsummer onwards to allow the flowers to seed. A summer-flowering meadow should be cut from early autumn and in the spring when growth starts. Leave summer and autumn mowings to shed their seeds before you collect them, but pick up the spring mowings straight away.
● When mowing a wildflower meadow, remember that it needs to be left longer than a lawn. Aim for a height of 8–10 cm. If your lawnmower will not adapt to this height and the area is fairly small, consider using a traditional method such as a scythe or shears. A whipper snipper will also do the job.

For centuries, colourful wildflowers have added grace and charm to grassy areas.

Bandicoots can dig holes in lawns as they search for grubs.

Setting out your boundaries

To block an unsightly view, create shelter or simply preserve your privacy, there are many reasons for enclosing a garden, and many ways of doing it. Whatever methods you choose, you can find an attractive way of protecting your garden from the outside world.

Consider the options

HOW HIGH CAN YOU GO? Any wall or fence that is built or extended over 1 m high will need planning permission from the local council. There may also be restrictions on height in the deeds to your house or in the local authority or highway regulations. Always check thoroughly before starting to build any walls or fences.

● The height of a gateway looks best if it is similar to that of the fence or wall. It extends the 'line' that you have created, giving an impression of harmony.

WHOSE RESPONSIBILITY? Boundary fences are the responsibility of neighbours, who jointly bear the cost of maintenance and repair. The style and quality of fencing should be determined by other fences in the neighbourhood. The extra cost for a more expensive style of fence may need to be borne by the neighbour who desires the more costly product. In cases of dispute over fences and boundaries seek legal advice or contact your local council.

RECYCLING IS BEST Stone walls are not cheap to build. To keep costs down, it is worth looking around for quantities of old stones in local demolition yards.

LAY THE FOUNDATIONS You will need to make a concrete footing for all walls, and this should be two or three times the width of your wall. About 40 cm is deep enough

for a simple, low wall. Put a layer of hardcore into a level trench, fill in with concrete and leave it to set for a couple of days.

QUICKER BRICKS Using 'combination bricks', which look like several bricks stuck together, will make building a wall much easier and quicker. Some are regularly shaped, others interlock for greater stability.

COPING A BRICK WALL To prevent water penetrating your wall, put a coping layer (a line of 'roof'-shaped bricks) on the top. It will also make the wall look finished. You can buy special curved coping bricks, but be sure to use ones that are wider than your wall so that they shed rainwater away from the bricks. Try pre-assembled coping in the form of sections of tiles or bricks already fitted together, and simply fix them to the top of your wall with cement.

With careful planting a wall is transformed from a boundary to a rugged and decorative garden feature.

WHAT TYPE OF WALL OR FENCE?

STONE OR BRICK WALLS The most solid way of enclosing your garden is a wall. But they are expensive and you may need professional help to build and repair them.

WOODEN FENCING Traditional paling fences are usually left to weather and grey with age. To enliven a paling fence consider using palings with decorative tops, painting the fence or substituting fibrecement panels.

METAL FENCES Many modern suburban gardens are now fenced with metal panels. Easy to erect, they can be pre-coloured and are termite- and weather-resistant. Metal fences also give instant privacy.

HEDGES A hedge can provide an attractive enclosure, an effective windbreak and shelter for wildlife. However, some types demand high maintenance and take up a lot of space. Hedges take several years to grow to size.

LATTICE PANELS Light lattice can be used with wooden fencing to open up a view, provide a framework for climbing plants or reduce the effects of wind.

CEMENT BLOCKS Small openwork blocks and cement panels can produce a similar effect to lattice. They are bulky and relatively expensive, but will last a long time. Cement fences that resemble wooden post and rail are also available. Although expensive they have the benefit of being long lasting, termite-proof and fire-resistant.

HOW TO IMPROVE THE APPEARANCE OF A CONCRETE WALL A wall made of concrete blocks is one of the strongest and most compact types of wall you can have. However, it does not look very attractive.
● Cover it with trellis or evergreen climbing plants such as star jasmine.
● Use a wooden cladding. Following the manufacturer's instructions, fasten the first row of cladding to the wall with screws. The following rows are then overlapped and held in place with the special fixings that are provided by the supplier.

A picket fence can be turned into a feature with the addition of an old-fashioned lichgate.

● Put the flat surface to good use and create a trompe l'oeil or false perspective effect. If you are artistically inclined you can paint one or, if you prefer, buy a ready-made trellis specially constructed to give this effect. If you add a judiciously placed mirror to an otherwise dull concrete wall you can give the appearance of space to your garden.

THE BENEFIT OF FENCES Fences require as much planning as walls, but are less expensive. They are quicker and easier to erect, require little specialised knowledge and it is easy to replace palings or panels later if necessary. Fences create a less solid effect than walls but can be decorative features in their own right. Many different types are available, from wooden paling to metal.

BUILDING A PALING FENCE A tumble-down paling fence isn't a good look for the backyard. If the fence posts and rails are in good condition then just replace the old palings with new ones. Consider unifying and updating the look of your fence with a coat of paint. An airless spray gun will make this a quick and easy job. If there's no fence to update, installing a new one is a job you'll need help with. Use treated timber rated for in-ground use, and remember to seal any cut ends. Fence posts should have the holes for the rails pre-cut.
● Put in the fence posts. Use a post-hole digger or an auger to dig a hole around 60 cm deep and the width of the post plus 20 cm all around to hold the cement.
● Put the posts in position, beginning with the end posts. Check all posts are straight (use a spirit level) and partially fill the hole

Raised beds add interest to the garden and are perfect for gardeners who find it difficult to bend to ground level. The good drainage raised beds offer is an added bonus. Remember that walls over 1 m high require engineering approval and should be built by a tradesman.

1 Mark out the area and calculate the number of bricks you need. Lay the first course on a thin layer of mortar spread on top of paving.

2 With a spirit level, check that the bricks are laid flat and adjust the thickness of the mortar if required. Leave gaps for drainage at intervals.

3 In the second course, place the corner brick endways on, for a strong bond. Stagger all joints for a strong wall.

4 Lay the top bricks upside-down for a neat finish. Allow the mortar to set, then fill with a drainage layer and good-quality garden mix.

with water. Tip in rapid-set cement, adding more water. The cement should reach the top of the hole. Hold posts in position until the cement sets (around 15 minutes).

● Run string lines between the two end posts and install the rest of the fence posts so the spaces for rails are level.

● Insert the rails through the posts. You will need to join the rails and these should butt together inside each post.

● Starting at one end, evenly space the fence palings. Secure with nails or screws and check each paling is vertical. Where a second layer of palings is being used, fence palings can be spaced 10 cm apart.

● Finish with a fence coping for a neat and weatherproof look.

MAKING HOLES FOR POSTS A pick or spade are the traditional tools but, if you can buy or hire a spade hole shovel (a spade with two blades and a scissor-like action) use it to dig a narrow straight-walled hole. Where there are many holes to be dug, or the soil is hard, use a hand or power auger.

POST HOLDERS As an alternative to digging a hole and filling it with concrete or stones, for wooden posts you could use metal post supports, known as fence spikes. The spikes must be driven into the ground perfectly straight, which is not always easy when the ground is stony or has roots growing across it. Make sure they are level before you put in the fence posts. Post supports are also susceptible to high winds so are really only safe to use in sheltered spots.

WATERPROOFING POSTS If your wooden fence posts have a flat end, shape the tops so that they come to a point, or make them rounded, so that water will run off and will not penetrate and rot the wood. Alternatively, fit ornamental caps to the top of the posts or seal cut ends with wood preservative.

CHECK YOUR PALINGS Fences are subject to extremes of weather and temperature. If you are building your own fence, inspect upright fence posts and palings carefully. Reject any that are warped or misshapen.

● If you buy wooden fence panels from a garden centre, check each one thoroughly. Avoid any that have broken, displaced or frayed slats. Buy posts in the same condition so that they all age at the same rate.

PAINTS AND PRESERVATIVES Modern wooden palings that are pre-treated with wood preservative need little maintenance. You can leave your fence to acquire a natural grey colour over the years, or apply a coat of varnish or paint.

● Bear in mind that you will probably have to renew varnish or paint every 3 to 5 years, which is not always easy after climbing plants have grown up it. Wood stains are a lower maintenance way of colouring fencing.

● Don't use creosote on areas that are likely to come into contact with human skin, as it is now considered dangerous.

● If possible, use a water-based, nontoxic wood preservative on trellis or other wooden fencing intended as supports for climbing plants, as this has few harmful effects.

LATTICE AS FENCING You can use lattice as lightweight, decorative fencing that stands up well to the wind, as long as it is securely fastened to upright posts. It can also be used fastened to the top of fences, or secured to walls to support climbing plants.

● For a totally natural appearance, make your own openwork lattice from any locally available pliable branches.

RUSTIC FENCING If you live in the country, unless you have young children or a dog, there is no need to use tall fencing or walls. A low fence will mark out your boundary and it will blend in with your surroundings.

● Picket fences, with their vertical, pointed wooden slats spaced evenly and fixed to horizontal rails, are traditional in country settings. They are popular in natural wood, or you can finish them with paint.

Retaining walls need drainage or weep holes so moisture doesn't build up leading to the collapse of the garden behind it.

YESTERDAY'S SECRETS

A LIVING WALL OF TURF
Use up spare turf to build a low retaining wall reminiscent of ancient times. First cover the turf to cut out the light or spray it with glyphosate, and leave it until the grass dies. Break the turf into strips 50 x 30 cm, and fold them in half along the short edge, with the soil on the outside. Lay these pieces like bricks directly onto prepared ground, sloping towards the area to be retained. You can even use the pieces to cover an existing low wall you wish to disguise. When the wall is complete, plant up the joints with ferns, ivy and primroses, adding compost in any gaps and watering well. You can also also add some stones for greater stability.

Dress up your wall or fence

TOP TIPS FOR DRAPING A FENCE Even if your fence already looks quite decorative, you may still wish to adorn it further with some pretty, light, climbing plants such as clematis or hardenbergia.

● **ADD WIRES FOR SUPPORT** Before your climbers start to grow, screw metal hooks or vine eyes into your fence posts or wall and stretch wire between them, keeping them taut so they can support the plants as they fill out and get taller.

● **AVOID IVY** All climbing plants whose tendrils can grow between the slats of a wooden fence can break them.

● **USE CONTAINERS** Containers can be suspended from a fence. Fence posts are usually the strongest points for anchorage.

● **FOR GOOD COVERAGE** Fast-growing annual climbers will quickly cover a new fence and don't have strong suckers or tendrils that could damage it. Suitable fast-growing plants are nasturtium, snow pea and sweet pea. For longer-term coverage, grow passionfruit vine, jasmine or golden hops. If you have room, you could instead try some of the shrubs that are suitable for training up a wall, such as ceanothus, *Cotoneaster horizontalis*, *Euonymus fortunei* 'Silver Queen' or sasanqua camellias.

This neatly painted picket fence covered in nasturtiums gives the garden a quaint and attractive rustic air.

PLANTING TO DISGUISE LONG, STRAIGHT LINES To shorten the appearance of a long, straight wall, break it up every 2 m or so with a group of plants with unusual shapes or foliage. The more a line is divided, the shorter it will appear.

● For shades of violet that produce a beautiful effect along a low brick wall, plant an edging of 'Johnson's Blue' geraniums, interrupted at regular intervals by clumps of mauve Siberian iris and a golden sedge with an upright habit.

● To complement most styles of fencing and a wide variety of flowering plants in the border, consider plants with grey leaves, such as dusty miller and lamb's ear, as well as aromatic herbs and species with purple or bronze-coloured foliage.

CHOOSE AN APPROPRIATE GATE Always choose gates that are in keeping with the style of your boundary fence. It would look odd if you installed a massive oak gate in a garden enclosed by a simple fence. But don't be afraid to mix, say, a painted wooden gate with an old brick wall.

A ROCKERY WALL Dry-stone walls have been a feature of the English country land-scape for centuries. If you are building one to create an old-fashioned country look, intersperse fist-sized blocks of polystyrene foam randomly between the stones. When the wall is finished, remove the pieces of foam and replace them with soil. You can then plant the pockets with rockery plants, such as aubrieta and saxifrage, which will add colour to the dry-stone wall and make it a point of interest.

The combination of wall and fence has been used to create a private and sheltered spot in which to sit and relax.

Add character to your front fence with shaped pickets and a gate that matches the fence.

CHAPTER 2

Flowerbeds and borders

Colourful bulbs for spring

Spring bulbs come in many colours, ranging from white, yellow and blue to pink, purple and orange. They awaken the garden from its winter sleep and usher in a new growing year. Whether they are in beds, naturalised in a lawn or displayed in pots, their colour delights the eye until the start of summer.

Best buys for bulbs

GO FOR QUALITY Sound bulbs are really essential for successful flowers. Choose your source carefully, avoiding places where you know the bulbs are exposed to humidity or excessive warmth.

● Buy bulbs as early as possible, preferably in March. This way you will have the widest choice and the bulbs will be healthier than end-of-season leftovers.

● Reject any bulbs that have started to grow – when they are showing a hint of white roots or a light green bud – or any that show signs of bruising, mould or insect pests.

● Pick bulbs whose outer skins are intact, as they will be better protected from disease. A split skin might be a sign that the bulb has dried out during storage.

FEEL THE BULB A healthy bulb should be firm and fleshy. Reject any bulbs that are withered or look dried out.

LARGE BULBS ARE BEST The greater the circumference of the bulb, the more nourishment it will contain for the bud inside, and the better the flower will be. Of course, larger bulbs are more expensive, but they are worth the price, especially if you want to grow them in pots or containers, where failed blooms would spoil the display.

● Hyacinths are the exception: keep the largest bulbs for growing indoors, as they produce heavy flowers that will not withstand outdoor conditions. For the garden, choose average-sized bulbs.

● To get good-quality flowers in the very first year of planting, choose bulbs with a circumference of around 8 cm for crocuses, 28 cm for hyacinths, 12 cm for narcissus and 11 cm for tulips.

SPECIAL OFFERS CAN BE TEMPTING
Bargain stocks of bulbs sold in bags often contain mixed varieties, predominantly the most common colours (for example, red and yellow tulips, or yellow narcissus). These bulbs usually differ in size, which means they will not all flower at the same time and will not produce a uniform visual effect. The smallest ones may not even flower at all. Take advantage of special offers like this only if you are buying bulbs for naturalising.

This old cherry tree is surrounded by stunning jewel-like ixias that have been allowed to naturalise for a spring show.

The bigger the bulb, the better its flower will be.

TAKE CARE WHEN YOU BUY LOOSE

Bulbs that are sold loose are often high in quality and large in size. You can find some interesting varieties, and buying in this way means that you can select the exact quantities you want. But be careful – it is all too easy to go home with a mixture of varieties because they can be difficult to differentiate. You could even end up with a mixture of species if you are not careful. If you are in doubt about the identity of any bulbs, plant them in rows in a corner of the vegetable garden and use them for cut flowers. Then any surprises will be pleasant.

Gardener's Choice

FOR A CONTINUOUS DISPLAY

Plan a succession of bulbs to flower from late winter to early summer. Spring bulbs are available in many colours, ranging from fresh white, bright yellow and blue to pretty pinks, purple and warm oranges. If you live in a very cold climate, there are many traditional bulbs to enjoy, but temperate and warm climates have their own selections.

LATE WINTER (cold climate): Crocus, cyclamen, snowdrop, winter aconite.

LATE WINTER (temperate climate): 'Erlicheer' daffodil, freesia, jonquil, snowflake **1**, narcissus.

EARLY SPRING: Bluebell, blue starflower (*Ipheion uniflorum*), daffodil, Dutch iris **2**, grape hyacinth, ixia, snowflake.

MIDSPRING Babiana, grape hyacinth **3**, tulip.

LATE SPRING: *Allium neapolitanum*, dietes **4**, *Fritillaria persica*.

SAVE MONEY WITH MULTIFLOWER

VARIETIES Some varieties of crocus, hyacinth, narcissus and tulip produce several flowers per bulb. Choose these varieties to increase the impact and length of the flowering period, as the individual blooms do not all open at the same time.

FIVE MONTHS OF BRILLIANT BULBS

For a continuous display of bulbs throughout the spring, plant a range of species and varieties. Begin with snowdrops, then move on to crocuses, hyacinths, narcissus and tulips, and try some unusual species too. By mixing the earliest and latest flowering varieties, you can enjoy a succession of flowers from June until November.
● Bring the wonderful spring atmosphere indoors by growing bulbs for cutting. If you have space, plant some in an out-of-the-way corner of the garden, and stagger them so you have cut flowers all spring.

Bulbs in your garden

A NATURAL EFFECT Plant bulbs in drifts about 30 cm wide, letting them meander between flowering shrubs and clumps of perennials. The spring growth of the other plants will hide the yellowing foliage of the bulbs after they flower.
● Try to mimic the way bulbs grow in the wild by scattering them at random over a patch of ground before planting, rather than arranging them in rigid rows.
● Leave a space of two or three times the width of the bulb between each one. Bulbs don't look cramped when planted closely; they look best in tight groups.

IN THE SUN BUT SHELTERED Bulbs that get too hot in the soil may flower while their stems are still short. This is often seen in bulbs like tulips and hyacinths that are growing in temperate climates. Keep bulbs cool by planting them at the recommended depth in the soil, covering the soil with a layer of mulch and selecting a spot so the soil is out of direct sun, particularly in spring, but the plants can grow up to the sunlight. Plants in pots should be crowded together to keep the pots cool.

Planting bulbs intended for display in a lawn into baskets, instead of directly into the lawn, has a number of advantages. It prevents the bulbs spreading into areas where they are not wanted and you can lift them and refresh the soil for the next year, or even change the bulbs completely.

1 Cut out a piece of turf the same size as your bulb basket and dig down to the depth required for your bulbs.

2 Arrange your bulbs in the basket, making sure that they are evenly spaced, then place the basket in the hole.

3 Fill the hole with fine soil and replace the turf. After flowering, remove the basket and store the bulbs indoors.

Eucharist lilies in bloom resemble daffodils but grow well in warm to tropical climates.

SETTLE IN THE BULBS If possible, plant bulbs as soon as you buy them or store them in a cool, dry place. Remember to wait until the soil has begun to cool off and the hot summer weather has passed – and you are sure autumn is here to stay. Depending on where you garden, spring-flowering bulbs are planted between late February and the end of April or very early May. Bulbs planted after early May or June will grow but may not reach their potential.
● Unlike seeds, which can be stored, spring-flowering bulbs need to be planted each year. Left unplanted they may shoot but fail to grow or simply rot away.
● Wait until mid-April to early May to plant out tulips. If you plant any earlier and the autumn is mild, they could start to show premature shoots, which would be very sensitive to frost.

FRITILLARIA AND LILIES LIKE DEEP PLANTING Unlike most bulbs, *Fritillaria imperalis* and lilies (except *Lilium candidum*, which requires shallow planting), should be planted a good 20 cm deep. Don't allow bulbs to dry out.
● When planting, tilt the fritillaria bulbs so they are not upright. If water soaks directly into the central growing point, the bulb will rot. You can identify the growing point of the bulb because it shows traces of the previous year's stem.

CYCLAMEN PREFER THE SURFACE Plant cyclamen close to the surface of the soil. If they are buried too deeply, they will not grow well and will not flower. Mulch them with leaf mould.

WHICH WAY IS UP? Bulbs should be planted with their tips uppermost. If you are unsure which end is which – and anemones can be quite confusing in this respect – it is best to lay the bulbs on their sides at the bottom of the hole.

USE A NATURAL FERTILISER If you do not have very rich soil, place the bulbs in a 2 cm deep bed of good compost or add a little blood and bone. This means you will not need to use chemical fertilisers, which often contain too much nitrogen and encourage foliage growth while weakening stems. Don't use fresh manure, because this will rot the bulbs.

GOOD BEDFELLOWS Spring bulbs go very well with country garden flowers such as forget-me-nots, foxgloves, pansies, primulas, violas and wallflowers.
● For the beauty of their evergreen foliage, also mix bulbs with perennials such as carex, *Phlox subulata* or saxifrage.
● In garden beds, the giant forget-me-not (*Brunnera macrophylla*), with its pretty heart-shaped leaves, is an excellent partner for the early-flowering bulbs, while the feathery inflorescences of lady's mantle (*Alchemilla mollis*) accompany the late-flowering bulbs particularly well.

PLANT EN MASSE To make a bold splash, create a bed using just one variety of bulb, all in a single colour. You will need to plant at least 20 bulbs, or even 50 to 100 if the area is large. For a more subtle but still dramatic effect, use different shades of the same colour, making sure that the bulbs will all bloom at the same time.

HIDE DYING FOLIAGE Once their display has finished, spring bulbs become rather unsightly. To hide their yellowing leaves and the empty space that follows, partner early-flowering bulbs with plants with thick summer foliage. In sunny spots, use species geraniums, *Nepeta* x *faassenii* 'Six Hill's Giant' and valerians. For semishade, use ferns, hosta and lamium.

NATURALISING BULBS IN YOUR LAWN Grass is the perfect setting for some bulbs. They adapt so well that they become naturalised, reproducing and forming ever-larger clumps of flowers. Once flowering is

For a natural look, scatter bulbs over the ground, then plant them where they fall.

Tulips prefer cool to mild climates with cold winters and make an impact when mass planted.

over, however, you must wait at least 7 weeks to mow the lawn, leaving the foliage to build up food reserves in the bulb for next year's flowers. Get around this by planting bulbs in areas you can develop as natural meadows, or around trees. Or choose bulbs that flower early in the season so that you can mow the lawn much sooner.

● If you have a sprinkler system on your lawn, avoid planting spring bulbs there. Frequent watering during their summer rest period will rot the bulbs.

● The spring bulbs that naturalise best in cool-climate lawns are bluebell, crocus, grape hyacinth, *Ornithogalum umbellatum*, *Scilla sibirica* and snowflake. Many species of narcissus also lend themselves to naturalising and are readily available, especially *Narcissus* 'Actea', *N. cyclamineus*, *N.* 'February Gold', *N.* 'Golden Harvest' and *N. pseudonarcissus*, the wild daffodil.

● In warmer climates try mass planting freesias, ixias and sparaxis in lawns or verges for a wild meadow look.

PROTECT TENDER NEW GROWTH From early winter onwards, it is not unusual for the tender shoots of bulbs such as anemones and tulips to start to just nudge through the surface of the soil. Protect them from pests

like slugs and snails by surrounding them with ash, crushed eggshells or sharp gravel known as horticultural grit.

● If the climate where you live is rather cold, protect your bulbs in winter with a layer of leaf mould. As well as being a good heat insulator, the leaves will absorb excess winter moisture, which could rot the bulbs.

DIVIDE AT THE RIGHT TIME Clumps of spring-flowering bulbs can be divided and replanted as soon as the leaves start to die back. However, the snowdrop (*Galanthus*) should be divided straight after flowering.

PLANT A BED OF BULBS

1 Choose an open spot that has nothing else planted in it. Mark out the edges of the flowerbed.

2 Remove the surface soil from this section to a depth of about 20 cm.

3 Lay out the bulbs pointing upwards. Replace the top-soil, covering the bulbs completely and firming down.

BULBS MAKE BEAUTIFUL CUT FLOWERS Using a sharp blade, cut flowers early in the morning or late in the evening. Take as few leaves as possible.

● **KEEP THEM COOL** Place the flowers in a bucket of cold water for several hours – they will soak up the water and will keep longer. But if you've ever wondered why tulips bend and droop in a vase, this is because they have become waterlogged. They need only a little water to keep them at their best.

● **SEPARATE NARCISSUS** Keep stems in their own bucket of water overnight so they release their toxic sap, which harms other flowers and makes them fade. They can be mixed with other flowers the following day. To be sure, change the water every morning.

● **ENCOURAGE LARGE FLOWERS** Spray with a foliar feed as soon as flower buds appear.

SCATTERED ON THE LAWN For a natural look, scatter several handfuls of bulbs over a mown lawn and use a bulb planter to plant them where they fall. Replace the plug of soil and turf extracted by the planter.

Growing bulbs in pots

CLAY OR PLASTIC? Clay pots dry out quickly so use them for bulbs that like well-drained potting mix, such as irises and tulips. Keep plastic pots for species such as bluebells that grow under trees or prefer damp soil.

PLANT CLOSE TOGETHER If you are planting bulbs of the same variety, go for a massed effect and pack them in tightly.
● Choose a pot that is at least 15 cm deep and as wide as possible, so that the pot doesn't hinder the bulb growth.

PLANTING IN STAGES For a container that's bright with blooms from the beginning until the end of spring, plant bulbs with complementary flowering periods, such as crocus, grape hyacinth, narcissus and tulip. The largest bulbs need to be planted at the greatest depth, so place narcissus at the bottom of the pot, followed by a layer of potting mix. Then space out the medium-sized tulip bulbs around them, making sure they are not directly over the ones beneath.

Cover with a layer of potting mix, then finish off with the small grape hyacinth and crocus, with a final 2 cm layer of potting mix.

WATER WISELY AND WELL Water regularly but moderately, giving a little more during and after the flowering period. As bulbs hate stagnant water, don't stand pots in saucers as this restricts good drainage.

Out of season flowers

ENJOY WINTER FLOWERS If you've seen tulips or hyacinths in full flower for Mother's Day or even earlier, you have probably wondered how they've been encouraged to flower completely out of season as these are spring-flowering plants. These bulbs are forced into flower by being exposed to artificially cold temperatures.
● Can forced bulbs be replanted for flower-ing again in spring? Sadly, most forced bulbs fail to reflower so are best discarded as their flowers die. If you want hyacinths or tulips to bloom again in spring, buy a packet of bulbs when you would normally buy your potted flowers in autumn.

Spring bulbs, such as narcissus, flourish in the dappled light beneath a cherry tree in blossom.

For a striking display of bulbs in a pot, arrange them very close to each other.

Enjoy the perfume and colour of hyacinths by planting a collection in individual pots for your windowsill.

HYDROPONICS MADE EASY If you grow a hyacinth or amaryllis bulb in a narrow-necked vase filled with water, leave a space at least the width of a finger between the base of the bulb and the liquid. The humidity in the air pocket encourages healthy root growth and the gap prevents the bulb from rotting.

GROWING HYACINTHS IN WATER

1 Select a light position for the glass holder, and fill it with water up to the neck.

2 Choose a good-sized, healthy bulb and place it in the neck, top uppermost.

3 The water should be 1 cm below the bulb so that it does not rot.

4 The bulb will put out roots and produce leaves and a flower.

CHINESE STYLE The Chinese method of growing bulbs on fine gravel lets you appreciate the root growth as well as the beauty of the flowers, as you can see the roots as they grow. The paperwhite narcissus or the yellow 'Soleil d'Or' will give good results as will colchicum.

● Choose a transparent glass bowl that is approximately 10 cm deep and then fill it with alternate layers of sand, gravel and clay beads. Make a bed of bulb potting mix over these layers and then position the bulbs close together on top. Support the bulbs by spreading a layer of fine gravel around them, just letting the tips show through. Finish by carefully filling the bowl to within 1 cm of the base of the bulbs with water containing crumbled charcoal, which will keep the growing medium sweet.

LIFE AFTER POTTING Although you can't regrow the same bulbs in this way year after year, you can get them to flower in the garden in subsequent seasons in the garden. Remove the faded flowers – but not the foliage – and feed the bulbs with a flower fertiliser every other watering. When the leaves begin to yellow, stop watering and feeding them. You can place the bulbs in the garden or repot less-hardy species, such as amaryllis, in new potting mix.

● You can even replant bulbs grown in water, but be patient. They usually take 2 or 3 years to flower again.

YESTERDAY'S SECRETS

HIGH ACHIEVERS
Some bulbs carry with them a certain cachet as they are known to be hard to grow. If you can grow these bulbs successfully fellow gardeners mentally award you with a 'badge of honour' as they recognise your gardening prowess. On this list are fritillaria, lily-of-the-valley and snowdrop, which all need a cool climate to grow well. In a temperate climate, gardeners with beds of long-stemmed tulips automatically get the nod of achievement from fellow gardeners.

Snowflakes (top) are the best choice in a warm climate – only attempt snowdrops (bottom) if you live in a cold or mountain zone.

Caring for bulbs when flowering is over

NOURISHING FOLIAGE Once your bulbs have finished flowering, remove the faded blooms to prevent seeds from forming, which exhausts the bulbs (see below left). Don't remove any foliage, as the bulbs need their leaves to restore their strength for flowering in the following year. You can help them by watering regularly and feeding with blood and bone or organic fertiliser to provide the necessary nutrients.
● While the foliage is still green, it is a good time to dig up and divide dense clumps of small bulbs such as anemones, crocuses, snowdrops and winter aconites.
● Only once the foliage has become yellow and dry should you cut it. When you do, cut close to the ground, and mark out where the bulbs are so you don't accidentally disturb them when weeding or digging in your garden. Lift the bulbs at this stage if you live in a humid climate or have poorly drained soil over the summer months.

PREVENT DRYNESS It may be necessary to water narcissus and wild daffodil bulbs during the autumn if it is very dry. The flower buds are formed during this period and a lack of water will dim the beauty of their late winter to spring show.

KEEPING DISEASE AT BAY A light sprinkling of flowers of sulphur before the summer rest period protects bulbs from disease and mould (see below centre). Also use it before planting – put the bulbs in a paper bag with the powder and shake it vigorously. You can buy flowers of sulphur from most garden centres and chemists.

SUMMER HIBERNATION If you prefer to remove bulbs once their flowers have faded to avoid the sight of yellowing foliage, lift them carefully with a fork, keeping the soil around the bulb.
● Dig a trench in a semishaded little-used corner of your garden and put a plastic net or wire mesh at the bottom, letting it overlap the ends of the trench.
● Set the bulbs in the trench and cover them with soil, leaving the foliage exposed.
● Water the bulbs thoroughly during dry spells. Once the foliage has shrivelled and faded, they can be lifted for storing. Simply pull out the net and shake off the soil, then remove the dead leaves.
● Dry the newly cleaned bulbs in a well-ventilated place for a few days, then place them, uncovered, on a bed of sand in shallow boxes.
● Store them in a dry, dark and cool room or garage until replanting in autumn. Never store bulbs that are damp or have dead or damaged skins.

BEWARE OF RODENTS To protect your stored bulbs from rodents, place the bulbs in old pantihose or stockings with some dry sand (see below right). Rats and mice hate synthetic fibre and are unlikely to attempt to nibble through it. Even so, check the bulbs regularly and remove any that show the slightest signs of rot or damage.

A WATER-FREE DIET FOR YOUR TULIPS Originally from mountainous regions of the Middle East, tulips like hot, dry summers in well-drained soil. These are difficult conditions to provide in mixed beds, so it is best to lift them as soon as the foliage has yellowed and store them in a cool, dry place all summer before planting out again in the autumn. To avoid this time-consuming chore, plant them under stone-fruit trees, which dry out the soil in summer.

1 After the foliage has dried completely, dig up the bulbs and place them on a layer of dry sand in a crate.

2 Space them out well and make sure none are touching and sprinkle them evenly with flowers of sulphur.

3 Cover the bulbs with another layer of sand until only their tips are showing.

4 When the bulbs are covered to their tips, store them in a dark, cool, dry place, safe and well away from rodents.

Far left: Remove spent flowers to stop seeds forming and allow all the plant's energy to be directed into the bulb and next year's blooms.
Left centre: Dusting flowers of sulphur over stored bulbs will reduce fungal problems.
Left: Store bulbs in a section of pantihose to keep rats away.

Bulbs for a spectacular summer and autumn

Bulbs that flower in summer and autumn are a magic ingredient in the garden. They extend the colourful show over many months and look fresh after other flowers have begun to fade in the summer heat. Plant them in spring and then sit back and enjoy the parade of blooms.

Planting and tending tips

HEALTHY PURCHASES Buy your bulbs as soon as they appear on garden centre shelves or market stalls. This way they have less chance of being damaged by poor storage.
● Although the largest bulbs are not guaranteed to produce the best flowers, don't buy bulbs that look unusually small or poorly developed in comparison with the normal-sized bulbs of the species. They may not have grown properly or they may have some type of disease. Choose bulbs that are plump, firm and uniform in appearance. They should not be marked and their skin should not come away easily.
● If gladioli corms are pink because they have lost their papery brown tunic, don't buy them. They may be damaged.

THE BEST SOIL Most bulbs like light, well-drained soil. If your soil is heavy and has a tendency to become waterlogged, improve it by digging in gypsum and organic matter such as compost. If the soil is still poor, create raised beds or grow bulbs in large pots.
● Soil that is too light and porous for other plants is ideal for growing bulbs. Plant them on top of a layer of garden compost or well-decomposed organic matter.

PLANT LILIES IN THREES For a beautiful show from the first year on, plant large lilies in soil enriched with plenty of organic matter such as leaf mould. Plant them in groups in flat-bottomed holes measuring

Crinum lilies, also known as spider flowers, produce striking summer flowers.

50–60 cm in diameter. In each hole, add a handful of coarse sand for drainage then put three bulbs in a triangle and firm them in. This guarantees an attractive arrangement.

SUMMER-FLOWERING BULBS
● **BLOOD LILY** This bold round flower gets its common name because of its vibrant red colour. Blood lily (*Scadoxus*) will grow in sun or light shade and flowers in summer.
● **CRINUM LILY** Although some species are native to Australia, where they are known as spider lilies, the spectacular garden varieties come from the tropics and subtropics. Plant in sun or part shade in a well-drained soil and protect flowers from snails.

AUTUMN-FLOWERING BULBS
● **AUTUMN CROCUS** Plant autumn crocus around the base of shrubs and at the bottom

Clumps of daylilies bloom throughout the summer months and into autumn.

Measurements marked on a trowel will guide correct planting depth.

Close plantings of lilies support each other and make a statement in any garden.

of slopes. They will then peep through grass or other foliage and make room for themselves between clumps of perennials. The flowers will appear before the leaves, which follow in early spring.

● **BELLADONNA LILIES** These bulbs are survivors. Long after the original house and garden has disappeared, a clump of belladonna lilies will still bloom each year with fragrant trumpets. Pink, or sometimes white, *Amaryllis belladonna* blooms appear before the leaves, which then grow through winter.

DEADHEADING TIPS Remove dead flowers from plants such as amaryllis, crinum and dahlia and they will grow back more vigorously. When deadheading dahlias, cut off the flower and its stem just above the first pair of leaves. For plants that bear flowers at the top of a floral spike, such as gladioli, remove individual flowers by pinching them off at the stem beneath the flower. Cut the spike at its base when the flowers have died.

TENDER OR HALF-HARDY PLANTS
Gardeners who live in temperate regions may be able to leave dahlias in the ground once they have finished flowering. However, in cold areas, the tubers must be lifted and stored in a dry, dark and frost-free room or garage, because the fleshy roots are very sensitive to cold and moisture in winter.

HOW DEEP SHOULD YOU PLANT?
Planting depths relate to the depth of the soil between the tip of the bulb and the soil surface, not the depth of the hole. As a rule of thumb, bulbs should be planted at a depth equal to at least twice their height. However, if your soil is very light, then plant them at

a depth equal to three times their height. You can gauge the correct depth by using a trowel marked with graduated measurements.
● Many summer-flowering bulbs prefer to be grown so that they are not completely buried in the soil.

Divide and multiply

NEW BULBS FOR FREE If a clump of bulbs becomes very congested, gently uproot it after flowering and divide it. This will give the mother bulb a new lease of life and generate a flush of new shoots. Shake the soil off gently and remove the young bulbs. These offsets should come away from the original bulb easily. If they don't, it is because they are not yet mature – in which case don't force them or you may end up damaging the plant. Replant the mother plant and its offshoots immediately.

ANOTHER METHOD OF MULTIPLYING
Some varieties of allium and lily, such as 'Enchantment', produce bulbils that appear on stems or in leaf axils during the summer

Gardener's Choice

TROPICAL CHOICES

Canna 'Tricolor' **1** has striped foliage and peach-coloured flowers. Shell ginger **2** brings an exotic touch to a warm climate garden. This red ball of flowers belongs to the blood lily, *Scadoxus multiflorus* **3**.

months. Carefully remove them, dust them with flowers of sulphur and put them in a plastic bag along with damp moss. Keep them cool but free from frost. In the spring, plant them in small pots filled with multi-purpose potting mix, and place them in a sheltered spot in half shade.

● Wait a year before replanting them in the garden and they will flower better.

● Crocosmias, crocuses and gladioli also produce offsets around their corm. Remove these and then replant them in a small box kept somewhere that is cool and sheltered. Water them in spring, then put the young plants in the ground. Crocus corms will flower the following year whereas gladiolus will take 2 to 3 years.

BE GENTLE WITH YOUNG PLANTS Use a dibber or small bamboo cane to set your new plants into the garden. The roots are fragile and the aerial shoots are easily broken if you are too heavy handed, but a dibber will make holes of the right size, into which you can easily insert the plants, firming lightly to remove any air pockets.

Solving common problems

CHEMICAL-FREE POT TRAPS Earwigs are one of the worst enemies of bulbs, damaging their flowers and leaves. Instead of spraying them with insecticide, try a simple, chemical-free trap. Cook a jacket potato, carefully scoop out most of the contents, leave it to cool and then place it among your plants. The earwigs will climb into the jacket shell to feast. All you have to do is remove the potato jacket with its occupants – but do it gently, because these small pests are quick to escape. Screwed up newspaper and upturned pots will also act as earwig traps.

WATCH OUT FOR SOFT ROT If your irises show signs of rotting at the base of the outside leaves, check your soil is draining properly. If the soil is too wet, damaged root stock can be invaded by bacteria, which attack rhizomes and leaves, causing them to rot. You can smell the decay. Destroy the plant immediately, then lighten the soil to improve drainage for other irises.

1 Cut the stems 15 cm from the ground and dig up the tubers. Label the plant if you have more than one clump.

2 Allow the tubers to dry for several days, then clean them gently with a brush, removing most of the soil.

3 Sprinkle the tubers with flowers of sulphur to prevent fungus from growing during storage.

4 Trim all the stems again, 10 cm from the tubers, to complete the preparations.

5 In a clean box, position the tubers. Cover with sawdust or dry sand to the base of the stems.

6 Ensure all the tubers are labelled and put the box in a cool, dark, well-ventilated, frost- and vermin-free place.

BEWARE OF SCORCHING Iris rhizomes protrude above the soil's surface and, because they are exposed, they are prone to damage. When mulching or top-dressing with animal manure, avoid covering them with organic material, even if it is well decomposed, as this will cause scorching.

BEAUTIFUL FLOWERS AT STAKE The weight of large dahlia blooms often causes the stems to bow down to the ground and snap. Three bamboo canes inserted in the

SUMMER BULBS AT THEIR BEST

DAHLIAS 1 The large-flowered hybrids are striking everywhere but are particularly so in big flowerbeds.

GINGER LILIES (*Hedychium gardnerianum*) **2** Fragrant heads of yellow or cream flowers (*H. coronarium*)

on tall canes give a touch of the tropics even to cool-summer gardens. Happy in the shade of trees, they like moist, rich soil. Prune after flowering.

IRISES 3 and **MADONNA LILIES** (*Lilium candidum*) **4** Imposing blooms will grace formal flower-beds in very late spring and early summer.

GLADIOLI 5 Their upright habit can make them difficult to grow with other bedding plants. They look their best in beds on their own.

DAYLILIES 6 These long-flowering lilies can bloom from late spring to autumn. There are evergreen and deciduous forms. Grow in full sun.

1 2
3 4

5 6

ground in a triangle around the clump and ringed with string or raffia two-thirds of the way up, will hold the foliage and flower stems together. Position the stakes before planting to avoid damaging the tubers.

DISBUD YOUR DAHLIAS To get the biggest blooms, remove secondary flower buds, leaving just one bud on each stem. If you are worried about losing your only flower in bad weather, disbud every other stem to still enjoy a dazzling display.

BANK UP YOUR GLADIOLI If you cannot stake gladioli or plant them in dense groups, build up a small mound of soil at their base for support or plant them in a sheltered area.

Bulbs for every setting

A SPLASH OF COLOUR BENEATH THE
TREES Autumn crocus and cyclamen are excellent for creating a carpet of flowers under tall trees. They naturalise readily and will eventually cover the ground entirely, which is a definite advantage in areas where grass struggles to grow.
● In spring, plant autumn-flowering crocus such as colchicum and *Crocus speciosus* with creeping bugle, for autumn flowers.

LILIES FOR DAMP SHADE Lords and ladies (*Arum italicum*) are planted in autumn. A handy filler for a shady area, this lily needs no maintenance and is very robust. It will naturalise spontaneously (indeed it can become weedy) and regrow year after year, spreading its beautiful green foliage marbled with white, which is renewed in autumn and lasts throughout the winter. As an added attraction, its flowers are replaced in late summer by clusters of decorative berries which turn bright red.
● Arum lilies (*Zantedeschia aethiopica*) come into their own in the damp or boggy areas of your garden, particularly in shade. They will also do well beside a pond. The species is weedy in some areas so it is a good idea to grow the compact 'Childsiana', the pink-flowered 'Pink Marshmallow' or the spectacular 'Green Goddess'. Plants flower in summer and can be divided in autumn.

The glorious pink flowers of nerines appear in autumn before the leaves.

PLANTING BULBS IN CREVICES The autumn-flowering crocus can grow through the sometimes dense foliage of rock-garden plants such as aubrieta, and in the small crevices created in dry-stone walls. Plant autumn-flowering crocuses in a little soil and cover them with gravel.

Arum lilies enjoy a moist, shaded spot in the garden.

DIVIDING RHIZOMATOUS IRISES

To ensure they continue to flourish, irises need to be divided approximately every 3 years in late spring after flowering, or during the autumn months.

1 Dig up the rhizomes carefully, using a fork to lift as much of the root growth as possible.

2 Take out the rhizomes intact, brush them off and cut the stem into 10–15 cm sections with a sharp knife.

3 Each division should have several roots and leaves, or a bud. Trim the leaves to half their length.

4 The rhizomes can rot where they have been cut. Avoid this by spraying the wound with flowers of sulphur.

5 Replant the rhizomes. In heavy soil, leave the tops exposed; in light soil, plant just below the surface.

6 Space them 25–50 cm apart, depending on the variety, and water each divided plant thoroughly.

DISCOVER IRISES All irises prefer a sunny position and can be grown from rhizomes or bulbs. Rhizomatous types prefer drier soils as damp soils encourage disease. Although their flowers are beautiful, they can be untidy when not in bloom. The dwarf forms of bulbous iris flower in early spring, while the taller Dutch or English varieties flower in late spring and early summer, and provide excellent cut flowers.

GROW CROCOSMIA FOR LATE COLOUR
The scarlet, orange or yellow hues of crocosmia will brighten up even partially shaded sites, if they are well drained and sheltered. These plants are prolific and spread rapidly and may become weedy. Divide them in spring.

PLANNING A FRAGRANT GARDEN
Plant the hardy regal lily (*Lilium regale*), which tolerates all growing conditions, at the entrance to your garden. For sweet scents in late summer and autumn, opt for *Lilium speciosum*, a large Japanese lily which is also highly perfumed, but needs to be planted in a sheltered position safe from the first frosts.

STAR PERFORMERS FOR SUMMER
Alliums and lilies get top billing for their performance and versatility. Hardy and easy to grow, they will grace flowerbeds, borders, pots and even the vegetable garden. All lilies prefer light shade, though Martagon lilies will naturalise in large spaces and meadows. Alliums flourish in full sun in any type of well-drained soil and prefer to be planted in autumn. The giant garlic (*Allium giganteum*), though a popular choice because it looks so spectacular, can grow to a height of 1.8 m, so if your garden is exposed and windy, it is better to choose a shorter option.

SHADE-LOVING LILIES Many lilies, such as *Lilium superbum*, flourish when lightly shaded by trees, allowing the plant to have its head in the sun but its roots in cool ground. If you don't have trees with light foliage, plant your lilies with perennials that will provide protective cover as they grow.
● Ensure that your lilies thrive for many years without artificial fertiliser by preparing the ground well for them. Add leaf mould to the soil, plus some sand if the ground is heavy. Mulch with well-decomposed compost every autumn.

Begonias will thrive in a trough and make a stunning display in the summer garden.

A LASTING BOUQUET Gladioli are perfect for cut flowers and can last up to 12 days in a vase – if you follow two basic rules. The first is to pick the flower spikes when the buds at the base of the stem are just starting to open. The second is to remove the two unopened top buds and pinch off dead flowers every day.

LATE BLOOMERS Some bulbs are planted in late spring and autumn for flowers at the end of summer and early winter. This is the case with the plants *Amaryllis belladonna*, colchicum, *Crocus speciosus* and nerine.

SUMMER STUNNERS If you like bold colour and form, then make room in your garden for dahlias. There are so many hybrids and colours available, flowering from summer to autumn, that there is one for every occasion. Combine them in groups of three or five with other late bedding plants. The dwarf species are ideal in pathside borders, flowerbeds and containers of all types, and large-flowered dahlias look good along walls. Give your vegetable garden some old-fashioned charm by planting rows of dahlias to provide spectacular flowers for cutting.

WINDOW DRESSING Summer bulbs are ideal for planters and window boxes. All they need to flower is some potting mix. Plant them singly in pots three or four times their size in diameter, or combine them with a flowering annual or a deciduous perennial in a larger tub. Tuberous begonias mix well with other summer plants.

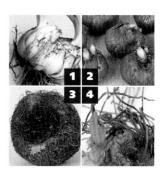

Year-round colour for your garden

Familiar to every old-fashioned gardener, annuals and biennials never fail to delight. These abundantly flowering, short-lived plants bring brilliant colour to lattices, arches, banks and flowerpots. They are easy and inexpensive to grow, and their innocent charm will take you back to a simpler, gentler time.

The art of sowing

GET OFF TO A GOOD START Conditions in the first 2 weeks after sowing will determine an annual plant's strength and beauty for the rest of the season. To help annual seeds germinate quickly and to ensure that the plants develop strong roots, sow them in mild weather, on moist, well-prepared soil. If the ground is poor and the weather is too warm, the seeds will produce spindly and feeble plants.

FOR CONTINUOUS FLOWERS Annuals have brief lives and need to be replaced at the end of their flowering period. For a regular supply of spring and summer flowers, sow seeds in trays at intervals of between 2 and 4 weeks, starting in late winter. Some gardeners use this method to replenish their borders several times a year.

SOWING SEEDS In warm and frost-free climates seeds from spring and summer annuals can be sown in either autumn or late winter to give flowers that will bloom in the spring and summer. In cold or frosty areas, sow seeds in early spring.

SOW BIENNIALS FOR SPRING COLOUR In late summer to autumn sow daisies, campanula, forget-me-not, foxglove, polyanthus, viola, wallflower and other biennials. Plant the seedlings out into their flowering positions in autumn. They will spend the first year producing leaves and will flower the following spring.

HARDY CHOICES FOR BEGINNERS Some species put up with all manner of mistreatment and still manage to germinate well. If you are new to gardening, start with these tolerant favourites.

- **COSMOS** From late spring to autumn, its graceful white, pink or deep red flowers are carried on long slender stalks 80–150 cm high. The foliage is delicate and feathery.
- **SCARLET RUNNER BEAN** As well as producing edible beans, this annual flowers from summer to autumn, thus earning its place in many cottage gardens. Its foliage is abundant, it puts out white or bicoloured flowers and the plant will climb to 1.8–2.4 m.

Annuals and biennials give a dazzling show of colour.

To protect freshly dug soil, stand on a board while sowing seeds into the centre of a garden bed.

ANNUALS FOR SUMMER DISPLAY

Many plants can be cheaply and easily raised from seed, either in punnets or sown straight into the ground (direct-sowing).

SOW IN PUNNETS

JULY–AUGUST Antirrhinum, begonia, cleome, cosmos, dahlia, gazania, gerbera, impatiens, limonium, petunia (below), phlox, portulacca, salvia and sweet pea.

AUGUST–SEPTEMBER Plant out frost-hardy seedlings from early August but frost-tender plants such as petunia should not be planted out until all threat of frost has passed.

IN AUTUMN Hardy annuals, such as candytuft, Californian poppy, cornflower, larkspur, linum, marigold (*Calendula*), nemophila, nigella, paper daisy, poppy (*Papaver*), rudbeckia, scabiosa, silene, sweet alyssum and sweet pea. Transplant directly in place when they reach 3–4 cm. They need to be sheltered. In spring these young plants have a feeble root system. Do not move them again or you might lose two-thirds of your crop in their final position.

DIRECT-SOW

AUGUST Anchusa, arctotis daisy, Californian poppy, *Chrysanthemum carinatum*, clarkia, cornflower, paper daisies, *Gaillardia*, lobularia, and marigold (*Calendula*).

IN SEPTEMBER Amaranthus, convolvulus, cosmos, paper daisies, godetia, love-in-a-mist, nasturtium, sunflower, Virginian stock and zinnia.

● **MALLOW** From summer to autumn, graceful, pastel cups stand out against the blue-green foliage of the mallow (*Lavatera*). Clusters of stems that can reach 60 cm in height make a handsome, branching clump.

● **MARIGOLD** The pot marigold (*Calendula*) is a favourite in the country garden for its pretty orange to yellow, sometimes pink-tinged, single or double flowers. The plants flourish for many months, even flowering throughout winter.

AVOID SEED MIXTURES Assortments are a bad idea. The pack may contain an odd mix of varieties called 'scented', 'wild', 'for shade' or 'for dry ground'. Often, the pack doesn't provide specific information on each variety, so you won't know the correct conditions for successful planting. The result tends to be disappointing, with one or two prolific varieties taking over. Instead, buy packets and make your own mixes.

DON'T USE FRESH MANURE Even if it is well decomposed, fresh manure contains too much nitrogen for seeds. This makes the plants produce too much leaf and stem growth, at the expense of robust flowers. Sow on ground that was manured 2 years previously, or follow a centuries-old gardening practice and enrich the soil with a green crop such as mustard or clover.

BUY SOME PLANTS IN PUNNETS Some plants are difficult to grow from seeds. Punnets are a better option for aster (*Callistephus*), bells of Ireland (*Molucella*), calceolaria, gerbera and lisianthus. *Begonia semperflorens*, busy lizzie (*Impatiens*), petunia and verbena are available as young plants.

NEWSPAPER ENCOURAGES SEED GERMINATION Seeds sprout more easily when they are covered during the daytime with damp newspaper, especially in very hot weather. Keep the paper in place with tent pegs or markers stuck in the ground. This covering will also prevent the birds from pillaging your seeds.

COOL-LOVING PLANTS Foxglove and primula seeds like to be covered with a fine layer of organic matter, such as leaf mould or garden compost, which keeps the soil cool and damp. Professionals use vermiculite, a light expanded mineral.

YESTERDAY'S SECRETS

GIVE YOUR PLANTS A HEAD START

If you live in cooler regions, start sowing a few seeds during the autumn and winter in a cold greenhouse or cold frame. Sow large seeds individually in plug modules and smaller seeds in pots or seed trays, then prick them out into individual pots later. Be sure to label all your seeds. You can also buy established plug plants from specialist nurseries or garden centres. Wait 24 hours after receiving them, then prick them out into trays or individual pots. Grow them on in frost-free conditions for about 4 weeks before planting out.

SOW AN ANNUAL BORDER FROM THE CENTRE OUT To sow a large bed without compacting the freshly dug soil, start in the middle. Stand on a plank and move it out towards the edges as you work. Rake over the flattened strips of soil left by the plank each time you reposition it.

● If you are growing annuals for cutting, sow seeds in rows. Sow four rows, then leave a space before sowing another four, and so on. The spaces will serve as paths so you can pick the flowers without trampling on them.

Planting out a seasonal display

THE BEST TIME TO PLANT The timing of planting out annuals varies with your climate. In warm, frost-free climates sowing and planting out in autumn and early winter makes the most of mild winters and early spring seasons. Use the spring for planting out summer annuals. In frost-prone areas, avoid planting out frost-tender annuals such as impatiens until the last frosts have passed. In cold climates most planting is done in spring with only the hardiest of plants being sown during the autumn months.

Blue salvias and yellow rudbeckias can be started in punnets in early spring while sunflowers can be direct-sown into the bed.

● Despite their sensitivity to cold as they age, petunias that self-sow, or are planted in early autumn in the garden, can survive mild winter frosts. The plants burst into bloom in late winter or early spring.

FOR A WINTER GARDEN In autumn, it is best to plant out biennials such as violas and pansies, which will first flower in the next month, and then again in late winter. For continual flowering from autumn until the end of spring, go for the antique bronze and pastel colours of pansy 'Antique Shades' or the deep velvety and almost black tones of 'Black Knight'. For big bold pansies, try 'Giant Supreme'. The pink or white daisy, *Bellis perennis* 'Galaxy', will also flourish throughout the winter.

EARLY COLOUR Autumn is the time to plant calendulas, wallflowers (*Erysimum*), primulas, polyanthus and others flowers that bloom in winter and early spring.

● Forget-me-nots are great companions for spring bulbs such as daffodils. To avoid the annoyance of seeds sticking to clothes and pets' fur, pull up forget-me-nots as soon as seeds begin to form, but leave a few plants to provide seeds for next year's show.

STAKE OUT TALL PLANTS Give larkspurs and other tall annuals support as soon as they are planted in the garden. Place twiggy branches among the young plants and the branches will support the growing stems as they rise through them. You can also use canes for support – fix growing stems to them either using traditional means such as soft string or raffia, or with modern metal or plastic ties. Make sure you do not tie so tightly that growth is restricted.

WORK IN COOL CONDITIONS In fine weather, don't plant during the hottest time of the day. To keep small plants from drying out as soon as they are put in the ground, work in the morning before 10 o'clock. Better still, wait until the end of the day, after 4 o'clock. The plants will then benefit from the coolness and humidity of the night.

WELCOME SUNSHINE While most annuals are generally undemanding about their soil as long as it is well drained, they do need a sunny situation. Several can cope in lightly shaded corners, though, including

1 Water the tray before removing the plants. Use a pencil or squeeze the base to push up the root ball from the bottom.

2 Make a small planting hole in the potting mix, and position the plant so that its neck is level with the soil.

3 Fill the space around the roots with more potting mix, and use your fingertips to firm the soil around the stem.

4 Water carefully to avoid disturbing the plant. Then seal in the moisture with a mulch of fine gravel or organic mulch.

Gardener's Choice

A RAINBOW IN THE GARDEN

Annuals and biennials come in nearly every colour imaginable. You can combine flowers and foliage in your beds and borders to make eye-catching combinations, to complement and contrast and to provide a theme for your planting schemes.

BLUE Ageratum, felicia, forget-me-not (*Myosotis*) **1**, linum, lobelia, love-in-a-mist, nemophila, nicandra and petunia.

GREEN Bells of Ireland (*Molucella*), euphorbia **2** and mignonette.

YELLOW OR ORANGE Calceolaria, calendula, chrysanthemum, coreopsis, cosmos (*Cosmos sulphureus*), eschscholzia, evening primrose (*Oenothera*), gaillardia, glaucium, golden eye (*Bidens*), limnanthes, marigold **3**, mimulus, nasturtium, nicotiana, paper daisies, portulaca, rudbeckia, sanvitalia, sunflower, tagetes, tithonia, ursinia, viola, wallflower (*Erysimum*) and zinnia.

PINK OR FUCHSIA Ageratum, antirrhinum, aster (*Callistephus*), bellis, clarkia, cleome, cosmos, dahlia **4**, *Dianthus barbatus*, dimorphotheca, geranium (*Pelargonium*), gomphrena, heliotrope, hollyhock, impatiens, lavatera, malcolmia, matthiola, mirabilis, nicotiana, paper daisies, petunia, *Phlox drummondii*, portulaca, silene and sweet pea.

RED Bellis, celosia, gerbera, godetia, linum, lobelia, monkey flower (*Mimulus*), nemesia, petunia, poppy (*Papaver*) and wallflower (*Erysimum*).

VIOLET Brachyscome, browallia, campanula, cornflower, convolvulus, gilia, honesty (*Lunaria*), larkspur, lisianthus, lobelia, pansy, petunia, phacelia, primula, salpiglossis, scaevola, torenia, verbena and viola.

WHITE African daisy (*Arctotis*), begonia, campanula **5**, cosmos, dimorphotheca, gypsophila, lavatera, linum, love-in-a-mist (*Nigella damascena*), nemophila, nicotiana, paper daisies, salvia and viola.

GREY AND SILVER Dusty miller (*Senecio*) **6** especially varieties such as 'Silver Dust' and 'Cirrus'.

campanula, catchfly (*Silene*), creeping zinnia (*Sanvitalia*), euphorbia, impatiens, mimulus, nasturtium and nemophila.
● Group together plants with the same requirements, such as impatiens, foxglove and torenia. These will all flourish in semishade, in a cool, well-drained soil.

PLAN BEFORE PLANTING Fill a bottle with sand and gently pour it out over the soil to mark out the boundaries of your plan.
● Line up the plants, in their pots, in staggered rows, every 15–30 cm depending on their spread, to decide on the final positions before planting.

YESTERDAY'S SECRETS

GOOD OLD SOAK Follow the old gardener's tip to make the planting out of seedlings easy, and soak the seed tray in water to ensure that the roots are well moistened. They will separate with ease and are less prone to wilting once planted.

WATCH OUT

TOXIC ANNUALS
Some wild or cultivated annuals and biennials are poisonous, and they are all the more dangerous when they spread through a garden. Contact with the sap of euphorbia or with the leaves of nicotiana can cause skin allergies. It is dangerous to eat the seeds of larkspur, *Solanum capsicastrum* or sweet pea. When buying *Primula obconica* look for varieties selected to be nonallergenic, as these beautiful flowers can cause irritation for many people.

ADVANCED SEEDLINGS MAKE IT EASY
Recently seedling growers have developed punnets with more growing space leading to large, well-developed seedlings that are easy to plant and quick to establish. For even faster colour, invest in small pots of bedding plants that are already in bloom. Sold in 140 mm pots they are usually called 'Bloomers' and are widely available from garden centres all year round.
● To help them to gain strength, you can plant individual seedlings in pots or in boxes before bedding them into their final positions several weeks later.

A GOOD SOAK FOR A QUICK
RECOVERY Half an hour before planting out, immerse punnets in a bucket of water until all the air has stopped bubbling out of the soil. Thoroughly water the hole in the ground before putting in the plant.
● Water around the plant until the soil is saturated. Turn the rose of the watering can upwards for a gentle shower that will not loosen the soil.

NOT TOO DEEP
The planting hole should be deep enough to allow you, after placing the seedling, to add a small handful of fine mulch, which reduces the danger of the roots drying out. The neck of the plant should be level with the soil surface to ensure moisture will be absorbed when the plant is watered.

The secrets of composition

VARY THE HEIGHT Mix three or four different heights to give a border structure with low-growing annuals at the front and taller plants at the back of the bed.
● **FIRST ROW (10–20 CM)** Gazania, limnanthes, lobelia, sanvitalia, sweet alyssum (*Lobularia*) and Virginian stock (*Malcolmia*).
● **SECOND ROW (20–50 CM)** Ageratum, arctotis, dusty miller, felicia, gomphrena, impatiens, love-in-a-mist, nasturtium, petunia, phlox, poppies, salvia and star of the veldt (*Dimorphotheca*).
● **THIRD ROW (50 CM–1 M)** Cornflower, clarkia, gypsophila, mallow (*Lavatera*), larkspur, lisianthus, marigold, nicandra, nicotiana, paper daisies and snapdragon.

● **FOURTH ROW (OVER 1 M)** Amaranthus, cleome, cosmos, hollyhock, sunflower, tithonia and *Verbena bonariensis*.

SIMPLE SPLASHES OF COLOUR Plant together annuals or biennials of the same type – the same height or flower shape, for example – in a group approximately 1 square metre. Start simply, restricting yourself to just two or three different colours at first. Some gardeners don't like to mix flowers of different yellow hues, or oranges with reds or yellows, or reds with blues. Others might find the result very pleasing.

A CURTAIN OF FLOWERS To hide an unsightly wall, train sweet peas or another quick-growing climber up a piece of garden twine. At a convenient height, stretch a horizontal piece of twine between two nails set 1.2 m apart, and insert two more nails along its length to hold it firm. Every 15 cm along this main cord, knot in vertical cords, leaving them free to trail to the ground. Place annuals in pots at the base. They will grow rapidly up the twine, and your wall will soon disappear behind an abundantly flowering curtain. Sweet peas also provide scented flowers to pick for indoors.

VALUABLE SPACE FILLERS In their first year of planting, shrubs and perennials will not fill all their allotted space. Use annuals to fill the gaps in your borders while waiting for the other plants to reach full growth.

SEASIDE GARDEN For a carefree garden near the sea, concentrate on plants that grow naturally in barren or windswept sandy areas such as mini agapanthus, echium, euphorbia

PLANTING BULBS IN A MIXED BED

1 Set out the plants at the correct planting distances, and plant them in firmly.

2 Place bulbs between the plants, spacing them evenly. Dig holes with a bulb planter or trowel.

3 Plant bulbs at the required depth. Push them gently into the soil at the bottom of each hole, pointing upwards.

4 Firm the soil lightly and water if it is dry. Insert a label to remind you of what has been planted there.

Fast-growing sweet peas are ideal for covering an unsightly garden feature.

and evening primrose. Some of these can become weedy control them by cutting the plants back after they've flowered.

PLANT A FLORAL CARPET To make a living mosaic, choose low-growing annuals that have interesting foliage or an unusual habit. Outline the shape of your design by planting two staggered rows around the edge. Make sure you allow for enough plants – you will need 12 to 16 cineraria for each metre, for example. Then, to complete the effect, fill in your 'frame' with a block of a single variety or mixed plants in a geometric pattern of your choice. Succulents also work very well in these patterns.
● **FLOWERS FOR COLOUR** *Ageratum houstonianum*, *Begonia semperflorens*, French marigolds, lobelia, lobularia and viola.
● **FOLIAGE** *Senecio cineraria* 'Silver Dust', for grey, and beetroot (*Beta* 'Bulls Blood') for purple. Feverfew (*Tanacetum parthenium* 'Gold Moss' or 'Plenum') has striking gold foliage with small white flowers.

COVER A SUNNY TRELLIS Many fast-growing climbers grow readily from seeds and can be grown as annuals or, in a warmer climate, many will establish as perennials. To quickly smother a fence or small trellis in one season, try planting seeds of asarina, cup and saucer vine (*Cobaea scandens*), moonflower, nasturtium, snail vine (*Vigna caracalla*), Spanish flag (*Ipomoea lobata* syn. *Mina lobata*), sweet pea – and annuals or perennials in the right climate.
● Canary creeper (*Tropaeolum peregrinum*) flourishes in summer to autumn with bright yellow flowers 2–3 cm in diameter. It climbs to a height of 2.5–4 m.

TO BRIGHTEN UP PAVING To jazz up your paving, haphazardly, here and there, scoop out the soil in the gaps between your paving stones, bricks or flagstones. Replace this soil with a mixture of multipurpose potting mix or garden soil and sow brachyscome or nemesia, or other small plants.

POPULAR WALL FLOWERS To soften a low, sunny wall, sow annuals and biennials in the crevices or on the top of the wall. Californian poppies, snapdragons and wallflowers will all thrive in this hot, dry situation. Fill the spaces between the stones with sandy soil supplemented with blood

and bone, or a mixture of equal parts of soil, coarse sand and leaf mould. Use a small fork to squeeze the planting mixture into the gaps and water liberally until the soil is soaked before sowing.

LIVING WIGWAM Make a circle of tall bamboo canes about 1 m in diameter. Push the canes into the ground to a depth of 40 cm, leaving a space about 50 cm wide between two of the canes for the door. Bind the canes about 15 cm from the top with raffia or wire. Then sow runner beans, snow peas or sweet peas at the foot of the canes. Water the plants regularly and as they grow up the bamboo canes, the sides of your wigwam will begin to take shape.

A NIGHT-SCENTED TERRACE To fill your patio or terrace with fragrance from summer to autumn, plant different species of stock (*Matthiola*) and flowering tobacco plant (*Nicotiana*). These are particularly good for entertaining areas as their scent is especially attractive during the nighttime.
● Moonflower (*Ipomoea alba*) has amazing white flowers that give out a sweet scent in the evening as they open. The plant is capable of covering any kind of fence or other support within a couple of months.

*A sober looking wall can be given some summer charm by planting a row of pink hollyhocks (*Althaea rosea*), or try sunflowers.*

Gardeners through history have made simple wigwams using canes or stakes to support climbing annuals.

Getting the most from your plants

WATER AND HOE REGULARLY Watering is vital, especially immediately after planting and during hot weather. Every 1 to 2 days check the potting mix in pots and containers to see if it has dried out.

● To avoid disturbing young plants, use a watering can or water breaker fitted with a fine rose, and hold it high above the plants.

● If watering with a hose, use a rose attachment and point the rose upwards over the plants. This prevents damaging the plants by watering with too much pressure.

● Hoe the ground regularly to get rid of weeds that will compete with your plants. Mulching well will also help reduce weeds.

PINCHING OUT FOR STRENGTH Encourage your young plants to develop into sturdy, bushy specimens by pinching out the tips of the growing shoots. Grasp the tip between your thumb and index finger, above a leaf or a pair of leaves. This light pruning will delay flowering slightly, but it will be all the more abundant when it does start. Regularly pinch out cosmos, godetia, heliotrope, petunia and sweet pea.

● The fragile stems of aster, campanula and rudbeckia are vulnerable in wind. Pinching out the tips restricts their development and helps them to remain upright.

THE RIGHT NATURAL FERTILISER To boost the flowering of annual climbers, feed them every 2 weeks with ash or an organic fertiliser high in potash suitable for geraniums, raspberries, roses or tomatoes. Avoid nitrogen-rich fertilisers as they encourage leaf rather than flower growth.

WATCH OUT FOR SPONTANEOUS RESEEDING Since they reseed themselves generously, calendulas, cosmos, forget-me-not, foxglove and other annuals or biennials are favourites with those who love cottage gardens, but they can wreak havoc in more formal schemes. Control their spread and prevent seeds from developing by removing the flowers as soon as they have finished. In some cases, it is best to remove the whole flowered stem or even the plant. As these plants are produced from cross-pollination,
their seeds may give rise to plants that are very different from the mother plant.

● If you want an orderly garden, it is a good idea to avoid calendula, Californian poppy, coreopsis, impatiens, larkspur, limnanthes, linum, nasturtium and nigella, or at least keep them firmly in check.

NATURAL PROFUSION If you like the informal jumble of a cottage garden, allow your annuals and biennials to develop and scatter their seeds before pulling them up. Forget-me-nots, foxgloves and honesty will spread themselves in semishade, and evening primroses will do the same in sunny places.

PROLONG FLOWERING Remove spent blooms to prolong flowering and prevent your annuals and biennials from exhausting themselves by producing unnecessary seeds.

● Many annuals will flower vigorously for a fortnight then dwindle to a few scattered flowers. Prune the stems that have finished flowering to stimulate further growth.

● Cut hollyhocks back to the base of their stems as soon as they have finished flowering. They will grow back and flower again over several years. If allowed to seed, a plant may not grow back the following year.

● Prune the principal stem of foxgloves as soon as they have finished flowering. New flower spikes, smaller but still worth having, will spring up from lateral stems.

BACK FROM SUMMER HOLIDAYS If you find that your window boxes or other containers have dried out on returning from holiday, you can easily refresh them with plants that can cope with early autumn chills, including aster, *Begonia semperflorens*, felicia, nicotiana, pot marigold (*Calendula*), rudbeckia, salvia and zinnia.

COLD-CLIMATE CLEAN-UP Pull out annuals – including climbers – as soon as their foliage begins to wither when cold and frost set in. To cheer up your empty pots with an immediate splash of colour, replenish them with polyanthus, primula or viola, which will last through the winter.

A WINTER OVERCOAT To minimise the danger of frost damage in cold areas, you should reduce watering. You can discard the winter protection when the weather gets warmer and all danger of frosts has passed.

Pinch-prune young seedlings once or twice during their first 4 to 6 weeks.

Have the secateurs ready to cut off spent flowers.

Collecting seeds for next year's plants

USE A CONE OF NEWSPAPER ... To gather seeds from the garden, roll up two sheets from a large newspaper to make a cone with a wide opening at the top. Fold and secure the cone at the bottom to stop the seeds escaping. Shake the seed-laden plant over the cone. Once you have your harvest you can simply fold over the newspaper, seal the top and label it with the name of the plant.

PAPER BAG ... Put a paper bag over flowers that have finished blooming and secure it around the stem of the plant with a piece of string, raffia or wire. Once the stems have dried out, cut just below the tie, turn the bag upside down and shake the plant so that the seeds fall into it. Label the bag immediately.
● Never store seeds in a plastic bag – it will not let air through and the seeds will rot.

... OR AN UMBRELLA To gather the maximum number of seeds in record time, shake seed-bearing stems above an upturned open umbrella.

DRYING IS ESSENTIAL To reduce the risk of mould, air-dry seeds thoroughly on newspaper before storing them.

SAFE, DRY STORAGE Old tablet bottles are perfect for storing seeds. The drying agent in the cap will protect them from damp. You could also use old film canisters, or put the seeds in envelopes or paper bags and peg them to a line in a dry, well-aired space such as a garage.
● Collect the little bags of absorbent silica gel that come with electrical or computer equipment, or in vitamin bottles. Drop them into the tightly sealed boxes in which you store your seeds.
● To keep off weevils and rodents, add a mothball to the storage container.

USE A FINE-MESH SIEVE For fine, small seeds such as snapdragons and petunias, put the ripe, dry flower heads into an old kitchen sieve. Rub gently over the mesh and the seeds will fall through.

Gardeners have always saved seeds for replanting. Gather your seeds before pulling out spent plants.

CHECK THE CUPBOARD Don't store your seeds in an MDF (medium density fibreboard) cupboard. MDF is a kind of manufactured timber made with a glue that emits formaldehyde, which can shorten the life of seeds.

Save seeds in a labelled envelope and store in a cool, dry spot until sowing time.

Gardener's Choice

SEEDS FOR COLLECTION
Many common garden plants set plenty of seeds, which are ready for collection when the pod or seed head dries out. Always collect seeds from the best specimens only.

SELF-SOWING ANNUALS Plants in this group that produce an abundance of seeds include forget-me-not (*Myosotis*), honesty, love-in-a-mist (*Nigella damascena*), pot marigold (*Calendula*) and poached egg plant (*Limnanthes douglasii*). Seeds from these plants are easy to collect before they fall and can be sown where you want to grow them, or given to gardening friends.

ANNUALS OR BIENNIALS Aquilegia, foxglove, nasturtium (*Tropaeolum*), nemesia, pansy, poppies and wallflower (*Erysimum*) all set good quantities of seeds, which can be sown when required.

PERENNIALS Seeds of cyclamen and primula are best sown as soon as they are ripe, when they will germinate quickly. If stored and dried, germination takes a long time. Evening primrose, lupin and Welsh poppy (*Meconopsis cambrica*) are often short lived and are best started from seeds every few years.

SWEET PEAS These plants also readily set seed, but remember that the offspring will not be exactly the same as the parent plant. This is particularly true when growing hybrid plants, which often have specific colours and forms only when the same parents are used. This plant variability is caused by cross-pollination by flying insects, such as bees. However, this has often resulted in the accidental production of a new improved variety, so there is no harm in seeing what comes up.

Beds and borders in full bloom

Inspired by the cottage garden, the most pleasing flowerbeds are usually dense and varied with a long flowering period. They may look natural, but in fact they need careful planning.

Good planning

ROUND OR SQUARE? The formality of straight lines or the charm of curves? It's up to you. A combination of the two designs gives excellent results.

ALLOW FOR SPACE A garden you are happy to be in is one where you feel you have room to breathe. Don't try to plant every bit of ground, for an overgrown atmosphere can be oppressive. The planted areas – hedges, shrubs and trees, flowerbeds and borders, and plants in containers – should take up no more than 50 per cent of your garden. Keep the rest unplanted and reserve it for lawns, paths, steps, terraces and patios to give a feeling of spaciousness.

MAKE A SKETCH If you have a large flowerbed or border in mind, draw up a plan of the proposed bed, taking the spread and height of each plant into account. Colour your plan, using the colours of the plants to give you a good idea of the overall effect.

MARKING OUT BORDERS You can mark out any shape you want by using sand. Scoop up a handful of dry sand and let it trickle out in a thin, even stream to act as a nontoxic, temporary guide for digging.
● To mark out a circle or semicircle, tie a length of string to a bamboo cane. Fix a sand-filled bottle to the other end of the string, pull it tight and 'draw' your curve.
● To help you mark out the corners of a rectangular bed, use an old wooden vegetable crate as a guide. This will help to ensure your right angles are accurate.

PLAN A FEW SURPRISES Add interest to your garden and break up the symmetry of flowerbeds and borders by planting a tree or a shrub at one end but not at the other. Strong elements such as climbing and taller plants lend greater weight to their particular part of the border and give a pleasing sense of drama and surprise.

GET OFF TO A GOOD START Although they look tempting, do not buy young plants in flower. Choose healthy, compact plants with vibrantly coloured leaves and well-branched stems. The base of the stem should be strongly attached to the root mass, not loose, and the root ball should be damp to the touch. Reject plants with either dry or saturated potting mix.

CHOOSE QUALITY, NOT QUANTITY The beauty of a flowerbed does not rely solely on the number of plants it contains, but on the harmony of their colour and shape, and

Use dry sand to outline planting areas in the garden.

Mark out a circular planting bed with a piece of string.

Iceland poppies and pansies flower together during late winter and early spring.

the balance of textures, heights and flower sizes that you use. The most successful arrangements comprise no more than about half devoted to flowers, combined with small shrubs or plants with attractive foliage.

GREAT HEIGHTS After the exuberance of spring, gardens can seem to fade away as summer warms up. Keep gardens colourful with a selection of heat-tolerant shrubs. For flowers, consider the stunning angel's trumpet (*Brugmansia*) or the oleander. In a small but sunny area, oleander can be pruned and shaped as a standard rather than be allowed to develop as a large shrub. Frangipani, agapanthus and hibiscus also bring colour to the summer garden. For attractive leaf colour and height plant cordyline, croton and dracaena. (Croton can be sensitive to the cold in cooler areas.)
● Do not keep summer bedding plants beyond autumn when they stop growing. Just pull them up and compost them.

EXPERIMENT WITH SHAPE AND TEXTURE Gardens are three dimensional, so make the most of the shape and form of plants by choosing a range of plants with different outlines – from spiky to feathery to bun-shaped.
● Plant compact perennials such as daylily (*Hemerocallis*), wood spurge (*Euphorbia amygdaloides* 'Purpurea') and yarrow (*Achillea ageratum*) among plants that are leafy or that have tall flowering heads, such as allium, iris, giant feather grass (*Stipa gigantea*) or *Verbena bonariensis*.

A PARASOL FOR PLANTS As summer warms up, some plants will suffer if they are positioned in full sun. To give plants, such as ferns, fuchsias, hostas and some of the euphorbias, winter and spring sun and summer shade, plant them under the shelter of small deciduous trees such as a crepe myrtle, frangipani, Japanese maple, pear tree or deciduous magnolia.

TOP TIPS FOR A FOUR-SEASON BED
It can be easy to have your garden looking good in spring and summer, but the art of good gardening is to have a garden with year-round interest. In cold climates, the four-season garden is a challenge. Include plants that produce berries, decorative foliage and bark, and flowers in autumn or winter.

● **FOR BERRIES** Try beauty berry (*Callicarpa bodinieri* 'Profusion'), crab-apple (*Malus sieboldii*), *Skimmia japonica* 'Reevesiana', snowberry (*Symphoricarpos orbiculatus*) and spindle tree.
● **FOR AUTUMN FOLIAGE** Plant American smoke tree (*Cotinus obovatus*), *Fothergilla major*, Japanese maple (*Acer palmatum*), purple chokeberry (*Aronia* x *prunifolia*), smoke bush (*Cotinus coggygria*) and spindle tree.
● **FOR DECORATIVE BARK** Consider ornamental raspberry (*Rubus cockburnianus* or *R. biflorus*) and red-barked dogwood (*Cornus alba*) both with decorative branches.
● **WINTER EVERGREEN** Try Christmas rose (*Helleborus niger*), heather (*Calluna*), pansy (*Viola*) and primula.
● **WINTER BULBS** For a good display in winter in a cold climate plant crocus and

Lovely petunias are among the longest-flowering of all the annuals, continuing to bloom right into autumn.

Gardener's Choice

INDISPENSABLE FOLIAGE
Don't underestimate the value of foliage when you are designing a garden. Don't only assess plants on flower colour – look for interesting foliage. Here is a selection of the best grasses and decorative foliage plants for your flowerbeds.

DELICATE FOLIAGE In a shaded area, amass a collection of ferns for an interesting foliage garden. In a sunny spot, grow the fine foliage forms of dusty miller, fennel (*Foeniculum vulgare* 'Purpureum') and wormwood (*Artemisia* 'Powis Castle') **1**.

TO GIVE MOVEMENT Include grasses like blue fescue (*Festuca glauca*), fountain grass (*Pennisetum setaceum*) **2**, *Lomandra* 'Tanika', lyme grass (*Leymus arenarius*), pony tail grass (*Stipa tenuissima*), quaking grass (*Briza media*) and zebra grass (*Miscanthus sinensis* 'Zebrinus').

TO ADD HEIGHT Tall foliage plants can be used like a living fountain in the garden with cordyline, dracaena, New Zealand flax and zebra grass (*Miscanthus sinensis* 'Zebrinus').

TO SOFTEN BRIGHT COLOURS SILVER-GREY Dusty miller, woolly lamb's ear (*Stachys byzantina* 'Silver Carpet') **3**; GOLDEN Bowles golden sedge (*Carex elata* 'Aurea'), hakone grass (*Hakonechloa macra* 'Aureola'); BLUE *Euphorbia myrsinites*, *Hosta* 'Blue Blush' or 'Hadspen Blue'; BRONZE OR PURPLE New Zealand flax (*Phormium tenax* 'Bronze Baby') and purple bugle (*Ajuga reptans* 'Burgundy Glow').

dwarf iris (*Iris reticulata*). In a temperate climate enjoy paperwhite narcissus and the golden flowers of jonquils.

BEDDING PLANTS The term *bedding plants* is interchangeable with annuals. They can be grown from seeds or purchased at garden centres as seedlings or potted colour (sometimes call 'Bloomers'). There are annuals available that flower in every season and die down after producing seeds. They are a great way to inject instant colour into a drab garden.

● Annuals will go through their best growth in a season. After a flush of flowers they can begin to look tired. If your plants are looking past their best, either pull them out to make room for new, vigorous plants, or cut them back, water and fertilise them for a second flush of growth and flowers.

Composition

A LAYERED EFFECT A flowerbed or border should be made up of three or four plant layers, getting gradually taller towards the back. This way, the bed will have interest and structure. Arrange the heights in a series of steps, working from low plants (under 30 cm) at the front, to the giants (1 m or more) at the back. Seed packets and plant labels should be consulted for the plant height.

*Create tiers of plants in deep borders: dwarf zinnias at the front, then African marigolds (*Tagetes erecta*) and cornflowers (*Centaurea cyanus*), with clumps of dahlias as a backdrop.*

A RESTRICTED PALETTE Create a bold effect by using just one or two dominant colours in your beds or borders. Add a third colour if it is white or black (dark violet, as black flowers do not occur in nature). Choose monochrome and complementary colours, such as those in the following suggested schemes.

● **FRUITS OF THE FOREST** Combine these deep pink and white flowers in full sun: *Achillea millefolium* 'Cerise Queen', bear's breeches (*Acanthus mollis*), ice plant (*Sedum spectabile* 'Brilliant'), *Verbena bonariensis*, matched with pink chrysanthemum and fleabane (*Erigeron karvinskianus*).

● **WHITE AND PEPPERMINT** Bergamot (*Monarda* 'Snow Witch'), cosmos, Jack-in-the-pulpit (*Arisaema sikokianum*), lesser periwinkle (*Vinca minor* 'Alba'), Mexican orange blossom (*Choisya ternata* 'Aztec Pearl'), plantain lily (*Hosta sieboldiana* 'Elegans') and spider flower (*Cleome hassleriana*) make a striking display in sun or partial shade.

● **BLUE AND GREEN** Deep shade is often very moist. The blues and greens of blue corydalis (*Corydalis flexuosa*), bugle (*Ajuga reptans*), giant forget-me-not (*Brunnera macrophylla*), lady's mantle (*Alchemilla mollis*) and plantain lily (*Hosta* 'Bressingham Blue') are a successful combination.

A SYMPATHETIC BACKDROP Shrubs make a good backdrop for a bed. So do climbers such as golden hop, jasmine and clematis, and giant perennials such as plume poppy (*Macleaya cordata*). Climbers have the advantage of occupying little ground space, which makes them useful if your bed is narrow or if your garden is short of space.

FOR A NATURAL LOOK Establish your flowerbed as an extension of some other existing feature in your garden. Merge it into another group of plants such as a hedge or a bed of shrubs. Or back it onto some hard landscaping such as a path, some steps, a low wall, a pergola or patio. A bed in the middle of the lawn will always look artificial.

A DECORATIVE MULCH In addition to preventing the growth of weeds, retaining moisture and slowing erosion caused by heavy rain, a mulch can also be decorative. Spread a layer of coloured gravel or pebbles between the plants to hide the bare soil and accentuate the flowers and foliage.

RAISING INTEREST Do you wish your flat garden was more interesting? A raised flower-bed can give your favourite plants a higher profile. Build low walls (15–20 cm high) on a concrete foundation buried about 10 cm below the surface. Use concrete, brick or stone for the walls, depending on your surroundings. Fill the bed with a mixture of garden soil and compost, coarse sand or gravel. Overlapping beds of different heights can look good when bordering a terrace.
● A raised flowerbed gives height to any planting scheme featuring perennials, bulbs, annuals and biennials.
● For anyone who has trouble bending down to ground level to weed and plant, raised beds can make gardening less of a trial. If you make the walls 50–60 cm high and 25–30 cm thick, you can even sit on them while tending the garden, making it an altogether more relaxing experience.

PLANNING A RAISED FLOWERBED
When selecting plants for a raised bed, make sure the bed is deep enough for them.
● If you need to use soil that is very different from the rest of the garden, for example if you need to use a potting mix for an acid-loving plant and your garden soil is alkaline, cover the bottom and inside walls of the bed with a porous membrane to prevent the soils from mixing together.

IMPROVE YOUR CONTOURS Give your garden height and your plants scale by building up a mounded bed. On a free-standing mound, put the tallest plants in the middle, with the smaller ones spreading down to the edges. If you create a slope against a wall, your tallest species, positioned at the back, will have even more impact.

TOP TIPS FOR EDGING There are several good ways to separate flowerbeds from the lawn or paving that borders them.
● **CONSTRUCT A HARD EDGE** Wooden boards, bricks or buried slates will hold back plants that tend to escape from the border into the lawn, such as plants with rhizomes.
● **PLANT A BORDER** Box, cotton lavender, geranium 'Johnson's Blue', lady's mantle and mondo grass all have evergreen foliage.
● **USE GROUNDCOVER PERENNIALS** The spreading ergenia and Japanese spurge (*Pachysandra terminalis*) will merge together to hide the bare earth.

● **GROW GRASSY PLANTS** Planting golden pearlwort (*Sagina subulata* 'Aurea') between paving stones at the edge of the border will create a natural, softening effect.

KEEP GRAVEL TIDY If you want to create a gravel path alongside a flowerbed, make sure the bed is slightly lower than the path to prevent soil, bark or other mulch material from spilling over onto it.

AN ACCESS PATH If you create a rectangular border of hardy perennials, put a path in front of it, however narrow. This will give you access for maintenance, allow spreading plants in the front row to attractively spill over, and ensure a smooth transition to the lawn that makes mowing easier.
● For really large beds, arrange a narrow path 40–50 cm wide along the back of the bed.

For a striking effect, combine two plants of the same colour (top) or just a single colour with green (above).

Gardener's Choice

NATURAL MULCHES
Mulches prevent moisture loss from the soil, suppress weeds and protect plants from winter frosts.

WOODCHIPS 1 These make a good, moisture-retaining mulch for the base of perennials and annuals. They are readily available, although a cheaper option would be to chip your own.

COCOA BEAN SHELLS 2 These are almost rotproof and fine enough to give good cover. They deter slugs, but unfortunately can be very harmful to dogs if they eat the shells.

GRAVEL 3 This makes an ornamental covering. For protection from slugs and snails for hostas and other vulnerable plants, sharp-edged gravel or crushed seashells or eggshells are best, although shell will gradually make the soil more alkaline.

LUCERNE AND SUGAR CANE These are easy to use and break down to feed and improve soil structure. They keep soil cool and moist.

GARDEN COMPOST 4 To add a balanced, slow-release fertiliser to your soil, in late spring spread well-rotted garden compost around the roots, making sure it is clear of the stems. Compost also improves the general condition of the soil.

MANURE Farmyard or stable manure is an invaluable aid for soil improvement. Most forms of these manures are useful but must be well rotted.

BARK Composted barks are a good moisture-retaining mulch. Coarse bark chips and flakes are best used for paths or areas without plants as they don't feed the soil and can lead to water-repellent soils.

Colourful flowers that will last and last

Mainstays of the old-fashioned flower garden, herbaceous perennials regrow from their root stock in spring after they have been cut back, so you do not need to replant them each year. Some perennials are evergreen, which means you can enjoy their attractive foliage all year round. Choose evergreens to keep your garden beds interesting when everything else has faded – a few even flower in the depths of winter.

Well-planted perennials

KEEP YOUR DISTANCE Plant labels and seed packets usually indicate how many plants you can grow in 1 square metre, enabling you to work out how many you will need to fill your flowerbed. Increase rather than decrease the recommended spacing between plants to permit adequate air circulation and to allow plenty of room for the plants to spread naturally. It is also important that you keep in mind the final height of the plants when planting them out in a bed – aim to keep them in the right proportion to their eventual width.

When setting out plants, make sure they are properly spaced to have room to grow freely.

GAIN A SEASON The traditional advice is to plant perennials in spring, but if you put them in at the beginning of autumn they will have time to settle in before the cold weather begins. Protect very young plants beneath a mulch of dry leaves or fern fronds, or cover them with sacking when there is a frost. By spring, the root stock will already be established and new growth will begin sooner. The new shoots will grow quickly and there will be more flowers in the first year of flowering.
● Perennials that are bought via mail-order are usually shipped in late autumn to winter while the plants are dormant. In all but the coldest climates it is safe to plant them out as soon as they are received. Mark the location of each plant with a stake or a label so you'll remember they are there.

BUY WELL-DEVELOPED PLANTS Speed up the time that it takes for plants to settle by buying established specimens of between 1 and 3 years old, in large pots. These will take much less time to develop dense growth than young or bare-root plants.
● Before buying any plant, check that it's in good condition and that the root stock is sprouting a number of young shoots.

AT ARM'S LENGTH When you create a bed of mixed perennials, consider its dimensions from a practical, as well as an aesthetic, point of view. You must be able to reach all of the plants in a flowerbed for pruning, clearing and cutting flowers. For this reason, the

Perennials are ideal plants to use for softening the edges of paving and brickwork. Spilling out onto pathways, they give a pretty, rambling and weathered old-world air to your garden.

length of your outstretched arm is the best yardstick for determining the width of a flowerbed. If you can reach the bed from behind, then you can allow two arm lengths.
● The longer the flowerbed is, the more effective it will be, although it's better to repeat sequences than to plant too many species. Three to five species is enough for a single-depth bed 5 m long. You will need twice as many if the area is double depth.

TRY OUT NEW PLANTS If you want to experiment with an unfamiliar plant, try planting two or three in different locations around your garden. After a year, you will be able to see where it flourishes and can move the other plants to the best location.

PLANT A VERTICAL GARDEN To make the most of the nooks and crannies in low dry-stone or lovely old brick walls, create a miniature vertical garden.
● Fill any gaps with a moistened mixture of soil and compost and plant out using seeds, seedlings or small plants. Choose the species that will tolerate dry soil and poor conditions, such as erigeron and saxifrage, and they will take root and multiply without any help from you. Water the plants during hot weather or in long periods of drought to prevent them from drying out completely.

● Plant trailing species on top of low walls. Choose plants that need the minimum of nutrition, such as cerastium and sedum. You can choose from a wider range of plants if you are prepared to add a little compost from time to time.

WATER BEFORE PLANTING Soak the planting holes and wait for the water to drain away before planting. This will make it easier to work the soil and the roots will be less likely to dry out. Water or, preferably, soak new plants before transplanting them. The potting mix will hold together better and the roots will quickly re-establish.
● If the weather is wet and your soil is already waterlogged, wait until it dries out a little before planting. Meanwhile, stand your plants outside in the rain.

BETTER DRAINAGE If you have damp or perpetually waterlogged soil, you will need to lay agricultural pipe (sold as 'ag' pipe) to improve drainage. Dig a narrow trench about 1 m deep with a slight fall away from the wet area, to assist drainage. Fill the base of the trench with blue metal, lay a length of pipe over the stones and fill in around the pipe with more blue metal and top up with soil. Select pipe that's enclosed in a stocking of geotextile fabric to exclude dirt particles.

A LIVELY OLD FRIEND
Mint is a very old favourite in flower and herb beds and is a natural insect repellent. But it will invade your whole garden in no time if the soil and location are to its liking. A traditional way of keeping mint in check is to plant it in a pot and sink it into the soil to prevent it from over-powering other plants in the flowerbed.

But be aware that the creeping rhizomes of mint can still sometimes climb over the rim of the pot or out through the drainage holes at the bottom. If you want a large clump of mint, it's a good idea to transplant several plants into a large pot and grow them on a patio or under a garden tap.

Mint can be invasive if left unchecked, but it can easily be contained in a sunken pot.

To give your plant a good start, water dry soil before planting to help it settle in.

- If you can't access storm water or other drains, allow it to drain to a rubble pit.
- Where the soil is heavy clay its drainage can be improved by digging in gypsum and plenty of organic matter.

FOR THRIFTY, PATIENT GARDENERS

Seeds cost less than plants, but even the fastest-growing perennials take 2 years to flower from seeds, while the slowest, like peonies, can take 6–8 years. The best plants to grow from seeds are those that are difficult to find in the nursery or garden centre, or that are expensive to buy in large numbers if you are planting a new garden.
- Seeds should be sown in early summer in a shady, out-of-the-way corner or in a cold frame. Sow thinly and add organic matter and sharp sand to improve the soil.

A good mix of colours and shades

AT HOME IN MOIST SOIL With their bright, varied colours, primulas are probably the prettiest perennials for moist soil. Many of the varieties sold grow well around ponds and in all damp ground. *Primula obconica* is spectacular for winter to spring flowers in shades of white, apricot, lavender and pink. Look for allergy-free varieties to avoid skin irritations. Japanese primrose (*P. japonica*) flowers in spring and midsummer and boasts flowers in a range of colours from pink, red and purple to white.

Patches of cool blue delphiniums contrast well with warm yellow achilleas and add interest when planted with other bright meadow flowers.

Single-colour flowerbeds can look very cool and sophisticated, like this lovely silver border of centranthus, foxglove and lamb's ear.

INSECT-REPELLING PLANTS Aromatic plants, such as artemisia, lemon balm, mint, sage and thyme, keep insects at bay with their strong fragrance. They also make attractive borders for flowerbeds and around a kitchen garden. Lavender and rue are said to help repel annoying flies and French marigold has been shown to keep soil free of nematodes.

TRIED AND TESTED COLOUR COMBINATIONS The wide variety of perennials available lets you be creative in your use of colour. A useful tip is that perennials in dark, vibrant colours are enhanced by paler shades of the same hue.
- **SINGLE-COLOUR PLANTINGS** Widen your range of colours for a better effect. Introduce green and silver shades to whites, add violet to blues, yellow to pale lemons, or heighten them with gold. Temper warm reds, which can be garish, with a more elegant crimson.
- **ONE PREVAILING COLOUR** To avoid any jarring, use a single colour per season as the main shade in multicoloured flowerbeds.
- **BOLD COLOUR MIXES** Mix red and orange using delicate flowers to lessen clashing.

LABOUR-SAVING SLOPES Grassy slopes, which can be hard to mow, can be planted instead with groundcover perennials, whose roots also keep the soil from sliding. Trailing lantana is one of the best perennials for this purpose, as are agapanthus and oregano. Also, creeping bugle, dead nettle and epimedium are unbeatable for under trees.

COTTAGE GARDEN OLD FAVOURITES

A cottage garden needs a lot of plants, try these tried-and-true treasures.

GOLDEN MARGUERITE *Anthemis tinctoria* **1** is long flowering and the flowers last well when cut.

PRIMULA *Primula bulleyana* **2**, one of the most charming of species, likes being in damp soil near water and prefers a cool climate. *P. sieboldii* has a bright white centre and deep pink, purple or white petals and enjoys a slightly acid, damp soil.

CORYDALIS *Corydalis flexuosa* **3** grows best in partial shade and acid soil. Try *C. ochroleuca* in a well-drained spot tucked against a wall or on a slope.

BERGAMOT *Monarda didyma* is a traditional cottage garden plant with many named forms. 'Cambridge Scarlet' **4** has red flowers while 'Croftway Pink' has bright pink blooms.

BUTTERFLY BUSH 'Siskiyou Pink' **5** is a compact, pink form of the popular and usually white perennial, *Gaura lindheimeri*.

FOXGLOVE *Digitalis purpurea* **6**, with its pink, purple or white flower spires, is a must for any cottage garden. All species thrive in shade.

1 2
3 4

5 6

BORDERS OF COLOUR Plants with tall flower spires bring height and long-lasting colour to the garden. Lupins, particularly the Russell hybrids, are popular in cooler climates for their height and colour range. First hybridised in 1890 they are a true old-fashioned plant for your garden. Many of the hybrids have two-tone flowers: 'Blue Moon' is rich purple and white while 'Queen of Hearts' is cream and red.

● Larkspurs bring shades of pink, white and mauve to gardens in spring and grow well in cool to subtropical gardens. Easy to grow from seeds, they are sown directly into a sunny, well-drained garden bed in autumn. Or plant seedlings in late winter or early spring. Larkspurs will self-seed.

● Verbascums also have very colourful and long-lasting spires of flowers. For an unusual apricot-flowered verbascum look for 'Helen Johnson'. These plants grow well in hot, dry spots, thrive in gravel gardens and they may self-seed into gravel paths.

A SCENTED GARDEN There are many scented and perfumed perennials. For a fragrance-filled garden, choose carnation, phlox, romneya, sweet rocket (*Hesperis*), violet and wallflower. Aromatic plants like anthemis, bergamot, lemon balm, mint, sage, santolina and verbena form a fragrant background to which you can simply add new plants each year. Although it is actually an evergreen shrub rather than a perennial,

You can tone down one-colour beds by simply adding white flowers, as has been done in this border, or flowers in the same shade but paler.

1 If it's dry, soak the plant in water while you dig a hole that is twice as large and deep as the root ball.

2 Add some compost to the bottom of the hole and mix it in, along with some slow-release organic fertiliser.

3 Water the planting hole. This helps your plant settle in and is essential if the soil is very dry in hot weather.

4 Place the plant in the hole and double-check that the top of the root ball is level with the ground.

5 Replace the soil around the root ball, firming it down to remove all air pockets. Water well. Top up soil if necessary.

6 Check the soil is moist, then spread a 5–7 cm layer of mulch around the plant to keep in moisture.

lavender is one of the most popular scented plants and it is fairly easy to grow. Position fragrant plants along garden paths so you can savour the smell as you pass by.

CLASSIC RESTRAINT, WITH A TWIST
A flowerbed made up of only one or two species is easy to maintain, but your garden could look static if this is the only style of planting it contains. There are several ways to add interest to these gardens.

● Give some extra pace to your flower-bed by introducing a few tall campanulas, delphiniums or lupins at irregular intervals.

● Experiment with colour by adding some contrasting touches to your garden. Introduce a bright shade if the flowerbed is dark, white if the blooms are red, and blue or deep violet if the bed consists of warm pinks, oranges, salmon or yellows.

● Combine these two approaches for a more striking effect. Plant several midnight blue delphiniums in a large flowerbed of yellow achillea, or let some crimson lupins emerge from a carpet of blue geraniums.

COMPACT PLANTS SAVE TIME Perennial borders can be a good idea for gardeners who are pressed for time. Opt for compact species that will retain their shape over the years

WATCH OUT

ALWAYS WEAR GLOVES
Never handle common rue (*Ruta graveolens*), giant hogweed (*Heracleum mantegazzianum*) or spurge (*Euphorbia*) (below) with bare hands. They are poisonous and can irritate the skin. It is essential to wear gardening gloves whenever you are planting, transplanting, cutting or dividing any of these species. In fact, it is a good idea to protect your nails and hands with gloves when planting or tending any perennials.

with little maintenance. The best species, from the smallest to the tallest, are bellflowers (*Campanula carpatica* or *C. portenschlagiana*), common rue (*Ruta graveolens*), which has dense grey-blue foliage, oregano (*Origanum vulgare*), perennial candytuft (*Iberis sempervirens*), which is covered in white flowers in spring and pinks and sweet William (*Dianthus barbatus* and *D. plumarius*). Taller species include geranium varieties such as *Geranium pratense*, *G. renardii* or *G. sanguineum*, common bistort (*Persicaria bistorta*) and catmint (*Nepeta nervosa*).

REDUCE YOUR WORKLOAD Cut down on your maintenance by planting perennials in large patches and restricting the number of species used. This means that in autumn

Gardener's Choice

THE HARDIEST PERENNIALS
Perennials thrive in difficult conditions and are remarkably long lived. Here are some of the most robust.

IN POOR AND DRY SOILS Achillea, anthemis, centaurea, erigeron, gaura, hollyhock, potentilla, valerian and wormwood (*Artemisia*).

IN SHADY GARDEN AREAS Acanthus, aconite, astrantia, bergenia, blue ginger (*Dichorisandra*), clivia, euphorbia, fox-glove (*Digitalis*), giant forget-me-not (*Brunnera*), ginger (*Alpinia*), lady's mantle (*Alchemilla*) and lungwort (*Pulmonaria*).

IN HOT SUMMER AREAS Achillea, agapanthus, anchusa, angelonia, aster, canna, ceratostigma, chrysanthemum, clivia, daylily, dietes, echinacea, gaura, gerbera, kangaroo paw (*Anigozanthos* Bush Gem series), lychnis, malva, penstemon, salvia, sedum, shasta daisy (*Leucanthemum*), thrift (*Armeria*) and valerian.

SOME LONG-FLOWERING PERENNIALS
Achillea, anthemis, bellflower (*Campanula*), bergamot (*Monarda*), centaurea, coreopsis, cranesbill (*Geranium*), delphinium, diascia, gaillardia, gaura, nepeta, penstemon, potentilla and verbena.

you can cut back the dying plants at the same time, using a pair of shears to work quickly across the entire bed.
● In frosty areas, wait until winter has passed before you cut back tender perennials such as salvia and verbascum. The dead stems not only protect the crown during bad weather but they can also look very attractive when covered with frost in winter.

SUCCESSFUL TRANSPLANTS Most perennials can be quite easily transplanted, as long as you prepare the planting area with a compost mixture and are careful not to damage the roots when you move them. The dormant season is the best time to transplant. If you don't have the chance to do this in the autumn or winter, wait to transplant until early spring, just before regrowth begins.

MOVING HOME-LOVING PLANTS
Hellebores, hostas and peonies do not like being moved and they can take a long time to establish themselves again. If you have to move them, make sure you take up the entire root ball and water them frequently during the first year until their roots have spread. However, flowering after transplanting can be unpredictable, so you may need to be patient.
● Be careful not to bury peony buds too deeply. Make sure they are planted just below the surface, or there is a chance that they will never flower.

PERFECT PERENNIALS FOR THE VASE
Many perennials will last well when cut and placed in a vase. For the best results, always remember to pick them early in the morning, just after they open and before the sun is too high in the sky and too hot. Some of the best perennials for cutting are agapanthus, anthemis, astilbe, bergamot (*Monarda didyma*), centaurea, cone-flower (*Echinacea*), crocosmia, delphinium, dicentra, epilobium, gaura, golden rod (*Solidago*), gypsophila, heliopsis, liatris, peony, phlox, primula, rose campion (*Lychnis*), salvia, shasta daisy (*Leucanthemum*), sunflower (*Helianthus*) and valerian.
● If you like arrangements of dried flowers, then grow achillea, anaphalis, chamomile, Chinese lantern (*Physalis alkekengii*), globe thistle (*Echinops*), honesty (*Lunaria annua*) and statice (*Limonium*).

1 Dig up the crown with a fork, while being careful to lift the root ball without damaging the roots. Shake to remove the soil.

2 Divide the clump into at least two sections, using your hands for small plants or a garden fork for larger ones.

3 Immediately replant these sections, selecting those with healthy roots and removing the middle sections of plants that are getting too old.

4 Replace the soil that was removed from the hole and firm it well with your hand. Add more soil if necessary, then water thoroughly.

Staking tall perennials is necessary for a weather-proof garden. Without a stake, tall plants become top-heavy as they bloom and can begin to flop, which often causes them to break, especially in strong wind or when rainwater gathers in the flowers. They can also smother their companions.

TOP TIPS FOR STAKING Some tall plants, or even plants with heavy flowers, can need staking to keep them upright.

● **PEONIES AND DELPHINIUMS** (top left) Insert twiggy branches or thin bamboo canes into the soil around the clump you want to stake and slant half of them inwards to support the centre of the plants. You can also buy specially designed cages or linked stakes, through which the plant will grow.

● **SINGLE STEMS** (top right) Insert a sturdy stake in the ground near the base when planting, being careful not to damage the root system, and attach the stem to the stake as it grows. The fastener should be flexible so it does not impede the growth of the stem.

● **MAINTAINING AN EDGE** (above left) If you would prefer a much more discreet form of staking, to go along the entire length of the garden bed, then place a thin wooden stake at each end of the bed and extend raffia, string or green plastic garden twine between them. This support will soon be hidden when the plants' foliage begins to grow.

● **STAKING CLUMPING PERENNIALS** (above right) Insert three or four thin plastic stakes or pieces of bamboo into the ground around the perennial and tie a length of string or

raffia around the stakes, about halfway up. You can now easily raise the height of the support gradually as the clump grows.

HOSE DAMAGE It is surprising just how much damage you can do to your flowerbeds by dragging your hose behind you when you water. Avoid this when setting out your beds by putting in some small wooden stakes to guide your hose safely past vulnerable plants.

OPT FOR EASY-TO-GROW SPECIES
Aquilegia, campanula, elephant's ear (*Bergenia*), Hattie's pincushion (*Astrantia*), hellebore, heuchera, lychnis, phlox, salvia, santolina, silene and tradescantia are all relatively undemanding.

FLOWERBEDS WITH GOOD EDGES
Protect your grass and make it easier to mow by creating a paved path about 30–50 cm wide along the edge of all your flowerbeds. The bushy foliage of the border plants will soon spill over onto the path to soften the sharp edges, which is much better than the foliage spreading out onto the lawn, getting in the way when you are trying to mow, and even killing your grass.

Extend perennials' flowering season

PLANT STRATEGIES FOR THE SUMMER

A perennial garden filled with flowers from spring to autumn requires strategies to help plants through hot and humid or hot and dry summers. Soil enriched with compost and well-rotted manure holds water efficiently so it's readily available to plants when days are hot. Regularly top up the soil around plants with organic mulch to keep the root systems cool, which reduces plant stress.

● In hot areas, avoid planting perennials in late spring or summer as they will not establish well. Make new perennial plantings in the cooler months. If gaps appear during summer, fill them with fast-growing, heat-tolerant annuals such as marigolds.

● Try to deeply water your garden late in the evening, or early in the morning as the day warms up, to provide lasting moisture. This will mean your flowers will last longer.

TWO FLOWERINGS ARE ALWAYS BETTER THAN ONE

Some perennials, such as gaura, penstemon and species geranium, can flower repeatedly if you take the trouble to cut them back as soon as their first flush has ended. Water freshly pruned plants liberally and feed them with organic fertiliser.

● To phase the flowering of your asters, nepetas and summer phloxes, cut back every other plant to about half its height in early spring. This will also help improve the stability of tall asters and keep them from flopping over. Dividing plants is another way to produce a lot more flowers and helps maintain healthy all-round plant growth.

HOLIDAY CLEARING If you are going away in summer for more than 2 weeks, remove all the blooms from your plants, even those that have not yet faded. This prevents them from going to seed in your absence.

A LITTLE BOOST Since perennials remain in place for years, give them a healthy dose of organic material when you first plant them. They will recover from their move quickly and establish with vigour. Before setting the plants in, mix leaf mould, garden compost or any well-decomposed organic matter into the bottom of the planting hole. In spring, spread garden compost around the base of the plants to stimulate regrowth.

ANNUAL CUTTING BACK At the end of autumn, cut back groundcover perennials to keep them thick and encourage young shoots to grow more vigorously. With bushy species, such as cotton lavender and thyme, cut back stems to two-thirds their height after flowering, or at the end of winter.

HERBACEOUS PERENNIAL CUTTINGS

1 Cut 15–20 cm sections from the year's young shoots or from any stems with no flowers.

2 Recut just below a node at the base of a bud, and remove all the leaves below.

3 Replant the cutting in a mixture of sand and potting mix, then water it liberally.

4 Keep the cuttings quite warm (15–18°C) under horticultural fleece or a plastic sheet that is suspended from stakes.

Add a burst of colour with late-flowering perennials in hot colours that will last until autumn.

Flowering leaf cacti like these epiphyllums and zygocactus combine well as a cascade of colour and texture when planted in a hanging basket.

● To ensure that clumps of plants continue to grow and regenerate, cut back one out of every three plants each year. This maintains appearance while encouraging regrowth.

JOY WITH GERANIUMS Ivy geraniums, zonal geraniums and pelargoniums are garden workhorses and all technically in the genus *Pelargonium*. They flower for many months, relish hot, dry times in summer and respond with vibrant flowers. Reward their perseverance with regular pruning. In spring, tip-prune from time to time to encourage a bushy shape. After the initial flush of flowers in spring, cut back lightly to encourage growth and flowers. Prune heavily in late summer or autumn. Use the best of these prunings for cuttings.
● Species geraniums (*Geranium* spp.), also called cranesbills, need little pruning other than removing spent flowers and cutting back invasive plants. Plants may be lightly sheared in late spring and summer to encourage more flowers.

HIGH AND DRY In summer, many perennials can succumb to fungal diseases, such as crown or root rot, if they are not correctly planted and cared for.
● Gerberas are susceptible to fungal problems as they grow from a structure called a crown. The crown of the gerbera needs to be grown at the surface of the soil in very well-drained, light soil. If the soil is poorly drained, create a raised bed. When planting, raise the crown 1–2 cm above the surface – never bury it under soil or mulch.

● When plants are in full growth they have a tendency to scramble over one another. Weaker or smaller plants can be smothered by over-enthusiastic neighbours leading to fungal and dieback problems. Regularly cut back plants that encroach on others to improve air circulation and prevent fungal diseases from occurring. Where your plants continually outgrow their space, consider moving them (or their neighbours) in the winter to an area where they will be able to grow without competition.

LAYER YOUR CARNATIONS Carnations often die out after 3 years of growth but regular layering provides young plants, which will gradually replace the old ones. Once plants that are 1 year old or more have flowered, take a side stem with no flowers and bend it down so that it touches the soil. Trim off the leaves, leaving several at the end. Make a very narrow slit in the side of the stem and insert this section in the soil, using a small wire hook to hold it down. Water with a fine spray. After 6 weeks roots will have formed, and it should be possible to separate the new plant from the mother plant with a sharp knife and transplant it. This is ideal for carnations in borders.

DIVIDE AND RULE When perennials are well established and happy in their environment, they have just one goal, which is to grow taller and bigger. This means that sooner or later they will have to be divided, before the most vigorous, such as alchemilla, artemisia and species geranium, overwhelm the less robust plants in your flowerbeds.

THINNING OUT Perennial seedlings should be thinned out (below) when the plants have reached a height of about 10 cm. Remove one out of every two or three plants, depending on their mature spread, and either discard or transplant them.
DISBUDDING Disbud any perennials with large flowers, such as chrysanthemums, to produce a showy single bloom. Wait until most of the side buds have emerged along with the central bud, then remove all but the central bud. The resulting flower will be magnificent.
PINCHING The opposite of disbudding, pinching forces the stems to branch out and produce a greater number of flowers. Pinching works well on perennials that branch easily, such as helenium and rudbeckia, and is best done when the plant has reached one-third of its height. Nip out the top 3–5 cm of the stems with your fingers or secateurs.

Versatile impatiens grown in hanging baskets bring colour and vibrancy to outside living areas such as patios and verandas.

By combining a variety of different propagation techniques, and choosing your plants carefully, you can very quickly and inexpensively achieve the look of a long-established garden at little cost.

• There are two key periods for dividing perennials. Divide spring perennials in summer or early autumn after they have flowered. Summer- and autumn-flowering perennials such as agapanthus can be divided at the end of winter, before spring growth occurs. Water the plants well during the weeks following division and, if necessary, remove some of the leaves to limit water loss.

• Remember: never transplant a perennial without dividing it first.

A NEW LEASE OF LIFE As they get older, herbaceous crowns become less vigorous, which means they often lose their central leaves. Give them a new lease of life by lifting them and cutting away the oldest parts of the plant, leaving the younger, outer sections intact. Proceed as if dividing normally but, instead of splitting the plant into smaller pieces, clean it by removing old and damaged roots. Without allowing the roots to dry out, replant immediately in well-loosened soil, then firm it down to remove any air pockets and water liberally.

DIFFICULT TO DIVIDE Acanthus, Japanese anemone and verbascum do not divide well because they have only a few fleshy roots, known as taproots. To get new plants you will have to take root cuttings.

• **ROOT CUTTINGS** Dig up a plant during its dormant period and remove a few root sections as thick as your little finger and 7–10 cm long. Replant the mother plant as soon as you have taken the cuttings. Make a slanted cut along the narrowest end of each cutting: this is where the new roots will grow. Plant each cutting upright in propagating mix or peat moss and sharp sand and cover with a fine layer of potting mix or sand. Finally, if you don't have a greenhouse, place the pot in a foam vegetable box and stand it in a sheltered spot such as on the veranda or porch. In spring shoots will appear from the root.

• **SELF-SEEDING** Aquilegias and lupins are difficult to divide, but they often seed themselves around the mother plant. When the plant has shed its flowers, leave the stems intact and, as the seeds ripen, harvest them for sowing or allow them to spread naturally.

HARVESTING SEEDS Collect seeds when the seedpod is mature, but before they are dispersed naturally. To avoid missing out, gather the seedpods when they are changing colour and drying out, or cover them with paper bags to catch the seeds as soon as the pods open. Shake the bags over a piece of paper to ensure that all of the seeds fall out, then leave them to dry in a sheltered place.

Beautiful and long-lasting foliage

Ornamental foliage plants adorn your garden for much longer than flowers. They brighten up shady spots, carpet the ground beneath trees and shrubs and in Victorian times were used in gravel gardens. Some are evergreen perennials while others take on striking winter tones.

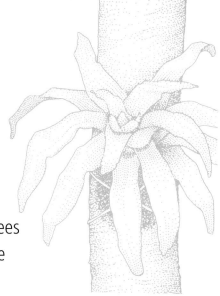

Large-leaved plants

A MAGNIFICENT SHOW These are shade-loving giants that flourish in cool positions and spread rapidly, which makes them useful as groundcovers where nothing else will grow. But it is important not to let their roots dry out during the summer months.
● In shady places, opt for filipendula, ligularia, macleaya, petasites and rodgersia.
● Acanthus, gunnera and ornamental rhubarb (*Rheum palmatum*) will tolerate sunshine and shade.
● Hostas develop into large clumps in east-facing gardens that enjoy morning sun and afternoon shaded warmth.

CONTROLLING SLUGS AND SNAILS These pests are very partial to hostas. Put an end to disappearing seedlings and leaves shot with holes by spreading a thick layer of wood ash, sawdust, sand or sharp gravel around the base of the plants in spring. Slugs hate anything that sticks to their mucus or slime.

FIND A SHELTERED HOME FOR YOUR RODGERSIA This plant's leaves are truly magnificent and similar to, although much bigger than, the leaves of the chestnut tree. Rodgersia likes very wet, even waterlogged, soil as well as an out-of-the-way sheltered position. Make sure you give it the protection it needs and choose a spot under deciduous trees where it will flourish. Water its foliage in very hot weather and make sure the soil does not dry out completely.

TAMING THE GUNNERA A work of art in its own right, gunnera has rounded, lobed leaves that are 1–2 m wide – and its leaf stalks are up to 2–3 m tall. Plant it in the spring, in moist or wet soil and full sun, ideally near the margins of a pond. In other locations, be sure to water it regularly.
● Allow a space of 3–4 m between the base of each plant. The gunnera takes root quite slowly and does not like being moved.
● In late autumn, fold the leaves down and over the plant. In cold areas, supplement this protective covering with a thick layer of dead leaves kept in place with conifer branches.

KEEPING GIANTS IN CHECK In small to medium-sized gardens, you can plant clumps of large-leaved perennials in big containers and plunge them into the soil. This will keep them from growing too big. You can also gradually uproot stems that are too invasive, particularly those of the winter heliotrope (*Petasites japonicus*). These plants spread by creeping rhizomes and eventually cover vast areas. Others, such as cow parsley, multiply by seeds. Cut off the flower stems before they produce seed heads; this will keep them from spreading across your garden.

Coloured leaves

ATTRACTIVE GROUNDCOVER Plant trailing perennials in bright colours under trees. Dead nettle, creeping bugle and persicaria lose no time in covering the ground. You only need four to six plants per square metre as they spread by runners or rhizomes.

Gunnera has giant foliage that looks stunning when grown next to water.

Stop snails the old-fashioned way, with a ring of ash.

COLOURFUL AND EVERGREEN Crimson and purple have a mellowing effect, while yellow adds zest and white lifts and softens contrasting colours. Scatter some evergreen perennials throughout your garden for year-round colour and interest.

A SPLASH OF CRIMSON OR PURPLE Species that don't need much maintenance when it's cold include bergenia, *Heuchera* 'Palace Purple' and 'Chocolate Ruffles', *Persicaria microcephala* 'Red Dragon' **1**, purple sage (*Salvia officinalis* 'Purpurascens'), various types of sedum that carpet beds, tubs and low walls, and the outstanding creeping bugle (*Ajuga reptans* 'Atropurpurea'), which spreads very quickly.

STATELY SPURGE This sculptural plant ranges from dull blue-green to bluish in colour, including *Euphorbia characias*, *E. polychroma* and *E. myrsinites*, which is good for groundcover. The most interesting euphorbia, known as chameleon spurge (*Euphorbia dulcis* 'Chameleon'), changes colour throughout the year and turns a rich purple in the winter.

WINTER FLOWERS AND FOLIAGE Hellebores make an excellent choice for winter. Corsican hellebore (*Helleborus argutifolius*) **2** is the most spectacular with its large, bluish jagged-edged leaves and creamy green flowers.

SUN-DRENCHED FLOWERBEDS For sunny borders, the creamy yellow foliage of oregano (*Origanum vulgare* 'Aureum') will certainly make an impact.

The brighter, variegated varieties, such as spotted dead nettle (*Lamium maculatum*) or variegated hosta, are your best choice.

BEWARE OF SUN SCORCH Avoid planting species with gold-coloured foliage in full sun. Because they are more sensitive to sun than green-foliage plants they may get sunburnt. Plants with grey, crimson and bluish foliage, however, will flourish in bright sunlight.

REVIVE YOUR BORDERS Bergenia adds beauty to borders and tolerates shade, full sun and all types of soil. Its red and purple colours are even brighter in poor soil.
● The only drawback is that bergenia spreads continuously by rhizomes. Divide every 2 or 3 years in late summer and replant only the newer outer sections.

Some attention-grabbing grasses

ORNAMENTAL SPECIMENS The large Poaceae or grass family has all the plants with long, narrow leaves, including cereals and grass that is grown on lawns and in meadows. Varieties have been selected generally for the colour, shape and unusual appearance of their leaves, although occasionally for the shape of their seed heads. Planted in isolated clumps, they provide an elegant focal point while, en masse, they form an attractive backdrop for flowering perennials.
● Wait until early spring to cut back dead foliage. As well as being ornamental – many species of Poaceae are colourful in winter – the foliage protects the roots from the cold.

GRASSES FOR WET SOILS Most varieties of evergreen carex, molinia (*Molinia caerulea*) and the graceful tussock grass (*Deschampsia cespitosa*) form dense clumps that eventually cover heavy, wet or boggy soils.

PERFECT FOR DRY AREAS There are two grass genera that are ideal for a full-sun spot with porous, sandy soil: *Pennisetum* and *Stipa*. The many species and varieties of *Pennisetum* and *Stipa* suit a variety of situations, and they have ornamental seed heads that look great in flower arrangements.
● The bright reddish *Imperata cylindrica* is a

Dead nettle makes an easy and colourful groundcover when it is planted in shade.

Enjoy grasses in winter but cut them back hard as the new growth appears in spring.

The long, arching sprays of miscanthus form an elegant contrast to the upright clumps of rosemary around it.

spectacular grass that sends up blood-red new shoots, which give it the common name of blood grass.

GRASSES SOFTEN AND SCREEN
Ornamental grasses cascade over rocks or garden paths, or they billow out to screen unwanted areas. Most will last until the end of winter before they need cutting back and many develop interesting colours and seeds.
● The slender leaves and small size of clumps of ornamental fescues are welcome in any garden (most are only around 15–20 cm tall). Blue fescue (*Festuca glauca*) has tufts of blue foliage that looks good all year round. For an Australian native alternative try mingo grass (*Themedia australis*).

AN ALTERNATIVE LAWN
In moist areas holcus (*Holcus mollis*) is a good alternative to a regularly mown lawn. Mow it just before flowering to ensure that its white foliage streaked with green remains thick and dense.

QUICK GROWTH
If you have a garden that has cool soil, fill it out quickly by planting miscanthus. This is a very fashionable grass – particularly the variety with striped foliage (*Miscanthus sinensis* 'Zebrinus') – and it forms tall ornamental clumps. Use it as a focal point or as an attractive windbreak at the back of a garden border.

DISTINCTIVE GROUNDCOVER
Plant mondo grass at the base of containerised perennials and shrubs for an attractive way to conceal the edges of the tubs. Ideal for this is dwarf mondo grass (sold as mini mondo), which grows in short, tufty clumps of around 10 cm high. Slightly larger, at 15–25 cm tall, but with distinctive narrow black leaves, is black mondo grass (*Ophiopogon planiscapus* 'Nigrescens'). This will arch over the edge of a pot. In the ground it makes an unusual edging plant. Both plants resemble grasses but are actually members of the lily family.

A GRASS TO STABILISE SLOPES
Choose aquatic grass (*Glyceria maxima*) for around the edges of a pond or river. This plant will stabilise sloping ground and it tolerates its roots being submerged in up to 20 cm of water. It grows to a height of about 80 cm and spreads rapidly by rhizomes.

FOR THOSE PLACES WHERE NOTHING WILL GROW
Hakone grass (*Hakonechloa macra*) is a highly ornamental member of the Poaceae family and is a good choice for shady city gardens and areas under trees, as it forms a dense carpet of variegated leaves.
● Knotted club rush (*Isolepis nodosa*) thrives in the moist soils near a pond or in gardens along the coast where salt air is a problem. It forms a spiky clump up to 1 m high dotted with round brown flower heads in summer.

BAMBOO FOR A DIFFERENT KIND OF HEDGE
Bamboo, a form of grass, forms clumps that are tall and readily produces new shoots. These emerge from the ground in spring, attain the height of last year's stems, then grow higher. The new stems increase the height of the clump every year until your selected species reaches adult size. Make sure you choose a species that is suitable for its position in the garden. If the clump becomes too bushy, cut off peripheral shoots as soon as they emerge from the ground.

Bamboos grown in pots provide excellent patio screening – and they rustle gently in the wind.

EXOTIC WINDBREAKS Medium and large clumping bamboos can look wonderful as isolated clumps and make excellent hedges. You can create a noise-reducing screen by planting two rows of species whose stems are completely covered in leaves, such as weavers bamboo (*Bambusa* 'Gracilis').

NATURAL WONDERS Dwarf bamboo species cover slopes, stabilise loose soil and will tolerate areas where grass would require too much attention. Clip only the smallest varieties, such as *Pleioblastus pygmaeus* var. *distichus*, twice a year – leave the other varieties to grow thicker unaided. Their irrepressible vigour makes them ideal for even the most inaccessible areas.

ELEGANT SCREENS For a balcony or patio, choose bamboo varieties that will not exceed 3 m high. Species with moderately vigorous rhizomes are also suitable for pots, but only if they are planted in sturdy tubs made of wood, concrete or brick – but not plastic. This is because their rhizomes are so strong they can easily split plastic tubs.

Fabulous ferns

TREE FERN TRICKS Tree ferns are tall, stately plants that add height and interest to a fern or shade garden. They respond well to overhead watering like a small dripper or micro-sprayer placed in the top of the plant.
● Spent fronds are unsightly. To keep these plants neat and tidy, regularly remove old fronds. Chop them into small pieces to spread under the plant as mulch.

FOR SHADY SPOTS Late 19th-century gardeners were enthusiastic growers of ferns, even building dedicated ferneries to provide ideal growing conditions. Ferns originated in dark prehistoric rainforests and so they tolerate even very dense shade. They thrive in a south-facing position in continually wet soil where other plants fail and they make ideal groundcover under trees, along with alocasias, clivias, hostas, irises or lady's mantles.

SET IN STONE Evergreen ferns are the ideal plant for shade and for planting in crevices of stone walls, beside steps and between the stones around ponds. Choose the Hart's

A bird's nest fern makes a dramatic foliage statement in any shady area in the garden.

tongue fern (*Asplenium scolopendrium*) with its slender green fronds, *Onoclea sensibilis*, whose delicate, pale green fronds dry out in winter, or maidenhair ferns.
● Very cool soil is good for the ostrich fern (*Matteucia struthiopteris*), or the lady fern (*Athyrium filix-femina*), which rapidly grows into clumps almost 1 m in diameter.
● The hardiest and least labour-intensive fern of all is the male fern, *Dryopteris filix-mas*, which will grow anywhere. It tolerates chalky soils and even drought.

PERFECT IN POTS Grow ferns in plastic pots to retain the moisture they love. To make a plastic pot look attractive, conceal it in a larger, decorative terracotta container such as an old urn. Put gravel at the bottom of the outer container before inserting the pot. If your terracotta urn is not large enough, line the sides with a plastic sheet and transplant the fern directly into it, leaving the bottom open for drainage. Once you have planted the fern, cover the surface of the soil with pieces of bark or other mulch to keep the potting mix moist. Remember to keep the pot well watered.

Ferns grow well in pots and can be clustered together to brighten up a dull spot.

Decorative plants are grown especially for their appearance, and pests should not be allowed to spoil their beauty. However, there are many ornamentals that are prone to disease.

Bulbs and roots

ARMILLARIA ROOT ROT

This fungus attacks the roots of flowering plants, such as the peony, most climbers and bulbs. See page 150.

BASAL ROT

● **SYMPTOMS** The leaves turn yellow and the roots or bulb give off a characteristic rotten smell. The underground parts of the plant lose colour and rot, and the outer skin withers. The rot is caused by a number of fungi and bacteria.
● **PLANTS AFFECTED** Most plants that grow from a bulb, rhizome or tuber.
● **TREATMENT** This persistent soil-borne disease is difficult to combat and spreads quickly.

It is best to carefully pull up and destroy affected plants as soon as the symptoms appear. Disinfect or discard infected soil. Replant with plants other than bulbs until the infection disappears, which can take several months. Prevent rot in overwintering bulbs and tubers by dusting with sulphur.

BLACK VINE WEEVIL

This weevil, whose larvae are more harmful than the adult insect, attacks a large number of flowering plants, such as the begonia, busy lizzy (*Impatiens*), fuchsia, pelargonium and primula. See page 151.

BLUE MOULD

● **SYMPTOMS** Reddish brown marks appear on the bulb, which are followed by a covering of bluish spores. The bulb then starts to rot. This is caused by a fungus that primarily attacks bulbs while in storage but it can also affect those in the soil.
● **PLANTS AFFECTED** Most types of bulbs including crocus, iris and tulip.
● **TREATMENT** Dust bulbs with sulphur as a preventive measure, then store in a dry, well-aired place that will not be affected by frost. Destroy bulbs as soon as the first symptoms appear.

CABBAGE MOTH

The caterpillar of this moth particularly attacks the roots of China aster, French marigold (*Tagetes*) and pelargonium. See page 205.

CROWN GALL

This bacterial disease is common in chrysanthemum, cineraria, dahlia, pelargonium, phlox and sweet pea. See page 150.

NECK AND ROOT ROT

● **SYMPTOMS** The stem goes soft and the rest of the plant withers and dries up. When violets are affected, purplish spores grow on their roots, which then rot and crumble. This rot is caused by a variety of fungi that grow vigorously in wet weather.
● **PLANTS AFFECTED** Busy lizzy, carnation, French marigold (*Tagetes*), lobelia, lupin, pansy, pelargonium, petunia, sage (*Salvia*), sweet alyssum, sweet pea, verbena and violet.
● **TREATMENT** Remove and destroy all affected plants. Replant with non-susceptible types and change your planting scheme every 2 years. Apply sulphur dust around the roots when planting, or at the base of the stems of healthy plants in infected areas. In bygone days, gardeners treated plants with milk spray and stinging nettle extract (see page 255) to protect plants at risk.

Stems

DAMPING OFF

● **SYMPTOMS** The seedlings seem to be growing well when, suddenly, their basal stems turn reddish and then black. The young plants wilt and die. Also known as black rot disease, damping off is caused by numerous fungi.
● **PLANTS AFFECTED** All seedlings.

● **TREATMENT** Use fresh seed-raising mix and store it in a cool, dry area out of direct sunlight. Disinfect all tools, pots and trays that are to be used for raising seedlings. Use a copper-based fungicide at first sign of attack.

NEMATODE (EELWORM)

● **SYMPTOMS** Leaves may wilt even though the plant doesn't need water. Infected stems twist, swell and burst. The leaves turn yellow, wither and become stringy. When bulbous plants are affected, the bulb turns soft and powdery and the plant dies. This is caused by microscopic nematodes (eelworms) that live in the soil and on plants. Nematodes can also carry plant viral diseases.
● **PLANTS AFFECTED** Many ornamental plants including chrysanthemum, hyacinth, narcissus, phlox and snowdrop.
● **TREATMENT** Pull up and bin the diseased plants, then remove the contaminated soil. If you notice the symptoms in your garden, lift and treat your bulbs by soaking them for 2 hours in water at a temperature of 40°C to prevent the disease from spreading to other plants. Plant French marigold (*Tagetes*) in infected soils as these plants are not attractive to nematodes and will starve them from the soil. Grow French marigolds near vulnerable plants to act as a deterrent.

XANTHOMONAS BLIGHT

● **SYMPTOMS** This bacterial disease produces brown patches on the stems of flowers, which eventually break, destroying flowers or seeds.
● **PLANTS AFFECTED** Poppy.
● **TREATMENT** Grow resistant varieties and avoid overcrowding

plants in the garden. Also avoid watering over the leaves. Use a registered fungicide and remove affected stems or plants.

Leaves

APHIDS

● **SYMPTOMS** The plant's growth slows and, if the infestation is large, its shoots wither and curl up. Aphids pierce the tissue and suck sap from the young leaves and stems, weakening the plant. Aphids may also spread viral diseases so should be controlled where possible.
● **PLANTS AFFECTED** Most ornamental plants.
● **TREATMENT** Apply a registered spray to the infested areas of the plant as soon as the pest is noticed. Garlic infusion and stinging nettle extract (see page 255) are traditional remedies which were used by earlier gardeners. Alternatively, introduce ladybird larvae into the garden or build a ladybird shelter to encourage these friendly insects to stay in your garden permanently.

BACTERIAL CANKER

● **SYMPTOMS** Circular spots appear on the leaves, and these are surrounded by a ring of yellow that is punctuated by little black raised points. These circular spots are sometimes semitransparent just before they turn brown or black. As the canker spreads, the leaves dry up and the plant will die. Also known as bacterial spot, this disease is caused by numerous bacteria that enter the plant through wounds.
● **PLANTS AFFECTED** Antirrhinum, delphinium and prunus species.
● **TREATMENT** Affected plants will need to be pulled up and destroyed. The only remedy is to prevent the disease by using disinfected soil, and taking care not to cause damage to plants when transplanting them.

BOTRYTIS

● **SYMPTOMS** Also known as grey mould, botrytis attacks the buds, leaves and fruits of plants. The buds become covered with a whitish powdery layer, which prevents them from opening. The leaves turn yellow and wither. The fruits change colour, go soft and eventually fall off. When the plant is shaken, it will give off a telltale white dust. Botrytis is caused by a fungus that attacks plants that are already damaged and weak.
● **PLANTS AFFECTED** Many ornamental species as well as fruit and vegetables.
● **TREATMENT** If the outbreak is serious, remove and bin any affected plants (do not put them on the compost heap). This disease can be prevented by good nutrition and air circulation around plants. Do not overcrowd plants. Remove infected growth as soon as it appears and spray with a registered fungicide.

CABBAGE MOTH

The yellowish brown or green caterpillar of this moth eats the leaves and shoots of pelargonium, stock and many other flowering plants. See page 205.

CABBAGE WHITE BUTTERFLY

The green caterpillars of this butterfly attack many ornamental plants including the geranium and nasturtium. See page 205.

CAPSID BUG

● **SYMPTOMS** There are so many holes in the leaves of plants affected by capsid bug that they seem to have been riddled by a volley of tiny bullets. The buds can also be affected, so that they fail to develop. There are raised brown marks on the fruits. Capsid bugs (*Lygus*) eat the leaves and inject a toxic substance into them, so destroying the cells.
● **PLANTS AFFECTED** Many plants, including chrysanthemum, geranium and sage (*Salvia*).
● **TREATMENT** Only in severe attacks spray with a registered insecticide such as pyrethrin and rotenone (Derris dust).

CYCLAMEN MITE

● **SYMPTOMS** Tiny insects infest the growing tips of cyclamen. They live and feed inside the leaf and flower buds causing the stem and leaves to become scarred and distorted into spoonlike shapes. Flowers fail to open.
● **PLANT AFFECTED** Cyclamen.
● **TREATMENT** No preparations are available to control these mites. Bin all infected plants.

FROGHOPPER

● **SYMPTOMS** Bright yellow or white streaks appear on the leaves. These are unsightly but do not actually damage the plant. During the nymphal stage, froghoppers hide inside a froth known as cuckoo spit. This pest belongs to several species of sap-sucking insect.
● **PLANTS AFFECTED** Busy lizzy, chrysanthemum, foxglove (*Digitalis*), marigold (*Tagetes*), primrose, sage (*Salvia*), tobacco plant and verbena.
● **TREATMENT** Pick off the insects by hand. If there are vast colonies, spray using an insecticide with a base of pyrethrin or bifenthrin. Apply a foliar feed at regular intervals during the summer to encourage new growth to repair the damage.

FUSARIUM WILT

● **SYMPTOMS** The plant seems to lack water even when it has been given the correct amount. Its leaves begin to wither and then go yellow and dry up. Sometimes they turn a pinkish colour and the base of the stem turns black. The roots can also be affected. This wilt can be caused by several different fungi. Damage occurs quickly in hot or humid weather.
● **PLANTS AFFECTED** Antirrhinum, aster, carnation, China aster (*Callistephus*), chrysanthemum, cineraria, sweet alyssum (*Lobularia*) and sweet pea.

● **TREATMENT** Pull up all affected plants and disinfect the soil. Replant with non-susceptible plants and dust the roots with sulphur when planting. Ensure good hygiene to prevent the fungi spreading.

GERANIUM RUST
● **SYMPTOMS** Yellowish marks appear on the surface of affected leaves and brown spores become visible on the underside. These are caused by a fungal infection that flourishes in wet weather.
● **PLANTS AFFECTED** Pelargonium. Other types of rust, which vary in colour, affect carnation, chrysanthemum, gypsophila, hollyhock, mallow, sweet william and all of the Malvaceae family.
● **TREATMENT** During damp periods, when geranium rust is most prevalent, spray affected plants several times, at fortnightly intervals, with products containing, for example, mancozeb. Alternatively, use stinging nettle extract or a milk spray (see page 255).

INKSPOT DISEASE
● **SYMPTOMS** Black spots or linear marks, caused by a fungal disease, appear on the leaves of kangaroo paws. Plants may die if not treated.
● **PLANTS AFFECTED** Kangaroo paw, especially *Anigozanthos manglesii* and its cultivars.
● **TREATMENT** Grow resistant varieties such as those in the Bush Ranger and Bush Gem series. Keep the plants free from overcrowding and grow in well-drained soil. Plants can be cut back to remove any affected growth. Treat with a registered fungicide.

LEAFMINER
● **SYMPTOMS** The leaves are mined by curving tunnels. If you place an affected leaf up against the light, you will be able to see larvae in these tunnels. These tiny larvae hatch from eggs laid in the leaf by adult flies. Severe leafminer infestations can result in the leaves dying. These flies can produce two or three generations in just 1 year.
● **PLANTS AFFECTED** Chrysanthemum, cineraria, columbine (*Aquilegia*), delphinium, gerbera, nasturtium and sweet pea.
● **TREATMENT** Pick off all badly affected leaves, or you can simply squash the larvae in their tunnels between your fingers. If the problem spreads, you may need to spray the foliage with a registered systemic treatment and repeat until it has been controlled.

LEAF NEMATODE
● **SYMPTOMS** Leaves begin to turn yellow then brown and finally die. Damage starts at the base of the plant. In tall-growing plants such as chrysanthemums its progression up the plant is obvious. The problem is caused by a nematode, which is splashed from the ground to the leaves.
● **PLANTS AFFECTED** African violet, chrysanthemum, coleus, ferns and other ornamentals.
● **TREATMENT** Remove all the affected leaves. Keep the soil well mulched and try to avoid disturbing the soil when watering. Stake chrysanthemums to avoid contact with the soil. Do not propagate from affected plants (particularly chrysanthemums). When you notice damage, spray with a registered systemic insecticide.

LEAF SPOT

● **SYMPTOMS** Round spots with yellow edges, which gradually spread and turn black, can be seen on the surface of the leaves. These spots may join together to produce large dead areas on the leaves. Stems and also roots, especially tubers, may be affected and rot. These symptoms are caused by a fungus that develops in summer and autumn when the atmosphere is very humid.
● **PLANTS AFFECTED** Many different plants are affected by this disease.
● **TREATMENT** This disease can spread rapidly, so at the first signs of attack, spray with a copper-based treatment and repeat as per manufacturer's instructions. Foliar feeding in the summer will aid recovery.

LILY CATERPILLAR
● **SYMPTOMS** This yellow, grey and black striped caterpillar feeds on the surface of the leaves and burrows into the leaf sheath at the base of the plant. The leaves may start to look tattered. Secondary rot may follow where the insects feed. Left unchecked, this caterpillar may kill plants.
● **PLANTS AFFECTED** Clivia, spider lily and other members of the amaryllis family.
● **TREATMENT** Squash visible caterpillars with your hands, or use a contact insecticide. Treat any secondary infections with a registered fungicide.

MEALYBUG

● **SYMPTOMS** Tiny soft-bodied insects appear on the undersides of leaves and at leaf axils (where the leaf stalk joins the stem). The foliage becomes sticky with a fluffy white wax that is excreted to cover the mealybugs and their eggs. Also attacks roots.
● **PLANTS AFFECTED** Plants in the greenhouse, potted plants and many garden plants, particularly if they are under stress due to lack of water or too much shade.
● **TREATMENT** Introduce ladybird larvae on the larger plants and a predatory mite on smaller ones. Use a systemic insecticide. If infestation is severe, destroy affected plants.

METALLIC FLEA BEETLE
● **SYMPTOMS** Round holes appear in the leaves. These then turn a whitish colour and dry up. The plant may die if it is a heavy infestation. These beetles thrive in warm, sunny weather in spring and summer. Beetles jump off when an infected plant is shaken.
● **PLANTS AFFECTED** Dahlia.
● **TREATMENT** White or yellow plastic containers with water and detergent or insecticide are attractive to these insects. Don't use if children or pets use the garden. If necessary, spray with a registered treatment and feed to aid recovery.

POWDERY MILDEW
A white powdery coating appears on leaves and young shoots. The

plant's leaves become deformed, its growth is stunted and its flowers do not set. This affects zinnia and many ornamentals. Avoid it by growing varieties that are resistant. Use milk spray (see page 255) or a registered fungicide. See page 253.

SHOTHOLE

Spots appear on the leaves, which then turn brown and eventually fall out, leaving the leaves looking like they've been peppered by tiny gunshots. This disease, which is caused by a number of fungi, bacteria and viruses, affects a wide range of plants. See page 253.

SLUGS AND SNAILS

● **SYMPTOMS** The edges of leaves, sometimes even whole leaves, have been eaten. A slimy trail indicates their presence. They come in many colours and sizes, and wet weather makes the situation worse as plants tend to rot.
● **PLANTS AFFECTED** Most garden plants and seedlings.
● **TREATMENT** Collect these pests by torchlight at night when they are most active and visible. Place traps at intervals around the garden and empty frequently. Tip the slugs into plastic bags, tie the tops and put them in the garbage bin. Use the traditional barriers of sharp sand, ash or one of the modern granular equivalents around plants that are at risk. Copper rings, tape and sprays were also used in bygone

days and are still available today. Encourage slug- and snail-eating wildlife into your garden – frogs, birds and lizards will all eat many slugs and snails.

SNAPDRAGON RUST

● **SYMPTOMS** Leaves start to yellow, and brown lumps begin to form on their undersides.
● **PLANTS AFFECTED** Snapdragon.
● **TREATMENT** Grow resistant varieties and avoid watering over leaves. Use a registered fungicide.

SOOTY MOULD

● **SYMPTOMS** The upper side of the leaves becomes sticky and turns a blackish colour, as if soot has fallen on it. Sooty mould is caused by a fungus that grows on honeydew, which is excreted by sap-sucking insects such as aphids, mealybugs and scale. It does not threaten the plant's life, but slows its growth by blocking out air and light.
● **PLANTS AFFECTED** All ornamental species attacked by sap-sucking insects.
● **TREATMENT** Wipe the leaves of affected plants to remove the mould, if practical, and spray foliage with a spray oil, soap spray or with a registered systemic treatment to control the pest.

STAGHORN BEETLE

● **SYMPTOMS** The tips of the fronds turn brown and holes develop in the fronds.
● **PLANTS AFFECTED** Elkhorn and staghorn ferns.

● **TREATMENT** Remove all visible beetles by hand. Trim damaged leaf tips to remove the feeding larvae. If necessary, spray with some diluted contact or systemic insecticide.

VERTICILLIUM WILT

● **SYMPTOMS** Leaves start to wither then turn yellow and dry up. The stems and roots lose colour. This wilt is caused by fungi that block the circulation of sap.
● **PLANTS AFFECTED** Antirrhinum, bellflower (*Campanula*), carnation (*Dianthus*), chrysanthemum, cineraria, gerbera, pelargonium, poppy and sage (*Salvia*).
● **TREATMENT** No chemicals can combat this disease. Pull up infected plants and bin them; do not put disease-infected plants on the compost heap. Disinfect tools that have had contact with infected plants, and replace soil in which they have been grown.

WHITEFLY

● **SYMPTOMS** A cloud of whiteflies that fly off when disturbed. Swarms of them can be found both outside and in greenhouses. They secrete honeydew on the leaves, causing a black mould to develop. Whiteflies lay their eggs under leaves, from which emerge larvae (scales), each with a covering of white waxy film that makes them look like mealybugs. These larvae live on the underside of the leaves and suck sap, which gradually weakens the plant.

● **PLANTS AFFECTED** Many garden plants including abutilon, busy lizzy, fuchsia, gerbera, pelargonium and many more.
● **TREATMENT** Use yellow sticky cards, to which the whiteflies get stuck (this also enables conclusive identification). It is possible to purchase 'scales' of *Encarsia formosa*, a tiny parasitic wasp that preys on the larvae. The temperature must be above 10°C for this wasp to survive. If necessary, spray with pyrethrin or an insecticidal soap in midsummer, paying attention to the undersides of the leaves. Repeat until cleared of the insect.

Flowers

BIG BUD

● **SYMPTOMS** The flowers of affected plants become distorted and may turn green instead of their normal colour. Stems may also become distorted and stiff or the plant may be more bushy than normal. The disease, a Mycoplasma, is spread by a sapsucking insect, the brown leafhopper, as it feeds on the plant. This problem is also called 'greening' or 'virescence'.
● **PLANTS AFFECTED** Aster, chrysanthemum, dahlia, geranium, gerbera, zinnia (as well as many vegetable crops including lettuce, potato and tomato – in affected fruiting plants, the production of fruit is reduced).
● **TREATMENT** Protect your plants by using a systemic spray or by squashing leafhoppers seen on plants. Remove badly affected growth or misshapen flowers. Keep the area free of weeds, which can also harbour the pest.

CHAPTER 3

Ornamental trees and shrubs

The beauty of roses

No flower is more a part of the quintessential cottage garden than the rose. Over the centuries, gardeners have celebrated it, nurtured it and developed hundreds of disease-resistant, repeat-flowering varieties. But the charming old roses have never fallen out of favour. These favourites of yesteryear have much to offer modern gardeners.

Plant your new rose successfully

SPECIAL VARIETIES FOR POOR SOIL
Even gardeners with very difficult garden conditions can grow roses. You can choose varieties that have been bred or hybridised to tolerate adverse conditions and even humid climates. Some rose growers actually toughen up their plants by growing them without fertiliser and pesticides, and by rationing water. This creates plants that are much better able to grow in poor environments.
● You can improve your soil to encourage even a tricky specimen to flourish. First, choose a site that has not been previously used for roses and dig in well-composted manure or garden compost to boost the organic content of the soil and feed the rose well at planting. Once established, dose regularly with dedicated rose feed and mulch with chopped lucerne or other organic mulch and regularly add a spadeful of old manure to the mulch under each rose.

Don't worry if you can't plant your new dormant rose bushes straight away. Simply find a shaded spot and keep their roots protected with a layer of garden soil so the plant doesn't dry out.

Roses and lavender make a fragrant pair and the lavender keeps aphids at bay and attracts bees.

THE BEST TIME TO PLANT Winter is the best time to plant roses as this is when they are dormant. From late autumn until the end of winter, good-quality bare-root roses are plentiful and often well priced.
● As roses begin to grow and flower they are sold in pots. Those planted between spring and autumn will need a little extra care and attention to ensure they establish well.

WAIT BEFORE BUYING Be careful not to buy bare-root roses too early in the autumn. If they are lifted before time they may start to sprout if the weather turns mild, and these shoots will be susceptible to frost. For the best results, wait until the natural resting period in late autumn or early winter, when they have shed their leaves and are dormant.

FRUIT AND VEGETABLES HELP ROSES THRIVE
Plant your roses close to the herb garden. Chives, lavender, lemon balm, rosemary, tarragon and thyme repel many garden pests.
● Chives help roses to combat powdery mildew because, like garlic, leek and onion, they contain sulphur compounds that are a natural enemy of powdery mildew.
● Old-time gardeners say banana skins improve the colour of roses. We now know that this is because they are high in starch and potash, which breaks down to feed the roses.

Lightly cover banana skins added to the soil around roses.

The soft colours of sweetly scented old roses fit perfectly into a traditional cottage garden setting.

Look out for new stocks of bare-root roses from mid-May or, if the weather is mild, wait until mid-June, when plants are less likely to regrow before spring.

CONTAINERISED ROSES ARE THIRSTY
If you buy roses in pots, plant them straight away. If you can't, then make sure you keep them well watered.
● Submerge the rose container into a bucket of water for half an hour before planting.

LET THE SUN SHINE IN
Don't forget the golden rule: roses love sunshine. For the best results plant them in a site where they will get as much sun as possible. At least 6 hours a day from early morning onwards is vital.

NOT TOO DRY, NOT TOO WET
Roses will not thrive in wet or waterlogged soils. If you have a heavy soil, then improve the drainage before planting your roses. Dig some gypsum and lots of good organic matter into the soil. Alternatively, you could make a raised bed of 30 cm to 1 m high and fill it with a very good-quality organic garden mix.
● Avoid areas close to walls or fences as these may prevent rain from reaching your plants.

AVOID WET WEATHER FOR PLANTING
If it has rained continually since you bought your roses or if there has been a hard frost, wait for the weather to improve before you plant them. Choose a spot at the base of a cool, sheltered wall or somewhere protected from the sun and dig a trench with a sloping side. Spread out the roots, lay them against the slope and cover them with soil up to one-third to one-half of their stems. Make sure that no two plants overlap.
● When the weather improves, prepare your site, dig up the roses, and plant them in their final positions. Do not leave the bare roots in the open for more than an hour.

SELF-SUFFICIENT ROSES
Contrary to popular belief, roses are actually drought-hardy plants. Don't overwater. A deep watering that soaks the ground, not the foliage, once or twice a week, is more than enough for producing healthy plants.
● Give roses extra water if they are newly planted, are in new growth or are coming into flower during a heatwave.

TIDY ROOTS
Before planting new roses, tidy up dense and tangled root balls. Use sharp secateurs to carefully remove some of the overgrown roots. This allows the remaining roots space to grow quickly into the new surrounding soil.

WAIT BEFORE TRAINING CLIMBERS
When planting climbing roses, tie the stems loosely to the lattice and wait for several days until the soil has settled around the new plant. When the ground returns to its original level, refasten the stems securely.

PLANTING A BARE-ROOT ROSE

1 Dig a hole 40–50 cm deep and loosen the sides and bottom with a fork. Mix a dedicated granular rose fertiliser into the soil in the planting hole before you position the rose.

2 Untangle the roots and cut off any that are damaged. Trim the others back to one or two-thirds of their length. If unpruned, cut back stems to one-third of their length and remove any that are dead, diseased or crossing.

3 Dress the roots by soaking them in a bucket of water and soil, with the addition of seaweed extract, to reduce transplant shock. Coating the roots in this solution will keep them from drying out when they are planted in the earth.

4 Build a small mound of earth, place the rose on it and spread out the roots. The graft union of the plant should be above the surface of the soil. Fill in the hole and tamp down with your hand, then water well.

Choosing the perfect roses for your garden

A RED, RED ROSE Red roses vary in colour and different reds may jar if they are planted together. They can be striking against a dark green background.

● For a bright, pure red rose you can choose 'Ingrid Bergman', 'Kardinal' or 'Altissimo', which is a climber with a single pure red flower. For a pink-red, 'Titan' is hard to beat and comes in a climbing form as well. The mantel for best orange-red is held by 'Fragrant Cloud', which also has a fabulous scent. Several roses vie for the title of best dark red including 'Kentucky Derby', 'Mr Lincoln', 'Oklahoma' and 'Papa Meilland'. 'Guinée' is the darkest of the red climbers.

● Red roses lose some of their charm in the heat of summer when their colour can fade or become sun-bleached. In the spring and autumn red roses are at their best. A little light summer shade can help improve colour.

OLD-FASHIONED ROSES If you like the old roses, there are hundreds to choose from. Nurseries stock a wide range of species and varieties, all with a proven track record. Try some of these old favourites in your garden.

● **BUSH AND SHRUB ROSES** 'Ballerina', light pink; 'Buff Beauty', yellow and buff; 'Cardinal de Richelieu', purple; 'Fantin Latour', soft pink; 'Félicité Parmentier', pinkish white with bluish leaves; 'Hansa', bright red; 'Mme Caroline Testout', satin pink; 'Mrs John Laing', a delicate pink; 'Reine des Violettes', rich purple, fading to lilac; 'Variegata di Bologna', crimson-striped white flowers.

● **WIDESPREAD GROUNDCOVER** 'Max Graf', bright pink flowers.
● **FOR POTS** 'Little White Pet'.
● **FOR HEDGES** 'Stanwell Perpetual' and 'Roseraie de l'Haÿ'.
● **CLIMBERS AND RAMBLERS** 'Blush Noisette', delicate pink; 'Cécile Brunner', pink; 'Dorothy Perkins', light pink; 'Félicité et Perpétue', white.

LATE COLOUR If you want a really low-maintenance shrub rose with glorious autumn hips to brighten your garden at the end of summer then consider *Rosa glauca*. It has beautiful blue-grey leaves, a mass of pink single flowers and bright red hips.

TOP TIPS FOR CHOOSING ROSES Roses are versatile plants, but some are more suited to particular situations than others.

● **SPECIES ROSES** These are vigorous plants found in the wild or bred close to the wild species as hybrids. They are used to brighten boundary hedges or in natural plantings.
● **OLD ROSES** Their gentle colours, sweet scent and the varied and appealing shapes of their blooms make them the perfect rose for cottage, country or period gardens.
● **HYBRID TEA ROSES** Highly scented and good for cutting. Team with old-fashioned flowers to soften their bright colours.
● **FLORIBUNDA ROSES** Ideal for creating blocks of colour in mass plantings. Their long flowering season suits a mixed border.
● **MODERN SHRUB ROSES** Bred to combine all the very best features of roses – fragrance, beauty and disease resistance.
● **CLIMBING AND RAMBLING ROSES** Use to clothe arches, obelisks, walls and lattice, or train along ropes for swags of flowers.
● **MINIATURE ROSES** Ideal for growing in pots or at the front of a mixed border.

Gardener's Choice

ROSES TO SUIT EVERY TASTE

COVER A POST, ARCH OR WALL If you want to grow climbing roses up a post, over the top of an arch or along a wall look for 'American Pillar' **1**, readily trained up a post, 'Handel' **2** for a wall or arch or the easy-going single pink climbing form of 'Sparries-hoop' for any wall.

COLOUR THROUGHOUT THE WINTER Single-flowered *Rosa moyesii* **3** is an ancestor of modern roses. It has ornamental hips, especially in cool climates.

TROUBLE-FREE FLOWERS 'Iceberg' **4** with its lightly scented white flowers is one of the easiest of all roses to grow. It is available as a bush rose but more usually seen as one of the tall-stemmed standards or climbers. Coloured varieties including 'Burgundy Iceberg' and 'Blushing Pink' are also available.

AN OLD ROSE 'Variegata di Bologna' **5** is a hardy Bourbon rose that simply oozes charm. It needs tying to supports.

FLOWERS TILL AUTUMN 'Centenaire de Lourdes' **6** is a wonderful floribunda with a particularly long flowering period.

Old-fashioned bush and shrub roses are full of charm and romance. Here are some favourites (from left to right): 'Ballerina', 'Félicité Parmentier', 'Max Graf' and 'Roseraie de l'Haÿ'.

1 2
3 4
5 6

MIX AND MATCH ROSES

SPRING DISPLAY Roses can be preceded in spring by a display of anemone, columbine, hellebore and primula.

HERBACEOUS PERENNIALS (below) Extend the rose flowering season by planting agapanthus, aster, campanula, hosta, iris, lilies, oenothera, salvia and species geranium.

DECORATIVE HERBS Fennel provides an excellent backdrop for shrub roses, and tarragon looks good under bush roses.

TALL BEARDED IRISES These tall plants can create wonderfully bold contrasts. Choose colours that highlight your roses, for example purple irises look stunning with yellow or orange roses. Irises and roses also enjoy the same growing conditions.

INTERESTING SHRUBS There are many shrubs that make good companions for roses, including abelia, ceanothus, clematis, eleagnus, hibiscus, honeysuckle, oleander, *Viburnum carlesii* and *V. mariesii* and weigela.

ATTRACTIVE BORDERS Plant an edging of dwarf box (*Buxus* 'Suffruticosa'), blue or white lavender, or nepeta to give your rose beds the perfect finish.

Fill your garden with the heady scent of roses

Climbing roses work their magic above other plants. The prolific 'Wedding Day' cascades over trees, walls and pergolas.

GROUNDCOVER ROSES Low-growing roses are available in many varieties from 30 cm to 1.2 m high. These plants spread outwards rather than upwards, and form wonderful carpets of flowers. Many can also be used to create hedges up to 1.2 m high and lose no time in covering banks, rock gardens and other inaccessible places. They can also form decorative mounds that can be used to hide unsightly garden features such as old tree stumps and manhole covers.
● Groundcover roses usually need little care and attention and are extremely hardy. This is particularly true of 'landscape' roses, a category bred for ornamental use in towns, parks and roads. Try to make the most of their sturdiness to protect vulnerable areas of your garden. For example, use a thorny variety such as *Rosa* 'Paulii' to stop animals getting into your flower garden.
● To keep the roses in their horizontal state, shear them regularly, and don't worry about cutting off the buds as new flowers will soon follow. Prune hard in winter.

CASCADING ROSES If you want to train roses over a high wall, choose the vigorous varieties such as 'Madame Alfred Carrière', which is white, flushed with pink. 'New Dawn' and 'Wedding Day' bloom profusely and will cascade nicely over pergolas or gazebos. 'Climbing Softee' has clusters of

YESTERDAY'S SECRETS

A LOOK AT ROSES THROUGH THE AGES

Today the noble rose is one of the most popular garden flowers, but traditionally it was more valued for its healing properties than for its beauty. Pliny listed over 30 medicines that could be derived from roses. *Rosa gallica* 'Officinalis' is thought to be the medicinal rose that was cultivated by the Romans and later adopted as the red Rose of Lancaster. The flowers were used by the Greeks, Romans and Egyptians in perfumes and in oils and were thought to help ward off the plague. The Victorians used rose petals in jellies, sandwiches and in tea.
● Garden lore says to plant a rose in any month with an 'r' in it, but, in the southern hemisphere, roses are best planted in the cold months from May to July.

small, cream flowers. It's a good choice to cascade near a path or sitting area as it has no thorns and can be trained as a short climber.

POTTED ROSES: THINK BIG If you are growing roses in containers, use large pots that won't restrict the roots. As a fairly rough guide, plant standard roses in 50 cm wide and 60 cm deep pots. A bush rose – hybrid tea or floribunda – will need a 40 cm wide and 50 cm deep pot. Miniature roses thrive in smaller containers, around 30 cm deep.
● Don't forget that these sizes are for young plants. As your roses grow they will need to be transplanted into progressively larger containers in winter.

SURROUND YOUR PONDS Ramblers and groundcover roses create attractive barriers around water. Plant them around the edge of a pond in large groups – in pots or in the ground about 40 cm apart – to stop children from leaning over the water and to discourage pets. Roses also attract a variety of wildlife to the water, making it a natural haven.

OVER-EXUBERANCE In days gone by roses were often encouraged to ramble wherever they pleased, which included often being left to scramble freely into trees. However, letting any climbing plant completely overrun a tree or shrub could soon lead to problems. For instance, branches may break or even die back, and the entire tree could gradually decline leaving an expensive tree surgery bill. If you want roses to scramble safely, grow them over a wall, lattice or pergola.

POSSUM MAGIC Possums do love roses, which can make growing roses in areas where possums are present a nightmare. Gardeners have developed some ingenious methods of deterring these furry nighttime visitors:
● Install motion-sensitive lights that turn on when possums approach.
● Block access to the roses by using a barrier around the main trunk or branches, or by covering them at night with shadecloth.
● Hang shiny discs such as unwanted CDs in among the roses.
● Spray new shoots and roses with a deterrent product such as D-ter.

MAKE BEDS MORE INTERESTING A bed that is home to only roses can look sparse for much of the year, when they are not in flower. To add some interest and 'clothe' the bare lower stems of large-flowered roses, plant perennials such as alchemilla, artemisia, dwarf potentilla, nepeta and sage.

1 For the best results plant roses in autumn or spring. Choose plants that have at least three healthy and well-balanced branches.

2 Before planting, water the root ball thoroughly. Either soak the pot in a bucket of water or pour water directly into the top of the pot.

3 If the roots are pot-bound, tangled and dense, then carefully tease them apart and thin them out if necessary.

4 After planting and watering, spread a thick layer of organic mulch such as composted bark, lucerne or sugar cane around the base to keep the soil moist.

Gardener's Choice

AUTUMN ROSES

Modern-day rose varieties include an increasing number that will reflower in late summer and remain in bloom until the end of May. These long-flowering varieties are available in all colours.

RED 'Alec's Red' **1**, 'Ena Harkness' and 'Tess of the D'Urbervilles' are good reds.

PINK 'Anne Boleyn' and 'Queen Elizabeth' **2** produce pink flowers.

ORANGE AND YELLOW 'Rusticana' has orange flowers, while 'Golden Wings' **3** is a light buttery yellow.

WHITE 'Anita Pereire' **4** boasts pure white flowers until winter, as does 'Iceberg', and 'Glamis Castle' reflowers with prolific white blooms.

FOLIAGE Some species roses and hybrid roses can be grown for the special appeal of their feathery foliage and attractive hips, in addition to their colourful flowers. Varieties in the Rugosa and Pimpinellifolia families have many tiny leaves which turn from lustrous bronze to orange, even red, in autumn, and many produce glossy hips. Roses with both ornamental foliage and hips include *Rosa rugosa* and *Rosa glauca*.

WEED SUPPRESSORS Covering the bare soil in a rose bed with groundcover plants will also smother the weeds. Lavender bushes make an attractive combination with roses, the silvery grey foliage is a wonderful foil to the colours of the blooms. The fragrance also repels some garden pests.

How can you get more from your rosebushes?

LEAVE THE SOIL NEAT AND TIDY Old-fashioned rose gardens were often rather drab: they were regularly hoed and weeded and the ground was left completely bare in a determined effort to avoid the invasion of aphids and other pests. Nowadays rose beds often contain other plants for added interest. But that does not mean you can relax about keeping the beds tidy. Garden pests can and will attack discarded plant material as well as a variety of weeds, so be sure to remove any waste and weeds, especially after pruning.

TOP TIPS FOR TRAINING ROSES Keep up with training your climbers and ramblers. Keep them tied in and tidy them regularly as they grow and mature; this will also boost flowering and make day-to-day maintenance easier. Otherwise the branches will become tangled and you may lose track of stems that should be pruned or removed.
● **LATTICEWORK AND PERGOLAS** Regularly check to ensure that new shoots have not grown through to the underside of the structure. Ensuring that a plant is growing on one side of the structure only will make it easier to take the plants down if you need to do any repairs. It will also make maintenance work and annual pruning and removing dead wood simpler.
● **HORIZONTAL WIRES** Use these to train roses up walls. Separate the upward-growing stems when you tie them in and gently curve them, which will generate a greater number of flowers on each stem.
● **VERTICAL TRAINING WIRES** To grow tall climbers and ramblers on high walls, use vertical wires for good support. On a two-storey house front, if you want to train roses up to the first floor, then position the wires

between ground-floor windows and fix the central stems to them. Then you can spread the central stems and train the canes horizontally below the first-floor windows.

PROLIFIC FLOWERS Climbing roses will produce more flowers if you bend their supple stems as they grow by attaching a weight to them, such as a small pot. For the best results, train the stems horizontally as much as possible. If you are growing a rose over a column, arch or pergola, choose small-flowered species because they will adapt more easily to the required shape.

NO MORE CHEMICALS Growing roses in ideal conditions reduces the risk of disease and increases the size and number of flowers. Full sun, regular deep watering applied to the roots, and good air circulation all help roses to be disease free. Regular treatments with spray oils and bicarbonate of soda (use 1 teaspoon of bicarb to 1 litre of water) reduces problems with black spot. Full-cream milk, diluted with 9 parts water, is an excellent spray to prevent powdery mildew.

Encourage profuse flowering by adding weight to stems.

Check plant ties regularly and adjust them if need be.

PEGGING ROSES TO PRODUCE MORE FLOWERS

This technique is suitable for hybrid roses that tend to grow long shoots with flowers only at the ends. By restricting growth, pegging encourages stems to produce more flowers.

1 During the latter part of autumn, clear the soil at the base of the rosebush and remove any dead leaves.

2 Cut off at ground level any stems that flowered during the current season and any that may hinder arching.

3 One by one, gently bend long, non-flowering stems until their tips are touching the ground. Space them evenly around the clump.

4 Hold them in place with hooks or pegs made of supple bamboo, at least 60 cm from the base.

5 Leave the bent stems pegged like this until the following autumn.

6 As the current year's new shoots emerge from the bent branches, the plant will start to look like a pincushion.

Caring for roses

GOOD TIMING FOR TREATMENT If you have to treat your roses, remember to choose a day when the weather is calm and not rainy or windy. This ensures treatments are applied exactly where they are needed and not blown onto nearby plants or washed off the plant and down into the soil. It is best to apply any garden treatment during the early morning or evening, out of the heat of strong sun.

DROUGHT TOLERANT Rosebushes are surprisingly drought-tolerant plants and they will thrive during dry conditions. To prevent flowers burning in the sun or plants wilting due to lack of rain, water roses deeply once or twice a week, avoiding watering over the leaves as this can promote disease.
● If you have a drip irrigation system, you will need two or more drippers for each rosebush; this will ensure the plants get even watering. Also, it doesn't take long to check how deeply the moisture has penetrated the soil – remember it should be watering the roots, not just the surface.

WINTER SPRAY Roses benefit from a spray with lime sulphur immediately after pruning in winter. This removes any persistent scale and destroys overwintering eggs and fungal spores. To treat effectively, saturate the stems and the soil around each rose. Don't spray if there are new shoots present as lime sulphur can burn tender growth.

MULCH IS A MUST Roses grow better when their roots are covered with organic mulch. Use 5–7 cm of lucerne, composted pine bark, sugar cane or compost. As the mulch breaks down it continually feeds the soil and promotes strong growth on the rose. To add extra nutrients mix well-rotted cow manure or pelletised chicken manure into the mulch. Mulch also keeps moisture in the soil and reduces soil temperatures in summer.
● Lucerne has been shown to reduce the incidence of black spot on roses and is recommended as the best mulch for roses.

PEST CONTROL Aphids are attracted to soft new growth on roses. As soon as the roses begin to send out new shoots, remember to check for aphids and either remove them by squashing them gently with a gloved hand,

A sunny wall is an ideal spot for a climbing rose, which can be trained to enhance a feature such as this window.

knock them off with a few strong squirts from the hose or spray them with a spray oil or other chemical that's registered for aphids.
● Plant nasturtiums around a rose bed. They will attract colonies of aphids to their stems and leaves, which can then be cut off and destroyed. The hardy nasturtium plants will quickly recover, and your roses will have been spared an aphid infestation.

THE RIGHT TIME TO WATER During the summer, only water your roses early in the morning and never in the middle of the day. Also avoid watering in the evening after a humid day as this will promote diseases, such as black spot, which develops in hot, wet atmospheres, and powdery mildew, which occurs when roses are grown in soils that are too dry.
● Apply water around the base of the plant and avoid using a fine spray, as roses weighed down with water will not last long. Overwet leaves may also burn in the sun from the magnifying effect of the droplets.
● Water the soil thoroughly before spreading liquid manure around the base of the plants, or do this after it has rained.

HOLES IN YOUR ROSEBUDS This is a sign that small caterpillars are living in your rose and that the flowers may soon be entirely eaten away. There are two natural solutions: simply remove all the affected buds, or plant

Water well at the base of the plant – a small mound of soil at the base will stop water draining away too quickly.

shrubs and flowers that attract small birds and wasps alongside your rosebushes. The birds and wasps will eat the caterpillars and keep them off your roses.

PREVENT POWDERY MILDEW Whitish, floury marks on the leaves and buds of roses are the symptoms of this disease, which often appears in mild, dry weather. The best way to prevent it is to water infrequently but profusely. This will encourage the plants to push their roots deep into the soil, and roses with deep roots are known to be able to withstand powdery mildew.
● Also reduce the incidence of this disease by growing roses in full sun and encouraging good air circulation around the plants by keeping competing plants from engulfing the rosebushes.

FIGHT FUNGAL DISEASE Treat your roses to a tonic of sulphur, a powder contained in most rose feeds. Sulphur helps to unlock inaccessible nutrients in the soil, gives your roses a boost and helps to combat black spot and powdery mildew.

Pruning and trimming for better flowers

WELL-PRUNED ROSES When pruning your roses, systematically remove all dead, diseased, stunted, damaged or broken wood. The pruning wound should be very white. If it is brown, cut slightly lower down into living stems. Remove any stems that rub together, cross over each other or look as if they are likely to cross in the future.

AIM FOR OPEN GROWTH Open up the centre of the plant as much as possible and cut off any suckers growing below the graft union, removing them at the stem. Retain only healthy stems and cut them back to a good length for the shape of your bush.

WHEN TO PRUNE Roses are generally pruned in winter but the timing of pruning really depends on your climate. In warm climates prune roses from June to early July. In cold or frosty areas it is a good idea to

This shows a healthy pruning cut that has removed old growth. Always sterilise your secateurs before moving on to the next plant.

prune in early August. This later pruning in colder areas delays the appearance of new growth shoots, which are likely to be burnt by frosts, until after the last frosts. Prune roses back by at least one-third, which will stimulate lots of new shoots for new spring and summer flowers.
● **EXCEPTIONS TO THE RULES** Don't prune roses in winter that only flower in spring such as banksia roses. A heavy pruning in winter will remove spring blooms, so prune these roses after flowering.
● **SUMMER PRUNE** Lightly pruning repeat-flowering roses at the end of summer will promote a good flush of autumn blooms. Cut back flowered stems as if picking a long-stemmed bouquet. Fertilise after pruning.

REMOVING SUCKERS

Suckers are stems that grow from the plant base beneath the graft union. A sucker tends to be bright green and has seven leaves. These shoots are from the root stock, so are different from the rose you are growing. Remove them or they will drain the rose's energy to the detriment of the rest of the plant.

1 Dig carefully around the base of the rose with a spade to uncover the point where the sucker is attached. This will be beneath the graft union.

2 Cut the sucker as close as possible to the stem from which it is growing, taking good care not to damage the stem. Remember: never remove suckers from above the ground.

3 Carefully replace the earth and water well. Keep a close watch on your rose so that you can take action if another sucker begins to grow.

The process of regularly removing spent flowers is known as deadheading.

PRUNING STANDARD ROSES TO PRESERVE THEIR SHAPE To maintain a well-balanced standard rose shape in the first year of growth, prune two-thirds of the main stems in the crown and remove any excess stems from the centre. In the subsequent years you can remove secondary stems level with the main stems and trim the others to about a half of their original length.

● Slope the angle of the cut away from the bud and, remember, the high side of the cut should be above the bud to prevent water from collecting in the bud and causing it to rot. It is also a good idea to leave at least 5 mm between the bud eye and the cut to avoid damaging it.

● Prune weeping standards lightly and not until after they have flowered.

ENCOURAGING NEW GROWTH ALONG THE RIGHT LINES Look closely at a rose stem and you will see the buds are alternately arranged along its length. When pruning a rose, make an angled cut, just above a bud, that faces in the direction you wish the shoot to grow. Usually this would be an outfacing bud – pruning to one of these opens up the centre of the rosebush and allows in life-giving light and air.

● **TOO EARLY TO SEE THE BUDS** If the buds are too small to see, prune the stem to the required height and then patiently wait for the nearest buds to show. As soon as you can see them, pick the one you want to encourage and prune above it with a neat, angled cut. Do not wait too late in the spring or the bud will not develop.

DEADHEADING Spent blooms can look unsightly and provide a refuge for pests. Remove them daily or as soon as possible.

● **LARGE-FLOWERED ROSES** Cut off spent flower heads just below the second pair of leaves, level with an opening bud.

● **CLUSTER-FLOWERED ROSES** For cluster-flowered roses, you can remove individual flowers just beneath the corolla as they fade. Then when all the flowers have died, cut off the whole cluster following the instructions for large-flowered roses.

● **SPECTACULAR NEW BLOOMS** If you deadhead in the proper way – for your type of rose – it will give the stems a new burst of energy. The bud that is nearest to where you cut off the bloom will now develop and produce new flowers.

Enjoy bigger blooms by cutting off all buds except the terminal one at the end of a stem.

● **PREVENT HIPS FORMING** Unless the hips (seedpods) are particularly attractive, do not allow them to form as they will divert vital energy away from the plant and will prevent the formation of further flowers that season.

HANDLE WITH CARE Tetanus is a serious and sometimes fatal disease. It is caused by a bacterium that lives in the soil and in animal intestines. Make sure your anti-tetanus vaccination is kept up-to-date and always wear protective gloves, especially when pruning. Even a tiny wound, such as a thorn prick from a rose, can become infected with the tetanus bacterium.

GET BIGGER FLOWERS You can encourage a large-flowered rose to produce even bigger blooms by removing all the buds adjacent to the main bud at the end of a stem and retaining only the end bud. This rosebud will take advantage of all the sap and bloom magnificently, although you will have fewer

DID YOU KNOW?

TO PRUNE OR NOT TO PRUNE

Although pruning bush roses, standard roses and climbers will generate new shoots, if you want, you can also let them keep their natural shape. As a result they will produce more foliage and slightly fewer flowers, but will only require a little maintenance. You will only need to prune about once a year to remove dead wood and any unhealthy, deformed or crossing branches. Occasionally you will also need to cut out some centre stems to open up the plant and improve air circulation.

Hedge roses that are difficult to reach, as well as climbers on fences and walls, will benefit from pruning, but this can be done with hedge clippers or shears. Standard roses, however, demand regular pruning to preserve their shape or habit and keep the stem free from shoots.

PRUNING REPEAT-FLOWERING ROSES

1 For bush roses, in your rose's first year, cut back the main stems to 12–15 cm from the ground.

2 To prune, using clean secateurs, make a sharp, slanting cut, just above an outward-facing bud eye.

3 From the second year, remove excess shoots in winter. Moderately prune vigorous outer stems.

flowers. Do not use this method on young or newly planted roses as you will not get enough flowers for a good display. Instead choose plants that have already reached a fair size and are producing numerous healthy stems for this type of pruning.

BEAUTIFUL STEMS Standard roses should be staked during their first 2 years because this will help them initially to take root more securely and develop a better shape.
● Disbud the main stem regularly. Because the graft union of a standard is at the top of the stem, some shoots of the root stock may appear along the trunk.

TIDYING UP YOUR ROSES AT THE BASE
Dead stumps left at the base of the plant will harbour disease and can encourage rotting. Remove these carefully with a sharp, clean pruning saw to reveal a smooth surface where rainwater cannot collect. At the same time, get rid of other debris and plant waste from around the base of the plant.

Growing new roses from old

PRODUCE NEW ROSES THE EASY WAY
Commercially grown roses are very often budded or grafted. However, many roses will grow from a cutting. Don't expect 100 per cent success, but in most cases you will have

Hardy and smothered in blooms throughout the summer, most floribunda roses are easy to propagate by taking cuttings.

success with strong stems that have already produced flowers. Many modern hybrids can be difficult to grow from a cutting.
● Rose cuttings can usually be taken any time between summer, when growth has hardened up. However, during the winter months, at pruning time, is the normal time to take cuttings.
● Cuttings can be grown directly in the ground or grown in pots. If you are growing them in a pot, select a 20 cm pot and fill it with a mixture of sharp sand and potting mix or peat moss in equal amounts. Insert several cuttings in one pot and it is a good idea, to avoid confusion, to only put one variety in each pot. Label each pot with the name of the rose and the date.
● Stand the pot in a sheltered spot. Rose cuttings may take months to form roots. When new growth is seen, move cuttings into individual 15 cm pots in potting mix.

BOUQUET CUTTINGS If you like a rose you are given as a cut flower by friends, ask them to take a cutting for you in the winter. Or you could try taking a cutting from the stem yourself. Don't take cuttings from florist roses. These are special varieties of roses, bred for greenhouse production, and may not thrive in a garden.

DIY RAMBLERS Save money and bulk up your garden plants by layering any of your roses that have long, flexible stems. In the spring, choose a healthy rose stem that is close to the ground. Leave it attached to the plant, but lay it horizontally on the soil. Remove the leaves where the stem touches the ground and carefully make an incision in the bark on the underside of the stem at this point. Cover with a few centimetres of soil, leaving the tip of the stem exposed. Peg the stem down with wire and remember to keep it well watered. In autumn, check to see that it has rooted into the soil. You can then cut the new rose from the mother plant and plant it elsewhere in the garden.
● To ensure you get strong-growing, bushy plants from your cuttings, be patient and do not allow the new rose to flower in its first season. Standard roses are grafted at the top of the main trunk. This graft is exposed to the cold and can be susceptible to frost. In winter cut back the stems at the top of the rose by about half their length and wrap the graft union to protect it.

NATURAL ROOTING HORMONE
In the summer, choose your favourite rose and cut off a vigorous non-flower-bearing stem that has not yet become woody. Remove the lower leaves with a knife, leaving a small part of the leaf stalks. Cut a cross in the base of the stem and insert a grain of wheat in the crack. Soak the stem in a glass of water overnight, and plant into a pot filled with a mixture of equal parts horticultural sand and potting mix. This treatment will help the plant become established.
● The modern equivalent is a plant-rooting hormone, which can be purchased at most nurseries.

Cuttings from roses can be grown directly in the ground or planted into pots.

Standard roses are grafted onto a tall stem of an understock. Remove any shoots that form below the graft union.

Enjoy the great versatility of roses

ORNAMENTAL HIPS Some varieties of rose produce attractive fruits that appear on the bush during late summer and will even last through autumn until winter – even longer for some species. Instead of cutting off the dead flowers, gently pull off the entire corolla to remove the petals, leaving the core intact.
● This is difficult to do with ramblers and roses that form dense hedges. Remove the petals where you can, but elsewhere the hips will develop unaided.
● Rose varieties with ornamental hips include species roses such as *Rosa rugosa* and several old roses such as 'Fru Dagmar Hastrup'. *Rosa pomifera* produces hips shaped like small apples and *Rosa glauca* develops bright hips in bunches. *Rosa moyesii* produces very long hips shaped like plump bottles, which look attractive for months.

THE SWEET TASTE OF ROSES Although rosehips – the fruit of roses – are edible, they rarely feature in modern recipes. This is a shame because they are very rich in vitamin C and have a pleasant, delicate taste.
● Make rose jelly and rose jam by picking the hips after the first frosts so that they are softer. Crush them in a food mill or blender and filter the pulp to remove the seeds and hairs. For each cup of rosehip pulp, add half a cup of sugar to the strained liquid. Cook and stir the mixture until it thickens, then pour into sterilised jars and seal them.
● Rose petals are also edible and can be used in salads, in desserts such as candied rose petals and rose sorbet and in savoury dishes such as lamb tajine and meatballs. Gather petals in the morning from newly opened, fragrant flowers.
● Rosehip tea, rich in vitamin C, is an age-old remedy for colds, made by infusing hips in boiling water for several minutes. Strain to remove the hairs and sweeten to taste.

FRESHLY CUT FLOWERS Choose rosebuds that are about to open or blooms that opened the night before. Take fairly long stems and cut just above a bud that is about to regrow.
● Before cutting roses, assess the general appearance of the plant so that you avoid creating an unbalanced shape.

USE THE RIGHT TOOL FOR A CLEAN CUT Rose stems must be cut very cleanly, not crushed. Use bypass secateurs (right), which give a very clean cut, in preference to a pair of anvil secateurs.

A LONG-LASTING VASE OF ROSES After cutting, strip off some of the leaves, otherwise they will rot in the water. Also remove the thorns as these small wounds will help the stems draw up more water.
● Keep your cut roses looking good for an extra couple of days by helping them draw in more water. Cut the stems at an angle or make a vertical cut in the base of each stem.
● If your roses are drooping, try standing the stems in hot water for a few seconds or recutting the stems under water.
● Don't stand the vase in direct sunlight, and top up every day with one-third fresh water. Remove flowers when they begin to fade.
● A soluble aspirin, a teaspoon of lemonade or a few drops of bleach added to the water may help prolong the life of cut flowers such as roses. Regularly changing the water also keeps flowers looking good for longer.

AN OLD HERBAL REMEDY Rosewater has soothing properties and is particularly effective in eye compresses. Make rosewater yourself by adding 500 g of freshly picked rose petals to 1 litre of previously boiled, cooled spring water. Leave the liquid to infuse for 3 or 4 days in a covered container, filter, then pour into a stoppered glass bottle and keep it somewhere cool.

To avoid crushing stems use sharp, clean bypass secateurs to cut stems.

To enjoy a good display of ornamental hips and provide winter food for the birds, don't deadhead your roses.

The glorious garden shrub

Shrubs are the backbone of your garden's structure, giving shape to flower gardens, providing dramatic focal points throughout the year and doubling as hedging and screening. From the pretty flowering shrubs of the cottage garden to modern hybrid Australian natives there have never been so many shrubs to choose from.

Choose well and plant well

GETTING THEM OFF TO A GOOD START

When you buy your container-grown shrub, it will probably have already spent some time in its pot, and the ball of potting mix around its roots may have dried out completely. If you plant your shrub in that condition, its roots will remain desiccated and even with copious watering it will not revive – and it will not survive. As a precaution, before planting, immerse the root ball and its pot in a bucket of water for at least 15 minutes, until bubbles stop coming to the surface.

LOTS OF WATER Immediately after you have planted your shrub, give it a watering can of water, even if it is raining. This isn't just an old gardener's tale, but a necessity to help it bed in and let the root ball make good contact with the soil.
● If the water does not soak in fast enough, create a small basin by building up a ridge of soil around the plant. Fill it with water and let it slowly ebb away, then repeat this process until your watering can is empty.

KEEP AN EYE ON THE ROOTS Shrubs are almost always sold in containers. Check the root system to make sure it will flourish once you get it home and take it out of its pot.
● Turn the plant over to check that the roots are not poking through the drainage holes, which is a sign that it has spent too long in the pot. Don't be afraid to take the plant out

of its container. It should have several white roots all around the root ball. If it doesn't, the plant has been recently repotted and may not be a good buy.

LOOK AFTER BARE-ROOT PLANTS

Sometimes you can find shrubs that are not sold in containers, but rather have been lifted from the soil where they are raised with bare roots. Plant these bare-root shrubs in winter while they are dormant.
● Before planting a bare-root shrub, make sure you prepare, or 'dress', the roots. Cut off any broken or damaged roots and trim larger ones, but do not touch little ones, as these will take up water from the soil.
● To plant, follow the same procedure as you would for a containerised plant. So that you do not plant too deeply, lay the handle of your spade across the planting hole. The neck of the shrub – that spot between the

Ensure that the root system of your pot-grown plant is wet before planting by standing it in water for 15 minutes.

Getting down to earth

Make sure you get the best shrub for your particular garden conditions. Before you choose – and pay for – your plants, it's always a good idea to assess your soil and test its acidity or alkalinity with a do-it-yourself kit from your local garden centre, or have it professionally analysed by a lab.

TYPE OF SOIL	SUITABLE SHRUBS
Dry earth for most of the year	Abelia, *Genista hispanica*, kerria, sea buckthorn, tamarisk and *Viburnum opulus*.
Moist or damp soil for most of the year	Bottlebrush, elder, hydrangea, mahonia and sacred bamboo (*Nandina domestica*).
Acid soil	Azalea, camellia, grevillea, hydrangea, calico bush (*Kalmia latifolia*), *Pieris japonica* and rhododendron.
Alkaline soil	Deutzia, forsythia and philadelphus.

Cotinus coggygria *is an eye-catching shrub that is remarkable for its stunning foliage, especially in autumn when it is at its most brilliant.*

roots and the trunk that you may be able to identify by a soil mark made when it was in the ground – should be at that level.

MISTAKES TO AVOID To give your shrubs the best chance, avoid these common pitfalls.
● Don't plant them too close together. They will become overcrowded after 2 or 3 years and you will have to dig some of them up just when they are settling in.
● Don't economise by buying shrubs that are too small. It is much better to buy just a few large, good-quality plants and to enrich the soil correctly when planting.
● Avoid autumn feeding. This encourages the formation of soft and sappy new shoots that may be damaged by cold or frost.

AUTUMN FOR PLANTING The best time to plant most shrubs is in autumn while the soil is still warm but temperatures are falling. This gives plants a head start in spring when their root system will be well established.
● Avoid planting frost-sensitive shrubs in autumn in cold climates – wait until spring.

GROWING ACID-LOVING PLANTS IN THE WRONG SOIL Don't attempt to grow acid-loving plants such as azaleas, camellias and heathers in alkaline soil by just filling a trench with some potting mix for acid-loving plants. These plants are not designed

for such conditions, and you simply can't beat nature. Even though initially this method may seem to work, it is only a temporary fix and creates an artificial environment that the plant will exhaust in 2–3 years when it will become stunted and sick.
● If you have alkaline soil (a pH of 7 or more), select plants that grow well in these conditions, such as correa, deutzia, eremophila, forsythia, philadelphus and westringia.
● If your soil is alkaline but you are really determined to grow an acid-loving specimen, consider growing it in a large pot filled with potting mix for acid-loving plants.

PLANTING IN A LAWN Any plant growing in a lawn will have to compete with grass for food and water. To reduce the drain on these resources, cut out a section of turf 3–4 cm deep and as big as the plant's root spread, where you wish to plant your shrub. This removes the grass that would otherwise grow right above your plant's roots. Plant your shrub as you normally would and surround it with an organic mulch.
● A better approach is to make a planting bed in the lawn that will hold several shrubs. This will be much easier to maintain and much less hassle when mowing the lawn.

Good buying: avoid pot-bound plants with roots growing from drainage holes (top); look for healthy white roots (above).

PLANTING ACID-LOVING PLANTS IN ALKALINE SOIL

To maximise your chance of success with a plant that is not suited to your soil conditions, use a lined trench. However, you will still need to renew the acid mulch from time to time.

1 Dig a hole 1 m deep – it might be a good idea to hire a mini-digger. Line the bottom and sides of the hole.

2 To line the hole properly, use a sheet of thick permeable membrane, which lets water drain but stops soils mixing.

3 Half-fill the hole with gravel, then part-fill it with potting mix for acid-loving plants, available at garden centres.

4 Immerse the plant's root ball in water for half an hour, then position it in the hole and fill with potting mix.

5 Firm in the plant and make a recessed area that will retain water around the base. Trim the membrane.

6 Water the plant in well, then spread a layer of an acid mulch such as pine bark around the base of the plant.

TEMPTED BY A SHRUB IN FLOWER?

Garden centres often entice gardeners to buy wonderful flowering shrubs in the middle of summer when they look their best. It's risky trying to plant containerised shrubs when they are in flower, but if you just can't resist, there are precautions you can take to ensure you get the best possible results.

● Plant your shrub in the desired location, but make sure it is watered daily, directing the water to the base of the plants, treating it as if it were still in a pot.

● Lightly prune the shrub after flowering, which will encourage healthy new growth.

● If you see a plant that you like while you are on holiday, in either a colder or warmer part of the country than where you normally live, make sure you ask about its heat and frost tolerance before you buy it and take it home – it may not grow in your garden.

● Mulch around the plant with a thick layer of composted bark, which will keep the soil fresh and reduce evaporation.

THE BIGGER, THE BETTER If you want to give your shrub the best possible start in life, make the planting hole at least twice as wide as the diameter of the root ball. This way the plant will establish much more quickly and perform to its full potential.

● Don't plant the shrub too deeply: the top of the root ball should be at soil level after planting. Break up the soil at the bottom of the hole with a fork to make it easier for the roots to penetrate and get a good hold.

Colours and scents

LATE-AFTERNOON FRAGRANCE Flowers are often at their most fragrant at around 5 o'clock in the afternoon. Plant them where you can appreciate their lovely scent – near windows, next to garden seats and along paths. Choose aromatic plants that flower during different seasons to keep your garden fragrant all year. Good examples include philadelphus (spring); gardenia and murraya (summer); buddleia (summer-autumn); brown boronia and daphne (winter).

SHRUBS AS PRESENTS Give a shrub to friends instead of buying a bunch of flowers. It is a present that will last for years and will be a steady reminder of your friendship.

Blue-flowering hebe is an evergreen shrub that brings a cool touch to the summer garden.

A COOL BLUE SUMMER To bring a fresh new feeling to your garden at the height of summer, plant shrubs with blue flowers. In all climates try hebe, pictured above. In cool or Mediterranean climates select blue forms of buddleia, caryopteris, ceanothus, *Hibiscus syriacus* and perovskia. In areas that are warm to subtropical, choose duranta, hydrangea and plumbago.

● These sun-loving species prefer sheltered sites with well-drained soil and in these conditions they are frost hardy. For good healthy plants, feed them with a complete fertiliser containing trace elements.

AN AUTUMN ON FIRE Many deciduous shrubs have wonderful, warm autumn hues, changing to yellows, oranges and bright reds. The best colours can be achieved in a cool climate after a good summer that is hot and dry, but not parched. For the best autumn-colour show, choose plants like *Amelanchier lamarckii*, *Cotinus coggygria*, *Enkianthus campanulatus* and *Euonymus alatus*.

GIVE SHRUBS AN EXTRA SPARKLE Some shrubs look superb in one season but pretty boring for the rest of the year. Here are a few great ideas to inject a bit of colour into a green garden. Try using your out-of-season shrubs as a green backdrop for the seasonal plantings of annuals and perennials, or even climbers trained on tepees. Azaleas, camellias or rhododendrons that stop flowering in late spring or during summer can be magically brought back to life with a vibrant border of summer-flowering impatiens.

The red berries of Euonymus europaeus *will add strong winter colour to your garden.*

● You can also invigorate a garden that is mainly shrubs by planting some with different coloured leaves. For a dash of gold grow *Abelia* 'Francis Mason' or golden diosma (*Coleonema* 'Sunset Gold'), or for a white and green variegated effect include euonymus or *Pittosporum* 'James Stirling'.
● Variegated plants can also illuminate a dark corner in the garden with a brilliant flash of gold or white.

SHRUBS TO DINE ON Birds are especially fond of shrubs with nectar-laden flowers and berries or seeds. By attracting birds to your garden, you will also reduce the number of pests, such as caterpillars and slugs. For year-round interest, make sure you plant a variety of native plants such as banksia, bottlebrush and grevillea for their flowers. Add to these

Lillypilly berries like these on Syzygium leuhmannii *are attractive in the garden and are eaten by native birds and small mammals.*

Snowberry not only looks great in your garden, but the white berries also provide food for birds.

some local wattle for seed and lillypilly for berries and you'll have a garden that is also a restaurant for the birds. For food all year round, select plants that bloom at different times of the year.
● It is not only native shrubs that attract birds. Camellias of all types have nectar for birds such as wattle birds and parrots and they flower from autumn through to early spring, providing much-needed nectar through the cooler months of the year.

UNDER CONIFERS Conifers create dry shade, which is a difficult environment for many shrubs to grow in. Prepare your planting area thoroughly and do not plant immediately underneath the tree. Try some of the following, according to your soil type: aucuba, azalea, buxus, euonymus, fuchsia, hydrangea, mahonia and rhododendron. These should all adapt well to this situation.
● Make sure the shrub gets enough water as conifers will compete for any available moisture in the soil.

COLOURFUL BERRIES Some of the berry-producing plants have now become weeds, but don't feel that you need to completely forgo the pleasure of growing berries in your garden. Berries on *Euonymus europaeus* (above left) and ardisia are ornamental only. Many also provide food for us, or the local wildlife, including blueberry, elderberry, lillypilly (left) and snowberry (above right).

AUTUMN DOES NOT MEAN THE END OF THE GARDEN There are several shrubs that will flower during autumn and even in the winter months, including many varieties of banksia, camellia, *Erica carnea*, garrya, hamamelis, japonica, reinwardtia (frost-free

climates) and viburnum. Plant them close to the house so they are visible from the main windows and you can enjoy them throughout the winter months.

COLOURFUL BRANCHES IN A BARE LANDSCAPE

In cold climates where many shrubs and trees are bare in winter, gardens can seem dull. Counteract these winter greys and browns with shrubs that have interesting white, yellow, orange or red stems, which contrast sharply with their surroundings. *Cornus alba*, despite its name, displays fiery red branches and *Rubus cockburnianus* creates a festive Christmas-in-July atmosphere with its arching white branches that give the impression of being covered in winter frost.
● The most colourful branches are those that have grown over the previous year. In spring, remove the oldest stems – those that have begun to lose their bright colour – from their base. This will encourage healthy new growth that will form next winter's colourful stems.

FOR FADED FLOWERS
Don't be too hasty in pruning hydrangeas and roses or you will miss the winter sight of red rosehips and the colourful pink and green tones of the 'dried' flowers of hydrangeas in autumn.

WHITE WEDDINGS IN SPRING
An abundance of unblemished white and soft pink flowers in spring is a pure delight. You can enhance your garden with shrubs that bear blooms brilliant enough for a white wedding display. Be adventurous and try a few of the more unusual ones such as *Cornus kousa, Exochorda* x *macrantha*, kolkwitzia, and *Viburnum plicatum* 'Mariesii' (right).

SUITABLE FOR DRY GARDENS
It is important to remember that, when growing any type of plant, it doesn't pay to try and fight nature. If you live in a dry area, you may need to tailor the plants you grow to the prevailing conditions – if the rainfall is minimal, grow plants that naturally occur in the Mediterranean and drier regions, such as broom, gorse, helianthemum, rosemary, santolina, tamarisk and yucca and, of course, natives. Shrubs with silver or grey foliage are better adapted to hot and dry gardens.
● Be sure to plant these shrubs properly. Prepare the planting hole and add garden compost or well-rotted manure. Plant shrubs in the autumn, to allow the roots to establish over winter before the onslaught of summer. Water thoroughly at planting and at regular intervals until the plant has established itself.
● Remember when watering that it is always better to soak the ground thoroughly but occasionally rather than to water superficially but frequently, such as on a daily basis.

Beautiful branches brighten up winter, from left to right: Rubus cockburnianus, Salix alba *'Vitellina', and* Cornus alba *'Sibirica'.*

WATCH OUT

POISONOUS OR DANGEROUS SHRUBS

There are certain shrubs you should avoid planting in your garden or treat with care if already growing. Heavily perfumed *Brugmansia* (formerly *Datura*) carries a hallucinogenic substance in its blooms. All parts of the yellow oleander (*Thevetia*) and common oleander (*Nerium oleander*) are poisonous. Many grevilleas can cause skin allergies at pruning time. Laburnum, a feature of cool-climate gardens, is poisonous in all its parts. Yew has poisonous fruits and the green fruit on brunfelsia is attractive to dogs. Pyracantha and berberis have sharp thorns.

Lovely white blossoms festoon the branches of Viburnum plicatum *'Mariesii' early in the flowering season.*

To keep your variegated plants more interesting, remove any green branches that appear.

SHRUBS THAT SEE RED Some shrubs have beautiful young leaves that contrast sharply with their older foliage. These are ideal for creating some mid-border interest as spring progresses. The leaves of *Photinia* x *fraseri* 'Red Robin' and *Pieris formosa* 'Forrestii' are a spectacular red at first, before turning to a more subtle shade of green in summer.

The striking evergreen pieris not only produces a stunning display of red foliage in spring but it also flowers profusely.

SHRUBS FOR NESTING Birds are one of the gardener's best friends, devouring a wide variety of insects and pests. Provide them with nesting sites and you may be lucky enough to have them stay in your garden.
● Birds particularly like evergreen shrubs, for guaranteed privacy, as well as shrubs with thick, prickly branches for protection. In an isolated corner of the garden, plant hakea, melaleuca and pyracantha to make good homes for your feathered friends.

Keeping your shrubs healthy

GREEN LEAVES ON A VARIEGATED SHRUB? A branch bearing totally green leaves can often develop in the middle of a shrub with variegated foliage. To keep the look of your shrub, remove the reverting shoot as soon as you notice it by cutting it out with secateurs from right at the base of the branch it is sprouting from. If you don't take prompt action, your shrub could revert to a solid green all over, which will make it much less decorative.

THE DANGERS OF SALT In coastal areas, sea spray and salt-laden winds can damage garden plants, clogging their leaves and stripping them of moisture. If your garden is in an exposed coastal location, choose plants that are able to withstand these conditions. Visit a local nursery for advice and take a look at what grows well in neighbouring gardens and in the wild. Plants such as coastal banksia, coastal myall, coprosma, escallonia, hebe, metrosideros, pittosporum, rosemary and westringia will normally thrive in these conditions.

TROUBLESHOOTING If a shrub is not growing well despite your best care, check for any of the following:
● It may be that the soil and planting hole were not well prepared before planting. If the soil is not properly broken up this can lead to air pockets where the roots are unable to make good contact with the soil. The soil might be poor quality or unsuitable for the type of plant you are trying to grow. It is a good idea to lift the plant and then replant it in good soil in winter.

Hebe x andersonii 'Variegata' is a variegated evergreen shrub for a sheltered position.

● The roots may have been damaged during planting or through staking too close to the shrub. If possible, lift the plant and cut out any damaged roots. Then replant it with care, gently teasing out the roots by hand and laying them over a small mound of potting mix in the base of a large planting hole.
● A hot or cold snap or a period of drying winds may have affected the growth of your plant. Give proper protection or move the shrub to a more sheltered spot.

TOP TIPS FOR POORLY FLOWERING
SHRUBS A disappointing display of flowers can often be easily remedied.
● **HAVE PATIENCE** The shrub may be too young. Some can take several years to flower.
● **GIVE NOURISHMENT** Choose a fertiliser that is high in potash to encourage flowers. A nitrogen-rich fertiliser boosts leaf growth to the detriment of flowers.
● **COVER WITH HORTICULTURAL FLEECE IN WINTER** The flower buds may have been damaged by frost in spring.
● **MULCH THE SOIL SURFACE** It is essential to maintain humidity and to protect roots from extremes of temperature. The shrub may have been too hot prior to flowering.
● **PRUNE CORRECTLY AND AT THE PROPER TIME** Spring-flowering shrubs often suffer if they have been chopped back in a winter garden tidy-up. Pruning late in the season

removes the shoots that form next year's flowers. Prune immediately after flowering and restrict winter pruning to a gentle trim.
● **PLANT IN A MORE SUITABLE SPOT** The shrub may be planted in the wrong position, suffering from too much shade or sun, or it could be in a draught. Dig it up during the following winter and move it.

A BANDAGE FOR DAMAGED STEMS
If a branch has broken or split due to wind, or perhaps a wayward ball, don't despair because you may be able to mend it. Use budding tape or a medical bandage to bind it up. Many branches can heal themselves if they are treated in this way. Keep it well watered and apply a regular dose of seaweed extract to encourage regrowth. Remove the bandage when the wound has healed.

PREVENT GRASS FROM GROWING
UNDER SHRUBS Trying to mow the grass around a shrub planted in the lawn can be a problem. The more grass is mowed, the quicker it grows, competing with the shrub for the available nutrients and water. Long grass may also harbour pests. Carefully cut away a circle of turf about 1 m wide from around the base of the shrub and apply a thick layer of mulch.
● Mulch with a 5–8 cm layer of organic mulch, which will gradually break down into the soil. Spread it around the base making sure it doesn't actually touch the stem of the shrub, and top it up every 2 or 3 months.

PRODUCE HEALTHY CUTTINGS
Many shrubs can be propagated using these traditional techniques. Start by trimming the new shoots that develop at the base of the plant in summer. These are called lignified stems and they are the best material for taking semiripe cuttings. Choose only healthy stems and remove about 15 cm of the shoot, cutting about 5 mm below a node. Trim the cutting carefully so that the cut is clean and straight, which minimises the risk of disease attacking the cutting through a ragged edge. Remove the lower leaves carefully and cut out the shoot tip. Fill a pot with equal amounts of sharp sand and peat moss, make a hole with a dibber and plant the cutting. Firm it in and water gently. Place the pot in a sheltered spot or in a polystyrene box to root, and plant the rooted shoot in the garden next spring.

WATCH OUT

WATER MAKES A DIFFERENCE
Watering a new plant well after planting is one of the most important parts of ensuring its survival and good growth. Water as soon as you plant, but don't forget to water the plant well in the following weeks, too.

It takes time for the plant to send its roots out into the garden soil. Until this occurs, new plantings need to be watered as frequently as any potted plant. Water well at the base of the stem to make sure the water soaks into the root system. Also take care to water new plantings thoroughly in particularly hot or windy weather.

Dehydration isn't just a summer problem. Evergreen shrubs and conifers continue to need water in winter, even though their growth slows down. Water only when the temperature is above freezing, paying special attention to shrubs that were planted less than a year ago.

To ensure the survival of your new shrub, water it copiously just after planting, even if it is raining at the time.

Pruning the simple way

TOP TIPS FOR PRUNING For the best results when pruning, make sure you use a good quality pair of secateurs. To really encourage your flowers to grow, choose a pair of bypass secateurs. These have a scissor action to make them easy to use, which means they will be gentler on the stems. Anvil secateurs have a flat jaw against which the cutting blade acts, minimising twisting, making them ideal for cutting out dead wood or removing undesirable growth such as suckers and thorns.

● **POSITION THE CUTTING BLADE CORRECTLY** The larger of the two blades should always be closer to the part of the stem you are retaining (below left). This will ensure that the cut is clean and neat so it will heal faster and reduce the risk of disease. If you cut with the smaller blade closer to the stem you are retaining, you are more likely to crush the stem tissue. It will take longer to heal and can dry out the stem.

● **ALWAYS CUT TO 1 CM ABOVE A NODE** This stops the sap from flowing further up the branch than it needs to and diverts it to the bud, which will quickly form a shoot.

● **USE AN ANGLED CUT ON VERTICALLY GROWING BRANCHES** Prune all vertically growing branches by making an angled cut. This will prevent water from stagnating on the wound and it speeds up the healing process and reduces the risk of disease. The slope of the angle should be away from the bud at the node, so that water will not run onto it. It is not essential to cut horizontal branches like this because any water will run off them naturally.

● **NOTE THE GROWTH PATTERN** Branches of shrubs form one of two patterns, which determine where the pruning cuts should be made. The branches either sprout in pairs from opposite sides of the stem joint, or from separate buds on alternate sides.

RENOVATION PRUNING Are your shrubs top-heavy with foliage and going bare at the base? If so the chances are they are not developing new stems from the base. In late winter or early spring, when the first buds begin to shoot, cut out about one-third of the oldest branches down to ground level. This will encourage fresh growth from the base without seriously reducing flowering. Next year remove another third of the oldest branches to ground level and repeat for the third year, when you should have a completely rejuvenated plant. This type of pruning will work well with leggy evergreen azaleas and with tibouchinas.

PRUNING A SHRUB WITH DECORATIVE STEMS Shrubs grown for their attractive winter stems need to be pruned in early spring before they start growing in earnest. Cut back any stems that are more than 2 years old, right down to almost ground level. Alternatively, choose the oldest central stems and remove these.

REJUVENATING A NEGLECTED SHRUB If you have inherited a shrub that is over-grown and needs restorative pruning, wait until it has flowered and then prune it hard.

Bypass secateurs work with a scissor-like action. Remember to always position the larger blade closest to the stem to be retained.

If you are growing shrubs for their stem colour, cut out older stems to encourage healthy new shoots with good colouring.

PRUNING A SPRING-FLOWERING SHRUB

1 Prune spring-flowering shrubs such as forsythia just after they have flowered, when the new leaves begin to appear.

2 Cut back old branches over 2 cm thick, which generally have grey bark. They clutter the centre of the clump and do not flower well.

3 To let air and light into the centre of the plant and stimulate growth, cut back lateral shoots and any that are rubbing or growing inwards.

4 Cut back all other shoots to 50 cm from the ground. This way, the sap will flow to all the remaining buds and turn them into new branches.

By simply shortening backgrowth after flowering you can stimulate lots of healthy new shoots.

● Select the oldest branches and cut these back to the base using a pruning saw. Make sure you are careful not to damage any of the neighbouring branches.

● Locate the other branches originating from the centre of the bush and cut these back to their base, or just above a secondary branch that is growing outwards. Finally cut back all the other branches by removing two-thirds of their length (above). Remember to make your cut 1 cm above an outward-facing bud to keep the structure of the shrub open.

BE BOLD WHEN YOUR ARE PRUNING YOUR SHRUBS
Amateur gardeners can often be afraid of hard-pruning their shrubs, preferring to prune them lightly into neat shapes. However, this is more likely to ruin the shrub's natural appearance because it encourages dense and tangled growth that prevents flowers and leaves from growing in the centre. It is much better to remove the oldest branches, recognisable by their dark, often gnarled bark. Cut them right back to the trunk, just before the growing season.

ECO-FRIENDLY TIP
Don't discard your shrub prunings; they make excellent natural supports for perennials and small shrubs. Alternatively you can put them through a shredder and mix them with equal quantities of green material in the compost heap.

● Once composted, which takes about 3 months, this will make an excellent mulch for your shrubs, retaining valuable moisture and adding to the fertility of the soil.

LATE-WINTER PRUNING
Evergreen hibiscus, *Hibiscus rosa-sinensis*, is pruned in late winter or early spring. This is done to stimulate new growth and strong flowering. Cut it back all over by about a third. Use this pruning time to clean up around plants, removing debris that has accumulated under plants such as spent flowers and leaves that may be harbouring pests and diseases. Cover the bare earth with a layer of organic mulch mixed with cow manure or garden compost.

● Fuchsias are also pruned in at this time, cutting back all old wood. Follow the hard prune after 6 weeks by pinching out the new shoots to encourage bushy growth.

LET SHRUBS BECOME ESTABLISHED
Most shrubs don't actually require a lot of pruning during the first few years after they have been planted out. To begin with, try to confine your efforts to removing any crossing branches that spoil the shape of the shrub, and to removing any unsightly dead flowers. However, remember to always cut out any damaged or unhealthy branches straight away: this will prevent the spread of diseases.

DO YOUR SHRUBS HAVE OPPOSITE OR ALTERNATE BUDS?
Before you decide just how to prune your shrubs, take a look at the buds on their stems. If the buds are growing in pairs, opposite each other, then prune straight across and above a pair of healthy buds. If, on the other hand, the buds are arranged alternately up the stem, then cut at an angle of 45°, just above a healthy bud, making sure that the lower point of your cut is just behind the bud, but not beneath it.

DID YOU KNOW?

WHY YOU NEED TO PRUNE SHRUBS TO MAKE THEM FLOWER
Spring-flowering shrubs normally flower on stems that are in their second year of growth. This means that to encourage plenty of flowers next year you need to stimulate the shrub to make new stems from the base this year. These new stems will mature and bear flowers in their second year.

Even though most shrubs will flower with no pruning, they will become woody and may start to go bare at the base. For the very best results, each year cut the oldest branches back as low as possible and just lightly trim the remaining branches, keeping the overall shape of the plant intact. Do this as soon as possible after flowering to allow enough time for the plant to generate some fresh stems that will flower next spring.

PRUNING A SUMMER-FLOWERING SHRUB

1 *Buddleia davidii* is a shrub that responds well to pruning. When the flowers at the tips of the branches have died back, cut them off to encourage the remaining flowers to develop.

2 After the flowering season is over, cut the branches back by about one-half and then early the next spring prune them hard, cutting right back to the growth point of the previous branches.

3 Keep the centre of the shrub open to let in lots of air and light. If the branches are tangled and overgrown, cut back the oldest ones to the base. Some new stems will soon regenerate.

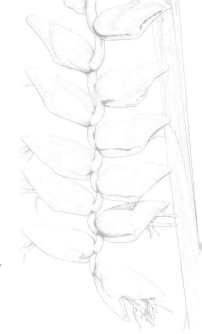

Living green walls and sculptures

A painstakingly clipped hedge or an intriguing piece of topiary was once the hallmark of a grand formal garden. Cottage gardeners also adapted the tradition to suit their more spontaneous style and, today, we can borrow from this past to use shrubs of all kinds to create boundaries, backdrops and focal points of distinction.

Grow a perfect, handsome hedge

BUY BARE-ROOT PLANTS Specimen shrubs are almost always sold in containers. This means that they can be planted all year round – except during very cold or very dry and hot weather – with immediate results. If you are planning to grow hedges, however, it is much more cost effective to buy younger plants in small pots or tubes. These will need planting in the autumn or spring and your hedge may take a couple of years to thicken out, but it will establish quickly and it will work out much cheaper.

● Nurseries generally offer discounts for bulk buys of 10 or more of the same plant, which makes planting a hedge more cost effective.

USE A MECHANICAL DIGGER If you have a long length of hedge to plant, you can save yourself some hard work by hiring a small mechanical digger to break up the ground. Plan to do your digging about 1 month before planting the hedge, then add quality organic garden mix, cover it with 10 cm of organic mulch and leave it to rest. The soil will settle down gradually during this period.

● When you are ready to plant the hedge, the earth should still be easy to work and you will only need to dig holes large enough for the root ball of each plant.

MULCHING IS ESSENTIAL Applying some mulch to the base of a newly planted hedge is essential to prevent the growth of weeds.

Remove perennial weeds and their roots, and then spread a generous 10 cm layer of any well-rotted organic mulch or compost along the base of the hedge.

AN ACCESS PATH IN FRONT OF YOUR HEDGE Hedges need regular maintenance, so remember to leave a path between the hedge and the flowerbed. Make sure there is enough room to move about comfortably, possibly with a wheelbarrow, or to erect scaffolding if the top of the hedge is too tall to reach from ground level.

SAVE SOME PRECIOUS SPACE Although hedges offer many benefits, they are greedy for space so, in a small garden, they may not be the best solution. If you do want a living

An old-fashioned garden with formal hedges and topiary can be a gardener's favourite fantasy. But even the grandest scheme can be the inspiration for less ambitious designs.

screen around the garden, consider erecting a lattice and growing climbers or, for a fruitful option, espalier and fan-trained fruit trees.

FAST GROWERS There are some shrubs, in particular some conifers, that will grow into a hedge fairly quickly. The disadvantage is that the vigour of these shrubs does not diminish at all once the hedge is established, which means you will have to cut them three or four times a year to keep them in check. The most rampant growers are the Leyland cypress and its cultivars, and false cypress (*Chamaecyparis* spp.).

SOME VERY NEIGHBOURLY CONCERNS
If your neighbour has a hedge that intrudes into your garden you can trim the parts that extend over the boundary. If you have some concerns about the height of a hedge blocking your sun, view or being a fire hazard, first discuss your concerns with your neighbour. If good neighbourly relations fail, contact the local council, who may direct your neighbour to prune the hedge.

A 'WILD' HEDGE A soft, natural-looking, informal or mixed hedge is made of several different hedging plants and it is not kept neatly clipped. It may not be as dense as a uniform evergreen hedge, but it looks attractive and needs much less attention. You may need to curb the vigour of some of the plants to leave room for the more timid ones.
● Plants that lend themselves to informal hedges include abelia, acalypha, banksia, bottlebrush, elder, grevillea, hakea, melaleuca and New Zealand Christmas tree. Some of the large roses, such as rugosa roses, make excellent wild hedges.

ABSORB POLLUTION WITH A HEDGE
If you want to reduce the noise from your street as well as the traffic fumes, choose from a variety of dense, evergreen hedge plants such as golden privet, Japanese euonymus or oleander.
● In cold climates, deciduous hedges of beech or hornbeam will also absorb sound, even during winter, as they hold onto many of their dead leaves during the colder months.

A PROTECTIVE HEDGE One reason for planting a hedge is to deter both human and wildlife intruders, and plants with prickles and spines are particularly effective. Berberis,

HOW TO PLANT A HEDGE THROUGH FABRIC

There are various specialist fabrics, such as weed mat, that are designed to suppress weeds yet let the rain permeate through to the plant roots below. Once the plants are in place, apply a mulch over the top and water well until they are established. A cheap, old-fashioned alternative to weed mat is to lay down thick layers of newspaper, overlapped and moistened.

1 Loosen the earth in the plot to 40 cm deep, add compost and level the surface. Dig a 10 cm deep channel round the planting area.

2 Place the piece of fabric over the plot, making sure you slide the edges into the channels and hold them down securely with soil or pegs.

3 Use a knife to cut crosses in the fabric where the plants will go. Fold their corners back and dig a hole large enough to take the root ball.

4 Set the root ball in the hole, fill it with soil, press it down, water, then replace fabric over the plant base. Cover with an attractive mulch.

bougainvillea, dog rose, elaeagnus, hawthorn and holly will all form a secure wall, either used alone or in combination, and they will be covered in flowers in spring. Some will also have berries for the birds in autumn.
● To create an impenetrable barrier, erect a sturdy wire fence before planting. Place your shrubs along this fence and, after a few years, they will cover the wire.

A NEW HEDGE EACH YEAR Give your garden added variety. Try growing annuals or herbaceous plants to create a different type of screen for each year. Hollyhocks, Jerusalem artichokes, sunflowers and sweetcorn can all be sown or planted as young plants in spring to create a tall, flowering, green hedge that will last for many months.

DID YOU KNOW?

TROPICAL COLOUR
Hedges don't have to be just green. Try looking for some boldly variegated plants such as acalypha (below top), or golden or lime forms of shrubs such as duranta, for a colourful hedge that will give your garden a tropical atmosphere. If you live in a cooler climate, the bright pink flowers of *Camellia sasanqua* (below bottom) make a bold and colourful hedge, which gains a new burst of colour after each pruning.

A HEDGE OF ROSES Several types of roses will make fine, old-fashioned hedges, even though they are bare during winter. The best all-rounders are the old roses because of their dense foliage and their long flowering period. Wild species roses, such as rugosa roses, are favourites in traditional cottage gardens and make a tough hedge that produces a very attractive display of hips in the autumn.
● If you want a hedge smothered in flowers, remember to prune the stems to different heights to ensure that the flowers appear all over the hedge instead of just at the top.

STAY WELL CLEAR OF WILLOW Hedges made from interlaced willow stems were once a feature of old-fashioned country life because they used to be widely available and they were easy to make. While today they are regaining popularity in Britain and Europe, willows are considered weeds in Australia and New Zealand so are not recommended.

BRIGHTEN UP A DULL CONIFER HEDGE
If you plant a hedge made entirely of conifers, it can look quite austere. To brighten it up plant a golden form of conifer or make a tapestry hedge by planting a mix of conifers, variegated hollies, pittosporums and other tall evergreen shrubs.
● Golden forms of conifers well suited to hedging include *Cupressus* 'Swane's Gold', which has narrow, conical growth and the large growing *Cupressus* 'Limelight', which has stunning bright lime foliage.

FOR AN EASY-MAINTENANCE HEDGE
Rather than planting vigorous conifers that expand sideways and have to be cut back regularly, plant a row that have an upward-growing habit and a spread that only rarely exceeds 1 m. Try the *Juniperus communis* 'Hibernica', *Juniperus* 'Skyrocket' or *Thuja occidentalis* 'Smaragd'. With these varieties, you will need to give the tops a regular trim but you won't have to worry about any excessive sideways expansion.

A GOOD WINDBREAK If you live in a windy, exposed area, you may need a hedge that will provide some protection from strong winds. The best sort of hedge to create an effective windbreak is one that filters the wind, rather than one that blocks it out completely. A solid hedge could be damaged or even totally uprooted in stormy weather,

whereas one that allows the wind through will still reduce the impact of the weather by as much as 75 per cent.
● A windbreak protects an area of ground equal to 20 times its height for every 1 m in length. This means that a hedge 1.8 m tall and 10 m long will protect 360 square metres. Check the height of the mature plants and how quickly they will grow when choosing the best ones to use.

A selection of suitable hedging plants

Use the table and its key to choose the type of hedge that will suit your needs.
KEY: D – Deciduous • E – Evergreen • Q – Quick-growing • SE – Semi-evergreen • ST – Subtropical

	COLD CLIMATE	TEMPERATE CLIMATE	COASTAL CLIMATE	TROPICAL AND SUBTROPICAL
SECURITY	Barberry (D) Blackthorn (D) Dog rose (D) Hawthorn (D/Q) Holly (E) Japanese quince (D) Rugosa rose (D)	Barberry (D) Bougainvillea (D/E) Japanese quince (D) Rugosa rose (D/Q)	Bougainvillea (E/Q)	Berberis (E/ST) Bougainvillea (E) Duranta (E)
SCREENING	Beech (D) Golden privet (E) Japanese quince (D) Photinia (E) Portugal laurel (E) Spindle tree (D) Yew (E)	Abelia (E) Aucuba (E) Bottlebrush (E) Escallonia (E/Q) Japanese spindle (D) Lillypilly (E) Murraya (E) Oleander (E) Photinia (E)	Coastal banksia (E) Coastal myall (E/Q) Elaeagnus (E) Escallonia (E) Metrosideros (E) Oleander (E) Olearia (E) Pittosporum (E) Portugal laurel (E)	Bamboo (E) Bottlebrush (E) Grevillea (E) Lillypilly (E) Melaleuca (E) *Viburnum odoratissimum* (E) Wattle (E)
WINDBREAK	*Cupressus torulosa* (E) Elder (D/Q) Golden privet (E/Q) Laurustinus (E) Lawsons cypress (E/Q)	Bottlebrush (E/Q) Lillypilly (E/Q) Photinia (E/Q) She-oak (E/Q)	Atriplex (SE) Coastal banksia (E) Coastal myall (E/Q) Metrosideros (E) Pittosporum (E) She-oak (E/Q) Tamarisk (E)	Bamboo (E) Sugar cane (E)
LOW DIVIDER	Box (E) *Lonicera nitida* (E/Q) Rosemary (E/Q)	*Duranta* 'Sheena's Gold' (E) Dwarf murraya (E) Italian lavender (E) Japanese box (E) Lavender (E)	Coprosma (E) Cotton lavender (E) Lavender (E) Westringia (E)	Agapanthus (E) Alternanthera (E) Ardisia (E) Liresine (E) Mother-in-law's tongue (*Sansevieria*) (E) Rhoeo (E) Ruellia (E)
NATURAL OR FLOWERING	Deutzia (D) Dogwood (D/E) Flowering currant (D) Forsythia (D) *Fuchsia magellanica* (E) Laburnum (D) Lilac (D) Spiraea (D/E) Weigela (D)	Abelia (E/SE) Gardenia (E) Grevillea (E) Hebe (E) Hibiscus (E) Murraya (E) Plumbago (E) Rose (D)	Escallonia (E/Q) Hibiscus (E) Hydrangea (D) Westringia (E)	Allamanda, flowering (E/ST) *Baeckia virgata* (E) Camellia (E/ST) Gardenia (E) Hibiscus (E) Ixora (E) Rondeletia (E)

Keeping your hedges trim

TRIMMING WITH CARE When using an electric hedge trimmer, remember to watch out for the electric cable at all times. As a safety precaution, pass it over your shoulder and behind you, well away from the cutting blades – this will avoid any chance of cutting through it. Always use a circuit breaker when using any type of outdoor power equipment.

KEEPING SAFE Before using your hedge trimmer, make sure it is in good repair.
● Modern power machines require both your hands to be on the machine to operate it: if you let go with one hand a blade brake stops the machine. Be extra careful when using machines that do not have this safety feature and can be operated with one hand.
● When buying a machine, make sure the blade ends are protected by blunt extensions so that if the blade falls onto your body it doesn't cut, it just bruises.
● Wear protective gloves and goggles, trousers, long sleeves and leather shoes.

A WELL-GROWN HEDGE If you want a hedge to be 2 m high, don't wait until it reaches this height before trimming it, as this may make the growth towards the base sparse. Trim the top of the hedge as soon as it reaches 1 m in height. This will make it thicken out at the base. Allow the hedge to grow by a further 15–20 cm each year until it has reached the desired height.

Remember to buy a hedge trimmer that is appropriate for the size of your hedge.

A GENTLE TRIM FOR THE LAUREL ...
The cherry and Portugal laurels grow quickly to form thick, evergreen hedges.
● Don't cut them with shears or a hedge trimmer, as slicing through the large glossy leaves will spoil the appearance. Instead, use secateurs, trimming individual branches to the required length one at a time.

... AND NOW FOR THE PYRACANTHA
In spring a pyracantha hedge becomes covered in tiny white flowers before it grows new foliage branches. Don't cut it back now, unless you live near bushland. After flowering, pyracanthas form red and orange berries that gain full colour in autumn. If you prune hard after flowering, the berry show will be diminished. In areas near bushland, where pyracanthas could become weedy, plants should be pruned after flowering to stop the berries forming. This way, there will be no chance of the plant becoming a weed outside your garden. To keep the hedge neat and retain the berries, prune off the new growth using secateurs.

WHEN TO CUT YOUR HEDGE Make the first trim of the year near the end of spring, some time in November. Do the second trim after the growth of early summer, in January or February. Species that grow fast, such as Leyland cypress, should also be cut at the start of spring and during the summer months. Other hedges should be trimmed as necessary, depending on how quickly they grow.

CUT THE SIDES AT A SLIGHT ANGLE
When cutting your hedge, start at the bottom and work your way up. If you start from the top and work your way down, the prunings will fall onto the lower branches, making it more difficult to cut the hedge.
● For a well-presented hedge that's green from top to bottom, cut the sides at a slight angle, tapering inwards towards the top – so that the top of the hedge is narrower than the bottom. What this shape does is make sure the bottom of the hedge will receive enough rain and more sunlight.

A HEDGE WITH A VIEW If you have a dense hedge that has established itself, you can cut a round window or an arched doorway in it to open up a romantic vista. This gives your garden some privacy and a view at the same time – it was a favourite design trick of landscape gardeners of the past.

CUTTING A HEDGE

1 A piece of string tied between pegs will help you cut a straight line. Use secure steps, rather than a ladder, to climb on.

2 Work safely and never try to cut above your shoulder height or stretch too far as you could lose control of your tools or fall.

3 For hedges that have small leaves use a hedge trimmer or a pair of shears. For hedges with large leaves cut branches one by one with secateurs.

4 Cut inside the line of the hedge so that the cut ends cannot be seen. Check frequently as you cut to make sure you are keeping a straight line.

COMPOST HEDGE CLIPPINGS Make the most of your hedge clippings by passing them through a shredder. If you place the shredder close to the hedge you can feed the clippings into it as soon as they are cut. Add the clippings to the compost heap to break them down before using them as a soil conditioner or mulch.

● To catch the clippings as you cut, spread a sheet along the base of the hedge. When you have finished cutting, the prunings can be bundled up and removed for shredding.

THE IDEAL WAY TO WATER A HEDGE
Use a weep hose that is made of a special perforated material that lets water pass through its walls. This allows you to water slowly and gives the water time to penetrate the earth properly and reach the roots. It is ideal for watering the base of a hedge. Trail the hose on the ground between the trunks or stems and attach one end to a tap.

● In areas where water restrictions limit hose types, make sure you select a weep hose that complies with your local authority's requirements or install a drip system.

● It's a good idea to always install a timer at the tap so you don't have to remember to turn the system off.

SPRAY CONIFER HEDGES Some conifer-hedge pests thrive in very dry conditions but can be deterred by spraying water into the hedge once a week in summer.

A WINTER CLEAN-UP FOR THOSE BARE HEDGES Tidy up a deciduous hedge during winter when the branches are bare. At this time it is much easier to cut out the dead wood and tangled stems and remove any unwanted climbing plants such as brambles. Keep an eye on the mulch at ground level and top it up if it has become thin.

A DEAD CONIFER When one plant in a coniferous hedge starts to die while the others around it remain quite healthy, it may be due to a root rot fungus, particularly in damp or waterlogged conditions. Remove the affected plant completely with as much of the root and surrounding soil as you can. Bin all the plant material instead of composting it. Treat the soil and the rest of the hedge with a phosphorus spray that can control root rot fungus. Also reduce the frequency of watering.

The fine art of topiary

AGE-OLD PRACTICE The art of topiary dates back to ancient Rome and has been a feature in gardens ever since. A clipped geometric shape adds a formal, period feel to the garden, while a whimsical topiary bird or beast recalls informal country plantings. Topiary is just one of many examples of how traditional skills can be used to great effect by today's gardeners.

TOPIARY PLANTS NEED NOURISHMENT To ensure you get the very best from your topiary plants, they need to be well fed, which encourages them to grow new shoots and dense foliage after trimming. Use an organic fertiliser that is high in nitrogen.

THE RIGHT TIME TO CUT TOPIARY PLANTS While the shape of the topiary is still being formed, cut it once a year at the end of spring, removing half the previous year's growth. This will encourage secondary branches to develop, which will form a dense

Gardener's Choice

THE BEST PLANTS FOR TOPIARY
Box plants were frequently used for topiary in the past and remain one of the most popular plants for crafting into sculpted forms, but any of the plants listed below will give you good results.

EVERGREEN SHRUBS Box, duranta, golden privet, holly and *Lonicera nitida* will give year-round colour and form.

DECIDUOUS SHRUBS Although *Berberis thunbergii* and hornbeam shed their leaves in winter, they are still worthy topiary subjects in cold climates.

CONIFERS Yew is a traditional choice that is today replacing privet as a cottage-garden favourite. Juniper is also suitable.

LOW PLANTS For small sculptures, try ivy, lavender, *Lonicera nitida*, muehlenbeckia, santolina or star jasmine trained over a frame.

Ready-to-use wire frames enable you to grow your own topiary, even in a pot.

1 Plant a young box in a container and remember that box likes well-drained, and even chalky, soil enriched with organic matter. Also, it dislikes being directly in the sun.

2 Cover the plant with a bamboo frame. Be patient: box grows very slowly. Allow it to branch out and fill the frame. Japanese box is faster growing and better suited to warm climates.

3 Cut off all foliage outside the frame with shears, trimming monthly if necessary. Repeated cutting will encourage the plant to get more bushy.

4 Water the pot regularly to keep the soil cool. When the shape is perfect, remove the frame. Break it and remove pieces to avoid damaging the plant.

growth. Once the desired shape has been obtained, the frequency of cutting varies according to the vigour of the species and the shape you have chosen – a complicated shape may need cutting every month to keep it precise. If an impeccable finish isn't important, then just cut it once a year after the spring growth, and again after flowering in relevant species. Never cut once autumn has started because new shoots will not have time to harden before the winter.

USE THE RIGHT STRUCTURE In order to create a simple, straight-edged shape, place a frame made of thin bamboo canes over the plant before cutting it. Once you have trimmed the plant to the required shape you can take the canes away.

● If you want to create a more complicated shape such as an animal, or a clear-cut geometric design such as a pyramid, cylinder,

ball or cone, make the shape first from wire netting. Fix the netting over the plant, secure it to the ground with wooden stakes and trim any foliage that passes through it.
● Once in place, don't remove the wire structure as it will eventually be covered by foliage and disappear.

TOPIARY IN POTS Box topiary shapes in pots can make a stylish feature for your patio, beside a doorway or even on steps, and being slow-growing, they require very little maintenance. When they are grown in containers, it is important to feed the plants well because they derive all their nutrients from the soil in the pot. Always use a good-quality potting mix and ensure there are good drainage holes in the base of the pot.

FOR PRECISION, USE SHEARS A hedge trimmer is too fast to use for really accurate cutting, so, if it is precision you want, use a pair of shears instead. They let you make a neat job of trimming and are also much easier to handle when dealing with complicated or rounded shapes.
● Invest in a quality pair and keep them in good working order with a sharp edge to the blade. If you cut a shrub with blunt shears you will maul its stems and cause lasting damage. This could result in yellow, brown and dead tissue that not only mars the look of the plant but can actually kill it.
● Shears with wavy blades are best to use on hedges with a finer foliage.

A DYING BRANCH If one of your topiary branches turns brown and appears to be dying, cut it off at the base, into the healthy, living wood. If the plant is well fed and watered, new shoots should appear on the old wood to fill the hole, though sometimes it takes years to restore the original shape. This should work on most plants but remember that conifers rarely regenerate when cut back into mature wood.

RESTORING AN ABANDONED TOPIARY If the plant has not been trimmed for some years, it is likely that the original shape has been lost. Cut back hard in the first year to approximately the original shape, then trim more carefully for the next 2 or 3 years to obtain an even, precise surface and restore the original form. Feed the plant well to encourage plenty of new shoots.

DID YOU KNOW?

MAKING A SPIRAL
Yew, box and lillypilly are particularly suitable if you want to create a spiral shape (below). It is not very difficult but you will need patience, as it will take 5–7 years to obtain a neat shape. You need to start with a slender plant 50–60 cm high, staked upright. In the second year, cut it to a cylindrical shape, forming a column about 10 cm in diameter. Cut it again at the end of summer to the required width.

Repeat this process in the third year. When the plant has reached a height of about 1.2 m, remove the stake and begin cutting the spiral shape with shears, starting at the base. Mark it out first using string or wire wound around the stem. Then gradually use secateurs to free the trunk from its stems and follow the shape around the plant.

Halfway to paradise

We have the humble cottage garden to thank for our love affair with climbers. There, where space was at a premium, these charming plants clambered over walls and trees to delight the eye and lead it upwards. In the modern garden, we still appreciate their ability to transform the smallest space with their colourful flowers and heavenly scents.

Well-planted and placed climbers

ALWAYS BUY IN CONTAINERS Unlike annual climbers, which are normally sold as seeds or as pots of seedlings, all shrubby climbers should be bought as mature plants in containers, or as smaller potted plants. These rooted climbers are in just the right condition to grow in your garden. Do not be tempted to buy climbers that are not suited to your climate.

Large-flowering clematis with climbing rose is an old-fashioned and stunning combination.

● When looking to buy a climber, remember that a healthy one will have several stems growing from the base and its foliage will be lush and healthy not dried or discoloured.

WHEN TO BUY Although plants in containers are available all year round, it is still best to buy a climbing plant in early spring or at the beginning of autumn. These are the best times to plant, which also means you will probably have the widest selection of healthy plants to choose from.

PRICES CLIMB, TOO Don't be surprised if you find that buying climbing plants is an expensive business. Of course, some plants will cost more than others, and this will depend on the size of the root ball and how many stems it has. As a general rule, the older the plant is the more expensive it will be. Some plants have been grafted onto a root stock and then grown on at the nursery for several years, and the price will reflect this extra nurture.

SHOULD YOU BUY A LARGE CLIMBER? Sometimes in garden centres you will find large climbers, 2 m or more tall, sold in large pots and often already in flower. You can buy them with confidence, but for the best results grow them in a pot where they will create an immediate decorative effect.
● For the garden, it is often better if you choose younger, smaller plants grown in containers, that are no more than 1.5 m tall. These will establish themselves more quickly than the larger plants, which may not flower for a year or two when they are planted out in the garden. The younger plants will grow so fast that in 2 years they will reach the same height as the larger climbers.

CLIMBERS AND THE LAW
If a wall belongs to your property entirely or is a party wall, you are perfectly within your rights to grow a climber on it. However, a plant should ideally not spill over the top of the wall into your neighbours' property without their agreement: they are within their rights to cut it back if it does. If you rent or live in a block of flats, you must get permission from the landlord or managing agent before planting a climber.

Also, prune climbers regularly to keep them from overhanging footpaths or blocking the entrance way.

Pyrostegia drapes over walls to give cascades of winter flowers.

WHEN TO PLANT OUT – IN SPRING OR AUTUMN?

Plants in containers can be planted out all year round, except during periods of frost, flood or intense drought.

● If at all possible it is preferable to plant out in autumn so that the roots have time to develop while the soil is still warm from the summer sun. This way the young plants will also get to benefit from the winter rain.

● In heavy soil that stays wet all winter, it is better to plant out in spring.

SOAK CLIMBERS BEFORE PLANTING

Plants that are sold in pots are often grown in a type of soil mixture that is very difficult to make wet once it has dried out – and even more so after planting out. Make sure you always immerse the plant in a bucket of water at room temperature before it is planted out into the garden. Soak for at least 15 minutes, or until there are no more air bubbles rising to the surface of the water.

CLOSE BUT NOT TOO CLOSE ...

If you want to train a climber against a wall, plant it about 30 cm away from the support. If it is any closer than this, then any rain or hose water that falls could be deflected by the wall, and the plant will not receive enough water to grow. Don't worry about it missing the wall, it will soon make the leap onto the support and start climbing – or give a helping hand if necessary.

KEEP IT VERY COOL

Most climbing plants like to have cool roots. You can easily achieve this by covering the soil around the base of the plant with a thick layer of mulch. However, make sure that the mulch does not build up around the stem of the climber or it may impede the circulation of air around the base and could cause stem rot.

● Provide shade by placing a tile or opaque screen at the base of the plant.

● Planting a shrub close to a climber will also create beneficial shade for its roots.

DON'T LAY LATTICE FLAT AGAINST THE WALL

Whether you are using lattice, metal wire or fishing wire as a support for your climber, it is essential to leave 3–4 cm between the support and the wall. This lets the stems of the plant twist around the support from all angles and it gives the roots some protection from the heat that will be generated by the wall in summer. The best

way to create this space is to place small pieces of wood or plastic spacers between the wall and the support.

● To make it easier to take the lattice down if you need to paint or repair the wall, don't fix it to the wall itself but instead attach it to hooks screwed into the wall. Then, when necessary, you can simply lift it up, with the plant in place, and lay it carefully on the ground beneath the wall.

CREATE A WATERING BASIN

Build up a small ridge of soil around the base of the plant, on top of the mulch, to create a watering basin. This will collect any water when it rains and from when you water the plant, and direct it so that it penetrates the soil around and above the root ball.

● Keep the basin intact for at least the first year after planting your climber. However, if you live in a particularly cold area of the country, you may want to remove the watering basin in winter, to avoid creating a frozen puddle around your plant.

SOIL CONDITIONS

Most climbers are tolerant of a variety of soil types. For best results make sure you mix in plenty of well-rotted garden compost in the planting hole. Specialist tree and shrub potting mix may also help. This will improve the water retention of the soil and add vital nutrients.

● In extreme alkaline conditions, wisteria plants may develop yellow (chlorotic) leaves. Try watering the plants with sequestered iron or use an acidifying mulch.

By removing a few screws, the antigonon and square lattice here can be removed to repaint the wall behind.

PLANTING A CLEMATIS

1 Dig a deep hole a little in front of the support. Lay the root ball in it so that the stems lean towards the support.

2 Fill up the hole, covering the root ball and the first 5 cm of the stem with a mixture of soil and well-rotted compost.

3 Water generously and firm down well to get rid of any air pockets and give the plant the best chance of taking root.

4 Protect the base to help keep the roots cool. Clematis love 'a warm head and cool feet'.

Which climbers would enhance your garden?

SCENTED CLIMBERS If you like fragrant flowers, then make some space in your garden for *Clematis montana* 'Elizabeth', which smells of vanilla in spring. *Jasminum officinale* is a favourite for aromatherapy, cosmetics and perfumes, while stephanotis has an entrancing scent in warm to tropical climates in summer. Also try wisteria and, of course, climbing roses such as 'Crépuscule', which has apricot flowers over many months.

CLIMBERS THAT CAN WITHSTAND THE COLD If you live in a region where winters are very harsh and the temperature plummets to extreme levels, choose your climbers with care. Among the hardiest climbing plants are deciduous clematis, honeysuckle, ivy, parthenocissus, rose and wisteria.
● Plants do not really become resistant to cold until their second or third year in the garden, so don't forget to protect them from any frost during the first few winters after planting. Take particular care at the base of the plant, where a generous layer of mulch would be beneficial.

A CARPET OF CLIMBERS Even without vertical support, climbers will continue to grow – horizontally. This means they can be used to carpet problem areas that are difficult to maintain or unpleasant to look at. Ivy and star jasmine will form a dense groundcover, but keep them trimmed so they don't invade other plants, especially trees.
● Dense climbers such as banksia rose, ivy geranium and pyrostegia can be used to hide ugly fences or outbuildings.

GOOD COMBINATIONS Whether they flower simultaneously or at different times, try planting two types of climbers next to each other. Roses intertwined with spring- or summer-flowering clematis are a popular choice. In warmer climates plant blue and white varieties of potato vine, such as 'Monet's Blue' (blue) and 'Alba' (white).
● Annual climbers such as nasturtiums and sweet peas, or even climbers usually seen in the vegetable garden, such as hops and scarlet runner beans, would make good summer companions for evergreen climbers. Pick your planting partners carefully to create the greatest impact.

COVER A WALL QUICKLY Bignonia and parthenocissus can grow up to 1 m in a year. For quicker results, plant several of the same species of plant along the length of a wall.

Shrubby climbers for walls

NORTH-FACING

- *Actinidia kolomikta*
- *Clematis armandii*
- Climbing roses
- Hardenbergia
- Mandevilla
- *Solanum crispum* **1**
- *Trachelospermum jasminoides*
- *Vitis vinifera* 'Purpurea'

EAST-FACING

- Carolina jasmine
- *Clematis montana*
- *Lonicera japonica* 'Halliana'
- Pandorea
- *Parthenocissus quinquefolia*
- Sollya
- Winter jasmine **2**

SOUTH-FACING

- *Akebia quinata*
- *Hedera helix* **3**
- *Hydrangea petiolaris*
- Large, light-flowered clematis
- *Parthenocissus tricuspidata*

WEST-FACING

- Bignonia
- Bougainvillea
- *Campsis radicans* **4**
- *Jasminum officinale*
- Passionfruit vine
- Summer-flowering clematis
- Wisteria

1 2
3 4

5 6

CLIMBERS FOR THOSE SHADY CORNERS

Some plants have interestingly variegated leaves, which can brighten up areas of the garden that are sheltered from the sun. Enjoy the seasonal tints of *Actinidia kolomikta*, which displays pink and white young leaves in spring, and *Ampelopsis glandulosa* 'Elegans', which has lovely pink shoots and leaves splashed with pink and white.

● Use variegated ivies such as *Hedera canariensis* 'Variegata', *Hedera colchica* 'Sulphur Heart' and *Hedera helix* 'Glacier'.

CLIMBING HYDRANGEA

The climber, *Hydrangea petiolaris*, is the understated cousin of the more flamboyant common hydrangea, which has large blue or pink inflorescences. *Hydrangea petiolaris* has flat white flowers that appear in December and are set against its beautiful dark green foliage. This hydrangea likes an east- or south-facing wall, but it needs light so avoid shade cast by neighbouring trees.

FAST-FLOWERING WISTERIAS

Some wisterias can take between 10 and 20 years to flower if grown from seeds, which can be enough to try the patience of any gardener. To prevent this problem, avoid buying un-named seedlings and try to buy wisterias that are already in flower when you buy them.

The flame lily, Gloriosa 'Rothschildiana', flowers in summer but dies down to a tuber in winter.

Climbing hydrangea thrives on an east- or south-facing wall where it clings using suckers.

Alternatively, choose grafted plants – make sure this is specifically mentioned on the label – which will flower in 2 to 3 years.

● Do not give nitrogen-rich fertiliser to newly planted wisterias, as this encourages energy to be used for the growth of the stem and leaves, and can actually delay flowering.

CLIMBERS ARE NOT SUITABLE FOR ALL WALLS

Be careful when choosing climbers to grow up a wall. Avoid climbers such as *Hydrangea petiolaris*, ivy and parthenocissus, that have adventitious roots or suckers, if they are to be grown up a soft-stone or half-timbered house, or any walls with cracks. These plants will worm their way into every nook and cranny, weakening the joints and increasing the risk of damp.

● Although ivy can damage old walls whose stones or bricks need repointing, it is virtually impossible for it to get a hold on a modern concrete wall in good condition, so lattice may be needed.

A WARNING ABOUT IVY

Although ivy is appealing when it is draped over walls, take care when pruning or removing it. Ivy harbours dust and mites, which can cause skin, eye and respiratory irritation. Make sure you wet it down before handling it, wear a hat, a long-sleeved shirt and a mask.

FLAMING GLORY

The deciduous climber *Gloriosa* 'Rothschildiana' grows from a large tuber to produce stunning red and yellow lily flowers (left). Grow it in a large container with support or against a wall. It needs full sun but you need to protect the roots using a layer of mulch to keep them cool. Snails love new shoots so protect the plant well in early spring. Always select the hybrid forms

DID YOU KNOW?

HOW PLANTS CLING Plants have many ways of scaling walls and other supports.

WINDING STEMS Akebia, honeysuckle, phaseolus and wisteria have stems that coil around their support.

ADVENTITIOUS ROOTS Campsis, *Hydrangea petiolaris* and ivy **1** have clinging roots that develop on the stems when they are in contact with the support, especially if it is rough and damp. These roots have no nutritive function.

STEM TENDRILS Some parthenocissus and passion-fruit **2** have stem tendrils that will coil around any support – nails, the stalk of a nearby leaf or a piece of metal wire. Clematis have twining leaf stalk tendrils.

SUCKERS Other types of parthenocissus **3** have stem tendrils that look like hands, with sticky pads, or suckers, at the end of each 'finger'. These suckers are extremely adhesive and can be difficult to remove.

THORNS Roses **4** and rubus climb by scrambling up supports with their thorns but will also need some additional tying and training.

as the species becomes a weed in warm and coastal areas. After the vine has died down leave it in the pot undisturbed.

DECIDUOUS OR EVERGREEN? Some popular climbing plants that are evergreen in warm climates may, when grown in cool or frosty winter gardens, lose their leaves to survive the winter chill. Banksia roses and bougainvilleas will lose their leaves in very cold climates while mandevillas may be cut back completely and should be grown with as much frost protection as possible.

HEAT INSULATION Climbers can help you run your home more efficiently. Evergreen climbers can actually play a role in insulating your house. In winter, air cavities between the plant and the outer wall form a useful insulating layer that helps to keep heat in. And in summer, the leaves block the sun's rays and help keep the house cooler.

Special effects for your climbers

TRAIN YOUR CLIMBER TO LOOK LIKE A TREE The vines *Hydrangea petiolaris* and wisteria (above right) can be trained to grow into little trees. To do this, plant them with plenty of space around them and drive a solid wooden stake into the ground near the base of the plant. Let the shoots run along the ground. Once the shoots are between 1 and 2 m long, lift them up and wrap them around the stake. The branches will then grow around it and thicken to form a straight treelike trunk, while any new shoots will grow from the top. You will need to be patient, but the final effect will be dramatic.

USE A MIRROR TO CREATE SPACE If you have a small garden, try placing a large mirror in a corner behind a climber growing up a post or narrow lattice. The climber won't take up much space but will appear to double its size, and your garden will seem larger.

GROW PLANTS WITH SUPERB AUTUMN FOLIAGE Some deciduous climbers display brilliant, fiery colours during autumn that can rival others' showy flowers. Boston ivy (*Parthenocissus tricuspidata* 'Veitchii') has

Strong, shrubby climbers, like this wisteria, can be trained on a stake to look like a small tree.

blood-red leaves in May and the leaves of *Vitis coignetiae* turn wine-coloured in late March before they fall.

● Deciduous vines such as grapevine and wisteria are a great choice to train over a pergola as, once their leaves have gone, the winter sun streams in.

TRAILING CLIMBERS Parthenocissus (right), passionfruit and pyrostegia will form a dramatic wall of colour. Just stretch a rope or chain between two structures such as a fence and a pergola, and these climbers will head for their new support. When they are unable to find anything vertical to cling to, the young shoots will hang down, forming elegant green drapes in the summer and a crimson curtain of colour in the autumn.

Caring for climbers

BLOWING IN THE WIND Be wary when covering wire netting with climbers. In many cases it is an ideal support for plants with twining stems or tendrils as it lets the air circulate. But the foliage can create a solid barrier to the wind, and in exposed areas a violent gust could wrench out the supporting posts and blow the netting down.

CONTROLLED FREEDOM Climbers with stems that wind themselves around their supports sometimes also need to be fixed

Create dramatic curtain-like effects with climbers. Here (above top) parthenocissus is a blaze of colour against a wall in autumn and (above) elegantly draping over a wall.

to them. However, don't strangle the stems by attaching them too tightly. Instead wind a flexible clip around the stem and fix to the support. Alternatively, tie garden string loosely around the stem and the support. You should be able to put your finger easily behind the stem where it is tied in.

RECYCLE OLD PANTIHOSE AND TIGHTS
Wash and then cut the legs off old pantihose and tights and then cut them into 4 cm wide strips that open out into circular bands. These are strong and will make excellent, flexible, easy-to-use ties with which to attach the stems of climbers to lattices and supports.

LAYERING CLIMBERS Producing new climbers by layering couldn't be easier. In spring, lay one of the soft shoots attached to the mother plant on the ground and cover with a 5 cm layer of potting mix so several buds – but no leaves – are beneath the soil. Hold it in place with a wire hoop. Then the following spring, when it has rooted, take out the hoop, cut the shoot behind the new roots that have grown, dig it out and plant it in its new site. You might have to wait a year but the result is a free plant.

CLIMBERS ARE A HAVEN FOR SMALL ANIMALS
Climbing plants offer shelter, food and sometimes breeding sites for all kinds of creatures. Insects and spiders will be the first to arrive and, if you are lucky, slow worms and lizards may follow, attracted by the natural supply of insect food. Then the birds will move in, finding in the foliage and the elevated position both safety and privacy for their nests and young ones.
● However, be careful when you prune or trim your climbers, in case you disturb a nest of young, or deprive birds of their safe home. Some birds nest as late as December.

STRONG-ARMED WISTERIA Wisteria stems can grow as thick as a person's arm and wind themselves around their support with such force that they can bend it or pull it out, even if it is metal. In order to avoid this problem, remember to choose a sturdy support that is in good repair.
● Other climbers can also be very heavy, especially when they are well established or when they are covered in fruit. Bear this in mind if you plan to erect a pergola and cover it with rampant growth.

PUT YOUR DELICATE PLANTS UNDER STRAW MATTING
If you have planted a climber against a wall and are not sure how well it will withstand the cold, protect it from frost by covering it on frosty nights with a bedsheet, a piece of cardboard or horticultural fleece. Also protect the root system with a layer of mulch.

CLIMBING FLOWER POWER Feed your flowering climbers with an organic fertiliser rich in potash, such as compost enriched with seaweed or comfrey. This encourages flowering and boosts growth. Pay particular attention to climbers growing in containers.

Some simple tips for pruning

PRUNE BEFORE PLANTING On climbers that have adventitious roots or suckers, such as ivy, climbing hydrangea and parthenocissus, only the new young shoots will cling to the support. There is no point struggling to get the stems of a plant you have just bought and planted to adhere to a wall because they will not oblige. Cut back the stems to about 10 cm from the root ball, above a bud, and the young shoots that will soon begin to grow will automatically, with no fuss, start to climb up the support.

Most climbers need regular tying to keep them trained.

Layering is an easy way to grow new plants from vines such as jasmine or quisqualis.

DID YOU KNOW?

MY CLEMATIS IS WILTING
Without warning, the flowers on one or more shoots of a clematis can turn black, dry out and die. This is called clematis wilt and is thought to be caused by fungus or bacteria present in the soil. There is nothing you can do to stop it, but you must act quickly and radically to save the plant. Cut the branches off completely, down to ground level, and clear the area around the base to a depth of around 10 cm. Replace the soil you have removed with healthy soil from another part of the garden. If your garden has a history of this problem, try planting the clematis deeper.

Make sure you choose your climbing supports with care. Remember they must be strong enough to support the plant when it is fully grown.

IS PRUNING NECESSARY? This depends on the type of plant. Many climbers quite happily grow without pruning, but some need pruning to encourage flowers. If your plant is outgrowing its space or becoming unmanageable it is time for the secateurs.

PRUNING FOR BETTER FLOWERS Make a note of when your climbers flower and the type of stem wood on which the buds grow, then you can prune them at the right time to encourage a spectacular display next year.

● **SPRING FLOWERS** Plants that flower in spring, such as *Akebia quinata*, *Clematis alpina* and other early clematis, form their flower buds on the previous year's growth, which is ripened and woody. The buds rest during winter until the start of the mild weather when they open. If you prune these stems in winter you will remove next year's flower buds and miss out on a spring display. Wait until your plant has flowered then cut the flowering stems back hard to encourage new growth that will flower next spring.

● **SUMMER FLOWERS** Plants that flower in summer, such as large-flowered clematis like 'Mrs Cholmondeley', climbing rose and passionfruit, form their flower buds during spring, on fresh shoots that grow from the end of winter. Don't prune the long spring shoots, as they carry summer flowers. Cut back the plant in winter or early spring to encourage the growth of new shoots.

● **WINTER FLOWERS** Winter-flowering plants, such as banksia rose and *Jasminum nudiflorum* form their flower buds on growth that is made during the spring and summer. Prune these plants after they have finished flowering to encourage new shoots that will mature and ripen during summer to bear next season's flowers.

PREVENT DAMAGE TO ROOFS Ivy and parthenocissus can be very invasive on house walls and can even get under roof tiles, causing leaks. To keep their growth under control, cut them back once a year to 50 cm below the level of the gutter.

PRUNE AND CONTROL Many climbing plants can simply outgrow their welcome, especially if they engulf neighbouring plants, walls or roofs. No matter what time of the year it is, if you notice a vigorous plant, such as quisqualis or wisteria, invading where it shouldn't, cut back the wayward shoots.

When to prune popular climbers

PLANT	WHEN	HOW
Campsis	Winter	Cut back the secondary shoots close to their base.
Clematis	Winter to early spring	Prune early-spring flowerers after flowering, midseason flowerers in early spring, and late-season clematis in winter and early spring.
Gelsemium	Spring	After flowering thin out old growth.
Grapevine	Winter	Cut off the young shoots from the previous year above the second bud.
Ivy geraniums	Autumn to winter	After flowering remove spent flowers and prune back any old growth.
Pandorea	Spring to summer	Light pruning to shape after flowering.
Parthenocissus	Winter	To rejuvenate the plant, cut back all the growth to ground level.
Passionfruit vine	Early spring	To rejuvenate the plant, shorten all the secondary stems, which shoot from the older, main stems, to 5 cm from the point at which they sprout from the main stem.
Port St John creeper	Autumn	Prune back outward or wayward shoots close to old wood after flowering.
Quisqualis	Early spring	Remove several older stems to allow for new growth. Remove spent flowers in autumn.
Rose (non-repeat-flowering)	Spring	Remove all the old stems after flowering.
Rose (repeat-flowering)	Mid to late winter	Cut out all the weak, diseased branches. Shorten the strongest branches by two-thirds.
Wisteria	Late summer	Once the main framework is established, cut off all the secondary shoots above the third bud in late summer.

Quisqualis is shrubby when young but quickly grows and fills out. It can spread to up to 10 m or more and has fragrant flowers that change colour from white to red.

The supporting roles in the garden

Styles in lattice, pergolas and arbours have changed little over the last hundred years. However, today they are available in modern materials or traditional wood, and there are options to suit not only every size and design of garden but every size and type of climber.

Versatile lattice

SPRUCE UP A WOODEN LATTICE An old lattice can be in poor condition, particularly if it has not been adequately treated against fungal rot and algae. Treat it with a water-based preservative about every 2 or 3 years, although this can be very tricky once it is smothered with climbing plants.

● Untreated wood can be used for all types of decorative purposes in the garden but, depending on the type of wood, it may deteriorate quite quickly.

● Once you have preserved the timber of your lattice, you can apply a variety of colour washes and finishes either to blend the lattice into the background or to add more colour and contrast to the garden. Many of these colour washes are water-based and can be used in conjunction with a water-based preservative. Read the instructions carefully and do not use any preservatives that will be harmful to your plants.

FIXING REMOVABLE NETTING TO A WALL

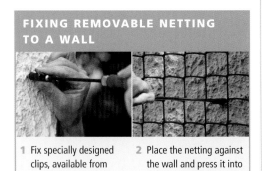

1 Fix specially designed clips, available from hardware stores and garden centres, to the wall at regular intervals.

2 Place the netting against the wall and press it into the clips, which will ensure the netting stays away from the wall.

Rejuvenate an old lattice by treating it with a preservative and a coat of paint.

PUT SPACERS BEHIND THE LATTICE
If you are fixing a lattice to a wall or fence to support climbing plants, use small blocks of wood to hold the lattice about 5 cm away from the wall. This enables the plants to twine in and around the lattice more easily and so supports the plant more securely. It also improves airflow around the wall and the foliage of the plant, thus reducing the risk of fungus.

NATURAL SOUND-PROOFING Town and city balconies can be screened off using a lattice that has been covered in evergreen climbing plants. Buy ready-planted containers complete with lattice, or combine plants with a lattice of your choice, and in a short time you will have an attractive living screen.

● A wall of plants will also absorb a certain amount of air pollution and reduce noise from nearby roads.

COVER AN UNSIGHTLY AREA Make a screen or enclosure from lattice panels fixed to posts, then train vigorous climbers over it.

NATURAL SUPPORT
Traditional gardeners used to coppice trees, particularly native eucalypts, by cutting the main stem to the ground and allowing a crop of fresh stems to develop from the base. The stems they cut were then used as supports in the garden and around the home.

After 1 or 2 years of new growth, the stems can be used as supports for your climbing plants. If you wait a while longer, they will grow thick enough to use for making an authentic rustic lattice for your garden.

Create a trompe l'oeil on a wall and an illusion of depth with a decorative lattice.

The graceful laburnum adds a charming, cascading effect to any cold-climate garden.

To quickly cover an eyesore in your yard, choose plants such as hardenbergia, potato vine or star jasmine. Prune regularly to keep them looking good. For a quick fix, cover the lattice with nasturtiums or sweet peas while a slower, permanent creeper gets established.

TRAIN THEM WELL Before you tackle the task of training a climber, remember that the base of a support or a wall is often set in concrete, and it is almost always in a rain shadow. To make sure the roots get enough moisture, position the plant at least 30 cm away from the support.

● Climbing plants are often sold with two or three stems attached to a thin supporting bamboo cane. After planting, carefully remove the bamboo cane, and gently position the stems against the support so they will grow vertically, securing them with ties.

● One year later, the stems will have made new shoots. Separate these secondary stems and train them to fan outwards across the support at a 45° angle.

● The following year the stems will have grown again and may even have developed lateral stems. Separate these and this time train them horizontally. Train these stems at a 45° angle, and so on each year.

● Remember to keep the plant ties quite loose and flexible. This will make sure that each stem is free to grow unhindered.

CREATE AN OPTICAL ILLUSION Use a decorative lattice specially designed to alter the perspective of your garden and make a small space appear larger (left). A lattice with

this 'trompe l'oeil' effect draws your eye into it to create the illusion of a deeper space. It is most effective when attached to a wall.

● Remember, however, that if you train a plant over this type of lattice you will lose the illusion of distance that it creates.

EXPANDABLE LATTICE Some lattice is sold without an outside frame and can be expanded to fit available space. The further you stretch, the more you open its structure.

Garden structures

CREATE A DRAMATIC ROSE UMBRELLA Train a climbing rose that has been grafted onto a standard root stock to form a cascade of flowers (above right). Simply fix an umbrella-shaped rose frame firmly into the ground and arrange the trailing stems over it.

RECYCLED FISHING LINE If your climbers are only growing up the vertical supports of your gazebo, use thick fishing line or wire stretched horizontally across the arches, to train the plants along. The line or wire is virtually invisible and once the stems have reached the other side it can be removed. Just make sure it is not used where it could catch someone unawares.

A weeping rose creates a living umbrella of blossom.

DID YOU KNOW?

TREATED WOOD
Garden timber products are usually pressure-treated with preservative chemicals. This treatment saturates the wood and protects it from getting damaged by fungal rot and other problems. If in doubt, double-check before you buy. Treated wood is usually guaranteed for garden use for quite a number of years. To avoid contact with preservatives, wear gloves when handling treated wood and paint treated wood structures, such as handrails and play equipment that may be regularly touched. If sawing treated timber, always re-treat cut ends with a timber preservative.

Lattice or openwork panels are perfect for the more delicate climbers such as clematis. This is because they let lots of light through.

A COVERED TEPEE If you have restricted wall space, you can still grow climbers on free-standing plant supports.
● Using tall bamboo canes, construct your tepee in your garden bed or in a large pot filled with potting mix. This tepee structure will support the more compact, slower-growing herbaceous clematis, like *Clematis* 'Arabella', or the smaller climbing roses.
● For heavier and more vigorous clematis, honeysuckles or roses, use stronger supports that are made from wood or metal that you can securely anchor to the ground among other plants in the garden.

LATTICE FENCING Lattice fencing in a criss-cross pattern has a natural, rustic look and is an ideal support for clematis, honeysuckle and nasturtium. Try using lattice to fence off different sections of the garden, such as the vegetable patch or the children's play area – its open structure will make the whole garden appear larger.

LATTICE PANELS FOR A TERRACE OR PATIO If you can't dig down into the ground to fix supports for a lattice, don't despair. You can get special brackets that screw onto hard surfaces, into which the posts simply slot and are held in place with screws. The lattice can then be easily attached to the posts. If this is not possible you can also build 'shoes' from bricks cemented to the patio, which will hold the posts in position.

ATTACKING RUST Some gardeners like the 'antique' effect of rusted metal in the garden.

If you don't, and there is something corroding in your garden, rub it down with a wire brush to remove the loose rust and paint on a coat of an anti-rust product that will form a protective barrier over the metal.

ELECTRICITY PYLONS AND POLES Don't be tempted to cover these with climbers, as this is dangerous and is not permitted.

Pergolas, arches and arbours

ORIGINS OF PERGOLAS Gardeners have used pergolas, arches and arbours to add interest and height to gardens since ancient Roman times – their artwork shows arching reed-lattice arbours adorned with vines and roses. Traditionally, the pergola is a wooden or metal structure that supports climbing plants, under which you can promenade or simply relax in comfort.

BUILD YOUR PERGOLA FOR LASTING For a pergola to really last the distance, the base of its uprights must be kept dry and secure. Soak the post base in preservative and sink it into holes filled with concrete.
● You can also use metal brackets to hold the posts. These are easy to install, they need no cement and they allow you to replace the posts easily. However, they are difficult to drive into hard or stony ground.

Gardener's Choice

TRADITIONAL MATERIALS FOR PERGOLAS

TREATED PINE This wood is strong and easy to work with. The posts should be at least 10 cm square and the horizontal crosspieces 5 cm thick. Use the material that has been appropriately treated for the way you will use it. For example H4 and higher rating is treated for in-ground use.

RECYCLED HARDWOOD Create a truly rustic look by building in old timber that has been salvaged from demolition work.

METAL You can also use a metal framework, but avoid a look of scaffolding. Metal structures can create a traditional effect, which is not surprising, as iron has been used for garden furniture for over 200 years. You can now buy ready-made, decorative wrought-iron or aluminium arches, and position them one after another to create a formal pergola as long as you like.

A PERGOLA WITH A ROOF For a shaded terrace next to your house, grow climbers over a pergola running alongside a wall. While you wait for the plants to cover the roof of the pergola, use split bamboo panels for shade and for protection from the rain.

● If you position a pergola next to your house, remember that the frame and the plants growing on it can block out a lot of winter light. Avoid structures that are too heavy, choose deciduous climbers and make the pergola high enough to let plenty of winter light into the house.

DECORATE YOUR PERGOLA WITH POTS
Though wooden lattice panels and pergolas are intended to support climbing plants, they can also hold baskets and pots. This means you can choose plants to extend the flowering season or add colour.

CREATE A COVERED WALKWAY For the best results possible, a pergola that goes over a path should be 2.5–3 m tall and wide. If it is wider than it is high, you run the risk of creating a 'tunnel effect'. Remember, two people, side by side, should be able to pass through easily, without ducking to avoid the plants: allow at least 60 cm overhead.

MAKE YOUR GARDEN SEEM BIGGER
The arch of a pergola, inviting you to pass underneath, has the effect of dividing your garden in two. So, if you have quite a small garden, a pergola may help to make it seem larger, particularly if you position it so that it appears to hint at wider vistas beyond. On the other hand, it will also make a long garden appear shorter.

● If you have a small garden, it's a good idea to choose a pergola with a framework that is not too chunky, or one that is painted green to blend in with the background. In a large garden, you have more room and can afford to draw attention to its structure or colour.

PERGOLA AND LATTICEWORK KITS
Even if you are not a do-it-yourself expert, you can still have a reasonably inexpensive pergola. Today, ready-to-build kits containing posts, arches and struts in treated wood make it easy to design and construct your own pergolas, arches, fences and many other garden structures. When you decide what you want, select the individual elements you require and tailor them to suit your plan.

1 Unpack and sort out all the components, including the posts, rafters, fixtures and fittings. Now fix the first upright.

2 Secure it to the base using the metal fittings provided in the kit, and use a spirit level to ensure that the upright is truly vertical.

3 Erect the remaining posts, ensuring that each one is vertical. Then add the cross-pieces, which will stabilise the whole structure.

4 For speed, strength and efficiency use an electric screwdriver to fix the main crossbeams to the uprights.

5 Once the posts and crosspieces are in place, position the rafters, slotting them into the main frame.

6 Your new pergola will now provide you with a secluded, shaded living space in which to relax in your garden.

THE POWER OF THE WIND Never underestimate the power of the wind. Choose your pergola and climbing plants with care if your garden is exposed to strong winds.

● A lightweight metal frame could twist and be damaged by wind, so build a strong wooden structure with posts set firmly and securely into the ground.

● Plants with heavy growth also make a structure vulnerable, creating a solid barrier that is more likely to be damaged by wind.

Think big: remember that the larger the pergola the more space there will be for plants to grow and display their colourful blooms.

DID YOU KNOW?

WOOD NEEDN'T ALWAYS BE BROWN
Get more from the timber in your garden by giving it a coat of colour. There is a huge choice of paints available, in both traditional 'heritage' colours and brighter, more modern hues, though tones of blue and green are always good. A colourful lattice or pergola will add interest to the garden in all seasons, but they are particularly attractive in the winter when many of the plants have died back and the garden is bare.

Gentle giants and lifelong friends

It's impossible to imagine a garden without trees. If you have had the good fortune to inherit one from 50 or even 100 years ago, you may have occasionally mused on its life. When you plant a new tree, you're investing in future generations and continuing a precious tradition.

Buy a healthy tree

CONSIDER THE TREE'S MATURE SIZE AND SHAPE Never buy a tree without first checking what height and spread it will reach at maturity, or at least after 10 years' growth. This will help you choose a tree that is neither too tall nor with too wide a spread, but a tree that is just right for your garden.
● Conifers and evergreens can cast a lot of shade, especially when the winter sun is low in the sky. Due to the density of this shade and the inhospitable soil conditions created by the fallen needles of most conifers, other plants are unable to grow beneath them.

THINK LOCAL Garden centres and many flower shows unveil magnificent new species every season. But try to resist the current fashion for rare varieties that need special care, unless, that is, you are already an experienced and knowledgeable gardener.
● Visit your local nursery for the best choice of trees to suit your garden. It's always useful to know a plant's common name as this can give you a clue to its place of origin and thus to its ability to adapt to your garden. In particular avoid plants that come from areas that are much colder or warmer than where you live. These trees may grow well initially but can be more prone to both pest and disease problems and will not prosper.

YOUNG TREES ESTABLISH QUICKLY
It's not always a good idea to buy plants that have developed into young trees. Those with a good-sized trunk and a spread of branches will already have spent several years growing

in a nursery bed or a container, and so transporting and transplanting them into your garden will cause them inevitable stress.
● If the tree has been field-grown, some of the root system may be left behind when it is uprooted, and the tree will have to regrow sufficient roots to anchor itself and absorb water and nutrients, while at same time trying to adapt to its new environment.
● In the long run, it may be better to spend less money and buy a younger, smaller tree that will settle in more quickly. It will soon catch up with the older tree, whose energy will be concentrated on establishing a good root system instead of making top growth.

The attractive foliage of Robinia 'Frisia' provides a pleasing backdrop for a herbaceous border and it also adapts well to a small garden.

BUYING ON A VERY GRAND SCALE

Semimature trees are grown by specialist tree nurseries. These will have been grown in open ground for anywhere between 5 and 10 years, sometimes longer. In days gone by, trees were grown in the ground and dug up, usually in winter, using a tree spade. The root system was wrapped in hessian or burlap for transport. Today, most are grown in the ground in a root control bag, a geotextile fabric that has been formed into a pot in the ground. The major roots are contained, but smaller feeder roots form in the surrounding soil. When the tree is harvested these smaller roots are broken off. However, this doesn't do any permanent damage because they will quickly regrow once the tree is replanted.

● Always remove the bag or covering from a tree's roots at planting time.

● Some trees are transplanted as mature specimens rather than being specially grown in a nursery. If you are buying and relocating a mature tree, do it during winter to reduce transplant shock.

BUYING AND PLANTING A LARGE TREE

The popularity of garden makeover television shows has created a market for large trees as gardeners demand an instant effect. There are drawbacks to buying large trees. Size indicates the length of time the tree has been growing in the nursery and the larger and older they are, the more expensive and the more difficult to handle. Unless you have access to special equipment such as heavy trucks and a crane, employ a landscape contractor to deliver and plant your tree.

It is not always best to buy a mature tree. A young tree is much less traumatised in the move and so it doesn't have to expend all its energy recovering.

● **DIG THE HOLE** Ensure that the hole dug is at least twice as wide as the root ball but only as deep as the root ball. A hole that's too deep will lead to the tree being too deeply planted and poor growth will follow.

● **TEST THE DRAINAGE** Most trees can't cope with wet conditions. If water drains slowly from the planting hole, dig in gypsum to improve drainage. If necessary, plant the tree into a specially prepared raised bed.

● **STAKE AND SECURE** If the tree is unstable or buffeted by wind, secure it between three stakes using adjustable tree ties. Remove the stakes and ties once the tree is growing well.

● **EXTRA SHADE** If the tree's roots have been cut or broken, it may be unable to supply enough moisture to keep the leaves healthy. Temporary shade over the foliage together with an anti-transpirant spray will reduce moisture loss while the roots are regrowing.

IS IT A TREE OR A SHRUB?

It can be difficult to define what a tree is. Broadly speaking, a tree has a trunk with branches that grow upwards from its crown. But some trees, notably conifers, grow branches along the whole length of their trunk. Other trees have supple branches that bend down to the ground, called weeping or pendulous trees. The branches of other trees grow along the ground, with no trunk at all. Even height is no guide, as some trees peak at 1 m, while some of the larger shrubs can, in maturity, reach 3 or 4 m. If you are in any doubt as to the eventual size and suitability of your chosen tree, seek some expert advice from staff at a specialist tree nursery.

Frangipanis are usually grown as small trees but in colder climates they could be considered to be large shrubs.

WATCH OUT

TRANSPORTING TREES: BEWARE OF DAMAGE

Tree purchases rarely fit easily into the family car and often end up poking out of the sunroof, tied to the roof-rack or even sticking out of the open tailgate.

Be very careful that you don't cause the tree undue stress on its journey.

Wrap up your tree well using plastic bubblewrap or cardboard to cover any exposed areas to protect them from wind damage.

Better still, have the tree delivered by the nursery in a covered truck.

BUYING OUT OF SEASON As long as a tree is containerised you can plant it at any time of year, but don't be tempted to plant a bare-root tree unless it is dormant.

● Even if a tree is container-grown it still needs regular care. If you plant in spring or summer, water regularly and ideally keep the soil cool, especially during hot weather.

SMALL IS BEAUTIFUL If you have a small garden, and if you have to plant trees near to buildings, restrict your choice to dwarf varieties or those that are particularly slow-growing. This will ensure that you are not in any danger of planting a tree whose roots will later undermine your house.

● If space is extremely restricted, consider using a small specimen tree planted in a large container, such as a half-barrel. You could try one of the smaller crab-apples or a bay tree (*Laurus nobilis*) – they are useful for culinary purposes as well as being an ornamental ever-green – but remember that trees housed in containers must be fed regularly.

Choosing a tree for your garden

FAST-GROWING TREES Trees take many years to develop their mature size and shape. If you are looking for trees that are fast growing then consider some of these, all of which can grow 1 m or more per year: birch, crepe myrtle, maple, paulownia, robinia or wattle. The tree-in-a-hurry, *Virgilia oroboides*, will grow rapidly to between 6 and 9 m but it is only very short lived.

GROW TREES THAT HAVE BEAUTIFUL AUTUMN FOLIAGE Canada, Japan and the United States are famed for their fabulous bronze-red autumn foliage, and you can achieve the same effect in your own garden.

● **GOLDEN** Try the maidenhair tree (*Ginkgo biloba*) or the tulip tree (*Liriodendron tulipifera*) for golden autumn leaves.

● **GOLDEN YELLOW TO PURPLISH-VIOLET** The sweet gum (*Liquidambar styraciflua*) has dramatic autumn colouring but remember to look for small varieties.

● **BLOOD-RED** The scarlet oak (*Quercus coccinea* 'Splendens') or the red maple (*Acer rubrum*) have deep rich red foliage.

DECORATIVE BARK Many can recognise the white bark of the common birch, but what about that of the Himalayan birch (*Betula utilis*), which is pale pink? Lots of trees are grown especially for their decorative bark, to brighten up the winter months.

● The plane tree is one example and so is the flowering cherry (*Prunus sargentii*). The Tibetan cherry (*Prunus serrula*) (right top) has walnut-brown bark that peels off in horizontal strips to reveal shiny red bark below, and the paper-bark maple (*Acer griseum*) has cinnamon-coloured bark that detaches by rolling up on itself.

● Other striking examples of decorative bark include the trees *Eucalyptus niphophila* (right centre) and *Betula nigra* (right bottom).

TREES FOR SCREENING In very windy and exposed locations, trees can be used as effective windbreaks. If you plant them densely they will form a screen that will shelter the rest of the garden.

● Remember that it is always better to filter the wind to diminish its force rather than to block it with a solid wall, which will create inevitable turbulence.

BLUE SHADES Some conifers have grey-blue foliage – not only the celebrated blue Colorado spruce (*Picea pungens* 'Hoopsii') (below) and the Lawson cypress (*Chamaecyparis lawsoniana* 'Pembury Blue'), but also the blue cedar (*Cedrus atlantica*) and the flaky juniper (*Juniperus squamata* 'Meyeri').

● The lovely bluish colour of these conifers changes, depending on the intensity and amount of available light and the concentration of humidity in the air. It also varies according to the tree's general state of health.

Above is a selection of some ornamental trunks (from top to bottom): Tibetan cherry, eucalyptus and birch.

You can see here why the delicate blue of the Colorado spruce is much sought after.

POPULAR TREES WITH CHARM

Trees are so varied that there is an interesting and attractive variety for any space you wish to fill, or any function you demand of it.

A CONIFER FOR YOUR COURTYARD

Italian cypress (*Cupressus* 'Swane's Golden')
Juniper including *Juniperus* 'Skyrocket' **1**
Juniperus 'Spartan'.

A WEEPING TREE

Beech (*Fagus sylvatica* 'Pendula')
Blue Atlas cedar (*Cedrus atlantica* 'Glauca Pendula')
Bottlebrush (*Callistemon viminalis* 'Captain Cook') **2**
Japanese pagoda tree (*Sophora japonica* 'Pendula')
Weeping ash (*Fraxinus excelsior* 'Pendula').

AN EVERGREEN

Holly (*Ilex aquifolium* 'Argentea Marginata')
Holm oak (*Quercus ilex*)
Magnolia (*Magnolia grandiflora* 'Little Gem') **3**.

A TREE WITH VARIEGATED FOLIAGE

Maple (*Acer negundo* 'Variegatum')
Variegated Japanese maple (*Acer palmatum*) **4**.

A TREE WITH PURPLE FOLIAGE

Beech (*Fagus sylvatica* 'Riversii')
Cercis (*Cercis canadensis* 'Forest Pansy')
Maple (*Acer palmatum* 'Atropurpureum') **5**
Prunus (*Prunus cerasifera* 'Pissardii').

A SCENTED TREE

Eucalyptus (*Eucalyptus gunnii*) **6**
False acacia (*Robinia pseudoacacia*)
Katsura tree (*Cercidiphyllum*)
Manna ash (*Fraxinus ornus*)
Paulownia (*Paulownia fargesii* or *P. tomentosa*).

A FLOWERING TREE

Flowering crab-apple (*Malus* 'Evereste')
Flowering dogwood (*Cornus florida*)
Judas tree (*Cercis siliquastrum*) **7**
Tulip tree (*Liriodendron tulipifera*)
Winter cherry (*Prunus subhirtella* 'Autumnalis').

A TREE WITH DECORATIVE FRUIT

Flowering crab-apple (*Malus*)
Maidenhair tree (*Ginkgo biloba*)
Mountain ash (*Sorbus aucuparia*)
Mulberry tree (*Morus*) **8** female specimen
Oriental plane tree (*Platanus orientalis*).

BEWARE FALLING OBJECTS The fruits of conifers are cones. Some are striking, such as those of the Korean fir (*Abies koreana*), which produces violet-coloured cones from an early age, or those of the blue Arizona fir (*Abies lasiocarpa*), which are red and pendulous, measuring 7 cm in length. Beware of parking or lying under a tree bearing cones.
● Especially large are the cones of the kauri pine, *Agathis robusta*, which can be 15 cm long and wide.

TREES FOR ALKALINE SOIL ... Although an alkaline soil definitely restricts the choices for your garden, there are many handsome species that tolerate it. Among the evergreens, choose holly, juniper and yew. Suitable broad-leaved trees include beech, linden, liquidambar and whitebeam (*Sorbus aria*).

... AND ACID SOIL Most trees will grow in slightly acid soil, but some need a soil that is completely lime free. These are notably Judas tree (*Cercis siliquastrum*), Katsura tree (*Cercidiphyllum japonicum*), Persian parrotia (*Parrotia persica*) and red maple (*Acer rubrum*).

INVASIVE ROOTS Some trees have extensive roots that can lift paths and terraces, or possibly even crack the walls of houses. Cedar, jacaranda, liquidambar, oak, poplar and weeping willow, among others, should not be planted close to buildings.
● You can help prevent roots from reaching too close to your paving and pipes, or even encroaching on shrubs and young trees, with a dedicated root barrier. Sink a rigid plastic panel into the ground about 2 m away from the trunk. These are the same panels that are used to keep bamboo under control.
● Never plant trees with extensive roots near your vegetable or fruit garden where you will need to dig regularly.

Planting a tree

BEST TIME TO PLANT Deciduous trees are rarely grown in containers but usually cultivated in open ground. Once their leaves fall, they rest during the winter. This is the best time to plant so they will be in good shape when the growing period begins in spring.
● For the best results plant bare-root trees between June and August.

PLANTING CONIFERS Always buy conifers with a wrapped root ball or one that is growing in a container. Plant them as you would a bare-root tree, following these tips.
● Do not put an upright stake in the hole before planting the tree.
● Soak the root ball in a bucket of water for about 15 minutes before planting.
● When the root ball is positioned in the hole, make sure that the neck of the plant is level with the surface.
● Once planted, water well, with at least 10 litres of water.
● Keep the tree in place by attaching it to one or several stakes positioned away from the roots around the planting hole.

DIG, BUT DON'T DIG TOO DEEPLY When planting, a tree should be positioned in the soil as it was where it was grown, with the neck (the zone between the roots and the trunk, often visible as a watermark on the tree) at soil level. To check, lay the shaft of a rake across the hole. The 'neck' of the plant should be at the level of the shaft.

WATERING BASIN When you finish planting and the soil has been replaced, there should be some soil left over. Use this to create a watering basin, a small ridge around the tree on the surface of the soil. Try to give it a diameter that corresponds to the size of the root ball so that the water pools over the root hairs. The ridge will help retain water in the correct area when you water the tree.

The autumn colouring of the tulip tree (Liriodendron tulipifera) *is just as attractive as its earlier foliage.*

1 Dig a large, deep hole. Ideally make it 80 cm square so that the roots will not grow around themselves if the earth is too hard.

2 Trim off broken, damaged or diseased roots just above the damage, cutting back into healthy tissue using a pair of secateurs.

3 Carefully position the tree in the middle of the planting hole, laying a straight edge across the hole to make sure it is neither too deep nor too shallow.

4 Fill the hole with well-prepared earth. When it is half-full, gently shake the trunk so that the soil settles in around the roots, then fill it up and firm it down.

5 Make a shallow trench around the tree and water. Fill the trench with water until the ground is saturated.

6 Fix two stakes, one on either side of the tree, 20–30 cm away from the trunk, taking care not to damage the roots.

7 Attach each stake to the tree with a tree tie. Take care not to overtighten the tie. Then loosen off or replace the ties as the tree grows.

8 After watering, spread a 5–7 cm layer of organic mulch, such as sugar cane or compost, over the planting site. It is now ready to grow.

TOP TIPS FOR PLANTING A TREE A tree should be planted for the long term and not moved again, so it's very important to give it every chance to get off to a good start.

● **HEEL IT IN** If you've bought a tree and find you can't plant it immediately, don't expose the roots to the air, but take a tip from professional growers and 'heel it in'. Dig a hole 30 cm deep with a sloping back, lay the tree on the ground with its roots in the hole, and cover them with well-tilled soil. The tree can spend several days, even weeks, like this before being planted in position.

● **ALWAYS KEEP A SAFE DISTANCE** Whether you are planting a row of trees or a single one, the rule is the same: if the mature tree will be over 2 m tall, the centre of the trunk should be at least 2 m away from any structure or other large plant.

● **DON'T CUT OFF THE ROOT HAIRS** Even though you should cut off any damaged roots before planting, take care not to damage the smallest roots, the root hairs, as they are the ones that will draw water and nourishment from the soil.

● **WATER IMMEDIATELY AFTER PLANTING, EVEN IF IT'S RAINING** The object is not so much to nourish the tree as to help the earth settle between the roots and to ensure good contact between the soil and the root system. Soak the planting area until the ground can take no more water.

● **THE SEAWEED SOLUTION** Water newly planted trees with a solution of seaweed and water. Repeat this fortnightly until new growth becomes apparent.

STAKING SHOULD BE FLEXIBLE Once you have planted the tree, fix it to a stake using a flexible tree tie to support it and to allow the new roots to establish themselves. This will allow for the movement of the soil as it settles around the base of the plant. During the first few weeks the newly planted tree may subside by several centimetres as it beds down into its new position.

STAKING AFTER YOU HAVE PLANTED If you need to stake a tree once you have planted it, use this old-fashioned method. Make a support consisting of three wooden stakes driven into the ground in a triangle 50 cm from the trunk, and attach the tree to this with flexible ties (above right). This method protects the roots and the root ball from damage.

Three stakes are certainly better than just one, but regularly check the ties and adjust if needed.

To attach a tree to a stake, use flexible ties (above top) that are available from garden centres, or ties padded with foam rubber (above).

● Another method is to use an angle stake. This is driven into the ground 1–1.5 m from the tree. It is angled away from the tree and attached halfway up the trunk. Use proprietary ties to fasten the tree to the stake.

STAKING ADVANTAGES A sturdy stake will support a tree when it is young but can also help protect the trunk from wind, whether cold or hot and drying, and from rain. It may also provide a little protective shade during the hottest time of the day.
● Be careful not to tie the tree too tightly to the stake, so that its growth is not hindered. Check ties regularly and loosen any that are too tight. Don't forget to remove the stake after about 3 years, when it will have outgrown its usefulness and can look unsightly.

Trimming and pruning trees

PRUNE YOUR TREE GENTLY Trees can struggle to recover from harsh treatment. It's more effective to prune lightly. The objective when pruning is to preserve the overall shape of the tree and to open up the canopy by removing some of the internal branches.

WHEN TO CUT A LARGE BRANCH You may need to remove a large branch from one of your trees that has become a nuisance or has been broken by the wind. Do this in spring when sap flow will accelerate healing.

USELESS SHOOTS Suckers are vigorous, growing shoots that generally don't produce flowers or fruit. They develop at the base of, or on, the trunk, and sometimes where there is a wound caused by lopping a branch. Cut them back as soon as they appear or they will drain the plant's energy.

THIN OUT LOWER BRANCHES You will find the filtered light very pleasing and it should encourage plants to grow underneath.

GETTING RID OF SPURS A spur is the remains of a branch that has not been cut close enough to the branch or the trunk that bore it. Apart from being unsightly, a spur inhibits the healing of the scar, dries out and rots, facilitating the onset of disease.

NEW STYLES FOR OLD TREES Conifers sometimes age badly by losing their foliage at the base. You can revamp them with lopping shears and cut them, Japanese-style, into cloud shapes. Cut away the side branches to reveal the trunk, retaining only the growth at the tip of the large leader branches, and trim these into ball shapes.

Ensuring a long life for your tree

WHEN A YOUNG TREE HAS NOT TAKEN WELL Protect it from the sun's heat and from excess evaporation with a protective screen. Using three stakes as a framework, wrap the trunk in protective sheeting such as hessian or polythene, and spray the trunk and foliage with water in the morning and evening during hot weather. Keep the ground above the roots cool by spreading a layer of bark mulch or cocoa shells around the trunk. Check that the staking is adequate and that the cloth is tied neither too tightly nor too loosely.

SWIFT ACTION FOR DAMAGED TREES A tree can be wounded in many ways. It may get a knock from a lawnmower or from a car bumper, or a branch may be torn off by the wind, or lost from disease. Most wounds will heal naturally and do not require excessive attention. Torn tissue should be tidied and trimmed with sharp pruning tools to reduce the area of the wound and prevent access for pests and diseases.

KEEP A GOOD EYE ON SCARS The bark of a tree is very much like its skin. As soon as a wound appears through an accident or a disease, the bark will close over the naked wood. This is a tree's internal healing mechanism and is designed to prevent penetration by moisture, disease or parasites. Between the bark and the wood is a very fine layer of tissue called the cambium, and as soon as the cambium is exposed to the air, for example when a branch is cut, it begins to generate lots of new cells. These rapidly form a ridge around the wound and gradually cover it over until the wound is closed and healed. You can speed up this process by keeping the wound smooth and clean.

1 Make a notch under the branch. Cut a third of the way through the branch with a saw, working from underneath, 3–5 cm closer to the tree than the place where you will make the final cut.

2 To help the cut to heal, you should always cut at right angles to the axis of the branch, as close as possible but not flush with the trunk.

REMOVING SUCKERS

1 Suckers are shoots that spring from a stump or a root and sap a plant's energy. To remove one completely, clear the earth around the base of the sucker.

2 Carefully cut the sucker back to the point where it grows from the main stem. Use a pair of good, sharp secateurs or a small pruning saw.

This lovely old tree has been given a new lease of life simply by supporting its branches.

A spiralling split in the trunk may be an indication that lightning has struck a tree.

DID YOU KNOW?

AVOID TREE DAMAGE
Over-eager lawn mowing and trimming can cause extensive damage to trees. Every time the bark at the base of the trunk is cut by a blade or a spinning line, it creates an entry point for fungal diseases. Severe and repeated damage ringbarks the tree and can kill it.

Stop trunk damage by keeping cutting implements away from the base of trees. Remove lawn and weeds and replace them with an organic mulch or gravel. Shade-loving groundcovers such as the pretty dichondra or pratia make a really terrific no-mow alternative to lawn.

WATER GENEROUSLY Even though plants in dry soil can tolerate a certain amount of drought, they should not be left entirely to their own devices. As your plant establishes its root systems it is able to locate and draw up water from within the soil. In extreme drought its roots may not reach deep enough to find this precious resource so you need to give a helping hand. As a general rule, trees that have been planted less than 3 years need to be watered copiously and often. Never neglect your newly planted trees, especially during hot summer months.
● For a tree that is adapted to dry soil, choose a conifer such as the bristle-cone pine (*Pinus aristata*), juniper, *Pinus halepensis* or the white spruce (*Picea glauca*). Among the broad-leaved trees, eucalyptus and false acacia are worth planting in dry conditions.

DRIP-WATERING You can sometimes see plastic pipes protruding from the ground beside trees in towns and cities. These pipes are pierced with holes and looped around the roots during planting, with the end left sticking out of the ground. The trees can be watered easily through the pipes to make sure the water reaches right to their roots. This encourages roots of newly planted trees to establish themselves much more quickly.

GUARD AGAINST LIGHTNING If your garden is home to an old, solitary tree in an exposed position, install a lightning conductor on your house. This will draw the lightning to the conductor and protect your tree.

● The species that are most often affected by lightning are, in order of their susceptibility, gum, oak, elm, pine, ash, willow, poplar, spruce and maple – especially if they are planted in sandy or normal soil.
● Trees struck by lightning usually die. Sometimes death is instant because the lightning causes the tree to explode. At other times the damage isn't quite so obvious but may show up as spiralling cracks running up the trunk (above). In these cases the tree will decline over 6 months or so. Call in a tree surgeon if you suspect lightning damage.

NEW LIFE FOR OLD TREES Old trees are a very valuable asset in the landscape and they deserve every care. If you have a large old tree, try and have it regularly inspected by a tree surgeon who is a member of a professional organisation. Proper pruning, fertilising, watering and, in some cases, support of limbs, can extend the life and the safety of favourite old trees.

TO REMOVE A DEAD TREE Forget the idea of attacking a dead tree with an axe. Begin by lopping off all the branches, then reduce the trunk to a manageable size. To remove the stump, don't resort to chemicals or burning, as previous generations might have done. Either hire a stump grinder or a winch, which you can use to pull the stump from the ground, or employ someone to do the job for you. Take advice from the hire shop and always use any safety equipment that is recommended.

A length of plastic ag pipe inserted at planting will water the tree's root system.

Controlling diseases on large trees and shrubs may sometimes require very drastic measures. Many species can support pest colonies without detriment.

Roots

ARMILLARIA ROOT ROT
● **SYMPTOMS** Foliage discolours, wilts and then dies back. The whole plant can die rapidly or it can hang on for years. Infected plants produce a white fungal-smelling growth beneath the bark at the base of the trunk. Black rootlike 'boot-laces' grow on the outside of roots, which is how the fungus spreads to other plants. Clumps of honey-coloured toadstools may also grow around infected plants, usually appearing in late autumn to winter.
● **PLANTS AFFECTED** Most woody plants. Box, buddleia, caryopteris, chestnut, fir, holly and monkey puzzle.
● **TREATMENT** Prevent attack by removing trunks, roots, old fence posts and debris before establishing a garden. Dig out and destroy the infected plants immediately, removing as much root and infected soil as possible. Replant with disease-resistant annuals or perennials. Although no fungicide is registered for control, biological controls include trichoderma, which is a benign wood-rot fungus. Add organic matter and reduce stress to existing plants by increasing watering in drought. Better drainage in wet conditions will improve plant survival rates. Valuable infected trees can be assisted by removing soil from the base of the trunk, hence exposing it to the air and allowing it to dry out.

CROWN GALL
● **SYMPTOMS** This bacterial disease enters the shrub through a wound and produces whitish swellings (galls) on top of the roots or at the base of the trunk. These turn black and block sap circulation, leading to death.
● **PLANTS AFFECTED** Currant, cypress, euonymus (spindle), rhododendron, *Ribes sanguineum* and rose.
● **TREATMENT** To avoid buying infected roses and fruit trees, buy only those that have been treated. If symptoms appear, remove and destroy the plants. Replace them with new stock treated with No-Gall or replant in new soil. Prevent the disease by improving soil drainage around the plant and feeding with a fertiliser high in phosphate and potash. Avoid root damage when transplanting.

CURL GRUB

● **SYMPTOMS** The larvae of many beetles feed on the roots of trees and shrubs. They are C-shaped and white, hence their name. After feeding on roots, the grubs move further down into the soil, pupate and emerge in spring or early summer as beetles. Some areas can have hundreds of grubs. Symptoms include plants that wilt although not in need of water, or that appear to be unthrifty. They may have little or no root system.
● **PLANTS AFFECTED** Many trees including eucalypts and seedling pines.
● **TREATMENT** Remove grubs that are found in soil or potting mix, squashing them or throwing them on the lawn for birds to feed on. Control beetles. See also African black beetle, page 206.

PHYTOPHTHORA (ROOT ROT)
● **SYMPTOMS** Bark becomes discoloured and blackish liquid oozes from wounds at the base of the trunk. On digging around the trunk, the roots show signs of fungal rot. The leaves turn yellow, then brown, and the shoot tips wither and the shrub finally dies.
● **PLANTS AFFECTED** Many.
● **TREATMENT** Drench the root system with phosphorus acid or a registered fungicide. Improve drainage and avoid damage to roots when transplanting.

Trunks and branches

ANTHRACNOSE
● **SYMPTOMS** Infected branches shrivel. Cankers appear at the base of shoots and on the leaves along the veins, making the leaves appear burnt.
● **PLANTS AFFECTED** Many shrubs and trees, such as cornus, plane, salix and walnut.

● **TREATMENT** Pick up all infected leaves, prune out seriously damaged branches and bin them. Spray the whole plant with a copper-based fungicide and repeat as per manufacturer's instructions if the disease continues to affect the tree.

BRACKET FUNGI
● **SYMPTOMS** Fungi develop in clumps on the tree trunk and branches. The tree weakens and its branches become brittle.
● **PLANTS AFFECTED** Ash, beech, larch, oak, pine, plane, *Robinia pseudoacacia* and yew.
● **TREATMENT** Scrape off minor infestations with a knife. When established, the fungi will have penetrated the tissue and felling is the only option.

CANKER

● **SYMPTOMS** Swollen-edged cracks form in the bark. Bark tissue is exposed and oozes a whitish substance, or resin in the case of conifers. The tree withers and dies.
● **PLANTS AFFECTED** Ash, beech, chestnut, conifer, haw-thorn, laurel, lime, plane, poplar, rose, sorbus and willow.
● **TREATMENT** Cut the diseased tissue back to healthy wood.

CYPRESS CANKER
● **SYMPTOMS** The branches turn brown and die, splits form in the trunk from which resin oozes and the entire tree dies. May

spread to neighbouring trees in a hedge or windbreak.

● **PLANTS AFFECTED** Cypress.

● **TREATMENT** Remove affected trees and replant with resistant species (including *Cupressus arizonica* and *C. lusitanica*).

FASCIATION

● **SYMPTOMS** The affected stem thickens, enlarges and flattens, forming an undulating ribbon, sometimes with curling edges. However, the plant will continue to grow and flower as normal. Fasciation is an accident of growth and not a disease.

● **PLANTS AFFECTED** Daphne, forsythia and many shrubs.

● **TREATMENT** There is no treatment for fasciation. If the plant becomes too unsightly, simply cut off the affected shoot.

LONGICORN BEETLE

● **SYMPTOMS** Sawdust appears at the base of trees under galleries bored in the trunk. The beetles may chew the leaves.

● **PLANTS AFFECTED** Many, especially stressed trees, including eucalypt, wattle and willow.

● **TREATMENT** Destroy the larvae by scraping the galleries with a piece of steel wire. Improve the health and vigour of trees with better watering and fertilising. Remove affected branches. If the tree is old and the attack is severe, remove the tree altogether.

WITCHES' BROOM

● **SYMPTOMS** Small clusters of dense, stunted shoots appear on the tips of branches, causing the foliage to yellow. If shaken, white dust will drop off.

● **PLANTS AFFECTED** Birch and carpinus.

● **TREATMENT** This disease is

more unsightly than dangerous. Cut off the 'brooms' and destroy the branches to prevent spores from spreading.

Leaves

AZALEA LACEBUG

● **SYMPTOMS** Yellow to brown or silver mottling appears on upper side of the leaves. The transparent insect can be seen under the leaf.

● **PLANTS AFFECTED** Azalea and rhododendron.

● **TREATMENT** Dust leaves with sulphur in spring or spray new growth with systemic insecticide.

BLACKSPOT

● **SYMPTOMS** Dark brown spots appear on foliage. These spots grow larger and finally join together. At the same time, the leaves turn yellow and fall, leaving the stalks entirely bare.

● **PLANTS AFFECTED** Rose.

● **TREATMENT** Collect up all the infected leaves. In spring, spray the whole rose plant and the surrounding soil with a registered fungicide and repeat as per manufacturer's directions. Well-mulched plants resist attack.

BLACK VINE WEEVIL

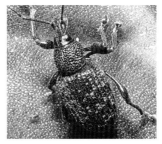

● **SYMPTOMS** Irregular nicks occur around the edges of the leaves and excreta can be seen on the leaf. Roots are sometimes devoured by white larvae, which leave deep gashes.

● **PLANTS AFFECTED** Many trees and shrubs, including euonymus, hydrangea, rhododendron, skimmia and yew.

● **TREATMENT** Drench the infested soil with the natural control nematode *Heterorhabditis megidis*, which parasitises the weevil larvae, or with a registered insecticide. Ring containers with grease bands to trap adults before they even lay eggs in the potting mix.

BOTRYTIS

This disease attacks flowers as well as leaves and fruits. It affects mostly weak, damaged shrubs. See page 97.

CALLISTEMON SAWFLY

● **SYMPTOMS** Shrubs become defoliated or their leaves are skeletonised by the larvae of the sawfly. Although this insect looks like a caterpillar with a large head and a tapering tail, it doesn't turn into a moth or a butterfly.

● **PLANTS AFFECTED** Bottlebrush (*Callistemon* spp.).

● **TREATMENT** Larvae cluster together and may be removed. Alternatively spray with contact insecticide. Prune off damage,

water and feed the shrub with a low-phosphorus fertiliser.

CUP MOTH

● **SYMPTOMS** Spiky green and boldly patterned caterpillars appear and feed on leaves. Pupa cases are cuplike structures on twigs or loose bark. The adult is a small moth. Hairs may fall from the insects feeding in trees and cause irritation to those below, including children playing.

● **PLANTS AFFECTED** Many Australian native trees including the brush box (*Lophostemon confertus*), gum tree (*Angophora* spp., *Eucalyptus* spp. and any related plants) and the water gum (*Tristaniopsis laurina*).

● **TREATMENT** If the infestation is really severe, the tree may need to be treated with an injection of a systemic insecticide. Avoid exposure to the irritant hairs.

DUTCH ELM DISEASE (New Zealand only)

● **SYMPTOMS** This disease caused the disappearance of most elms in many parts of the northern hemisphere. The leaves change colour, turn yellowish and dry up. The branches wither and die, followed by the tree. The bark is covered in brown blotches and peels off. A cut branch will reveal a brown ring at the centre.

● **PLANTS AFFECTED** Elm.

● **TREATMENT** There is no remedy for this disease. Control the elm leaf beetle, which can spread the fungus to healthy trees. Use registered insecticide in a spray program and trunk banding to control elm leaf beetle. Cut down and dispose of trees affected by Dutch elm disease to limit disease spread.

FIREBLIGHT
(New Zealand only)
● **SYMPTOMS** The leaves crumble and look burnt. The bark splits and exudes a whitish ooze. The tissue inside turns red. Contamination of nearby trees is swift.
● **PLANTS AFFECTED** All the members of the Rosaceae family, such as cotoneaster, hawthorn and pyracantha.
● **TREATMENT** Prune out infected growth to healthy wood and spray with a copper-based fungicide. Disinfect tools after use.

FULLERS ROSE WEEVIL

● **SYMPTOMS** Damaged foliage, buds and flowers due to the feeding of adult weevils.
● **PLANTS AFFECTED** Many shrubs including camellia and rose.
● **TREATMENT** Hand-remove the adult weevils and spray with a registered insecticide.

GALL

● **SYMPTOMS** The undersides of leaves are covered in white

spots that turn brown. The leaves blister and become covered in red raised bumps, or galls.
● **PLANTS AFFECTED** Many ornamental trees and shrubs.
● **TREATMENT** Cut off any affected growth. Spray with a systemic insecticide.

GOLDEN MEALYBUG
● **SYMPTOMS** The affected leaves are covered in black and gold insects, which develop a mealy wax covering. These insects are active in the spring months. Sooty mould may form on the honeydew – the sticky exudate that is produced by insects as they feed. Golden mealybug slows growth.
● **PLANTS AFFECTED** Bunya pine and Norfolk Island pine.
● **TREATMENT** Encourage ladybirds, which feed on pests. (Note that the ladybird larvae may resemble those of the pests they feed on, but are more active.) For severe infestations, spray with contact insecticide or inject with systemic insecticide.

HAWK MOTH
● **SYMPTOMS** Leaf edges are chewed, especially in summer.
● **PLANTS AFFECTED** Many ornamental trees and shrubs.
● **TREATMENT** Remove the large caterpillars by hand.

LEAF BEETLE
● **SYMPTOMS** In spring and summer, the leaves are pierced with holes, although the veins are unaffected. The leaf tops may also be cut off and can take on a shrivelled appearance.
● **PLANTS AFFECTED** Elder, lavender, poplar and willow.
● **TREATMENT** Where practical, pick off the adult beetles by hand and destroy.

LEAF BLOTCH

● **SYMPTOMS** Grey swellings with brown edges appear on infected leaves. The marks grow larger with the centres turning red and drying up.
● **PLANTS AFFECTED** Chestnut and vines.
● **TREATMENT** There is no cure for this disease. To control the spread, collect and bin all infected leaves and prunings. Improve drainage around the plants and feed regularly to aid recovery.

LEAF-CUTTING BEE
● **SYMPTOMS** The margins of leaves are cut out in circular shapes with regular contours.
● **PLANTS AFFECTED** Rose.
● **TREATMENT** Damage to the plant is actually more unsightly than harmful. Treatment is not necessary, especially since the leaf-cutting bee is also a pollinator.

LEAF GALL
● **SYMPTOMS** Tumours appear on leafy stems, often around the veins. These roundish swellings have a white covering that turns brown and shrivels.
● **PLANTS AFFECTED** Azalea, camellia and rhododendron.
● **TREATMENT** Cut off and bin all affected parts. Spray with a copper-based fungicide.

LILLYPILLY PSYLLID
● **SYMPTOMS** Pimple-like lumps appear on the upper surface of new lillypilly growth, which are

caused by the feeding of the nymph of psyllid. The lumps look very unsightly.
● **PLANTS AFFECTED** Lillypilly (some varieties are more susceptible than others).
● **TREATMENT** Trim off affected growth and spray new growth with oil or systemic insecticide. Plant new and alternative species such as *Acmena smithii* var. *minor* which may be less susceptible.

LOOPER
● **SYMPTOMS** Leaves develop skeletonised patches or holes caused by distinctive small caterpillars which can usually be found on the plant. The caterpillars are fine green or light brown and move with an arching or looping movement. Droppings may be more obvious than the caterpillars themselves.
● **PLANTS AFFECTED** Many shrubs, including rose.
● **TREATMENT** Squash the caterpillars with your fingers if you see them. If necessary, spray these caterpillars with *Bacillus thuringiensis* (sold as Dipel) or a registered insecticide.

METALLIC FLEA BEETLE
Small holes appear in the leaves. Affected plants are abutilon, grapevine, members of the hibiscus family (Malvaceae), including lavatera and mallow, and fruit trees. See page 98.

MOSAIC VIRUS
Serious infection causes foliage to deform and the plant to wither. Roses and other ornamental shrubs are affected. Prune the affected parts. See page 206.

PAINTED APPLE MOTH
The hairy caterpillars of this moth form colonies in woven cocoons

and spread out to feed or to take over new plants. The moth affects apple, wattle and many ornamental trees. See page 252.

PEAR AND CHERRY SLUG

These sluglike insects are larvae of the sawfly. They chew the leaves of crab-apple, flowering quince, pear, plum and related plants. See page 252.

PROCESSIONARY CATERPILLAR

● **SYMPTOMS** The leaves are devoured. Large cocoons can be seen on the tips of the branches.
● **PLANTS AFFECTED** Many trees.
● **TREATMENT** Prune out the cocoons before the caterpillars emerge. If they become active, spray with *Bacillus thuringiensis* (sold as Dipel) or a registered insecticide.

ROSE RUST

● **SYMPTOMS** Orange-yellow patches develop on the upper leaf surfaces, with pustules on the undersides causing leaves to fall prematurely.
● **PLANTS AFFECTED** Rose.
● **TREATMENT** At the first sign of attack, spray the leaves with a registered fungicide.

SCALE

Black or brown spots are visible on the underside of leaves and stalks. If pressed, a hard covering can be felt. A waxy or cottony discharge can also be seen. Sooty mould is also a characteristic sign. Many species of shrubs and trees are affected. See page 250.

SILVER LEAF

● **SYMPTOMS** Leaves take on a silvery tinge. As infection spreads, the tree withers and dies back.
● **PLANTS AFFECTED** Members of the Rosaceae family.
● **TREATMENT** There is no treatment for this disease. Prune back all affected growth to healthy white tissue (infected wood has a dark stain) in the summer only.

THRIPS

● **SYMPTOMS** This pest leaves whitish specks on leaves, which form a silvery marbling.
● **PLANTS AFFECTED** Palm, privet and many ornamental fruiting tree and shrub species. Gladiolus is also affected.
● **TREATMENT** In your greenhouse, introduce the predatory mite *Amblyseius*, or hang up sticky boards to trap the thrips. Plant *Nicotiana sylvestris*, whose sticky leaves act as a trap.

TWO-SPOTTED MITE

● **SYMPTOMS** The leaves become dull and turn yellow with blotches, and then fall. The undersides of leaves are covered with a fine web and eggs.
● **PLANTS AFFECTED** Many ornamental trees and shrubs.
● **TREATMENT** In a greenhouse, introduce the predatory mite *Phytoseiulus persimilis* or lacewing larvae, the two-spotted mite's natural enemies, as soon as the pest is noticed. Outdoors, spray with a registered fatty acid or oil-based treatment.

VERTICILLIUM WILT

This fungal disease attacks catalpa and *Robinia pseudoacacia*, causing the foliage to yellow and wither away. See page 99.

WEB-FORMING CATERPILLAR

● **SYMPTOMS** These caterpillars eat leaves and buds and form woven, hanging, silky nests. Insects may feed in the webbed foliage or move out to other leaves. Many feed on only one plant genus.
● **PLANTS AFFECTED** Cotoneasta, Illawarra flame tree (*Brachychiton acerifolius*), kurrajong (*B. populneus*) and other trees.
● **TREATMENT** Carefully prune out and bin the nests containing the caterpillars. If the caterpillars become active, spray them with *Bacillus thuringiensis* (sold as Dipel) or a registered insecticide.

Flowers

AZALEA PETAL BLIGHT

● **SYMPTOMS** The flowers wilt and later become brown and dry and remain on the shrub.
● **PLANTS AFFECTED** Azalea and rhododendron.

● **TREATMENT** From bud colour in spring or autumn, spray with a registered fungicide. Two to three treatments are usually needed. Shear over plants after flowering or hand-pick affected flowers and those that have dropped and place in a bag in the garbage. Avoid overhead watering during the flowering period.

BOTRYTIS

Also known as grey mould. Buds turn brown and rot. Flowers fail to open or develop brown spots. On light-coloured flowers, concentric pink rings can be seen. Roses are often affected. See page 97.

HIBISCUS BEETLE

● **SYMPTOMS** Small holes appear in the flowers, and buds may fall without opening. The beetle is small, black and swarms inside the flower, feeding on the pollen.
● **PLANTS AFFECTED** Hibiscus (especially *Hibiscus rosa-sinensis*) and magnolia.
● **TREATMENT** Remove affected flowers and fallen buds. Spray with registered systemic insecticide. Place a white plastic ice-cream container under affected plants to attract the beetles. Fill the container with water and methylated spirits or an insecticide. This is not suitable for gardens where children or pets could have access to the container.

PLAGUE THRIPS

Flowers become brown and dry due to the feeding of tiny black insects that can be seen among the petals. Many flowering shrubs and trees are affected, including New South Wales Christmas bush and rose. See page 253.

CHAPTER 4

The vegetable garden

A well-planned and planted vegetable plot

The old-fashioned kitchen garden is a productive food factory. Follow a few traditional planning principles to get your vegetable plot off to a good start and use age-old gardening wisdom to reap a rich harvest.

Begin with basics

CHOOSING A SITE It is common sense that some sites are just not suitable for growing vegetables. Steep slopes, boggy or flood-prone areas, shady sites and locations too far from your water supply are not worth trying. Instead choose a site in full sun, one that is sheltered or can be sheltered from drying wind and, if possible, is free of weeds and debris. Avoid anything less than 10–20 m away from large tree roots.

SHAPING UP Vegetable gardens come in all shapes and sizes, but squares or rectangles are most practical for the production of a range of different vegetables with differing requirements and growing seasons. The size of your vegetable plot depends on the overall size of your garden and your vegetable needs.

PATHS ARE ESSENTIAL If you trample on soil you will compact it, which means water won't drain away easily – although plants need water, they certainly don't want to be waterlogged. A system of paths between beds is the solution because it makes access and maintenance much simpler.
● You can plant vegetables on either side of a central path, but make sure it is at least 90 cm wide, so you can push a full wheel-barrow between the vegetable beds.
● Put down a thick layer of bark mulch or lay paving slabs to reduce weeds on the path. Pouring boiling salted water from pasta or vegetables on weed seedlings will kill them.

PLANT VEGETABLES IN BEDS OR ROWS? Remember to choose the system that suits your own space and your style of garden.

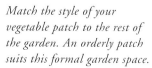
Match the style of your vegetable patch to the rest of the garden. An orderly patch suits this formal garden space.

● **RECTANGULAR BEDS** Some gardeners like to divide their vegetable gardens into neat rectangular beds no more than 1.2 m wide and separated by narrow paths about 30 cm wide. Beds are clearly marked and you can reach the centre from the access paths without stepping on the soil.
● **STRAIGHT ROWS** If you are growing vegetables to feed a large family you may prefer to grow them in long, straight rows, grouping them by type. In row gardening it is not so easy to work without stepping on the soil, so lay down planks and walk on these when you need access to your crops.

WORK OUT THE CORRECT SPACING FOR VEGETABLES There's a clever trick to working out spacing when you are growing a mixture of vegetables. For example, if you are sowing two types of vegetable in one small bed, work out the spacing needed between the rows by adding the amount of space required by each crop and then dividing the total by two.

YESTERDAY'S SECRETS

LABEL IT
It is good practice to label everything you plant. In the olden days, gardeners would lovingly handwrite their own labels. However, empty seed packets make excellent row markers – attach them to sticks and sink them firmly into the ground, then cover the packets with a plastic bag or a jam jar to protect them against bad weather.
● If you've still got seeds left in the packet, make a separate label. Most garden centres sell a variety of labels and row markers.

SOIL NEEDS You can grow your vegetables in most types of garden soil. You should dig the ground over in autumn or spring – if your soil is compacted and hard to dig by hand, you may need to use a rotavator – and work in lots of well-rotted compost.

● If the soil is sandy, you may need to add bulky organic material to it. Improve the soil over the longer term by growing a green manure (see page 269). These are annuals like alfalfa, mustard or phacelia that are dug into the soil just before they flower and, as they decay, they enrich the soil with humus.

GETTING STARTED Remove any waste material and weeds from the patch, and use a hoe to break down the soil to a depth of several centimetres. Rake the soil, removing stones and debris.

● Do this in mild weather, when the soil is neither too wet nor too dry to work. Then broadcast the seeds of the green manure crop over the whole area.

HAVE WATER ON TAP A handy source of water is essential for the vegetable garden. Make sure your hose reaches the garden so you can water thoroughly every day.

● If your shed is near the vegetable patch, put a water tank in place to collect rainwater from the roof. Keep the tank covered to prevent build-up of algae and other water-borne diseases that might affect young plants.

TOOLS ON HAND A garden shed is vital for storing tools, seeds and other garden para-phernalia. Always store your tools in the shed so they are in a convenient place ready to use each time you garden. Never leave your tools outside to be ruined by the weather.

● Hardware stores sell sheds in flat packs that are relatively simple to erect.

DISPLAY YOUR VEGETABLES Raised beds are particularly useful if you want to avoid bending over to work. They look good, too. Constructed from natural wood, raised beds become an attractive feature, displaying low-growing vegetables as if they were decorative plants in their own right. Raised beds also solve the problem of digging into poorly drained soils.

DESIGN A PLOT TO SUIT YOUR NEEDS Don't forget to take into account the time and energy you have at your disposal – allow

half a day's work per week for a plot up to 10 square metres, less if you have access to a cultivator to break up the soil.

● **10 SQUARE METRES** You can grow a good selection of vegetables, enough for a single person or a couple.

● **50 SQUARE METRES** You have the space to grow ample vegetables for two people or for a small family.

● **100 SQUARE METRES** Your plot is big enough to support a large family.

FLOWER BORDERS WITH OLD-FASHIONED CHARM If you would like to give your vegetable plot the feel of a lovely old traditional cottage garden, where you can grow practical and decorative plants side by side, try putting aromatic flowers and plants around the borders. Culinary herbs such as parsley, sage, summer savory and thyme can provide a double benefit as they are both attractive in the kitchen garden and useful in cooking. Plant brightly coloured flowering plants, including calendulas, dwarf dahlias, sweet williams and marigolds, that are both colourful and traditional.

● If you prefer a more formal look to your vegetable garden, try using a low box hedge instead of flowers to edge the garden beds or paths. Box hedge is slow-growing and has densely packed, small green leaves that can – with regular clipping – be kept in a neat geometric shape.

'PIONEER' CROPS When you start a new vegetable garden, you may not have time to dig over the entire area and improve all the soil before planting or sowing your first

With a little planning, a mixed bed of herbs and vegetables in clumps and rows can make an attractive garden feature.

Place your paths so they will give you plenty of all-weather access to the vegetable garden.

Raised beds will end back-breaking work, add height and structure to your garden and solve drainage problems.

Include flowering plants with your vegetables, they look great and attract beneficial insects.

Mixed cropping in the vegetable garden

Some gardeners believe that certain vegetables grow better when planted with particular neighbours. Here are some traditional 'friends and foes' for mixed or companion planting schemes.

PLANT	GOOD COMPANIONS	BAD COMPANIONS
Asparagus	Leeks, parsley, peas, tomatoes	Beetroot
Beetroot	Cabbages, celery, lettuces, onions	Asparagus, tomatoes
Broad beans	Lettuces, parsnips, potatoes	
Cabbages	Beetroot, celery, cucumbers, green beans, lettuces, parsnips, peas, potatoes, tomatoes	Leeks, onions, radishes
Carrots	Green beans, leeks, lettuces, onions, parsnips, peas, radishes	
Celery	Beetroot, cabbages, cucumbers, green beans, leeks, peas, potatoes, tomatoes	Parsley
Cucumbers	Cabbages, celery, green beans, lettuces, peas, sweetcorn	Potatoes, tomatoes
Green beans	Cabbages, carrots, celery, cucumbers, leeks, lettuces, peas, potatoes, radishes, sweetcorn, tomatoes, zucchinis	Onions
Leeks	Asparagus, carrots, celery, green beans, lettuces, onions, tomatoes	Beetroot, cabbages
Lettuces	Beetroot, broad beans, cabbages, carrots, cucumbers, green beans, leeks, onions, peas, radishes, turnips	Parsley
Onions	Beetroot, carrots, leeks, lettuces, parsnips, tomatoes	Cabbages, green beans, peas, potatoes
Parsley	Asparagus, radishes, tomatoes	Celery, lettuces, peas
Parsnips	Broad beans, cabbages, carrots, onions	
Peas	Asparagus, cabbages, carrots, celery, cucumbers, green beans, lettuces, potatoes, radishes, sweetcorn, turnips	Garlic, onions, parsley, tomatoes
Potatoes	Broad beans, cabbages, celery, green beans, peas, tomatoes	Cucumbers, onions, sweetcorn
Radishes	Broad beans, carrots, cucumbers, green beans, lettuces, parsley, peas, spinach, tomatoes	Cabbages
Spinach	Most vegetables	
Sweetcorn	Cucumbers, green beans, peas, zucchinis	Potatoes
Tomatoes	Asparagus, cabbages, celery, green beans, leeks, onions, parsley, potatoes, radishes	Beetroot, cucumbers peas
Turnips	Lettuces, peas	
Zucchinis	Green beans, sweetcorn	Cabbages

crops. Dig over what you can in the time available and then use some vegetables as 'pioneers' to help you prepare the soil.

● Jerusalem artichokes and potatoes will break up the soil as effectively as digging will. Cabbages, pumpkins and zucchinis will cover the soil well, suppressing the growth of weeds. These are surface-rooting crops, as are celery, leeks and tomatoes, so you don't need the soil to be well worked to succeed.

● It is more difficult to sow the small seeds of carrots, lettuces and onions into rough ground. Carrots need well-dug soil so they can produce straight, deep-growing roots. French beans, runner beans and lettuces need well-dug soil that has been allowed to settle, as their roots are prone to attack from insects that can penetrate air pockets.

MANURE – THE VITAL INGREDIENT

Manure is the essential ingredient to the fertility of your vegetable garden. It provides the nutrients that plants need and it improves the structure and drainage of the soil with the humus that it produces.

● If you are starting from scratch, work in at least 50 kg per 10 square metres over the entire area. Every year after, add 30 kg per 10 square metres to a third of the garden. Rotate and work on a different third each year.

● Always use well-rotted manure – never fresh. Save money and buy it in bulk.

COMPANION PLANTING You can follow

traditional practice and attract beneficial insects that feed on aphids, caterpillars and other garden pests by planting flowers alongside your vegetables in the kitchen garden.

● The most attractive flowers and herbs include angelica, the orange- or yellow-flowered calendula, coriander, cosmos, dill, marigold, nasturtium and poached egg plant (*Limnanthes douglasii*).

INTERCROPPING Intercrop plants with

short growing cycles with those that have longer cycles. Plant lettuces (short cycle) between rows of cabbages (long cycle) or, in late summer, plant radishes among strawberries.

Rotate vegetables

SIMPLE ROTATION If you grow the same vegetables in the same piece of ground, year after year, the soil becomes overworked. Pests and diseases are likely to become established and, as a result, vigour, health and yields are likely to decrease. So it's best to move the crops around. The simplest way to do this is to have a 3- or 4-year plan and divide your garden into three or four sections, each at a different stage of rotation. Follow a plan like this for each of the sections:
- **YEAR ONE** Add manure or compost and then grow greedy feeders, such as cabbages, celery, leeks, potatoes, pumpkins, tomatoes and zucchinis on the composted area.
- **YEAR TWO** Plant beetroot, carrots, onions and turnips.
- **YEAR THREE** Plant green beans and peas.
- **YEAR FOUR** Grow the crops grown in year one or, better still, plant artichokes, strawberries or other perennial vegetables after adding more manure or compost. After 2 or 3 years, stop growing these perennials and start a new rotation cycle after adding more organic matter.
- There are some crops that you can use to fill in any gaps, such as green salad, radishes, spinach and turnips – you can grow these in whatever stage of rotation you like.

'HAPPY FAMILIES' Crop rotation can get quite complicated, especially when you are just starting out, but if you group plants together according to their botanical families, their form or their soil and nutrient requirements, you can't go far wrong.
- Plants belonging to similar families – for example, Apiaceae, which includes carrots and celery, and Brassicaceae, which includes broccoli, cabbages and cauliflowers – are best grown together.
- Plants that develop the same form – for example, leafy vegetables, fruiting vegetables, or bulb and root vegetables – are also usually grown together in the same section of the plan.

THE 'SPINACH' METHOD This is another form of old-fashioned companion planting. Instead of planting rows of associated vegetables, sow 50 cm wide rows of spinach, and leave rows between them for other vegetables. The spinach seedlings act as a nurse crop, shading and protecting the interplanted

seedlings. The spinach can be harvested to eat or hoed off and left on the soil surface to provide a mulch and, if hoed into the soil, it is a perfect green manure.

EXTENDING THE ROTATION If you find that for some vegetables and groups of vegetables, such as brassicas and potatoes, diseases and pests are a persistent problem in your garden, it may be necessary to keep them in a longer rotation cycle to get good yields and healthy crops. If this is the case, you will need to add some extra sections in your vegetable garden to carry out the ideal rotation plan.
- Strawberries are even more demanding. You need to move the bed every third year and avoid returning to the original section within 6 or 7 years.

GIVE THEM LOTS OF SPACE TO GROW
Even though mixed planting uses every bit of soil, vegetables should never be cramped. You still need to allow plenty of space between the rows. Here is a spacing guide for a few commonly grown crops.
- Trailing pumpkins – 2 m.
- Artichokes, cardoons, cucumbers, eggplants, melons, tomatoes, zucchinis – 1 m.
- Climbing French beans, runner beans, tall peas, New Zealand spinach – 75 cm.
- Potatoes – 60 cm.
- Cabbages, dwarf French beans, dwarf peas, Jerusalem artichokes, strawberries – 60 cm.
- Beetroot, broccoli, capsicums, celery, parsnips, silverbeet and sweetcorn – 50 cm.
- Broad beans, chicory, endives, fennel, leeks – 40 cm.
- Beetroot, carrots, dandelions, garlic, kohlrabi, lettuces, onions, shallots, spinach, salsify – 30 cm.
- Corn salad, parsley, radishes – 20 cm.

By rotating the vegetables in your garden beds, you get to produce healthier crops without the need for chemicals and pesticides.

Dependable brassicas and other tasty greens

Cabbages and leafy 'pot herbs' such as silverbeet and spinach were among the first vegetables to be cultivated in Europe and other parts of the world. These plants are very attractive, as well as edible, which has meant that they have enjoyed a recent rise in popularity, reviving the tradition of growing vegetables among the flowers.

Cabbages and brussels sprouts

USING SEEDBEDS OR MODULES

Cabbages need to be carefully transplanted or their growth will be checked.

● Sow cabbage seeds into modular cell trays and transplant them only when the seedlings have developed really strong roots, and then harden them off before you plant them out into the garden. Seedlings that have grown in modules will have well-developed roots and should continue to grow well.

WHAT DO YOU DO WITH A HEADLESS

CABBAGE? The cabbage head is formed from layers of leaves folded over each other and is, in effect, a large bud. If a cabbage fails to heart up or make a head, don't leave it to become tough and inedible, remove it and use its foliage as spring greens.

● Don't settle for second best, if some seedlings have not formed proper growing points,

The head of a cabbage is a leaf bud. However the head of a broccoli is actually a flower bud.

Some cabbages can be just as attractive as they are productive. Plant them with flowers among your tomatoes in the vegetable garden.

it is best to simply get rid of them and then replace them with healthy, strong seedlings that will heart up successfully.

● If cabbage plants receive irregular watering or experience hot temperatures when they are still young, they will bolt – meaning flowers will form instead of cabbage heads.

● Chinese cabbage is a fast-maturing cabbage, it forms a loose head in 8–10 weeks.

● Grow other fast-maturing varieties such as 'Emerald Acre' that can be grown to maturity throughout winter, thereby avoiding problems of bolting and splitting.

EAT UP ANY UNWANTED SEEDLINGS

Sow cabbage seeds into a seedbed, then prick out the seedlings and transplant them into their growing site in the garden, where they will have space to develop.

MAKE THE MOST OF MODULAR TRAYS

Commercial cabbage growers have long used plug plants, and now home growers can raise seedlings in modular trays as well. The plastic cells are ideal for encouraging plants to develop strong and compact root systems so that, when they are transplanted, there is minimal root disturbance and they get off to a good start in your vegetable plot. This means that they can usually be harvested earlier than other types of transplants. Growing your own strong plants from seeds will also help avoid bringing diseases into the vegetable garden from other sources.

● It's a good idea to plant a few extra seedlings so you can take one or two before they mature and use their leaves for spring greens.

SUCCESS WITH SEEDLINGS Plant your seedlings to the same depth they were in the seedbed or modular tray. Just before you plant, soak the roots of each plant in a mixture of soil and water. When they are growing well, earth them up by drawing soil around the base of each plant. This ensures the stability of young plants as it encourages them to make new roots along their stems.

GET A DOUBLE CROP Instead of pulling out the stumps that are left in the ground after harvesting cabbages, use a sharp knife to make a cross on the top of each one. Four or five loosely formed heads will then sprout from each cross, giving you a second crop.
● The green sprouting broccoli, or broccoli Calabrese, will yield a double crop for you. Regular picking ensures the continual production of heads. Harvest the central head first, well before the buds open into flowers.

PREVENTING CLUB ROOT Club root is a disease that is triggered when a microscopic fungus that lives in the soil – and can persist there for decades – finds a host plant to live on. To avoid this it is imperative that you lift any diseased plants carefully and destroy them. Never add plants with club root to your compost heap, or you will simply recycle the disease. You can combat club root with the following cultivational methods.
● **ROTATION OF BRASSICAS** This is the simplest method, depriving the fungus of an appropriate host.
● **RAISE THE pH LEVEL OF THE SOIL** The fungus thrives in moist, acid soils, so if you achieve a pH level of 7 or 7.5, it will be too high for the club root fungus to survive. Regularly enrich the soil with lime in the form of dolomite lime. Apply it in autumn, so it acts on the soil before the next growing season begins.
● **IMPROVE YOUR DRAINAGE** A few months before planting out brassicas, prepare the soil for good drainage. Dig in one barrowload of well-rotted manure per 1 square metre. To lighten heavy soil, add gravel.

TOP TIPS FOR GROWING BRASSICAS Ensure your brassicas have the best possible care by following a few basic rules.
● **ROTATE THEM** Rotate brassicas so they are never on the same patch in your vegetable garden more than once every 3 years. If you grow them in the same spot year after year, you are likely to see a build-up of club root, black rot and black leg. Because they are greedy feeders, the soil needs enriching after they have grown there.
● **STAKE THEM** Stake individual brussels sprouts plants and rows of broccoli and kale. Support top-heavy ballhead cabbages and cauliflowers to stop them lying on the ground.
● **PROTECT THEM** Some plants, including tomatoes, are said to repel cabbage white butterfly, so regularly place the suckers you have pinched out from tomato plants, or fresh sprigs of broom or fern, onto cabbage leaves. Butterflies dislike the smell of these and, it is said, will avoid your cabbage patch.
● **UNDERPLANT THEM** Underplanting your cabbages with a green manure crop may distract insects that would otherwise lay their eggs on the cabbage leaves.

HOMESPUN REMEDIES Cabbage leaves have an age-old reputation as cure-alls for all sorts of everyday ailments, which include colds, minor burns and wounds that are proving slow to heal.
● To make a compress, choose three to five clean, fresh leaves that have good colour, remove large veins and crush with a rolling pin. Place the leaves on the affected area,

Always plant the seedlings to the same depth in the ground as they were in the punnet.

CABBAGE SEEDLINGS

1 Carefully remove a seedling from its punnet or seedbed, use a dibber or trowel to make a hole, and lower the seedling into the planting hole, taking care not to damage the roots.

2 Water the seedling in and use your fingers to firm the soil around the roots. Water well at the base of each plant.

3 Protect young plants from the wind and the sun by covering them with a crate or with some shadecloth. Some gardeners cut back leaves by half to reduce evaporation and water loss.

Cabbages all year round

Cabbages adapt well to different climates and in warm northern areas they can be grown at most times of the year, as long as it is not too wet. To ensure a year-round supply, stagger your plantings and plant a few different varieties so they don't all mature at once.

VARIETY	HEAD WEIGHT	DAYS TO MATURE
FAST-MATURING VARIETIES		
'Earliball'	3.5–4 kg	100–128
'Eureka'	3.5–4 kg	100–128
'Sugarloaf'	1.5 kg	70–90
SAVOY TYPE		
'January King'	6.8 kg	110
'Savoy Hybrid'	4.5–5 kg	120
OLD-FASHIONED (HEIRLOOM) VARIETIES		
'Emerald Acre'	1.6 kg	53
'Red Drum Head'	3.3 kg	110

If using a knife to harvest brussels sprouts, be careful not to damage the other sprouts nearby.

and change twice a day. Those who use this remedy say it is more effective if you warm the leaves with an iron before applying them.
● Cabbage leaves also make an excellent face mask. Wash the leaves well before using.

NO MANURE FOR BRUSSELS SPROUTS
Leafy members of the cabbage family need to be planted in well-manured soil, but not brussels sprouts since too much nitrogen, which is one of the main nutrients in manure, will produce open heads, rather than those tightly budded sprouts you are aiming for. If your soil is naturally fertile, you will not need to add any manure to the planting area. If the soil is infertile, however, add a little well-rotted garden compost.

REMOVING SPROUT TOPS
Although brussels sprouts are tightly packed along the stem, you can twist the buttons off by hand. If you use a knife, take care not to damage the smaller sprouts nearby (above).
● When picking a small quantity, take them from the base of the stem and work upwards, the sprouts higher up the stem will be smaller and mature later than those lower down.
● The leaves at the tops of the sprout stems are good to cook and eat as greens. This is beneficial also because, if you remove these green tops, you are depriving aphids of any potential resting and feeding places.

THREE CHEERS FOR THE FORGOTTEN KALE!
Kale is a leafy, cabbage-like vegetable that is widely grown in countries throughout northern Europe, but it is often neglected in our southern hemisphere gardens, where it is also known as borecole. However, it is well worth making space in your garden for this plant because it is frost hardy, colourful

and decorative through autumn and winter. Although whitefly can be a problem, it is relatively unaffected by aphids, caterpillars and other pests. Kale is also less prone to club root than cabbage.
● Sow your kale in spring to early autumn. The leaves will be ready to harvest according to your needs after the first frosts, and from then on throughout the winter.

Cauliflower and broccoli

CAULIFLOWERS ARE GREEDY FEEDERS
Cauliflowers thrive in deep, fertile soil and need to be watered regularly. If you live near the sea, gather seaweed and spread it on the ground before digging over. Or, enrich every 10 square metres of soil with 50 kg of compost, 1 kg of blood and bone or another natural manure rich in organic nitrogen. Proprietary fertilisers containing seaweed extracts are available.

GROW PURE WHITE CAULIFLOWERS
If a cauliflower head is overexposed to light and bad weather, it will lose its pure white colour. To protect it and preserve its whiteness, bend the largest outer leaves so that the leaf spine cracks, and fold them over and fix them to cover the head (below).

ROMANESCO GAINING IN POPULARITY
For variety, try this delicately flavoured Italian cauliflower. It has an unusual conical shape with pointed, yellow-green florets, but it is cultivated like other cauliflowers.

Protect the white curds of cauliflowers by bending the leaves over the head and securing them.

1 2
3 4
5 6

PICKING AT THE RIGHT MOMENT

For a double crop of broccoli, you need to harvest it at exactly the right time – when the flower heads are well formed, but before they open. To harvest the broccoli, cut the heads off at the top of the stalk. Once you cut off the heads, don't pull up the plant because the buds in the axils of the remaining leaves will develop and provide another crop of smaller, but just as tasty, heads.

Take your pick of greens

LETTUCES OF EVERY DESCRIPTION

The word 'lettuce' usually conjures up lovely images of crunchy green summer salads. Add more interest to your salads by combining the range of different lettuce types available. There are so many different varieties to choose from, you could eat a different one for each day of the week.

- **BUTTERHEAD TYPES** These have soft leaves that heart up into crisp centres, and can be all green or have red-tinged leaves.
- **COS (OR ROMAINE)** Lettuces with a long conical head which produces a crisp yellow heart and has deep green outer leaves. Sometimes these are red-tinged.
- **ICEBERG TYPES** These crisp, full-hearted lettuces are the most commonly grown and eaten salad lettuces. They are descendants of the European Batavia lettuce 'Chou de

Water lettuces around the base of the plant and not into the heart. If the heart of the lettuce is soaked, water may sit for too long and eventually the heart may rot.

Vary your summer salads with different varieties of lettuces such as butterhead and looseleaf types, and, pictured in the centre, 'Lollo Bionda'.

Naples'. Today's garden varieties include the 'Crisphead', 'Great Lakes', 'Greenway' and 'Winter Triumph' lettuces.
- **LOOSELEAF** These lettuces include salad bowl and oakleaf types. They can be used as whole heads, or picked by the leaf.
- **MIXED SALAD LEAF SEED COLLECTIONS** Mixed seed collections are definitely a good option for the indecisive. These are attractive in the ground as well as in salad bowls.

TOP TIPS FOR GROWING LETTUCE

To make sure your lettuces are tender and juicy, follow these guidelines.
- **PROVIDE MOIST SOIL** Grow lettuces in a moisture-retentive soil to prevent the plants from bolting. To increase its water-holding capacity, add compost or manure annually.
- **USE AVAILABLE SPACE** If you're short of space, plant lettuces as a quick crop between sowings of cabbages. The lettuces will be ready to harvest before the cabbages grow and take up all the space.
- **GET RID OF WEEDS** Use a hoe to keep garden rows of lettuce weed free. In fact, there's an old saying, 'Hoeing once is the equivalent of watering twice'. This is because hoeing actually loosens the soil and lowers the rate of evaporation of moisture and, as weeds are competitors for water, getting rid of them gives the lettuces a better chance.
- **PICK AT THE RIGHT TIME** To test whether a hearting lettuce is ready to pick, feel the heart – it should be nice and firm. If it is not, leave the plant in the ground for a few more days before testing again.

AN EARTHY TOUCH FOR FLOWERBEDS

Cabbages needn't be limited to the vegetable garden. Give flowerbeds a robust charm by using some of the many plants in the cabbage family to add colour and texture to your borders. In recent years, the tradition of growing vegetables for decorative and practical purposes has gained in popularity in many ordinary kitchen gardens and stately homes alike, harking back to a time when good husbandry demanded that every bit of land was cherished.

Ornamental cabbages are especially suitable, and as temperatures drop in autumn, their colours intensify. 'Tuscan Black', a kale also known as the palm cabbage, is a truly spectacular plant with a bouquet of dark, blue-green leaves that can reach a height of up to 2 m. Kale is frost hardy and is especially decorative when its frothy, blue-green or purple leaves are edged with frost.

When leafy greens such as cabbage or lettuce develop flowery stems instead of hearts, they are said to have 'bolted'.

LETTUCES ON THE LEVEL When you prick out lettuces, don't plant them too deeply. The point at which the rosette of leaves joins the stem should be above the surface of the soil. It is hardly necessary to firm them in, just water them in lightly.

● If you are planting lettuces from punnets, plant the base of the seedling just level with the surface of the soil.

PRODUCING YOUR OWN SEEDS In the past, gardeners often saved seeds from their favourite and strongest-growing plants. Lettuce seeds are particularly easy to collect, but don't bother with F1 hybrid seeds as they will not come true to type. To harvest seeds, leave one or two plants to go to seed. Ripe seeds look tufty and start to disperse in the wind. At this stage pull up the plant and hang it upside-down in a cool, dry place. Peg large paper bags over the flower heads to catch any seeds. Collect all the remaining seeds by shaking or knocking them into the bag. Clean the seeds, carefully removing any dust, earth or other pieces of debris, and store in a cool, dry place ready for use.

SUCCESS WITH SEEDLINGS Sow seeds into punnets, trays or cells filled with seed-raising mix, and water them. When the seedlings appear, keep the soil moist.

● When seedlings are properly established and they have good root systems, transplant them into the garden or into larger pots.

● Look for disease-resistant varieties when planting. 'Winter Triumph' lettuce, for example, is resistant to downy mildew.

● You can sow seeds early in the growing season to get an early harvest. As soon as the soil warms and the weather improves, harden the seedlings off in a cold frame. If it is an overwinter crop, plant into a cold frame.

CORN SALAD – AN EASY SALAD CROP
To learn the secret of cultivating corn salad, or lamb's lettuce (variety 'Jade'), it is worth knowing its origins. This plant was a weed that grew among crops and was gathered by country folk working in the fields. The seeds germinated after harvest on the hard straw-covered soil. If it wasn't picked, the rosettes ran to seed in spring and continued their cycle in the next crop.

● Although this suggests that corn salad needs very little attention, it does best if it is sown into a reasonably fertile soil in an open, sunny site. If you sow in autumn and winter, it will need protection from severe frost while in hot climates it needs careful watering and light shade to survive summer. Sow it either in the growing position or into punnets, and transplant when the seedlings are large enough to handle.

● You can use corn salad as a cut-and-come-again salad crop. Water it well during dry periods, and you will be able to harvest it within 4–12 weeks of sowing.

QUICK AND EASY: CUT-AND-COME-AGAIN LETTUCES Mixed salad leaf seed collections are useful for colour and variety. They take up less space than other lettuce sowings, and you can get three to four cuts from each one of the plants. Grow them in

1 Use a trowel to very gently lift the young seedlings from an outdoor seedbed.

2 Hold the seedlings by the leaves and treat the root very carefully. Some gardeners trim the leaves to avoid water evaporation.

3 Use a dibber to make a hole and lower the seedling into it, so that the leaves are just level with the top of the soil.

4 Use your hands to gently firm down the soil around the plant and water it in thoroughly.

Salad throughout the year

By growing a large range of lettuce varieties in your vegetable garden, it is easy to have fresh leafy green salad vegetables in the garden all year round. This means you can try a different lettuce each week, or even each day of the week.

VARIETY	PLANTING TIME	COMMENTS
Butterhead lettuce	All year round	Soft-hearted lettuce
Chicory, radicchio	Autumn to spring	Bitter tasting; harvest individual leaves only
Cos	All year round	Upright lettuce
'Crisphead'	All year round	Full-hearted iceberg-style lettuce
'Great Lakes'	Summer	Full-hearted iceberg-style lettuce
'Greenway'	Late winter to spring	Full-hearted iceberg-style lettuce
Mizuna	All year round	Loose form of lettuce
Rocket	All year round	Wonderful nutty flavour; may bolt in hot weather
'Winter Triumph'	Autumn to winter	Full-hearted iceberg-style lettuce

a partially shaded site and keep the plants well watered. Sow seeds continuously and harvest as you require the tender young leaves. Try 'Mignonette', 'Red Coral' (also called 'Lollo Rosso') or 'Red Oakleaf'.

EASY OPTIONS For quick and easy lettuces, plant soft-hearted varieties such as 'Butter-crunch', 'Lollo Bionda' and 'Oakleaf'. Red-tinged varieties, for example, 'Red Coral' ('Lollo Rosso') and 'Red Velvet', are more heat tolerant and so they are easier to grow.
● To keep a continuous crop going, stagger your plantings so all your crop doesn't mature at once and harvest the leaves of soft-hearted varieties as they are needed. Only harvest the entire lettuce if it's mature.
● For an easy mix, look for seed mixes sold as mesclun mix. These contain chicory, corn salad, endive, rocket and soft-hearted lettuce. Make successive plantings.

Chicory, endive and radicchio

FOR SOME SHARP-TASTING SALAD LEAVES Chicory, which is also known as Belgian endive or witlof, is lifted and forced into producing smooth-leaved, tightly packed heads. Endive has deeply cut and loose foliage, which, in the colder climates, is blanched by covering with soil or tying the leaves up around the heads.
● Radicchio, or red chicory, has marbled red and white foliage, which is less bitter after forcing. 'Red Traviso' is a frost-resistant form.

PREVENTING BITTERNESS IN ENDIVE
If you want to produce an endive that isn't bitter, you will have to prevent the leaves of the heart from turning green. To do this, protect them from light for about 10 days before harvesting. This technique is called blanching. Make sure the endives are dry, so the heart doesn't rot, then tie up the head with raffia or rubber ties. Alternatively, place a cloche or dish over the heart of the plant.

EUROPEAN HERITAGE The bitter flavours of endive, radicchio and chicory have been greatly enjoyed in European countries for many years. These flavours are now begin-ning to become much more popular and are

Sugarloaf chicory is a bitter relative of lettuce and is grown as a cold-season crop.

enjoyed in our own restaurants and gardens. Chicory in particular is enjoyed as a forced leafy vegetable, called witlof, which is savoured for its sweet white leaves.

CHICORY IS ESSENTIALLY A ROOT
The edible part of chicory is the large bud that develops after forcing. Sow chicory seeds in spring, in soil that has been well dug over and broken down. It is not advisable to add manure or compost to the area where you grow chicory, since, as with carrots, organic matter, as well as any hard lumps of earth, will cause the roots to fork and become misshapen. The aim is to produce regularly formed roots that look like parsnips.

EASY-TO-GROW CHICORY 'Pain de Sucre', or sugarloaf chicory, named after the shape and size of its head, is an extremely reliable variety. This chicory does not need to be lifted and blanched, and it will heart up in situ and can be harvested and eaten without additional blanching. It produces tender, pale yellow and slightly bitter leaves during autumn and for some part of winter. Keep in mind that the outside leaves will go mushy if temperatures fall below –5°C, but you can remove these by washing them off, and the centre should still be edible.

EAT A SALAD AND DETOXIFY YOUR BLOOD Chervil, corn salad, cut-and-come-again oakleaf lettuce, dandelion, radicchio and wild herbs were traditionally made into a salad at the end of each winter to purify the blood and balance the digestion ready for the coming spring, after the sluggish winter months indoors.

Spinach, silverbeet and cardoon

SPINACH OR SILVERBEET The word 'spinach' is applied to two different vegetables. True spinach, also called English spinach, grows best in a cool climate or in the cooler parts of the year in a warm climate. It can be used in salads or cooked as a vegetable. Silverbeet is a tall-growing, leafy plant that produces leaves all year.

ALL YOU WILL EVER NEED TO KNOW ABOUT ENGLISH SPINACH It's simple to grow spinach in soil that is lightly dug, but there are a couple of things to bear in mind.
● Spinach's worst enemy is damping-off, a disease caused by the parasitic fungus *Pythium debaryanum*. This lies dormant in the soil waiting for damp conditions and the right host – spinach seedlings. Formerly gardeners tried to prevent this by sprinkling powdered charcoal in the drill when sowing seeds, but it can be avoided by spacing the seedlings so that there is a good current of air.
● English spinach grows best in spring and autumn, but it is often grown through winter with seeds sown from late summer to spring.

EASY TO GROW New Zealand spinach (*Tetragonia expansa*) has distinctive diamond-shaped leaves. Sow in late winter to early spring after soaking the seeds for 24 hours. Plant three or four seeds per module, or in planting holes in the ground spaced 70 cm apart. The plants will spread and produce continuously. Harvest the leaves carefully without damaging the main stem.

BEAUTY AND THE BEET Silverbeet, which is also called leaf chard or leaf beet, is a large leafy vegetable which can be grown as an ornamental in the vegetable and flower

The best way to harvest tender spinach leaves is to pick them carefully, one leaf at a time.

garden – and it is delicious in cooking. The leaves and stalks have a pungent, earthy flavour and are delicious served with a white sauce or butter. When you harvest the leaves, remember to twist the stalk as you pull.

SPACE INVADERS The cardoon or artichoke thistle is classified as a weed in some areas. Where it is grown, it is the leaf stalk that is blanched and cooked like celery. In all areas, remove flowers to prevent seeding. Sow in spring, planting three or four seeds in each planting hole. Allow at least 1 m between the holes, in all directions. Thin out the seedlings 2 weeks after germination and leave one plant per hole. While they are small, you can grow lettuces and radishes between cardoon seedlings.

ENRICH YOUR SOIL WITH NITROGEN Take advantage of silverbeet's and spinach's production of nitrogen in its leaves and use any surplus seeds or plants as an alternative green manure. Sow spinach at the end of summer in any uncultivated areas of the vegetable garden. The first frosts will kill the plants. Then simply dig them in just below the surface, and the nitrogen in the spinach leaves will enrich the soil.

DID YOU KNOW?

STRANGE RELATIVES
Silverbeet is a tall-growing vegetable that is a variety of the same species as beetroot; however, it is grown for its leaves and not for its roots.
● Harvest silverbeet leaves as they are needed, but always allow around six leaves to remain for strong regrowth and leaf production.

Silverbeet comes in a range of stem colours. 'Fordhook' (far left), the most commonly grown variety, has creamy white or green stems; 'Rainbow Chard' has stems in orange (left centre), yellow, pink, white and bicolour; and 'Red-stemmed' (left) has crimson stalks.

Generous legumes and greedy sweetcorn

Beans and peas belong to a large group of vegetables known as legumes, which have long been cultivated by gardeners as useful soil improvers because of the way they absorb nitrogen. They fix it in nodules on their roots and so feed the soil when they rot. Sweetcorn, on the other hand, is a relative newcomer and a greedy feeder.

Beans for every garden

GET TO KNOW YOUR BEANS There are many plants called beans. Green beans are widely known on the vegetable plate and in the kitchen garden. They are harvested and eaten whole and are easy and very rewarding to grow. They are known by many names, including climbing beans, French beans and pole beans – just to confuse the issue, there are also dwarf-growing varieties.

● Runner beans are perennial beans that grow well in the cooler climates. Best known and most ornamental of these beans is the scarlet runner, which has attractive red flowers. Also attractive is the 'Painted Lady' runner bean with red and white flowers and large pods.

● In the general category of beans are the borlotti, broad and lima beans. Their pods are harvested and split for the beans inside. Broad beans are grown through winter and are harvested in spring.

FULL OF BEANS To ensure that your plants provide you with a good harvest follow these time-honoured tips. Beans are frost sensitive so grow from spring to autumn in cool and temperate gardens but grow them year round in the tropics and subtropics. Begin sowing seeds in spring for fast germination.

● For healthy growth, beans need the nutrients potassium and nitrogen as well as a regular supply of moisture. Dig in compost and well-rotted manure ahead of planting and ahead of adding fruit and flower fertiliser

Dwarf beans make the most of a small space and produce delicious crops through the summer months.

that's high in potassium, or add potash. Keep the soil moist and provide a sunny lattice or tepee for climbing varieties.

EARTHING UP Old-fashioned gardeners found that earthing up dwarf green beans (below) helps to support the stems. It also maintains moisture around the roots.

To retain moisture around young dwarf beans, mound up soil or add a layer of mulch.

DID YOU KNOW?

STRINGLESS BEANS
Runner beans have 'strings' running down their pods, which can become very tough with age. New varieties, that include 'Pioneer', are today becoming especially popular because they are stringless. 'Bountiful Butter', a yellow-skinned variety, is a tasty, stringless waxpod bean. A good choice for early or late sowing is 'Gourmet's Delight', which is well suited to early or late sowing. Many of the new varieties are resistant to diseases including anthracnose, common bean mosaic virus and halo blight.

SOW GREEN BEANS IN SUCCESSION

Green beans are sown from early spring to late summer and harvested from late spring. If you sow in succession you will have regular crops, rather than needing to harvest everything at once.

● The time between sowing and harvesting varies, depending on the type of bean, but allow 8–12 weeks. Using this yardstick you can gauge how many sowings you need to make during the growing season.

● For faster results, select a dwarf variety of bean – these are dwarf plants, not dwarf fruit, and are ready to harvest in 8 weeks.

RUNNER BEANS

RUNNER BEANS Runner beans are best grown in cool climates and don't set fruit in warm climates. Sow from spring to summer and harvest from summer. They die at the end of summer but regrow in spring.

● Pick regularly to keep runner beans cropping throughout summer.

● Water runner beans regularly also to make sure they keep cropping.

SAVING BEAN SEEDS Allow the last beans on each plant – those that are too high to harvest – to ripen fully. The pods will turn yellow and look dry and shrivelled (below). Pick them and remove the beans from the pods. Store them in paper bags in a cool, frost-free, dry place. Label the bags with the name and sow them the following year.

● You can save seeds from broad beans and peas, but seeds taken from F1 hybrids will not grow true to type.

FEED BEANS ON WASTE As they produce their own nitrogen, runner beans are able to digest uncomposted material. In early spring, when you are tidying the garden, fill a trench with the soft greenery and harmless weeds you have just cleared from elsewhere on your plot.

If you want to replant your own seeds, allow the last of the crop to mature for next year's sowing.

● At planting time, chop these cuttings with your spade, cover with compost-enriched soil, and sow seeds or plant young seedlings.

CONSERVING MOISTURE Preparing the soil by digging in uncomposted green waste and well-rotted manure helps to keep the ground damp, but take other measures to further reduce the need for watering in dry spells, for example, a mulch of compost will help lock in the moisture.

GETTING THE BIRD Legume seedlings are attractive to birds, so protect them until they have grown into good-sized plants. Horti-cultural fleece is useful for protecting a row of seedlings and bird netting is effective.

● Homemade 'humming lines' fashioned from twine strung across the vegetable bed and stretched tightly on canes deter birds.

● Alternatively, unwanted CDs can be hung around the garden as shiny bird scarers.

Broad beans

SIMPLE SOWING Broad beans are very easy to grow in most soils, and sowing is simple. They grow best in cool to temperate climates and are planted in autumn and winter.

● Broad beans are sown directly into beds. They need lots of space so grow them in rows, each row spaced 60–75 cm apart. Plant seeds into damp soil 5 cm deep and space 20 cm apart. Seeds take 10–14 days to germinate.

● If you apply fertiliser to the row at planting, more is usually unnecessary. Too much ferti-liser, especially one high in nitrogen, will promote leaf growth over flower production.

SUPPORT BROAD BEANS Tall-growing varieties of broad bean may need support if they are grown in exposed sites. Tie the bean plants to individual canes or, to support a whole row of beans, use two stakes with a fork at the top, inserted firmly into the soil at either end of the row. Lay a bamboo cane across from one fork to the other and tie it in. At intervals, tie upright canes into the horizontal cane and these will support the beans as they grow.

A BONUS CROP Thrifty wartime gardeners cut broad bean stalks back to 10–15 cm after harvesting. Shoots from the base of the stalks

1 Beans can be sown where they're to grow. Sow in seed holes, usually three to four per hole, 30 cm apart.

2 Don't sow the beans too deep, no more than 3 cm. Hoe or rake over soil to cover the seeds.

3 Water well to settle the soil in the planting holes and moisten the beans.

4 Once the first leaves have appeared, earth up slightly with a hoe and remember to keep the plants well watered.

Broad bean 'Aquadulce', growing here with string support, can be sown in autumn for spring crops.

then form bushy stems, and produce a second, smaller crop. While waiting for the second crop, grow lettuces as a quick crop.

PINCHING OUT TOPS Broad beans are well known for attracting aphids. Some gardeners feel that pinching out the tops, where the youngest and tastiest shoots are found, will rid plants of the pest. Pinching out will also stop the plants from getting leggy.

PEST ALERT A good tip to enable you to have pest-free crops is to grow the delicious herb, summer savory, alongside your broad bean rows. Its aroma is said to deter pests from the beans and the herb can be used to flavour cooked bean dishes.

Perfect peas

A COOL CROP Peas are a prolific crop for the cooler months. For a fast crop, select sugarsnaps or snow peas. Both these peas are eaten pods and all, so they don't require a long time waiting for the peas in the pod to mature before harvesting.
● **TROPICAL AND SUBTROPICAL AREAS** Sow seeds from March to July.
● **TEMPERATE AREAS** Sow seeds from February to August.
● **COOL CLIMATES** Sow pea seeds from June to late September, and in early October.

SOW PEAS DEEP The first two seed leaves develop below ground, which means peas have to be sown at a depth of about 5 cm in order to develop a good root system. They also need to be densely planted, so sow seeds close together, no more than 1–2 cm apart.

MAKE THE MOST OF SPACE Peas are produced on dwarf plants as well as tall climbers. Dwarf peas can be grown just about anywhere in the garden – even in pots. Where space is at a real premium, tall-growing varieties can be trained onto a wall, lattice or over a garden arch. Peas are good crops for children to grow because they get fast rewards and kids can pick and eat the peas straight from the garden.
● **FAST PRODUCTION** 'Earlicrop Massey' is a fast-cropping dwarf form that is ready to pick in 12–14 weeks.
● **LONG PRODUCTION** If you can wait, the climbing variety 'Greenfeast' takes some 14–16 weeks to bear, but it will continue to produce for 3–5 weeks. Pick every few days to keep new flowers coming.

THE ART OF STAKING PEAS All types of peas are climbers and need support for their twining tendrils. Small bamboo canes make excellent supports for all types of climbing peas as do twiggy branches.
● It is easier to stake and harvest peas if they are grown in double rows 50–75 cm apart, depending on the variety.

MICE AND PEAS Mice will enjoy rearranging your pea seeds under the ground, although deep planting may put them off the scent. Old-fashioned gardeners

Peas are easy to sow and rewarding to grow. Sow the seeds to a depth of 5 cm and 1–2 cm apart.

STAKING PEAS WITH A NATURAL SUPPORT

1 Use stakes that grow in your garden to support your peas. Break up twiggy branches or use bamboo canes to support them when their tendrils start to develop.

2 Place the twigs at intervals of 25–30 cm and about 5 cm away from the plants. Angle the sticks so that they meet above the centre of a double row of plants.

3 Encourage plants towards the sticks and soon they will begin to use their tendrils to climb up and gain support against windy and rainy weather.

used to dip their pea seeds in paraffin – the strong smell was said to ward off mice.
● An alternative way to avoid problems with mice is to plant your peas in lengths of guttering about 1 m long. Fill guttering with soil and keep it in the greenhouse or in a cold frame. When the plants are well established, dig a trench, push them out of the guttering along its length and plant them in the ground, firming the soil around the roots. You may also need to earth up the plants so the roots are all well covered.

Succulent sweetcorn

PLANT YOUR SWEETCORN IN BLOCKS
To produce juicy sweetcorn, it must be wind-pollinated. The plant is adapted for this by having two sets of flowers: male flowers are the long tassels at the top of the plant, and female are the 'silks' below which the cobs develop. Pollen is blown from the long tassels of the male flowers to pollinate the female, so planting in blocks rather than rows favours pollination.

WARM-WEATHER FRIENDS
Sweetcorn needs warm weather to get established. Direct-sow corn once the soil has warmed up, from August in temperate zones, and October in cooler climates. In subtropical and tropical zones sweetcorn can be grown year round. Since the carbohydrate-rich kernels are susceptible to attack by fungi, insects and slugs, it needs the warmth to enable it to germinate quickly, before it is attacked.
● Sow two or three seeds into holes that are about 3 cm deep and 25–30 cm apart. For greater success, sow two or three kernels in a pot, and transplant the seedlings out into the garden when all danger of frost has passed.
● As plants grow, lateral roots may develop at the soil surface. Leave them in place, they anchor the plants and provide nourishment.

HARVEST TIME
The 'silks' will tell you when it is time to harvest. The cobs develop inside a sheath made of several leaves known as bracts or spathes, and only the silks – all that remains of the flower styles – are visible from the outside. Initially, the silks are green and when they have turned dark brown, and

This ripe sweetcorn shows how the 'silks' at the top of the cob have dried out and turned brown.

look and feel dry, the cob is ripe. You can check the ripeness of the cob by peeling back the bracts. Immature kernels are milky and translucent. When ripe, they are plump and tender and, depending on variety, bright yellow, pale cream or black.

FROM GARDEN TO TABLE
There's an old saying in the American South: 'You can walk down to the garden to pick your corn, but you have to run coming back'. This means that, to capture its sweetness, you can't keep sweetcorn for very long before cooking it. Boil the husked cobs in unsalted water, as salt will harden the kernels.

To enhance wind pollination of sweetcorn and to ensure the best results, grow them in blocks.

A cob of sweetcorn develops below the female flower, or the 'silk' of the plant.

DID YOU KNOW?

SWEETCORN AND GREEN BEANS IS A WINNING COMBINATION
Sweetcorn and green beans were both introduced from the Americas where they are widely cultivated. They make excellent companions in a mixed bed, because sweetcorn is a greedy feeder and benefits greatly from the nitrogen fixed in the soil by the beans. The beans, in turn, use the upright-growing sweetcorn as support. The two crops also complement each other nutritionally and are often eaten together.
● If you want to grow beans alongside your sweetcorn, wait until the sweetcorn has two or three leaves, then sow a few bean seeds in spaces between the plants. Choose from dwarf or nonvigorous varieties, such as 'Gourmet's Delight' or 'Pioneer'.
● To grow sweetcorn with pumpkins, which is another traditional US partnership, sow the sweetcorn when you plant out your pumpkins.

Fruiting vegetables in the summer sun

At the onset of summer, melons, tomatoes and zucchinis swell with the promise of a succulent maturity. As the summer progresses, so too does the size and flavour of these fruiting vegetables that are ready for delicious summer salads and refreshing snacks.

Red, ripe and delicious tomatoes

THESE SEEDS NEED WARMTH Tomato seeds need warmth to germinate and they germinate readily in the natural warmth of spring, or for much of the year in tropical and subtropical areas. Gardeners in cool and temperate climates who want to have their tomatoes ripe before Christmas need to use a few tricks to get them growing ahead of spring. Sow seeds into small pots or cell trays in late winter in a warm place such as in a heated propagator, a foam box or even on top of your hot water system.

SEEDLING CARE Tomato seedlings can be planted out once they have reached the stage of having three to four leaves and all threat of frost has passed. If the early spring weather is unpredictable in your area, then transplant tomato seedlings into individual pots and keep them in a warm sheltered spot for a few more weeks.
● Old-fashioned gardeners in areas of the Mediterranean have been known to protect their young tomato plants with two terracotta roof tiles propped together.

STAKING PLANTS Push the stakes firmly into the ground, leaving 60 cm between each one, so that the plants have enough room to grow. Make a planting hole about 10 cm in front of each stake and place the plants into the holes, angling them slightly towards the stakes. Water the plants and then gently firm the soil around them, being careful not

to damage the stems. As the plants grow, you can begin to tie them against the stakes to give them the support they need.

WATER RESERVOIRS Tomato plants need regular and copious watering. To make sure they get enough, sink a small flowerpot into the ground near the base of each stake. Pour water into this every day so that it fills up and then slowly drains into the soil near the plants. Another method is to remove the top from the neck of a 2 litre plastic bottle, cut the bottle in half and sink the neck into the ground. Fill it with water every day.
● During the growing season, tomatoes need regular feeding, so use this water reservoir for applying water-soluble fertiliser. You can also feed the tomatoes with liquid manure made from nettle or comfrey (see page 269).

Home-grown, vine-ripened tomatoes are delicious. Pick them regularly as they ripen.

Tomatoes are thirsty growers. Sink a pot up to its rim at the base of each plant. Fill each morning, being careful not to wet the fruits or foliage.

THE PICK OF THE TOMATO CROP

Varieties of tomatoes differ in size, shape, flavour, texture, colour, type of skin, picking time and mildew tolerance. So how do you choose between all the tomatoes available?
● If you like stuffed tomatoes, go for the large-fruited varieties.
● If you are adventurous, try growing the lesser-known and more unusually coloured or shaped 'heirloom' varieties, which add extra interest to your summer salads.

BEEFSTEAK A large, smooth, blemish-free fruit with thick meaty flesh.
BLACK RUSSIAN An heirloom variety with a dark skin and good-flavoured flesh.
BRANDYWINE Another heirloom, a large-fruited, beefsteak-type with good flavour.
BROAD RIPPLE A very prolific cherry tomato that produces large trusses of yellow oval or pear-shaped fruit.
GARDENER'S DELIGHT A late variety with small, very tasty fruits.
GREEN ZEBRA Green, apricot-sized fruit that ripens to yellow. Produces until winter.
GROSSE LISSE A reliable producer, even for inexperienced growers.
MORTGAGE LIFTER Beefsteak variety from the US has large, often 1.8 kg, fruit. In the 1930s, selling at a dollar a plant it enabled its grower to pay off his mortgage in 6 years.
ROMA 1 An elongated plum tomato, ideal for making tomato sauces and pizzas.
ROUGE DE MARMANDE 2 AND SUPER-MARMANDE Early-producing varieties with large fruits.
SUMMERTASTE Prolific, disease-resistant variety and a good choice for warm climates.
SUPER MARZANO F1 A giant, disease-resistant pear-shaped fruit.
SUPER SWEET 100 F1 One of the cherry tomatoes that produces red 3 or yellow, sometimes pear-shaped, fruit.
TINY TIM A compact variety that's excellent in pots. Small, tasty fruit.

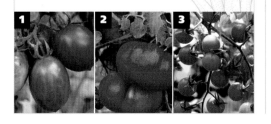

MULCHING IS ESSENTIAL Like many other crops, tomato plants need to be very well spaced because of their volume. It is always a good idea to cover the soil at their base with mulch. Use lucerne, sugar cane or composted bark, in a layer up to 5 cm deep. This suppresses weeds and helps prevent any excessive water evaporation from the surface of the soil. Remember to mulch only on damp soil to keep the existing moisture in, otherwise it will prevent rain reaching the roots and ensure that dry soil stays dry.

STAKES AND TEPEES Tomato plants have a naturally trailing or climbing habit and most need some form of support. Training them upwards not only means they take up less space, but they also escape the adverse effects of damp soil, which promotes the development of diseases.
● Use tomato stakes 1.5–2 m long, and push them into the ground near the base of each plant. As the plants grow, use raffia or string to tie the stems to the stakes.
● One way to ensure that the stakes are stable is to arrange them in groups of three or four, angled towards the centre, and tie them firmly at the top to form a tepee shape for the plants to grow on. This can be the best solution especially if your tomatoes are growing in an ornamental garden.

BUSHY TYPES Some varieties of tomato, such as the 'Roma' and 'Tiny Tim', have a bushy habit and don't need staking. However, in the garden, it's always a good idea to keep these varieties off the ground to prevent their fruits from rotting. You can simply support them on an upturned crate.

MIXED CROPPING Tomatoes grow well with asparagus, cabbages, celery, green beans, leeks, onions, parsley and potatoes.
● Tomatoes don't grow well with beetroot, cucumbers, fennel and peas.
● Plant marigolds (*Calendula*) around them to reduce infestations of whitefly.

THE 'COPPER WIRE' TIP In the past, some European gardeners have claimed to protect their tomato plants from mildew by piercing the young plants with copper wires at two points along, and at right angles to, the main stem. Though not scientifically proven, it is possible that copper compounds form in the sap and attack the fungi that cause mildew.

A LITTLE BIT OF REGULAR CARE AND INSPECTION
A well-tended vegetable patch like the one below (top) looks like hard work, but the key to success, as yesterday's gardeners knew, is regular care. Don't leave a vegetable patch unvisited for days. Check your plants in the early morning or early evening – it will only take a few minutes a day.

Regular chores include: water anything that's dry, have a quick look for signs of pests or diseases, remove dead leaves or unwanted shoots and harvest anything that's ready. For example, tomatoes benefit from the regular pinching of the small shoots that appear in the leaf axils (below, bottom). Top growth can also be pinched back to control the overall height of the tomato bush.

TRIMMING AND PINCHING OUT Check tomato plants regularly during the crucial stages of their development, and pinch out all the little shoots that appear in the axils of the leaves. If they are not pinched out the tomato plant will use its energy to become bushy and fruit production will be reduced. Do not pinch out the side shoots on bush tomatoes, as they will eventually bear fruit.
● In very hot regions, leave some axil shoots to create a slight shade for the tomatoes, which will reduce sun scald damage to fruit.

A BOOSTER SHOT FOR THE TOMATOES When your tomatoes begin to bloom, mix two large spoonfuls of Epsom salts in 5 litres of water and pour onto the soil around the plants. The magnesium and sulphur in the salts encourage healthy fruits.

HOW TO HASTEN RIPENING In the late summer and early autumn months, remove any foliage that may be shading the fruit from the ripening effects of the sun.
● When sunshine is at a premium, follow the old-fashioned practice of using backing boards to reflect sunlight onto your sun-loving tomatoes. Simply cover a board with aluminium foil, prop it against a support and angle it so it catches the sun's rays and bounces them onto the ripening fruit.

MAKING THE MOST OF YOUR TOMATO SUCKERS You may notice that a tomato's suckers, like the other green parts of the plant, have a very pungent smell. This is released – at the slightest contact – as a smelly, coloured substance from many tiny glands on the surface of the plant. Some gardeners say that this property can be used to protect other vegetables against garden pests. For example, it is said that if you place tomato suckers on the leaves of cabbages or other brassicas, the smell of the tomato will disorientate cabbage white butterflies and cabbage moths. This prevents them from laying their eggs on the leaves and protects your brassicas from caterpillar damage.

A WIDE RANGE OF COLOURS Many of the old heirloom-type tomatoes taste much better than modern varieties and their varied hues can be used to add interest to the salad bowl. In recent years, yellow, orange, green, pink, purple, black and even striped tomatoes have become increasingly popular.

PRODUCING YOUR OWN TOMATO SEEDS IS SIMPLE Almost nothing could be easier than producing your own tomato seeds, provided they come from a traditional variety and not from an F1 hybrid. First, put the pulp of a ripe tomato into a bowl and add a little water. Soon, a whitish bacterial film will form on the surface of the liquid. After about 36 hours, add more water and stir the mixture – this fermentation process separates the seeds from the pulp, and the seeds will sink to the bottom. Strain off the liquid through a sieve, rinse the seeds under the cold tap and then leave them to dry on a piece of paper towel.

Pumpkins, squash and zucchinis

ALL IN THE FAMILY The pumpkin, gourd (non-edible), squash and zucchini are among the more widely grown members of the gourd family, Cucurbitaceae.
● Pumpkins come in a range of shapes, sizes, colours and flavours and are generally harvested in autumn. Hard-skinned varieties such as 'Queensland Blue' and 'Jarrahdale' have excellent storage abilities. They'll last through winter stored in cool, dry conditions. Their flesh is rich in Vitamin C.
● Zucchinis are harvested earlier in the growing season and do not keep the same way that pumpkins do. Their soft skins and their bland flesh need to be picked while the fruit is still young and small. In the peak of summer a tasty zucchini can become large and tasteless in as little as 4 days.

EASY-TO-GROW ZUCCHINIS Sow zucchinis and pumpkins in situ, allowing 1 m between plants in all directions and 2 m for trailing varieties. Sow to a depth of about 2 cm. In cold climates, don't be tempted to sow until spring, when all danger of frost has passed. In warm, frost-free tropical and subtropical zones these and other cucurbits can be sown for most months of the year.

LONG-SEASON ZUCCHINIS Make the most of your zucchinis and make sure you have plenty of fruit during the summer months. Sow them in succession between the months of September and December.

Zucchini seeds are usually sown directly into the vegetable garden but can be started in a tray or punnet.

TWO'S COMPANY Zucchinis are extremely prolific, so it's not worth planting out more than two at a time. Remember to create a small hollow around the base of young plants for watering. This will hold the water and ensure that it gets to the right spot, preventing water stress.

MULTICOLOURED ZUCCHINIS Zucchinis are available in a range of skin colours. The traditional favourite has a dark green skin, but you can also grow zucchinis that are light green or yellow in colour. They all taste similar and, if cooked unpeeled, look good when served together.
● For something totally different, look for heirloom varieties called crookneck summer squash, a form of zucchini with a bulbous end and a narrow neck. Crookneck summer squash have yellow skin and can develop warty, thick skin. The fruit matures slightly more slowly than that of most other zucchinis.

GETTING OFF TO AN EARLY START Instead of seeds, buy punnets of seedlings and advanced seedlings to give you a head start on crops like zucchini and pumpkin, but be careful not to plant them out too early if you live in a frost-prone district.

KEEPING WEEDS DOWN If you plant trailing or sprawling varieties of pumpkins, squash and zucchinis, they will soon grow and they will cover a vast area with their extremely abundant foliage. Plan for this unusual spread and reap the benefit of the foliage keeping the weeds down.

LADDER OF SUCCESS To give pumpkins somewhere to trail and to keep them out of the way, place an old wooden ladder – one past its best for practical use – against a fence or wall. Plant trailing varieties at its feet, and they will climb up the rungs.

EASY NEIGHBOURS Pumpkins, squash and zucchinis will grow anywhere, even in the most poorly prepared of soils. If you are starting a new vegetable garden and have not had the time to prepare the ground properly, it's still possible to get a good crop of these vegetable fruits. As long as you can add well-rotted manure to the soil they will thrive almost wherever you plant them.
● All of these vegetable fruits will do best if planted in a sheltered, sunny position.

Butternut pumpkins are decorative, easy to grow and keep well when picked at maturity.

SOWING ON THE COMPOST HEAP
Pumpkins, squash and zucchinis need lots of organic matter and thrive if they are sown or planted directly on the compost heap. Sometimes they even grow without the help of the gardener since the seeds in kitchen waste often germinate unaided. As an added bonus, the foliage of most pumpkins and squash provides a natural covering to keep the compost heap shaded and moist. If the seeds are from F1 Hybrids the results may be variable, but usually still delicious.

TOP TIPS FOR THE CARE OF PUMPKINS AND SQUASH Many of these tips will work for tomatoes and cucumbers too.
● **ENCOURAGE FRUITS** To promote the growth of lateral shoots and female flowers, nip out the growing tips of the main shoots of trailing plants when they are 45 cm long.
● **HELP POLLINATION** If the fruits are not setting well, pollinate the plants by hand. Use a small brush to transfer pollen from the male flowers to the female, which you can identify by a swelling just behind the bloom.
● **REMOVE SOME LEAVES** As soon as a small pumpkin develops, it's a good idea to remove some of the leaves from the fruit-bearing stem. Leave two or three just above the fruit.
● **FOIL PESTS** If you spread aluminium foil on the soil around the base of the plants, you can prevent viruses transmitted by thrips and aphids. You can deter cutworm by wrapping stems in a sleeve of aluminium foil, making sure the sleeve is buried 2–3 cm in the soil. Taping foil behind the plants, on a fence or on a wall, not only increases the light but is great for confusing pests.

WATCH OUT

SPACE INVADERS
If you have a small garden, then you'd be well advised to avoid trailing pumpkins and squash that take up too much space. Most varieties spread for several metres on either side of the main plant and will smother other plants with their huge leaves. Check on the seed packet whether varieties are trailing or not.
● Most pumpkins are trailing, but if you have a small space try 'Golden Nugget', which is a bush form. Plant these pumpkins 1 m apart or grow them in a large pot.
● Butternut pumpkin will trail but it can also be trained onto a fence or lattice to save some valuable space.
● Zucchinis grow on large, leafy bushes.

Pumpkins like 'Queensland Blue' and 'Jarrahdale', shown here, have thick skins and keep for a long time.

A tile keeps pumpkins from rotting where they touch the ground in wet summers and autumns.

Harvest zucchinis when they are small, or they will become tasteless; 10–15 cm long is ideal.

ON THE TILES Place a tile, a small board or a flat stone under the pumpkin fruit to keep it off damp soil and avoid pests and possible rotting. The tile will absorb heat from the sun and will ripen the fruit more quickly.

WHEN TO HARVEST? Fruiting vegetables will be ready to harvest at different times and in varying quantities.

● ZUCCHINIS Harvest zucchinis when they are 10–15 cm long for best flavour. The more you pick the more fruits the plant will produce, and if they are picked at this size they will be very tasty. Any larger and they are halfway to becoming marrows and will have a watery flavour.

● PUMPKINS The fruits are ready to pick when they've coloured well and developed a hard skin. Give them a tap, and if they sound hollow they are ready to pick. Another indicator of ripeness is that the foliage begins to turn brown, as does the stem where the fruit joins the plant.

CURING PUMPKINS After picking pumpkins, you should keep the harvested fruit in a warm, sunny place. In hot districts cure pumpkins in a sheltered but airy spot, such as under the house or tank stand. If you are curing them outdoors bring them indoors if frost is forecast.

STORING PUMPKINS Harvest and store pumpkins for up to 3 months in an airy, frost-free place. Many old-fashioned gardeners stored their prize pumpkins in nets hung up in sheds to keep them from coming into contact with other fruits in storage.

● Pumpkins store best and longest in a frost-free environment. Avoid storing in damp areas. For maximum protection, store them on wood, cardboard or several layers of newspaper rather than cold surfaces such as stone or cement.

LIVING JACK-O'-LANTERNS You can add some fun to growing pumpkins, and delight the children, if you make a carving on the skin of a baby pumpkin and watch it grow with the fruit. Mark out a pattern or a face on a young fruit – a large nail is a good tool to use – and then be patient for a few months. Don't remove the fruit from the plant as it needs to carry on growing. By autumn, the pattern will have expanded and grown into a life-sized face.

THE STRANGE SPAGHETTI SQUASH Confound dinner guests with this curiosity from the pumpkin family. This heirloom variety is cooked whole for around 30 minutes. When the skin is opened, the flesh forms long, spaghetti-like strands. It grows like a pumpkin and seeds are available from heirloom seed specialists.

The trailing varieties of pumpkin will make good use of any neglected or wild areas in your garden. They can spread for up to several metres away from their planting point.

Gardener's Choice

SOME EYE-CATCHING PUMPKINS

BUTTON SQUASH or 'Patty Pan' **1**. The decorative scalloped shape and yellow, green or white skin of this tasty squash variety conceal flesh that tastes best when picked small.

PUMPKIN The 'Cinderella' type **2** is an old French favourite, popular because of its deep orange skin and heavy ribbing, although it is also good to eat. However, the sweet butternut pumpkin **5** is the classic cooking pumpkin, good for soups, pies and casseroles.

TURK'S TURBAN 3 This highly coloured and shapely squash has a tasty flesh, but it is normally grown for its unusual appearance.

'QUEENSLAND BLUE' 4 AND 'JARRAHDALE' are the traditional backyard pumpkins with excellent keeping abilities.

HUBBARD SQUASH 6 When roasted, this great-tasting squash has a superb nutty flavour. It keeps well.

1 2
3 4

5 6

Cucumbers and melons

COOL AS A CUCUMBER Cucumbers need a warm growing period to thrive. In tropical and subtropical areas they survive just about all year round, but in cooler and more temperate areas they are confined to spring and summer plantings. For year-round production in these cooler climates, cucumbers can quite effectively be grown in heated greenhouses or igloos during the winter.

CUCUMBERS COME IN ALL SHAPES AND SIZES The traditional cucumber is long and dark green, while some varieties are round or apple-shaped with light green or white skin. 'Crystal Apple' is one of the most popular varieties of round cucumber varieties and has smooth, white skin.

TRAINING YOUR PLANTS Cucumbers can be grown up canes, lattice or along the ground. Remove growing points of stems regularly to encourage bushy growth and better fruit setting.

MALE AND FEMALE FLOWERS Many greenhouse hybrids are all female and therefore must be unfertilised to prevent a bitter flavour. However, most cucumbers have separate male and female flowers on the one cucumber plant. It is the female flowers that develop the fruit. Lebanese cucumbers can have male and female flowers on separate plants, so always sow several plants at one time to make sure you get fruit.

STRAIGHT AND NARROW Glasshouse cucumbers were a favourite of the 19th-century gentry, whose gardeners grew them in glass sheaths to keep them of a uniform shape, straight and tender.

HARVEST CUCUMBERS FOR THE BEST FLAVOUR Harvest cucumbers when they have reached a good size, 15–20 cm long, but before they turn yellow.

GREAT GHERKINS Gherkins are actually long cucumbers that are picked when they are still immature, at only 5–10 cm long. At this stage they can be pickled. Good varieties for gherkins are 'Gherkin' and 'Pickling'.

GROWING MELONS Sweet melons, which include rockmelons and watermelons, are trailing plants that grow much like pumpkins. They need an open, sunny and warm situation with plenty of organic matter and compost added to the soil before planting. In cool and temperate zones they may take 14–16 weeks from planting until the fruit is ready to pick.
● **ROCKMELONS** Look for mildew-resistant varieties such as 'Hales Best'. Rockmelons are ready to pick when the stem comes easily away from the vine.
● **WATERMELONS** There are many watermelon varieties including the red-fleshed 'Candy Red'. For small melons look for 'Minilee'. The most recently developed are seedless varieties such as 'Viking Seedless Hybrid'. Harvest when the side of the melon that touches the soil turns yellow and the melon sounds hollow when tapped.

WHEN TO SOW MELONS Sow melons in the spring and the early summer months, directly into the soil. Remember the seeds need a minimum temperature of 16°C to germinate. They will thrive if a temperature of 20°C can be guaranteed.

WATERING Melons need regular, and lots of, water especially when in flower so that they develop good fruit. They need plenty of nutrients so use a tomato fertiliser with added magnesium.

HOTBEDS This old-fashioned method gives all fruiting vegetables, including pumpkins and cucumbers, a good start. Before planting, dig out a bed and fill it with organic matter which, as it decomposes, releases heat and helps plants develop. (In the old days,

These vigorous telegraph cucumbers naturally develop the desirable long, narrow cucumber shape.

Gherkins are immature green 'ridged' cucumbers that are picked when they are young and sometimes pickled.

From seed, rockmelons can take up to 4 months to grow to harvest size and they need full sun all this time.

Watermelon grows readily from seed and it particularly appeals to children who enjoy its sweet, juicy summer fruit.

fresh manure would have been used as it was widely available, but any organic matter will work.) Cover the organic matter with a good layer of soil, and sow or plant into that. The soil cover prevents heat loss from the hotbed and protects the young plants, which might otherwise rot due to the heat and moisture produced by the heap.

Eggplants and capsicums

EGGPLANTS As a native of the tropical regions of Asia, eggplants (or aubergines as they are also known) require warm temperatures to flourish and fruit. Some can also be grown in large pots. Growing conditions are similar to those for tomatoes.

● Eggplants are best known for their large, egg-shaped fruit produced by varieties such as 'Bonica', 'Blacknite' or 'Long Purple'.

Eggplants make a decorative and delicious backyard crop. The beautiful 'Blacknite' has large, glossy oval fruit.

● If the traditional eggplant is too big, look for the smaller 'Black Gnome' which fruits 11 weeks from planting and so suits pots and cooler areas with limited growing times.
● For a curiosity, look for white eggplants. 'Ghostbuster' has small, finger-sized white fruit while 'Long White Streaked' has white and mauve fruit.

RESTRICTING GROWTH FOR AN EARLY HARVEST If your growing season is short, you need to force eggplants into producing flowers as early as possible. To do this, pinch out the growing point once the plant has produced up to five leaves, taking it above the fifth leaf. Soon, the lateral shoots will produce flowers, which you should also pinch out above their fourth leaves. This second pinching out will force the plant to put all its energy into producing fruit, which you will be able to harvest earlier than if the plant was left to grow its own way.

PEPPER POTS Capsicums and chillies need warmth and, in cool and temperate zones, they are planted in spring after any threat of frost has passed. In tropical and subtropical areas, capsicums can be grown year round. Use a foliar feed of dilute seaweed solution and guard against slugs, which love the fruit.
● If you have a balcony or small garden with a warm spot, try a capsicum plant in a 30 cm pot supported by a cane.
● For the largest capsicums grow 'Big Bertha', or try 'Californian Wonder' or 'Canape'.
● Many chillies are cold tolerant and will grow for several seasons. For a small ornamental plant look for 'Thai' chillies with fruit in colours of white, purple and red.

Gardener's Choice

STARS OF THE PEPPER FAMILY

The pepper, can be divided into two types: the sweet (capsicum) type and the hot (chilli) type. The larger sweet capsicums have a milder taste. Grow all types in a warm sunny spot. Water them well in hot weather.

CHERRY PICK 1 This produces small, round fruits, on vigorous, disease-resistant plants.
CORNO DI TORO This is a long chilli which is red or yellow. It is great stuffed, stir-fried or eaten raw.
HABAÑERO A very hot chilli used in curries and other spicy dishes.
JALAPEÑO 2 This long hot chilli is often used on pizzas.
MINIBEL This is a newly developed variety.
PURPLE BEAUTY 3 This capsicum has an unusual deep purple colour and is sweet and juicy straight off the plant.

GARDENING BY THE MOON CALENDAR
According to old-fashioned gardening wisdom, the intensity of the moon's light at different stages in its cycle encourages the germination and growth of plants.
● When the moon is waxing, or growing larger, some gardeners sow and plant species they want to be vigorous. They also gather medicinal herbs, root and fruiting vegetables, including tomatoes, pumpkins, zucchinis and capsicums (below).
● When the moon is waning, they sow and plant those species whose leaves they want to restrict, such as fruiting vegetables. This is because restricted leaves results in larger fruits.

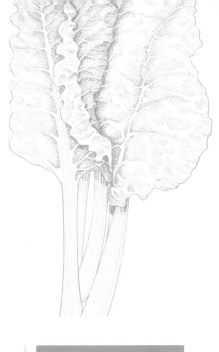

Enjoy vegetables that last year after year

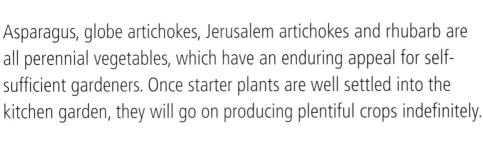

Asparagus, globe artichokes, Jerusalem artichokes and rhubarb are all perennial vegetables, which have an enduring appeal for self-sufficient gardeners. Once starter plants are well settled into the kitchen garden, they will go on producing plentiful crops indefinitely.

Planning for the long term

ASPARAGUS GROWS BEST IN LIGHT, SANDY SOIL Create the ideal environment for asparagus by lightening the soil with non-acid river sand, available at garden centres.

- To plant asparagus in winter or spring, prepare the soil in autumn by digging over and adding compost or well-rotted manure (about 50 kg per 10 square metres) and a complete organic fertiliser (30–40 g per square metre). Remove all weeds because asparagus plants must never have any competition, but do not hoe around them or they will not thrive.
- After harvesting, spread some compost or manure on the bed and cut back old stems to soil level once they turn yellow or brown.

Asparagus is harvested just below ground level when the tips are about 7–10 cm above ground.

CHOOSING THE SEX OF ASPARAGUS Asparagus is a dioecious perennial, that is, the plants can have either male or female flowers. Male plants produce more vigorous shoots, but you'll have to trust your supplier, since the only way to distinguish female plants is by their red berries in summer.

DON'T BUY DRY ROOTS Asparagus roots must be fresh before planting. If you can't plant the roots immediately, cover them with a damp cloth, sacking or sand to preserve them in the interim.

HARVESTING ASPARAGUS The knack to harvesting asparagus is to cut it off at an angle with a sharp knife, just below ground level. Asparagus is ready to harvest in early spring when the tips of the young green shoots are approximately 7–10 cm above the ground.

- Asparagus is best harvested after the plant's second or third year, when the roots of the plant have become well established in the soil. If you start harvesting the shoots too soon, you'll weaken the plant and possibly affect the next year's harvest.

NUTRIENTS FOR ASPARAGUS Asparagus loves sulphur and calcium, so look for fertiliser rich in these nutrients.

START OUT WITH GLOBE ARTICHOKE OFFSHOOTS Nurseries and garden centres sell young artichokes in pots. However, you may be able to find a gardener who grows them and ask for some offshoots during spring. To remove these from the clump, simply separate some of the stronger-looking

PLANTING ASPARAGUS

1 Dig a trench and position a stick every 50 cm to mark the position of each plant. Heap soil around each stick.

2 Place an asparagus root on each mound of soil, making sure it is well spread out over the mound.

3 Fill in the trench with good-quality soil and compost or manure, and earth it up slightly, retaining the sticks to mark the position of the roots.

shoots from the main plant with a garden spade. It is essential that the shoots have rootlets at their base. Cut back the leaves to half their length and plant them immediately, leaving 80 cm between plants.

THE FOREVER FAITHFUL JERUSALEM ARTICHOKE Once planted, Jerusalem artichokes are in the garden for ever. When you harvest them, it is impossible to remove all the tubers, and so some will always stay in the ground, ready to be next year's crop. Jerusalem artichoke plants are relatively tall, growing to 3 m, so it is best to plant them where you have space for a permanent stand. You can make the most of these plants' height and get double value from your plants by using them as a sheltering windbreak in your vegetable garden.

DEPENDABLE PERFORMERS Jerusalem artichokes grow well in most soils and in sun or shade. Plant the tubers in the spring, to a depth of 10–15 cm, and about 30 cm apart. You should be able to harvest them from late autumn through winter.
● Jerusalem artichoke 'Fuseau' has long, white tubers that resemble some potato varieties. 'Dwarf Sunray' produces tubers that do not need to be peeled. You can grow Jerusalem artichoke tubers bought from the fruit and vegetable shop or saved from your own stock if you have grown them previously.

GROW INSTANT RHUBARB Rhubarb can take 12–18 months to reach full production from crowns that are planted in the winter. However, if you want to be able to harvest rhubarb soon after planting, don't buy plants sold in pots at garden centres and nurseries because these will take some years to mature. Instead, in spring, ask a gardening friend who already has an established patch of good-quality rhubarb for some healthy pieces of root with one or two buds for propagation. Dividing the roots of old clumps of rhubarb revives and reinvigorates them, so this will keep everyone happy.

KEEP THEM COOL Rhubarb grows well in a cool, moist soil in a position in full sun or with part shade. Keep the soil cool and moist by using organic mulch and watering regularly. Rhubarb is hardy so it doesn't need protection against frost during winter, even in the coldest regions.

Harvest rhubarb with a twist-and-pull action, discard the leaves and only cook the stems.

HARVESTING YOUR RHUBARB It is easy to harvest rhubarb without breaking the stems by using the following method: twist the stalk slightly and pull it gently.
● If you harvest rhubarb regularly it won't flower. The flowers are not unattractive, but the plant puts all its energy into producing them rather than the leaf stalks.

NEVER EAT RHUBARB LEAVES! Rhubarb leaves are actually poisonous – so never be tempted to eat them.

RED STEMS Rhubarb can have green or red stems but it seems from the reactions of gardeners and rhubarb fanciers that red stems get the thumbs up. The red stems also add colour to the vegetable patch. Red-stem colouring is better in cold-winter gardens, but if you want guaranteed red-stemmed rhubarb, select a red variety such as 'Sydney Crimson' or 'Wandin Winter'. Green stems are safe to eat.
● If your rhubarb is green and you want it to be red, an old-fashioned tip is simply to add a few drops of red food colouring while cooking or better still, add some strawberries.

FLOWERING RHUBARB Rhubarb is a leaf crop so flowering is not encouraged. If, however, flower stalks do appear, cut them off at the base and give your rhubarb clump a dose of high-nitrogen fertiliser as a side dressing or a liquid feed. Increase watering as the plants may be stressed.

Satisfying winter root vegetables

Once upon a time, provident gardeners were judged on the richness of their winter reserves. Given this, it is hardly surprising that the nutritious, delicious and easy-to-store beetroot, carrot and turnip were, and still are, popular mainstays of the kitchen garden.

The winter-hardy beetroot

ROUND OR LONG? The two main varieties of beetroot are globe and long rooted.

● **GLOBE BEETROOT** The familiar round, or globe, beetroot is less prone to bolting than other varieties and can be sown several weeks earlier to provide roots from early summer. 'Boltardy', 'Derwent Globe' and 'Globe' are recommended. For later sowings, which will provide roots for harvesting in the autumn and the early winter months, sow the small-rooted, quick-growing 'Baby'.

● **LONG-ROOTED BEETROOT** These varieties are still quite frequently used today as a main crop. They are matured in the ground before being harvested and stored in early winter. 'Cylindra' is a good long-rooted variety that is easy to prepare for cooking, which can be simply steamed, or it can be pickled.

TRADITIONAL CULTIVATION Beetroot thrives on light soil, but will also grow successfully in most fertile, well-cultivated vegetable garden beds. Sow the seeds thinly in rows that are 30 cm apart. Barely cover the seeds with soil and water them in well. Thin out the seedlings as they develop to a spacing of 15 cm between plants.

● In tropical and subtropical areas, beetroot can be sown all year round, although rot can become a problem during the wet season. In temperate gardens, you can sow between July and March, making successive plantings to stagger the harvest. In colder climates, try to restrict plantings to spring and summer.

Long-rooted beetroot varieties such as 'Cylindra' and 'Forono' are easy to cut, and they produce uniform slices with little wastage.

A HARVEST YOU CAN LEAVE IN THE GROUND Beetroot is grown for harvest any time from early summer right through to early winter, depending on the variety.

● As soon as the roots are large enough to cook, usually after 20 weeks, you can pull early globes whenever you need them.

● Your main crops for winter use can be left in the ground until they are required. In very cold regions you may need to cover them with straw to protect them from frost.

● To store harvested beetroot, cut the tops off the roots, being careful not to cut too

close to the crown or the root will bleed. Open-store them in a cool spot or keep them in the fridge for several weeks.

A VISUAL FEAST If you like very decorative dishes and a touch of originality, grow yellow beetroot, such as 'Golden', or even two-tone beetroot with concentric circles of red and white, such as 'Pink Chioggia'. You'll be able to buy the seeds from most good vegetable seed catalogues. The 'Albina Vereduna' is an unusual white heirloom variety.

Grow carrots for all seasons

A FINE TILTH For the best results possible, grow carrots in light or sandy soils. The soil needs to be carefully prepared before you can sow the seeds. Fork the soil over and rake out all stones and debris that you can find. Also remove any perennial weeds.
● Carrots can develop very long taproots, depending on the variety, and they need to be able to grow uninterrupted, straight down into the soil. If you don't prepare the soil properly, the result will be carrots that are forked or otherwise misshapen.

GET AROUND POORLY DRAINED SOIL
You can get around the problem of heavy or poorly drained soil in your garden beds by growing short or intermediate varieties of carrot in raised beds. Break down the soil with the back of a rake, and then build up long ridges about 10 cm deep and 30–40 cm wide. Sow the carrot seeds, preferably coated as they are so small (see page 187), into their ridges. You may also need to install a leaky hose or drip system for economical watering as these ridged beds dry out very quickly.

Carrots thrive in a friable soil with a fine, uniform texture and no stones or hard lumps.

CARROT SHAPES There are short-rooted, almost round carrots that you can grow in even the smallest spaces, intermediate carrots and long-rooted carrots with tapering roots. Short-rooted carrots are harvested relatively early. They are tender but less productive than the other types.
● Short-rooted carrot varieties (also known as round) include 'Early Chantenay' and 'Mini Round' (also called 'Paris Market'). Short-rooted varieties suit shallow soils and can be harvested as soon as the root reaches 2 cm in length.
● Baby carrots are pulled when finger sized. Look for 'Baby', which is sweet and tender.
● Long-rooted carrot varieties include 'Majestic Red' (an Australian-bred carrot), 'Top Weight' and 'All Seasons', which are disease resistant.
● For a traditional cylindrical carrot look for 'Manchester Table'.

PRE-GERMINATION TREATMENT Cover your carrot seeds with warm water and leave them to soak overnight. If you have a sprouting jar for mung beans, you can use it to 'pre-germinate' the seeds for 48 hours and then sow immediately – don't let them dry out.

If you are running late with your seed sowing, you can soak carrot seeds in warm water to give them a helping hand to germinate.

Carrots come in all shapes and sizes including short-rooted (far left) that are ideal for pots, intermediate (left centre) and long-rooted (left). The growth time varies depending on the size of the carrot. Many reach a good size by about 50 days but need 90–126 days to reach their full size.

TRICK THOSE WEEDS Carrots are slow to germinate and weeds can soon take over the bed. This is why carrots have a reputation for being a 'messy' crop. It can be tricky pulling up weeds without uprooting the carrots.

● There is a partial solution to this problem, which is to make mock sowings. Prepare the soil as if you were going to sow your carrot seeds, but don't actually sow them. Wait for it to rain and for the weeds to come through. As soon as the soil dries out, uproot the young weeds with a rake. Repeat the process a few days later, when the soil is dry, then sow your carrot seeds for real.

SOWING SPARSELY According to an old saying, if you sow seeds thickly you'll harvest sparsely. This is particularly true of carrots, whose fine seeds are difficult to sow evenly in the drill. The ideal spacing would be one seed every 5 cm, but you need to sow more to allow for those that don't germinate.

● To sow sparsely, hold the seed packet fairly high above the drill, which should be about 8 cm wide. As you move slowly along the drill, tap the packet to release the seeds. However, don't do this if it's windy or the seeds will blow all over the garden.

● So that you're not too heavy handed when sowing carrot seeds, mix the quantity of seeds required – 4 g per 10 square metres – with some dried coffee grounds. It is much easier to scatter this relatively bulky and clearly visible mixture in the drill. It is also said to protect the crops from insects.

● Alternatively, mix the seeds with sand and you will also be able to sow the seeds more evenly. You will still have to thin the seedlings to give the plants enough space.

To make the most of the valuable space in your vegetable garden, why not sow fast-cropping radishes with long-growing carrots.

SOW CARROTS WITH ONIONS AND LEEKS Carrots, onions and leeks are all attacked by specific garden pests that are attracted to their host plants by smell. Planting alternate rows of carrots and onions, or leeks, disorientates and discourages pests.

MIX CARROT AND RADISH SEEDS If you sow these crops together then, because radishes germinate much more quickly than carrots, they will mark out the rows for you and enable you to see where you should hoe. You will have harvested the radishes before the carrots need the space.

● You can also mix carrots with aromatic herbs, especially coriander, dill and rosemary. These plants have the advantage of providing a certain degree of protection against pests.

PRECISION WEEDING Removing weeds from a row of carrots is an extremely delicate operation. Old-fashioned gardeners even suggest it is best done with a knitting needle!

FORKED ROOTS Carrots can be deceptive. Their large necks, which look full of promise, may emerge above the soil but, when it's time to lift them, the carrots revealed by your garden fork are often a disappointment because the root has stopped short after a few centimetres and given rise to new taproots. These are known as forked roots.

● The fault lies in the soil. Forked roots are caused by a deeper, compacted layer of soil (the result of working the soil to the same depth each year), by poorly structured soil with hard lumps or by the presence of some partially rotted manure. They can also be caused by insects and other disease-causing parasites. Just make sure you dig the soil more deeply and more thoroughly next year.

GOODBYE, PETER RABBIT Some gardeners have had success in deterring rabbits with the old-fashioned practice of poking matches, head down, into the soil near each carrot.

HARVESTING CARROTS Usually, if you try to pull a carrot by the foliage, you'll end up with the leaves in your hand and the root still firmly in the ground. Before you pull, push the carrot gently into the soil – this enlarges the hole, breaks the rootlets that anchor the root in the soil and makes it easier to pull the carrot up.

1 Wait until the seedlings have two or three true leaves, apart from the cotyledons, before thinning them out.

2 Leave one plant every 5 cm. Save time and energy by pulling up weeds as you thin out the carrots.

3 Old-fashioned tip: use the point of a knitting needle to help in delicate weeding jobs.

Try mixing carrot seeds with sand or ground coffee to make sowing more even.

The roots of carrots can become forked in stony soils or when too much mulch or manure is used.

AN OLD-FASHIONED CLAMP In the past in cold climates, beetroot, carrots, parsnips, potatoes and turnips were stored during the winter months in an outdoor clamp to protect them from the weather. Vegetables had to be retrieved with care and any gaps in the clamp were closed to avoid unbalancing the heap. It was recommended that the heap was opened only at noon so that the sun's rays would prevent that part of the heap from being frozen.

● Alfred Smith, a market gardener in the 19th century, wrote about the traditional construction of a clamp, which was placed high in a sheltered place where the ground was well drained. A shallow pit 30 cm deep and 1.5 m square was dug in the soil and covered with a thick layer of straw. The vegetables were then arranged on the bed in a ridged heap 90–120 cm high. Another layer of straw was placed over the vegetables, at least 30 cm thick, followed by a 30 cm layer of the soil dug from the pit. Funnels of straw were then made in the sides or at the top for ventilation, to prevent rotting.

● Carrots were piled up to form a cone shape, their top ends facing outwards, and covered in sand only, not straw or earth. Potatoes were piled this way, too.

DRYING OUT IS ESSENTIAL Once you've pulled or lifted your carrots, leave them on the surface of the soil for a day or two to ensure that they keep well. This process is known as 'drying out', and it firms up the skins and is essential before they are stored in a clamp or in a cool cellar over the winter. When carrots have been lifted, cut off the foliage just above the neck – the point where it joins the root.

STORING CARROTS IN THE GROUND

The best way to store main-crop carrots is to leave them in the ground over winter. But if the temperature drops below –5°C, they may be damaged by frost. A 5 cm layer of dead leaves or straw, which needs to be held in place with horticultural fleece, offers some degree of protection.

USING CRATES Line a wooden fruit crate with hessian. Remove excess soil from the carrots, taking care not to damage the roots, but do not wash them. Place one layer of carrots into the box, on a generous layer of insulating material: compost, sand, sawdust or leaf mould. Cover with the insulating material and layer again. Store the crate where the temperature will be a constant 0–4°C.

Before long storage, carrots should be left to dry then shaken free of any soil.

DID YOU KNOW?

TO FERTILISE OR NOT TO FERTILISE?
Before you plant out or sow vegetable seeds, the ground needs to be well prepared and well-rotted organic material added. It is preferable to do this soil preparation in autumn, so that the organic matter is broken down in the soil and the nutrients are released, ready for the plants to use next season. If the soil is really well prepared in this way, it is unlikely that you will need to add fertilisers during the growing period.

Root crops don't have the same nutritional needs as salad greens or tomatoes. Although they need nitrogen to promote a good yield and early cropping, too much nitrogen will produce watery roots that don't store well. They also need phosphorus and potassium to promote the build-up of reserves in the root and to help produce good-quality vegetables, as well as the magnesium and trace elements essential for human health.

If you haven't been able to prepare the soil in advance, don't worry, all of these elements are available in commercial organic fertilisers.

STORING ROOT VEGETABLES IN A CRATE

1 Store root vegetables in a cool, damp, frost-free place at 0–4°C. A wooden crate is an ideal storage container for your vegetables.

2 Remove the tops, cover the base of the crate with a layer of sand or sawdust and place the dried-out but unwashed root vegetables on it.

3 Cover the vegetables with a layer of sand or sawdust and make more layers. When the crate is full, seal with an airtight lid.

Nice and spicy radishes

CHOOSE RADISHES FOR A QUICK CROP

The radish, with its colourful skin and white flesh, is one of the spiciest roots you'll find in the kitchen garden. Radish seeds can be sown all year round in most areas but successive sowings from spring to autumn will provide a regular harvest for salads. Seeds sprout in 5–8 days and the delicious peppery radishes can be harvested from 6–8 weeks from sowing. Sow a little and often. If you sow into short rows every fortnight, then you will have a supply of radishes all summer long.
● Radishes are often used as a starter plant for children, who like to see quick results. They also grow well in containers.

COLOURFUL CROP Radishes are white on the inside but their skins can be white ('Long White Icicle'), red ('Salad Crunch'), or red and white ('French Breakfast'). 'Black Spanish Round' has black skin. Radishes are a rich source of calcium, iron and vitamin C.

RIGHT SHAPE, RIGHT DEPTH Although radishes are commonly round or globe-shaped, they can also be tankard-shaped (sometimes called intermediate) or long. The long radishes such as 'Long Scarlet' and 'Long White Icicle' can reach 15 cm in length and need to have well-prepared soil.
● Sow radish seeds in 50–100 cm long rows, 10–15 cm apart at a depth of around 5 mm. Sow evenly to avoid erratic germination.

PROTECT EARLY SOWINGS Radishes dislike root disturbance and need to be sown in situ. In cold climates, those sown early, from August, will need protection. Use a horticultural fleece or a plastic cloche to protect the seedlings from frost.

SUN OR SHADE? Full sun for early and late sowings will mean your radishes do well, but a little shade is needed for those sown in midsummer. Radishes prefer well-drained, light soil, but they should be well watered to grow succulent and tasty roots.

GETTING THE BEST OUT OF RADISHES For juicy well-shaped radishes, sow them in moist soil and water the growing plants well

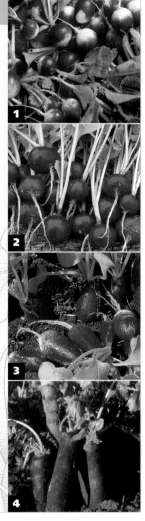

Gardener's Choice

THE LONG AND SHORT OF RADISHES
Grow fast-growing round radishes from spring to summer and use them raw to add extra colour and bite to salad dishes. Long radish can be slower to mature than round, and it may not be harvested until winter – just in time to be cooked and added to hearty winter soups and stews.

ROUND OR GLOBE RADISHES
ROUND RED radishes include 'Sparkler 3' **1** and the tankard-shaped 'French Breakfast', both with a white tip. 'Round Red', 'Scarlet Globe' **2** and 'Salad Crunch' are round red forms that grow reliably. 'Fluo F1' **3** is halfway between long and round and is often called intermediate. 'Gentle Giant' earns its name from its large size (up to 6 cm round) but it has only a delicate, not peppery flavour.

LONG RADISHES
MULTICOLOURED 'Long White Icicle' (white skin), 'Long Black Spanish' (black skin) **4** and 'Long Scarlet' (red skin) develop tapering roots that are up to 15 cm long. 'Easter Egg' has oblong roots in tones of pink, purple or white.
JAPANESE RADISH or daikon is becoming better known by vegetable gardeners. For the best results, sow Japanese radish in spring or autumn. It grows well in cool to temperate climates and the roots can weigh as much as 5 kg or more.

once the seedlings are established. Thin the seedlings to 2 cm to avoid the overcrowding that results in lanky plants.

RADISHES FOR INTERCROPPING AND QUICK CROPPING As radishes mature so quickly, they are particularly useful for intercropping: sowing between other crops while they establish themselves. They are also very useful as quick crops in between plantings of main crops. In midsummer, sow radishes as a quick crop or intercrop – they will benefit from being shaded by the other plants, preventing them from bolting in the heat.

EDIBLE LEAVES It is a shame to discard the leaves of freshly picked young radishes, and it is completely unnecessary, as chopped, fresh young radish leaves make a delicious garnish or salad ingredient. There is even a variety of radish called 'Rat's Tail', which is grown especially for its hot seedpods.

The fast-growing radish makes an ideal quick crop for planting between main crops of slower vegetables.

Old-fashioned salsify, scorzonera and horseradish

SATISFYING SALSIFY, THE OYSTER PLANT
Salsify is a biennial root vegetable that produces attractive mauve flowers, which are also edible. Salsify's roots are long and brownish in colour, with wrinkled skin and a distinctive, delicate flavour that is often compared to oysters or asparagus. It needs an open site and does best on light soils. On heavy clay, it is best to sow into a trench filled with compost or loam. Don't apply manure just before sowing; rather sow into a soil that was manured for a previous crop, as salsify doesn't do well in ground that has been freshly manured.

● Sow the seeds of salsify in situ in spring for an autumn to winter harvest. The roots keep well in the ground, but once they're harvested they should be eaten promptly, because they tend to shrivel quickly.

SCORZONERA, A DRAMATIC ROOT
Scorzonera is an old-fashioned perennial vegetable that is rarely grown by today's vegetable gardeners although it is still a favourite in many Mediterranean countries. It produces smooth, black-skinned roots which can be left in the soil to grow to a larger size for a second season. They are easy to grow; simply sow the seeds into open sites

Scorzonera, although similar to salsify, is fleshier and has a more delicate flavour.

Horseradish is grown for its strongly flavoured root but the young leaves are also tasty.

in sandy soil. If the soil is heavy, trench as you would for salsify. Sow to a depth of 1 cm and thin seedlings to 10 cm.

● When you harvest the roots, take special care not to damage them as they tend to bleed if their skins are broken.

● Look for the variety named 'Russian Giant'.

HORSERADISH, A CLASSIC
The hardy horseradish is grown for its long taproots, which have a pungent, peppery flavour.

● Dig and manure the bed in winter. In late winter or early spring, purchase horseradish roots, known as thongs, about 25 cm long and finger-thick. Plant them vertically so their tops are 5 cm below the surface.

● Lift the roots as required during summer. In winter, lift and store them. To save on storage space, borrow a technique from old-time gardeners and lift a root from the winter garden, cut off a piece to use, then replace the root in the soil for another day.

● The long roots are difficult to eradicate, so horseradish should be grown as a perennial in a corner where it can be left undisturbed, or dug up each year and replanted in spring.

● A traditional way of controlling invasive horseradish plants and coaxing them into putting down long, straight roots is to plant them in galvanised drainage pipes. Sink the pipe up to the rim in a deep hole. Fill it with compost-rich soil, insert the horseradish, gently firm down and water thoroughly.

Turnips, parsnips and swedes – the old stand-bys

A TRADITIONAL WINTER CROP Turnips were once grown only as winter vegetables, but today you can sow fast-maturing types, such as 'Purple Top Milan' and 'Snowball', which you can eat as soon as they reach a suitable size, normally in around 50 days. However, turnips are easiest to grow if they are sown in late summer or early autumn, to grow throughout the winter. In some cold areas turnips can be sown in spring.
● Later-maturing types such as 'Green Globe' can be stored to eat over winter. Crops can be harvested most of the year.

TEMPTING TURNIPS The fleshy white roots of the turnip have a delicate mustard flavour. The leaves are also used as a green vegetable and their young shoots, when blanched, can be eaten. Grow quickly and, except for the winter-cropping varieties, they can be a quick crop, grown between plantings of longer-growing vegetables.

CHOOSE YOUR SHAPE Turnips come in globular, flattened and long-rooted types.
● 'Aramis' and 'Model White' are flat-rooted varieties suitable as an early crop.
● For summer crops, the globular 'Snowball' or 'Tokyo Cross' are recommended.
● 'Gilfeather' is pure white. 'White Globe' is a white, ball-shaped turnip with a deep rim of red at the top.
● For a winter crop, choose the globular 'Golden Ball', which has sweet yellow flesh and particularly hard roots that store well.

STARTING EARLY In cold climates sow turnips in cell trays in a sheltered spot in late winter. Once all threat of frost has passed, transplant into rows 25 cm apart, spacing plants 10 cm apart. In frost-free climates, sow the seeds directly where they are to grow.
● For autumn to winter storage, sow seeds in rows in mid to late summer, 30 cm apart, then reduce this to 15 cm. Sow seeds in succession every 21 days.
● Turnips grow well in light, fertile, well-manured soil. Bury the manure deeply or the roots may fork and have an earthy flavour.

TURNIPS NEED LOTS OF WATER Turnips need regular water throughout their growing season or their centres become woody. In dry seasons remember to water them well. Lack of moisture later in the season, especially for midsummer-sown turnips, can result in stunted, woody plants, bolting and pests.

THE SWEDE, A CHUNKY VEGETABLE The swede is a winter-hardy crop grown for its sweet yellow flesh. It stores well over winter. Sow seeds in spring to a depth of 2 cm and thin out to 25 cm.
● An open, sunny site in light, well-drained, fertile soil suits this root crop, with regular watering. 'Champion Purple Top' is reliable.
● The swede's bad reputation is totally unjustified, probably a legacy of its overuse in rationing during World War II. This hardy vegetable, which matures in 3–4 months and is exceptionally trouble free to grow, deserves its place in our kitchens and in our vegetable gardens.

PARSNIPS IN THE WILD In its natural state, parsnips are part of the flora of Europe. Before carrots and potatoes took over vegetable gardens in the 19th century, the parsnip was the main root vegetable eaten and was mainly used in soups. Its long ivory roots are tender and full of flavour.
● There are several good varieties to grow that are canker resistant. Tried and tested favourites include 'Gladiator', 'Hollow Crown Improved', which has been grown since 1820, and 'Tender and True'.

TOP TIPS FOR GROWING PARSNIPS Parsnips do best in sunny, open sites and, although light soil is best for root formation, they will grow in heavy soils as well. Prepare the soil ahead of planting.
● **SOW THINLY** Sow parsnip seeds from winter to late summer (in tropical areas, sow in the dry season). Sow groups of two to four seeds to a depth of 2 cm. They are slow to germinate, but when necessary, thin out the seedlings leaving 15–20 cm between plants, depending on the size of roots required.
● **AVOID DROUGHT** During the growing season keep weeds under control and water in dry periods or the roots will split.
● **HARVEST TIPS** Parsnips take 18–20 weeks to mature and can be harvested over many months. As a root vegetable, parsnips can be stored in the soil, particularly over winter.

'White Globe' is a popular ball-shaped turnip variety with a purple-rimmed top.

'Golden Ball' is a winter-crop turnip with sweet-tasting yellow flesh that stores well.

The old-fashioned parsnip is a favourite to accompany a traditional Sunday roast.

In frost-prone areas, the arrival of the first frosts damages the foliage but is said to improve the flavour of the parsnips.

● **LEAVE YOUR PARSNIPS IN THE GROUND** Parsnips can be left in the ground, in whatever weather, as this is where they will keep best. Alternatively, store them in the fridge.

KOHLRABI – NOT EXACTLY A TURNIP

The kohlrabi, or turnip cabbage, is a member of the cabbage family and produces a swollen, edible stem. Although it is not a root vegetable, it has a similar taste and use to the turnip, but is easier to grow. It is also drought tolerant. So long as the soil is well manured, with a high pH level to lessen the likelihood of club root, kohlrabi will grow equally well in either sandy or heavy soil.

AN EARLY DEVELOPER Kohlrabi is the vegetable to plant into your vegetable garden in late summer or autumn as your summer crops are removed. In cool climates, it can also be sown in early spring but these seedlings will bolt if soil temperatures are below 10°C. Seeds are directly sown and harvested within 8–10 weeks. The roots are ideal for autumn soups and stews, so don't grow kohlrabi too early in the season or it will develop too rapidly – before the soup season.

Gardener's Choice

KOHLRABI

One of the lesser-known vegetables, kohlrabi comes in a wide range of varieties, both classic and new. If you happen to come across seeds for 'Superschmelz', don't miss this great opportunity to grow some truly phenomenal vegetables. This variety has huge globes, which reportedly weigh as much as 20 kg.

LANRO This is a new strain of the classic 'White Vienna' **1**, and as such is still one of the most reliable varieties of kohlrabi.
PURPLE VIENNA 2 This is another reliable classic, as is 'Purple Globe'.

● Sow heavily and thin out rather than transplanting, to avoid root damage. Prick out when the plants have a few leaves, and space them at 25 cm between each plant.
● Harvest as soon as globes are well formed so you can enjoy them while tender. If left, they become hollow and fibrous, and split.
● A useful tip: earthing up slightly as the globes begin to form will keep them tender.

HAMBURG PARSLEY This parsley has roots that look and taste similar to parsnip. It has smaller roots, but the foliage stays on the plant throughout winter and can be used as a parsley substitute.
● Hamburg parsley grows well in full sun in light or heavy soils. Sow seeds during spring and summer, to a depth of 2 cm and thin out the seedlings to 15–20 cm.
● Harvest the roots from the end of summer as and when you need them. Store them over winter in the ground or in crates of sand.

Celery-flavoured celeriac

CELERIAC NEEDS AN INTRODUCTION

Celeriac has long been popular in Europe, but is increasingly grown in our own backyard, where it contributes admirably to the traditional self-sufficiency of the winter kitchen garden. Celeriac is cultivated for its thick roots, which are used as an autumn or winter vegetable. The plant resembles celery, but at ground level it develops a swollen root similar to a turnip. Apart from the edible roots, which have a celery flavour, the leaves can also be used fresh for flavouring.

CELERIAC PREFERS AN OPEN SUNNY SITE Plant seedlings in fertile soil and water copiously during the growing season. You can leave mature plants in the ground to harvest as you need them.

LOOKING AFTER CELERIAC For large celeriac with a good shape, give the plants plenty of room, with rows 45 cm apart and plants spaced at 30 cm. Remove any faded lower leaves to expose the top of the stem, and use a knife to cut off any rootlets that develop above the surface of the soil. A good variety to choose is 'Snow White'.

DID YOU KNOW?

A LONG GROWING SEASON FOR CELERIAC
Expect celeriac to have a growing season of at least 26 weeks from sowing, in order to produce good-sized roots. This means it should ideally be started out under glass, if the winter is cold. Germination can be slow and erratic, so keep an eye on seed trays. In cooler climates, sow into a heated propagator in late winter or early spring. When the seedlings are large enough to prick out, move them on into 8 cm pots. Harden them off when all danger of frost is past and weather is uniformly warm. Sudden drops in temperature cause the plants to bolt. Plant out in later spring or early summer.

To help the celeriac develop a good shape, remove its lower leaves (above top) and cut away any rootlets that are above soil level (above).

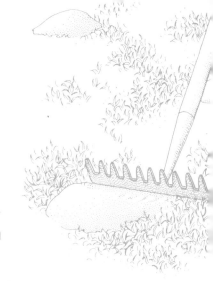

Easy-growing bulbs, stalks and tubers

Yesterday's gardeners depended on their vegetable patch for survival. They paid particular attention to vegetable crops that could be grown or harvested and stored through the colder months, such as onion, garlic, shallots, celery and that old favourite, the potato.

The aromatic onion, garlic and shallot

FOR BEST RESULTS Garlic, onion and shallot bulbs are easy to grow, and you can produce good yields from year to year if you follow a good rotation system. Allow a gap of 2–3 years before you grow any other member of the onion family on the same piece of ground. Rotation lessens the likelihood of a build-up in the soil of pests and diseases that affect these bulbs, which means the plants will be healthy and your harvest from them successful.

PREPARE THE SOIL WELL IN ADVANCE If you add manure to the bed destined for onions too close to planting time, the bulbs are likely to rot off in the ground. And if they do grow, they probably won't be very good for keeping. Avoid planting onions in soil that is high in nitrogen, which promotes leaf growth at the expense of the bulb.

SECRETS OF SUCCESSFUL PLANTING Garlic, onions and shallots are all planted in the same way. Hold the bulb between your thumb and first two fingers and push it into soil that has been well broken down, so that the point is uppermost and slightly lower than soil level. This will protect the bulbs from birds that might pull them out.
● Sometimes the bulbs are pushed out of the soil by the developing roots a few days after planting. Prevent this by planting each bulb

in a narrow but fairly deep hole made with your finger or a dibber. If the bulbs are pushed out of place, they will need to be repositioned, otherwise the roots will grow sideways rather than downwards.
● You can buy garlic, onion and shallot sets for planting from your garden centre. Just remember to choose plump, healthy sets.

KNOW YOUR ONIONS Onions can usually be grown in most areas, particularly throughout winter. Onion varieties are known by the maturing times, which relate to the length of day, or the amount of sunshine, they need to induce bulb formation. This is important because sowing the wrong variety of onion at the wrong time may lead to bolting rather than to bulb formation. Always sow Early Season varieties first, followed in succession by later-maturing varieties.

After lifting onions, leave them to dry on the ground for a few days before bringing them indoors for storage. This drying process firms the outer skins, which helps them keep.

For successful planting, use a dibber to prepare a deep planting hole for garlic.

Harvest onions when the tops bend over and die back. Leave the foliage to yellow.

1 The foliage and heads of the garlic must be completely dry. Start with three heads and plait their foliage together.

2 Introduce new heads as the plait lengthens, so that the new foliage continues where the previous foliage ends.

3 Continue to plait until you reach the required length, then tidy up any loose ends.

4 Hang your garlic plait in a cool, dry place. This will keep you supplied with garlic for an entire season.

● **EARLY SEASON** (also called Short Day) Sow from February to May in tropical and subtropical areas. In temperate climates sow in autumn and in cold climates sow these onions in late autumn. Varieties include 'Early Barletta', 'Gladalan', 'Hunter River Red' and 'Hunter River White'.

● **MIDSEASON** (also called Intermediate) Sow in temperate and cool areas in early to midwinter. Varieties include 'Sweet Red'.

● **LATE MATURING** (Long Day) Suitable for cool, southerly areas only and sown in late winter to early spring. These late-maturing varieties have the best keeping ability. Varieties include 'Creamgold' (also called 'Pukekhoe'), 'Mild Red Odourless', which is an heirloom variety, and 'Spanish Red'.

PLANTING ONIONS Onions are grown from seeds or from small onion bulbs called sets. Sets speed up harvest times to around 12 weeks from planting and can be sown in spring. Seeds can be started in seed trays or direct-sown, which reduces double handling by cutting out the transplanting stage.

● Onion seeds are sown at a depth of 5 mm with plants thinned to 10 cm apart. Space rows 20–30 cm apart. Keep well weeded.

● 'Shallot Salad Onions' is a variety grown for its leaves only. It can be sown all the year round and harvested in 8 weeks.

WHEN THE LEAVES COLLAPSE, THE ONION BULBS CONTINUE TO SWELL

As onions reach the end of their growing cycle, the necks appear to collapse and fold over the bulb, sideways. They will also begin to turn yellow and dry off. All plants should do this at about the same time, to ensure uniform harvesting. If they collapse late, you can give nature a helping hand by gently drawing a rake – prongs upwards – across the onion bed, or fold the necks sideways by hand. Leave the onions in the soil to mature.

WHEN TO HARVEST Harvest garlic, onions and shallots when the foliage has all turned yellow, and when the weather is sunny and dry. Don't remove the foliage: when it has dried out completely, the bulbs can be stored in crates in a cool, dry place. Alternatively, you can plait the dead foliage and make a string, or store the bulbs in clean cut-off old stockings or pantihose – simply tie a knot between each bulb to prevent contact and hang them for the winter.

● Before harvesting garlic, some gardeners suggest that you tie a knot in the green stems. The theory goes that, deprived of sap, the leaves will dry out more quickly and force the bulbs to swell. If you do this take care not to break the stems.

TASTY VARIETIES OF ONION AND GARLIC

ONIONS 'Ailsa Craig' and 'Brown Spanish' are globe-shaped brown onions. 'Creamgold' ('Pukekhoe') is a globe-shaped white onion that is available as seeds or sets. 'Red Shine' forms attractive red onions.

SPRING ONIONS (*Allium fistulosum*) 'Antilla Red' is a red multi-stalked cultivar for harvesting as required. 'Evergreen Long White Bunching' produces many stems from each plant. 'Straightleaf' is an upright variety.

PICKLING ONIONS 'Pearl Picker' is a white early onion that is suited to pickling when sown at 1 cm apart. Don't thin these onions.

SHALLOTS 'Matador' keeps well. It forms globe-shaped bulbs, with a red skin and pale pink flesh.

GARLIC 'Cristo' is a classic French variety, with pink cloves. 'Elephant' garlic is the biggest bulb of them all. It grows up to 10 cm across and produces juicy cloves with a mild sweet flavour. 'French' garlic has a strong flavour. 'New Zealand Purple' garlic has rosy red skin.

There are actually quite a few varieties of garlic. Pictured here are 'Thermidrome' garlic (left), 'Sultop' (centre) and the large 'Elephant' garlic (right), which is also sold as Russian garlic.

THE SECRETS OF SHALLOTS As these onion-like plants (also called eschalots) don't form a large bulb, they're one of the quickest and easiest onion-type crops to successfully grow. To add an onion flavour to food, harvest and chop the leaves of shallots – without waiting for the bulbs to mature.
● Shallot seeds are planted in spring, while small bulbs or sets are best planted in autumn.

GROW YOUR OWN PERFECT GARLIC
In autumn or early spring, plant cloves of garlic straight into the ground, spacing them about 10 cm apart.
● When planting cloves of garlic, make sure you use the largest cloves on the outside of the head. This will give the best results as those on the inside tend to be less successful.
● If you leave two or three heads of garlic in the ground when harvesting, you can use cloves from these for your new garlic crop. Plant them individually when they begin to produce little green shoots. As they already have roots, they will grow quickly.
● Beware: some garlic heads imported from overseas may be treated to stop or to inhibit sprouting and are unsuited to planting.

PREVENTING ROT Garlic is prone to rot in damp soil. Avoid this by planting into light, sandy soil. Some traditional gardeners used to space the rows widely to 30–40 cm. Once the cloves start to shoot, use a hoe to clear some of the soil from around the bulbs.

Leek, fennel and celery

ENJOY LEEKS THROUGH THE YEAR
In cool and temperate climates, successive sowings of leeks every 4–6 weeks will provide you with leeks that are ready to harvest for much of the year. They are not a crop for impatient gardeners because, like onions, they take many weeks to mature. They are, however, worth the wait and are particularly useful in autumn and winter. Leeks will flower and set seed in their second spring.
● In tropical and subtropical gardens, grow leeks in late summer to take advantage of the cool, drier times of the year.
● In temperate and cool gardens, leeks can be sown from spring to autumn.

NAMED VARIETIES In colder parts of the world leeks can take months before they reach maturity and can be planted as early, midseason and late varieties. There isn't such a large range of varieties available in this country because leeks grow readily in our warmer climates. Named garden varieties include 'Jumbo' and 'Welsh Wonder', which produce thick, white stems. 'Welsh Wonder' is fast growing and immature stems that have grown to around 2 cm across can be harvested 12–14 weeks from planting. 'Elephant' is a tall-growing heirloom variety with blue foliage and thick stems. It takes around 20 weeks to reach harvest but produces a stem that's a weighty 6 cm in diameter.
● **BONUS CROP** Some leeks form small off-sets at the base of the stem called 'pearls'. If transplanted with care these 'pearls' will grow into a bonus crop.

A TOUCH OF WHIMSY Some gardeners protect their leeks against stem and bulb eelworm by using eggshells turned upside-down on sticks inserted along the rows of leeks. Whether the eelworm moth is disorientated by these strange objects is difficult to say, but they do seem to work.

FOR SNOWY WHITE LEEKS Plant leeks deeply if you want them to be really white. Use a hoe to make a furrow 5 cm deep in a 30 cm deep trench that has been prepared with well-rotted manure. Then plant young leeks using a dibber pushed into the soil as

Leeks are a useful crop that earns its place in any vegetable garden. By growing many different varieties, you can harvest them all year round for constant use in your kitchen.

Using upside-down eggshells is said to protect leeks against stem and bulb eelworm.

PLANTING OUT YOUNG LEEKS

1 Leeks are ready to plant out when they have reached about the size of a pencil. Snip off part of the green foliage, which will reduce the plant to about 20 cm long.

2 Make a hole with a dibber and then plant the leeks so that 10 cm, or about half their length, is in the ground.

3 Water into the planting hole formed by the dibber, leaving the leeks to find their own level. Check them daily while they're establishing, and replant any that birds pull out.

far as possible. About 1 month after planting, draw 3–5 cm of the soil back into the trench and around the stems.

● Repeat this process each month until there is a ridge of soil on either side of the stems that reaches just below the base of the leaves. Tie collars made from corrugated cardboard around the stems before earthing up, which will keep grit off the leeks.

● When you hoe off weeds, leave the dead weeds in the furrow to cover the leek stems. They will rot down when covered by the soil in the ridge as it is built up, and will help to 'blanch' the leeks as they grow.

TIPS FOR GROWING GREAT LEEKS
The keys to success with leeks are regular watering, good drainage and generous feeding. Apply either a side dressing of a high-nitrogen fertiliser or water over the young leek plants with a liquid fertiliser every 2–3 weeks and keep them clear of weeds.

● Because they grow in winter, you can plant leeks where early peas and salad crops have already been harvested.

SOME BENEFICIAL ASSOCIATIONS
Many old-fashioned gardeners knew, from much trial and error, that there were good and bad combinations of vegetables to plant in the vegetable patch. For example, some associations that appear to be very mutually beneficial are leeks with any one of the following vegetables: carrots, celery, corn salad, fennel, onions and tomatoes. These pairings seem to work because the plants need the same nutrients and sometimes protect each other against predators.

Harvest the mature fennel bulbs in the autumn. However, the leaves can be picked during the summer to add to salads or meat dishes.

FAITHFUL STAND-BY Leeks are very hardy vegetables and they will sit steadfastly in the ground throughout autumn and winter, hardly growing but not deteriorating as long as the temperature stays cold. Leave them in the ground and lift as required.

FLORENCE FENNEL NEEDS THE SUN
Sow the annual Florence, or globe, fennel in spring to early summer into a sunny spot with well-drained soil. Thin seedlings out so they are spaced 30 cm apart. Fennel needs regular watering during its growing period, and if you earth up the soil as the plants begin to fatten up, the resulting bulbs will be whiter and more tender.

● Choose annual fennel for its squat, bulbous edible stems and sweet, tender leaves, rather than the tall perennial kind, which is often found in the herb garden.

A DIFFICULT NEIGHBOUR Probably due to its powerful aroma, fennel is particularly aggressive when grown next to a number of other vegetables. Apparently, only celery and leeks are able to live in the same vicinity.

FIT AND READY FOR THE HARVEST
Fennel will be ready to harvest in early to late autumn. Cut the bulb off the stem at ground level, and if you are lucky some flavoursome shoots will regrow from the stump. If you notice that the bulb is beginning to elongate, harvest at once. This is a sign of bolting, which means that the plants will go to seed and the edible parts will be too tough to eat. There are a number of bolt-resistant varieties becoming more available, including 'Argo', 'Amigo F1' and 'Zefa Fino'.

EASY-TO-GROW CELERY Celery is a delicious stem that needs blanching, though you can also find self-blanching or green celery. It needs a sunny site and a well-prepared

Improve celery's taste and tenderness by blanching it. Wrap the stems in newspaper or cardboard and mound up the earth around it.

loam soil. Celery seeds should be sown into punnets or trays and either transplanted into blocks in the vegetable garden or into pots to be grown on to a larger size before planting out. 'Greencrunch' and 'Stringless' are popular stringless varieties. Stems can be harvested as needed.

● Celery grows best in cool to mild climates where it is planted in spring. Keep the shallow roots well watered throughout summer.

● In warmer areas start celery in late summer or autumn to grow through the winter.

BLANCHING CELERY Once the stems are growing well you need to earth the plants up, or enclose each plant with a tube of cardboard. This keeps the stems clean and blanches them at the same time.

● Self-blanching varieties include 'Golden Self-Blanching', 'Greensleeves' and 'Lathom Self-Blanching'. They are all ready for harvest from late summer to autumn.

● If you have sown self-blanching celery, make sure you space the plants 25 cm apart. Trenching varieties need 20–25 cm spacing between the plants.

WHY BOTHER TO BLANCH? The purpose of blanching is to tenderise and sweeten a plant's edible parts. Plants that are naturally bitter when grown in full light are usually more palatable when light is restricted.

Storing and eating potatoes through the year

POTATOES FOR REPLANTING? You can always replant small potatoes from last year's crop, to give you next year's crop, but there is no guarantee that the new crop will be disease free – they may have been contaminated by a virus or they could be carrying blight spores. A much more reliable option is to buy seed potatoes that are certified as disease free – look for this on the label. You can also buy seed potatoes in cheaper, larger quantities.

GROWING POTATOES Versatile potatoes can be grown in all climates if you select the optimum planting times.

Potatoes and runner beans happily grow together. They have similar soil requirements and like the same positioning in the vegetable garden.

● **TROPICAL TO SUBTROPICAL** In warm, frost-free gardens grow potatoes year round. However, the optimum months for planting are January to August to avoid the wet season.

● **TEMPERATE** Enjoy two crops a year by planting in late winter for a spring crop and planting in late summer for an autumn crop.

● **COLD AND FROSTY GARDENS** Plant from August to December to avoid the cold and frosty winter conditions.

CHITTING THE POTATOES Potatoes naturally produce sprouts, or chits, and these produce the new plants. Place your seed potatoes in a box or tray in a light and frost-free room to chit them. The sprouts should be short and firm. Several sprouts may develop on each tuber; some gardeners suggest you remove all but three.

● Try sprouting your seed potatoes in an old egg carton. Set them fattest-end-up, as this end produces the best sprouts.

NATURAL DIEBACK OF FOLIAGE
Potatoes will come into flower as the tubers ripen. Soon after, you will notice that the foliage begins to turn yellow and drop off. This is a natural process, and you should leave it until you are ready to harvest the tubers from the ground.

● To harvest new potatoes, burrow under the plant 3–4 weeks after flowering as the lower leaves begin to yellow.

A NOURISHING SEAWEED MULCH
Seaside gardeners have long valued seaweed as a mulch and feed for potatoes. For a

1 Plant potatoes to a spade's depth of 30 cm, leaving 50 cm between plants in all directions. Cover the tubers.

2 When the foliage appears, heap the earth around the base of the plant so that it hides the stems and forms a mound from which the leaves emerge.

3 Continue to earth up along the entire row. This enables the tubers to form in a compact cluster and protects them from early-season frosts.

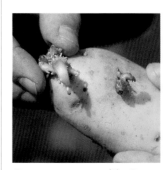

Potatoes sprout readily. On each tuber, several sprouts or 'chits' may develop, but it is best to remove all but three.

trouble-free potato patch, fill your trench with seaweed, plant up the potatoes and then cover with another 15–20 cm of seaweed.

THE POTATO HARVEST Lift potatoes in fine weather and leave them on top of the soil for 24 hours to harden the skins. If you have to harvest in rain, keep them in a dark but warm, well-ventilated place for a few days, letting them dry out properly. Don't store any that are damaged or blemished.
● Take care when digging potatoes as cuts or bruises made to the tubers can develop rots such as gangrene, which destroys the potato or reduces its storage time.

USE THE BEST TOOL FOR THE JOB The potato hook, or Canterbury hoe, with two long, slightly curved prongs, is much better suited to lifting potatoes than the garden fork. If you stand at right angles to the row, you can sink the prongs beneath each plant with a single blow. Then all you have to do is pull on the handle of the hoe and any stems above the surface of the soil.

SAFE STORAGE You can transfer your potato harvest to the basement, shed or storeroom, if it is frost-free and dark. A root cellar was a popular old-fashioned place for storing root crops, potatoes and apples.
● Potatoes must not be exposed to light. If they are, they will turn green and build up a bitter and toxic alkaloid known as solanine. Store them in wooden crates or sacks. Avoid storing potatoes in plastic, which will make them sweat and rot.

PREVENTING POTATO BLIGHT There is no miracle cure for potato blight which, if the season is wet, can ruin the whole crop.
● If your garden is in a region with wet summers, then make sure you choose a potato variety that is blight resistant.
● Use only well-rotted manure on potato beds as new manure will encourage disease.
● Spray plants with Bordeaux mixture or a copper oxychloride base in an organic culture. Carry out the first treatment when plants reach a height of 30 cm and then spray every 2–3 weeks, or every 10 days in very wet weather.
● If symptoms appear, remove the badly affected foliage to prevent contamination of the tubers. Dispose of the affected foliage, but do not put it on the compost heap.

NOT A TRUE POTATO The sweet potato, a close relative of convolvulus, grows as a sprawling vine. It needs a warm, frost-free climate to crop. To get started in spring, buy sweet potato tubers and let them sprout as for potatoes. Cut the tubers into small chunks for planting. Alternatively, plants can be grown from cutting. Sweet potatoes enjoy the same soil preparation as potatoes but, as they are trailing plants, need room to spread. Place sprouts or cuttings 50 cm apart in rows 100 cm apart.
● Harvest when the vine begins to yellow (usually in autumn). Leave the tubers to cure in the sun before storage.

The sweet potato, a close relative of the morning glory, grows as a sprawling vine.

Know your potatoes

Potatoes have interesting skin colours and some have unusual flesh colours, ranging from white to yellow and even purple. Different potato varieties also have different keeping abilities and perform differently when cooked. To distinguish between them, varieties are broadly classified as all-purpose, waxy or floury. All-purpose potatoes can be cooked as desired, waxy varieties are ideal for baking, chip making and in potato salads, while floury varieties are good for mashing. Many are now available commercially and are sold by name in fruit and vegetable shops and in the vegetable section of the supermarket. Look for named potato varieties to grow in your garden.

VARIETY	COOKING	COMMENTS
Bison	All-purpose	Red skin, white flesh
Coliban	All-purpose	White skin and flesh
Crystal	All-purpose	White skin and flesh, good in pots or small spaces
Desiree **1**	Waxy (not for frying)	Pink skin and yellow flesh, high yielding
Kennebec	Waxy (good for chips)	White skin and flesh, large, grown commercially
King Edward	All-purpose/waxy	Old favourite, pear-shaped, available for gardens
Kipfler	Waxy (dry texture)	Finger-sized, pale yellow flesh, gourmet potato
Nicola	Floury (good for mashing)	Yellow flesh, good disease resistance
Otway Red	All-purpose	Australian variety with red skin
Pink Eye	Waxy	Cream flesh, some pink, prolific, good garden form
Pink Fir Apple **2**	Waxy (good in salads)	Heirloom variety, long tubers, pink skin, yellow flesh
Pontiac	All-purpose (not for frying)	Red skin, commercially grown, early maturing
Sebago	All-purpose	Grown widely commercially, white flesh, high yield
Shine	All-purpose	Australian bred, quick growing
Spunta	All-purpose	Prolific, good backyard choice
Toolangi Delight	All-purpose (good for chips)	Purple skin, white flesh, gourmet potato

Protecting your vegetable crops

The main enemies of growing vegetables are winter frosts, cold spring temperatures and summer drought. Over the centuries, gardeners have learned to deal with these threats by finding ways to protect the soil and their vegetables from inclement weather.

Covering the soil

A TRADITIONAL MULCH Past gardeners used mulch made partially of rotted manure. It is easy to break down and ideal for mulching. A thin layer spread over a seedbed will promote germination by helping the soil retain moisture. A slightly thicker layer helps recently planted cabbages, celery, eggplants, leeks and strawberries to establish.

TOP TIPS FOR EFFECTIVE MULCHES
Anything that covers soil and protects it from light and heat can be used as a mulch. Lots of materials make ideal mulches and are free. They all reduce the evaporation of moisture and keep the weeds down.
● **GRASS CLIPPINGS** Clippings can be spread on the ground once they've dried out or been composted. Spread thinly, even if it means renewing regularly – you should still be able to see the soil. If the layer is too thick this mulch tends to form compact lumps that will eventually go mouldy and attract slugs.
● **FLAT STONES** These make good mulch and allow you to walk on them freely. Used around trailing vegetables such as pumpkins, they help prevent rotting on cool, damp soil.
● **PAPER AND CARDBOARD** Newspaper that is folded in half or in quarters and corrugated cardboard, with sticky tape and staples removed, make a practical mulch for widely spaced vegetables. Cover with a scattering of dried grass for a more pleasing aesthetic effect.
● **SUGAR CANE, LUCERNE AND PEA STRAW** Depending on where you live, local organic mulches are an excellent choice to protect and improve the soil in your vegetable plot.

Dried grass cuttings make an economical and effective mulch, as long as there are no weed seeds.

● **FOREST BARK** Tree bark is a very popular mulch in the ornamental garden, but is not really very suitable for a vegetable garden, except when it is used for pathways and strawberry beds, because strawberries like its acidity and the drainage it provides. If you do use bark as a mulch, it's a good idea to select composted fine forms, not chips, as these can debilitate the soil. Add fertiliser to the soil when you dig it over for another crop and it will improve the structure.

RETAINING MOISTURE Mulching helps to prevent the moisture in the soil from evaporating. The best time to mulch is in spring, when the soil is warm but still moist, and any time after it rains. However, never mulch when the soil is dry, because all this will do is prevent the rain getting through and just keep the ground dry.

Give protection from the weather

CLOCHES TO KEEP OUT FROSTS AND COLD WIND In cold or variable climates, use these transparent covers to protect seeds that have been sown in situ, cuttings and young plants from rain, cold snaps and frost. They also maintain moisture in dry spells. Place them in position about 1 week before sowing and planting to warm up the soil, and use them to overwinter hardy crops, such as lettuces and carrots.

PROVIDE LIVING SHADE AND SHELTER A living screen of sunflowers growing along the western side of your vegetable patch will protect vulnerable crops such as lettuces from sun and wind damage by providing late afternoon summer shade. Sunflowers also add a cheery, old-fashioned cottage-garden feel to your garden. When the seed heads mature they can be fed to the birds.

PRACTICAL POLYTUNNELS If you don't have the time to be on permanent 'cloche duty', a polytunnel – like the ones used by commercial growers – will protect seeds that are sown in situ and early seedlings from the last frosts. These tunnels consist of plastic sheeting, which is stretched over a framework of metal hoops. The ambient temperature under polytunnels is more moderate and easier to regulate than in cloches.
- A polytunnel can also be used to hasten the ripening of strawberries. Remove it as soon as external temperatures are high enough or your crops are well established.

USE COLD FRAMES FOR SMALL-SCALE GREENHOUSE GARDENING A cold frame was an indispensable item in our grandparents' gardens. It consists of a wooden frame that covers a piece of ground, and is lower at the front than at the back, plus a glass cover. It is ideal for germinating seedlings such as cabbages and lettuces, which are then pricked out into their final positions. A cold frame is also a good home for young plants pricked out for the first time

KEEP YOUR VEGETABLES FROM DRYING OUT Newly pricked-out plants such as artichokes, beetroot, cabbages, lettuces and

Tall plants, such as sunflowers, make a living screen for shade and shelter for vegetables.

tomatoes are particularly susceptible to being dried out by the sun and cold winds in spring. Protect them by floating over a layer of horticultural fleece, which acts as a barrier.
- Alternatively use shadecloth vertically to shade new plantings from the heat of the afternoon sun. Remove the barrier when the plants are well established, in cool and temperate climates, but in hot zones, leave it in place to continue protecting your crop.
- In most climates gardeners are advised to remove lateral branches on tomatoes but in very hot-summer climates, the extra leafy growth should be allowed to grow to shade the crop and protect it from sun scorch.

MAKING A COLD FRAME FROM AN OLD WINDOW

1 Remove the parts you don't need – bolts, weatherboard, handles, hinges – and give the frame a coat of paint.

2 Fix metal handles to an outside edge – you will be able to use this to open and close the lid.

3 Make a bottomless rectangular frame, lower at the front than the back, and the same size as the window.

4 Treat the frame with wood preservative to prevent the wood from rotting, and then give it a coat of paint.

5 Attach the window to the frame, ideally using hinges as this will make the structure more solid.

6 Place your cold frame in a north-facing position so that the sun can warm up the plants inside.

Fresh herbs at your fingertips

Imagine an old-fashioned garden and you will most likely picture a sunny bed of herbs. Growing these aromatic plants, which have always been highly prized for their culinary and medicinal qualities, has a long and ancient tradition we still value today. Fortunately, herbs are very easy to grow and positively thrive in poor, dry soils.

Herbs to sow annually

DILL AND CARROTS MAKE VERY GOOD PARTNERS Dill is an aromatic annual that is ideal for sowing among carrots (one or two seeds per 1 m along a row) as it is said to act as a deterrent to carrot fly.
● Its aromatic summer leaves add flavour to omelettes and fish dishes, especially salmon.

BASIL COMES IN UNUSUAL VARIETIES
Basil is a highly aromatic herb. It is grown as an annual in most gardens. Most people know the large, floppy foliage of lettuce-leaf basil but there are many other varieties to choose from, such as 'Dark Opal', which has purple leaves. Basil is useful in salads as well as in cooked dishes.
● If you get the chance, try planting anise basil, bush basil, which has masses of tiny leaves, cinnamon basil and lemon basil. Add

Pinch or snip out tips to encourage bushy plants in the garden or in a pot on the windowsill.

a touch of purple to the vegetable garden and your cooking with one of the purple basils such as 'Purple Ruffles'.
● Cut out the growing tip of the basil shoot to encourage the plant to bush out.

NASTURTIUM An easy-going plant for the flower garden, nasturtium is also a plant for the herb garden. Easy to grow from seeds its leaves add a peppery taste to salads while the flowers can be tossed into salads.
● Other edible flowers for the herb garden include calendulas, roses and violets.

ANISEED FOR FLAVOURING CAKES
Aniseed is usually grown as an annual. Sow seeds directly into the soil when all danger of frost is past. Aniseed needs full sun, some shelter and well-drained soil to thrive. By late summer the seeds are ready to harvest and use in the kitchen.
● The ripe seeds are ideal for flavouring cakes and pastries, and the feathery foliage, which you can cut all through the growing season, is delicious in salads.

BORAGE ADDS A TOUCH OF BLUE
The star-shaped flowers of borage are a very pretty sky-blue colour. They are highly ornamental in the garden and at the table. The grey-green leaves are thick and hairy. However, borage is best known as a medicinal plant and will also attract bees for honey production and pollination of other crops.
● Once you have introduced borage into your garden, it will be there for ever, as it self-seeds copiously. If it appears where you don't want it, treat it as a weed and pull it up.

DID YOU KNOW?

GROW YOUR HERB GARDEN IN POTS
If you don't have very much space in your garden and you want to grow herbs, then remember that there are many that will happily grow in containers, such as the strawberry pot above.

Plants that will thrive in confined spaces and will grow well in pots and window boxes include basil, bay (which needs a large pot), chervil, chives, dill, lavender, lemon balm, lemon verbena, marjoram, mint, parsley, rocket, rosemary, sage, tarragon, thyme and winter savory.

The traditional herb garden will have a good mix of plants for culinary, household and medicinal uses.

Use chervil fresh from the garden as it doesn't dry well.

Chives are actually perennials but they also grow quickly and easily from seeds.

PERENNIAL ONIONS TO SOW Welsh onions are useful all year round. A small clump will bulk up over time to form a large clump. Lift and divide the clumps in spring to make more plants, or if you leave a few flower heads to set seed, the seeds are easy to gather and sow to make more plants.

THE SUBTLE TASTE OF CHERVIL Chervil has aniseed-flavoured feathery foliage. It is a hardy biennial, although it is usually treated as an annual. Sow seeds in spring, summer or early autumn. Where it is sown directly into the ground, thin seedlings to 25 cm. Chervil seedlings are very delicate and need careful handling when planting.
● It's best to grow chervil in partial shade, with regular moisture, otherwise the plants will bolt and run to seed.

CHIVES FOR THE BORDER Chives are perennials and are productive year round in all but the coldest climates where they die down over winter. Sow seeds in spring, summer or early autumn either in punnets or trays or directly into the garden or pots. Alternatively, you can buy small plants from garden centres or herb specialists. Their pink flowers are attractive in the front of a border.
● To ensure the plants are vigorous and healthy, divide the clump into smaller sections every 2–3 years, in early spring. Plant the smaller sections 25–30 cm apart in rows. You can divide in summer and, if you do, cut them back to 5 cm above ground level and they will grow well.

● Garlic chives are a good alternative to real garlic. The pungent garlic flavour is found in the distinctive broad, flat leaves.

CORIANDER – LEAVES OR SEEDS? For the best results, sow coriander directly into its growing site when all danger of frost is past. If growing for leaf, look for varieties selected for leaf production. In cooler climates, coriander can be sown from spring to summer. In full-sun situations or in hot-summer climates, coriander often bolts into flowers and seeds. Avoid this by growing in spring or autumn, or planting in light shade. Keep well watered. If you are growing it primarily for its seeds, give the plants adequate space and plant them in early spring or in autumn.

TASTY CUMIN AND CARAWAY SEEDS Cumin and caraway are herbs that produce masses of seeds that will lend a distinctive taste to many spicy and fragrant dishes.

Try not to grow coriander in very hot weather or it will bolt to flower and seed production.

YESTERDAY'S SECRETS

NATURAL PROTECTION
To make use of every last bit of space in the garden, cottage gardeners planted practical and ornamental plants together. They noticed that certain herbs seemed to protect both vegetables and flowers. They planted chives around the base of rosebushes to combat aphids and blackspot, a scourge of garden roses. Dill was grown to protect carrots from carrot fly, winter and summer savory were thought to keep aphids away from broad bean plants, and horseradish was used by these gardeners to combat fungus disease in fruit trees.

Tarragon is grown for its leaves and likes a well-drained, sunny spot, and can be grown in pots.

Sorrel can reach 60 cm high – it can be eaten like spinach or its leaves can be used in salads.

● Cumin is a frost-tender annual originally from the Mediterranean region. In the cooler climates, sow cumin in spring after all threat of frost has passed. It can be direct-sown in a sunny spot or it can be raised in a punnet or seed tray and planted out later.
● Caraway is a hardy biennial. Sow seeds into rich loamy soil in spring. Caraway grows well in full-sun conditions. You can also sow it in early autumn to overwinter.

TARRAGON FOR WHEN A DELICATE FLAVOUR IS CALLED FOR
Tarragon is a perennial but is often grown as an annual for its licorice-flavoured leaves. It can be raised from seeds in spring or summer and it can also be grown from cuttings taken in the early summer. Select a well-drained spot in full sun for the best possible growth. Tarragon can also be grown in large pots.
● In colder climates tarragon rarely produces flowers or sets seed.

THE EVER-USEFUL SUMMER AND WINTER SAVORY
Summer savory is an annual that is often grown with broad beans. Summer savory is also said to deter aphids from attacking the bean plants. Winter savory can be used in a similar way. It is a hardy perennial and provides good flavour in winter cooking. Savory is grown from seed planted in punnets or seed trays.

USE SORREL LIKE SPINACH
Sorrel is a hardy perennial whose large leaves can be lightly cooked and used in the same way as spinach. The lemony young leaves can also be added raw to salads or as a tasty addition to savoury white sauces. Common sorrel (*Rumex acetosa*) may become very invasive, so you may prefer to grow the ground-covering buckler-leaf sorrel (*R. scutatus*), which has silvery green, shield-shaped leaves and will not become invasive. Sorrel grows well in partial shade in well-drained soil.

POPULAR PARSLEY
Iron-rich parsley is a must in any vegetable and herb garden. Today, there are many varieties of curly and flat-leaf parsley to choose from.
● Flat-leaf parsley has the most flavour. A good one to try is the variety 'Giant Italian'.
● Curly-leaf parsley, such as 'Moss Curled', is less aromatic than flat-leaf parsley but very tasty, with a crunchy texture.
● Sow seeds into trays in the greenhouse in the spring or in the ground when the soil has warmed up. It takes 3–4 weeks to germinate, but germination is not difficult.

KEEP YOUR PARSLEY TO USE LATER
Parsley stores and freezes well. To keep for a few days without freezing, wash it and place in the fridge in an airtight box. To freeze parsley, wash it, pat it dry and put it in plastic bags in the freezer. When you use frozen parsley, simply crumble it into the dish or pot before it thaws out.

RUNNING TO SEED
Parsley is a biennial, and in its second year it sends up flowering stems and produces seeds. To make sure you have parsley for cutting, sow from early spring to autumn and treat it as an annual. When the plants go to seed, it is best to dig them up and use the space for other plants.

Gardener's Choice

AROMATIC AND DECORATIVE
Growing a selection of herbs will add colour to your vegetable garden and bring traditional tastes to your table.

SAGE (*Salvia officinalis* 'Tricolor') **1** Sage needs warm sun to develop the oils that provide its distinctive flavour.

LEMON VERBENA (*Aloysia triphylla*) **2** Their scented leaves and tiny flowers make these old-fashioned shrubs a real delight.

BORAGE (*Borago officinalis*) **3** Bees love the blue flowers of borage whose young leaves emit a delicate cucumber fragrance.

CHAMOMILE (*Chamaemelum nobile*) **4** You can make tea with the lovely flowers of this mat-forming evergreen perennial which prefers a cool climate.

PEPPERMINT (*Mentha piperita*) **5** No garden should be without mint, and this variety has a particularly good flavour.

PURPLE BASIL (*Ocimum basilicum* 'Rubin') **6** Grown as an annual, basil is the quintessential Mediterranean herb.

1 2
3 4

5 6

Herbs happy to be in the shade

SWEET CICELY A large plant with feathery, fernlike foliage, this stately herb grows to a height of over 1 m. Once established, it thrives in most conditions. Its freshly picked leaves, with their lovely aniseed aroma and slightly sweet taste, are ideal for sweetening and flavouring desserts. The seeds are also very tasty and were once used to freshen and sweeten the breath. They were also used as sweets in Tudor times.

SCENTED LEMON BALM Though it smells of lemon, lemon balm is botanically close to mint and its leaves have a soothing effect when rubbed on insect bites or nettle stings. It is also used to flavour sauces for chicken and fish and in herbal teas.
● Lemon balm is a perennial that makes a strong clump in cool, damp soil and can be invasive. Plant a root fragment or a small pot plant. It will seed itself readily.
● If you plant the variegated form and allow it to seed, only green-leaved plants will appear, as it does not come true from seeds.

LOVE FLAVOURSOME LOVAGE This unusual hardy perennial has a strong flavour, similar to celery. Lovage grows best in partial shade or sun, in well-drained soil and spreads to form large clumps. Top-dress with well-rotted compost in autumn.

ARCHITECTURAL ANGELICA This giant herb is a biennial that can grow 2 m. The stems of second-year plants are used in confectionery and baking. Macerate a few pieces of angelica in white wine to make an aromatic wine cup, or use it to flavour cakes and cooked fruit. Angelica produces a huge amount of seeds, which will copiously self-seed if you leave them all on the plant.
● Once angelica has set seed, the plant dies and you need to remove it. Hoe off unwanted plants in spring, leaving a few to develop.

HORSERADISH – STRONG SENSATIONS GUARANTEED Horseradish is a perennial plant that produces large, elongated leaves and a head of white flowers in summer. The plant is grown for its white roots, high in vitamin C, calcium and magnesium.

● The variegated form of horseradish is particularly decorative. Horseradish spreads from root cuttings, so when you dig it out, take care not to leave behind pieces of root.

OLD-FASHIONED HORSERADISH FUNGICIDE Gardeners used to steep chopped horseradish leaves in water, then filter the liquid and use it to spray fruit trees for the brown rot that attacks them. It was thought that if it was used early enough, this spray would help to combat the fungus.

TOP TIPS FOR MINT There are many species and varieties of mint. Low-growing types, such as Corsican mint, are best grown as groundcovers rather than for culinary uses. Here are a few of the most popular and better-known varieties.
● **SPEARMINT** A mild-flavoured mint, this is used to flavour cucumber, tabbouleh and yoghurt, and to make mint tea.
● **PEPPERMINT OR BLACK PEPPERMINT** More strongly flavoured than other varieties, peppermint is used to make infusions.
● **EAU-DE-COLOGNE MINT** A mint with green, purple-veined foliage, it is highly prized for culinary use.
● **PENNYROYAL MINT** This strongly scented wild mint has medicinal properties.
● **BOWLES MINT** This is the best mint for making a strongly flavoured mint sauce.

KEEP MINT IN CHECK Mint is well known for its vigorous, invasive habit, spreading by means of creeping underground stems. To prevent it from taking over completely, plant it in a large pot with drainage holes – if the pot does not have drainage holes the mint

1 Harvest marjoram early in the day, when the dew has dried. Use sharp secateurs to cut through the twiggy stems.

2 Arrange the stems in small bunches and tie them securely with a piece of ribbon or string.

3 Use the ends of the ribbon to make a loop that will be used to hang the bunches.

4 Hang on a line in a dry, well-ventilated room such as an attic or a sunroom.

Angelica grows to a height of 2 m so it needs very careful positioning to avoid it overwhelming other plants.

will become waterlogged and rot. Sink the pot into the ground so that its rim is just above the surface of the soil. Check the rim of the pot from time to time and cut off any runners before they escape into the garden.

KEEP FLIES OUT A sprig or two of mint added to a glass of water is said to be a good way to keep flies out of a room. You will also find that the mint takes root very quickly in the water and in no time you will have extra plants to give your friends.

Sun-loving perennial herbs

THE FACTS ABOUT TRUE AND FALSE CHAMOMILE Chamomile is an evergreen perennial herb. Apart from common, or Roman, chamomile, which is used as a sweet-smelling lawn, there is German chamomile, which has medicinal properties. Feverfew is also regarded as a chamomile, and it is said to be effective in treating migraines and headaches. It has pale green, sometimes golden, foliage and lots of tiny white flower heads with yellow centres. It also has a strongly aromatic foliage and its flowers are thought to be beneficial in deterring insect pests from invading other garden plants.

THAI HERBS ADD FLAVOUR If you enjoy the flavour of Thai or other Asian cooking, include some authentic herbs in your garden to spice up your cooking.
● Ginger (*Zingiber officinale*) can be grown in temperate to tropical climates from a rhizome. In cooler zones plant ginger in spring or early summer and harvest the root in the autumn (or in the dry season in the tropics) although it is best left for several years to form a large strong clump.
● Lemon grass (*Cymbopogon citratus*) forms a huge grassy 1 m high clump and likes a sunny well-drained spot in the garden. It can also be grown in a large pot. Harvest the leaves for tea or the mature stem to add to curries. Sow seeds in spring.
● Vietnamese mint (*Polygonum odoratum*) is not a true mint but has the same rampant growth habit. Keep plants young and productive by cutting back regularly. It grows easily from cuttings in sun or light shade.

The evergreen leaves of the bay tree can be used fresh or dried. Harvest them using sharp secateurs.

MARJORAM OR OREGANO? These are both species of *Origanum* and are tough, aromatic plants that tolerate cold winters. If drainage is poor, particularly in areas where winters are wet, grow them in pots.
● Oregano thrives in full sun and well-drained soil. To encourage new leaf growth, cut back the stems after flowering. Divide established plants in autumn or spring.
● Marjoram is usually grown as an annual. Sow seeds in spring or autumn spacing plants about 20 cm apart. Select a well-drained spot in sun. Don't allow plants to dry out.

GROWING BAY Prized for the flavour of its evergreen leaves, bay laurel grows well in the ground and in containers and works well clipped into topiary shapes. It is fairly slow-growing but in the ground it can grow to a large tree of up to 15 m. If you don't have space for such a large plant, cut it back, but wait until all danger of frost is past.
● Trim bay annually to keep well shaped.
● The golden form (*Laurus nobilis* 'Aurea') looks good when it is grown in combination with the green form.

SATISFYING SAGE Forming a shrubby plant in the garden, sage is one of the best-known culinary herbs. There are several sage varieties with different-shaped, coloured and aromatic evergreen foliage.
● Purple sage (*Salvia officinalis* Purpurascens Group) looks attractive in the flower border.
● Narrow-leaf sage (*S. lavandulifolia*) has pretty narrow leaves and strong blue flowers.
● Harvest the leaves for cooking just before the plant flowers – this is when they are at their most fragrant.

WATCH OUT

BAY WATCH! Although the leaves of sweet bay or bay laurel (*Laurus nobilis*) are used in cooking, never eat the berries as they are poisonous. There are a number of plants with leaves that can be mistaken for sweet bay. However, they are not safe to eat. Watch out for these.
● Cherry laurel or common laurel (*Prunus laurocerasus*) is an ornamental – and poisonous – laurel, with large, thick, glossy leaves. It is widely used for hedges.
● An attractive but poisonous shrub, oleander (*Nerium oleander*) has elongated leaves and pink, apricot or white flowers. It is often grown as an ornamental plant in a pot.

DID YOU KNOW?

LET THERE BE LIGHT Some herb seeds need light to germinate. Basil, savory and sorrel are among the herbs that need to be sown on the soil or potting mix surface so that the light can reach them. Before sowing, water the potting mix or soil, then sow seeds onto the surface. Cover with a light sprinkling of vermiculite, and if seeds are in pots or trays, place in a sunny position. They will germinate much more quickly this way.

Although sage is usually grown for its foliage, its flowers are very attractive and can also be used to perfume drawers. Cut back your sage plants after flowering to encourage a compact shape.

PROPAGATING SAGE Although you can increase your stock of sage plants by taking cuttings in the usual way, you can also use a traditional layering technique. In spring, fix a trailing stem from your sage plant into the soil and cover it with plenty of soil. Wait until late in the summer for the new plant to root and then cut it free – you now have a new plant. You can do this as often as you need.

THYME TO CHOOSE Thyme is a native of the Mediterranean scrubland and is one of the most versatile herbs in both the garden and the kitchen. Most thymes are hardy perennials, but thrive in full sun in a light, well-drained soil.

- There are many different thymes to choose from, and each one boasts a different leaf and flower colour and aroma. Some thymes grow as small woody shrubs, such as caraway-scented (*Thymus herba-barona*) and common thyme (*T. vulgaris*), and the lemon-scented thyme (*T.* x *citriodorus* 'Silver Queen'). Others are spreading, mat-forming plants that flower at ground level, such as *T. serpyllum*, which has small pinky-mauve flowers, and *T. s.* var. *coccineus*.
- Use upright varieties of thyme, such as *T.* x *citriodorus*, as small edging plants for your formal borders or herb garden. For a very decorative effect, plant mat-forming varieties in cracks in the paving and foot-paths, or let them tumble over rockeries.
- Give your shrubby thymes a light trim straight after flowering – this will encourage a bushy, compact shape.
- As well as pleasantly scenting the garden, thyme can be used throughout the year in salads and in cooked savoury dishes.

EASY THYME CUTTINGS Simply cut a sprig or two from the mature plant, then remove the lower leaves from each stem, and plant so that two-thirds of the stem is in the soil. Water well and the cutting should take root in 3–4 weeks.

HYSSOP IS AN UNDERRATED HERB
Hyssop was highly prized by our ancestors and is mentioned in the Bible. During the

17th century, it was used to dress wounds. Today, it tends to be widely – and unjustly – ignored. Its flowers attract bees and butter-flies to the garden and the bitter, minty taste of its leaves is ideal for making infusions and flavouring dishes.

- Hyssop is a hardy herbaceous perennial that is native to the mountainous Mediterranean regions, where it thrives in the arid, stony soil. It is fully hardy in this country, as long as it is kept in full sun and well-drained soil. Its needs are similar to those of catmint, lavender and rosemary, and it is a good idea to grow hyssop with these plants.
- Grow hyssop from seeds sown in autumn or from softwood cuttings taken in summer. This herb needs to be cut back annually to prevent it from becoming too woody.

ROSEMARY SHAPES UP Rosemary is an evergreen shrub native to the Mediterranean scrubland. It responds well to shaping into pyramids, cones, balls and spirals, or trimmed into a fragrant hedge. Trim rosemary often and cut it back in spring, removing damaged or dead branches. Do not let the plants get leggy. There are prostrate forms available that will cascade over walls or over the edge of your herb garden.

- Rosemary grows best in full sun, in very well-drained soil, producing small flowers in spring and summer. It needs shelter from harsh winter winds and it does not tolerate winter wet at its roots.

LEMON VERBENA This fragrant shrub grows well in warm, frost-free gardens. Trim to keep it bushy. Use the leaves in herbal tea or in pot pourri. Lemon verbena grows well from cuttings taken in summer.

The lemon-scented thyme (Thymus x citriodorus) has attractive light green foliage and combines well with the flowers of common thyme (T. vulgaris).

TAKING ROSEMARY CUTTINGS

1 In spring, cut the young shoots about 15–20 cm long. Remove the lower leaves.

2 Plant the shoots in trays filled with a multipurpose potting mix with added grit.

3 Water sparingly. After 4–6 weeks check to see if roots have developed. Plant them out in situ the following spring.

Pests and diseases of vegetables

Organic growing techniques produce strong and healthy crops resistant to pests and diseases. However, if your crops do get infected, use natural remedies where possible. But if you spray, make sure you observe withholding periods.

Leafy vegetables

APHIDS

Green and black aphids collect in colonies on the stems and flower heads of many leafy vegetables. Companion planting can help combat these pests. Chervil, marigold, nasturtium and savory are all considered effective deterrents. See page 97.

BACTERIAL LEAF SPOT
- **SYMPTOMS** Leaves develop spots that can become large and brown. In some vegetables, this can lead to total leaf collapse or, in lettuce, total plant rot.
- **PLANTS AFFECTED** Cucumber, lettuce, pumpkin and squash.
- **TREATMENT** Use healthy seeds. Reduce overhead watering and improve air circulation and drainage. Practise crop rotation. Apply a copper-based fungicide.

BACTERIAL SOFT ROT
- **SYMPTOMS** Soft, slimy and often smelly rots appear on the fleshy stems and the leaves of various vegetables. These may sometimes be secondary infection after insect damage.
- **PLANTS AFFECTED** Celery, lettuce and many brassicas. May also affect potato tubers, which may not show symptoms of rot until after harvest.
- **TREATMENT** Reduce watering, store harvest in dry conditions.

CABBAGE MOTH

- **SYMPTOMS** The leaves of cabbage-moth infested plants are covered with varying-sized holes made by yellowish brown or green caterpillars. On cabbages, these caterpillars bore into the heart of the plant and ruin the edible parts with their excrement.
- **PLANTS AFFECTED** Cabbage and other brassicas, and swede and turnip.
- **TREATMENT** Check brassicas regularly and remove any eggs, which are laid in groups of 20–100 on the undersides of the leaves – also remove the caterpillars. If the larvae are numerous, before they burrow into the heart leaves, spray with *Bacillus thuringiensis* (sold as Dipel), a bacterium that will kill the caterpillars within a few days, or with a registered insecticide. Spray both the upper- and undersides of leaves.

CABBAGE WHITE BUTTERFLY

- **SYMPTOMS** The leaves are ragged and full of holes, and the heart of the cabbage becomes riddled with tunnels. Inside are the blue-green or greenish yellow caterpillars, which are responsible for the damage. If you do not act quickly, only the veins will remain.
- **PLANTS AFFECTED** All members of the cabbage family, including broccoli and brussels sprouts.
- **TREATMENT** Take action at the first sign of attack, before the caterpillars burrow into the heads of the plants. Use an insecticide containing rotenone (Derris dust), natural pyrethrins or *Bacillus thuringiensis* (sold as Dipel). Remove and crush any eggs that have been laid.

CLUB ROOT

- **SYMPTOMS** Roots become swollen and deformed. This is caused by a soil-borne fungus, which penetrates the plant and forms swellings. The leaves turn yellow and wilt in sunny weather. Spores released by the swellings can remain in the soil for up to 10 years before becoming active.
- **PLANTS AFFECTED** All members of the cabbage family.
- **TREATMENT** Crop rotation is essential to prevent the disease recurring year after year. Treat young plants with a registered treatment before planting out. Lift and bin any affected plants. Make sure that the soil is limed and well drained as this fungus flourishes in very acidic conditions. Before planting, check that the roots of bought brassicas and related plants are healthy. Improve soil drainage by deep digging and incorporating plenty of humus.

CORN EARWORM

Corn earworm caterpillars may attack leaves of cabbage and other brassicas. See page 209.

CUTWORM

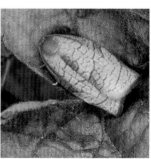

- **SYMPTOMS** The roots are eaten away, severed or riddled with holes. The leaves turn pale and acquire a papery texture. Finally, perforations appear, revealing the presence of green or yellowish brown caterpillars. These are the larvae of a number of moths, including bogongs, that may flutter under your outdoor lights on summer evenings. They live in the ground, where they feed on roots, but also come to the surface at night to devastate the lower leaves and sever plants at ground level. The plants weaken, wither and soon die.

● **PLANTS AFFECTED** Artichoke, cabbage, lettuce and many vegetable seedlings.
● **TREATMENT** Remove all weeds. *Bacillus thuringiensis* (sold as Dipel) is a very effective solution to use, destroying the caterpillars by stopping them from eating. Alternatively, you can pick off the caterpillars by hand at night when they are at their most active. Maintaining humidity levels in dry weather also hinders their development. When this pest is active, spray the affected plant with a registered insecticide. Hoe soil around the plants during the danger months of spring and early summer, and pick up and destroy any caterpillars that you see.

DOWNY MILDEW
● **SYMPTOMS** A pale grey fungus appears on the leaves, flowers and young shoots, and the plant beneath the mildew yellows. These symptoms worsen under cool, damp conditions.
● **PLANTS AFFECTED** Artichoke, brassicas, celery, leek, onion, salad greens and spinach.
● **TREATMENT** Remove and bin all affected parts, then spray with Bordeaux mixture. Practise crop rotation, avoid overcrowding when planting and limit humid conditions – avoid splashing the leaves when watering. Be sure to promptly remove any plant debris and all damaged plants.

EARTH MITE
● **SYMPTOMS** In the cooler months these insects feed at night on leaves, resulting in mottling, or the leaves as a whole can become grey or white before they brown and die. Young plants can die.
● **PLANTS AFFECTED** Beetroot, brassicas, lettuce and silverbeet.

● **TREATMENT** Remove weeds such as capeweed. Spray with a registered systemic insecticide.

MOSAIC VIRUS

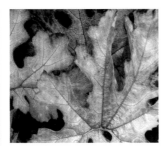

● **SYMPTOMS** Infected leaves become discoloured with yellow or pale green mottling. The plant's growth becomes stunted and deformed and it eventually dies.
● **PLANTS AFFECTED** Lettuce. Also bean, cucumber and pea.
● **TREATMENT** Lift and bin any affected plants to prevent the virus from spreading further. Spray the crops with a registered insecticide to control the aphids, which carry this disease from infected plants.

RUST
Characterised by orange blotches on the leaves, rust affects beans, chicory, leeks, roses, spinach and stone fruit. Cabbages are affected by white rust (or white blister). See pages 153, 209 and 252.

SCLEROTINIA ROT
This brown rot spreads in the stems of affected plants and may lead to a range of symptoms, such as wilting in lettuce. Plants affected include cabbage, cauliflower and lettuce. See page 208.

SLUGS AND SNAILS
These pests attack most vegetables, especially young plants with tender leaves. Don't throw slugs into your compost heap. Instead, kill them by dropping

them in salty water or simply squashing them. See page 99.

THRIPS
These tiny winged insects attack mainly leeks, causing silvery mottling on the upper surface of the leaves, while the undersides appear dirty. Use sticky traps to eradicate pests from the greenhouse. Frequent watering may also help as thrips prefer dry conditions. See page 153.

WHIPTAIL
● **SYMPTOMS** Infected leaves have small, narrow ribbons. Some plants may show yellowing or twisting of leaves. This is caused by a molybdenum deficiency.
● **PLANTS AFFECTED** Brassicas, including brussels sprouts and cauliflower.
● **TREATMENT** Lime soil before planting brassicas and apply a complete fertiliser with trace elements including molybdenum.

Root vegetables and bulbs

AFRICAN BLACK BEETLE

● **SYMPTOMS** C-shaped white beetle larvae feed on the roots, which causes wilting even though plants are not in need of water. Plants may be loose in the soil due to lack of roots.

● **PLANTS AFFECTED** Beetroot, potato and many other vegetables, including cabbage, cauliflower and corn, as well as grasses and ornamentals.
● **TREATMENT** Remove grubs from soil, treat lawns and gardens with a spray based on eucalyptus and tea tree oil. Turn off outdoor lights to avoid attracting the beetles. Treat any severe larvae infestations with a registered chemical that is watered over the soil. In spring, use an insecticide registered for beetles to reduce adult beetle population.

ALTERNARIA LEAF SPOT
● **SYMPTOMS** Causes grey or brown circular patches of more or less dead tissue on leaves. The leaves dry up and, in some cases, a fungus forms.
● **PLANTS AFFECTED** Carrot, chicory and potato.
● **TREATMENT** Limit the spread of this disease by removing and binning all affected leaves as soon as possible. Spray any plants that have become infected with a fungicide that contains mancozeb.

BEET LEAFMINER
● **SYMPTOMS** Leaves become marked with fairly large brown spots. The tiny white grubs of a fly burrow inside the leaves and can cause considerable damage.
● **PLANTS AFFECTED** Beetroot and spinach.
● **TREATMENT** Pick off and destroy affected leaves or squash the larvae in their burrows. Spray the foliage with a registered systemic insecticide at regular intervals until the pest is cleared.

COMMON SCAB (POTATO SCAB)
● **SYMPTOMS** Small brown dots appear on tubers. These

grow to form raised or pitted areas that may cover the entire tuber.

● **PLANTS AFFECTED** Beetroot, potato and turnip.

● **TREATMENT** Use prevetion rather than cure. Buy disease-free tubers and avoid alkaline soils. Practise crop rotation and avoid watering late in the afternoon.

CUTWORM

The stems on small plants are severed by these earth-coloured caterpillars that gnaw away at the outer membranes at soil level. Plants affected are carrot and potato. See page 205.

GANGRENE

● **SYMPTOMS** Brown patches appear on the skin and flesh at the ends of the potato tubers, and around the eyes and lenticels (small openings on the skin). This diseased area then continues to enlarge until most of the potato tuber becomes decayed and shrunken. The bacterium responsible mainly attacks the areas damaged by forks when lifting potatoes.

● **PLANTS AFFECTED** Potato.

● **TREATMENT** Plant only undamaged, certified seed tubers. Take care when lifting potatoes and remove any damaged tubers. Store only healthy tubers in an airy, frost-free place and discard any that appear to be infected.

LATE BLIGHT

● **SYMPTOMS** Dark patches and some whiskery white fungal growth appear on the leaves of plants affected with late blight. The infection spreads to the stem and tubers, damaging the crop on the skin and on the inside.

● **PLANTS AFFECTED** Potato (sebago shows resistance).

● **TREATMENT** Select disease-free tubers for planting. If the leaves are affected, it is best to remove them before harvest. Discard affected tubers. Use registered fungicides when symptoms are first noted.

METALLIC FLEA BEETLE

These beetles are found on the seedlings of beetroot, brassicas, radish, swede and turnip. They pierce small holes in the leaves, which turn yellow. See page 98.

NEMATODE (EELWORM)

● **SYMPTOMS** The main roots of the affected plant bear either tiny white cysts (potato cyst nematode) or large yellow or brown swellings (root rot nematode). The lower leaves turn yellow and wither. The plants often die before the end of the summer and, consequently, the tubers may be particularly small.

● **PLANTS AFFECTED** Onion, potato and tomato.

● **TREATMENT** Lift and bin affected plants and tubers, and practise crop rotation. African or French marigolds (*Tagetes*) planted near susceptible crops will help to keep nematodes at bay. Do not grow potatoes, tomatoes or onions in infected soil for at least six years. With potatoes, try growing resistant varieties, such as 'Pentland Javelin' and 'Maris Piper'.

PARSNIP CANKER

SYMPTOMS Red or brown discolouration appears on the upper part of parsnip roots, which may become depressions or cankers and lead to the rot of the entire vegetable. Leaves develop silvery spots that turn brown, and may drop off.

PLANTS AFFECTED Parsnips,

sunflowers and some weeds in the carrot family.

TREATMENT This disease is worse in wet or poorly drained conditions so improve the soil before replanting. Remove all affected plants as soon as the disease is noted. Practise crop rotation (waiting at least 3 years before regrowing parsnips in this area). Use disease-free seeds.

POTATO LEAF ROLL

SYMPTOMS Leaves become thick and stiff and roll up. The plant is stunted and the crop is reduced.

PLANTS AFFECTED Potato.

TREATMENT As this virus is spread by aphids, make sure you control aphids on your potato crops. Use only virus-free seed potatoes when planting. Remove and destroy affected plants.

POWDERY SCAB

● **SYMPTOMS** Flat, raised or concave patches appear on the surface of the roots or tubers of affected plants. Common scab is brown, while powdery scab has corky patches that release a brown powder. Scab is caused by bacteria that thrive in light, sandy or very chalky soil.

● **PLANTS AFFECTED** Potato.

● **TREATMENT** Use prevention rather than cure. Dig in compost but do not lime the ground before planting potatoes. Practise crop rotation, increase the acidity of chalky soils and grow scab-resistant varieties. Do not grow

'Desirée' as it is susceptible to powdery scab. Make sure you plant only healthy seed.

TARGET SPOT (EARLY BLIGHT)

● **SYMPTOMS** Dark spots on leaves show a target-like pattern of concentric circles. Older leaves are affected first but the fungus spreads to stems and fruit.

● **PLANTS AFFECTED** Capsicum, eggplant, potato, tomato and weedy related plants.

● **TREATMENT** Select disease-free seeds and plants, remove any affected growth and weeds, and practise crop rotation. Spray with a registered fungicide when the symptoms are first noted.

TWO-SPOTTED MITE

This minute insect attacks celeriac, cucumbers, green and runner beans, peas, pumpkins, tomatoes and zucchinis. It causes mottling of the leaves, which subsequently turn yellow, wither and die. Spraying leaves with water will help as the mites thrive in dry conditions. See page 153.

WIREWORM

● **SYMPTOMS** Roots and tubers are riddled with narrow tunnels bored by a thin yellow grub 20–30 mm long. The grubs are the larvae of the click beetle (*Agriotes*, family Elateridae), which can live for 5 years before turning into an adult. A major infestation can destroy an entire crop.

● **PLANTS AFFECTED** Asparagus, beetroot, carrot, potato, pumpkin and many other vegetables.

● **TREATMENT** It is quite easy to pick up the larvae by hand when digging over the soil. Keep the soil well cultivated to expose any wireworms to the birds. Traps are also effective. Place small pieces of carrot or potato on spikes and bury them in the soil, at a depth of about 50 mm, to lure the grubs. Inspect and replace the traps regularly. Lift the potatoes when they are mature to prevent attack. Wireworms can be more of a problem on old pasture land.

Fruiting vegetables

BEETLES AND BUGS

● **SYMPTOMS** Leaves, flowers or fruit are damaged by the chewing or rasping of insects among the plants or in the leaf litter. Beetles and bugs commonly seen include twenty-eight-spotted ladybird, green vegetable bug, which gives off a noxious smell, harlequin bug (pictured), which are flat and multicoloured, and pumpkin beetle, which is orange with black spots and has an elongated body.

● **PLANTS AFFECTED** All vegetables but some beetles and bugs target specific crops such as cucurbits (pumpkin beetle).

● **TREATMENT** Remove and squash any insects, particularly on young plants. Pests may damage foliage on older plants but the crop is usually okay. Water and fertilise for vigorous growth. Dust with vegetable dust such as rotenone (Derris dust) weekly. Severe attacks can be treated with a systemic insecticide.

BLOSSOM END ROT

● **SYMPTOMS** A brown leathery patch appears at the base of the fruit (where the flower was) and gradually spreads. The fruit may rot. This condition is brought on by a lack of calcium and water stress either through too little or too much water.

● **PLANTS AFFECTED** Capsicum and tomato.

● **TREATMENT** Water crops regularly (once or twice daily), lime the soil and add organic matter before planting a crop where this has occurred before.

FRUIT FLY

The skin of the fruit becomes marked by puncture wounds where eggs have been laid. Rots develop as the eggs hatch and maggots feed within the fruit. The fruit may drop. Affects all soft vegetables. See page 254.

FUSARIUM WILT

The plant's growth will be affected and it may wilt and die. Affects cucurbits like rockmelon and watermelon. Remove affected plants, practise crop rotation and buy resistant species. See page 97.

GUMMY STEM BLIGHT

● **SYMPTOMS** Dark grey, sunken spots appear on the fruit.

The fruit splits and gum oozes from the cracks. Mould develops on the surface of the gum. As the blemishes heal, corky tissue forms around the edges. The damage is caused by a fungus.

● **PLANTS AFFECTED** Rockmelon and watermelon.

● **TREATMENT** Bin all diseased fruit. Grow resistant cultivars. Spray with a copper-based treatment to prevent spread.

MOSAIC VIRUS

Many vegetables are affected, including cucurbits (especially cucumber). Mosaic-like or mottled patches appear on the leaves, which become deformed and reduced in size. Young shoots curl, and the plant may be stunted and die early. On some plants, flower colour is affected. See page 206.

PEA AND BEAN WEEVIL

● **SYMPTOMS** Seeds bear small round holes, while the larvae can be seen on the surface of the soil, feeding on the first leaves. Light brown patches may appear on the seed coat. The larvae bore into the pods, then into the seeds. They are active while the plant is growing, but they can also wreak havoc among your stored vegetables.

● **PLANTS AFFECTED** Broad, green and runner bean, and pea.

● **TREATMENT** Established plants can usually tolerate weevil damage. Only act if the weevils are eating young plants. Either

use a registered insecticide or cover with fleece to prevent the pest from getting to them.

ROOT ROT

● **SYMPTOMS** The roots show signs of rot, the base of the stem changes colour and shrivels, and the plant dies fairly rapidly.

● **PLANTS AFFECTED** Beans (broad, green and runner), capsicum, cucumber, eggplant, pea, pumpkin, squash, sweet pepper, tomato and zucchini.

● **TREATMENT** Dig up and discard all infected plants and remove the surrounding soil to prevent the spread of infection. Maintain good hygiene and use only sterilised compost to prevent root rot outbreaks.

SCLEROTINIA ROT

● **SYMPTOMS** A white cottony mould is visible on the leaves and fruit, which becomes discoloured, turns brown and rots. The stems become discoloured and covered in dense fungal growth. Large black sclerotia (fungal resting bodies) are embedded in the fungal growth.

● **PLANTS AFFECTED** A wide range of vegetables, including beans, capsicum, cucumber, eggplant, pea and zucchini.

● **TREATMENT** The best treatment is to avoid sclerotinia with crop rotation.

STEM ROT

● **SYMPTOMS** This disease primarily affects the leaves of the plant, but it can also attack the stems and the fruit of members of the squash family. Slimy brown patches will appear along the edge of the leaves, which turn yellow. Stem tissue dies and the end of the fruit shrivels as it rots from the inside. Stem rot is caused by a fungus that also attacks certain ornamental plants such as chrysanthemums, fruit bushes and raspberries.

● **PLANTS AFFECTED** Cucumber, melon, squash and tomato.

● **TREATMENT** Feed the crop with liquid nettle manure (see page 269) to strengthen growth. Dig up and bin badly affected plants. Do not throw the plant remains onto the compost heap, but bin them. Clear up all crop debris at the end of the season and grow crops on a fresh site each year.

THRIPS

These tiny winged insects deposit whitish specks on leaves, which form a silvery marbling. Affected plants include capsicum, cucumber, eggplant, tomato and zucchini. See page 153.

TOMATO RUSSET MITE

● **SYMPTOMS** Mites feed on the leaves, which become dry and die from the base of the plant. The stem becomes brown and may crack, and fruit may drop or be scorched due to lack of foliage.

● **PLANTS AFFECTED** Capsicum, eggplant, potato, tomato and related plants.

● **TREATMENT** Remove the lower foliage, use mulch to prevent infestation to begin with and practise crop rotation. Dust with wettable sulphur (but not in hot weather) and spray with a systemic insecticide from when pest is first noticed.

WHITEFLY

Whiteflies attack fruiting vegetables and gradually weaken the plants by sucking their sap. See page 99.

Pods and cobs

ANTHRACNOSE

A fungal disease, anthracnose attacks peas, and green and runner beans in wet weather. Dark brown cankers form on stems, leaf ribs turn pinky brown and sunken brown spots appear on the pods. See page 253.

BEAN BLOSSOM THRIPS

● **SYMPTOMS** Dark 1.5 mm-long brown insects feeding in blossom lead to distorted and twisted beans which may also bear rusty marks or lumps. Leaves may pucker and their edges curl.

● **PLANTS AFFECTED** Bean.

● **TREATMENT** Remove affected plants after harvest and rotate crops. Spray the plant with a systemic spray or spray the infested flowers with contact spray (spray when bees are not active).

BEAN FLY

● **SYMPTOMS** Yellow spots appear on leaves and young plants wilt. Plants may become brittle.

● **PLANTS AFFECTED** Bean (not broad bean).

● **TREATMENT** Keep plants well watered. In affected areas use a registered systemic pesticide from the time you plant.

BEAN RUST

● **SYMPTOMS** Yellow pustules cover the upper surfaces of the leaves, and distort the underside of the leaves as well, and eventually affect the pods. The pustules turn brown, then black. This strain is caused by the *Uromyces appendiculatus* fungus, which develops during hot, wet weather.

● **PLANTS AFFECTED** Green and runner beans.

● **TREATMENT** Grow your bean crop in well-manured ground and feed it regularly with liquid nettle manure (see page 269). At the first sign of attack, spray your crop with a registered sulphur-based fungicide.

CORN EARWORM

● **SYMPTOMS** As the caterpillars feed they create holes and tunnels in fruit such as tomatoes or beans and may damage and tunnel in tips of sweetcorn cobs. The striped caterpillars continue to feed inside the fruit and this may then lead to the complete collapse of the fruit.

● **PLANTS AFFECTED** Bean, sweetcorn and tomato.

● **TREATMENT** Remove caterpillars by hand. Use a vegetable dust regularly. Control is difficult once the caterpillar enters the fruit. Sweetcorn cobs are usually edible if the tip is removed prior to cooking.

HALO BLIGHT

● **SYMPTOMS** Greasy, water-soaked spots appear on the leaves and pods. Those on the leaves become surrounded by a greenish yellow 'halo', while the spots on the pods exude a pale cream or silvery bacterial ooze. Infected pods become discoloured and shrivel, and the seeds become contaminated. This blight is caused by a bacterium that becomes active in wet, windy conditions that turn dry and hot during the flowering season.

● **PLANTS AFFECTED** Broad beans, and green and runner beans.

● **TREATMENT** Spraying with copper may protect plants from the disease. Lift and bin diseased plants, practise crop rotation and do not soak seeds before planting.

SMUT

● **SYMPTOMS** Sweetcorn seeds turn black and release a black powder when the cob is opened. Brown patches appear on the leaves of leeks. Different genera of fungi are responsible for this disease and are spread by rain splash or watering.

● **PLANTS AFFECTED** Leek, onion and sweetcorn.

● **TREATMENT** Lift and bin plants at the first sign of this disease. Do not plant the same crop where the previous one was infected. Fungicides have no effect. Make sure the plants are actively growing.

CHAPTER 5

Fruit from the garden

The strawberry – queen of the garden

Strawberries can be grown in almost any climate and you don't even need a garden bed! Juicy red strawberries can be raised in pots and hanging baskets, as well as in the traditional garden strawberry patch.

The strawberry wants it all

HOW BIG A PATCH WILL YOU NEED?
This really depends on how many strawberries you want. A single 6 m row will keep a family fed through the season, or if you're on your own, plant up a strawberry pot.

PLANT EARLY IN THE SEASON You can plant your strawberries any time between mid-autumn and late winter, but remember that the earlier you plant, the sooner your strawberries will start cropping.
● Packaged strawberry crowns are available in winter, while the young potted plants are available from nurseries during the warmer months. Alpine-type strawberries can be grown from seeds sown in spring or autumn. New plants can also be produced from the stolons, or runners, from the parent plants. These can be replanted from your strawberry patch from mid- to late summer.
● Always plant strawberries that are certified virus-free and never replant your strawberries in the same patch each year. Rotating your crops will help prevent the spread of any soil-borne diseases that may be in your patch.

PLANT AT THE RIGHT DEPTH Strawberry plants should never be planted deep in the ground. Ensure that the crown, which is the boundary between the roots and the head of leaves, is just above the soil surface. Dig a fairly wide hole, and spread out the roots before covering them with soil and packing it down. No matter how many strawberries you have to plant, don't be tempted to use a dibber because the holes will be too narrow.

DELICATE SEEDLINGS When uprooted from the ground, young strawberry plants are quick to dry out, so don't leave them lying around in the hot sun. Instead, put their roots straight into a mixture of potting mix and water, and plant them in the garden again as soon as possible.

PLANT ON A RIDGE If the soil in your garden is heavy and wet, it will not be the ideal situation for growing strawberries. Therefore, when you prepare your patch, make sure that you provide well-drained soil for the plants' roots. If you're growing a double line of plants, build up a flat-topped ridge of soil about 20 cm high and 1 m wide, and set the plants in that.

AT HOME IN THE WOODS Originally strawberries grew in forest clearings, which is why they particularly like the rather acid qualities of tree humus. Fertilise your strawberry patch by spreading a generous

When picking strawberries, leave some stalk attached to the fruit, or the berries will lose their freshness.

Don't plant strawberries too deeply – set the crown just above ground level.

A bed of straw will protect your strawberries from grey mould and slugs.

layer of leaf mould over it. A reliable old-fashioned tip is to cover the soil between the stalks of the plants with conifer needles, ferns and ground pine bark or, failing that, a good layer of straw. This porous carpet has the added advantages of discouraging weeds and purifying the surface of the soil so your strawberry plants will be less vulnerable to grey mould and slugs.

PATIO STRAWBERRIES All is not lost if you only have a balcony or a patio. You can grow strawberries in specially designed pots, which have honeycomb cavities, in a graduated stack of terracotta pots, or in large tubs or barrels filled with peat-enriched potting mix. Place them in a lightly shaded spot, make sure that they never lack water and regularly remove the stolons so the plants don't become exhausted. Enjoy the harvest, but don't expect to have enough for jam.

DAY LENGTH Most strawberries flower and fruit in response to increasing day length, so most produce their main crop in spring and early summer. Some crop later in spring than others, so to guarantee fruit for many months, grow late and early varieties. The Australian-bred variety 'Alinta' produces fruit all year round as it is 'day-length neutral', that is, it is not triggered by changing day length. For year-round fruit, 'Alinta' needs full sun, regular fertilising and deep watering.

TAKE OFF LEAVES Leaf diseases strike strawberries during late autumn. So, as soon as possible after harvesting, clip off the leaves, cutting high enough not to touch the heart of the plants. These plants will then soon start to grow healthy new leaves.

SUSCEPTIBILITY TO WEEDS One of the big problems with growing strawberry plants is their vulnerability to vigorous weeds such as couch, kikuyu and oxalis. The plants can be suffocated by these weeds, their fruit deprived of sunlight and their soil can lose its richness. If weeds start to become a problem in your strawberry patch you may want to consider moving it to a new, weed-free site.

COMBINATION PLANTING Use the soft, loose soil between two rows of strawberry plants for a line of English spinach, lettuces or white onions: crops that aren't greedy and won't rob the strawberry plants of nutrients.

KEEP THEIR HATS ON Never hull strawberries before washing them or the berries will soak up water and spoil their flavour.

REDISCOVER SOME OLD FLAVOURS
Study specialist catalogues and track down those old-fashioned strawberry varieties that were created above all else to please the palate. Their tender fruit is best savoured fresh from the garden. Old varieties of strawberries include the 'Redgauntlet', 'Tioga' and 'Torrey'.

MODERN VARIETIES More recent varieties have been specially bred to grow vigorously, resist disease and improve fruit appearance. When well grown their flavour is still very delicious and sweet. Tasty new varieties include 'Alinta', 'Hokowase' and 'Zdana'.

'Redlands Crimson' is an old favourite prized for its sweetness.

Tempting berries from the bush

Filling a basket with raspberries, blueberries, currants, gooseberries or blackberries is a joyful reminder of simpler times, and once you have grown a few you'll be hooked. You don't need a large garden to grow these fruits, but you'll have more success if you live in a mild climate.

Blueberries and raspberries

BLUEBERRY HISTORY The American blueberry (*Vaccinum corymbosum*) is a modern variety, and is much more productive than the smaller European species (*Vaccinum myrtillus*), although some say it has less flavour. The European blueberry, or bilberry, grows wild in many European countries. It is extremely difficult to grow outside its natural habitat, so the American blueberry is a better choice for your garden.
● The American blueberry reaches 1–2 m high and produces 1–3 kg (and sometimes as much as 10 kg) of fruit per bush. It is very decorative when its leaves turn red in autumn.
● Unlike the European blueberry, which grows happily in woodland, the American variety only fruits well in full sun, so choose its position carefully.

BLUEBERRIES NEED ACID SOIL Like its wild counterpart, which grows on peaty heaths, the cultivated blueberry needs an acid soil in which to thrive.
● Use a pH kit (available from nurseries) to identify your soil type, or simply check out the flower colour of hydrangeas in your area. Pink flowers are indicators of alkaline soils, while blue-mauve flowers tell you that the soil in which they are growing is acid.
● If you don't have the right soil, blueberries can be grown in a large container filled with some acid potting mix.
● When planting blueberry bushes, dig a hole 50 cm across and fill it with a mixture

of equal parts ericaceous compost, leaf or pine-needle mould and well-rotted garden compost. Leave 1.5 m between plants.
● Give the plants an annual top-dressing of moss peat or acid leaf mould to enrich the soil. Alternatively, feed them with an ericaceous plant food.

ALWAYS PICK BLUEBERRIES BY HAND
Don't be tempted to use any of the contraptions which are available for gathering blueberries. Apart from the fact that they gather as many leaves as they do berries, they will also damage the berries of the large-fruited cultivated varieties. There is really only one solution and that is plenty of patience and picking by hand.

POLLINATING PARTNERS Highbush blueberry varieties, such as 'Blue Rose', 'Brigitta', 'Denise' and 'Northland', do not require a crosspollinator. However rabbit-eye varieties like 'Delite' and 'Tiff Blue' need a pollinating partner to ensure a good crop of fruits. Rabbit-eye varieties are suitable for warm climates and for coastal gardens.

Always pick blueberries by hand – put them in a large, shallow basket or container so that they do not get crushed.

DID YOU KNOW?

SUMMER- AND AUTUMN-FRUITING RASPBERRIES
The raspberry is a perennial plant that sends up new shoots from its underground roots at different times of the year, depending on whether the variety is summer- or autumn-fruiting.
● Summer-fruiting varieties: These fruit once a year, in summer. As some of the shoots bear fruit, others are growing and developing. The new shoots will bear fruit the following year, while the current fruit-bearing shoots will die off.
● Autumn-fruiting varieties: The fruit on these varieties appears from March until the first frosts, on canes that have developed in the current year.

MULCH THE SOIL FOR A GOOD CROP

The raspberry is a woodland plant that appreciates a mulch of partially composted dead leaves, twigs, straw, tree bark, wood shavings, pine needles or any other woody debris. Added on a regular basis, these materials will decompose and create the acidity that the plant needs to grow. Mulching also provides protection against diseases such as spur blight – a major problem in some areas – and helps to keep weed growth down.

RASPBERRIES NEED SUPPORT

Raspberry stems, or canes, are extremely supple and are liable to be flattened by wind, rain and the weight of the fruit. It is essential to provide some kind of support; for example, a post-and-wire system.

● Sink two posts into the ground at either end of the row of canes, reinforcing each one with an angled strut.

Gardener's Choice

EASY-GROWING RASPBERRIES

BOGONG This cultivar has large, firm fruit with good flavour.

CHILCOTIN Dual-cropping variety with bright red, good-sized fruit.

CLUTHA Summer-fruiting, good-yielding variety with red, firm and shiny fruit.

DINKUM Autumn-fruiting variety. It has medium-sized fruit with excellent flavour.

EVERBEARER A late variety producing large berries with good colour and flavour.

HERITAGE 1 Autumn-fruiting variety. The fruit is medium-sized with good flavour.

NOOTKA Midseason raspberry producing high yields of medium-sized berries. Nootka is resistant to fruit rot.

SERPELL'S WILLAMETTE 2 Hardy, dual-cropping variety with thornless canes and tasty fruit.

SKEENA Almost thornless variety with good rot resistance and a low tendency to sucker.

● Stretch galvanised wire between the posts, at a height of about 1.7 m. Tighten one end with a straining bolt.

● Tie each cane to the wire with a plastic tie, garden twine or a length of pantihose.

PRUNING RASPBERRIES Regular pruning ensures a succession of healthy new canes and good fruit production. When and how you prune depends on the raspberry variety.

● **SUMMER-FRUITING VARIETIES** Once fruiting is over, cut the canes that have just fruited down to ground level. Tie in canes that have grown during the current season. The following spring, cut back the tips on the new canes to a healthy bud.

● **AUTUMN-FRUITING (HERITAGE) VARIETIES** Prune in late winter, cutting all the canes down to ground level.

COMBATING PESTS AND DISEASES

The most common pests of raspberry plants include wingless grasshoppers, Rutherglen bugs, rose scale and Queensland fruit fly. These insects can all cause significant damage to plants, so control programs may be necessary. Methods include hand removal and spraying with insecticides, as well as fruit fly baits and traps.

● Fungal diseases such as cane spot (anthracnose) and spur blight can be readily controlled with an appropriate fungicide. Infected canes should be removed and destroyed. Phytophthora root rot is a more serious disease, causing leaves to die back and young canes to wilt. Planting resistant varieties, as well as good drainage, will help to avoid root rot.

Raspberries appreciate a mulch such as leaves, bark, straw, twigs or compost.

A very simple post-and-wire support is ideal for your raspberry plants.

PLANTING RASPBERRY CANES

1 Plant raspberry canes in autumn or winter. Add well-rotted manure to the base of the planting hole and, if your soil is dry, mix in a quantity of acid potting mix or peat.

2 Plant the canes only about 10 cm deep and spread the roots out. Planting too deep inhibits the development of beneficial suckers. Firm the soil around the base of the canes.

3 Leave a hollow around the base of each plant, and water well. Once the plant has settled in, cut down the canes to 25 cm above the ground, cutting at an angle above a bud.

Currants and gooseberries

PLANTED TO PERFECTION Redcurrants and blackcurrants require a high chill factor over late winter and early spring. Plant young bushes deeply. If the neck of the plant – where the roots join the branches – is 5–10 cm below the surface of the soil, it will produce a number of suckers that will later become the important framework branches.
● Twelve is the ideal number of branches for a blackcurrant or redcurrant bush to encourage maximum fruiting.

PLANT CUTTINGS IN SITU If a friend has a currant bush, why not ask for a cutting? In early spring, clear and break down the soil in the spot chosen for the new bush and push two 25–30 cm long cuttings or sections of branches, taken from the previous year's growth, into the ground. These cuttings should be pushed into the soil at an angle, about 10 cm apart, with one bud showing.
● Planting cuttings directly in their growing positions will encourage the plants to put out deep roots. This will make the young bushes less susceptible to drought than if they are transplanted as baby bushes.

TURNING A CUTTING INTO A FRUITING BUSH When growing a new bush from a cutting, cut it back every winter for 3 years before allowing it to fruit.
● **THE FIRST WINTER** After planting, cut back new shoots developed to two buds.
● **THE SECOND WINTER** Cut back any new shoots to three buds, and any suckers to 15 cm above ground level.

You can outwit bothersome birds by netting your currant bushes (left) or by fooling them and growing white (right) or pink varieties.

● **THE THIRD WINTER** Cut back the shoots to four buds above their base and suckers to 15 cm above ground level. The next year, your currant bush will be ready to produce fruit.

WATCH OUT, BIRDS ABOUT It won't take long for the local bird population to spot your new fruit bushes – and work out how to get them. They can quickly rob the plant of its fruit or strip buds from the branches, leaving bare, unproductive wood.
● There are bird deterrents such as vibrating tape, which is effective, but only for a few days. It has to be changed regularly or the birds simply get used to it.
● If you are growing a number of different fruit bushes, it is well worth going to the trouble of building a fruit frame and covering it with netting to keep the birds away.
● Birds love soft, red fruit, but you can outwit them by choosing white- and pink-fruiting varieties of currant, such as 'White Dutch'. White varieties are often simply labelled 'white currant'.

NEW VARIETIES OF BLACKCURRANT Many of the very old varieties of black-currant have been overtaken by new introductions. Most older varieties flowered and produced fruitlets in early spring. As a result, they were often damaged by frost and their yield was variable. To solve this problem, plant breeders introduced the 'Ben' group, which flowers much later and is less prone to frost damage. These newer varieties, such as 'Ben More', have made growing black-currants much easier. This variety has large, black shiny fruits with a sweet acid flavour, high in vitamin C, and with a resistance to pests and diseases.

A STANDARD CURRANT If you'd like a currant that can be picked standing up, doesn't take up a lot of space and is easy to weed around the base, turn your cutting into a standard bush.
● Remove all the buds from the lower half of the cutting, so the shoots don't develop below ground level. Push the cutting vertically into the ground at the chosen position.
● Once it has rooted and new shoots have developed, tie the strongest shoot to a bamboo cane and remove the rest.
● Allow the stem to grow to about 1 m, then prune the tip. Side shoots will grow from the top three or four buds.

1 2
3 4
5 6

REJUVENATING CURRANT BUSHES The simplest way to give new vigour to an old currant bush is to cut all the branches back to ground level in winter. The following spring, a number of suckers or shoots will emerge from the soil and develop during the summer. They should then begin to bear fruit the following year.

GROWING GOOSEBERRIES Like currants, gooseberries give the best results when grown in cool to cold climates. They are very easy to grow in any type of well-drained but moisture-loving soil. They thrive in full sun or partial shade, but do not plant them in frost pockets – they flower in early spring and may be damaged by a severe late frost.

SIMPLY PRUNING GOOSEBERRIES
You will need to wear leather gloves when pruning all but the thornless gooseberries. You should do the main prune during autumn or winter, but if birds are likely to damage buds, delay pruning until bud-burst so they do not strip the few remaining buds.
● Cut out dead wood and any crossing branches, and cut back by half any new growth shooting from the main branches.
● During the early summer cut back all newly produced side shoots to four or five leaves from the base.
● Aim to create a plant with a goblet shape, to make picking easier, and with space in the centre of the bush so that air can circulate around the fruit, helping to prevent disease.

GOOSEBERRIES WITHOUT THORNS To make picking less painful, look for thornless varieties such as 'Captivator'. This variety is also resistant to powdery mildew, a disease that often affects gooseberries.

FOR COOKING OR FOR EATING? There are two types of gooseberry – culinary and dessert. Culinary varieties are ideal for cooking but are too sharp to eat fresh. Dessert gooseberries are sweeter and can be eaten fresh. If you don't have much room, choose a dessert type as younger fruits can be used for cooking and ripe fruits for eating fresh.

STRANGE FRUIT An inquisitive nurseryman hybridised the blackcurrant and the gooseberry, which produced the Worcesterberry (*Ribes divaricatum*), a small black 'gooseberry' that tastes of blackcurrant.

Blackberries

PAIN-FREE BRAMBLES The thornless blackberry is a cultivar, or cultivated variety, of the familiar wild blackberry. It is the product of genetics and pure chance, since the 'thornless' gene does in fact exist in several species of wild American blackberries. By hybridising various combinations of these species, breeders produced thornless varieties. Although blackberries are roadside weeds in many areas, these cultivated forms are worth growing. The fruit of the cultivar doesn't taste as sweet as that of the wild bramble, but it is larger and easier to pick. There are now named varieties available from nurseries and by mail-order from specialist growers. However, many are still simply labelled 'Thornless Blackberry'.

THEY'RE NOT FUSSY Blackberries can be grown in most conditions. If you have had trouble growing berried fruit in the past then these are the ones to try, especially as they are tough and will even put up with a bit of shade, making them ideal for gardens which are surrounded by overhanging trees.
● As blackberries do not flower until spring, they can even be planted in a frost hollow.

THE GROWING CYCLE – THE KEY TO PRUNING During the first year of a blackberry's development, the root stock produces shoots that emerge from the soil and put on several metres' growth. Then the

1 Prune in early spring. Start by cutting out 2-year-old stems at the base. Then remove spindly growth from the end of new canes.

2 If you have few new canes, leave some old canes in place to fruit again. Cut back any damage on these old canes to a healthy bud.

3 Remove damaged and diseased wood and any canes that you feel will obstruct paths.

4 Carefully tie in the new year-old stems as these will produce the most fruit. They'll be cut off at the base the following year.

Don't pick blackberries as soon as they turn black. Leave them for a few days when they will taste sweeter.

following year, lateral shoots appear on the long climbing stems. These shoots will flower and produce fruit during the summer and then die off in the winter. During this time, other vigorous shoots will develop from the root stock and they will produce fruit the following year, and so on.

● When pruning your blackberry, cut out any dry, dead stems at the base. Leave all the visible new shoots because these will produce the following summer's fruit. See right for how to prune, step by step.

SUPPORT REQUIRED Even the modern compact variety of blackberry can put on several metres' growth in a single season. It's essential to provide its supple climbing stems with support so they don't sprawl all over the ground – but you can wait for a year after planting before putting a system in place.

● Sink wood or metal stakes at least 2 m long into the ground at 5 m intervals and, if possible, support each one with an angled strut. Then stretch three lengths of thick, galvanised wire horizontally between the stakes at a height of 1 m, 1.3 m and 1.6 m above the ground. Tighten each wire at one end with a straining bolt and, finally, plant the blackberries along the support system at intervals of 2.5 m.

● As the shoots grow, tie them to the wires at an angle using soft, pliable ties that won't damage the young stems. You can buy practical, reusable ties from garden centres, or use strips of fabric or old nylon pantihose.

KEEP OUT OF THE SUN Once blackberries are picked, they tend to turn red and hard if left in the sun. Cover your crop with a tea towel while you are picking, and keep them in the refrigerator until you use them.

Lillypillies and mulberries

FRUIT FROM THE RAINFOREST The lilly-pilly is a very beautiful Australian native tree. One of its features is its glossy, evergreen foliage, but it also has attractive pink or red new growth, fluffy cream-coloured blossoms followed by masses of red, pink, white, blue or purple berries ranging in size from 1 cm diameter up to 10 cm in diameter and the

size of a small apple. Each berry has a single, hard central seed with the more tasty berries having small seeds and larger, fleshy berries. While lillypilly fruit is usually edible it is actually mostly tart or else it is simply lacking flavour. The fruit does however make very tasty jellies and preserves.

● Lillypillies are very popular in the home garden because they make wonderful hedge, topiary and screen plants. They range from large shrubs about 1 m in size, to big rain-forest trees over 10 m tall.

● Lillypillies in flower and in fruit are also excellent plants to have because they will attract native birds and animals to your garden. Lorikeets in particular are attracted to the flowers while cassowaries are known to eat fallen fruit.

GROWING LILLYPILLIES Lillypillies grow in all but the coldest and driest climates. They are tough, hardy plants that tolerate most soils and require little maintenance, apart from extra watering during dry spells. Lillypillies also grow better if protected from hot, dry winds. Regular pruning encourages compact shape and flushes of new growth. If fruit is desired, prune after fruit is harvested.

● Even though most lillypillies are easy to grow and virtually trouble-free, some are prone to attack by insects called psyllids (*Trioza eugeniae*). These tiny little creatures

Acmena smithii produces clusters of pink lillypilly fruits. Trees can reach 12 m in height.

DID YOU KNOW?

A TREAT FOR SOFT FRUIT
Gooseberries, currants, raspberries and blackberries all benefit from added compost, as a source of humus. Add a couple of shovelfuls of this precious enriching organic material around the roots of each bush or plant in autumn and the earthworms will drag it into the soil.

burrow inside the leaves and feed on them, causing unsightly lumps, or pimples, to form. Control measures include spraying with a systemic insecticide, pruning off affected foliage and planting resistant varieties. Some varieties that show resistance to the lillypilly psyllid include riberry (*Syzygium luehmannii*) and *Acmena smithii*.

STRANGE HABITS Some of the lillypillies found in rainforests and seen in parks and gardens produce fruit in a strange way. Instead of forming on the tips of branches, the flowers and fruit can be found clustered along the main trunk and branches. This odd habit is called 'cauliflorous' and can be seen in the rose apple (*Syzygium moorei*).

BACKYARDS OF OLD In the not-so-long-ago past, Australian backyards nearly always featured a Hills hoist and a mulberry tree. The two weren't really compatible, as birds feasted on the fruit and then deposited purple droppings on the clean washing! In those days kids enjoyed swinging on the clothes line, eating mulberries and collecting mulberry leaves for their pet silkworms. However, modern backyards are too small for a normal mulberry tree, which can grow up to 10 m tall and 5 m or more wide, but there are smaller varieties available today including dwarf weeping mulberries.

Gardener's Choice

BEST MULBERRY VARIETIES

BLACK ENGLISH This variety produces delicious, long black fruit in late spring.

DWARF BLACK This little mulberry grows to only around 5 m, so it is an excellent mulberry for small gardens.

HICK'S FANCY Has red berries in late spring.

SHAHTOOT This variety has long, cream fruit on a small tree. Shahtoot is also a good mulberry for smaller gardens.

WHITE MULBERRY Has greenish-yellow berries in late spring. The weeping form, 'Pendula', is a smaller tree and is ideal for small backyards or street planting.

Mulberries are one of the easiest of fruits to grow in the backyard but the fruit can stain paving, outdoor furniture or washing on the line.

EASY-TO-GROW OLD FAVOURITE The mulberry is a wonderful deciduous tree with huge, heart-shaped leaves. The white spring flowers are followed by delicious red, purple-black or white fruit during mid-spring and summer. Mulberries are not particularly fussy about soil either, and they will grow anywhere from cool temperate areas right through to subtropical climates. They will also grow in arid areas if watered well. These lovely trees are self pollinating and they have few pest and disease problems, apart from birds and bats, which love eating the fruit.
● Plant mulberry trees in winter or in early spring when the trees are dormant. Make sure you select a sunny, open situation away from areas where the falling mulberry fruit could become a nuisance. Mulberries are ideal for new gardens as growth will be rapid and fruit will be produced on young trees.
● To remove mulberry stains, rub over the stain with a green mulberry.

MULBERRIES FOR SILKWORMS One of the traditional uses for mulberries is to use their leaves to feed silkworms. The species planted widely in groves around silkworm factories was the white mulberry, *Morus alba*. All mulberry leaves can be used to rear silkworms, which today are mainly kept as children's pets in spring.

LOGANBERRIES
In 1881, James Logan of Santa Cruz, California, a judge and an occasional plant breeder, created a new plant with conical red berries while attempting to hybridise two varieties of blackberry. One of the parent plants was in fact a nearby raspberry whose pollen had accidentally fertilised one of the blackberry flowers. Varieties such as 'Thornless Loganberry' are cultivated in the same way as the blackberry. It is not frost hardy and its fruit, which is harvested at the end of summer, tends to be rather hard and tart. This makes it more suitable for making jam than eating raw, although it also freezes well.

Fruits of the vine

Vines such as grape, kiwifruit and passionfruit are easy to grow. They don't take up very much space in the home garden and they provide excellent crops of delicious fruit for harvesting.

Sweet and succulent grapes

GROW A VINE IN A POT Fill a large pot 35–40 cm in diameter with a good-quality potting mix suitable for acid-loving plants. Plant a young vine whose climbing stems can be trained up a pergola or trellis. It will do well on your patio in a sunny position. At the end of the summer you can pick a few bunches of delicious table grapes.
● Repot the grapevine every 2 years, if this is possible, otherwise top up the container with fresh potting mix.

DO YOU LIVE IN A VINE-GROWING REGION? Like all cultivated plants, the grapevine has particular climatic requirements, especially when it comes to summer temperatures. While vines can withstand extremely cold winters, they do not like late-spring frosts, which destroy the buds, and they need warmth and baking sun during the summer months to ripen the fruit. Grapevines grow best in Mediterranean-style regions, which have hot, dry summers, cool to mild winters, low humidity and moderate annual rainfall (mostly falling in the cooler months). In subtropical areas, look for low-chill grape varieties such as 'Flame Seedless'.

VINES FOR WINE The cultivation of grapes began in Australia when seeds and cuttings arrived with the first fleet. Governor Phillip had established over 1 hectare of grapevines at Parramatta, west of Sydney, by 1791. The wine-making industry as we know it now began in the 1840s, and today, Australia is the seventh largest wine-producing country in the world. If you are thinking about making your own wine at home, you will probably need more than one vine (a single vine will only produce about 2–4 kg of

fruit). Grapevines need plenty of attention, so they often become a specialist hobby for some gardeners. A well-loved vine will produce grapes for decades but it can take up to 4 years to give you a substantial crop.
● If you don't have enough grapes from your own vine for making wine, get together with others for a neighbourhood vintage.

THE BEST TIME TO PLANT GRAPE-VINES Plant vines during winter. Whether the plants have a root ball or are bare-root, make sure the point where they have been grafted onto the root stock is about 4 cm above the level of the soil.
● Always choose varieties that are suitable for your area and your needs.
● Remember to grow varieties that are resistant to pests and diseases.

Given a sheltered spot, plenty of sun and good support, a grapevine will happily live in a large trough.

To protect your ripening grapes from wasps and troublesome birds, wrap them in paper bags that have been pierced with holes.

Gardener's Choice

TOP GRAPE VARIETIES

Grapes can be black (which are sometimes described as red) or green. Red wine is made by leaving in the skins.

CAROLINA BLACK ROSE This is an excellent home-garden variety, which has very high disease resistance.

FLAME SEEDLESS An early-season seedless variety with a firm, red skin.

LADY PATRICIA This is an early- to mid-season variety with golden-yellow skin. It has sweet, slightly astringent flesh.

MUSCAT HAMBURGH 1 A classic Muscat variety which has large, dark red fruit.

PINK IONA 2 This is a sweet variety with pinkish skin and good disease resistance.

- Train your grapevine to grow on a fence, on lattice or over a pergola.
- Water the vines well from late winter right through to harvest time.
- Avoid wetting the leaves and fruit to help prevent fungal diseases such as anthracnose, downy mildew and powdery mildew.

REJUVENATING AN OLD VINE Once a vine reaches 20–25 years old it becomes less productive. Hard pruning will promote new vigour, but should be carried out over 2 years so that it is less traumatic for the vine.

- During your grape's first summer, make sure you concentrate on the vine's leaf- and grape-bearing shoots that originate near the base of the vine – these are the ones you will keep. Train them in the best direction by staking and by using lattice.
- In winter, cut out some of the vine shoots, leaving those produced by the branches that you have decided to keep.
- The following winter, use a saw to cut the vine stock, or trunk, just above the shoots to be retained. Smooth off the cut with a well-sharpened knife or pruning knife and seal it with candle wax to prevent infection from pests and diseases.

PROTECT YOUR GRAPES Here's an old-fashioned tip that can improve the quality and quantity of your crop. Before your grapes ripen, protect them from wasps and birds by carefully wrapping them in paper bags that you have pierced with holes.

SOME TOP TIPS FOR A GOOD GRAPE HARVEST To get plump, perfectly shaped dessert grapes, thin out the bunches when the fruit first appears. Do this by using nail scissors to remove damaged, diseased or mis-shapen grapes. You don't need to thin the grapes that are being grown for wine because any shape or size will do for this purpose.

- **LET THE SUN IN** As the fruit ripens, tie back or remove some of the foliage so that the sun can reach the fruit.
- **PICK ON TIME** When the stem that attaches the bunch of grapes to the vine starts to go brown, the fruit is ready for picking.
- **CUT A BRANCH** Take the whole bunch, not individual grapes – this way they are easier to store and should last a lot longer.
- **STORE WELL** Put your harvest in a box with a soft lining and store it in a cool and shaded place for up to a month.

PRUNING A VINE IN LATE WINTER

1 Cutting cleanly and at an angle, remove all the branches that bore fruit the previous year.

2 Cut back the spurs you are keeping to the second bud. The upper bud will produce this year's fruit.

3 Cut back a long lateral shoot to 20 cm and tie it carefully to the training wires. This will extend your vine.

4 De-bud the vine later in the year by removing surplus shoots during the summer.

Kiwifruit and passionfruit

WEIRD BUT WONDERFUL The strange-looking hairy fruit known now as kiwifruit but once called Chinese gooseberry is a deciduous, twining vine native to the Yangtze River valley of northern China and the Zhejiang Province on the coast of eastern China. In the early 1900s, missionaries took some kiwifruit seeds with them from China to New Zealand, where the vine soon became popular in backyard gardens and where it gained its modern name. It has tough, quite leathery leaves, fragrant cream flowers and delicious, oval fruit with pale green flesh.

BEWARE OF CATS Once you've planted your kiwifruit, you may notice local cats rolling near the base of the plant – cats are wild about the aroma released by the roots. They're only a serious threat to your plants if they sharpen their claws on the trunks, so it might be worth using protective sleeves.

HEAVY STUFF Kiwifruit can be surprisingly vigorous, a fact that you really should bear in mind when building a pergola to support this fruiting climber.
● Make sure the structure is solid. The shoots can grow several metres a year, which not only means there is a lot of foliage to catch the wind, but also that the plant is extremely heavy and capable of damaging the structure.
● Ideally, pergolas should be 2.5 m high and 3 m wide, with wires spaced 60–75 cm apart to support the laterals.

CULTIVATION Kiwifruit grows best in a sunny position with protection from strong winds. It prefers mild or temperate climates without late frosts or burning heat. The vines like a well-drained soil that is slightly acid, with plenty of added organic matter.
● The kiwifruit has male and female flowers on separate plants, so both a male and a female vine are needed for pollination and fruit production. One male is needed for every eight to nine female plants. The best time to plant is during winter when the vines are dormant. Female vines start to bear after about 4 years, and will continue bearing for about 20 years. In winter, prune laterals back to a few buds beyond the previous season's growth.

The passionfruit flower is remarkably ornamental, such as this flower of Passiflora edulis.

PASSIONFRUIT FROM THE SOUTH The passionfruit is a vigorous climbing vine that originates from South America. The plant gets its name from the way it could evoke Christ's Passion, that is, from the threadlike appendages that recall the crown of thorns; the stamens, the sponge steeped in vinegar; and the stigmas, the nails of the cross.

GROWING PASSIONFRUIT Passionfruit grows well in subtropical and temperate climates. It likes a well-drained soil with added organic matter and a warm, sunny position protected from strong winds. Plant your passionfruit in spring. If you live in a cool area you might have some success if you plant your passionfruit vine next to a north-facing masonry wall.
● You can train your passionfruit vine to grow along a fence, lattice or pergola. Make sure you fertilise regularly and mulch well. Prune back after fruiting to encourage new growth, remove dead wood and keep the vine tidy. Vines take 12–18 months to reach fruiting size and usually become unproductive after a few years, so it's a good idea to start another one in a different spot in the garden as a replacement after 4–5 years.

ONE OR MORE? Some passionfruit will only produce fruit if there is another vine nearby. The golden passionfruit and the granadilla need two vines for fruit but the widely grown black passionfruit (which is usually grafted on to *Passiflora caerulea*) fruits well even if there's only one vine – so this is better suited to a garden.

The fruit garden of your dreams

Few gardens today have the luxury of the space for an orchard devoted exclusively to fruit trees. Remember, though, if you don't have very much room, with careful planning you can still have a fruit garden that will take you through the seasons.

Using space wisely

THE BEST POSITION FOR YOUR FRUIT GARDEN In today's smaller gardens, all fruit plants, including trees, bushes and climbers alike, are often planted together. Fruit gardens and orchards should, as far as possible, occupy an open space in your garden that is neither too wet nor susceptible to spring frosts.

● The best positions are on a north- or east-facing slope, just below a wall or hedge.

● The worst positions are in a frost pocket or on waterlogged or frequently flooded ground – for example, on a slope just above a high wall, a tall hedge or a group of trees.

● Avoid the area to the north of your vegetable garden, otherwise the tall fruit trees will cast shadows over your crops.

● If possible, don't choose a site that is at all isolated from other gardens. If you do, you are likely to suffer from more than your fair share of fruit-plundering birds, and your trees won't be pollinated by other fruit trees in your neighbourhood.

WHAT TO PLANT WHERE Plant fruit trees in a lawn or paddock, but remember to leave enough space to allow you to mow the grass between the trees. Don't forget height either, as some trees, especially cherries, can grow to 15 m, whereas dwarf fruit trees may be so low that you have to duck when mowing, which can make it a better option to plant them in a border on their own.

● Plant espalier vines and trained soft fruit bushes against a sheltered, sunny wall.

● It's a good idea to plant cordon and fan gooseberries, blackcurrants and raspberries

around the edge of your vegetable garden or in a fruit frame. Strawberries will also go well in the vegetable garden.

CHECK THE HEIGHT AND SPREAD A tree is a long-term commitment, so try not to plant one that will take up a lot of space in a small garden. You, or your successor, will be forced to cut it down prematurely as it outgrows its space. This is particularly true of mango and walnut trees, both of which can eventually grow to at least 15 m tall and spread to between 10 and 18 m wide.

ASK THE NEIGHBOURS There's nothing better than taking a good look around the neighbourhood when you are planning a

You don't need a huge garden to grow fruit – you can grow trees and soft fruit among your vegetables, like this pretty espalier pear tree.

small orchard or fruit garden. To find out which species and cultivars thrive in your area, ask neighbouring gardeners for their recommendations as well as their advice on what should be avoided. Local farmers' markets also reflect what grows well in a region and may help you choose trees and fruit bushes that will be happy and that are sure to produce fruit in abundance. But that doesn't stop you experimenting, trying some old varieties and using a bit of imagination.

SAVING SPACE IDEAS Don't plant large-growing fruit trees that will take up all the space in your garden when they mature. By using some clever space-saving options, you'll make room to try some of the more unusual species (see the table below).

● **DWARF** There are 'true' dwarfs, which are just naturally small, or ordinary fruit trees grafted onto dwarf understocks. When full-sized tops are grafted onto dwarf root stocks, they produce full-sized fruit.

● **MULTI-GRAFT** A multi-graft is one where several varieties of one type of fruit are grafted onto one plant, with each graft growing independently and its fruit retaining its own characteristics. Multi-grafted apple, citrus, pear and stone fruit trees are all widely available today. A fruit salad tree has different but compatible fruits grafted on to one plant such as several citrus or a mixture of stone fruits.

● **TWO PLANTS, ONE HOLE** Plant two or even more fruit trees of similar size and vigour in the one hole. This is ideal where a pollinator is needed but space is tight.

● **ESPALIER** This is a tree that is trained flat against a wall on a framework of wires, with pairs of branches stretched out horizontally every 40 cm or so like a ladder. This is a very formal way of training.

THE ULTIMATE SIZE OF A TREE Before planting a group of fruit trees make a note of their eventual spread. When they mature they will suffer if they are planted too close together. Fruit trees do, however, appreciate a pollinating partner nearby so that bees can dance from one tree to the next. You will get far more fruit if trees are planted in groups.

Planting your fruit tree

BUY YOUR TREES IN WINTER Today the fashion is for container-grown trees that can be bought all year round. However, at certain times of year nurseries offer a wide choice of bare-root trees, which is a more traditional way to buy fruit trees. Although they are available throughout the period when the trees are dormant, they are best bought and planted in winter. They will then have the entire winter to put down the new roots they'll need to get away in spring.

● If possible, visit the nursery and choose the trees yourself. Select only those with shiny bark, a good root system and well-balanced branches in good condition.

LONG-LASTING STAKES Stakes are vital if you do not want your young trees to blow over in the first gust of wind. Choose a stake that is as thick as your arm and long enough to sit just below the crown of the tree once it is hammered into the ground. Char the part that will be buried to prevent rotting.

A PRECIOUS STONE Before you plant your tree, place a large stone or mound of earth in the bottom of the planting hole. It will serve as a wedge that prevents the tree sinking when the hole is filled in and the soil firmed down. It is bad for the roots to be planted too deeply – the uppermost roots should be almost level with the surface of the soil.

IN WET SOIL, PLANT ON A MOUND There's nothing worse for the roots of fruit trees than to be in permanently wet soil. You can create good drainage in heavy,

Trees to suit your garden

SPECIES	POLLINATION REQUIRED	HEIGHT
Avocado	Better fruiting	8 m
Black Sapote	No	6 m
Custard Apple	Yes	7 m
Feijoa	Better fruiting	5 m
Grumichama	No	3 m
Guava	No	5 m
Jaboticaba	No	6 m
Papaw	Yes	5 m
Persimmon	No	6 m
Tamarillo	No	4 m

waterlogged soil by building up a mound of soil to which you have added some well-rotted compost. Then plant the tree in the mound so that its neck is about 10–20 cm above the surrounding ground level.

RECYCLE OLD PANTIHOSE In a fruit garden you always need ties for securing a young trunk to a stake or for training or supporting a branch. A perfect and a very inexpensive solution is to use old pantihose. They form a wide, soft tie and will not cause damage to the growing trunk.

GREAT EXPECTATIONS? In some years, spring frosts and rain can result in a poor yield, especially for stone fruit trees.
● Standard apple trees tend to alternate their yield naturally, producing fruit one year and then none in the next.
● Strong winds in spring and summer can impede the movement of pollinating insects and damage young fruits and young shoots, reducing the yield. Improve shelter for your fruit trees on any exposed sites.

TO GRASS OR NOT TO GRASS Grass is a practical way to cover the ground in your orchard, since it provides a secure footing, even after it has rained, and it offers a soft landing for any falling fruit. Grass will also enrich the soil by continually manufacturing humus. Finally, it does away with the never-ending chore of weeding. All you have to do is cut it regularly (much less often than an ornamental lawn) and you can even leave the grass cuttings on the ground. However, don't grow grass right up to the trunk or you may damage it with your lawnmower.
● However, there is a downside to grassing your orchard. The covering of meadow grass will compete with your trees by absorbing

Old pantihose are an inexpensive way to train or support branches (left). If your orchard is grassed, be sure to leave enough room between rows for the lawnmower (right).

Increase your fruit production and fill your garden with the gentle hum of bees by keeping a few beehives in your orchard.

moisture from the soil, so it is best to grass between the rows and leave an area of bare soil around the base of the trees. In dry areas, you can cover the soil with a mulch of leaf mould, bark or gravel to limit evaporation.

PROTECT THE BARK OF YOUNG TREES AND BUSHES The bark of newly planted trees and bushes is very susceptible to frost, and especially to thaws. If you live in a frost pocket, use this old-fashioned method of

WATCH OUT

SPARE A THOUGHT FOR YOUR NEIGHBOURS

Avoid planting trees less than 2 m from the boundary of your property. If the branches of your fruit trees overhang your neighbours' garden, they can legally gather any fallen fruit and can cut back any branches or roots that encroach on their property. You will not be able to gain access to pick fruit from over-hanging branches or prune without permission.

Over and above the strict legal aspects, avoid planting a vigorous tree in a position where it is likely to block your neighbours' view or cast a shadow over their house.

How much fruit will you get?

The amount of fruit produced by a tree will vary depending on its planting position and variety.

SPECIES	PRODUCTION PER TREE/BUSH/PLANT
Apple (tall)	Irregular: from nothing to over 100 kilograms
Apricot	Irregular: from nothing to several dozen kilograms
Blackberry	Regular: several kilograms
Blackcurrant	Regular: 1–2 kilograms
Cherry	Irregular: from several kilograms to several dozen kilograms
Grapevine	Regular: several kilograms
Hazelnut	Irregular: from nothing to several kilograms
Kiwifruit	Regular: several kilograms
Peach	Irregular: from nothing to over 10 kilograms
Pear (small or medium)	Irregular: from several kilograms to several dozen kilograms
Pear (tall)	Regular: several dozen kilograms
Plum	Irregular: from nothing to several dozen kilograms
Quince	Irregular: from several kilograms to several dozen kilograms
Raspberry	Regular: several kilograms per 10 square metres of canes
Redcurrant	Regular: 1–2 kilograms
Walnut	Irregular: from nothing to over 100 kilograms

protection. Wrap the tree trunks with straw, or paint them with a mixture of water and earth that has the consistency of a batter mixture. By simply adding some milk to the mixture it will help it stick to the trunk.

An ecologically friendly fruit garden

WORKING WITH NATURE You can easily improve the health and productivity of your fruit garden naturally, by planting shrubs, colourful flowers and herbs among the trees to attract beneficial insects, birds and bees.

GROW A FRUITFUL HEDGE Recently published scientific research has shown that certain trees and shrubs actually have a favourable effect on nearby orchards by providing a habitat for beneficial insects and birds that help to keep pests under control – something our forebears knew all along.
● If you would like to enclose an orchard with an attractive flowering or fruiting hedge, choose several different species from this list: abelia (*Abelia* x *grandiflora*), bay laurel (*Laurus nobilis*), crab-apple (*Malus* spp.), grevillea (*Grevillea* 'Robyn Gordon' and 'Superb'), heath banksia (*Banksia ericifolia*), Indian hawthorn (*Raphiolepis indica*), lillypilly (*Acmena smithii*), NSW Christmas Bush (*Ceratopetalum gummiferum*), sacred bamboo (*Nandina domestica),* sasanqua camellia (*Camellia sasanqua*) and viburnum (*Viburnum tinus*).

KEEPING BEES Because they play such an essential role in pollination, bees have been a feature of the orchard for centuries. In days gone by, it was the lucky orchard owner who had a hive under the trees. Beekeeping is a specialist hobby, but if you do want to take it up it will benefit your fruit trees and give you a supply of delicious honey.

ATTRACTIVE PLANTS Plants that attract beneficial insects include buddleias and lavenders for pollinating bees; colourful, open-centred flowers for ladybirds; and marigolds (*Calendula*) and French marigolds (*Tagetes patula*) for lacewings and hoverflies.

PROVIDE SOME WINTER SHELTER FOR GOOD FRIENDS Green lacewings, with their iridescent wings, can sometimes be seen on window panes during winter. Lacewings and their larvae are formidable predators when it comes to aphids, caterpillars and other common orchard pests. There are many things you can do to keep lacewings in the garden to continue their good work, and one of these is to provide them with natural shelter, especially in winter.
● Fill a flowerpot with straw and hang it in a tree to provide a winter retreat for lacewings.
● Some shrubs, such as mallow (*Lavatera* hybrid cultivars), provide a good habitat for the very beneficial ladybirds to overwinter.
● Try to encourage blue-tongue lizards, which will keep snails under control, by piling up a few logs or large stones in a quiet corner of your garden so they can bask in the sun and hide from predators.

KEEP FOUR-LEGGED LAWNMOWERS Few of us have large enough orchards for keeping sheep, but years ago sheep used to graze the grass underneath fruit trees and did away with the need to use a lawnmower. One or two would happily keep an orchard trim, but if you do keep them, make sure the boundary around your property is secure.

DID YOU KNOW?

ALWAYS ADD SOME NATURAL NUTRIENTS When you plant fruit trees, add plenty of organic matter to the planting hole in the form of homemade compost or some well-rotted farmyard manure and blood and bone. Water it in with a seaweed solution. If these aren't available, use a proprietary tree and shrub compost.

PLANTING A FRUIT TREE

1 Dress the roots by soaking the entire root system in a mixture of well-rotted garden compost and water for about an hour.

2 Cut out a circle of turf from where you intend to plant the tree, that measures about 1 m across, and then remove the topsoil.

3 Dig out a 50 cm deep hole and arrange the lumps of turf upside-down in the bottom. Trim any damaged roots from the tree.

4 Position the tree with the neck just above soil level. If necessary, put some topsoil back in the bottom of the hole to raise it a little.

5 Shovel some soil over the roots, gently shaking the tree so that it settles. Hammer in a stake between the roots, near the trunk.

6 Attach the tree to the stake, wedging a handful of straw between tree and stake where they touch. Fill in the hole and water well.

Appealing apples, pears and quinces

If you were lucky enough to grow up with an apple or pear tree in your garden, you will probably want to continue the tradition. There is a shape to suit even the smallest space, and today's disease-resistant varieties make growing such fruit easier than ever before.

Getting the right size and shape

TRAINED FOR SMALL GARDENS When trained flat against a wall or some lattice, fruit trees such as apples can take up little space. Stretching the branches out horizontally produces an espalier tree (see page 225), while fanning them out from the main branch produces the fan. A cordon is a form of trained tree with a central trunk and branches that are trained at a 45° angle.
● This type of structured shaping requires the regular work of pruning and training to maintain the desired shape.

SAVE TIME ON PRUNING If you do not want to prune every year and only have a small space, plant trees that have been grown on dwarf root stocks. Apples are available on dwarf root stocks such as M27, which affect tree size but not the fruit size.
● By selecting a columnar variety of apple or crab-apple such as the Ballerina series you can grow them even in a courtyard. These trees grow only 30 cm wide but 3–4 m high. They can grow in a large container or in the garden.

TRY NATURALLY PRUNING Today, most commercial fruit growers don't hard prune apples. They prefer to manage their trees more naturally, an example you could easily follow.
● Allow the fruit-bearing branches to produce fruit naturally and then prune a few each year by cutting back to just above a young lateral branch that will replace them. This is known as renewal pruning.

● If the spur bearers have a lot of fruit buds, you can also prune these to limit the amount of fruit that will be produced.

THE QUINCE REVIVAL Favoured by the Victorians, the quince is a beautiful, modest tree, which is often used as a root stock for pears. Quinces provide a light shade and they produce magnificent flowers and aromatic, apple-like fruits used in making preserves. 'Champion' is an all-round variety that lives up to its name.

PICKING A PEAR Fruiting pears become tall, spreading trees up to 15 m tall and 6 m wide and are an excellent choice as a multi-purpose garden tree. The pear gives shade, it is ornamental when in spring flower and in autumn leaf, and it has truly delicious summer to autumn fruit.

This small apple tree is growing on a dwarf root stock – as you can see it is laden with full-sized fruit.

An old-fashioned favourite, the quince is also a long-lived garden fruit tree that needs little maintenance.

An espalier pear is an ancient, formal shape (far left). A cordon apple is suitable for growing in the smallest of gardens (left).

● Most pears need cross pollination, however, the old variety 'Williams' (syn. 'Bartlett') is self-fertile although you will grow better crops with 'Beurre Bosc'.

SUPPORT FOR THE BRANCHES In heavy-cropping years, apples, pears and quinces can be quite literally weighed down with their fruit. When this happens there is a risk of some of the framework branches breaking.
● Prevent this by carefully lifting the branches and propping them on forked supports pushed into the ground (see page 241).

Beautiful flowers, bountiful fruit

WHERE HAVE THE FLOWERS GONE?
The most common reason for a tree failing to flower is overpruning. If you want your trees to flower and produce fruit, then put away your secateurs. At the very most, prune lightly, leaving at the very least six buds on each young branch. However, because they are pruned only occasionally, quinces don't tend to suffer from this problem.
● There is another, natural, reason for a tree not producing blossom – it may simply be too young. It takes 2–3 years for fruit trees to produce fruit, and some take longer.

THIN OUT IN STAGES Always thin out your fruit trees in two stages so that you do not traumatise the tree – a surge of sap to the remaining fruits could make them drop.
● Thin out pears first when the fruitlets are

the size of hazelnuts, keeping only one on the edge of the cluster. Thin out a second time when they are the size of walnuts.
● Apples should be thinned out about a month after flowering. A second thinning should follow about a fortnight later. Keep the fruitlet in the centre of the cluster.
● If you only thin out your trees once, make sure you do it when the fruitlets are the size

Gardener's Choice

BEST BACKYARD APPLE VARIETIES

ANTIQUE VARIETIES Apples have been grown for centuries and many of the varieties popular in yesteryear are firm backyard favourites. 'Cox's Orange Pippin' and a host of others are available from specialist growers.

BALLERINA This is a modern apple that has revolutionised backyard production with several named varieties including 'Waltz' and 'Bolero'. They are tall and very narrow and ideal for a tiny space or a narrow hedge.

GALA This is a round red apple with a self stripe. It is an early to midseason variety.

GRANNY SMITH This is a green apple raised in Sydney during the mid 19th century. It is a late-season variety.

PINK LADY This apple is a late-fruiting red variety developed in Australia. 'Pink Lady' doesn't need thinning.

Apples are thinned out about a month after flowering and again about a fortnight later.

Thin pears, when they're the size of small walnuts, by cutting unwanted fruit in half.

A fan-shaped apple tree is perfect for a sunny wall and won't take up much valuable space.

of walnuts. Do not remove the fruit at the peduncle, or stalk, but cut the pear or apple in half, leaving part of the fruit on the tree.
● Quince trees will fruit very well without any thinning out at all.

DON'T FORGET ABOUT POLLINATION
Unlike the self-fertile quince, many apple and pear trees need pollinating. To produce fruit, the blossom on these trees must be fertilised by other very specific species that flower at the same time and whose pollen is transferred by bees and other pollinating insects such as butterflies.
● Ensure surrounding plantings contain bushes and hedges that will attract bees.
● Attract pollinating and attractive butterflies to your garden by providing a saucer of water and a bit of sugar for them to feed on during the flowering period.

PREVENTING THE DREADED 'CORKY'
APPLES There is nothing more unpleasant when you bite into a freshly picked apple than coming across brown 'corky' patches in the middle of the fruit. These blemishes are caused by a lack of the trace element called boron. By using completely natural manures or organic fertilisers you will help to prevent these patches in your fruit, which can often be the result of adding large quantities of lime and potassium to the soil.

● If the deficiency is already apparent, try a rescue remedy of seaweed, which is rich in boron. Seaweed is available in powder and liquid form, the powder form for spreading around the base of the tree and the liquid for spraying on the leaves.

WEIGH DOWN BRANCHES TO GET
MORE APPLES The formation of fruit buds depends on the circulation of sap, which is in turn dependent on the angle of the branch. A vertical branch is more likely to make new wood than fruit. To reduce the circulation of sap and encourage fruit buds to form, reduce the angle of vertical branches by attaching weights to them such as baskets filled with pebbles or by tying them down with string attached to tent pegs. Try to get them as close to horizontal as possible.

AN ANTI-CATERPILLAR BELT In spring,
the codling moth lays its eggs on the leaves or on the young fruit of apple, pear and quince trees. Its larvae – tiny caterpillars that tunnel into the fruit to eat the seeds – will leave your crop incurably worm eaten.
● Prevent a second codling moth infestation by simply tying a strip of corrugated cardboard around the trunk of each of your trees.

Traditional gardeners placed weights in baskets hanging from apple branches as horizontal branches form more fruit.

Gardener's Choice

SEASONAL PEARS
There are three types of pear, based on the season when they are ripe and ready to eat, and their keeping qualities. Summer and autumn pears don't store well. Winter pears are picked in autumn, but will keep until late winter.

SUMMER PEARS These ripen in late summer. The best-known varieties are 'Docteur Jules Guyot' and 'Williams Bon Chrétien' (old variety) **1**.

AUTUMN PEARS These are ripe from March to April. This is the largest group of pears and includes 'Beurré Hardy' (old variety) **2**, 'Concorde', 'Doyenné du Comice' (old variety) and 'Joséphine de Malines' (old variety).

WINTER PEARS These ripen in April, but keep throughout the winter months, provided they are stored well. 'Conference', 'Olivier de Serres' and 'Winter Nelis' are all old varieties of dessert pear; 'Catillac' **3**, a culinary pear, is long keeping.

To encourage your apple tree to produce an abundance of beautiful apple blossom, do not overprune it.

● After feasting on your tasty apples, pears and quinces, the caterpillars will make their way down the trunk towards the ground where they will nestle in the cardboard, which is an ideal place for the larvae to turn into moths. In the late winter, before they emerge from their chrysalises, remove the cardboard and burn it. In this way you can control the moths by destroying the next generation.
● Another method of attracting and trapping codling moths is to hang sticky traps in the trees. These traps are available in various colours, with each colour attracting different pests, and some have a pheromone scent that makes them even more effective. These traps attract the codling moths, which then get stuck and can be disposed of.

Storing fruit

THE RIGHT TIME TO PICK It's time to pick your fruit when the first few ripening apples or pears fall – this is not counting the ones that fall prematurely because they have been eaten by caterpillars. Fruit is ripe if it comes away from the branch when twisted slightly.
● Quinces are ripe when their downy covering can be rubbed off easily by hand.

A VERY USEFUL GADGET The fruit picker (right) is a handy piece of equipment to have. It will save you having to climb or use a ladder when picking apples, pears and quinces at the end of the tallest branches of your fruit trees. Available from garden centres, it consists of a canvas or plastic bag that is fitted onto the end of a 3–4 m handle. These bags have pliant prongs around the edge that catch the fruit stems and, with a gentle pull, the fruit drops into the bag.

HANDLE THEM WITH CARE Pick apples and pears carefully to avoid bruising them, otherwise they will not keep. Cup the fruit in your hand as you twist it from its branch.

Use a specially designed fruit picker for safe harvesting. The fruit falls into the bag.

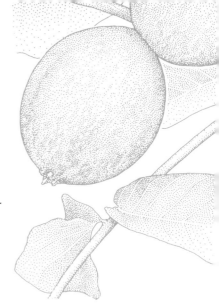

The secrets to success with citrus

No backyard, however small, should be without a citrus tree. Whether it is a cumquat in a pot or a lemon tree down the back, you'll enjoy the colourful fruit, fragrant flowers and year-round glossy leaves, and that's all before you've plucked a single fruit.

Golden cumquats and the grapefruit

GREAT IN CONTAINERS If there is one citrus that thrives in a pot, it's the cumquat (*Citrus japonica* syn. *Fortunella japonica*). All you need is to find a sunny space and a container that's at least 40 cm across and you will have a pretty and productive addition to your garden. Cumquats produce clusters of small orange fruit. 'Nagami' has oval fruit while 'Marumi' has rounded fruit. For year-round decoration look for a variegated form, which has cream and green striped leaves.
● This pretty fruit tree will grow in a large pot for many years. Just remember to fertilise each month through the growing season (spring to early autumn) with a handful of citrus food and, from time to time, add a little well-rotted manure mixed with organic mulch as surface mulch. Repot the cumquat

when the soil levels slump or if the plant appears to be stressed. In very hot weather potted cumquats may need daily watering.
● Train a standard cumquat by selecting a cumquat with a main stem and removing any side growth. The top of the plant can be clipped into a ball. You can underplant cumquats with herbs or mini mondo grass.

GOOD ENOUGH TO EAT Although many gardeners use cumquats for their decorative value only, the fruit, which ripens through winter, is great for bottling or for making into a delicious marmalade. The skin of the fruit is sweet and can be eaten with the flesh.
● The cumquat is considered lucky in some cultures and these golden-fruited plants are sometimes given as gifts to commemorate Chinese New Year.

CALAMONDIN CONFUSION This fruit resembles the round cumquat but has larger fruits that almost look like small mandarins. Calamondin (*Citrus* x *microcarpa*) is a hybrid of a cumquat and a mandarin. It grows well in pots or in the ground and the fruit can be used in the same way as cumquats. If it is left unpruned it becomes a dense shrub of around 2.5 m tall and 1.5 m wide.

GIANTS OF THE CITRUS CROP Grapefruit (*Citrus* x *aurantium* syn. *C. paradisi*) is among the largest of the citrus fruits. Most provide bountiful crops with little work from you. The main need is to thin over-generous fruit clusters to reduce the stress on branches. 'Wheeny', a cold-tolerant variety suited to cool winter areas, is heavy cropping. 'Marsh' is a seedless grapefruit.

A heavy crop of grapefruit can break branches, so thin out bumper crops early, or provide support for branches.

Cumquats produce decorative, long-lasting fruit even when grown in containers.

The biggest of all citrus fruits are pomelos, or shaddocks (*Citrus maxima*), which prefer a subtropical to tropical climate where they can reach the size of a small watermelon. In frost-free temperate gardens fruits have thick skin and pith and tart flesh but they are excellent for making marmalade.

COLOURFUL TINTS If you think of grapefruit as bitter and always yellow, it is time to rethink. New varieties are sweet and may have pink or red-tinged flesh. The pick of the crop is the ruby grapefruit (including 'Red Blush' and 'Ruby'), which has delicate pink flesh that's sweet to eat or juice.

Lemons and limes

A TOP CHOICE Lemons (*Citrus* x *limon*) are the most widely grown of all citrus fruit trees, and this is probably because they are so versatile. Lemons can be grown in tubs or espaliered against a warm wall if space is tight. Given ample room, you can grow a lemon as a small but attractive and productive tree in any sunny, well-drained soil. Lemons store well on the tree, which enables the crop to be treated as a larder and picked over many months.

TRENDY CHOICES FOR YOUR GARDEN

Once a rare sight in gardens, limes are now vying with lemons for a place of prominence in our backyards. The small, round, yellow to green fruit is substituted for lemons, and lime trees are prolific bearers. The most popular lime choice is the Tahitian (*Citrus* x *latifolia*), which grows in frost-free, temperate to tropical gardens. The main crop is ripe in autumn and winter but the fruit holds well on the tree.

Australian limes (*Citrus australis*) and finger limes (*C. australasica*) are native fruits from the *Citrus* genus, once known only to bush-food experts but now available to gardeners. The fruit of the Australian lime is round; the fruit of finger limes is elongated and about 6 cm long and carried on thorny stems. Both grow as tall shrubs or small trees up to 5 m high and they can be substituted for limes or lemons. Like most citrus these are best in a frost-free area. In dry or inland areas look for the desert lime, *C. glauca*, which has tiny but tasty fruit and is drought tolerant.

Meyer lemons are small, very pretty, spreading trees with good cold tolerance.

DID YOU KNOW?

FRUIT OR FOLIAGE?
Most citrus are grown for their edible fruits but kaffir limes (*Citrus hystrix*) are grown mainly for their leaves (below), which are traditionally featured in Malaysian and Thai cooking.

Pick the leaves for flavouring curries or stir-fries, or shred them finely to garnish a hot meal or toss in a salad. The fruit of the kaffir lime is small, wrinkled and dry inside. It is sometimes used as flavouring.

Mandarins and oranges

CHILDREN'S CHOICE A backyard mandarin (*Citrus reticulata*) is a sure-fire way to encourage kids to eat fruit. The trees are trouble free and crop heavily in a sunny spot. Encourage your kids to pick and eat mandarins as this citrus crop doesn't store well on the tree and is also very easy to pick and to peel. Once the crop ripens it will fall if not harvested. Overripe fruit spoils and loses its sweet flavour.

BIENNIAL BEARING Many citrus trees produce a heavy crop one year, followed by a lighter crop the second year. This habit, which is called biennial bearing, is marked in mandarins. To even out the crops, thin the young fruit in the heavy-bearing years.

KEEP IN TRIM Mandarins, especially the popular 'Emperor Mandarin', develop into large trees. Keep them trimmed to an easy height (around 2–3 m) for ease of picking. Pruning is best done at the end of winter.

SOME SWEET CHOICES The sweetest of all citrus fruits is the sun-ripened orange (*Citrus x aurantium* syn. *C. sinensis*). Like cumquats, lemons and grapefruit, oranges store well on the tree and can be harvested over many months. Oranges tend to be sweeter the longer they remain on the tree in the sunshine. The main cropping period is autumn to late winter but an orange can even be found when the tree is blooming with its next crop of flowers.

BLOOD ORANGES The red tinge seen in some grapefruit is also found in selected orange varieties. Blood oranges have a red blush to the skin and to the fruit and the squeezed juice is pink to dark red.

Citrus care

THE BEST CONDITIONS All citrus thrive in full sun (at least 6 hours a day is a minimum requirement) with well-drained soil enriched with organic matter. Citrus trees do not like poorly drained soil and most garden plants

are now grafted on understock that is more tolerant of poorly drained soils. This provides some extra protection against root rot fungal problems. Keep the area under your citrus trees clear of weeds and free from competing plants. To deter weeds, cover the root area of the tree with a 5–7 cm layer of organic mulch, and make sure you top it up regularly.

● Ragged or torn leaves and crop losses can be an indication that trees are grown in areas that are overly exposed to winds. Always provide a sheltered spot for your citrus trees and this will get the best results.

Gardener's Choice

CITRUS TREES TO GROW IN POTS
Some varieties of orange and lemon trees can be grown in large pots on a sunny veranda. In some very cold areas citrus are overwintered indoors.

CALAMONDIN This tree is a hybrid of a cumquat (*Citrus japonica*) and a mandarin. The oranges are small but perfect for jam. The tree requires a temperature of 13–15°C in winter and 18°C when the fruit is growing.

CUMQUAT This is a very decorative shrub, which is fairly resistant to the cold. It produces small, elongated fruits that can be eaten raw, skins included.

MEYER LEMON TREE One of the most common varieties, with fruit the size of an egg. It needs a minimum of 10°C.

An orange tree makes a handsome and productive addition to any garden.

DID YOU KNOW?

ORANGE OR MANDARIN?
As all the citrus fruits we enjoy are closely related to one another, there are some fruits that are hard to place as they are crosses between two different species. One of these oddities is the tangelo (*Citrus x tangelo*). People often ask if it is a mandarin or an orange. The red- to orange-coloured fruit peels like a mandarin, but has a tart orange flavour and, like oranges, it is good for juicing. Crops are ripe in late winter to spring. Protect from frost and grow in an open sunny spot to promote ripening.

Gardener's Choice

ORANGES FOR GARDENS

NAVEL Almost seedless with a distinctive bump at the base of the fruit (hence the 'navel'). 'Washington Navel' is a good backyard choice with fruit ripening in late autumn and winter.

RUBY A blood orange with red tones and sweet flesh. While not widely grown, this is a good choice for an unusual backyard citrus and a good choice for juicing.

SEVILLE A sour orange prized for its tart flesh and thick skin for marmalades. Seville oranges have better cold tolerance than other oranges. Cropping season is short, from autumn to early winter.

VALENCIA (below) Held on the tree ripening over many months, this is a good choice for a steady harvest. Fruit held in summer change from orange back to green and orange indicating ripe fruit.

REGULAR FEEDING GOES A LONG WAY

Citrus trees are very productive plants that produce the best and sweetest crops when they are given regular doses of fertiliser. As a general rule of thumb, fertilise all citrus trees in late winter, or in early spring in colder zones, and again during the late summer. For the best results, alternate between a complete citrus food, which is sold at nurseries, and an organic pelletised chicken manure.

● If your citrus fruit is tart even despite a long ripening period, it could indicate that you have a lack of trace elements in your soil. These are elements that are needed in only very small amounts and they can be bought at nurseries and added to the soil.

Mandarins are easy to grow and are great favourites with children. The delicious fruit can be eaten straight from the tree.

READING THE LEAVES A lack of nutrients shows up as a distinctive veining or patterning of the leaves. These indicate nutrient deficiencies that can be identified by the patterning. You can correct any nutrient deficiencies with applications of complete citrus food or by adding the missing element.

● **IRON DEFICIENCY** Green leaves fade leaving only the veins green and the remainder may be yellow or bleached to almost white.

● **MAGNESIUM DEFICIENCY** Leaves yellow from the edge but the centre remains green.

● **MANGANESE DEFICIENCY** Young leaves are pale green or they may appear to be yellowish between the veins.

● **ZINC DEFICIENCY** Leaves are smaller than normal and they may develop some yellow discolouration between the veins.

COMMON CITRUS PESTS As citrus are widely grown and tasty they are subject to a range of pest problems including aphids, scale and bugs such as bronze orange bug and spined citrus bug. Silver trails in new growth are the work of the citrus leaf miner. While none of these pests will kill citrus trees, they take their toll on the tree's vigour and on crop production. Regular spraying with horticultural spray oil during flushes of new growth and in winter when pests are in juvenile stages of development reduces the need to use harsher chemicals.

AGE-OLD PRUNING TIPS

Gardeners of the past knew that pruning was all about commonsense. In the case of citrus trees, where pruning isn't needed to produce a crop, cuts are made to solve growth problems and restrict height. Avoid pruning in summer as exposed wood may become sunburnt.

● Heavy crops can cause the lower branches to drag on the ground and actually split or break. A pruning technique, called skirting, removes the lowest branches leaving it clear and improving its air circulation.

● Neglected trees can be hard pruned in spring, cut back to a skeleton to rejuvenate growth. Follow hard pruning with regular deep watering and an application of fertiliser to maintain regrowth.

● Suckers – growths from below the graft union – are an indication that the tree is under stress. Suckers may be thorny and, if left, will produce unpleasant fruit.

● Remove the suckers, clear away any weeds and increase watering and fertilising.

Stone fruit – the taste of the sun

By growing an apricot, cherry, peach or plum tree you are bringing succulent summer delicacies to your garden. These luscious fruits were commonly grown in the past and deserve room in the modern garden.

Choosing a stone fruit

THE RIGHT CONDITIONS Stone fruits thrive in cool and Mediterranean climates and some varieties are suitable for coastal areas. There are even low-chill varieties that fruit in subtropical zones.

● Apricots (*Prunus armeniaca*) grow well in southern gardens, particularly in those with a Mediterranean-style climate with a long, hot, dry summer.

● Cherries (*Prunus avium*) do their best when grown in southern and mountain gardens, which have cold winters and mild summers.

● Peaches and nectarines (*Prunus persica*) grow in all but tropical areas. In the warmer areas, make sure you select low-chill varieties.

● Plums thrive in all but the very tropical gardens. In warmer areas, grow Japanese plums (*Prunus salicina*) but in cooler gardens you can enjoy succulent European plums (*Prunus domestica*).

SUN-RIPENED APRICOTS Apricots thrive in full sun and nothing quite equals the flavour of an apricot picked fresh from your own backyard. To grow apricots to perfection requires a cold winter – apricots need around 800 hours of chilling – followed by a warm to hot summer for ripening. Apricots are self-fertile, which means that only one tree is needed for fruit production. Additional watering produces plump juicy fruit.

● Although apricots enjoy the cold, their late-winter or early spring blossoms and small fruit can be damaged by late frosts. If frost is forecast and your tree is in bud or bloom, cover it with horticultural fleece.

Fruiting cherries are as attractive as ornamental species and often have colourful foliage and bark.

APRICOT CARE Apricots are not hard work. Good air circulation is a must, as is regular, deep watering in spring and summer. Pruning is best done in autumn to remove any dead or diseased wood and to reduce the tree size.

● Some varieties produce heavy crops one year with little or no fruit the following year. To avoid this feast or famine cropping, thin fruits during the productive years.

THE CHERRY TREE – FAMILY MATTERS There are two main types of cherry, which differ in their fruit and overall appearance. Do you want to make jam, or to eat fruit straight from the tree? Make sure you know so you can avoid planting the wrong type.

● **SWEET CHERRIES** The descendants of the wild cherry tree produce sweet, large fruit that tastes delicious straight from the tree. The trees are often too large for modern or town gardens but if you have room they are

Cherries are always handpicked and tall trees are often accessible only by standing on a ladder.

very decorative. Popular varieties include 'Starkrimson' and 'Stella', which are both self-fertile and act as pollinators for other popular cherries including 'Bing'.

● **SOUR OR CULINARY CHERRIES** These acid-tasting fruits with pink, red or white flesh are excellent for jam. They are descendants of the morello (self-fertile) cherry (*Prunus cerasus*).

SMALLER CHERRY One of the drawbacks of cherry trees is their size. A mature cherry can be 10 m high and wide, making netting, harvesting and pruning difficult. 'Compact Stella' is a small sweet, self-fertile variety.

CRACKED FRUIT Cherries will split if they receive too much rain or water at ripening and cracked or split fruit can easily become diseased. In rainy areas, choose varieties that are known to be less liable to burst. Varieties that produce large fruit and cherries grown in areas with hot or humid conditions are

Know your plums

EUROPEAN	JAPANESE
Compact trees	Large trees
Smooth bark	Rough bark
High chill (700–1000 hours)	Low chill (500–900 hours)
Late spring-flowering	Spring-flowering
Yellow, sweet flesh	Yellow or red (blood) plums
Green, yellow or blue skin	Red to purple skin
Crosspollination	Crosspollination (except 'Santa Rosa')
Light pruning	Heavy pruning

more prone to splitting or cracking than small, early-ripening varieties.
● Modern cherry cultivars including 'Starkrimson' have a much better resistance to cracking and bursting in wet weather.
● To avoid causing bursting yourself, never water cherries just as they are ripening, or just after they have ripened.

PEACHES AND NECTARINES These closely related stone fruit suit a range of backyards. Peaches have furry skin, while nectarines have smooth skin. Both grow well in warm and coastal climates, are small to medium trees that can fit many backyards and most are self-fertile. Like all stone fruit, peaches and nectarines need full sun, regular deep watering and good air circulation. Late frosts in spring and high humidity in summer can lead to problems with fruit production and quality.
● Prune after fruiting to encourage lots of new wood for high fruit production.

PEACHES IN A POT Dwarf peaches and nectarines are small enough to be grown in large pots or in a mini-orchard. Although the trees are small (only growing to around 1–1.5 m high and round) the fruit is normal-sized – and delicious as well. 'Nectazee' is a dwarf nectarine while 'Pixzee' is a dwarf peach. Both have pink flowers from winter to spring.
● Before the development of true dwarf varieties, peaches were dwarfed by grafting on to blackthorn root stock.

LOW-CHILL PEACHES Chilling requirements for peaches can vary from as little as 150 hours up to more than 1000 hours. Chilling hours are the number of hours that plants are exposed to temperatures below 7°C. Low-chill varieties are best for coastal and subtropical gardens so look for varieties such as 'Anzac', 'Beale', 'Flordaprince' and 'Sherman's Early'.

PLUMS Not all plums are sweet. Some varieties are best bottled, stewed or used in a pie. 'D'Agen' is a prune and is best dried. Mirabelles and damsons are great for cooking.
● The cherry plum (*Prunus cerasifera*) is a small ornamental with tart but edible fruit in spring. It's grown for its purple leaves and white spring flowers as well as its fruit and can be used as a hedge or windbreak.

EASY PLUMS There is a plum variety for just about any backyard. For ease of growth in a backyard, select the self-fertile 'Santa Rosa', which will also fertilise most other varieties that flower at the same time.
● Japanese plums are the best choice in warm climates as they have lower chilling needs than their European counterparts. Good backyard varieties include 'Mariposa', 'Narrabeen', 'Santa Rosa' and 'Satsuma'.
● In the cooler areas the European plum is preferred but most need a crosspollinating variety nearby and long hours of chilling. Home-garden varieties include 'Angelina', 'Green Gage', 'King Billy' and 'President'.

POLLINATION TIP While some varieties of plum can be planted in isolation, most plums need to have another variety growing nearby for crosspollination. But if pollinators have been slow to bloom or are damaged, it is possible to trick the bees. Branches of another variety that's in flower can be placed under the tree. The bees will then happily visit both the cut blooms and your tree.
● Plant herbs such as Italian lavender nearby to attract plenty of bees to the orchard.

The best fruit

HOW MANY YEARS? Once planted, a stone fruit tree needs to develop its framework of branches before its young shoots can become fertile. This means that you will have to wait 3–4 years before the first fruit appears, but it will take 5–10 years, depending on the species, before you obtain a substantial yield.

JUICIER APRICOTS Apricots will be bigger and juicier if you give your tree regular deep watering from spring to autumn, particularly while the fruit is forming in late spring and early summer and if the weather is dry.
● Water in line with the active roots, that is, in a circle under the extent of the foliage.

A CHERRY-PICKING TIP The first cherries ripen about 40 days after the tree has blossomed, and for a single variety the harvest lasts for about 3 weeks. When picking them, avoid tearing off the cherry stalk because this is where the buds that will produce next year's fruit will grow.

Dwarf peaches have large clusters of flowers or fruit and are an ideal choice for small gardens.

BARREN PLUMS If your plum tree is not producing plums, the first thing to consider is whether it is bearing blossom – there can be no fruit without flowers.
● Most plums need another plum tree close by to provide pollen. This tree needs to be in flower at the same time. 'Santa Rosa' is a reliable crosspollinating variety.
● Plum trees are insect-pollinated so there also need to be plenty of bees foraging in your trees to spread the pollen from flower to flower. One old-fashioned tip to attract bees to your tree is to spray several branches with a weak sugar solution. Apply the spray when the tree is about 75 per cent in bloom in early spring. It is not necessary to spray the entire tree but it may be necessary to repeat the spray after 2–3 days.
● Bad weather, including wind and rain, at flowering time or when the fruit is small may also reduce the crop size.

THINNING FOR PERFECT FRUIT If the branches of your plum tree are overloaded with fruit, you will need to consider thinning out the overloaded parts to ensure that the remaining fruit develops normally.
● A certain amount of fruit drop will occur naturally when the fruit is still small. If the crop is still too heavy, gently shake the branches and some fruit will fall. A smaller crop will mean that the fruit will be larger.
● Any fruit that is awkwardly placed or particularly small should be the first to be thinned out. Only keep six to ten fruits per 1 m on the main branches.

1 2
3 4
5 6

Pruning stone fruit trees

PRUNING WISDOM It is possible to grow productive stone fruit with little pruning. In commercial orchards or where large crops are needed, hard pruning is carried out annually in late winter or early spring to control the size of the crop and to open the centre of the tree to encourage good ripening. By contrast, most home-garden pruning is done in late summer or early autumn after harvest.

THE RIGHT TIME TO PRUNE A CHERRY
If you cut large branches off your cherry tree, you risk exposing it to pests and diseases.
● Help the wounds heal by pruning in late summer or early autumn, after harvest, when the sap is descending. Never prune in winter as disease may enter via pruning cuts.
● If you forget to loosen the ties attaching a young cherry tree to its support, the trunk may look quite deformed. Loosen the tie and the trunk will gradually return to its normal shape. If you leave it for too many years the trunk will be scarred for ever.

AUTUMN CLEARANCE
After the leaves have fallen, remove all fruit that has been 'mummified' by disease and still on the trees. These shrivelled fruits carry disease and are potential sources of further contamination.
● Diseased and pest-affected fruit should always be gathered into a bag, sealed and placed in the garbage bin.

TIPS FOR PRUNING PEACHES
When you buy a new peach or a nectarine tree, select a well-balanced specimen with at least four healthy laterals. This will make it much easier to do the essential early pruning, and you will end up with a better-shaped tree.

Mummified fruit results from the fungal disease brown rot. Remove fruit in autumn and spray.

● **AFTER PLANTING** In the first spring cut back the main leading shoot just above a strong lateral, leaving at least four healthy laterals. This will discourage tall spindly growth and encourage a neat rounded tree.
● **REMOVING SHOOTS** Take out any shoots that have grown below the main head of the tree, cutting flush with the trunk.
● **SHORTENING LATERAL SHOOTS** Cut back by two-thirds to an outward-facing bud. Remove any weak or damaged laterals.
● **ANNUAL PRUNING** In the second spring, prune the main laterals and sublaterals by half to an outward-facing bud. Hard annual pruning keeps the tree's growth in check and ensures it doesn't become bare in the centre.

PRUNE WHEN IN BLOOM With a mature, fruiting tree (usually more than 3 years old), this is the best way of seeing where to prune, as it is the presence and number of blossoms that determines where to cut. As you cut away sections of branch with blossom on it, you are thinning out the future fruit, so the fruit that remains will be bigger and better. Alternatively, backyard trees can be pruned after harvest.

CRUEL TO BE KIND To ensure fruit doesn't grow at the ends of the stems on a peach, making them spindly and weighing them down, cut off early buds that appear at the tips of the previous year's shoots. Spare the fruit-bearing buds at the base of the shoots and you'll get a good crop and a tidy tree.

THE EASY-CARE PLUM The plum does not need to be pruned to produce lots of fruit and does not like having its branches cut back, because this causes it to discharge gum.

Left: Peaches can either be pruned while in flower or left until after the fruit harvest.

Heavily laden branches may split or break as your crop develops. A forked stick helps support the heavy branches.

DID YOU KNOW?

PLANNING YOUR PLUM HARVEST
When you're choosing plum trees for your garden it is worth thinking about when they fruit. If you regularly holiday during summer (when most plums ripen) you'll need to plant early or late fruiters, as the fruit won't wait to be picked and you'll lose your crop.

● You only need to prune lightly to keep your plum tree in shape when the sap is falling, between harvest and leaf fall.

PROPPING UP AN OVERLADEN BRANCH
In a year when your tree is fruiting heavily, the branches may become bowed down with the fruit. Unless these branches are supported, they are liable to break under the weight.
● Rest the branch on a forked piece of wood or strap it to the top of a support, and prop it up against level ground.
● For a branch on a low tree an inverted rake can make a good improvised support.
● Props are not very secure, so watch they don't collapse when the branches are being buffeted by strong winds.

Grow healthy trees

A BITTER TASTE FOR APHIDS Rue has a reputation for being bitter. Take advantage of this characteristic by planting this perennial at the foot of your stone fruit trees. It will protect them from aphids, which establish their colonies on young tender shoots. It is thought that a bitter constituent from the rue passes into the tree's sap through its roots, and this repels the aphids.

A BARRIER AGAINST ANTS Did you know that it is usually ants that bring the aphids to fruit trees? Ants actually 'import' aphids so that they can consume the sweet honey-dew that the aphids secrete when sucking the sap from their host plant. Wrap grease bands, which are available from garden centres and hardware stores, around the tree trunks to keep the ants and other pests at bay.
● Check the manufacturer's information for the age of the tree the grease can be used on. This is important as young trees may absorb the substance through their developing bark.

PRECIOUS CALCIUM Calcium helps fruit stones to form, which is why apricot, cherry, peach and plum trees always benefit from fertiliser that is rich in calcium, unless the soil is naturally chalky and already rich in calcium carbonate.
● Make a series of holes 25–30 cm deep around the base of the tree, and pour into each hole one or two handfuls of a calcium or lime-rich fertiliser, such as powdered

bone, natural phosphate or ground chalk. Water well. Most modern plant feeds have calcium as an ingredient.

BEWARE THE BROKEN BRANCHES
Often, large branches will break off at the base, particularly on the cherry and plum tree. This is usually because too many large branches were left on the tree when it was young, a problem made worse by the branches rubbing against each other. Prune a tree into shape during the first 3 years of its life and keep only those branches growing at an angle away from neighbouring ones.

PROTECT PEACHES FROM LEAF CURL
This disease causes leaves to thicken and distort and is seen in late spring and summer. The best control is provided by spraying trees before the leaf buds open in late winter or early spring. Use a copper-based spray. If the problem persists, use a follow-up spray in autumn. Certain plants have a protective effect on fruit trees. Plant garlic, nasturtium or tansy, a yellow-flowered member of the daisy family. These old-fashioned plantings are said to help overcome leaf curl.
● Some trace elements help trees to stay healthy. Zinc, for example, is good for peach trees. Gardeners of old would spread a few zinc filings around the foot of their peaches, and rainwater would draw the beneficial metal down to the roots.

CONTROL YOUR WHITEFLY NATURALLY
Plant ornamental tobacco plants among your fruit trees to attract whitefly. The sticky flowers and the foliage are a natural trap.

PROTECT YOUR APRICOT TREES Apricot trees are prone to verticillium wilt. To help prevent this problem, do not plant them close to vegetables or dahlias, which can harbour the germs. In case of attack, which produces a sudden withering of the leaves, cut off and burn the affected branch or branches as soon as you see the symptoms.

ARE WHOLE BRANCHES FROM YOUR APRICOT TREE FAILING? This can often happen, and it does not mean that your tree is lost. To help it recover, cut back the old branches so that only a few centimetres are left, and preserve any suckers. The stumps will soon start growing again and they will produce new branches.

Use grease bands to keep ants out of your fruit trees and reduce the spread of aphids.

Old-fashioned fruits of the Mediterranean

With a renewed interest in healthy diets, all things Mediterranean, from olive trees to sun-warmed figs, have found new favour in the garden – and they add a little Mediterranean sunshine to your garden.

Growing a fig tree

A SUCCESSFUL CROP The good news about growing figs is that the commonly grown varieties do not need a pollinating partner and they can grow in nearly all soils, as long as they are free draining. Also, pests and diseases rarely affect them.

FIGS FOR ALL CLIMATES There are many fruiting figs and often names are confused or not even provided.

● **BROWN TURKEY** The most commonly sold fig is the vigorous 'Brown Turkey'. It is cold tolerant, crops over a long period and may have two crops – a late spring or early summer crop known as a breba crop, followed by fruit from late summer into autumn. The fruit has dark brown skin with pink flesh.

● **BLACK GENOA** This is a tall fig with purple-skinned, red-fleshed fruit in autumn. A light spring crop may also be produced.

● **WHITE GENOA** The variety of choice in cooler areas, this may have a light summer crop as well as an autumn crop. The fruit has green to yellow skin and reddish-pink flesh.

PLANTING A FIG Figs are planted in winter when they are dormant. Make sure the site is in full sun and well drained. In hot-summer climates figs will tolerate some light shade.

● Figs thrive on neglect but respond well to a dose of fertiliser such as pelletised chicken manure in spring and deep regular watering.

LOW-MAINTENANCE FIG PRUNING
Mature figs need very little pruning – simply remove any shoots that are crowding each other out and preventing a good airflow around the tree's branches.

Wear gloves when picking figs: the sap in their leaves and leaf stalks irritates the skin.

● After the first crop on a new tree, pinch out the lateral shoots, leaving a shoot with four leaves. This will encourage replacement fruit-producing stems.

THE PICK OF THE CROP Figs will let you know how ripe they are. As the fruit matures and sweetens, the neck of the fruit begins to droop. This is the best time to pick. Figs get sweeter the longer they are left on the tree but are most susceptible to splitting and to fungal disease at this time.

● To dry figs, leave them on the tree as long as possible for maximum sweetness.

● Cover the tree with bird netting extending to the ground. Check the net regularly for any trapped birds or even small lizards.

TAKING CUTTINGS FROM A FIG TREE
In winter cut off one of the previous year's shoots complete with its heel – a fragment of bark – and a terminal bud. Plant out the cutting, protecting it from frost with dead leaves or straw.

DID YOU KNOW?

FIGS AND WASPS
Many figs will only produce fruit if they are pollinated by a little wasp, known as the fig wasp. It is usually found inside wild figs, known as caprifigs. The figs that need pollination by the wasp are the Smyrna figs, which produce only female flowers. To ensure that the small wasps carry pollen from caprifigs to Smyrna figs, you need to hang branches of caprifigs in among the Smyrna figs. The female wasps emerge from the caprifigs and are coated with pollen. They fly to the female flowers transferring pollen as they go. This tradition of hanging branches of caprifig in a fig orchard dates back to the times of the ancient Greeks and Romans. Luckily for home gardeners and modern-day fig fanciers, the commonly grown figs (which are classified as Adriatic) are self-fertile.

● Fig wasps shouldn't be confused with fruit flies, which can sting figs in late summer leading to infestations of maggots and rotten fruit. If fruit flies have ruined your fig crops in the past, spray with a registered fruit fly spray as the fruit matures.

Olives ripen in autumn. Those grown for eating need to be first soaked in brine to remove bitterness.

Olives, medlars and pomegranates

FRUIT OR THE GOOD OIL? Olives are grown either for fruit (called table olives) or oil. If your aim is home-grown olive oil select an oil-producing variety such as the 'Barnea', 'Frantoio' or 'Mission'. If you want to preserve your own fruit, look for a large fruit such as 'Kalamata'. 'Manzanillo' and 'Sevillano' are grown for pickling while 'Verdale' is a good all-rounder.
● Although olives are self-fertile, crops are larger and more reliable where several varieties are grown nearby. Olives are wind pollinated so the crosspollinator should be within about 30 m.

CLIMATIC CONSIDERATIONS Olive trees will grow in a wide range of climates but the optimum choice is an area that's frost free but with a cool winter and a long, hot summer. At temperatures below –5°C olive trees may be damaged or even killed. Low temperatures (around –2°C) may also damage developing fruit but once the fruit has ripened to black it isn't susceptible to frost.

BEST POSITION FOR YOUR GROVE Olives are traditionally grown in groves but they can be planted as a single feature tree. They need full sun, well-drained soil and, if more than one tree is being grown, they should be spaced at least 3 m apart. Olives may be associated with stony dry slopes but they grow faster and produce a better crop in deep loamy soils with additional applications of fertiliser in spring and autumn. Level land makes harvesting and maintenance easier.

OLIVES ARE GREAT IN A TUB If space is at a premium in your garden, an olive tree can be grown in a large tub to lend a Mediterranean flair to your courtyard or patio. Don't expect a heavy olive crop but you will get some fruit each year.

AN AUTUMN HARVEST Olives mature in autumn and are ready for harvest. They can be picked when the green fruit begins to change to a yellow green, or left to mature to black. If they are to be pressed for oil the fruit should be left until it ripens thoroughly to maximise production.
● The traditional way to harvest olives is to spread nets under the trees and then hit or shake the tree to release a torrent of fruit. Fruit can also be handpicked and this is preferred for table olives.

PICKLE BEFORE EATING Olives can't be eaten straight from the tree. Before they are edible they need to be soaked in a caustic soda solution to remove the bitter flavour. After soaking, the olives are transferred to a brine of salt, vinegar and water.

FRUITING TREES FROM ANOTHER AGE Your great grandmother might have had one of the following trees in her garden.
● **MEDLAR** The medlar has a cultivated cousin called the large-fruited medlar. It is self-fertile and flowers are borne in spring or summer and the fruit (above right) follows in autumn. Wait until the first frosts have softened the fruit before picking.
● **POMEGRANATE** This fruit (below right) thrives in a Mediterranean climate. It needs full sun but adapts to all conditions – even the tropics. For a good crop, water well, particularly between flowering and harvest.

The hardy medlar makes delicious jams and adds a certain charm to your garden.

The wonderful pomegranate both looks decorative and is a very productive fruit.

Fruits from the tropics

Where climates are warm and frost free the productive garden can be filled with tasty tropical fruits. Some are rare and unusual, but others, like avocado and mango, are part of our everyday diet. Many tropical fruit trees have good foliage and are excellent shade trees.

Avocados add a tropical flavour to gardens and are attractive in fruit.

Avocados for everyone

GROWING SEED Some gardeners begin their love affair with avocados when they decide to grow a plant from the large single seed found in the fruit. Avocados (*Persea americana*) grow readily from seed but can take 7–10 years or more to reach maturity and begin to produce fruit. The fruit quality from seedlings may also be variable and not necessarily the same as the fruit from which the seeds were extracted. For a faster result, seek out grafted, named varieties guaranteed to crop within a year or two of planting.
● Place seeds in a 15 cm pot filled with potting mix, or in the neck of a bottle of water, to germinate. Avocados make handsome short-term pot plants but are unlikely to produce any fruit until they are transferred into the garden. Even in cool climates avocado trees can reach 10–15 m or more in height.

LIKE AVOCADOS AND LEMONS Despite their tropical origins avocados can survive quite low winter temperatures. As a general rule of thumb, if you can grow lemons, you can have success with avocados as well. Just remember that young avocado trees will need some frost protection to ensure they survive their first few winters.

LOOK FOR TOP NAMED VARIETIES Named varieties not only produce better quality and more reliable fruit, they are also grafted onto root stock that is much more resistant to disease. Named trees are also more regular in size and in shape, growing to around 10 m tall. Look for 'Bacon', which is a good cool-climate choice, and 'Fuerte' or 'Hass' for good results in home gardens.

GIVE THEM GOOD DRAINAGE Avocados need plenty of water and a deep, rich soil, but good drainage is the most important factor for the best growth. Where soils have become waterlogged, trees are likely to succumb to root rot disease. Grafted trees have better tolerance to root rot.

DID YOU KNOW?

MALES AND FEMALES
Avocado flowers have both male and female parts. In warm climates, flowers can be female in the morning and reopen in the afternoon as male. Some open in the afternoon as female, and reopen the next morning as male. However, they do not self-fertilise, so a mixture of trees is still needed. In cool climates, however, flowers are not as strict in their timing so male and female flowers will be open at the same time on a single tree allowing pollination and fruit production to occur when only one tree is grown.

The fruit from an avocado tree remains firm until it is picked and ripened off the tree.

Other delights

MAGNIFICENT SPREAD Mangoes (*Mangifera indica*) in the tropics are tall, spreading trees that drip with fruit. Trees can reach 30 m. In cool to mild climates they are 3–6 m tall and narrow, with only a few fruit. The best crops are grown in climates with a warm, dry winter and spring followed by a hot summer with good rains. Young trees are frost sensitive but older plants will weather the cold. Mangoes are stunning in spring when they are flushed with reddy-brown new growth.

CHOICE MANGOES Mangoes have been grown in tropical Australia since the 1870s and there are many seedlings and a host of local varieties including 'Kensington Pride' (also sold as 'Bowen Special') and the modern 'R2E2' which are commercially available.
● Mangoes are picked as the skin turns from green to gold and the flesh around the seed becomes a deep yellow. The picked fruit may still feel hard but will continue to ripen.
● For good fruit production, feed mangoes with a high potash fertiliser in spring.

MANGO DAMAGE Mangoes attract bats, birds and small animals when fruiting but where crops are bountiful there's still plenty left to harvest. Smaller trees in cooler climates should be netted to protect the crop.
● Black spotting of mango fruit is caused by the anthracnose fungus. To combat, spray regularly with a fungicide from flowering time until the fruit reaches maturity.

BANANAS Bananas are usually called trees, but are really tall herbaceous plants. As well as the usual fruiting, or Cavendish, banana (*Musa* spp.), there is a host of related species,

The delicious tropical mango ripens from green to lovely yellow or golden tones.

many of which are ornamental. Abyssinian bananas (*Ensete ventricosum*) have lush green leaves with prominent pink midribs. They tolerate cooler temperatures than *Musa* spp. and give a tropical feel to a temperate garden.
● In cool areas, grow bananas against a warm, north-facing wall. Encourage strong growth by applying compost and well-rotted manure around the base of plants.

RESTRICTIONS Laws strictly control the cultivation of bananas in areas where they are produced commercially. Check with your local agriculture department or council.

GOOD SUCKERS The sucker is a flowering stalk that has the pendulous flowering stem appearing from the crown of leaves. The tip of the stalk, or bell, is where the male flowers are. The female flowers cluster along the stem where the fruit forms a 'hand'.
● The growth and ripening of bananas takes from around 9 months in the tropics to 18 months or longer in cooler districts.
● Once the hand is ripe it is cut down. Also cut down the sucker as it will not flower again. New shoots will provide the next crop.

PAWPAWS Also called papayas, pawpaws (*Carica papaya*) are best grown in the tropics and subtropics but will occasionally thrive in temperate areas with good drainage and frost protection. Fruit production needs male and female plants. Male flowers cluster on long stalks while female flowers are seen on the trunk among the leaves where fruit later forms. At least one male is needed for every 10 females. Fruit takes around 8 months from planting or as long as 18 months in cooler climates. Adding to the confusion are tropical pawpaws that produce hermaphrodite flowers.

Pawpaw makes a highly productive and healthy addition to a warm garden.

Nuts for the harvest

Once upon a time, no well-stocked garden would be without a nut tree. They have fallen from favour, but you can revive this tradition by planting a tree that will yield a hearty crop for decades to come.

The mighty walnut

AN ACT OF FAITH Walnut trees (*Juglans regia* and *J. nigra*) do not produce nuts for 15–20 years and achieve their best yields after about 60 years, and they can live for 300 years. Trees grafted onto the American walnut tree, or hickory, produce faster but their life expectancy is shorter.

HARVESTING WALNUTS For pickling, gather the nuts in autumn, before they harden. Otherwise, gather after they drop. Remove the husk, clean the nuts carefully and dry them in an airy room. Store in containers, between layers of sand or sprinkled with salt.
● To avoid getting stained by the husks, spread sacking under the tree then knock down the nuts with a pole. You will be able to carry away the crop without touching it.
● The time-honoured way of removing walnuts from their husks is to pile them on hard soil and rake through them every day. Soon the husks split and fall off. Then simply spread the walnuts out in the sun to dry.

GROWING FROM SEED Strangely, one of the easiest ways of propagating walnuts is by seeds, that is, by sowing the nut itself. However, the new tree is often not quite the same.

TAKE CARE OF THE FRAGILE ROOTS
The walnut tree grows well and it seems that only high altitude and extreme summer drought can trouble it. However, it is seldom a good idea to transplant a tree grown from a seed, because its taproot system means that it is not certain to recover. It is better to leave seed-grown trees in place, so the taproot can dig deep down into the soil.

The walnut tree takes time to produce its first fruit, but it can live for 300 years.

Hazelnuts and almonds

SAFE KEEPING To prevent the residual dampness in the shells from causing mould that would spoil the taste of your hazelnuts (*Corylus avellana*), remove the nuts' little cuplike shells straight after harvest. Then every day for at least 1 week, spread the nuts out on a piece of canvas in the open and in the sunshine, bringing them in at night. When fully dry, store the hazelnuts in a dry place.

Freed from their green husks these walnuts are now ready for eating.

DID YOU KNOW?

A GRAND OLD TREE
If you inherit an old walnut tree that's in bad shape, remove any damaged branches with a sharp saw to avoid introducing pests and diseases. It is important to note, especially in a small garden, that walnut tree roots produce a toxic chemical that will poison nearby fruit trees.

PLANT TWO TREES FOR A PLENTIFUL HARVEST A good crop of hazelnuts depends on crosspollination. Be sure to have two complementary varieties close together so the pollen from the catkins is carried from tree to tree by the wind. 'Cosford Cob' is a good pollinator for most other trees, and 'Gunslebert' pollinates 'Cosford Cob'.

ALMONDS FOR MEDITERRANEANS Almonds (*Prunus dulcis*) are related to peaches with a similar, early-spring blossom. They are grown for the nut inside a fruit that ripens in autumn. They are well suited to gardens with a Mediterranean-style climate.

SUCCESS WITH ALMONDS Most almonds will produce more fruit if they are planted with another almond nearby. Avoid planting in ground that gets wet in winter and choose the sunniest spot in the garden. The most popular variety is 'Phoebe', which has pink blossoms and is resistant to peach leaf curl.

Macadamias and pecans

A NATIVE NUT Macadamias (*Macadamia integrifolia* and *M. tetraphylla*) are native to the east coast of Australia and have been long grown as a decorative and productive tree in backyards. They have spiky leaves, hanging clusters of pretty white or pink flowers in winter and spring followed by very tasty nuts. Trees grow to 15–20 m tall.
● Backyard crops are often attacked by rats, possums and birds such as cockatoos. To protect your crop, cover the tree with a bird net and deter animals from climbing up the trunk. Animals and birds will attack the crop when it is still green.

GROWING TIPS Macadamias need excellent drainage to avoid root rot disease. They will tolerate light shade, especially when the trees are young, and are best planted in spring. Keep the area around the tree weed free and lightly mulched with leaf litter. Make sure you use a low-phosphorus fertiliser applied in small amounts from spring to summer.
● Pruning is only required to shape the tree or removed damaged wood. Early pruning will delay fruiting.

Pecans are the nut of choice for hot, inland areas but they do need regular watering in summer.

IN A NUTSHELL The most difficult part of eating home-grown macadamias is freeing them from their shells. Macadamia nuts are carried in a green outer husk. When removed from the husk, the hard shell around the nut must still be opened. The best way to do this is to dry-roast the nuts in a warm oven for 12–24 hours. When the nuts are ready they will rattle in their shells. Use a macadamia nut cracker or follow the old-fashioned way of placing the nut in a vice or in a depression in a brick and hitting it with a hammer.

MACADAMIAS TAKE THE BISCUIT Macadamias are delicious raw but can also be used in cooking. Try them in biscuits, cakes or as a crust on fish or meat. Use them instead of other nuts in recipes.

PECANS (*Carya illinoinensis*) These are large trees reaching 30 m in time. Pecans are handsome deciduous trees for large gardens with deep, rich soils. They thrive in hot inland climates where water is available for irrigation. Plant pecan trees in winter while dormant leaving at least 10 m from other trees or buildings to allow for its natural spread. Fertilise regularly with a complete fertiliser and water regularly, particularly in summer.

Macadamias grow in green husks (far left) which split on ripening, releasing the nut (left). However, it needs to be freed from its hard outer case.

New plants from old

Before the rise of garden centres, a self-sufficient, old-fashioned gardener took it as a point of pride – if not necessity – to propagate new plants at home. All that is required is a little know-how and some patience. Here are a few traditional tips to make it simpler.

Cuttings take root

WHAT IS A CUTTING? A cutting is usually a 15–30 cm section of young stem taken from just above a leaf joint or node on the parent plant, then trimmed just below a node.

NATURAL ROOTING HORMONE Whether cuttings take root or not depends mostly on vegetable hormones. To help roots grow, make a notch in the base of the cuttings and insert a seed of corn, or any cereal. This will germinate on contact with the soil and spread growth hormones into its immediate area, which will help cuttings produce new roots.

BURY DORMANT CUTTINGS UPSIDE-DOWN Hardwood cuttings are usually taken outside the growing period, which is not the best time to plant them. Keep them until spring by burying them completely in the ground. An old trick for encouraging future root growth is to bury them vertically, upside-down. Mark the spot so you can dig them up and plant them in spring.

PLANTING AT AN ANGLE If you have enough room, designate part of your garden as a nursery bed. When you plant cuttings in the bed, position them at an angle with only the topmost bud above ground. This will ensure they have a good start.

DISENTANGLE ROOTS IN WATER If the roots of cuttings growing in the same pot become entangled, remove as much earth as possible and soak the mesh of roots in a bowl of water. Once the soil has fallen away, you will be able to see the roots better and untangle them without causing damage.

Propagating by other means

A QUICK START FOR RUNNERS To make sure that your runners establish quickly, do not leave them attached to the mother plant for too long. If you do, they will develop too many roots and you will find it hard to dig

Layering is an easy way to grow new plants.

A corn kernel inserted into cuttings will germinate and help produce new roots.

Methods of propagating fruiting plants

SEED	CUTTINGS	SUCKERS	DIVISION	LAYERING	SHIELD GRAFTS
Apricot (some)	Currant	Cherry (morello)	Currant	Blackberry	Almond
Avocado	Fig	Hazelnut	Raspberry	Blackcurrant	Apple
Peach (some)	Grapes	Raspberry		Fig	Apricot
Plum (some)	Kiwifruit	Strawberry		Gooseberry	Cherry
Walnut	Passionfruit			Grapes	Citrus
				Hazelnut	Medlar
				Kiwifruit	Peach
				Loganberry	Pear
				Passionfruit	Plum

1 Cut a young branch from the tree and select a healthy bud. Detach the leaf, leaving the leaf stalk, and slice under the bud, cutting a strip of bark without penetrating the wood.

2 Choose a place on the stock somewhere between 5 and 10 cm from the ground, where the bark is quite smooth. With your knife, cut a T-shaped slit that is no deeper than the bark.

3 To enable the graft to be easily slipped inside the T-shaped slit, very carefully lift up both sides of the slit bark with the rounded tip of your knife.

4 With one hand, lift the bark with a knife and with the other introduce the shield graft into the T-slit so that the bud is pointing upwards, as it would naturally.

5 Very carefully ease the graft all the way into the T-slit and then fold over the two flaps of bark you created previously so that the graft is now fully enclosed, or shielded.

6 Wind some raffia several times around the cut area. If, 10 days later, the leaf stalk on the graft comes off easily, this shows that the operation has been successful.

them out without damaging them. Runners produced in spring should be severed and planted out in early autumn.

● Remove all the leaves from the section of runner to be buried or they will rot in the soil. This will delay, if not prevent, the formation of roots and new plants.

SUCKERS WILL CREATE MORE SUCKERS

A sucker is a new tree or bush developing from the roots of an older one. If a plant is growing on its own roots, that is, they are not grafted, it can make a new plant. Don't be confused by the idea that suckers suck the goodness out of the plants as they don't.

● Dig up the sucker complete with some roots and then simply replant it where you want it to grow in your garden. Propagation with suckers is usual for hazelnuts, morello cherries, strawberries and raspberries.

YOU HAVE TO DIVIDE TO MULTIPLY

Division means separating a mother plant into pieces, and each piece is complete with roots, so that you can replant them as smaller, but separate plants. Division should take place during the dormant period between late autumn and late winter, but not in frosty weather. This technique is particularly suited to currant and raspberry bushes.

● Take a flat spade and drive it down into the soil between the young shoots emerging from the rest of the mother plant. Then dig out one part of the divided clump with your spade and replant it, making sure you preserve as many roots as you possibly can.

● Alternatively, you can lift out the entire root from the ground and then split it.

Grafting trees for the garden

WHAT IS ROOT STOCK? Root stock is simply the stem and roots into which you implant a bud or a fragment of stem, which is the graft, that has been taken from the plant variety you want to reproduce.

GRAFTING EQUIPMENT Traditionally, grafting was done with a special knife called a budding knife and the binding was raffia. Some gardeners now simply use a craft knife and adhesive or special polythene grafting tape. Wipe your knife clean with methylated spirits to prevent the spread of infection.

EASY GRAFTING If you have not done grafting before, try shield-budding, sometimes known as T-budding. This involves inserting the graft – a strip of bark with a dormant 'eye' or bud on it from the variety you wish to propagate – under the bark of the root stock. This is one of the easiest grafts, as long as the stock is compatible.

Suckers can be a source of new garden plants when severed from the parent plant.

There is nothing more satisfying than growing and eating your own fruit from the garden. How- ever, the enjoyment of biting into your home-grown fruit can be considerably compromised if there is a bug inside!

Roots

COLLAR ROT
● **SYMPTOMS** Collar rot is a soil-borne fungal disease that attacks roots with the damage moving up to the trunk, which shows splitting and oozing. Die- back of some branches or leaf tips may occur. Trees may die. The fungus may enter trunk wounds in the case of macadamias.
● **PLANTS AFFECTED** Avocado, citrus, macadamia and many ornamental plants.
● **TREATMENT** This disease spreads through damp soils and waterlogged conditions. Improve soil drainage or grow susceptible plants in raised beds. Some citrus root stocks are resistant so select grafted plants, and ensure graft is planted above soil level. Avoid ground where plants have died before. Apply a fungicide drench such as phosphorus acid to affect not only infected plants, but those growing nearby. Clean the trunk wounds and paint with a copper-based fungicide paste.

CROWN GALL
This bacterial disease causes whitish swellings on the roots of trees and at the base of the trunk. The swellings can actually grow to be as large as footballs, then turn black and rot. The tree's vigour is not affected and there are no signs of disease on the leaves or shoots. The bacteria enters the tree through a wound. See page 150.

Trunks and branches

CANE SPOT (ANTHRACNOSE)
● **SYMPTOMS** Grey sunken spots appeaer on fruit canes. Spots may be surrounded by a purple edge and spread – they may damage large areas and crops are reduced.
● **PLANTS AFFECTED** Loganberry and raspberry.
● **TREATMENT** Remove all old canes and young infected canes. Disinfect pruning tools. Also pick up fallen leaves. Spray at the 'green tip' stage with a copper- based spray. Spray again with a registered fungicide as the canes develop. Some raspberry varieties, such as 'Lloyd George', are highly susceptible to this fungal disease.

CANKER
Cracks form on the bark, which become gradually wider and sometimes form raised edges. The diseased tissue from underneath will appear and a whitish gum will ooze from the cankers. The diseased branch, and sometimes the entire tree or bush, will eventually wither and die. See page 150.

CITRUS GALL WASP

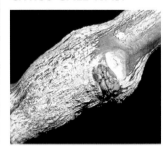

● **SYMPTOMS** Brown lumps, or swellings (known as galls) appear in the stems and twigs of citrus trees. Adult wasps lay their eggs inside the stems in spring, and the larvae feeding in the stems cause the galls. The galls grow larger during the summer. Trees that are constantly attacked are weakened and fruit- ing may cease.
● **PLANTS AFFECTED** Citrus.
● **TREATMENT** Remove the galls by pruning them off before the end of winter (wasps emerge in September and October and lay their eggs, which begins the cycle of infestation again). Old galls can be identified by the presence of exit holes. Put your prunings in a sealed bag and place it into the garbage bin.

GRAPEVINE SCALE
● **SYMPTOMS** Shiny dark brown scale appears on old or rough-barked stems. Young scale move about the plant in spring, feeding on leaves. Sooty mould may affect fruit quality.
● **PLANTS AFFECTED** Grapes.
● **TREATMENT** Remove all infested stems during winter pruning and spray with spray oil. Also spray foliage in summer, if necessary, with contact insecticide.

GUMMOSIS
● **SYMPTOMS** A sticky, viscous, yellowish brown gum oozes from a wound on the tree's trunk or its branches. Stem and leaf lesions may also develop, but these are less common. This fungal disease may be caused and spread by a simple insect sting, and the affected trees and bushes will gradually wither and die. The oozing gum is the tree's response to an attack of gummosis. Cool, damp conditions in your garden will encourage this disease.
● **PLANTS AFFECTED** Apricot, cherry, peach and plum.
● **TREATMENT** Avoid damaging the tree. Prune it at the height of the growing season. Scrape off the gum, and paint the resulting wound with a product that will protect the scar while it is healing. Prune out all infected growth to healthy wood. Spray the affected tree with an approved copper-based fungicide and feed it with liquid nettle manure (see page 269) to strengthen new growth.

SCALE
● **SYMPTOMS** Brown, black or white waxy spherical or elong- ated lumps on stems and branches or under the leaves. Under the waxy covering is a soft-bodied insect, which sucks sap and does some serious damage to plants and fruit. Scale may also attract ants. There are many types of scale – some feed specifically on one plant while others attack a range of plants.
● **PLANTS AFFECTED** Citrus and other fruiting trees.
● **TREATMENT** Spray oils will remove the waxy covering and smother the insect beneath. For persistent attack, follow with a contact insecticide or a systemic spray. Treat deciduous fruit trees and ornamentals with a winter spray of oil or lime sulphur. Bar ants from affected plants with

barriers around the stem or use an insecticide registered for ants.

WHITE WAX SCALE
● **SYMPTOMS** White waxy lumps develop on stems, concealing the soft body of the scale insect. Eggs are pink and laid in profusion. Ants may also be found on plants along with black sooty covering on leaves known as sooty mould.
● **PLANTS AFFECTED** Citrus (also bay).
● **TREATMENT** Remove all old scale with a small stiff brush. In early- to midsummer, when the young scale are feeding on foliage, spray the infected plant with spray oil. This will also remove the sooty mould. If the problem persists, continue spraying with the oil, but add a registered insecticide as well. Deter ants by banding the trunk of the tree with two sticky bands, 50 mm apart.

WOOLLY APHID

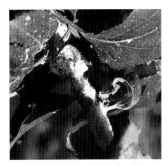

● **SYMPTOMS** The bark of the affected tree becomes split and swollen and a cottony, white 'wool' appears on the trunk and the branches. The reddish brown aphids (*Eriosoma lanigerum*) are about 2 mm long and are sometimes visible. The aphids first appear during spring and suck the sap from cracks in the bark and from young shoots. These pests' ability to reproduce by parthenogenesis (without fertilisation) means that a single aphid can produce as many as 100 offspring, which hibernate inside crevices in the bark.
● **PLANTS AFFECTED** Apple.
● **TREATMENT** Encourage natural predators, such as ladybirds, lacewings and birds, that feed on this aphid, into your garden. Use a forceful water jet to wash off the woolly cover, then spray the plants with an approved treatment as soon as the aphids appear in spring.

Leaves

APHIDS
The aphid's dark colour makes it easily visible against the plant's foliage. Colonies tend to collect at the ends of branches on a number of fruit trees, feeding on sap and eventually distorting their growth. Spray with a combined solution of rotenone (Derris dust) and pyrethrin. See page 97.

BLACK VINE WEEVIL
Adult weevils feed on the leaves at night and hide in the leaf litter at the base of the plant. Larvae damage the roots, and young plants may wilt and die. This weevil attacks a large number of flowering plants, such as apple, blackberry, blackcurrant, gooseberry, grape, olive, raspberry, strawberry and many ornamentals. Look for these insects during the night and destroy them. Use registered soil drenches to control the larvae. See page 151.

BROWN SPOT OF PASSIONFRUIT
● **SYMPTOMS** Brown or papery patches will appear on the plant's leaves and stems. This damage may kill the affected leaves and even entire branches. Also, dark, water-soaked patches develop on the fruit, which become brown and sunken. The fruit may shrivel or drop off the vine.
● **PLANTS AFFECTED** Passionfruit vine (including wild and ornamental forms).
● **TREATMENT** In winter, spray the vine with copper oxychloride. Thin out heavy growth in spring, and follow up the first winter spray with a spray of a registered fungicide. Remove and discard all affected fruit.

CAPSID BUG
The leaves of trees and shrubs affected by this bug look as if they have been riddled with tiny bullet holes. See page 97.

CITRUS LEAFMINER

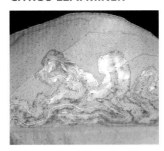

● **SYMPTOMS** Silver lines appear in the leaves and the leaves become distorted as tiny larvae burrow and feed in them.
● **PLANTS AFFECTED** Citrus.
● **TREATMENT** Remove the affected growth. Treat any new growth with spray oils. Systemic insecticide is needed to control the larvae feeding in leaf.

DOWNY MILDEW
This fungal disease widely affects vines and can completely destroy several vine stocks. Remove and bin all affected parts and rotate the crops. See page 206.

FIREBLIGHT (New Zealand only)
Fireblight is a serious disease that affects apples, pears and quinces. It causes the foliage of these fruit trees, and then the branches, to dry up completely. It is highly infectious, and the bacteria that cause it are easily spread by rain splash or on pruning tools. Lift and dispose of all affected trees. See page 152.

GREEN PEACH APHIDS

● **SYMPTOMS** Although its colour allows this aphid to blend well with the green of the foliage, the effects of its presence are very obvious and unmistakable. The afflicted leaves become deformed, curl up, turn yellow and then fall off. However, because green peach aphids generally attack in early spring, there is usually time for the leaves to grow back after they have had treatment.
● **PLANTS AFFECTED** Most fruit trees are affected.
● **TREATMENT** Use natural predators, such as ladybird larvae, which are widely available through mail-order. If aphids become a serious problem, treat them with a spray of rotenone (Derris dust) or pyrethin. Once treated, feed the plant with liquid nettle manure (see page 269). This will help the plant recover and strengthen.

LEAF SPOT
Brown or dead spots appear on leaves of various plants. Plants

affected are rhubarb and many fruiting plants including banana, blackcurrant, mulberry, pea and strawberry. If necessary, spray with a registered fungicide. See page 98.

OLIVE LACE BUG
● **SYMPTOMS** Leaves turn mottled and yellow, and then fall. It is caused by the feeding of tiny 3 mm long bugs with lacy wings. The entire tree may be defoliated if left untreated.
● **PLANTS AFFECTED** Olive.
● **TREATMENT** Spray with a contact or systemic insecticide. Water well and fertilise to encourage leafy regrowth.

ORIENTAL FRUIT MOTH
● **SYMPTOMS** The caterpillars tunnel into shoots, killing leaves and twigs starting from the tips. Gum is visible around the sites of attack. The fruit may also be attacked and damaged.
● **PLANTS AFFECTED** Apple, nectarine, peach and stone fruit.
● **TREATMENT** Cut back twigs that are damaged in spring. In early summer, wrap the tree trunk with some corrugated cardboard, hessian or a similar covering. This will trap the caterpillars when they go looking for a place in which to pupate. Remove the covering and squash the caterpillars with your fingers. Also remove any infested fruit. Keep the area around the base of the tree clear of loose bark and weeds. Spray with a biological control, *Bacillus thuringiensis* (sold as Dipel), which is meant for caterpillars that develop into moths or butterflies, or with another registered insecticide. Begin spraying *Bacillus thuringiensis* in mid-spring.

PAINTED APPLE MOTH

● **SYMPTOMS** Leaves become skeletonised by a brown caterpillar with tufts of hairs along its back. Cocoons are impregnated with caterpillar hairs. Adult female moths are wingless, so outbreaks are very localised.
● **PLANTS AFFECTED** Apple.
● **TREATMENT** Remove cocoons and caterpillars (hairs may be a skin irritant). Spray with *Bacillus thuringiensis* (sold as Dipel), a biological control for caterpillars that develop into moths or butterflies, or other insecticides.

PASSIONVINE HOPPER

● **SYMPTOMS** The leaves wilt, and the fruit shrivels and may fall. The insect is a clear-winged leafhopper, which sucks the sap of host plants. The passionvine hopper flies up when disturbed.
● **PLANTS AFFECTED** Citrus, kiwifruit, passionfruit, peach, some vegetables (beans, pumpkins) and some ornamental shrubs (jasmine and wisteria).
● **TREATMENT** Hose off the insect. Treat the plant and the surrounding soil with a registered contact or systemic insecticide. Water and fertilise to encourage strong plant growth.

PEACH LEAF CURL

● **SYMPTOMS** The leaves curl up and change colour from green to yellow, then to bright red or purple. These symptoms are accompanied by the appearance of characteristic leaf curl blisters. The leaves drop off and young shoots become deformed. Gum oozes from the affected area. Peach leaf curl is caused by a fungus of the genus *Taphrina*. It develops in early spring when cold, wet weather follows a mild winter.
● **PLANTS AFFECTED** Almond, cherry, nectarine and peach.
● **TREATMENT** Spray with a copper-based fungicide in late winter. As soon as the buds begin to swell in early spring, spray with Bordeaux mixture to prevent spores from entering the buds. Repeat 2 weeks later and again just before the leaves drop. Erect plastic covers over fan-trained trees to keep off rain.

PEACH RUST
● **SYMPTOMS** Leaves develop spots particularly in late summer and autumn, which start out pale yellow and then turn brown. The underside of each spot is a rusty patch of brown spores. Leaves may fall and twigs and fruit can also be affected. Trees are weakened and crops may be reduced or fail to mature.
● **PLANTS AFFECTED** Nectarine, peach, plum and stone fruit trees.

● **TREATMENT** Spray with copper oxychloride at bud swell. If the infestation is severe, spray with registered fungicide at petal fall with follow-up sprays at 4 and 8 weeks later in spring.

PEAR AND CHERRY SLUG

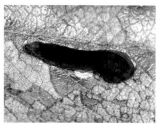

● **SYMPTOMS** The leaves become skeletonised by black, sluglike grubs (actually maggots), which are the larvae of sawflies. They drop to the ground after feeding, pupate in leaf litter, emerge as adults and lay eggs in the leaves.
● **PLANTS AFFECTED** Apple, cherry, crab-apple, pear, plum, quince and many other flowering fruit trees.
● **TREATMENT** Hose off the slugs or remove them by hand. Spray with an insecticide.

PEAR LEAF BLISTER MITE
● **SYMPTOMS** Red pustules form on the leaves, which are caused by the feeding of tiny blister mites. The blisters are around 3 mm across and they become brown with age. Trees affected are generally weakened and the crop will probably be reduced or malformed.
● **PLANTS AFFECTED** Apple, pear, quince and many ornamental plants.
● **TREATMENT** Spray with lime sulphur at the end of winter. If the infestation is severe, spray with a registered contact insecticide in spring.

POWDERY MILDEW

● **SYMPTOMS** The upper surface of the young leaves, shoots and flower trusses are covered with white powdery mould, which is caused by a fungal disease. The foliage becomes deformed and growth is stunted. Infected flowers do not set. Affected fruits may crack and split because they are unable to expand normally. They may also develop brown patches and the leaves will fall.
● **PLANTS AFFECTED** Apple, grape, gooseberry, melon, peach, quince and vines.
● **TREATMENT** Remove and put in the garbage all affected leaves and shoots. Spray the infected plants once a fortnight with Bordeaux mixture at the very first sign of the disease and repeat this treatment several times. Space the plants well to prevent them being overcrowded and to avoid creating humid conditions.

SHOTHOLE

● **SYMPTOMS** Tiny brown fungal spots followed by holes throughout leaves as if peppered by tiny gunshots. Leaves drop.
● **PLANTS AFFECTED** All prunus including plum.
● **TREATMENT** Spray in winter with copper-based fungicide.

SILVER LEAF

Silvery grey patches appear on the leaves of a few branches and they then gradually spread to the rest of the foliage. The infected tree will eventually wither and die. This fungal disease mainly attacks plum trees, but it can also affect trees in the Rosaceae family, such as apples, cherries, peaches and plums. See page 153.

SMALL CITRUS BUTTERFLY

● **SYMPTOMS** The leaves of citrus trees are devoured by a large black and patterned caterpillar with a voracious appetite. When disturbed, the caterpillar may release a smell from a protrusion on its head. The adult is an attractive black, white and red butterfly.
● **PLANTS AFFECTED** Citrus and related ornamental species.
● **TREATMENT** It is often very effective to simply remove these caterpillars by hand but, if large numbers threaten the life of the tree, you may have to spray them with a registered insecticide.

SOOTY MOULD

This problem appears as a black sooty substance on leaves. It is a secondary infection and is an indicator of the presence of either aphids or scale – or both. Sooty mould is common on citrus trees. See page 99. See also Aphids, page 97, and Scale, page 250.

TWO-SPOTTED MITE

These tiny mites, which are easily recognised by their bright red colour, are found on most species of fruit tree in hot dry weather. Affected leaves turn yellow and become covered with greyish-coloured mottling. The leaves of affected plants eventually wither and fall. See page 153.

Flowers

FROST DAMAGE

● **SYMPTOMS** Damaged flowers will fail, crops will also be affected and twigs die back.
● **PLANTS AFFECTED** All fruit trees in frost-affected areas can be affected.
● **TREATMENT** Late frosts can strike early while plants are still in bud or in bloom, causing the flowers, and sometimes also the shoots, to die. Without flowers the crop is sparse. The successful pollination of other crops may also be affected. If you live in an area prone to frost, avoid growing early-flowering varieties. Use protective anti-transpirant sprays and cover all vulnerable plants on frosty nights and water frost-affected growth before sunrise. Where automatic spray systems are available, set the timers to run the watering system at night and early in the morning to keep lines open (water can become frozen).

PLAGUE THRIPS

● **SYMPTOMS** Petals start to brown, the buds may fail to open and the fruit fail to form. Blobs of excrement are visible on the petals and tiny insects can be seen in the flowers.
● **PLANTS AFFECTED** Many fruiting plants.
● **TREATMENT** Water the flowers – plague thrips prefer hot, dry conditions. If the infestations are particularly severe and damage affects cropping, spray with a contact insecticide or use a soap spray.

RUTHERGLEN BUGS

● **SYMPTOMS** Small 5 mm long bugs feed on the buds and flowers. Strawberries may fail or become misshapen.
● **PLANTS AFFECTED** Strawberry.
● **TREATMENT** It's a good idea to encourage predatory insects into your garden. If you have severe infestations, use a contact insecticide spray. Avoid spraying when bees are active.

Fruit

ANTHRACNOSE

● **SYMPTOMS** This disease affects stored fruit. Blisters will appear on skin lesions, caused by a fungus that enters the fruit via the pores on lesions.
● **PLANTS AFFECTED** Apple, pear and quince.
● **TREATMENT** Avoid storing damaged, marked or bruised fruit. At the first sign of anthracnose, remove and bin all affected fruit to prevent spreading.

APPLE DIMPLING BUG

● **SYMPTOMS** Indentations or dimples appear on the fruit. These are caused by the feeding of a pale green bug that sucks the sap from the base of the flowers and developing fruit. If this type of damage is accompanied by corking in the fruit, then it is a boron deficiency (see over).
● **PLANTS AFFECTED** Apple (particularly 'Delicious' and 'Granny Smith' varieties).

● **TREATMENT** Damage is usually not serious and may be tolerated. If infestation is severe, use a registered spray from flower-bud stage.

BANANA SPOTTING BUG

● **SYMPTOMS** Sunken spots on the fruit of various subtropical fruits caused by the feeding of 15 mm green bugs and their nymphs, which are pink. The damage may extend into the fruit or it may be associated with cracks or sap exudate. The bugs may also feed on new shoots and will try to hide if disturbed.

● **PLANTS AFFECTED** Avocado, banana, citrus, custard apple, guava, lychee, pawpaw, passionfruit, pecan and others.

● **TREATMENT** Damage, even by a few insects, can be severe so inspect trees during flowering and fruiting and spray with a registered insecticide if seen.

BORON DEFICIENCY

● **SYMPTOMS** The fruit develop pitting, sunken or spongy areas and browning of the core. Twigs may die back, and leaves may be smaller and thicker than usual. This is caused by boron deficiency in soils and made worse by erratic watering.

● **PLANTS AFFECTED** Apple and pear.

● **TREATMENT** Apply borax evenly around the tree. The rate of application varies depending on the size of the tree (usually around 100–300 g per tree). Local agriculture departments recommend application rates. Conversely, too much boron can also cause problems.

BOTRYTIS

Also known as grey mould, this disease causes fruit to become covered with a whitish furry fungus, while the flesh becomes soft and then dries up. The fruit eventually rots. See page 97.

BRONZE ORANGE BUG

● **SYMPTOMS** The fruit will drop or it will become dry with a brown discolouration beneath the skin. Juvenile bugs are round and flat with orange or green colouring. Adults are a bronze colour and may cluster under branches or among foliage on hot days.

● **PLANTS AFFECTED** Citrus, especially orange.

● **TREATMENT** Spray in winter with spray oil to kill juvenile forms on immature fruit. Bugs fall to the base of plants when disturbed so remove them by tapping infested branches with a stick and catching the insects in a container of water with insecticide added. This insect emits a liquid that can injure eyes, so wear eye protection when near an infested tree. Use a systemic spray.

BROWN ROT

● **SYMPTOMS** Fruit, whether on the tree or in storage, bears signs of rot in the form of concentric circles with pale beige blisters. Rot gradually spreads and eventually affects the whole fruit. Brown rot is caused by a fungus that is carried by rain, wind, birds and insects. The mycelium (a strand of fungal growth) enters the fruit via an insect bite or a blemish.

● **PLANTS AFFECTED** All trees whose fruit contains pips or stones.

● **TREATMENT** Bin all rotten fruit and, to avoid re-infestation, do not put the dead leaves on the compost heap. Treat infected trees with a registered fungicide spray in the spring and repeat as directed in the autumn.

CALIFORNIA RED SCALE

● **SYMPTOMS** Flat red or orange scale appears on the fruit and leaves of citrus and other fruit trees. Leaves can become yellow and the twigs die back if infestations are severe.

● **PLANTS AFFECTED** Citrus, mango, olive, passionfruit and other ornamental trees and shrubs.

● **TREATMENT** Spray oils should be used in the summer covering all parts of the tree. Keep your trees well watered.

CITRUS SCAB

● **SYMPTOMS** Spots appear on leaves and warty growths develop on the stems or the fruit, although the inside of the fruit may be undamaged. Young fruit may drop. Lemons may be very large.

● **PLANTS AFFECTED** Citrus, especially lemons.

● **TREATMENT** Spray in spring, as petals are falling, with a copper-based spray, and again in late summer with a registered fungicide.

CODLING MOTH

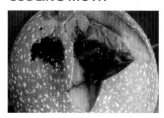

● **SYMPTOMS** Fruit ripens and falls prematurely. The flesh is riddled with tunnels made by the larvae of the codling moth (*Cydia pomonella*). The openings where the caterpillars enter the fruit are marked by very small piles of dark brown, sawdust-like pellets of insect excrement. The pale pink, brown-headed caterpillars bore into the centre of the fruit and feed on its flesh. When it is time to pupate, they leave the fruit and burrow underneath the bark.

● **PLANTS AFFECTED** Apple, peach, pear, plum, sweet chestnut and walnut.

● **TREATMENT** Hang pheromone traps in tree branches to attract the moths and reduce attacks. The moths are attracted by the smell of the sticky boards, and get stuck and die. Treat with an insecticide containing bifenthrin, spraying several times at 3 weekly intervals.

DRIED FRUIT BEETLE

● **SYMPTOMS** Brown, 3 mm long beetles infest ripe or spoiled fruit. Attacks are often followed by fungal infections.

● **PLANTS AFFECTED** Stone fruit and tomato.

● **TREATMENT** Pick up and destroy fallen and damaged fruit. Spray fruit trees with insecticide.

FRUIT FLY

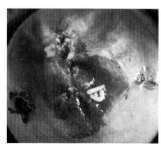

● **SYMPTOMS** Fruit shows puncture wounds where the eggs have been laid, followed by rot as the eggs hatch and the maggots feed within the fruit.

- **PLANTS AFFECTED** All soft fruits, including fig, nectarine, peach, plum, raspberry and strawberry.
- **TREATMENT** Use fruit fly traps, baits and sprays. The fruit can also be covered with paper or calico bags while still on the tree in the final stages of ripening. Tomatoes can be harvested green and ripened indoors.

FRUIT SPOTTING BUG

- **SYMPTOMS** A sap-sucking, green 15 mm bug, which is also active in nymphal stage, feeds on leaf stalks and young fruit, sucking sap. Fruit may fall or show gumming.
- **PLANTS AFFECTED** Many tropical and subtropical fruits including avocado, guava, macadamia, mango, pawpaw and pecan nuts.
- **TREATMENT** The fruit spotting bug is often seen in areas adjacent to native bush. The pests may not spread rapidly but they will hide when disturbed making control difficult. Spray them with a registered insecticide if necessary.

GRAPEVINE MOTH

- **SYMPTOMS** Vines are attacked in spring and summer by hairy caterpillars that may reach 50 mm in length. They are black with white and yellow stripes and have pink dots along their sides. Left unchecked, the caterpillars can defoliate a vine and attack developing fruit.
- **PLANTS AFFECTED** Grapevine (also Boston ivy and some native Australian plants).
- **TREATMENT** Spray with *Bacillus thuringiensis* (sold as Dipel) or an organic insecticide containing pyrethrins or rotenone (Derris dust).

SCAB

- **SYMPTOMS** Fruit becomes cracked, allowing parasitic infestations to enter, and is covered with dark brown scabs. Fruit is sometimes deformed and the infected part feels harder to the touch. Leaves can also be affected. This disease is caused by a fungus.
- **PLANTS AFFECTED** Apple and pear.
- **TREATMENT** Treat with a registered copper- or sulphur-based fungicide.

SPINED CITRUS BUG

- **SYMPTOMS** Clusters form on the fruit leading to dry patches and gumming. These are caused by a 20 mm green bug with hornlike spines on the shoulders. Fruit loss may occur.
- **PLANTS AFFECTED** Citrus.
- **TREATMENT** Hand remove bugs or spray with a registered insecticide.

WOODINESS OF PASSIONFRUIT

- **SYMPTOMS** Tree produces deformed fruit with a thick rind and very little pulp. The leaves may be pale green or mottled with yellow. Leaf damage is obvious in winter or early spring, before fruit forms. It is a viral disease spread by aphids and leads to the death of the vine.
- **PLANTS AFFECTED** Passionfruit.
- **TREATMENT** Remove all affected plants.

HOMEMADE PREVENTION

Yesterday's gardeners used many homemade but effective herbal remedies to discourage pests and diseases from attacking their precious plants. Remember, it is not always necessary to resort to chemicals in the garden.

EUCALYPTUS OIL FOR COMMON GARDEN PESTS

- 1 tsp eucalyptus oil
- 1 tbsp liquid detergent
- 500 ml water

Put the eucalyptus oil and liquid detergent into the water and stir. Dilute 20 ml of mixture in 1 litre of water and spray around the base of plants every 3 days.

GARLIC INFUSION FOR COMMON GARDEN PESTS

- 90 g garlic cloves
- 2 tbsp vegetable oil
- 1 litre hot water
- 30 g pure soap

Chop the garlic and combine with the oil. Allow it to stand overnight. Dissolve the soap in the water and add the garlic and oil mixture. Allow it to cool and then strain the liquid through a sieve. Dilute 20 ml of mixture in 1 litre of water and spray on any plants that are susceptible to aphids every 2–3 weeks.

MILK SPRAY FOR FUNGUS

- 1 cup whole milk (or the equivalent of powdered milk)
- 9 cups water

Dilute the whole milk or mix the powdered milk thoroughly with the water. Spray this mixture over the foliage of any plants that are affected with fungal diseases such as powdery mildew. Repeat every 3 days until the mildew disappears.

For treating black spot on roses, add 1 teaspoon of bicarbonate of soda to the milk mixture.

STINGING NETTLE EXTRACT

- 200 g fresh stinging nettle leaves
- 2 litres water

Chop the leaves and place them in a bowl. Pour the cold water over them and keep them submerged by placing a weighted plate on top. Leave to infuse for 24 hours. Strain the liquid through a large sieve. Dilute the extract with water (1:5) and spray on your plants as soon as you notice a pest.

Garden basics

The life of plants

Without the benefit of modern science, yesterday's gardeners had to develop an intuitive understanding of how their plants grew and what they needed to survive and to thrive. By combining a basic knowledge of plant biology with some useful tips from the past, you can learn to work with nature to grow a garden full of vigorous, healthy specimens.

The more you know, the better they grow

SLEEPING BEAUTIES All seeds need very specific, and often different, conditions to trigger their germination: warmth or cold, moisture, air and, in some cases, light. Without these, seeds can actually lie dormant for centuries, buried deep in the soil and only springing to life when the right conditions occur, like the poppy seeds stirred up by warfare in the fields of Flanders.
● To stimulate germination of large seeds such as walnuts and hazelnuts, store them in cool, damp sand over the winter months before sowing (see page 247). This treatment is called stratification.

LEAVES NEED TO BREATHE AS WELL
Plants absorb air through minute pores on the underside of their leaves. Rainfall washes off dirt and dust from plants in the garden, but indoor plants need regular cleaning to prevent blocked pores impeding growth.
● Beer and milk are often recommended for cleaning and shining the leaves on indoor plants, but these leave a sticky surface that will trap dust instead of giving a clean fresh leaf. Use plain, soft water, possibly mixed with just a tiny amount of washing-up liquid. Alternatively, stand your plants outside in the rain – or stand them in the shower and give them a cool watering.

PLANTS NEED LIGHT Without light, plants cannot produce the energy they need to sustain life, a process called photosynthesis.

Some plants need lots of light while others, such as some indoor plants like ferns and the indestructible aspidistra, can survive in the shade. A loss of green colour indicates that a plant is getting insufficient light.
● **ARTIFICIAL LIGHT** Special 'daylight' bulbs are available to help to foster photosynthesis, but a 100-watt bulb works nearly as well.
● **REFLECTED LIGHT** You can boost the light for sun-loving garden plants. Paint exterior walls white and plant up adjacent borders to create a Mediterranean-style garden.

KILL WEEDS WITH DARKNESS A simple but effective way of controlling unwanted plants is to stop their growth by blocking out their light. Cover them with a piece of old carpet, cardboard, newspaper or weed mat.

THIRST FOR WATER Plants take up water from their roots. It moves up through the stems and, on reaching the leaves, evaporates from the surface, then it draws more water

Ensure success by choosing plants to suit the conditions in your garden. In acid soil and semishade, grow azaleas or rhododendrons.

DID YOU KNOW?

PHOTOSYNTHESIS
The green pigment in a plant's leaves – chlorophyll – uses light to produce sugars, which plants consume as fuel. During this process, called photosynthesis, water combines with carbon dioxide from the air, releasing oxygen back into the atmosphere. The gases are then exchanged through pores called stomata on the underside of leaves. At night, the process is reversed and carbon dioxide is given off. Traditionally, plants were discouraged in bedrooms because of this – especially if anyone was sick – but the amount of carbon dioxide given off by a few plants is much too small to do any real harm.

from the soil. This process will continue as long as there is water in the soil. If the ground becomes dry and roots cannot take up enough water, the stems and leaves will wilt and photosynthesis will cease. Some plants, however, are well adapted to survive in very dry conditions – cacti and succulents can store water, and have prickly spines or hairy leaves that reduce water loss.

PLANT FOOD Plants need a balanced diet. Lack of fertiliser results in poor growth and leaves may become yellow, stunted and fall. Plants growing in containers are at high risk and depend on you to replenish the nutrients in the soil at regular intervals. Leafy plants need high levels of nitrogen (N), root crops need high levels of phosphate (P) and flowering and fruiting plants need extra potassium (K). Make sure you use a fertiliser that offers the best balance of nutrients for each type of plant. The label will give the NPK balance.

TOP TIPS FOR WATERING POT PLANTS

Mains water is not ideal for plants as its fluoride salts interfere with the absorption of nutrients. If possible, use rainwater collected in water tanks linked to the guttering from the house, shed or greenhouse. Alternatively, there are several old recipes for protecting and nourishing container-grown plants – in the home and garden – as you water them.

● **VINEGAR TONIC** Every month, mix a spoonful of cider vinegar in a litre of water and give your plants a good soaking to counteract the effects of fluoride salts.
● **LEFT-OVER TEA** Add stewed tea or used tea bags to the watering can to make a nitrogen-rich feed for foliage plants. Chamomile tea is antibacterial and fungicidal and so counteracts mildew, and green or black tea is good for acid-loving plants.
● **COFFEE PERK** Acid-loving plants also appreciate a top-dressing of coffee grounds every month or so, and they keep snails away.
● **VEGETABLE BROTH** Cool down the water in which you have cooked your vegetables and water your plants with it.
● **FISH STEW** Smelly aquarium water is full of nutrients and trace elements. Whenever you clean the aquarium, use the water to feed your plants.

HEALTHY ROOTS The root system takes up minerals that are dissolved in water in the soil. Without water this process stops

and the plants fail. However, too much water can have the same effect because it saturates the soil, driving out the air and suffocating the roots. Good drainage is vital to keeping your garden soil aerated.
● Many indoor plants die from overwatering. To prevent this, stand your pots on feet or on gravel to allow them to drain. Don't allow any pots to stand in saucers of water.

THE IDEAL ENVIRONMENT Bear in mind the origins of plants before introducing them into your garden. There is no point trying to cultivate a tropical plant in a cold mountain garden. It may survive a hot summer but will need cosseting indoors in winter. Plants are very adaptable, however, and many that have been introduced from around the world are now regulars in our gardens.

PLANTS NEED A REST TOO! Your plants naturally go through a period of dormancy during the winter, when growth slows down or when it stops altogether.
● Indoor plants also benefit from a rest around this time, during which they need very little water and no feeding. Start feeding them again when growth resumes in spring.
● 'Resting' outdoor plants can be lifted and moved during winter, but only at times when there is no risk of severe cold.

Gardener's Choice

PLANTS THAT TOLERATE DRY CONDITIONS

Many plants that originate from the dry regions of the world need much less water to help them absorb the nutrients they require from the soil.

TREES Albizia, crepe myrtle (*Lagerstroemia indica*), eucalypts, fig, Judas tree (*Cercis siliquastrum*), linden (*Tilia tomentosa*), olive, pine, pistachio (*Pistacia chinensis*), wattle **1**, yew and ziziphus.

SHRUBS Callistemon, ceanothus, cistus, coronilla, cotinus, escallonia, genista, Japanese flowering quince, lantana, lavender, photinia, rosemary and tamarix **2**.

ANNUALS, BULBS AND PERENNIALS Acanthus, achillea, agave, cleome, euphorbia, gaura, helianthemum, iris, kniphofia, narcissus, nepeta, pennisetum, phlomis, portulaca, ruta, santolina, sempervivum, valerian **3**, verbascum, verbena and yucca.

Buying the best

Successful gardening starts with strong healthy plants. While the old way was to raise plants from seeds and cuttings, the variety of plants now available from nurseries and garden centres, by mail-order and over the Internet grows each year. Here are a few tips to help you make the right choice and buy the best plants from the best sources.

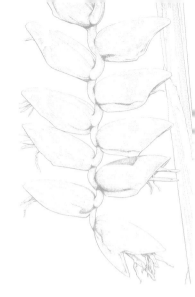

Where to buy

USE YOUR LOCAL NURSERIES AND GARDEN CENTRES Nursery people are passionate about plants and how they are grown, and they will always be pleased to give you good advice. Discover what grows well in your area and, therefore, what plants will be ideal for your own garden situation, by visiting local nurseries and garden centres and talking to the experts.

GET THE FRESHEST PLANTS Look for nurseries and garden centres that renew their stock frequently, and find out when they get their deliveries. Plants in such places will be fresher, and there will be a greater choice.

MAKE THE MOST OF MAIL-ORDER Ordering by mail or over the Internet is an ideal way to buy special and unusual plants that you cannot find locally. (But remember quarantine restrictions make it difficult to bring in plants from overseas.) But always remember that catalogues aren't accurate all the time. To avoid being tempted by misleading photos and descriptions, look up the true plant details for yourself, preferably in a reputable illustrated gardening book, before finally placing your order.
● Contact the supplier to check the availability of the plants you want to buy, and the best time of year to order them. Check the suitability of the plants for your own garden, soil type and conditions – and find out when and how the plants will be delivered.
● Unpack your delivery as soon as it arrives, water the plants and place them in a light spot to overcome transport shock. Once they have recovered, plant out as soon as you can.

Avoid weekend crowds in the garden centre if you can. This way staff will have more time to answer your queries.

GUARANTEE IS SECURITY Reputable companies guarantee the quality and success of their plants, as long as the planting and aftercare instructions are followed.

BUY SEEDLINGS This is a cost-effective way of buying many plants, particularly annuals and biennials for mass planting. Plants are grown from seeds in punnets divided into compartments, or cells. They come with a root system ready for transplanting. Although they are not very impressive at first, they will quickly grow on to full-sized plants.

UNDERSTAND PLANT LABELS Read plant labels carefully before you buy. They contain key information you need to achieve the best possible results from your plants – including when they will flower or produce a crop, the ideal growing conditions and lots more.
● Make sure you note down the size that a plant will eventually grow to and mark out the extent in your garden – this way you will avoid overcrowding.

Read the label before you buy. This allows you to check plant size and growing needs.

Some plants, such as fruit trees, need a pollinating companion to produce a crop. Others are self-fertile and produce crops on their own – check labels for this sort of detail.

WHEN TO BUY AND PLANT Wait until a plant's dormant period so it can recover from planting shock before the growing season.

MAY TO JULY These are the best months to buy bare-root deciduous trees, shrubs and roses. Avoid buying in periods of severe cold, when planting out is difficult.

SPRING OR AUTUMN Plant conifers, evergreen trees and shrubs in these months. Moist soil encourages them to root and establish.

EARLY AUTUMN OR EARLY SPRING This is the ideal time for planting herbaceous perennials and biennials. In very cold areas, wait for spring when the soil has warmed up and dried out, particularly for the more delicate plants such as the summer- and autumn-flowering anemones and some grasses.

SPRING When the risk of frost has passed it is time to plant summer annuals and plants for baskets and containers. Try not to be tempted to buy these plants too early in the year – they will have been forced and struggle to grow when planted out into cold soil.

CHECK THE ROOTS A poor root system will produce a weak plant. Before buying try to check the condition of the roots. A healthy root system will almost fill the container that it is growing in with loose, white, fibrous growth. Avoid plants with roots that show any of the following symptoms:

Small, underdeveloped roots that come away from the potting mix when removed from the pot will not sustain the plant. The root ball should hold soil in a unified clump.

'Pot-bound' roots, where the root growth is a solid, tangled mass, indicate the plant has been kept in the container too long. Avoid any plants where the plastic pot has burst with the amount of root growth (above left).

Roots escaping from drainage holes (above right) and growing into the soil beneath are also pot-bound. Do not try to untangle the roots or cut them out of the container. These plants are unlikely to do well.

TIP-TOP BEDDING PLANTS Annuals and biennials are useful to use as bright and colourful bedding plants and can be bought in punnets and small pots. When buying bedding plants look for:

Split pots (left) and roots protruding from drainage holes (right) mean plants are a bad buy.

Plants with sturdy green growth, with plenty of shoots and flower buds.

Well-rooted plants which can be removed from the punnet or pot in one piece.

Punnets or pots that are not too wet and not too dry – just moist is ideal.

Trays of the same colour – mass planting has more impact than a mixture of colours.

Plants growing in clean potting mix – don't buy plants that have algae and moss growing on the surface as these are old stock.

TAKE SOME INTERIM CARE While waiting to plant out bedding plants, keep them cool, moist and out of hot winds. Small punnets and pots dry out quickly, so water frequently without saturating the mix.

BARE ROOTS CAN SAVE YOU MONEY Dormant plants with bare roots are sold by some specialist nurseries, and sometimes via mail-order, during the autumn and winter months. They are an inexpensive way of buying deciduous trees and shrubs, fruit trees and bushes, roses and hedging stock. Here are a few tips to keep in mind.

The root structure should be really well branched and fibrous, and the largest root should be no thicker than your thumb.

Do not allow the bare roots to dry out completely. To avoid this, wrap the roots in damp newspaper or a similar covering and transport in a plastic bag.

Always try to plant out within 3 days of buying or receiving the plants. If this is not possible, you can 'heel them in'. Dig a trench with one sloping side, lay the plants in the trench so they are supported against the slope, then refill the trench with moist soil, covering the roots. Firm the soil, then cover the plants with straw to protect the roots from severe cold (right). They can be kept in this way for weeks or even months before planting in their final position.

Before planting, soak the roots in a mixture of soil and water for a few hours.

Bare-root plants sold in winter while dormant are good value for money.

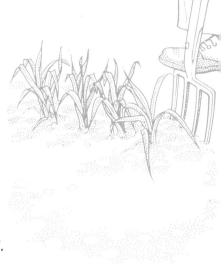

Feeding the soil

Each soil type has its benefits and its drawbacks and gardeners have a saying, which goes something like this, 'A clay soil will break your back, but a sandy soil will break your heart.' However, remember that there is a lot you can do, using traditional methods, to balance and enrich your soil to provide the right conditions for most plants to grow.

How to identify your soil type

SOIL TYPES Garden soils vary considerably, but all soils will be a mixture of ingredients such as clay, sand, limestone and humus in varying proportions. You can identify the composition of your own garden soil type by observing and feeling it. Dig out samples from several areas around your garden, at a depth of 20–30 cm below the surface, and mix them together. Rub wet and dry samples between your fingers and note the difference.

CLAY SOIL This looks shiny and feels smooth, sticky and slippery when wet. It is either brown, yellow or grey in colour. Its fine particles bind together to form solid, heavy clods. In summer the surface hardens and cracks. In wet weather, puddles stay on the surface and take time to drain. These soils become muddy, heavy and sticky to work with.

CLAY SOIL TEST Moisten a handful of soil, squeeze it into a ball and then roll it into a sausage shape, about 1 cm in diameter. The

Even though this garden has sandy soil, a wide range of plants has been grown.

longer the sausage can be stretched, the greater the clay content. If you can bend it into a ring without cracking it, this is a very clay soil. If the sample breaks up when rolled it is likely to have a high sand or possibly peat content. Many gardens have a mix of different soil types.

CHALKY OR LIME SOIL A yellowish-white soil, this is also sticky to the touch, although it has a crumbly texture and does not bind together when it is wet. Chalky or lime soil contains fragments of limestone, can be stony, drains freely and dries out in summer.

PEATY SOIL This black and crumbly soil contains high levels of organic matter and humus and does not clump together. Peaty

By doing a simple, old-fashioned soil test, you can quickly tell whether you have clay soil (left) or soil with a high sand content (right).

soil soaks up water like a sponge but also dries out and crumbles rapidly. It is fibrous to the touch, with a spongy texture, and does not stick together.

SANDY SOIL Between yellow and red in colour, sandy soil is gritty to the touch. Light and easy to work with, it is well drained and does not hold water, making it dry out rapidly and lose nutrients. Sandy soil tends to break up easily and it also feels very coarse and gritty to the touch.

Improve your garden's soil

SOIL IMPROVEMENT HAS ITS LIMITS It is preferable to match your plants to your soil type, rather than trying to modify your soil to suit the plants you want to grow. It is still possible to cultivate plants that will not tolerate your garden soil by growing them in containers with the right potting mix.

HEAVY CLAY SOIL Clay soil can be very fertile, but it is dense and often very poorly drained. It may become waterlogged during winter and so dry that it cracks in summer. These features make clay soil hard to dig and difficult for plants to grow. However, it can be improved and made into a top-rate soil.
● **ADD GYPSUM** Gypsum will improve and break up the heavy structure of clay soils. Before starting a garden in heavy clay soils spend time digging in gypsum (also sold as claybreaker). Dig to at least a spade's depth or hire a rotary hoe to ensure the gypsum is worked in well. Follow-up treatments may be required on an annual basis or when new plantings are made.
● **ADD PLENTY OF ORGANIC MATTER** Well-rotted manure, garden compost, mushroom compost and other organic matter works wonders on clay soil. Dig it in well and then continue to add it to the surface as a mulch.
● **GREEN MANURE CROPS** These are a good way of adding organic matter to soil in any unplanted areas of the garden. Sow rye grass, clover, comfrey or mustard seed in autumn. Dig it in when it has grown to about 20 cm in height but before it flowers.
● **ADD LIME** Lime will reduce the acidity of clay garden soil. Spread about 150 g per

Hydrangeas, like the lacecap pictured here, have blue flowers where soils are acid but they will become pink if grown in neutral to alkaline soils.

square metre over the bare soil and dig it in. Do this every 2 or 3 years. This will keep your soil acidity at an ideal level for growing most types of garden plants. Just remember to always allow at least a month before planting or sowing. Mushroom compost contains a lot of lime so it can be used instead of lime to boost soil alkalinity.

LIME SOIL Where soil has a pH over 7, you have a high alkaline soil. This high alkalinity can cause a yellowing of leaves, known as chlorosis, on plants intolerant of lime. It can also be shallow and can lack many nutrients.

It doesn't matter what type of soil you have in your garden; adding organic matter will always improve it, making for better plant growth.

● **LOWER THE PH** Do this by incorporating acidifying materials, such as well-rotted manure, garden compost, leaf-mould or flowers of sulphur and acid fertilisers.

● **ADDING SOME ORGANIC MATTER** This should be done each year to replenish your soil's nutrients and improve its water-holding capacity. Dig in plenty of rotted manure or compost, or grow a green manure crop in your uncultivated beds. In established garden beds, mulching the surface of the soil around plants will also incorporate organic matter, but without disturbing the plants.

PEATY SOIL This humus-rich soil retains water well but has a poor structure and can be poorly drained. Dig in coarse, sharp sand or pea shingle to improve the drainage. If it becomes acid, add garden lime or chalk.

SANDY SOIL A light soil that warms up quickly in spring, sand is excellent for grow-ing early crops. It has an open, free-draining

structure, however, which allows water and nutrients to be lost, and fertility drops rapidly if they are not replaced regularly.

● **MATURE MANURE** Well-rotted manure, garden compost or any other composted green waste should be incorporated each year. They will act as a natural sponge to soak up and retain water. Dig in a 2–3 cm layer of manure or compost.

● **GREEN MANURE** Dig this into empty beds and use as a surface mulch around plants to help to conserve water.

TOO ACID Few plants do well in an overly acid soil with a pH of 4 or less, but many Australian natives, azaleas, camellias and hydrangeas will grow in a pH of 4–5.5.

● **ADD GARDEN OR DOLOMITE LIME** Add garden lime in autumn. The amount you need to add will depend on how acid the soil has become. If the pH of the soil is 6–6.5 add 150 g of garden lime or other lime-rich products per square metre. For pH 5–6 add 200 g per square metre, and for pH 5 or less, add 300 g per square metre.

● **AND ADD PLENTY OF ORGANIC MATTER** To improve your soil's nutrients, feed your soil well, and dig in some organic matter in spring. Do not apply manure at the same time as you apply lime as they react together to produce ammonia – a pungent gas.

THE IDEAL SOIL

THE RIGHT BALANCE The ideal soil is called a loam and is a mixture of approximately 20–25 per cent clay, 30–35 per cent lime or chalk and 40–50 per cent sand. It is also rich in humus, such as compost or leaf mould. This mixture combines large and small particles of clay, lime and sand that, with the humus, bind together, holding onto moisture and nutrients while also draining freely.

POROUS AND OPEN A well-aerated soil allows strong, deep plant root growth. It also encourages healthy micro-organism activity that decomposes organic matter into humus, releasing nutrients into the soil. Excess water can drain away freely, avoiding waterlogged conditions that can damage roots, inhibit growth and cause plant failure.

pH PREFERENCES The majority of plants grow best in a slightly acid soil, around pH 6.5. Azaleas, conifers and hydrangeas are acid-loving plants that need a soil around pH 5.5. Asters, cotoneasters and forsythias are examples of some of the plants that prefer an alkaline soil, above pH 7.

Giving feed the right way

CHOOSING THE FERTILISER Whether you are using a natural fertiliser, or an artificial one, make sure you are treating your plants properly. For example, are you remedying a general soil problem, or feeding a particular plant to make it flower more profusely? Once you've decided which fertiliser to use, you have several ways to apply it.

FEEDING YOUR TREES PROPERLY The spread of tree roots is more or less equivalent to the spread of the branches, which means that the absorbent roots will usually be well away from the trunk, at a point that is directly below the outer limits of the branches. Apply the feed in this area. If the soil is compact, make a hole in the ground (right) and water in the application.

Improve sandy soil in your garden by frequently digging in well-rotted compost.

Garden lime will help raise the pH of acid soil, but remember to dig it in well.

To get fertiliser to the tree root, make a hole in the ground at the drip line.

DIGGING IN GREEN MANURE

1 Green manure is ideal for using in your vegetable patch before planting. Cut it down before it flowers.

2 When you've cut it down, leave your green manure cut crop lying on the ground to dry for several days.

3 When the green manure crop has dried out, go over it with a lawnmower without the catcher on, to chop up the dry remains.

4 Dig in the manure to a depth of 10–15 cm. Allow 1 week before planting out seedlings and 3 weeks before sowing seeds.

FEEDING SHRUBS Spread the fertiliser around the base of each plant and rake it into the top 2–3 cm of soil. Unless the soil is very wet, always water in the feed.

FOLIAR FEEDING Spraying a dilute liquid fertiliser onto the leaves of plants is a quick and effective way of direct feeding, particularly during periods of dry weather when the roots are less active. Foliar feeding is a great tonic for struggling plants and will give them a quick boost, but don't do it when the plant is in direct sun.

FLOWERPOT SPECIAL Flowers that are grown in pots need extra nutrients to grow and bloom well. This is because the pot plant quickly uses up the goodness in the small amount of potting mix in the container. Feed your potted plants regularly with liquid fertilisers or add slow-release pills (or pellets). These are scattered on to the surface of the pot and will feed plants for 3–9 months depending on the formulation selected.

USE NATURAL FERTILISERS You can buy natural fertilisers, such as the fish, blood and bone meal used by our forebears. These

substances are broken up in the soil, which encourages good microbial activity and improves the health and texture of the soil. This is an advantage organic fertilisers have over straight inorganic fertilisers, which are a compound of the pure nutrients nitrogen, phosphate and potassium plus some trace elements. Inorganic fertilisers are absorbed immediately by the plants for instant success, such as bigger blooms, but they do little to improve the soil long term.

NPK – THESE ARE THE INITIALS TO REMEMBER Nitrogen (N), phosphate (P) and potassium (K) are the essential chemical nutrients that all plants need. Proprietary fertiliser packs display the amount and ratio of N:P:K they contain. For example, an 18:8:8 fertiliser contains 18 parts of the nutrient nitrogen and 8 parts each of phosphate and potassium. When buying a fertiliser, choose one with the best balance for your particular plants – and look out for ones that also contain essential trace elements, such as magnesium and copper.

● **NITROGEN** This promotes the growth of green leaves and stems, and is ideal for lawns and leafy plants.

● **PHOSPHATES** Use phosphates to stimulate the growth of your plants' roots and flower buds and to improve general plant health.

● **POTASSIUM** This nutrient will give a boost to your plants' resistance to pests and diseases and will encourage good flower and fruit development, ripening and colour.

LIQUID FEED When you're using proprietary liquid fertilisers, follow the directions carefully. In general, feed every 2 weeks in the growing season, reducing to half the amount in the first and last months.

● To avoid burning your plant's roots, make sure the potting mix is moist before applying the feed. Water plants 15–30 minutes before feeding if the potting mix is dry.

DID YOU KNOW?

ORGANIC MATTER

Bulky organic material is the lifeblood of any soil and it must be replaced regularly, whether it is applied as manure, garden compost or green manure. By improving the structure and water content of your garden soil, you are encouraging root growth and increasing a plant's uptake of nutrients from the soil. At the same time, earthworms and micro-organisms in the soil digest the organic matter into rich humus, slowly releasing nutrients in the process, which plant roots draw on over time as they need them.

Slow-release fertiliser is convenient for pots (far left), while liquid feeds (left) will give your plants a quick and very effective boost.

The gardener's black gold

Well-made garden compost is the best source of organic matter: it is the lifeblood of a fertile soil. Compost breaks down slowly, releasing a steady supply of nutrients for strong, well-fed, disease-resistant plants. A boon to gardeners in years gone by, it plays just as important a role today, enabling us to recycle waste for the good of the garden.

Making and using compost

THE IDEAL COMPOST BIN Making good compost is really not very difficult if you just follow a few golden rules, starting with the design of the compost bin.

● Build or buy a good-sized bin – a 1 m cube is the ideal size. What this volume does is to allow high temperatures to develop inside the heap – and you need high temperatures to begin the breakdown process.

● The traditional compost bin is very effective and is made from treated wooden slats with 2 cm gaps between the slats to allow air into the heap. The top is left open for adding material but it must be covered to keep out the rain. One side can be left opened to allow you to dig out compost.

● Bins that are constructed from sections of reinforced chicken wire, or modern plastic bins can be equally effective.

● If you have the space, try using two or three bins for different composts, which are at varying levels of maturity.

MAKING YOUR OWN TRADITIONAL WOODEN COMPOST BIN Recycle old wooden pallets, or use new treated timber to build a structure that lasts.

● You will need four uprights for the corners of the bin and planks cut to 1 m lengths for the slats. Simply screw the slats between the uprights, making sure you leave gaps of around 2 cm, until you have a box shape.

● Unscrew the bottom planks for access to the compost. Cover the top with a piece of old carpet to keep the rain out.

THE GOLDEN RULES FOR SUCCESSFUL COMPOST-MAKING The secret to good composting is to produce a high temperature in the heap that breaks down a variety of plant waste from your garden and kitchen. Mixing moist, soft plant waste with drier, more fibrous material helps keep the heap well aerated and damp, which in turn will encourage decomposition.

● As you make the heap, activate the compost by adding small amounts of finished compost between the layers and watering with nettle–manure solution, simply made by steeping chopped nettles in water. Add a handful of dolomite or horticultural lime to balance the heap's acidity.

● Tread the heap from time to time, to firm it down and to remove any large air pockets.

● Test the temperature by inserting a wooden stick into the centre – when you bring it out, it should feel hot to the touch.

● Aerate the heap by turning it regularly, so that all material spends time in the middle where microbial activity is greatest.

SHREDDING WOODY WASTE Chopping or shredding your material for composting, particularly woody cuttings, speeds up the process of breaking down. Recycle your newspapers and plain cardboard boxes by shredding them before adding to the heap.

● Make sure you chop up any large items so they rot at the same rate as other materials.

DID YOU KNOW?

MAKING YOUR COMPOST Composting is the way that nature converts plant waste into dark brown, crumbly organic matter called humus. In a well-made, mixed compost heap, the bacterial activity that starts breaking down plant material will heat up the centre to a staggering 50–60°C. Soil microbes will continue the process when the heat cools down, which will produce humus.

Compost is ready for use when it has become a firm, dark brown, crumbly and odourless material. It can take from 6–12 months to produce 1 kg of humus from 10 kg of plant waste. Dig the finished compost into your garden to improve its water-holding capacity, boost its microbial content and increase its nutrients.

1 To ensure the bottom of the heap has good ventilation, spread a layer of branches at ground level.

2 Cover this with a layer of decomposed organic matter. This will activate decomposition in your compost heap.

3 Make up the third layer in the heap from your garden and kitchen waste. This layer should be about 30 cm thick.

4 Alternate soft wet waste (grass clippings or peelings) and dry waste (dead leaves or straw) or make a mixture.

5 Water regularly. Moisture evaporates as the heap warms up, and this can affect the decomposition process.

6 Do not add too many loads of grass cuttings at first. Mix them with drier material to keep the process working.

7 Activate the heap with manure, comfrey leaves, or a nettle manure solution (see page 269) about every 7 cm.

8 Cover to prevent the heap from drying out or being rained on. Rain washes away nutrients and cools the heap.

WHAT YOU SHOULD NOT PUT ON YOUR COMPOST HEAP

Don't add weeds with strong roots or the seed heads that will sprout. Meat or fish scraps attract vermin, and bread, pasta and rice can form moulds that attack the bacteria responsible for the decomposition. In the old days, these would have been used to feed the dogs or chickens.

QUICK ACTION

To accelerate the break-down process and maintain the temperature, turn the compost heap frequently to move the less-rotted material to the centre.

TOO DRY OR TOO WET

Spray the heap with water if it becomes dry – keep it moist but not soggy. If a white mould appears on the outside of the heap, then it is too dry.
● If your compost has the smell of ammonia, then it is too wet and not aerated enough. Remake the heap, adding more absorbent and fibrous material, such as shredded paper or sawdust, which will increase aeration, and also turn it more often.

THE BEST WAY TO USE YOUR COMPOST

Dig a liberal amount of well-rotted garden compost into the soil in early spring, around 5 kg per square metre. Spread a further 5 cm layer as mulch over the soil's surface in late spring. This will help control weeds, conserve soil moisture, protect roots against frost and add more organic material to the soil.
● Partially rotted compost will burn the roots and stems of most plants, but you can use it safely with cucumbers, gourds, potatoes, pumpkins, tomatoes and zucchinis. Mix a few forkfuls with soil in the planting hole and spread more over the soil surface around the plant – but not touching the stem.

COMPOST IS A NATURAL PROPAGATOR

Place trays or pots of seedlings and cuttings on the surface of a half-made compost heap, but make sure it's not a very hot new heap. This extra warmth will encourage your new seedlings and cuttings to grow.

AN IDEAL PLANTING MIX

Make an excellent planting mixture, to use for pricking out or potting on, by sieving equal parts of compost and soil through a fine wire-mesh sieve. You can make your own garden sieve by simply removing the base from a wooden box and firmly fixing some fine wire mesh over the base area.

Making compost is a natural, ecologically friendly way to recycle your green waste.

Use a shredder to chop up woody cuttings before adding them to the compost heap.

A well-prepared soil

Preparing the soil is the indispensable first stage for a successful garden. Although we tend to dig less today than gardeners used to do, the time and effort expended will bring ample rewards.

The importance of digging

HOW OFTEN SHOULD YOU DIG?
Digging breaks up and aerates the soil, it also buries the weeds and exposes soil pests to be eaten by the birds or killed by frost. However, digging too often can upset the ecological balance of soil by interfering with its micro-organism activity, which helps break down organic matter and aids the absorption of nutrients by the plant roots. Thorough digging once a year is generally all that is needed.

WHAT IS THE BEST TIME TO DIG?
It is best to dig during autumn to bury old weed growth and incorporate organic material. If a green manure crop is to be grown over winter, then dig the soil during late summer and sow the green manure crop immediately.

● Avoid digging when the soil is too wet, which can damage its structure and cause it to compact. A simple test is to squeeze a handful of the soil. If it crumbles it's fine to dig, but if it sticks together it's too wet.

DIGGING TECHNIQUES
Simple digging, that is, lifting out a spade's depth of soil and turning it over, is adequate when you are working on cultivated beds, but if you're preparing a new bed or digging in a lot of organic matter, single or double digging is preferable. These traditional techniques involve digging a series of trenches to a single or double spade's depth, and filling each empty trench with soil from the next as you dig. All this hard work will increase the depth of the topsoil, break up compacted layers in the soil and improve its drainage.
● On shallow soils, dig down to the subsoil and incorporate small amounts of topsoil into the subsoil to increase the depth of cultivated ground.

WATCH YOUR BACK
Do not overreach yourself by tackling too large an area or by attempting to take up too much earth with each spadeful – you should be able to lift it without difficulty. Bend knees and elbows, rather than your back, while lifting the spade. Spread out the work – 2 hours a day, or digging about 20 square metres of soil that is neither too heavy nor too stony, is enough. Any more and you will wear yourself out.

SPRING DIGGING AND WEED CONTROL
Digging during the spring can bring thousands of weed seeds to the surface, which will then germinate.
● To avoid a mass of weeds among your seedlings, hold off sowing until the weeds have grown and you have cleared them to produce a clean seedbed. If the soil is dry, watering it will stimulate weed growth and speed up the process.

Spiking your garden beds with an aerator is a great way to improve your soil's surface drainage.

THE 'LAZY' NO-DIGGING METHOD

When conditions are dry, digging in a light soil can cause valuable moisture to be lost. Instead of setting to the hard work of digging, an alternative is to cover the soil with a thick layer of well-rotted compost or manure. This layer protects the soil from water loss and compaction, and is gradually drawn into the soil by worms. Their busy activity helps drainage and aeration.

● If you do not make your own compost, buy some soil-conditioning organic material such as composted bark, composted wood or farmyard manure from a garden centre, or contact your local authority composting centre for a supply of recycled green waste.

Getting ready to plant

CONTROLLING WEEDS Bare, weed-free soil is much easier to cultivate than ground covered with growth. Weeds take nutrients out of the soil, encourage pests and diseases and make the garden look untidy. It is important to keep on top of weeds and prevent them from taking hold.

● Keep freshly cultivated soil clear of weeds by covering the area with old carpet. Leave it in place until you are ready to use the ground. On smaller areas, use newspaper or recycle your flattened cardboard boxes and cover

Gardener's Choice

WHICH GREEN MANURE CROPS?
It can be hard to choose a green manure crop to suit your particular situation, as there are many you can grow and each one has its particular benefits.
TO ENRICH THE SOIL AND ADD NITROGEN
Cowpea, fenugreek, lablab, lupin, mung bean, subclover and woolly pod vetch.
TO SUPPRESS WEEDS Buckwheat, cowpea, lablab, lucerne and sorghum.
FOR UNDERSOWING Cowpea, lucerne, subclover and woolly pod vetch.
TO BUILD BULK ORGANIC MATTER
Buckwheat, oats and sorghum.
TO ATTRACT BENEFICIAL INSECTS
Buckwheat and lupin.

them with a layer of soil. The cardboard controls the weeds and slowly rots to add organic matter to the soil.

● If weeds somehow have been allowed to develop, make sure you mow them down straight after they have flowered. If you let them go to seed, you will have to contend with generations of hardy survivors.

BEFORE YOU SOW OR PLANT Dig only well-rotted compost and manure into the soil before you plant. Fresh material should be left in a heap to decompose before it is dug in, while partially broken down material can be spread over the soil surface as a mulch that will gradually rot and be taken into the soil by worm activity.

● You can enrich a mulch with wood ash, poultry manure, phosphate-rich bone meal, nitrogen-rich dried blood, or blood, fish and bone meal, a balanced general feed. You can also use a liquid manure, which can be made by soaking green weeds such as nettles in a bucket of water (right).

DON'T FORGET GREEN MANURE Green manure crops can be used at any time of the year to improve and enrich the soil. These quick-growing crops are cut down and dug in at the height of their growth, just before flowering. Their top growth protects the soil surface from erosion and prevents weeds, and the roots improve drainage and aeration. When the crop is dug into the soil, it adds organic matter, which slowly breaks down to release valuable plant nutrients.

RAKE OVER THE SOIL Before sowing your seeds or planting out your small seedlings, it is important to break up the soil surface into a fine crumbly texture so that plant roots will establish quickly. Rake over the surface with a soil rake until any large clods of earth are broken down to a fine, level finish, which is called a fine tilth. Remove large stones and any remaining weeds.

HOE LIGHTLY Avoid hoeing more than 5 cm deep. This shallow action will cut off new weed growth near the soil surface and avoid bringing up more seeds from lower down. Weed seeds buried below 5 cm are unlikely to germinate and grow.

● Keep a hoe in a handy spot, ready to take with you whenever you walk around your garden, so you can 'worry away at the weeds'.

MAKING NETTLE MANURE

1 Half-fill a bucket with chopped nettles or other weeds and add rainwater (10 litres of water to 1 kg of chopped nettles).

2 Cover the bucket and then leave the mixture to infuse and ferment for 3–4 weeks.

3 The mixture will now have a strong odour. Filter it before using. To use, dilute 1 part infusion to 4 parts water.

4 Use the diluted solution to water the roots of plants, to enrich the soil or spray it on as a foliar feed.

Sowing seeds and planting out

There are as many tips and tricks for sowing, thinning, potting on and planting out as there are gardeners to recommend them. These gems have been gleaned by trial and error or passed on by word of mouth.

Successful sowing

TESTING THE SEEDS The capacity of seeds to germinate diminishes over time and the expiry date on the packet can sometimes be too optimistic if the seeds are not stored correctly. Once the packet has been opened and the seeds exposed to heat and humidity, their condition will deteriorate rapidly. Try these traditional tests for success.
● To sort the viable seeds from the others before sowing, soak them in a glass of water. Within half an hour the good, or viable, ones will sink, while the others, which are less likely to germinate, will float on the surface.
● To test germination, place 10 seeds on a couple of layers of moistened paper towel on a saucer and seal them, and the saucer, in a plastic bag. Put the bag in a warm, but not hot, place and wait for the seeds to sprout. If eight or more of the 10 seeds sprout, then the germination chances for the rest of the batch are good. Seven or less is a poor result and the seeds can still be sown, but you should add some extra to compensate.

A CHILLING EXPERIENCE Seeds of many species from alpine regions and some species from cold temperate and desert regions need to be exposed to a period of cold before they are able to germinate.
● The traditional method of doing this is to make drainage holes in a box or other container, place the seeds between layers of sand and bury the pot near a south-facing wall. In early spring, dig it up and plant the seeds.
● Another way is to put the seeds in a closed container that is filled with moist vermiculite or a similar medium and put in the fridge for up to 3 months.

SOME TIPS FOR EARLY SOWERS Most seeds need a nighttime temperature of at least 13°C to germinate. There are some that will sprout at lower temperatures, for instance carrots will germinate at 9°C, and lettuces and radishes will sprout at 10°C.
● Warm the soil up by one or two degrees before sowing and this will give you an early crop. Cover it with a cloche or a piece of old carpet or ground sheet weighed down at the edges with bricks or soil.
● After sowing, cover the seeds with a cloche or a homemade mini-greenhouse made out of a large plastic bottle with the base cut off. Leave the top open. This protection will also prevent mice, snails, rabbits and pigeons from nibbling the young shoots.
● Do not sow in frozen or very wet ground.
● Sow cold-sensitive plants that need a longer growing period, such as begonias, eggplants, geraniums, melons and tomatoes, in pots or trays and put them in a cold frame for an early start.
● Speed up germination indoors by placing seed trays or pots on a plank of wood on top of a heater or other warm place like the top of a clothes dryer.

THE APPLE TREE AND THE LILAC In cool climates, follow the rhythms of nature and read the signs around you. Sow vegetables and cold-resistant flowers when the apple blossom opens. With more delicate species, wait for the lilac to flower.

PERFECT SOIL FOR SOWING Fine, rich soil is an excellent choice to use for sowing and potting mix or for using as a top-up for your pot plants. To make your own fine soil, pass some soil from your garden borders through a 2 mm mesh sieve.

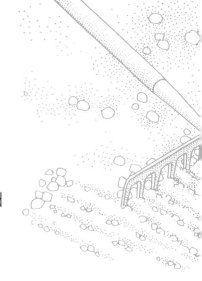

Convert a large plastic bottle into a mini-greenhouse.

A homemade seed dispenser helps you avoid backache.

A simple piece of chicken wire that is placed over the seed tray makes an excellent template for making sure you sow large seeds evenly.

WASTE NOT, WANT NOT If you buy your eggs in old-fashioned cardboard egg cartons, you can separate the sections and use them as plant pots. Put them directly in the soil when the seedlings are ready to plant out and the cardboard will gradually decompose in the ground, adding organic matter.

SOW WITH THE RISING MOON In times gone by gardeners followed the moon and many gardeners continue this tradition today. When the moon is in the ascendant, plant energy is said to be drawn upwards, making germination more likely. On the other hand, planting out should take place in the descendant phase, when lunar energy encourages the growth of new roots.
● Sow in the morning when the warming conditions will benefit seed germination.

AVOID BACKACHE A seed dispenser will help you to sow rows of seeds without back-breaking bending. Improvise with a piece of plastic tubing about 1 m long. Drop the seeds down the tube and into the drill.

SOWING SMALL SEEDS Fine seeds, such as begonia, lobelia and petunia, may stick to your fingers and be difficult to spread out. Mix the seeds with some dry sand or coffee grounds in an old flour shaker and shake the mix lightly over the soil. Or you can use a piece of folded card and tap it gently to keep the mix flowing. Just make sure you don't go back over already seeded areas.

A PENCIL TIP Spread moistened seed-raising mix in a seed tray, take an ordinary pencil and dip the lead tip into the mix to make a small hole. Then use the moistened tip to pick up a tiny seed – the moisture makes it stick – and poke it into the hole. Use the blunt end to cover the seed with mix.

SOWING LARGE SEEDS EVENLY When you are sowing broad beans, green beans, peas and other large seeds, place a piece of ordinary chicken wire over the seed tray and sow one seed per hole.

GOOD INSURANCE Sow seeds in pairs to avoid blank pots and to make sure you have enough plants. If both seeds grow, cut out the weaker one at soil level.

DO NOT SOW TOO DEEPLY In nature, seeds fall to the ground from their parent plants and, generally, nobody buries them. Remember this when you do not have any instructions for the sowing depth of seeds. Small seeds should be close to the surface and only just covered with soil. This used to be done using a feather, but an artist's paintbrush works well, too.
● Bury large seeds, such as nuts, at twice the depth of their largest dimension.
● In lighter soils, bury the seed a little deeper to encourage better rooting.
● In less fertile soils, sow seeds more thickly, which will allow for poor germination and development. Thin growth can encourage the invasion of annoying weeds, which might smother tender seedlings.

ALWAYS SOAK HARD SEEDS Plants of the Fabaceae family, such as haricot beans and peas and even eucalypts and wattle, have very thick skins. To aid germination, soak them for 24 hours in warm water or over-night in a cup of hot tea so they swell and soften before sowing.

GIVE HARD-SKINNED SEEDS A HELPING HAND TO GERMINATE Although soaking hard seeds often works, you may have to break into the seed coat on very tough seeds to let in enough water for germination to take place. Making a small nick in the outer shell of the seed with a clean sharp knife or small hacksaw is a tried-and-tested tech-nique. Another one is scarification, which involves rubbing the seeds against sandpaper or another rough surface. Seeds that benefit from scarifying include camellia, ceanothus, hawthorn, sweet pea and wisteria.

Protect your precious seeds from hungry birds by covering them with netting, or news-paper that is kept moist. Keep an eye on the seeds and when they begin to germinate remove the newspaper.

DISCOURAGING BIRDS To keep birds at bay, a good idea is to cover your seedbeds with netting, fleece or a single layer of pegged-down damp newspaper. Or you could cover the soil with a thin layer of fine gravel.

● Prickly branches such as bougainvillea and rose, tied to strings that are suspended across the seeded area, can also deter birds.

● Threading strips of kitchen foil or unwanted CDs on string stretched across the bed is a tried-and-tested deterrent.

PROBLEM PAWS Very prickly prunings or a mulch of gravel may also deter cats from digging in your beds. Simply remember that anything that is uncomfortable on their paws should keep them away.

NEW FORMS OF SEEDS FOR GREATER SUCCESS Coated, or pelleted, seeds can be used to further encourage seed viability. These seeds are covered in a layer of clay that contains agents such as bird and animal repellent and fertiliser that stimulates growth and protects from diseases.

SELFISH GENES F1 hybrid seeds are more fertile than those bred by more traditional selection methods. They do not pass on this genetic potential so the seeds produced by F1 hybrid plants will not be as fertile as the parent plant. To grow hybrid varieties, it is necessary to buy the specially bred seed each time you need it.

MARKER SEEDS When sowing outside, plant stronger, faster-germinating seeds next to tiny ones to break the soil crust and help the little ones push through. Victorians used radishes as marker seeds for carrots, evening primroses and poppies.

ON THE EDGE Cucumber, marrow, melon, squash and zucchini seeds like to be planted edgeways, not flat on the soil.

COLLECTING YOUR OWN SEED In days gone by, collecting seed from flowers and vegetables was very often the only means of guaranteeing more plants the following year. Today, it still makes sense to save seeds from annuals and biennials, and from salad crops, but you will need to purchase new seeds every few years to maintain quality. To obtain healthy seeds:

● Collect seeds only from the healthiest, disease-free plants.

● Keep the plant well watered while flowers and seed heads are forming and stake if necessary to keep them off the ground.

● Allow seeds to dry naturally on the plant.

USING POTTING MIX The *Legionella* bacteria occurs naturally in soil, compost and potting mix. While most people will not get Legionnaires' disease from using potting mix, it is important to take precautions when using potting mix:

● Wear gloves and wash your hands well after handling potting mix.

● Use potting mix in open, well-ventilated areas and moisten dry mix.

● Avoid breathing in the dust when opening the bag and, if necessary, wear a dust mask.

TRANSPORTING SEEDLINGS There are many gardeners who swap plants with their friends, which sometimes means that seedlings and cuttings must make long journeys.

● Transplant seeds into egg cartons (right) so you can transport seedlings easily. Close the carton for the journey for extra protection.

● For short journeys, cuttings can be pushed into holes made in a half potato, which will keep them moist. Wrap the potatoes in damp newspaper so they don't dry out.

Some seeds, such as melon, like to be planted edgeways.

Use egg cartons and potatoes to protect your seedlings and cuttings while in transit.

SOWING SEEDS IN TRAYS

1 Mix 1 part fine sand with 2 parts potting mix and then fill a seed tray with the mix.

2 Level the mix, then tamp it down with a block of wood to 12 mm below the lip of the seed tray.

3 Moisten this thoroughly with a spray or fine rose, and be careful not to displace the mixture.

4 Sow the seeds evenly over the surface using a seeder or a folded card. Mix fine seeds with dry sand.

5 Cover the sown seeds with a fine layer of well-sifted potting mix.

6 Then cover the tray with glass and put it in a well-lit room out of direct sun. Wipe the glass clean occasionally.

Looking after your seedlings

HEALTHY SEEDLINGS All seedlings will grow towards the light. Turn the tray each day to ensure their growth is balanced.
● Do not put seedlings in full sunlight, especially if it's from a large window, where they may be scorched.
● Give plants a good watering at least 1 hour before you transplant them. They will retain the water and survive the shock of being moved much better. Keep transplants in a plastic bag as you plant them out.
● Plant out in the cooler part of the day.

THINNING FOR STRONGER PLANTS
Thin out seedlings when they have produced two or three well-formed leaves. Larger seedlings will become crowded and will be harder to separate. They may grow tall and spindly and turn pale: all signs of weakness in young plants that cannot be rectified.
● If seedlings become overcrowded, do not thin them out by pulling on their stems as this may damage the roots of the seedlings that remain. Instead, cut the unwanted seedlings off at the base with pointed scissors and they will die naturally.

HARDEN OFF YOUR SEEDLINGS FOR PLANTING OUTSIDE When the temperature outside is still very low, place trays of seedlings into cold frames, an unheated greenhouse or a sheltered porch for a week or two, to harden them off. For a few seedlings, dig a trench in the ground to hold the tray and cover with a pane of glass. Remove the glass whenever conditions are warm. You can then transplant seedlings out into the garden, but cover them with a tent of newspaper if there is a risk of frost.

DAMPING OFF To avoid damping off, which is a seedling disease, make sure the top 1 cm of the potting mix contains at least 50 per cent good drainage material, such as sharp sand. The lower layer should be straight potting mix, which is more nutritious and encourages the seedlings to form a strong root system. Avoid letting the potting mix become waterlogged.
● Keep the potting mix around the seedlings well aerated, and provide plenty of light and

'Pots' made of rolled newspaper decompose in the soil, so you will be able to plant out the seedlings without disturbing their roots.

fresh air. Lightly watering the seedlings with chamomile tea is an old herbal remedy used to prevent damping off.

NEVER LET SOIL DRY OUT Seedlings need to be kept moist but not wet. The difference is small, but by observing when they droop, and testing the potting mix with your finger, you will soon learn through experience how much water they need. The best way to avoid damping off disease is to spray the compost lightly or to dribble water from a sponge to moisten but not drench the surface.

SOW INTO THE SOIL Californian poppy (*Eschscholzia californica*), clarkia, cornflower (*Centaurea*), love-in-a-mist (*Nigella*) and many plants of the Fabaceae family such as broom and lupin do not transplant well. Once all danger of frost has passed sow these directly into the garden.

PROTECT YOUNG PLANTS Seedlings and small plants can be damaged by harsh weather or even hot, direct sunlight. When they're at risk, cover the plants with a dampened dust-sheet draped over a frame. This protects, but allows rainfall and light to pass through.

HANDLING SEEDLINGS Lift out seedlings carefully with a dibber or an old pencil or pen, and hold them by the leaves rather than the stem or roots. Plants such as beetroot, radish, and other root vegetables may be set back by transplanting.

Easily keep seedlings moist using a spray bottle or sponge.

Hold seedlings by the leaves, not the stems or roots.

Watering your garden

We take our modern plumbing for granted, but water has not always been available simply at the turn of a tap. No wonder gardeners have learned to guard it jealously and use it wisely, and they have been devising all sorts of strategies for coping with both floods and drought.

Watering wisdom

THE BEST TIME TO WATER Never water during the heat of a sunny day. The water will evaporate before it can soak into the soil and benefit the plants. A plant's leaves may also be scorched by the magnification of the sun's rays through any droplets of water that are resting on them.

● Avoid watering in the early evening after a hot day, as the cool water will vaporise on the warm surface of the soil, creating a humid atmosphere around the plants that can then encourage fungal diseases.

● If the weather is very hot, it is better to do your watering in the cool of the early morning or later on in the evening when the soil temperature has cooled down.

NOT TOO LITTLE AND NOT TOO OFTEN
It is better to soak the soil from time to time than to water sparingly every day.

● Soaking the soil to a good depth encourages your plants to grow deeper, stronger root systems, capable of tapping reserves of water during periods of drought.

● Light watering does not penetrate down into the soil, and this encourages the roots to look for water at the surface, producing a shallow-growing root system that is vulnerable to drought: one that will suffer if you forget to water when it is hot.

WATER DELIVERS SOIL'S NUTRIENTS
Water carries soluble nutrients to plant roots that grow deep in the soil. However, excessive rainfall or heavy watering can wash away nutrients from the soil's surface, especially on sandy soils and slopes. Replace nutrients regularly by adding garden compost or similar organic material to the soil and by applying fertilisers when needed.

SEASONAL WATERING In spring, autumn and winter, make sure you water your plants in the morning rather than in the evening. This will protect them from the cold when the temperature drops at night, which could cause droplets of water on the leaves to freeze.

PREVENTING SOIL EROSION Heavy rainfall or excessive watering on sloping ground can wash away topsoil and create furrows in the surface. Stabilise slopes by building level terraces to plant into.

● A retaining wall at the foot of a terrace is the best way to hold soil in place. It will encourage water to soak into the soil and benefit the plants, too. Planting a low hedge along the wall line is an attractive way of edging the terrace.

● As an alternative to terracing, you could always sow a groundcover of plants to stabilise the soil and keep it from slipping. Very good groundcover plants for banks and

There are two golden rules for watering: never water in the heat of the day, and water thoroughly but not too often.

DID YOU KNOW?

ABOUT YOU AND YOUR ENVIRONMENT
With drought conditions in many areas of Australia, water restrictions are becoming a normal part of daily life. Some areas prohibit the use of sprinklers on lawns and gardens, as well as the washing down of any hard surfaces and vehicles. But rainfall is free, so collect and store as much of this water as possible, particularly in the summer months when water can be scarce and restrictions are in force. All types of plants thrive on rainwater. Contact your local water authority or your council to get some information on rainwater collection systems.

Water your plants with a gentle spray (left) or use a seep hose (right), which will apply a trickle of water exactly where it is needed.

slopes include agapanthus, dietes, prostrate grevillea varieties, grasses and clumping perennials like daylily and liriope.

● Another, more modern, way of holding the soil in place is to use a synthetic semipermeable groundcover fabric. Lay the fabric at an angle to the slope to reduce the risk of it being dislodged by downward drag, and peg it securely to the ground at regular intervals along its length.

● Once the groundcover fabric is in place, it will absorb water and help to prevent the soil underneath it from washing away. You can then plant your shrubs and your groundcover plants through the fabric. Then, in time, as the plants grow their roots will also help to stabilise the surface.

HOEING TO REDUCE WATER LOSS

Hoeing not only controls weeds, which compete with other plants for water, it also makes the soil surface crumbly, which allows water to soak in quickly to nourish the plants' roots. Take care not to hoe too deeply to avoid damaging surface roots and stems.

MULCHING TO CONSERVE WATER

By mulching the surface of the soil when it is moist, you can reduce the loss of moisture through evaporation. A mulch also prevents weeds growing, which means that your plants get all the moisture there is available.

A HOMEMADE WATER RESERVOIR For thirsty vegetables, or for any plants that need a lot of water, sink a terracotta pot, or a large plastic bottle with drainage holes punched into the bottom, into the soil next to your plant. When you make your plant-watering rounds, remember to fill the container with water, which will then slowly soak into the soil without any waste.

Hose know-how

REMEMBER, GENTLY DOES IT Water with a gentle spray. Better still, use a soaker hose, which will automatically produce a constant light spray, or a seep hose (left) which will apply a trickle of water where it is needed. These systems are traditionally left in place all during summer. Seep hoses can even be disguised under a mulch around permanent plantings so that they can get their water to the base of plants unnoticed. If you attach either of these simple systems to a timer, it will make watering the garden all the more discreet and easy.

● To make an improvised soaker hose, take an old hose and make small holes along its length using a bradawl to puncture the surface. Clamp or block one end of the pipe and attach the other to a tap. Turn on the tap gently to achieve a seep.

A COORDINATED WATERING SYSTEM

Wherever possible, buy your hose, attachments and any component parts from the same manufacturer. This way you make sure they all fit together well. Invest in a thick, durable, good-quality hose that will not kink. A coloured wall reduces the amount of light that penetrates the hose, preventing algae growth on the inside.

AVOID PRESSURE Do not use a strong, forceful spray when watering your garden plants. The weight of water can cause stems and branches to break off and flower petals to be damaged. Water at the base or keep to a light spray, arching the water over the plants so that it falls naturally from above.

● A similar technique is a quick way of oxygenating ponds that have fish in them during the heat of the summer. Play the hose at least 60 cm above the water and this will carry oxygen into the pond.

WELL-BEHAVED HOSES Use old, small terracotta pots to make sure your hoses behave properly. Stack two pots on the ground at the edge of a flowerbed, with the narrow bases facing to make an hourglass shape, then push a dowel through the centre holes into the soil. This makes a good-looking hose guide that will prevent your hose dragging over vulnerable flowers in the border and damaging them.

1 To concentrate water where it is needed most, build up a ring of soil 30–50 cm away from the stem of the plant.

2 Scoop out some soil from around the stem to create a well. Firm the edge, sloping it towards the stem.

3 Gently fill the well with water, avoiding damage to the retaining wall. Repeat the watering until the soil is soaked.

4 The water will eventually seep into the soil around the roots, ensuring the shrub or tree is kept well watered.

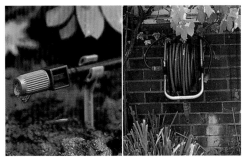

Drippers (left) come in many forms and are used to reduce water loss during irrigation. A hose reel mounted on a wall (right) keeps hoses tidy.

● You can also use a large, up-ended terra-cotta pot to wind your hose around for storage and to keep it from kinking. Once you have wound it, push the nozzle end in the pot drainage hole to keep it in place. There are convenient hose-reel winders you can buy to attach to the wall of your house next to the outdoor tap – or there are ones you can wheel around the garden.

AUTOMATIC DRIP-FEED WATERING

To save time watering, install an automatic drip-feed system. Unlike a seep hose, which delivers water all along its length, automatic drip-feed and trickle systems consist of a tube and individual nozzles which can be positioned to direct water where it is most needed – to individual plants, for example, that need more water than others. A variety of nozzles is available to produce sprays or trickles, and the system can be expanded using connectors and additional tubes.
● Use seep hoses to water individual containers on patios and balconies, window boxes, hanging baskets and plants that are placed in inaccessible parts of the garden.
● Do not be overly ambitious and keep the system manageable. The nozzles need regular cleaning to prevent blocking. Install an in-line filter, or soak the nozzles in vinegar overnight to keep them clear.
● An automatic timer will complete the system. It makes it easy to water regularly at the best time of day and means your garden gets watered when you are on holidays.

GARDEN SPRINKLERS
Less efficient than microspray seep hoses or drip-feed systems, sprinklers are still useful for delivering a fine spray over a specific area of the garden, such as a lawn or vegetable patch. However, they do use a large volume of water and some

local authorities prohibit their use. If you are allowed to use sprinklers, run them in the cool of the evening to reduce evaporation.

DUST OFF THE LEAVES When it is very dry and dusty, conifers and evergreens that are not in bloom will benefit from a regular spray with water to clean the leaves and help to deter pests such as two-spotted mites, which hate getting wet.

Watering plants indoors and under glass

CONTAINERS, PLANTERS, POTS AND TROUGHS Potted plants can dry out very rapidly, particularly in warm weather. They therefore need regular watering to keep their roots healthy. There are also a few simple rules to remember.
● **WATER TWICE** Water once and then wait for 15 minutes to allow the water to soak through the potting mix, then water again. This will ensure that the complete root ball and potting mix is moist throughout.
● **USE WARM WATER** Let water warm up to ambient temperature before use. Applying cold water from the tap to a warm root system can cause the plant to go into shock and suddenly wilt. If you are in a hurry, add a little hot water to the watering can to quickly warm up the contents.
● **GET GOOD DRAINAGE** Check that the drainage holes in the base of pots are kept clear to allow excess water to drain away. Make sure that all containers are raised off the ground using pot feet or bricks, or are standing on gravel if they are in saucers. This will prevent water from building up in the pot and avoids damage to the roots.

RULE OF THUMB It is not always easy to gauge when and how much water your pot plants really need. One way to find out is simply to insert a finger into the potting mix, and if it feels moist, do not water. If it is dry, water well to moisten all the potting mix, but allow excess to drain out of the pot.
● The weight of the pot is also a good guide. Pick it up – if it feels heavy it will still be moist, if it is light then water well.

Rainwater

NATURE'S GIFT Do not waste valuable rainwater. Instead, collect it in well-placed water tanks around the garden. The earliest water tanks were simply barrels or other containers placed wherever water would be needed for plants. They allowed the water to warm up as it stood, and many gardeners believe warm water is best for plants.

WATER FROM THE ROOF Purpose-built water tanks can be connected to the drainage pipes and gutters of your house, greenhouse or outbuildings so that you can collect the runoff from the roofs. They are durable and hold a good volume of water, which can be tapped off from the bottom. Make sure you raise the tank off the ground on bricks or a platform sold with the tanks, so you can get your watering can under the tap.
- Disguise tanks by growing shrubs or climbers around it. Avoid rampant plants or those with thorns as you'll need to be able to get to it easily year after year.
- Keep the water clean by putting a lid on the tank to exclude light and to prevent small creatures and leaves from falling in.
- At regular intervals, add a little charcoal to keep the water clean and fresh.
- Place a plug of fine wire mesh at the top of the downpipe to stop debris polluting the tank. Clean the wire from time to time to prevent build-up from blocking the downpipe.
- Make sure you have an overflow pipe from the top of the tank or you'll have to drain off some water from time to time.

TANKS FOR SMALL AREAS For small gardens and patios, choose a compact tank that will not be an eyesore. It should have a strong, durable design that will not leak.
- If you live in a flat, ask the residents association or property manager if you can divert rainwater from a downpipe into a tank for you and others to use.

MOST PLANTS PREFER RAINWATER If your tap water is hard (alkaline), use rainwater to keep your lime-hating plants healthy.
- If you have to use tap water, then add potting mix for your acid-loving plants, or leaf mould, to the soil surface from time to time to increase its acidity. Or make some acid water (see page 259) or add a little bit

To prevent water loss through evaporation, the best time to water the garden is early in the morning or late in the evening.

of vinegar to the water in the watering can. These measures will all help you to create the acidic environment that plants demand for good health.

UNPOLLUTED RAINWATER When it rains after a dry spell, the first flush of rainfall is likely to be laden with dust and pollutants. You can divert the polluted rainfall easily by attaching a small bypass pipe to the end of your drainpipe, a temporary measure that will dispose of unwanted rainfall down the drain. Do not forget to remove the bypass after the first flush of rainfall so you can continue collecting the clean rain.

SEEK ADVICE FIRST Your water authority or local council can advise you on local regulations for installation of rainwater tanks. Seek their advice before going ahead.
- Before making any modifications to your downpipes, check regulations with your plumber and local council.

COLLECTING YOUR OWN RAINWATER
Rainwater is a precious resource that has been collected and used for centuries. It is a lifesaver in times of drought but, in addition, rainwater has a slight acid content which is ideal for most plants.

Follow in the footsteps of gardeners of the past by installing a rainwater tank. Look for easy-to-install DIY water tanks and pipes to connect to the gutters of your house, garden buildings and greenhouse. There are also complete ready-made systems that can be plumbed in straight away. If space allows, link a number of tanks together so that no rainfall is wasted.

Above: The traditional tank-stand elevated tanks to increase water pressure and was usually disguised with plantings or lattices.

A narrow tank fitted beside the house is unobtrusive.

Tools for gardeners

Many of the tools we have today were familiar in Roman times. But modern materials make them more effective and easier to use than ever before. Invest in the best quality you can and look after them.

A well-stocked tool shed

SPADES, SHOVELS AND FORKS Choose your spade carefully, as you will use it more than any other tool. It is said that you can do every garden job with a good spade so you need one you can use comfortably. Select one with a short blade to make light work of digging. A 'lady's spade' is perfect for many gardeners – small and light, it puts less strain on the back – but those gardeners who have the strength for heavier work will want a heavier duty tool.

● **SPADE OR SHOVEL?** A spade has a flat, sharp blade; a shovel has curved edges and is used for scooping up material. It tends to be larger and heavier.

● **THE FORK** Choose to suit your strength. You will need a fork for breaking up heavy and stony ground, preparing soil, turning a compost heap and forking up debris.

SHARP SHEARS Straight-edged shears are best for cutting through soft growth. For woody material, shears with a serrated blade will grip and cut more effectively.

● Angled, long-handled edging shears make edging lawns an easy job, but check that the handles are the right length for you before you buy. They can be as short as 90 cm or as long as 110 cm. On large lawns, cordless electric edge trimmers or petrol-driven whipper snippers make short work of this task.

GOOD-QUALITY SECATEURS This is a hard-working tool where quality is important. Strong, sharp secateurs cut through plant growth cleanly without causing damage and are effortless to use. Invest in the very best, with hard steel blades that can be sharpened easily and replaced when worn. There are types of secateurs available that

have self-sharpening blades, which should always give a clean cut.

● Sharp scissor-action secateurs are the best for pruning soft growth with a clean cut. Anvil-action blades, which cut down on a soft metal plate, are best for cutting through hard, dry, woody material. Invest in a good-quality sharpening kit to keep your blades razor-sharp at all times.

HAND HOES AND CULTIVATORS
Available in various designs, the hoe is one of the most useful tools in the garden.

● A digging hoe is used for controlling weeds and breaking up small areas of hard ground.

The days of large teams of hired gardeners are long gone, but tools still need to be stored well – it doesn't matter how many you have.

- The Dutch hoe is perhaps the most, or one of the most, common, with a flat, thin blade that is pushed and pulled through the soil to loosen the soil crust and chop off weeds without damaging the plant's roots.
- The angled draw hoe is used for chopping off heavy weed growth, for earthing up and for making seed drills.
- The hand cultivator has three curved and narrow prongs that are dragged through compacted and clogged soil to break it up.

IMPROVISED RULER On the handle of a wooden rake or hoe, make small notches every 5 cm and highlight them with some coloured paint. Then you'll always have a ruler for measuring distances between drills and seeds after raking or hoeing soil.

READY TO HAND Stand large pots at key places around the garden for your tools when working. This avoids misplacing them and finding the rusty remains months later. Or wear a belt that holds small tools, or invest in a tool caddy or trug to keep all your small tools to hand as you work.

MANICURED LAWN Lawn can be a source of pride and you need a pair of long-handled lawn shears for cutting grass in areas that are inaccessible to a lawnmower, such as along edges and under shrubs. These give a neat result and are easy to control. The alternative of a whipper snipper is speedy but you may damage shrubs and tree trunks.

IMPROVISED KNEELERS Really get down to it and garden on your knees – taking care to avoid straining your back and making your knees sore. To make a very comfortable, soft kneeling pad, fill an old hot-water bottle with sawdust or sand and cover it on one side with a piece of old carpet.

RAKING AND SWEEPING There are two types of garden rake. A soil or garden rake has a head about 40 cm wide with short fixed tines. Use it to break up the soil surface. A spring-tine rake is for clearing lightweight debris such as leaves and is essential for raking lawns clear. Find one that has wooden, rather than metal, tines as it will be much springier and lighter to use.
- **A GOOD STIFF BRUSH** That well-tended look to paths and patios is achieved only with a thorough sweep.

A SHARP EDGE A half-moon edging iron with a sharp blade set into a straight handle gives a military neatness to lawn edges.

OFF TO THE COMPOST HEAP Treat yourself to a good-sized wheelbarrow with an inflatable tyre. Pneumatic tyres ride over irregular garden surfaces more easily than solid tyres and spread the weight of the load, reducing soil compaction. Buy the biggest wheelbarrow you can for fewer journeys, but don't overfill it with heavy material.

FROM THE KITCHEN CUPBOARD Use old spoons, ladles, forks and whisks to transplant seedlings and mix up homemade solutions. An apple corer is an excellent dibber for tiny bulbs, and a colander makes an inexpensive trug. Keep them in the garden shed or the laundry so that these recycled implements do not end up back in the kitchen.

Tools for a lifetime

PROTECT SECATEURS Plant sap and rotting vegetation corrode the blades of secateurs. After each use, wipe the blades with an oily rag to remove residue and protect the metal. To sterilise the blades, simply wipe them with methylated spirits.
- Sharpen shears and secateurs regularly by rubbing the cutting edge, round side down, with a sharpening stone dampened with water or oil. Blunt blades cause damage and possibly dieback.

CLEAN TOOLS To maintain your tools in good condition and to prolong their life, wash or wipe off soil and other residues with newspaper or a rag after using them. Use a small piece of wood to scrape off earth but never use metal, which can scratch. With a rag or fine steel wool, soaked in engine oil, wipe all metal parts. Do this after every use, or at least several times each season.
- Keep oil in a hand-soap bottle with a plastic plunge dispenser for ease of use.

TAKE CARE OF TOOL HANDLES Protect wooden handles by treating them once a year with linseed oil. Before you put the tools away for the winter, smooth the wood with fine sandpaper to remove rough areas and dirt, rub on the oil and leave it to soak in.

INDISPENSABLE
Use a trowel (below) to set out small plants and seedlings without damaging their roots. It is easy to use and ideal for small jobs in restricted spaces. Trowels are often sold in sets with a small fork and hand hoe, which are designed for container gardening. They come in a variety of materials, including very durable plastic, coated steel and carbon steel. If you use them frequently, think about investing in a stainless steel set – they are attractive and will never rust. Bind the handles with fluorescent tape or mark them with spray paint so they'll stand out from your garden plants and soil colours.

Fill an old hot-water bottle with sand and you have an instant kneeling pad.

NATURAL RUST CONTROL Use an onion that you have cut in half and sprinkled with caster sugar to rub down rusted metal parts. Just change the onion when it gets dirty.
● If you can afford it, invest in polished stainless steel spades and forks, which are easier to use and to clean, and do not rust.

INSTANT PROTECTION Keep the metal parts of your tools from rusting by plunging them into a bucket, at least 30 cm deep, that has been filled with a mixture of sand and a little lubricating oil. The abrasive sand will remove harmful residues and the oil coating will prevent rusting. Do this after each use.

IN PLAIN VIEW Wrap brightly coloured tape around the handles of all your garden tools. This will not only protect the handle and give you a smoother, more comfortable grip but it will help you to see any tools you may have mislaid in the garden.

NEW USES FOR OLD When they are past their best in practical terms, old tools can be decorative too. Fix an old trowel to the door of your shed to make a good-looking and easy-to-grasp handle. Don't throw away 'antique' wooden spades, forks and hoes that are too heavy and rotten to use. Paint them and hang them along a fence.

HARD-WEARING HANDLES Traditional gardening tools such as rakes and hoes are mounted on strong, hard-wearing ash or beech handles. Unlike plastic, woods stays cool and dry in your hands. When you choose a wooden handle, look for one with a straight grain. A grain that is crooked or knotted will make the handle less durable.
● The cheaper, varnished, softwood handles will not last very long.
● Some modern tools are attached to strong polypropylene handles that will be long-lasting and worth the money.
● Choose the right length of handle. If it is too long it will feel unbalanced, too short and it will leave you with a backache. Long-handled spades and forks are generally more comfortable to use and give greater leverage.
● However, never use a handle as a lever as it might break and cause injury.

COMFORT TIPS Try out the different shapes of handle before buying tools: many people find a D-shaped handle more comfortable than a simple T. And if any handle feels too hard, wrap it in flexible rubber tubing, such as the kind used to insulate pipe work.

CARE FOR HOSES Hoses that are left lying across the driveway or in the hot sunlight will deteriorate quickly and will eventually split or break. Always put hoses away out of the sun. A handy hint is to run the hose along the edge of a footpath out of harm's way, doubling back so the hose end is near the tap – the shade from overhanging plants will protect the hose from the sun.

Using power tools

SAFETY FIRST Always use protective equipment when using any power tools. Goggles, gloves and steel-capped boots are essential when operating rotavators and whipper snippers. Even when using a power mower you should wear leather boots.
● When you work with any electrical equipment in the garden, guard against shock by using a circuit breaker.

GROUND CLEARANCE Powered whipper snippers are invaluable tools for cutting down light and heavy plant growth.
● A range of models is available, powered by electric, 2-stroke and 4-stroke petrol motors. You don't have to buy your own – simply hire one when you need it.
● Whipper snipper heads have a rotating thread or wire for cutting soft growth. For tougher jobs, a solid cutting disc with saw teeth can be used to cut hard wooden growth up to 1 cm thick. Take great care when using.
● Larger models come with a body harness to take the weight of the machine and make working more comfortable.

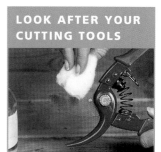

1 After each time you use your secateurs or shears, clean and sterilise the blades with alcohol or methylated spirits.

2 Sharpen blades regularly with a stone to maintain a clean cutting edge that will not damage plants when pruning.

3 Before putting secateurs away, oil all parts making sure oil flows around the blade and the cutting mechanism.

If you take good care of your tools it will lengthen their life, and save you money. Bright or even fluorescent tape (far left) that is wrapped around the handles of your tools makes them obvious in the garden. After using a tool give it a thorough clean. For example, always remove the dirt that is left in the tines of your garden fork (left).

A lawnmower is a piece of power equipment, so always wear protective footwear when using one.

MAKING A MOWER CHOICE The old-fashioned push mower is ideal for a small city lawn and modern versions are available. These are quiet, easy to store and need no fuel. However, if you need to mow a large area of lawn, you will probably prefer to use a powered lawnmower.

● A rotary mower (either 2-stroke or 4-stroke) is the usual choice for gardens. These mowers cut with a scythe action and will cut all kinds of grass including rough and long growth. Two-stroke mowers require added oil but 4-stroke mowers use unleaded petrol.

● A mulching mower does away with a grass catcher and is an excellent choice as it mows and mulches at the same time, returning the cut grass back to the soil.

● Ride-on mowers are an excellent choice for managing large properties and include safety features that make them safe to use even on slightly sloping land. The wider the cutting deck, the faster it will be to complete the job.

A RELIABLE MOWER For 4-stroke petrol mowers, record the time the machine is in use so that you know when you need to change the oil. Do the first oil change after 2–5 hours of use and thereafter about every 25 hours or at least once a year.

● Keep the inside of the mower clean and free of grass and soil residue, which might block the blade. Sharpen the blades at the beginning of the season and at regular intervals to maintain a sharp cutting edge.

● Clean the spark plugs at least once a year and replace every 100 hours. Change air filters every 50 hours.

● For safety's sake, deactivate the mower by disconnecting the spark plugs before cleaning or working on the machine.

A tool for every task

PREPARING THE GROUND

Cultivator	Loosening soil surface and breaking up clods.
Digging hoe	Controlling weeds, loosening soil, making furrows, working soil in small areas.
Flat spade	Digging, edging borders, making large planting holes.
Fork	Digging in hard and stony soil. Moving and piling up plant material.
Mattock	A pickaxe for breaking up heavy ground, loosening soil at the base of planting holes.
Rake	Levelling the ground, removing clods and stones.
Shovel	Removing earth from planting holes, moving heaps of material such as compost, gravel and manure.

SHAPING, CUTTING, PRUNING

Loppers	Cutting inaccessible branches up to 3 cm thick.
Pruning knife	Taking cuttings from woody plants.
Pruning saw	Cutting out medium-sized branches.
Secateurs	Cutting stems up to 1 cm thick; long-handled secateurs or loppers to cut high branches up to 3 cm thick.
Shears	Trimming hedges and grass edges.

WEEDING

Draw hoe	Chopping out strong weeds and roots, earthing up.
Dutch hoe	Chopping off weeds, loosening and ridging up soil.
Pronged weeder	Removing individual strongly rooted weeds.

PLANTING

Bulb planter	Planting bulbs, tubers and corms, planting naturalised bulbs in grass.
Dibber	Making planting holes for small plants, seedlings and potato tubers.
Trowel	Digging small holes to plant out or dig up young plants.

WINTER STORAGE For a problem-free spring beginning, make sure you clean everything scrupulously before storing for winter, as dirty metal parts can corrode very quickly. Always drain fuel from tanks before storing the lawnmower away.

● Provide dry shelter under canvas or an oilcloth. Avoid plastic covers, which can lead to condensation.

LAWNMOWER SERVICE The best time to have your lawnmower – or any other garden equipment – serviced is during the winter months when you are less likely to need it and mechanics are less busy. In spring, there is likely to be a long wait for servicing and you may not have the lawnmower when you want to use it.

Use protective equipment when using power tools. Wear protective goggles when using a whipper snipper.

Gardeners' friends

Lizards, frogs and birds feed on many pests that attack our plants. They are valuable allies, as are worms that work hard underground. Bees and butterflies pollinate flowers and ladybirds are aphids' enemies.

The birds and bees

WELCOMING FOOD PLANTS When you are designing your garden, include some plants for seed- and fruit-eating birds. Blueberry ash (*Elaeocarpus reticulatus*), lillypilly (*Syzygium* and *Acmena* spp.), umbrella tree (*Schefflera actinophylla*) and wild cherry (*Exocarpos cupressiformis*) all provide plenty of edible berries for fruit-eating birds, while the seed capsules of banksias, casuarinas and wattles are attractive to seed-eaters such as black cockatoos.

WINTER FEEDING Birds like honeyeaters and lorikeets eat nectar, and they will be regular visitors to your garden if you plant a range of native plants for them. Grevilleas such as 'Superb' and 'Robyn Gordon' flower year round, while banksias such as *Banksia ericifolia* and the hairpin banksia (*Banksia marginata*) are a great autumn to winter food source for many birds.

NEST BOXES Many birds can be attracted to gardens by carefully positioned and styled nesting boxes. Nesting boxes are also used by small mammals such as possums and bats.

Nectar-feeding birds like the striking-looking lorikeets are regular visitors to grevilleas.

With the disappearance of many natural nest sites, specially tailored nest boxes can help a wide range of birds to survive in the suburbs.
● Different-sized birds require different-sized nest boxes, with entry holes and perches that match the size and needs of the target bird.
● Try to position nest boxes at least 5 m above ground to make them safe from predators.
● Most nest boxes require drainage holes. Drill at least three 5 mm drainage holes in the base of a nest box.
● If possible, inspect nest boxes regularly to remove the nests of introduced pest birds. Watch for bees that invade and build hives.
● Nest boxes are available from some nurseries and through bird societies.

CLEAN, FRESH WATER Fresh water is essential in a bird-friendly garden. Ideally, birdbaths should be around 50 mm deep and have sloping sides. It's also a good idea to place some rocks or pebbles in the birdbath, to provide a foothold for little birds.
● Position the birdbath so that it can be seen from the house, and so that it is well out of the reach of cats and other predators. Tall or thorny shrubs nearby provide a perch, and look out point for birds visiting the birdbath.

SHELTER Include a variety of plant sizes and types to provide shelter for a variety of birds.
● Include some small, dense shrubs where small birds can nest, as well as some tall trees if you have room for them.
● Parrots build their nests in tree hollows, so if possible retain old trees with hollow limbs.
● Many birds are partial to fruit-tree pests such as aphids and codling moths. Put a nest box in your orchard and birds may protect your trees while raising their brood.

ENSURE A GOOD HARVEST Bees and butterflies are valuable to the gardener. They feed on nectar and pollen from flowers, and in so doing pollinate numerous plants,

A bird feeder hung among trees is a safe place for birds to visit for food or water.

DID YOU KNOW?

MOSQUITO CONTROL
Goldfish and small native fish are welcome additions to any pond or lake, as they eat mosquito and other insect larvae that live in the water. Koi carp have even bigger appetites, feeding not just on these larvae, but also on slugs and other undesirable pests. However, koi carp themselves are regarded as an environmental threat and keeping them is prohibited in all states except New South Wales and Western Australia.

particularly fruit trees, ensuring a good harvest. Attract pollinating insects by growing plants that yield a rich nectar source.
- **PERENNIALS** Candytuft, catmint, mallow and yarrow.
- **AROMATIC PLANTS** Lavender, rosemary, and thyme, as well as chamomile, garden myrrh, hyssop, lemon balm, marjoram, sage, and savory. In the vegetable garden, angelica, dill, fennel and sunflower.
- **TREES AND SHRUBS** Plant buddleia, camellia, lilac and wattle, along with shrubs or small trees bearing small fruit, particularly lillypilly. Small gums such as the 'Summer Beauty' and 'Summer Red' are rich in nectar and flower during late summer.

DISCOURAGE MEAT EATERS Don't be tempted to feed meat-eating birds such as butcherbirds, currawongs, kookaburras and magpies. They will drive away or kill little birds like finches and wrens.

Other friendly creatures

EARTHWORMS Earthworms are essential for fertile soil as they bury and digest plant waste such as leaves, stems and dead roots, drain the soil by digging tunnels, and strengthen soil structure. They're usually found in the top 15 cm of the soil, but they can dig down to 1.8 m. During winter, they burrow below the level of soil affected by frost and break up dense layers. Their aeration of the soil supplies some much-needed oxygen and encourages the growth of good bacteria. A million or more earthworms can be found in just one paddock. Avoid cutting up worms with equipment by working in the middle of the day when they are deeper in the soil, and using a fork rather than a spade.

FREE PLANT FOOD Earthworms eat the equivalent of their body weight every day. They produce mounds of material on the soil surface, called worm casts, which are highly nutritious and can be collected to feed your pots, window boxes and tubs.

A HOME FOR LIZARDS The blue-tongue lizards are large members of the skink family. They can often be found in gardens where

Remember to always keep birdbaths topped up with clean, fresh water to prevent the spread of disease among our bird life.

there is a plentiful supply of one of their favourite foods – snails! Encourage blue-tongues to stay in your backyard by providing them with some large, flat rocks to sit on to bask in the sun. They also appreciate places to shelter and hide from predators, like under rock ledges, inside hollow logs and pipes, or amongst low, spiky shrubbery. Cats and dogs can chase or kill these lizards so discourage your animals from hunting lizards. Don't use snail baits if you want to see lizards. The baits, or even the poisoned snails, may poison your blue-tongue lizard.
- Also keep in mind that any garden that is attractive to lizards could also attract snakes.

ENCOURAGING LADYBIRDS Ladybirds are one of the best allies the gardener has against insect pests, including aphids, scale insects and two-spotted mite. Encouraging them will reduce the need for other control measures. Colonies of ladybirds will build up in your garden and soon devour large numbers of aphids, up to 50 per day, each.
- Allow several clumps of nettles to grow in your garden. It may be an unpopular weed, but it harbours an aphid that will not attack your other plants and is an excellent food source for ladybirds. Ladybirds will build up and attack other aphids on your flowers, vegetables and fruits.

ATTRACTING FROGS, TOADS AND OTHER WILDLIFE There is nothing better than a pond for attracting wildlife into your garden. Frogs, toads and dragonflies will flock to water, and will eat insect pests and grubs that can be damaging to your plants.

Currawongs are always on the lookout for food and will find grubs in the lawns.

Spring

Buds are bursting, seeds are ready to be planted, green shoots are everywhere, and gardeners can't wait to pick up their tools. But although spring days are mild, beware of frosts at night.

ERADICATE THOSE BOTHERSOME SLUGS AND SNAILS As the weather warms, it is important to take precautions to protect tender young shoots from slugs and snails. Tried-and-tested solutions include scattering crushed eggshells, bran or sharp grit around the base of vulnerable plants or installing ingenious slug-and-snail traps, such as a jar, saucer or hollowed-out grapefruit of beer sunk into the ground.
● You can also hand-pick slugs and snails during the nighttime, but be prepared to stamp on them: they will return if you don't.

THIN EXCESS OXYGENATING PLANTS
Rake floating plants from the pond, taking care not to puncture the plastic liner with the metal prongs of the rake. Lift out container-ised plants and trim back a few stems before replacing them. This will prevent the plants from becoming invasive.

PREPARE THE SOIL FOR EARLY PLANTINGS In the kitchen garden, spring is the perfect time to replenish your soil. The first job is to clear up perennial weeds, then dig some organic fertiliser, such as rotted manure or compost, into your soil.
● Or, remember to grow a green-manure crop over the winter months and it will be ready to be dug in in spring.

CONTROL MOSS IN YOUR LAWN Moss is most common in wet, shady lawns and in underfed grass. Treat it by covering it with lawn sand in spring and then rake out the dead moss. This is just as effective and much more ecologically friendly than using a chemical moss killer.
● If the problem recurs, aerate the soil to improve drainage and feed regularly for strong growth. In dense shade, replace the lawn with groundcover plants.

DID YOU KNOW?

ANALYSING YOUR SOIL
A balanced, nutritious soil is essential for healthy plant growth. Modern home-testing kits give you a reliable indicator on the health, nutrition and level of acidity, called pH. The ideal level for most plants is 6.5. Once you have the test results you can take the appropriate steps to improve your soil and correct any imbalance. Test your soil every three to four years. If you don't want to do the test yourself, you can send your soil samples to a laboratory for professionals to analyse.

September

TREES AND SHRUBS

Water young trees and shrubs Retain moisture by mulching with well-rotted manure, bark or an attractive layer of gravel or stones.

Feed the garden Scatter complete fertiliser and water well. Add well-rotted manures to mulches.

Protect new shrubs Erect temporary windbreaks.

Protect rhododendrons and azaleas Protect flowers from petal blight by spraying with a registered fungicide when the buds show colour. Repeat fortnightly. Avoid overhead watering.

Care for your hibiscus Prune hibiscus (*Hibiscus rosa-sinensis*) by one-third in early September. Renew the mulches and feed with a complete fertiliser.

Prune shrubs Cut back summer-flowering shrubs and tip-prune fuchsia and geranium.

Trim shrubs Prune off all spent bottlebrush flowers (above) to encourage bushy growth. Give diosma, mint bush and other spring-flowering shrubs a light trim as flowering ends.

LAWNS AND PONDS

Prepare and treat new lawns Sow seeds or lay new turf on a prepared surface. Feed with lawn-starter fertiliser and water regularly to encourage strong and healthy growth.

Aerate established lawns Rake the lawn to remove dead grass and moss. Spike the soil with a garden fork to aerate it.

Mow for the first time Set the lawnmower blades on high. Mow when the grass has reached about 8 cm tall.

Watch for fusarium patches in lawn These are irregularly shaped areas of grass that turn brown in spring due to poor drainage. Treat with an appropriate fungicide, then take action to improve drainage of the lawn.

Remove algae from ponds Use a net or rake to do this.

Top-dress waterlily Use a good soil mixed with fertiliser for top-dressing. Mulch with a layer of grit or small gravel to help keep soil around roots and to discourage fish from dislodging soil and exposing roots.

Cut back marginal plants Remove any faded top growth from these plants.

KITCHEN GARDEN

Prepare beds Prepare soil early for cucumber, pumpkin, squash, tomato and zucchini.

Plant seeds and seedlings In frost-free areas plant seeds or seedlings of most summer vegetables including cucumber, eggplant, pumpkin, tomato and zucchini.

Protect frost-tender plants In cold areas protect vegetables overnight or delay planting until all threat of frost has passed.

Stake tomatoes At planting, insert sturdy wooden stakes to support your tomatoes. Always use new stakes to stop pests or diseases passing from one crop to the next.

Harvest asparagus Cut and harvest asparagus stems when they are 7–10 cm high.

Prune passionfruit Trim some stems on overgrown passionfruit vines to allow more light to penetrate to the centre of the vine and encourage ripening of fruit.

Care for strawberries Water well and keep plants mulched (above) as the first fruit appears.

FLOWERS AND BULBS

Top-dress established beds Sprinkle old beds with a general organic fertiliser.

Sow annuals from seed When the soil warms sow seeds for annuals, such as begonias, pansies and petunias. Remember that frost-tender annuals should be protected.

Plant summer annuals In cold or frosty areas delay the planting of frost-tender annuals, such as petunias, until after the threat of frost has passed.

Water perennials and watch for snails New growth that is very attractive to snails will appear from perennials awakening from winter dormancy.

Feed spring bulbs Spring-flowering bulbs make leafy growth in the spring, feeding next year's flower growth before dying down. Feed now with a complete fertiliser or bulb food. Don't cut down the leaves until they die back naturally.

Plant out bulbs In mild areas, now is the time to plant summer-flowering bulbs.

Deadhead daffodils (above) Repeat for other early-flowering bulbs and winter-flowering plants.

October

TREES AND SHRUBS

Plant evergreen trees and shrubs Establish these before the heat of summer. Mulch well.

Top-dress container-grown trees or shrubs Replace the top 5 cm of potting mix. Add water-retaining granules and slow-release fertiliser. Finish off with a decorative mulch.

Select trees for summer shade Plant named varieties that have known height and spread to avoid future problems.

Prune prunus Flowering prunus, such as ornamental flowering peach, should be pruned after flowering to remove inedible fruit. Cut back *Prunus glandulosa* to ground level.

Fertilise established fruit trees Give these a boost with a fruiting fertiliser. Water well.

Lightly prune shrubs that have finished flowering (above) These include early-flowering clematis and Japanese quince. Hard-prune forsythia.

Trim lavender Lightly trim winter- and spring-flowering lavender as blooms end.

Water and mulch new roses

Feed established roses Use a rose fertiliser and mulch with well-rotted manure. Continue to feed and deep-water.

Check roses for aphids At the first sign of these pests, pick them off and squash with your fingers or spray with an insecticide that won't kill beneficial insects.

Tie in new shoots of ramblers and climbing roses Make the plant as horizontal as possible to produce more flowers. These shoots will replace last year's flower stems.

Deadhead azaleas Do this by lightly shearing the shrubs. Remove fallen flowers. Spray new growth for pests such as azalea lacebug and two-spotted mite. Repeat the spray.

Remove seedpods on camellias Lightly prune camellias, especially sasanquas, removing apple-like fruits, which are the seedpods.

Boost your gardenias As these plants prepare to flower their leaves may yellow. Feed the plant with a complete fertiliser, top up mulch with well-rotted manure and deep-water. Yellowing of foliage can be an iron or magnesium deficiency, so feed with iron chelates or Epsom salts (for magnesium deficiency).

LAWNS AND PONDS

Sow new lawns and lay turf Water well.

Roll new lawns lightly This will help to firm the surface. Mow when necessary (usually about 6 weeks after sowing, depending on the weather) with the blades raised high.

Treat established lawns Aerate, scarify and feed lawns.

Control annual weeds Regular mowing will reduce the number of annual weeds in the lawn as it stops flowering and seeding.

Remove perennial weeds Dig out perennial weeds by hand, pulling out the roots. Only use a chemical spot treatment as a last resort.

Re-seed patches suffering from damage Top-dress with loamy soil or handfuls of spent potting mix.

Top up pond Regularly top up ponds (above) to replenish water lost through evaporation.

Keep ponds aerated Install a small fountain to allow ponds to be better aerated and reduce the likelihood of algae.

Prepare new ponds for planting Cover the base and the marginal shelves with a layer of rich, neutral to alkaline soil. Make sure you do not plant up until the soil has settled.

Plant deep-water and marginal aquatics At the end of the month, place floating plants on the surface. Weight underwater oxygenators with stones and gently drop them into the pond.

Divide and replant marginal aquatics Do this at the end of the month. Place gravel on the top of each pot to weigh down the soil (above).

Transplant self-sown seedlings Many deep-water floaters and marginal plants self-seed, so transplant the new plants to avoid overcrowding.

Propagate waterlilies Lift, divide and replant overgrown waterlilies. Cut the rhizomes into pieces, making sure each piece has a growing point.

Reduce water weeds Manually remove floating weeds with a net. They will break down quickly in a compost heap. Wash any new plants to remove unwanted weeds that may be attached to the stem or roots.

KITCHEN GARDEN

Hoe the vegetable patch
Frequent hoeing helps keep the
weeds down. Work in between
rows to avoid digging up seeds
and disturbing seedlings.

Grow beans from seeds Bean
seeds (above) can be planted this
month. These are a great introduction to vegetable growing for
beginners. Sow them beside a
fence or lattice.

Water seedlings Remember to
water the vegetable patch daily.

**Thin vegetable seedlings
sown last month** Plant more
seeds for a succession of
vegetables that will ripen
through summer.

Earth up your potatoes Do
this as they grow to prevent
'greening' of tubers.

Remove flowers from rhubarb
Do this as soon as they appear,
before plants are robbed of energy.

Sow salad leaves Plant seedlings of soft-hearted lettuce,
rocket and leafy herbs, such as
basil. Spring is an ideal time
to plant all herbs.

Plant dwarf tomatoes In small
gardens, plant tomatoes in pots
for a summer harvest.

Propagate thyme (above) Layer
creeping stems and then sever
the new plants when the roots
have fully developed.

Mulch strawberries Keep straw
mulch around plants and under
the strawberry fruit to keep the
plants moist and the fruit free
of fungal rot.

**Check newly planted fruit
trees** Make sure ties are secure
and firm the ground if any trees
or bushes have been lifted by
spring winds.

Prune stone-fruit trees
Pruning is especially important
for morello cherry trees. Cut out
crossing branches. On fan-trained
trees, remove branches growing
towards or away from the wall.

Mist open peach flowers Spray
the flowers with water. This helps
the fruit to set.

**Protect open flowers on fruit
trees and bushes** If a heavy
frost is forecast, place a layer
of horticultural fleece over
susceptible plants.

FLOWERS AND BULBS

Keep down the weeds Hoe
regularly between the more
established plants, avoiding root
damage. Give your garden beds
extra water during dry weather.

Stake perennials Support
perennials, particularly delphiniums and peonies, which are
prone to weakened stems.

Plant perennials Now is the
time to plant out late-flowering
perennials. Make sure they are
kept well watered.

Propagate perennials
Propagate by lifting, dividing and
replanting healthy outer sections
of plants such as helenium, Mich-
aelmas daisy and rudbeckia.

Awaken dormant plants
Increase watering of fuchsias and
pelargoniums (above). Also
liquid-feed every fortnight.

Feed chrysanthemums Sprinkle
a general fertiliser around each
plant, carefully raking it into the
soil. Insert wooden stakes to
secure the plants.

**Prepare for stunning summer
colour** Sow seeds or plant seedlings to take over from your
spring-flowering annuals. Plant
them into the garden and into
movable containers.

Remove spent annuals Spring-
flowering annuals, such as
pansies, will be reaching the end
of their show and they could
develop pest or disease problems.
Pull them up rather than spend
time and money on chemicals.

**Begin to check for lily cater-
pillars** Remove and squash all
adults and any young caterpillars
that you find hiding underneath
the leaves.

Look out for snails After the
first spring showers, it is a good
idea to watch for snails and slugs
on newly planted annuals.

Plant out your tubers In warm
areas, plant out arum lilies,
chrysanthemums, dahlias and
gladiolus (above) at the end
of the month.

Pot up cuttings Rooted dahlia
cuttings and tuberous begonia
can be potted up now.

**Rejuvenate your early-
flowering plants** Remove all
dead and faded flowers from
early-flowering bulbs and from
spring bedding plants. This will
promote continued flowering
and prevent seed formation.

November

TREES AND SHRUBS

Provide heat protection In hot weather, put shadecloth screens on the western side of plants, or cover new plantings with shade-cloth. Also provide additional water to cope with sudden hot spells, including hot winds.

Conserve moisture Spread a thick layer of shredded bark around young trees and shrubs (above). This will also keep weeds at bay.

Enjoy the jacaranda show Take in the display jacarandas make on the tree and on the ground. Sweep paths and paving to make sure they're safe underfoot, but enjoy the purple carpet on lawns until the next mowing is due.

Tidy flowering shrubs Deadhead faded flowers on spring-flowering shrubs, such as bottlebrush, diosma and mint bush (*Prostanthera* spp.). Trim long shoots on deutzia and Mexican orange blossom (*Choisya ternata*) and thin old wood from shrubs such as flower-ing currants, kerria, may (*Spiraea* spp.) and philadelphus.

Boost rose beds Underplant formal rose beds with both bedding plants and annuals for summer colour. Tall bearded iris are good companions for roses.

Prune hedging plants Cut back newly planted hedges. Clip box and murraya hedges into shape. If you have privet in your garden, clip it before or during flowering to discourage berries forming. The unpleasant fragrance of the flowers can cause allergies in susceptible people.

Clip topiary to shape (above) Trim standards and topiaries as soon as the growth begins to appear uneven.

Watch for pests Check azalea and rhododendron foliage for signs of azalea lacebug under the leaves. Silvering will be seen on leaf surfaces with frass and insect activity on the undersides. Dust under leaves with sulphur or treat with a systemic insecticide. Provide a foliar feed of fertiliser to encourage strong new growth.

Care for hydrangeas Deep-water hydrangeas on hot days for healthy bud development. Flowering begins in December.

Feed hibiscus Use a complete plant food for hungry hibiscus.

Look after gardenias Water and fertilise gardenias to combat yellow leaves and to encourage summer flowers.

LAWNS AND PONDS

Care for new lawns Water new lawns in dry weather (above).

Aerate lawns Improve water penetration by aerating with a garden fork or a powered aerator. Fill the holes with coarse sand.

Remove weeds from lawn Prick out perennial weeds using an old kitchen knife.

Mow areas naturalised with early-flowering spring bulbs Mow grass as soon as the bulb leaves die down.

Neaten edges Stop border plants from flopping over the lawn and creating bare patches. Support plants or edge the lawn with stones or bricks.

Use grass clippings Now the hot weather is here, leave clip-pings on the lawn to break down naturally. If you insist on catching them, don't place them on beds or around trees but add them to the compost heap with additional dry matter.

Feed turf Rain leaches nutrients, making turf yellow. Apply a high-nitrogen fertiliser.

Start regular lawnmowing (above) Fine lawns need mowing at least once a week, and coarser grass once a fortnight.

Continue to plant up ponds Plant deep-water aquatics, bog and marginal plants in and around the pond.

Propagate marginal pond plants If you haven't already done so, divide and replant overcrowded plants.

Maintain bog gardens In dry weather, flood the bog garden to keep plants moist.

Grow cannas Cannas make a striking addition to ponds. Look for bold-flowering forms or try to find variegated ones such as 'Tropicanna'.

Continue to top up ponds If the weather has been very hot or windy, top up ponds and other water features as water loss will be high. If water levels drop pumps may run dry.

Consider installing a night light As the nights become balmy, and more time is spent outdoors in the evening, low-voltage lighting in your pond or water feature will turn it into a garden feature night and day.

KITCHEN GARDEN

Plant out seedlings In warm areas, plant out brussels sprouts, cauliflower and other brassicas. In colder areas, however, wait another month.

Tie and pinch tomatoes Tie up tomatoes and pinch out lateral shoots (above) to avoid too much top growth.

Help tomatoes mature early Tomatoes ripen more quickly if you encase them in a brown paper bag.

Sow summer crops Towards the end of the month, sow green beans and runner beans, long-rooted beetroot, sea kale, salsify and sweetcorn.

Prolong the harvest Make further sowings of salad crops.

Keep the crops coming Continue to plant vegetables such as capsicum, cucumber, eggplant, squash, tomato and zucchini.

Plant sweet potato This ground-covering plant will form a crop by autumn if planted now. Buy tubers from nurseries, or your fruit and vegetable shop, and allow to sprout. Cut into chunks and plant in a sunny spot with room to spread.

Defend against caterpillar attack Watch for caterpillars on vegetable crops and remove and squash any that are seen. Regular dusting with rotenone (Derris dust) protects crops or directly spray caterpillars with *Bacillus thuringiensis* (sold as Dipel), a bacterial caterpillar control.

Thin out herb seedlings Plant out or pot up basil seedlings. Take cuttings of pot marjoram, rosemary, sage and thyme. Divide straggly mint and thyme.

Plant sunflowers Get the children in the garden by planting sunflower seeds. Sunflowers can also be planted to shade and shelter summer vegetables.

Spray and feed fruit trees and bushes Make sure that they are well watered in dry periods as the fruit is swelling.

Strengthen newly planted fruit trees Remove the blossom from new trees to direct the plant's energy into producing strong new wood that will subsequently bear fruit.

FLOWERS AND BULBS

Water your newly planted perennials Regularly water to give them a good start.

Add some support Continue to stake tall-growing perennials, such as delphiniums (above) and border carnations, before they flower in summer and are in danger of stem damage.

Sow annuals For summer annuals, finish sowing seeds.

Brighten up shady spots Plant shade-loving summer annuals such as impatiens and torenia.

Transplant half-hardy annual seedlings If all danger of frost has passed, plant out seed-raised half-hardy annuals after hardening off.

Move overwintered plants outdoors In cold areas, plant out fuchsia and pelargonium that have been overwintered and hardened off.

Look out for rust on fuchsia Early detection and removal of affected leaves can reduce the problem. Remove spent flowers and fallen leaves that can catch on foliage encouraging disease problems. If necessary, spray with a registered fungicide.

Prepare for summer bedding Lift spring-flowering narcissus and tulip bulbs from your garden beds if you need extra space for summer bedding. Heel in the narcissus and tulip bulbs until the foliage has withered.

Look after tubers If you haven't already done so, plant out and stake chrysanthemum and dahlia tubers (above).

Choose hippeastrum Look for these interesting and colourful additions to your garden in bloom now at nurseries. The flowers appear before leaves and bloom in gardens or pots.

Make the most of your spring bulbs Give them a new lease of life by removing dead foliage.

Refresh and enliven window boxes Towards the end of the month, empty your window boxes and other containers of their spring bulbs and any other spent plants. Replant the containers with summer bedding.

Plant up hanging baskets Use a water-retaining polymer and add slow-release fertiliser. Protect the baskets in a sheltered spot for about 2 weeks before hanging outside.

Summer

Early summer is a busy time. Weeds grow rapidly, as do most plants. By mid- to late summer, you can enjoy the results of your efforts; just make sure plants don't go short of water.

TRAIN CLIMBERS The long, flexible stems of climbers grow at their fastest during the summer months and often need support. Wrap self-supporting tendrils around wire supports, spiralling the stems upwards. Tie more substantial stems against posts or lattice using garden twine or raffia.

WATCH FOR PESTS AND DISEASES Warm, wet summers encourage pests and diseases to multiply rapidly. Treat aphids, blackspot and powdery mildew before they take hold. Avoid some problems in the first place by choosing disease-resistant plants and starting them out well.

PROPAGATE SOFTWOOD PERENNIAL CUTTINGS New summer growth is perfect propagating material. Look for strong, pliable stems and cut off the top 10 cm or so below a leaf joint. Trim off all but the top two pairs of leaves, then insert into pots of potting mix. Water the cuttings lightly and keep the mix moist by placing a plastic bag over the top of each pot.

WATER THE GARDEN As summer gets hotter and drier, it is essential to water well. Water in the early morning and evening to minimise evaporation. Water precise areas thoroughly rather than giving the whole garden a sprinkling and avoid wetting leaves as the sun may scorch them. Installing water tanks means you will have more water if there is a water shortage or water rationing.

PLAN FOR THE FESTIVE SEASON Start getting your garden in shape for outdoor entertaining. Remove spent annuals and deadhead shrubs that finish flowering. Plant advanced pots of summer-flowering annuals in dull corners to brighten the garden.

DID YOU KNOW?

VISITING BEETLES
The black and brown beetles that bash against windows and flyscreens on warm summer evenings will disappear overnight into cracks and crevices to lay eggs that in turn produce the white curl grubs that feed on plant roots in the soil. You can deter the beetles by turning off outside lights.

December

TREES AND SHRUBS

Remove weed seedlings Take out self-sown seedlings of trees such as camphor laurel, liquidambar and maple.

Prune deutzia Cut out the flowered shoots.

Trim photinia hedges

Remove faded blooms Take off faded flowers and thin out weak shoots. Cut back hard after flowering (avoid old wood).

Take softwood or semiripe cuttings Take cuttings from side shoots from deutzia, fuchsia and philadelphus.

Disbud large-flowered bush roses Remove buds near the main bud at the end of the stem for extra-large blooms (above).

Reduce water loss Mulch moisture-loving plants.

Water hydrangeas well Encourage long-lasting blooms on your hydrangeas by deep-watering. Potted plants and those exposed to heat or wind may need daily watering.

Buy Christmas colour Add seasonal colour to your garden with pots of Christmas bush.

LAWNS AND PONDS

Spike lawns Make small but deep holes to enable rain to penetrate to the roots.

Mow regularly During dry spells, raise the mower blades and leave clippings on the grass. This helps to conserve moisture.

Lay turf This is a good time to lay turf as it will settle down quickly, but water well through-out the growing season.

Use some dry-weather strategies Stop all weedkiller treatments and feeding during dry spells, unless you can water the lawn regularly.

Continue to maintain water levels of ponds Top up with plenty of fresh, clean water.

Reduce floating plants This will allow more light to filter through to deep-water plants.

Flush out and drown aphids Waterlily buds can be attacked by aphids, but there is no need to spray. Instead, use a mesh net to immerse the afflicted plant in the water for several days and drown the pests (above).

KITCHEN GARDEN

Lift potatoes Lift varieties that are ready for harvest.

Harvest your early tomatoes Early-maturing varieties planted in spring will be ready to harvest by the middle of December. Make new plantings to extend crop-ping until autumn.

Start planting out Plant out sweetcorn in cool zones. Continue to sow old-fashioned favourites, such as beetroot, chicory and silverbeet. In the herb garden continue to sow or plant seedlings of basil, chervil and dill.

Pick herbs regularly Harvest all herbs including annual herbs, such as chervil. Regular picking keeps them bushy (above).

Tie in long, vigorous shoots of cane fruits The shoots are soft, so be careful not to damage or snap them.

Protect bush and cane fruits from birds Use fine netting or a wire cage.

Watch out for fruit fly With all the summer fruit around now, put fruit fly traps near fruiting trees to see if it's time to start spraying for this pest or to har-vest fruit for indoor ripening.

FLOWERS AND BULBS

Pinch out growing tips of perennials Late summer- and autumn-flowering perennials, such as chrysanthemum and dahlia (including the giant tree dahlia), can be tip-pruned now to encourage bushy growth later.

Propagate pinks Take side shoot cuttings.

Turn hanging baskets Do this regularly so plants grow and develop evenly on all sides. On sudden hot days, take down hanging baskets in the morning, water thoroughly and place in a cool, sheltered spot to prevent baskets drying out during the day. Rehang in the evening, or when the hot spell has passed.

Promote bushy annuals Pinch out the growing tips of annuals to induce side-branching and a fuller shape (above).

Maintain thriving containers Fill in any gaps in your garden with annuals bought from the nursery in advanced punnets.

Cut flowers early Pick flowers from your garden for use indoors early in the day, and place the stems in water to avoid wilting.

January

TREES AND SHRUBS

Remove suckers from grafted plants Pay particular attention to citrus, robinia and rosebushes.

Prune shrubs Cut back long stems of choisya, jasmine and philadelphus after flowering. This will help maintain a good shape and stop spreading. Tip-prune New South Wales Christmas bush as colours fade in bracts.

Propagate shrubs Root semiripe cuttings of *Buddleia alternifolia*, callicarpa, deutzia, euonymus and viburnum in a pot. Also take heel cuttings from choisya, hibiscus and *Jasminum officinale*.

Feed roses Use an organic rose fertiliser. Spray against aphids, blackspot, mildew and rust at the same time if necessary.

Deadhead faded roses Remove the flowers on modern bush roses and climbers as they fade. Cut back to a leaf bud. Deadhead hybrid tea and floribunda roses to encourage a second flush of flowers (above). In late January, summer-prune repeat-flowering roses for a new flush of flowers.

Plant ferns Find shady spots to grow these plants.

LAWNS AND PONDS

Aerate compacted lawns Aerate and water thoroughly during prolonged dry weather.

Maintain regular mowing Continue to mow the lawn at least once a week, except during periods of drought.

Neaten edges After mowing, use long-handled edging shears to trim the grass overhanging the edge of the lawn.

Watch out for fungal diseases These diseases are most prevalent during hot, humid weather and must be treated immediately.

Limit damage to scorched lawns Avoid walking on grass that has been scorched. You may damage the healthy shoots that remain and create bare patches.

Remove excess leaf growth from waterlilies (above)

Weed the bog garden Water regularly and make sure that the soil does not dry out.

KITCHEN GARDEN

Harvest crops Harvest gherkins for pickling while small. Bottle or dehydrate tomatoes, summer fruits and other excess crops.

Plant late-summer crops Sow beetroot, broccoli, chicory, endive, radish, silverbeet and summer salad crops.

Shade new plantings Use temporary shade over new plantings of lettuce until root systems are well established.

Lift shallots Spread out in a shed to dry before storing. Lift onions at the end of the month and leave on the ground to dry.

Limit damage In windy gardens, earth up or stake broccoli and brussels sprouts.

Protect tomatoes In hot areas, leave bushy growth to prevent sun scald on fruit. Increase watering if plants are wilting.

Thin apples and pears Remove all but one of the fruitlets in a cluster – the one in the centre for apples (above) and the one on the edge of a cluster for pears.

FLOWERS AND BULBS

Keep your borders looking neat and tidy Cut back early-flowering perennials and tie in plants that have tall flower spikes. Daylilies (above) will produce a succession of blooms over many days.

Cut back perennials for a second flush Prune achillea, delphinium, gaura, lupin, *Salvia* 'Superba' and species geranium (*Geranium* spp.) all the way to the ground.

Deadhead your agapanthus Remove the spent flowers to prevent seeds forming.

Plant autumn-flowering bulbs Plant *Amaryllis belladonna*, autumn crocus, nerine and sternbergia for a prolonged border-colour show.

Disbud dahlias Pinch out the side buds growing below the terminal bud on each young dahlia plant. The remaining bud will develop into a larger bloom.

February

TREES AND SHRUBS

Trim hedges (above) Give your hedges a late-summer prune to keep them dense. Deep-water them once or twice a week.

Prune shrubs after flowering Shorten the stems and thin out old wood on shrubs, including ceanothus, escallonia and New South Wales Christmas bush (if not done last month).

Prune wisteria Prune your wisteria by cutting off all the secondary shoots above the third bud.

Take semiripe cuttings Propagate deciduous and evergreen shrubs. Root the cuttings in pots in a sheltered spot.

Keep a watch out for mildew In periods of prolonged dry weather, watch for mildew on hydrangeas and roses.

Summer-prune roses for an autumn flush After pruning all flowered stems and removing dead or crossing growth, apply rose fertiliser or some well-rotted manure and water thoroughly to encourage a new flush of growth. Keep a watch for aphids on new growth and treat as soon as you notice them.

LAWNS AND PONDS

Prepare the ground for turfing and sowing Fork over the soil, tread it down well, and then rake in a low-nitrogen lawn fertiliser (above). One week after feeding, sow lawn seeds, ensuring that they are sown evenly and that they are protected from birds by netting.

Continue to mow established lawns regularly Water well and fertilise to encourage strong summer growth.

Cover bare spots Use the runners from the edge of the lawn to cover any bare spots. Before turfing, fork over and water in a soil-wetting agent.

Replenish the pond Maintain the water surface at a specified level to avoid causing stress to both pondlife, such as fish, tadpoles and frogs, and plants.

Clean and top up birdbaths They should be cleaned and topped up on a daily basis.

KITCHEN GARDEN

Take cuttings of herbs Place root cuttings of herbs, such as bay, lavender, mint, rosemary, rue and sage, in a sheltered spot in the garden. Lift, divide and replant chives.

Avoid bolting crops Sow fast-growing leafy crops, such as coriander and rocket, in shade to avoid rapid growth, flowering and early seeding.

Harvest ripe crops Pick sweetcorn and tomatoes (above). Harvest self-blanching celery. Pick early apples and plums.

Protect ripening grapes Cover your vines with netting to protect them from birds and other pests.

Prune stone fruit trees Cut out dead, diseased, broken and crossing branches when the harvest has finished.

Water tropical fruits Keep mangoes and other tropical fruits well watered especially in areas where fruit is still ripening.

FLOWERS AND BULBS

Watch ginger lily (*Hedychium gardnerianum*) Look closely for stem borers and, if you find them, remove all affected stalks. Cut spent stems after flowering.

Maintain your border plants Tie in and feed chrysanthemums and dahlias. Make sure you keep your late-flowering perennials well watered and weed free. Deadhead faded flowers (above).

Prune untidy plants Pinch back trailing plants, such as ivy-leaved pelargoniums, that are beginning to become straggly.

Plant bulbs Plant jonquils and narcissus in February ready for early-winter colour.

Divide iris Lift, divide and replant clumps of iris that have overcrowded rhizomes.

Avoid fungal diseases Late-summer humidity causes fungal diseases in leaves and roots. Try to avoid this by clearing weeds and vigorous growth from around lavender, rosemary and other plants to ensure better air flow. Water at the base of the plants to keep leaves dry. Use a fungicide to control root diseases.

Autumn

As temperatures drop and humidity decreases, you and your garden will get a new lease of life. It's a great time to plant and to enjoy flowers, ripe crops and autumn foliage.

COLLECT AND STORE SEEDS Choose a sunny day to collect seeds, and make sure they are dry before putting them in storage. Place the seeds in envelopes or in brown paper bags (do not use plastic bags). Label each item and store it in a cool, dry, dark place. Seeds tend to lose their reliability to germinate after 1 year.

PREPARE THE POND FOR WINTER WEATHER As leaves fall from the trees, they will clog up ponds. They sink to the bottom and decompose, which causes harmful by-products. Gather up all fallen leaves regularly and remove any that have dropped into the pond using a rake. To prevent leaves from falling in, place a fine-mesh netting across the top of the pond and secure it at the edges with bricks. Remove the netting every fortnight, collect the fallen leaves and replace the netting securely.

MOVE, DIVIDE AND TRANSPLANT PERENNIALS Early autumn, while the soil is still warm, is a good time to move perennials as the plants prepare for the dormant season. Water the roots well before planting, soaking them in a bucket for about an hour. Prepare the planting hole by forking over hard soil to create a crumbly texture that the roots can easily penetrate. Add plenty of organic matter to get the plant off to a good start. Give shrubs an initial prune after planting and stake if necessary.

HARVEST CROPS WHEN RIPE Most vegetables are ready for picking from early autumn onwards. Harvest onions on a dry day. Once pulled, lay them on the ground, or hang them in a shed, for 10–14 days with intact leaves. Onions will rot if not dried before storing. Dry garlic the same way but don't harvest until the leaves have faded.

DID YOU KNOW?

GROW TRADITIONAL FRUIT TREES
Many old fruit tree varieties are too large to grow in today's small gardens. However, when these are grafted onto dwarf root stocks, gardeners can enjoy their wonderful flavour without the spreading boughs. Citrus, dwarf peaches and nectarines are all now available to fit even the smallest gardens.

March

TREES AND SHRUBS

Prepare the soil Autumn is the best time to plant evergreen and deciduous trees, shrubs and hedging. Dig in well-rotted manure or compost and a handful of blood and bone.

Lightly trim hedges Give established hedges a final cut.

Propagate shrubs Take hardwood cuttings of deciduous and evergreen shrubs. Root the cuttings in pots.

Divide suckering shrubs Thin the top growth of suckering shrubs, such as philadelphus.

Check supports and ties Early autumn winds can cause damage to young plants, so make sure ties and supports are secure.

Fertilise roses To help new wood harden and protect late developing shoots, top-dress with a handful of sulphate of potash.

Prune rambling roses and climbers Cut back flowered shoots to ground level. Prune flowered shoots of weeping standards back to main stem.

Water azaleas Keep spot-flowering azaleas watered but watch for petal blight. Spray with fungicide if flowers are affected.

LAWNS AND PONDS

Scarify established lawns Remove dead grass from lawns by raking vigorously with a spring rake (above).

Improve drainage Fork deeply over the lawn with a hollow-tined fork. Fill the holes by brushing in sharp sand or use some old potting mix.

Lay turf Water new turf in thoroughly and then make sure that it does not dry out.

Re-seed worn and damaged lawn Add sandy loam to level the damaged part with the rest of the lawn. Sow grass seeds over the damaged section and water well.

Continue to mow the lawn Raise the blades on the mower for a lighter cut.

Clear and tidy the bog garden Remove decaying foliage from bog plants that die back naturally after frost.

Feed fish sparingly Use a high-protein fish food.

Remove ferny azolla Scoop out this floating weed and other pond weeds.

KITCHEN GARDEN

Sow seeds for early crops Start sowing broad bean, cabbage and carrot seeds.

Pick tomatoes Pick any remaining tomatoes and bring the unripe fruit indoors and place with a banana to ripen fully.

Grow year-round lettuce Lettuce can be sown all year round so keep planting it to keep this handy crop available in the vegetable patch all year.

Harvest apples for storing Pick apples (above) and pears before they are fully ripe.

Pick autumn raspberries

Order bare-root plants Study nursery catalogues and advertisements in gardening magazines for information on mail-order fruit trees, shrubs and berries for winter planting. Place orders with mail-order specialists or ask your local garden centre to order plants for winter.

Plant autumn herbs Herbs that bolt in hot weather, such as coriander and rocket, will grow more slowly if planted in autumn.

FLOWERS AND BULBS

Tidy borders Clear beds of summer annuals and cut back fading perennials.

Plant hardy bedding plants Include forget-me-not, pansy, polyanthus and wallflower.

Sow winter annuals Sow drifts of candytuft, cornflower, larkspur, love-in-a-mist and poppy in blank spaces left in borders.

Remember St Patrick's Day This is the traditional planting date for sweet pea (above). Sow in pots, baskets or garden beds and add lime. In warm areas, delay for a month.

Propagate as you prune Take cuttings of daisies, fuchsias, lavender and pelargoniums.

Plant dutch iris Choose a sunny, well-drained position with alkaline soil.

Put bulbs in the crisper Put spring-flowering daffodil, hyacinth and tulip bulbs in the crisper of your fridge for 6–8 weeks before planting in late autumn.

April

TREES AND SHRUBS

Plant container-grown trees and shrubs Stake and tie in trees to prevent movement in autumn winds.

Prune deciduous trees and shrubs Cut out crossing and badly placed branches.

Top-dress azaleas and rhododendrons (above) Add a thick layer of leaf mould or lime-free mulch at the base of plants.

Transplant evergreens Prevent roots from drying out by soaking them in water before replanting.

Plant new hedges Enrich the planting holes with organic matter. Space 30–60 cm apart and mulch after planting.

Propagate shrubs Continue to take hardwood cuttings from your shrubs.

Prune berry shrubs Prune the berries from cotoneaster, hawthorn, holly and pyracantha that can become weeds if you live near bushland.

Continue to deadhead roses Don't prune them until winter.

Water tibouchina Keep them well watered especially during dry times.

LAWNS AND PONDS

Lay turf This is the ideal month for laying turf for a new lawn (above). Keep well watered.

Rake up fallen leaves and stack them for leaf mould This is particularly important on newly sown lawns as fallen leaves can raise the humidity around young grass shoots. High humidity can lead to fungal infections which can kill the grass.

Scatter wormcasts These are ideal sites for weeds to germinate. Brush them into the soil with a stout broom.

Mow with raised blades This is especially important if you want to naturalise bulbs in lawn.

Keep ponds clear of leaves Scoop out any fallen leaves and secure netting over the pond to catch further leaf fall. Thin out underwater oxygenating plants. Cut off any dead waterlily leaves.

Lift, divide and replant bog-garden plants

Continue to feed fish sparingly

KITCHEN GARDEN

Prepare the soil for winter Dig vacant ground and incorporate well-rotted manure or garden compost.

Harvest the end of the crop Lift and store beetroot and winter radishes. Lift potatoes. Pick the last tomatoes and cut down the plants.

Plant out cabbage seedlings (above) Make sure that they have sufficient moisture until they are well established.

Cut down bean and pea stalks Make sure you leave the roots in the ground.

Plant spinach Plant English spinach for winter greens.

Plant perennial vegetables Plant crowns of asparagus and artichoke suckers for long-producing crops. In cold climates delay asparagus planting until late winter.

Plant strawberry runners

FLOWERS AND BULBS

Cut down and lift dahlias After drying off the tubers, store in a frost-free place. In mild areas tubers can be left in the ground.

Plant up borders for next year Plant hardy perennials and biennials. Plant daffodil, hyacinth tulip and crocus bulbs (above).

Propagate perennial plants Lift, divide and replant overgrown clumps.

Add some potted colour Plant schizanthus in pots and baskets for winter blooms.

Trim aster These flower for many months. Trim them as flowers finish.

Plant groundcovers Plant seeds of Virginian stock at the same time as you plant bulbs, for a groundcover around spring-flowering bulbs until they begin to grow.

May

TREES AND SHRUBS

Cover the bases of tropical trees with straw or sacking Also protect graft unions of citrus trees in frosty areas.

Buy colourful autumn trees Select deciduous trees for planting while still showing autumn foliage colour (above).

Protect tender trees and shrubs Erect windbreaks using sacking or plastic. Don't prune frost-sensitive plants until spring.

Plant bare-root deciduous trees and shrubs Continue to plant container-grown specimens.

Protect frost-tender shrubs Place fleece or another light cover over frost-sensitive shrubs in the late afternoon if frost is forecast. Remove mid-morning as temperatures warm.

Water camellias Lack of water causes blooms to brown and fall.

Look for flowering natives Native plants in bloom provide nectar for birds.

Prevent wind damage Trim back bushy top growth of clematis in tubs. Prune in spring.

LAWNS AND PONDS

Prepare the ground for sowing a new lawn in spring Dig over the soil and leave it until spring.

Continue autumn lawn care Aerate, improve drainage and rake leaves from both new and established lawns. Finish laying turf as soon as possible.

Continue to mow the lawn How often you mow depends on how warm the weather is and how much the grass is growing. Mow soft-leaved buffalo to remove purple tips.

Continue to rake fallen leaves Add fallen leaves to compost heaps or straight to garden beds.

Oversow warm-season lawns Use perennial rye or other cool-season grass seeds for green winter lawns.

Maintain pond hygiene Continue to remove fallen leaves from the pond and thin out oxygenators to freshen up the pond.

Continue feeding fish until the end of the month (above)

KITCHEN GARDEN

Plant snow peas and sugar-snap peas

Protect tender crops In cold areas cover overwintering root crops with straw to protect them against frost.

Detach suckers from globe artichokes Pot up and overwinter in a cold frame.

Plant bay trees Evergreen bays (above) will grow in the ground or pots, and provide leaves for the kitchen.

Prepare holes for new fruit trees Plant bare-root fruit trees during mild, dry weather. Insert support stakes before planting. Mulch the ground.

Remove mummified fruit Also spray for brown rot.

Keep planting strawberries Plant in a sunny spot.

Prune soft fruit Shorten the leading shoots by half and cut side shoots.

Inspect fruit cages Check for tears in fruit-cage netting so that it is secure against birds.

FLOWERS AND BULBS

Tidy up for the winter months Finish digging new borders and leave the soil rough. Continue to tidy flowerbeds and borders by deadheading and cutting back unsightly top growth to ground level. Remove, clean and store stakes and canes.

Condition soil Mulch with green waste or leaf mould to improve soil condition without encouraging plants to grow.

Water winter annuals Annuals such as pansy, poppy and primula need watering in winter. Also watch for aphids.

Increase colour Place potted annuals in your garden. Buy advanced seedlings or plant them from punnets.

Protect your indoor plants Protect from draughts and central heating. Mist regularly to increase humidity around plants.

Prepare tubers for storing Check chrysanthemum stools and dahlia tubers. Discard any that are rotting. Clean gladiolus corms, discarding old corms and separating bulbils for storing and growing the following spring.

Winter

There are always jobs to be done in the garden, but winter is a good time for planning and leafing through catalogues and gardening books. Prepare now and your garden will never lack interest.

PLANT BARE-ROOT ROSES Soak roots in water for 1 hour. Cut out damaged growth and remove crossing stems. Dig a hole wide enough to hold the roots and deep enough for the graft union to be 2 cm above ground level. Add compost and a handful of blood and bone. Set the plant in the hole and spread out the roots. Refill the hole and firm the soil to remove air pockets. Finish by early winter, or before the ground gets too cold.

PLAN FOR NEXT YEAR Order seed catalogues so that, when the weather is not suitable for going out into the garden, you can make up a list of crops to purchase for sowing in the new year.

SHOP FOR COLOUR Don't settle for a drab winter. Choose from a range of camellias, subtropical plants and Australian native shrubs, such as banksias and wattles.

SOW SEEDS IN THE WARM SPOT Start sowing seeds in midwinter, but only if you can provide sufficient warmth for the seeds to germinate, and a well-lit position to put the seedlings in after germination. If you are not lucky enough to have a warmed greenhouse, don't be put off – simply select a sunny windowsill or a sun-warmed patio.

READ THE WEATHER Don't be lulled into a false sense of complacency by sunny winter days. Sunny days often spell cold nights and the likelihood of frost. Learn to read the weather and listen for frost warnings. Protect vulnerable plants by covering them at night.

CLEAR SNOW IN COLD AREAS If you live in a cold area, don't let snow weigh down your conifer branches. Brush it off immediately. Or, tie the branches together with twine to preserve the plant's shape.

DID YOU KNOW?

TRADITIONAL TIMINGS
Some people still plant and harvest their crops according to a traditional timetable. Seasonal dates were often handed down through families or passed from professional gardeners to their apprentices. Some traditional planting dates downunder are sweet peas on St Patrick's Day (17 March) and dahlias on Melbourne Cup Day (the first Tuesday in November).

June

TREES AND SHRUBS

Limit frost damage Protect graft unions on citrus trees by wrapping them with cardboard or weed mat.

Reduce shade Prune deciduous trees if long branches overhang herbaceous borders.

Prune established trees and shrubs In frost-free weather, prune dead, damaged and diseased branches (above).

Prune deciduous climbers and hedges Hard-prune old shrubs while dormant. Mulch afterwards.

Plant bare-root roses Use a mixture of compost and blood and bone. Prune twiggy side shoots and cut back damaged roots to healthy tissue. Add a layer of organic mulch.

Stop reversion Cut out green or yellow reverted shoots on variegated evergreen shrubs.

Propagate shrubs Take root cuttings of aralia, clerodendrum and *Rhus typhina*.

Water winter bloomers Camellias and magnolias need continued winter watering.

Prune poinsettia Cut these to the ground level after flowering.

LAWNS AND PONDS

Continue to mow occasionally Set the lawnmower blades at high, and mow only if growth demands it.

Protect the grass Constant walking over a lawn during the winter when soil is wet causes compaction and impedes drainage. Avoid walking across the lawn by the same route every day. Alternatively, build sunken stepping stones (above) or a path.

Clean and overhaul machinery Clean and oil all movable parts before storing under a water-proof cover or in a shed. Empty the fuel tanks of petrol-driven lawnmowers.

Treat bindii and clover Treat these weeds when plants are just beginning to appear among the grass. Use a registered herbicide but keep it away from trees.

Maintain swimming pools Keep pools free of algae over winter by running filtration systems regularly. Pools, even if covered, should be regularly checked and have leaves or debris removed.

KITCHEN GARDEN

Harvest winter vegetables These include brussels sprouts, winter cabbage, cauliflower, leek and parsnip.

Plant vegetables now Continue planting broad beans, peas and spinach. In frost-free tropical and subtropical areas the dry season is good for planting most vegetables.

Protect cauliflower Shade curds (the white heads) from direct sun, which causes dis-colouration. Tie the leaves to form shade. Pick the cauliflower when the heads are tight.

Protect Mediterranean herbs Protect marjoram and rosemary with mulch.

Clear annual herbs from beds and pots

Harvest rhubarb Grasp the outer leaf stalks and twist as you pull (above). Now is also the time to plant crowns where they can grow undisturbed.

Prune new apple and pear trees Reduce leading shoots by up to two-thirds.

Plant kiwifruit For fruit, buy at least one male for every one to eight female vines.

FLOWERS AND BULBS

Keep up winter maintenance Finish tidying beds and borders. Check stored tubers.

Create bushy seedlings Pinch out tips of sweet pea seedlings when three pairs of leaves develop to encourage side shoots. If flowering, pick blooms regularly to encourage more flowers.

Plant up early colour Cram window boxes and containers with winter-flowering pansies and ornamental cabbage (kale).

Pick pansies and violets Cut regularly to encourage flowering.

Provide winter protection Plants that are growing in pots or hanging baskets are more susceptible to cold damage than those same plants in the ground. Move frost-sensitive potted plants such as Marguerite daisy into shelter in cold climates.

Reveal hellebore (above) These flower from now into spring. Remove yellow leaves to reveal the flowers.

Keep cyclamen cool They will flower longer if kept cool at night so don't keep them in heated rooms. Water regularly and remove spent flowers by twisting them from the corm.

July

TREES AND SHRUBS

Continue to prune established trees and shrubs Remove any dead wood or diseased branches. Remove seedpods from wisteria.

Check for wind damage Firm trees and shrubs that have been loosened by the wind and stake if necessary (above).

Remove invasive climbers Check deciduous trees for invasive climbers, such as ivy and wisteria, and remove with care. Seek professional advice if considering pruning large or mature trees.

Protect plants from possum damage Magnolia buds may be eaten by possums. Protect new shoots on roses after pruning by watering with deterrent products such as D-ter.

Take chrysanthemum cuttings Midwinter is the best time to take hardwood cuttings, as they root easily.

Prune roses Cut them back hard to encourage new growth. Spray with lime sulphur after pruning to combat pest and disease problems. In frosty areas, delay pruning until next month.

LAWNS AND PONDS

Clean garden tools Disinfect all your pots and hand tools so they are ready for spring planting. Sharpen your spades, secateurs and all other cutting implements. Make sure all tools are cleaned, oiled and in good repair (above).

Prepare for the spring garden Order top-dressings and seed mixtures for spring sowing.

Improve lawn aeration and drainage Note where the water remains on the surface of the lawn after a heavy rainfall. Continue to spike the lawn if the weather permits.

Treat your lawn for weeds Treat bindii if it was neglected last month. Clover is often obvious in lawns in winter. It will add nitrogen to soil and provide welcome winter colour so don't feel you have to remove it. Clover will die down in warmer weather and as lawn grasses begin growing in spring. Green tufts of grass in lawns are probably winter grass. Avoid using herbicides, since it will die back naturally in spring. Its seeds also provide food for birds.

Clear fallen leaves from your ponds and water courses

KITCHEN GARDEN

Harvest your winter crops Pick beans, broccoli, brussels sprouts, winter cabbage, Jerusalem artichokes, leeks and silverbeet (above).

Check vegetables and fruit in storage Discard any that show signs of rot.

Prune fruit trees Prune established trees except stone fruits, such as cherries and plums. Newly planted fruit trees should be lightly pruned to give them shape, reducing all leading shoots by one-half.

Prune soft fruit Cut back new cane fruits, such as raspberries, to within 25 cm of the ground.

Spray deciduous fruit trees Spray nectarines and peaches with copper oxychloride before bud burst to eliminate later pest and disease problems.

Spray citrus trees These may be infested with the nymphal stages of the bronze orange bug. Spray the trees thoroughly with a spray oil to reduce their numbers.

FLOWERS AND BULBS

Weed borders In mild weather, fork over the soil between established perennials to remove weeds. Use a hand fork around smaller plants.

Plant perennials Late winter is the time to plant perennial phlox and, in colder climates, Russell lupins.

Look for pests on plants Check flowers and bulbs regularly for signs of pests, such as snails, around the bulb and around the perennial shoots.

Deadhead winter-flowering pansies This will ensure they will continue to flower freely.

Add some colour to the garden Look for pots of polyanthus or primula in flower.

Plant out forced bulbs Transplant hyacinth (above) into your garden when they have finished flowering indoors.

August

TREES AND SHRUBS

Prepare sites for spring planting of evergreens

Prune crab-apple trees to shape Remove any inward-growing shoots and badly shaped branches.

Thin out weak shoots from climbing shrubs Hard-prune shrubs if they are neglected and misshapen.

Start hedge trimming Give deciduous hedges their first trim by the end of the month, if the weather is frost-free.

Cut back established hamamelis after flowering (above) Remove all straggly branches to reshape the shrub and encourage next year's flowers.

Transplant shrubs This is a good time to transplant shrubs growing in the wrong place.

Remove invasive grass Remove grass, such as kikuyu, from deciduous shrubs while they are still bare.

LAWNS AND PONDS

Aerate an established lawn Go over the lawn with a spiked roller or shoes (above). If moss is a real problem, reduce shade cast on the lawn, improve drainage and reduce compaction rather than applying moss killer.

Avoid wet-lawn mowing Do not mow if the grass is wet.

Feed birds on the lawn If you do not have cats, feeding birds on the lawn will encourage them to eat lawn pests. Watch how much food you scatter, as too much could attract pests.

Feed lawns In warm climates apply lawn food after rain or thorough watering. Wait until spring in cooler climates.

Propagate bog plants Sow seeds of bog primula in boxes of seed-raising mix. Leave the boxes outside to expose the seeds to frost, but protect them from heavy rain.

Clean out ponds prior to spring growth

KITCHEN GARDEN

Keep harvesting winter vegetables Cut savoy cabbage and other brassicas.

Plant potato tubers Tubers are planted now in all areas.

Plant vegetables Sow the seeds or plant the seedlings of parsnip, spring onion and the first of the sweetcorn. Plant out tomato in frost-free areas.

Feed citrus trees (above) Feed trees ahead of their spring growth spurt with a complete citrus food. Remove weeds from around the tree base and renew the mulch.

Plant strawberries Strawberries can be grown in garden beds or in pots and they make a great treat for children.

Provide wet-weather access If the soil is wet and access to the vegetable patch is difficult, it is a good idea to lay down planks or bring in a load of gravel to form convenient footpaths.

FLOWERS AND BULBS

Prepare the soil for sowing Complete digging and manuring your sites for sowing annuals and biennials.

Plant petunias These pretty annuals, and other summer annuals, can be planted in warm, frost-free gardens. Delay until next month in cool areas.

Divide herbaceous perennials Lift and divide perennials (above) before new growth appears. Late winter is also a good time to divide those perennials that stay green all year such as agapanthus and mondo grass.

Check clivia for pests Watch for snails and caterpillars around clivia flowers.

Check tuber stores Discard chrysanthemum stools and dahlia tubers that are rotten.

Transplant bulbs Plant bulbs that have been flowering indoors or in pots in a sheltered spot in your garden as they finish flowering. Liquid feed.

Feed spring bulbs Feed these bulbs with a complete fertiliser to encourage good flowering the following year. Don't remove foliage until it dies down.

Glossary of gardening terms

ACID SOIL Soil with a pH below 7. Suitable for most plants, but particularly good for growing rhododendrons and many Australian native plants.

ADVENTITIOUS ROOTS Roots that grow from the aerial stems of plants, not from other roots.

AERATION Loosening the soil to allow air and water to penetrate. Spike a compacted lawn with a garden or hollow-tined fork to a depth of about 8 cm. A large area of compacted soil can be aerated using a spade or rotary hoe.

AERIAL ROOTS Roots that grow above the ground straight from the plant's stem. They absorb moisture from the air and help to support climbers, such as ivy, against walls and fences.

ALKALINE SOIL Soil with a pH level above 7. Most plants and vegetables grow well in slightly alkaline soils.

ALPINE Small plants that grow in mountainous areas between the tree line and the snow line.

ANNUAL A plant that has its entire life cycle within one growing season. It germinates, grows, flowers, sets seed and then dies.

AQUATIC A plant that grows in water, either totally submerged or with just its roots underwater and its flowers and leaves on the water's surface.

AXILLARY A bud that grows in between the stalk and stem or branch, rather than at the tip.

BIENNIAL A plant that lives for 2 years. It germinates and forms leaves in the first year, and then produces a flower stem, flowers, sets seed and dies in the second.

BLANCHING A technique for excluding sunlight from vegetables in order to maximise tenderness and flavour. Earth up the vegetables, wrap them in thick paper or cover them with upturned terracotta flowerpots. The stems of celery and leeks, and leaves of chicory, are all commonly blanched (see **Earthing up**).

BOG GARDEN An area in the garden where the soil is waterlogged, either naturally or artificially. Plants that prefer their roots to be around water or in moist soil, such as primula or lysichiton, grow best in this position.

BOLTING When vegetables prematurely run to flower or seed. Bolting can often be caused by poor soil quality or lack of water. Lettuce, spinach and coriander are all prone to bolting.

BRACT A modified leaf at the base of a flower or flower cluster. Bracts can be brightly coloured, large or small and scalelike.

BUD A condensed shoot that is protected by overlapping scales. Leaves or flowers develop from inside the bud.

BULB A modified stem, which acts as a storage organ. Usually found underground and produces roots, shoots and flowers every year. It is made up of fleshy scales wrapped around each other.

BULB FIBRE The perfect potting mix for growing indoor or outdoor potted bulbs. Bulb fibre contains peat or a peat substitute, crushed shell and charcoal, which keeps the mix 'sweet' and helps to prevent the bulbs from rotting.

BULBIL A small immature bulb that forms at the base of a mature bulb. The bulbil can be removed and potted up to form a new plant. In some lilies, the bulbils form on the stems above ground.

CALYX The name given to the outer protective covering of a flower. It is made up of a number of green sepals, fused together to form a bowl, funnel or tubelike structure (see **Sepal**).

CANE A tough, thin woody stem with a hollow centre, such as that of bamboo or raspberry.

CATCH CROP A fast-growing crop planted between slower-maturing crops. Alternatively, a catch crop can be grown in the interval between harvesting one crop and planting another.

CHALK A soft limestone. When ground into powder form, chalk is used to neutralise acid soil.

CHLOROPHYLL The green pigment responsible for light absorption and photosynthesis in plants.

CHLOROSIS A condition that arises when a plant cannot produce sufficient amounts of chlorophyll, resulting in the leaves losing their green colour and, in some cases, turning brown and dying.

CLAMP A device made up of thick layers of straw and soil for storing harvested root vegetables. Pile up the crop, such as carrots or potatoes, on the soil, then cover with a 30 cm-deep layer of straw followed by a 25 cm-thick layer of soil. Firm and smooth the soil so that rain will run off, then make a hole in the top and fill it with straw to provide ventilation.

CLAY SOIL A heavy soil that is predominantly made up of tiny mineral particles, forming a sticky mass when wet, and hard, compacted sods when dry. To improve clay soil, dig in plenty of organic matter.

CLOCHE A shelter, traditionally made from glass or tough clear plastic, that protects early crops outdoors or warms up the soil prior to planting.

CLONE A plant raised from a single parent plant by means of vegetative propagation (cuttings, division, layers or grafting) and not sexual propagation (seeds). A clone is identical to the parent plant and other plants raised from the same plant in this way.

COIR Processed coconut fibre that is used in seed and potting mixes to completely or partially replace peat. By using coir mix, gardeners will help to lessen the destruction of wetland habitats due to excessive peat harvesting (see **Peat**).

COMPOST Brown and crumbly humus that is formed by rotting down garden clippings and kitchen waste which is used to improve and nourish the soil.

CONIFER A tree or shrub that bears its seeds in cones. Conifers are usually evergreen.

CORDON A restrictive pruning technique used to train fruit trees into one main stem.

CORM A rounded underground storage organ and stem that looks similar to a bulb. A bud at the top of the corm produces shoots and new roots. Crocuses and gladioli grow from corms.

CROCKS Small pieces of broken clay pot traditionally used to cover the drainage holes in planting containers and facilitate soil drainage, but now no longer required when using modern pots and potting mixes.

CROP ROTATION An organic technique for growing vegetables on different sections of a plot on a 3- or 4-year cycle. Crop rotation helps to reduce the build-up of pests and diseases in the soil and prevent the soil from being stripped of particular nutrients by one crop.

CROSS POLLINATION The process whereby pollen from another plant, often another cultivar, is transferred to the receptive stigma of a flower to form fruit and seeds. Usually carried out by pollinating insects, birds or small animals but can also be done manually, for example by using a small paintbrush.

CROWN The base of a herbaceous perennial. The roots and shoots grow from the crown.

CULTIVAR A plant variety that originates from cultivation, not from the wild. The term cultivar is actually an abbreviation of 'cultivated variety'.

DAMPING DOWN A technique used to increase the humidity and lower the temperature in a greenhouse on a hot day. To damp down, spray the floor and staging with water using a hose or watering can.

DEADHEADING Removing dead or faded flowers from plants to tidy them up. Deadheading will also promote further flowers on the plant by preventing seed formation. Plants that need to be regularly deadheaded are roses, peonies and pansies.

DECIDUOUS A plant, usually a tree, climber or shrub, that sheds its leaves during winter, or in the dry season in areas with tropical and subtropical climates.

DIBBER A pointed tool, traditionally carved from wood, used for making holes in soil when transplanting seedlings. The end of a pencil makes a good alternative to commercially available tools.

DISBUDDING A technique to remove all but one bud on a plant's stem. This concentrates a plant's energy into producing fewer, but larger, blooms and high-quality fruit.

DIVISION A form of propagation where the roots and stems of a herbaceous perennial are teased or cut apart to make more than one plant. Each division of the separated clump can be planted to form a new plant.

DORMANT A state in which a plant's growth slows down or ceases temporarily. This usually occurs in late autumn and winter, but can also occur during the dry season in some climates.

DOUBLE-DIGGING A cultivation technique that improves soil drainage, aeration and fertility, and allows plant roots to penetrate more deeply. When double-digging, make sure that the soil is dug at least two spits deep (see **Spit**).

DRILL A shallow, straight and narrow furrow in the soil, in which seeds are sown or seedlings planted.

EARTHING UP A technique for protecting plants, especially potatoes, from frost, sun or disease. Gently draw the surrounding soil up around the base of the stem using a spade. This technique is also used for blanching vegetables (see **Blanching**).

ESPALIER A pruning technique for training fruit trees or ornamental shrubs against walls or fences. To create an espalier, trim the branches and train them horizontally to form matching pairs on either side of the main plant stem.

EVERGREEN A tree or shrub that retains its foliage through the year.

FAN A pruning technique used to train a fruit tree or ornamental shrub into a fan shape against a wall or fence.

FERN A nonflowering plant that reproduces by way of tiny spores that form on the undersides of the leaves (fronds).

FORCING A technique for encouraging plants to grow, flower or fruit before their natural time. To force a plant, place it in a dark place, such as under a large clay pot, or stand the plant in a heated greenhouse. Early crops, such as lettuce or rhubarb, or indoor pot plants, are all commonly forced.

FUMIGATE To use poisonous fumes to eradicate pests and diseases either in a greenhouse or in garden soils.

FUNGICIDE A chemical that kills fungi, which are flowerless plants that possess no chlorophyll. Fungi are parasitic and many are responsible for various plant diseases. Others form part of the natural decay cycle in the garden.

GENUS (pl. GENERA) A group of closely related plants that are linked by a range of common characteristics. For example, all species of wattle are grouped under the genus *Acacia*.

GERMINATION The first stage of a plant's development, when a shoot sprouts from a seed, spore or bulb to become a new plant.

GRAFTING A propagating technique for joining a stem or bud of one plant on to the root or stem of another, forming a new plant. Grafting is often used by rose or fruit tree specialists.

GRAFT UNION The point at which the scion and rootstock are joined.

HARDENING OFF Gradually accustoming plants that have been raised in shade or sheltered conditions, such as a shadehouse or greenhouse, to positions with more sunlight and exposure. To harden off a plant move it gradually into a more exposed situation.

HARDWOOD Fully ripened wood of trees and shrubs, from which cuttings are taken.

HARDY A term to describe plants that can withstand cold winter temperatures, including frosts. Also used to describe plants that tolerate extremely hot or dry conditions.

HEEL The expanded base of old wood or a small heel of bark on a side shoot when it is pulled away from the main stem of a plant.

HERBACEOUS A term for a plant that does not form a woody stem. Herbaceous plants usually die down in winter and grow up again in spring from basal shoots. The term herbaceous is usually applied to perennials, although it also applies to annuals and biennials.

HUMUS Dark brown, sweet-smelling, crumbly vegetable matter that has decayed, such as compost or leaf mould.

HYBRID A plant that is derived from crossing two different species, varieties or cultivars, often of the same genus. The new plant has some of the genetic characteristics of each parent.

INDIGENOUS PLANT A plant that originates or grows naturally in a particular location or environment.

INORGANIC A chemical compound that does not contain carbon, which is derived from animal matter, such as excrement or dead plants. Inorganic fertilisers can be mined or chemically produced.

INSECTICIDE A substance used to eliminate garden insect pests. Insecticides are available as aerosols, granules, liquid or powder and are applied to plants or soil in accordance with written instructions that accompany each product.

INTERCROP A fast-growing vegetable crop raised between rows of slower-growing crops.

JOINT The part of a plant's stem from which leaves, buds and shoots grow. The joint is sometimes slightly swollen, as on rosebushes. A joint is also known as a node.

LATERAL A side shoot or stem of a plant, growing from a bud on a larger stem.

LAYERING A propagation technique where a plant's stem is induced to form roots by laying the stem on the soil. This technique is particularly good for making new plants from azalea, honeysuckle and rhododendron.

LEACHING The washing away of soluble plant food and important trace elements from the topsoil by water drainage.

LEAF MOULD Compost made from dead or decaying leaves.

LIME A soil conditioner sprinkled over acid soil to neutralise it, and over heavy clay soils to improve the texture. Calcium, the chief chemical element of lime, is also an essential plant food.

LOAM A soil that contains a mixture of clay, sand, humus and silt. Loamy soil is well aerated and free-draining.

MARGINAL A plant that requires a constantly damp or wet soil, such as occurs at the edge of a pond, in order to thrive.

MULCH A layer of material that is spread over the soil around plants in order to conserve moisture, enrich the soil, suppress weeds or warm the ground. Manure, garden compost and bark chippings all make beneficial organic mulches.

NATURALISE To grow bulbs or other plants in a simulated natural way in the garden.

NEUTRAL SOIL Neither acid nor alkaline, with a pH level of about 7.

NITROGEN A natural element, occurring in the soil and air, which is absorbed by plants primarily to make green foliage.

NODE See **Joint**

NPK The chemical symbols for nitrogen (N), phosphorus (P) and potassium (K), the three major nutrients in fertiliser.

ORGANIC Substances, such as manure and compost, that are derived from either animal or vegetable remains. Organic fertilisers contain carbon and are made from formerly living matter.

OXYGENATOR A submerged aquatic plant that releases oxygen into the water in a pond.

PARASITE A plant that lives on another plant, and takes all its nourishment from its host. An example of a parasite is mistletoe.

PEAT Organic matter that is formed when dead plants from bogs (sphagnum peat) or heath-land (sedge peat) are prevented from decaying past a certain point through lack of oxygen. Peat is traditionally used for growing plants and improving soils. However, gardeners are now turning to peat-free alternatives because they realise that peat is not an infinite resource.

PERENNIAL A plant that lives for at least three seasons. The term can refer to trees and shrubs, but it is mainly applied to herbaceous plants that die down in winter and emerge again the following spring, such as phlox and peonies.

pH A scale running from 1–14, used to measure the acid-alkaline balance of soil. A reading of 7 is neutral, while those below mean that the soil is acid, and those above are considered to be alkaline. Most garden soils are within the range of pH 4.5–8.

PHOSPHORUS A major nutrient essential for plant growth. Sometimes also referred to as phosphate.

PINCHING OUT A technique for removing the tip, or growing point, of a stem to encourage branching or to induce bud formation. Growth is removed using the fingers.

POLLARDING A pruning technique for cutting a tree back to its trunk and the stubs of the main branches. Willow trees are often pollarded to provide young shoots for basket-making. Eucalyptus trees are often pollarded to provide a crop of juvenile foliage that is harvested for the florist trade.

POLLINATION The introduction of pollen to the stigma in order for the seeds and fruit to form.

POTASSIUM A major nutrient essential for plant growth. Sometimes also referred to as potash.

POTTING MIX A composted blend of barks and other materials designed for the growth of plants in pots. In Australia a rating system for potting mixes exists known as the Australian Standard.

POTTING ON Transferring a plant to a larger container. Plants are usually potted on when their roots become pot-bound and need more soil space to grow.

POTTING UP Placing a plant and potting mix in a container.

PRICKING OUT Transplanting seedlings from their initial containers into larger ones. To avoid plant damage when pricking out, do not touch the seedlings by their stems, but instead hold the leaves gently.

PROPAGATION The increase of plants, either by seeds or vegetatively, by means of cuttings, such as division, grafting or layering.

PRUNING The technique for controlled cutting back of plants to restrict their size, train or shape them, promote the growth of flower or fruit buds, or remove damaged, diseased or dead wood. Pruning is usually carried out on plants with woody stems, such as roses, fruit bushes or trees (see also **Pinching out** and **Thinning**).

RESTING PERIOD A time in the annual cycle of many plants when they are dormant and do not put on any growth.

RHIZOME A thickened, underground horizontal stem with roots and leaves or shoots. A rhizome acts as a storage organ when a plant, such as a geranium or an iris, is dormant (see also **Bulb**, **Corm** and **Tuber**).

ROOTSTOCK A propagation term for a rooting plant onto which another plant is grafted. The graft takes on some of the attributes, in size and vigour, of the rootstock plant. Fruit trees are often grown on rootstock.

RUNNER A stem that roots at the tip on contact with moist soil and forms a new plant. Runners are commonly found on strawberries.

SCION A shoot or bud cut from one plant to graft onto a rootstock of another.

SEEDLING A young plant after germination, with a single, unbranched stem.

SELF-FERTILE A term applied to a plant that will set fruit and seed when fertilised with its own pollen. It usually applies to fruit trees.

SELF-STERILE A term applied to a plant that requires a pollinator of a different clone to produce fruits. See also **Cross pollination**.

SEPAL Derived from modified leaves, these surround and protect a flower in bud.

SOFTWOOD The young shoots of shrubs and perennials from which cuttings are taken from spring to early summer. Also called soft tip.

SOIL IMPROVER Organic matter, such as manure and leaf mould, and inorganic material, such as chemical fertiliser, dug into the soil to improve soil drainage, structure and fertility.

SPIT A term used to denote depth of digging; the length of a spade's blade, or about 25–30 cm.

STAKING Supporting top-heavy plants with canes or wooden supports. Some young trees also need to be staked until they are established. This prevents the tree from rocking in the wind and becoming uprooted.

STANDARD A plant trained on a straight stem from which lower growth is removed. The top of the stem is then pinched to encourage branching and clipped to form a pleasing, usually geometric, shape.

STIGMA The female part of the flower that receives pollen.

STOLON See **Runner**

STRATIFICATION The period of either warmth or cold (depending on the plant) required by some seeds to trigger germination.

SUBSOIL The layer of soil that lies below the topsoil. It is easily recognised by its marked difference in texture and colour from the layer above, although its depth may vary.

SUCKER A shoot which sprouts from below ground at the base of a plant. If the sucker has sprouted from a grafted plant, it must be torn off at the source to prevent the rootstock from taking over the scion. Plants such as roses frequently produce suckers (see also **Rootstock** and **Scion**).

SYSTEMIC INSECTICIDE A chemical compound that is sprayed onto the foliage of a plant or watered over the root area that enters the sap in order to poison sap-sucking insects.

TAPROOT The main anchoring root of a plant, particularly in trees, which grows vertically down into the soil. The term taproot also applies to long root-formed vegetables, such as carrots and parsnips.

TENDER A term to describe plants or leaves that are vulnerable to frost, cold, drought or heat damage.

TENDRIL A thin, curling stemlike growth that twines around supports to help a plant to climb.

TERMINAL A bud that grows at the tip of a stem or branch.

THINNING The removal of some seedlings in a batch to improve the growth of the remaining plants. The term also describes the removal of a number of flower or fruit buds on a plant to prevent overcrowding and to encourage better results.

TREADING Firming soil that has recently been cultivated by walking on it. This is done before preparing it for sowing or planting, such as when planting a lawn. This technique is also used when transplanting shrubs or trees to remove air pockets from the soil and to make sure that the soil can be packed around the roots.

TRENCHING A deep-digging technique where soil is cultivated to a depth of three spits, or 75–90 cm (see **Spit**).

TUBER A thickened fleshy root or an underground stem, such as a potato, that serves as a food store and produces shoots.

VARIEGATED Leaves and flowers that are marked decoratively in a contrasting colour or colours. Variegated foliage is usually green mixed with yellow, gold, cream, white or pink or a combination.

WEED A plant that is growing where you do not want it. The term commonly refers to non-ornamental species that are fast-growing and will take over an area if they are not removed. Perennial weeds are more difficult to eradicate than annual weeds.

WINDBREAK A hedge, fence or wall that shelters plants by diminishing or diverting the wind.

WITHHOLDING PERIOD The length of time that must elapse between applying a pesticide (such as an insecticide or fungicide) and harvesting fruit or foliage. The period may vary from plant to plant and is stated on the pesticide label.

Measurements

LINEAR		WEIGHT		VOLUME		TEMPERATURE	
METRIC	IMPERIAL	METRIC	IMPERIAL	METRIC	IMPERIAL	CELSIUS	FAHRENHEIT
2 mm	$^1/_{16}$ in	5 g	$^1/_8$ oz	30 ml	1 fl oz	−10°C	14°F
5 mm	$^1/_4$ in	10 g	$^1/_4$ oz	50 ml	2 fl oz	−5°C	23°F
10 mm/1 cm	$^1/_2$ in	15 g	$^1/_2$ oz	75 ml	$2^1/_2$ fl oz	0°C	32°F
15 mm/1.5 cm	$^5/_8$ in	20 g	$^3/_4$ oz	90 ml	$3^1/_4$ fl oz	5°C	41°F
20 mm/2 cm	$^3/_4$ in	50 g	$1^3/_4$ oz	100 ml	$3^1/_2$ fl oz	10°C	50°F
50 mm/5 cm	2 in	100 g	$3^1/_2$ oz	125 ml	4 fl oz	15°C	59°F
5.5 cm	$2^1/_4$ in	150 g	$5^1/_2$ oz	150 ml	5 fl oz	20°C	68°F
10 cm	4 in	200 g	7 oz	175 ml	6 fl oz	25°C	77°F
20 cm	8 in	250 g	9 oz	200 ml	7 fl oz	30°C	86°F
30 cm	12 in	500 g	1 lb 2 oz	250 ml	9 fl oz	35°C	95°F
40 cm	16 in	750 g	1 lb 10 oz	500 ml	18 fl oz		
50 cm	20 in	1 kg	2 lb 3 oz	750 ml	1 pint 7 fl oz		
75 cm	2 ft 6 in	1.25 kg	2 lb 12 oz	1 litre	$1^3/_4$ pints		
100 cm/1 m	3 ft 4 in	1.5 kg	3 lb 5 oz	1.2 litres	2 pints		
1.5 m	5 ft	1.75 kg	3 lb 13 oz	1.5 litres	$2^3/_4$ pints		
2 m	6 ft 8 in	2 kg	4 lb 6 oz	2 litres	$3^1/_2$ pints		
5 m	16 ft 8 in	2.5 kg	5 lb 8 oz	2.5 litres	$4^1/_2$ pints		
10 m	11 yd	5 kg	11 lb	5 litres	$8^3/_4$ pints		
20 m	22 yd	7.5 kg	16 lb 8 oz	7.5 litres	$13^1/_4$ pints		
50 m	54 yd 2 ft	10 kg	22 lb	10 litres	$17^1/_2$ pints		

Index

Italic page numbers refer to illustrations.

A

abelia 19, 106, 114, 125, 126, 227
Abelia 'Francis Moon' 118
Abelia × grandiflora 227
Abies balsamea 'Nana' 120
Abies koreana 145
Abies lasiocarpa 145
abutilon 20, 22, 99
Abyssinian banana 245
acacia *see* wattle
acalypha 125, *125*
acanthus 87, 91, 92, 259
Acanthus mollis 80
Acer griseum 144
Acer japonicum 34
Acer negundo 'Variegatum' 145
Acer palmatum 79, 145
    'Atropurpureum' 145, *145*
Acer rubrum 144, 146
achillea 19, 28, 87, 259, 292
Achillea ageratum 79
Achillea millefolium 'Cerise Queen' 80
acid-loving plants 44, 115, 146, 259, 277
acid soil 114, 116, 146, 161, 214, 263
    improving 264
acidifying materials 264
acidifying water, for indoor plants 259
Acmena smithii 219, *219*, 220, 227
Acmena spp. 282
aconite 87
    winter 22, 63
acorus 34, *34*
Actinidia kolomikta 132, 134
adiantum 36
adventitious roots 134
aeonium 23, 36
aeration, lawn 47, 285, 286, 288, 292, 300, 301
African black beetle 206
African daisy 73
African marigold 207
African violet 36, *36*, 37, 44, 98
agapanthus 28, 43, 74, 79, 84, 87, 91, 106, 126, 275, 292
Agathis robusta 146
agave 259
ageratum 73, 74
Ageratum houstonianum 75
Agriotes 207
Ajuga reptans 80
    'Atropurpurea' 93
    'Burgundy Glow' 79
akebia 134
Akebia quinata 132, 137
albizia 259
alchemilla 90, 107
Alchemilla mollis 58, 80, 87
algae 35, 285, 299, 301
alkaline soil 114, 115, 116, 146, 214, 263, 295
alkaline water 259, 277
allamanda 126
Allium fistulosum 191
Allium giganteum 69
Allium neapolitanum 57
allium 69, *69*, 79
almond 29, 247, 248, 252
    'Phoebe' 247
alocasia 95
Aloysia triphylla 200, *201*
alpine plants 24
Alpinia 87

alstromeria 59
alternaria leaf spot 206
alternathera 126
Althaea rosea 75
alyssum 23, 25, 45
    sweet 71, 74, 80, 96, 97
amaranthus 71, 74
amaryllis 38, 62, 65, 98
Amaryllis belladonna 65, 69, 292
Amelanchier lamarkii 116
American blueberry 214
American smoke tree 79
Ampelopsis glandulosa 'Elegans' 134
anaphalis 87
anchusa 71, 87
anemone 58, 60, 63, 106
    Japanese 91
angelica 158, 202, *202*, 283
angelonia 87
angel's trumpet 79
Angophora spp. 151
Anigozanthos Bush Gem series 87
Anigozanthos manglesii 98
animal manure 263
animal pests 197, 245, 247
anise basil 198
aniseed 198
annuals 70–7
    as bedding plants 261
    best choices 70–1, 73
    bushy 291
    collecting seeds 77
    dry-tolerant 259
    fast-growing 19
    pinching out 76, *76*
    planting out 72–4
    poisonous 73
    prolonging flowering 76
    sowing 22, 70–2, 285, 287, 289, 301
    spontaneous reseeding 76
    spring 28, 70, 287
    summer 28, 29, 70, 285, 287, 289, 295
    transplanting 289
    watering 76
    winter 295, 297
anthemis 87
Anthemis tinctoria 84, *85*
    'E. C. Buxton' 22
anthracnose 150, 168, 209, 215, 245, 250, 253
anthurium 36
antibacterials 259
antirrhinum 71, 73, 97, 99
ants 241, 251
aphelandra 36
aphid 35, 97, 199, 205, 207, 227, 235, 241, 251, 253, 255, 282, 283, 286, 290, 291, 292, 293
apple dimpling bug 253–4
apple 153, 226, 228, *228*, 248, 251, 252, 253, 254, 255, 295
    pruning 228, 229–30, 299
    root stocks 228
    storing 231
    training for small gardens 228
    'Ballerina' 229
    'Cox's Orange Pippin' 229
    'Delicious' 253
    'Gala' 229
    'Granny Smith' 229, 253, 273
    'Pink Lady' 229
apricot 226, 236, 237, 238, 241, 248, 250
    'Alfred' 237, *237*

'Caselin' 237
    'Glengarry' 237
    'Moorpark' 237
    'Trevatt' 237
April activities 296
aquarium water 259
aquatic grass 94
aquatic mint 34, *34*
aquatic plants *31*, 32–4, 284, 286, 288, 291
    dividing 35, *35*
    floating plants 32–4, *32*, 35
    oxygenators 34
    potting 34
    see also water lily
aquilegia 28, 77, 88, 91, 98, 106
Arabis 25
arbours 140
arches 140
Arctotis 73, 74
arctotis daisy 23, 71
ardisia 126
Ardisia crenata 120
Arisaema sikokianum 80
Armeria 87
armillaria root rot 96, 150
aromatic plants 28, 84, 283
Aronia × prunifolia 79
arrowhead 34, *34*
artemisia 28, 29, 84, 87, 90, 107
Artemisia 'Powis Castle' 79, *79*
artichoke thistle 167
artichoke 158, 159, 181, 197, 206, 296
    globe 29, 180–1, *297*
    Jerusalem 125, 158, 181, 300
artificial light 258
Arum italicum 68
arum lily 68, *68*, 287
asarina 75
ash 150
    blueberry 20, 282
    manna 145
    mountain 145
asparagus 158, 173, 180, 208, 285, 296
aspidistra 36
Asplenium scolopendrium 95
aster 19, 20, 22, 45, 71, 73, 76, 87, 97, 99, 106, 296
    Chinese 96, 97
astilbe 32, 87
Astrantia 87, 88
Athyrium filix-femina 95
atriplex 126
aubrieta 25, 53, 68
aucuba 20, *21*, 118, 126
August activities 301
Auranticarpa rhombifolia 20
Australian lime 233
Australian native plants 23, 44, 297, 298
    see also specifics, e.g., bottlebrush
Australian native violet 25
automatic drip-feed watering 276
automatic watering in the greenhouse 276
autumn activities 294–7
autumn bulbs 64–9, 292
    best choices 65
    dividing and multiplying 65–6
    for different settings 68–9
    pests and diseases 66
    planting 64, 65
autumn colour 22, 135, 144
autumn-flowering trees 297
autumn flowers 22
autumn roses 107
autumn shrubs 116, 118–19
avenue of trees 15

avocado 225, 244, *244*, 248, 250, 254, 255
    'Bacon' 244
    'Fuerte' 244
    'Hass' 244
azalea 20, 34, 36, 114, 115, 118, 151, 152, 153, 285, 286, 288, 293, 296
azalea lacebug 151, 286, 288
azalea petal blight 153

B

babiana 57, 58, *59*
Bacillus thuringiensis 205, 206, 252, 255
bacterial canker 97
bacterial leaf spot 205
bacterial soft rot 205
Baeckia virgata 126
bagging (fruit) 231
balloon flower 24
balm, lemon 84, 86, 152, 198, 202, 283
bamboo 94, *94*, 126
    containing *94*
    dwarf 95
    for windbreaks 95
    sacred 114
banana passionfruit 223
banana skins 152
banana spotting bug 254
banana 245, 252, 254
    Abyssinian 245
bandages 121
bandicoots *49*
banksia 118, 125, 132, 298, 300
    coastal 120, 126
Banksia 'Giant Candles' 20, *21*
Banksia ericifolia 227, 282
Banksia marginata 282
banksia rose 137
barberry 126
bare-root roses 102–3, *103*, 297, 298
bare-root shrubs 114–15, 124
bare-root trees 144, 225, 261, *261*, 295
    looking after 146, 261
    planting 147, *147*, 297
bark 20
    decorative 144
    for mulch 81, 196
    forest 196
basal rot 96
basil 28, 198, 203, 287, 289, 291
    anise 198
    bush 198
    cinnamon 198
    lemon 198
    purple 200, *201*
    'Dark Opal' 198
    'Purple Ruffles' 198
bats 245, 282
bay laurel 29, 144, 198, 203, *203*, 227, 251, 297
bean blossom thrip 209
bean fly 209
bean rust 209, *209*
bean 26, 168–70, 206, 209, 252, 287, 289, 296, 300
    borlotti 168
    broad 158, 159, 168, 169–70, 208, 209, 295
    dwarf 168, *168*
    French 158, 159
    green 158, 159, 168, 169, 170, 171, 173, 207, 208, 209, 289
    lima 168
    runner 75, 158, 159, 168, 169, 170, 207, 208, 209, 289

Acknowledgments

Abbreviations: *t* = top; *c* = centre; *b* = bottom; *l* = left; *r* = right

Front cover: *c* Lorna Rose; *tl* RD; *tc both* Lorna Rose; *tr* N. & P. Mioulane/MAP. **Spine:** Clive Nichols/ Garden Picture Library. **Back cover:** *l* N. & P. Mioulane/MAP; *cl* Glen Threlfo/Auscape; *cr* Jerry Harpur/Auscape; *r* M. & J.C. Lamontagne. **1** Lorna Rose. **2** Clive Nichols - Lord Leycester Hospital garden. **3** Lorna Rose. **4–5** Lorna Rose - Garden: Jill Morrow, Wagga Wagga, NSW. **6** *t* C. Andrew Henley/Auscape; *c (above)* A. Schreiner/Horizon; *c (below)* A. Descat/MAP; *b* Glen Threlfo/Auscape. **7** Lorna Rose - Garden: "Foxglove Spires", Tilba Tilba, NSW. **8** *t & c (above)* Lorna Rose; *c (below)* M. & J.C. Lamontagne/Horizon; *b* Jerry Harpur/Auscape. **9** Lorna Rose - Harrington Garden, Balmain, NSW. **10** M.& J.C. Lamontagne. **11** Lorna Rose; *c (above)* V. Klecka - Latour-Marliac/Rustica; *c (below)* A. Descat/MAP; *b* Ivy Hansen. **12** *l* F. Marre/MAP; *r* F. Lamarque/MAP. **14** A. Schreiner/Horizon; *br* N.& P.Mioulane - Design: Sonny Garcia/MAP. **15** *tl* Lorna Rose - Garden: Cherry Cottage, Mount Wilson, NSW; *br* C. Nichols - Design: Sonny Garcia/MAP. **16** Marcus Harpur - Wendy Wetherick, Croydon, S London. **17** *t* M.& J.C. Lamontagne; *c* N. & P. Mioulane/ MAP; *b (1-6)* A. Schreiner/Horizon. **19** *tl* A. Schreiner/Horizon; *tr (1-4)* F. Lamarque/MAP. **20** C. Nichols/MAP. **21** *tl* A. Descat/MAP; *tr, bl & br* Lorna Rose; *cl* A. Descat/ MAP; *cr* C. Nichols/ MAP. **22** C. Nichols - Eastgrove Cottage/MAP; *c & b* A. Descat/MAP. **23** *t* Ivy Hansen; *b* S. & O. Mathews. **24** *(1-6)* Anness Publishing. **25** *t & b* Lorna Rose; *bl (1)* M. & J.C. Lamontagne; *bl (2)* A. Descat/MAP. **26** M. Faver-Maltaverne/Rustica. **27** *tl* F. Didillon/ MAP; *tr* Ivy Hansen; *cl* Noun - Jardin de Luré/MAP; *cr* Y. Monel - Jardin de curé de Wy-dit -Joli-Village/ MAP; *bl* A. Descat/ MAP; *br* RD/David Kirby - Garden: Barbara Wicks, Chapel Hill, Qld. **28** *tl* Jerry Harpur; *tr* John Glover. **29** *tl & tr* M. & J.C. Lamontagne; *tc* Garden World Images; *br (1)* A. Descat/MAP; *br (2)* RD; *br (3)* Richard Surman/RD; *br (4)* F. Didillon/MAP. **30** C. Nichols - Brook Cottage, Oxon/MAP. **31** *t* N. & P. Mioulane - 'Danse avec les carpes', Festival des jardins, Chaumont, 1997/MAP; *b (1-6)* N. & P. Mioulane/MAP. **32** *tl* P. Glemas/Horizon; *bl* Lorna Rose; *br* V. Klecka - Latour-Marliac/Rustica. **33** *tl* M. & J.C. Lamontagne; *tr* Garden World Images; *cl* C. Nichols/Chelsea/MAP; *cr* N. & P. Mioulane - Roots and Shoots, Hampton Court 01/MAP; *bl* F. Didillon/MAP; *br* John Glover. **34** *t* Lorna Rose.

cr N. & P. Mioulane/MAP; *b (1)* Lorna Rose; *b (2)* J. Y. Grospas/MAP; *b (3)* N. & P. Mioulane/MAP; *b (4)* M. & J.C. Lamontagne. **35** *tr (1-4)* Anness Publishing; *bl* N. & P. Mioulane/MAP. **36** *t* Lorna Rose; *c & b* F. Strauss/MAP. **37** *tl* Lynne Brotchie/ Garden Picture Library; *tr & b (1-4)* N. & P. Mioulane/MAP; *cr* M. & J.C. Lamontagne. **38** *l (1-3)* RD; *r (above)* John Glover; *r (below)* N. & P. Mioulane/MAP. **39** *all* F. Strauss/MAP. **40** *bl* Lorna Rose - Don Garden, Revesby, NSW; *br* Lorna Rose. **41** *tl* Lorna Rose - Garden: Wannan, Paddington, NSW; *tr* Lorna Rose - Garden: Betteridge, Annandale, NSW; *b (1 & 3)* RD; *b (2 & 4)* Lorna Rose. **42** RD/David Kirby - Garden: Dennis Hundscheidt, Sunnybank, Qld. **43** *t* Lorna Rose - Garden: 'Ayrlies', Whitford, NZ; *b* Ivy Hansen. **44** *t* Ivy Hansen; *b* Lorna Rose. **45** *t* JS Sira/ Garden Picture Library; *b (1 & 2)* M. & J.C. Lamontagne; *b (3)* Lorna Rose. **46** Jerry Harpur. **47** *(1-4)* N. & P. Mioulane/MAP. **48** *t* Michael and Lois Warren/Photos Horticultural; *b (1-6)* A. Schreiner/Horizon. **49** *t* Jerry Harpur; *b* Jean-Paul Ferrero/Auscape. **50** Lorna Rose. **51** *tl* RD/David Kirby - Garden: Barbara Wicks, Chapel Hill, Qld; *tr (1-3)* RD. **52** Ivy Hansen. **53** *t* Lorna Rose - Garden: Wilkinson, Tas - Designer: Torquil-Canning; *bl* M. & J.C. Lamontagne/ Horizon; *br* Ivy Hansen. **54** Lorna Rose. **55** *t* C. Nichols/MAP; *c (above)* Ivy Hansen; *c (below)* M. & J.C. Lamontagne; *b* Y. Monel/MAP. **56** *t* Lorna Rose; *b* M. & J.C. Lamontagne. **57** *tr (1-3)* N. & P. Mioulane/MAP; *bl (1)* C. Nichols/MAP; *bl (2 & 3)* M. & J.C. Lamontagne; *bl (4)* Lorna Rose. **58** Lorna Rose. **59** *tl, cl & cr* Ivy Hansen; *tr* Lorna Rose. **60** *t both* N. & P. Mioulane/MAP; *b (1-3)* F. Marre - Jardin Le Bois Pinard - Stylist M. Marcat/Rustica. **61** *t* A. Schreiner/ Horizon; *b* RD. **62** *tr* John Glover; *bl (1-3)* N. & P. Mioulane/ MAP; *bl (4)* A. Descat/ MAP; *br (above)* C. Nichols/MAP; *br (below)* RD. **63** *tr (1-4)* N. & P. Mioulane/MAP; *bl* J. P. Praderes/ Rustica; *bc* N. & P. Mioulane/MAP. **64** *tl* Lorna Rose; *tr* Ivy Hansen; *br* M. & J.C. Lamontagne. **65** *tl* F. Didillon/MAP; *b all* Lorna Rose. **66** *(1-5)* M. & J.C. Lamontagne; *(6)* Garden World Images. **67** *tl* F. Strauss/MAP; *tr & br* Lorna Rose; *cl* A. Descat/MAP; *cr & bl* M. & J.C. Lamontagne. **68** *tl* Lorna Rose; *tr* M. & J.C. Lamontagne; *b (1-6)* N. & P. Mioulane/MAP. **69** *t* M. & J.C. Lamontagne; *b (1)* A. Descat/MAP; *b (2 & 3)* N. & P. Mioulane/MAP; *b (4)* J. P. Delagarde/SRD. **70** *t* Photos Horticultural; *b* M. & J.C. Lamontagne.

71 *tr* N. & P. Mioulane/MAP; *bl* Lorna Rose. **72** *tr (1-4)* Noun & Gaëlle/MAP; *bl* A. Descat. **73** *l (1)* A. Guerrier/MAP; *l (2 & 4)* A. Descat/MAP; *l (3)* F. Didillon/MAP; *l (5 & 6)* N. & P. Mioulane/MAP; *r* Noun & Gaëlle/MAP. **74** *tr (1-3)* F. Marre/Rustica; *tr (4)* F. Strauss/MAP; *b* Lorna Rose. **75** *t* A. Descat/ MAP; *b* W. Watson/ BIOS/Garden Picture Library. **76** *t* A. Descat/MAP; *b* F. Strauss/MAP. **77** *both* M. & J.C. Lamontagne. **78** *tr* F. Strauss/MAP; *cr* J. P. Delagarde/SRD; *bl* Jerry Harpur/Auscape. **79** *t* F. Didillon/MAP; *b (1)* M. & J.C. Lamontagne; *b (2)* Y. Monel/MAP; *b (3)* A. Schreiner/Horizon. **80** F. Didillon/MAP. **81** *t (above)* C. Nichols - RHS Garden, Wisley, Surrey/MAP; *t (below)* F. Didillon/ MAP; *b (1)* Noun & Gaëlle/MAP; *b (2)* M. & J.C. Lamontagne; *b (3)* Garden World Images; *b (4)* Lorna Rose. **82** A. Schreiner/ Horizon. **83** *t* Jerry Harpur; *cr* Noun & Gaëlle/ MAP; *br* M. & J.C. Lamontagne. **84** *both* Noun/ MAP. **85** *tl, cr & br* M. & J.C. Lamontagne; *tr & cl* A. Descat/MAP; *bl* Globe Planter/MAP. **86** *t (1-6)* Noun & Gaëlle/MAP; *b both* M. & J.C. Lamontagne. **87** *(1-4)* N. & P. Mioulane/MAP. **88** *tr* Boucourt - Jardin de Miromesnil/Rustica; *tr & cr* N. & P. Mioulane/MAP; *cl* Noun & Gaëlle/MAP; *br* N. & P. Mioulane/Paul Dyer; Hampton Court/MAP. **89** *tr (1-4)* N. & P. Mioulane/MAP; *bl* John Glover. **90** *tl* Ivy Hansen; *bl* John McCammon/Auscape; *br* M. & J.C. Lamontagne. **91** *t* C. Nichols/MAP; *br* Garden World Images. **92** *t* Jerry Harpur; *b* M. & J.C. Lamontagne. **93** *tr* A. Schreiner/Horizon; *bl (1)* Globe Planter/ MAP; *bl (2)* A. Descat/MAP; *br* M. & J.C. Lamontagne. **94** *tl* A. Schreiner/Horizon; *tr (1-4)* Noun & Gaëlle/MAP; *bc* F. Strauss/MAP. **95** *tr* Lorna Rose; *tr (1-3)* N. & P. Mioulane/MAP; *tr (4)* Heather Angel/Natural Visions; *bc* Ivy Hansen. **96** Garden World Images; *r* N. & P. Mioulane/MAP. **97** Garden World Images; *c* N. & P. Mioulane/MAP; *r* M. Duyck/MAP. **98** *t* Denis Crawford/Graphic Science; *r* A. Descat/MAP. **99** *t* A. Descat/MAP; *c* Denis Crawford/Graphic Science; *r* G. Ken/Horizon. **100** Lorna Rose. **101** *t* Photos Horticultural; *c (above)* Ivy Hansen; *c (below)* & *b* Lorna Rose. **102** *t & bl* A. Schreiner/Horizon; *br* M. Viard/Horizon. **103** *tl* John Glover; *tr (1-4)* A. Schreiner/Horizon. **104** *l & cr* M. & J.C. Lamontagne; *cl* M. & J.C. Lamontagne/Horizon; *r* N. & P. Mioulane/MAP. **105** *tl, tr & bl* A. Descat/MAP; *cl* A. Petzol - Roseraie de l'Haÿ-les-Roses/Rustica; *cr* Lorna Rose; *br* F. Didillon/MAP. **106** *t* V. Vitis/Horizon; *b* Photos Horticultural - Designer: Lady Xa Tollemache.

107 *l (1)* Photos Horticultural; *l (2)* A. Descat/MAP; *l (3 & 4)* M. & J.C. Lamontagne; *r (1-4)* Noun & Gaëlle/MAP. **108** *all* M. & J.C. Lamontagne. **109** *t* Andrew Lawson; *b* Rustica. **110** *tl* Rustica; *tr (1-3)* Noun & Gaëlle/MAP; *bc* F. Marre/Rustica. **111** *t* N. & P. Mioulane/MAP; *b (1-2)* N. & P. Mioulane/MAP; *b (3)* A. Descat/MAP. **112** *l* Michael & Lois Warren/ Photos Horticultural; *r (above)* A. Schreiner/ Horizon; *r (below)* Howard Rice/Garden Picture Library. **113** *tr* F. Lamarque/MAP; *b* C. Nichols/ MAP. **114** F. Boucourt - Le Bois Pinard/Rustica. **115** *tl* A. Descat/MAP; *tr both* Hebe/ Rustica; *b (1-6)* N. & P. Mioulane/MAP. **116** Lorna Rose. **117** *tl* N. & P. Mioulane/MAP; *tr, cr & bl* A. Descat/MAP; *cl* V. Vitis/Horizon; *br* Ivy Hansen. **118** *tl* P. Nief/MAP; *tr* A. Descat/MAP; *bl* Lorna Rose; *br* Charles Hawes/Garden World Images. **119** *tl* N. & P. Mioulane/MAP; *tc* C. Nichols/MAP; *tr* A. Descat/MAP; *b* Y. Monel/MAP. **120** *t* M. & J.C. Lamontagne; *bl* Garden World Images. **121** *tl* A. Descat - Création Timothy Vaughan/MAP; *br* N. & P. Mioulane/MAP. **122** *tr (1-4)* N. & P. Mioulane/MAP; *bl* F. Lamarque/ MAP; *bc* A. Descat/ MAP. **123** *tl* Noun/MAP; *b (1-3)* N. & P. Mioulane/ MAP. **124** Jerry Harpur/ Auscape. **125** *tl (1-4)* N. & P. Mioulane/MAP; *br (below)* Lorna Rose. **126** *tl* N. & P. Mioulane/MAP; *bl* Ph. Asseray/ Rustica. **128** N. & P. Mioulane/MAP. **129** *tl (1-4)* N. & P. Mioulane/MAP; *br* V. Klecka - Latour-Marliac/MAP; *br* Ivy Hansen; *tr (1-4)* Noun & Gaëlle/MAP. **130** A. Descat - Jardin de Bagatelle/MAP; *br* Lorna Rose. **131** *tl* Ivy Hansen; *tr (1-4)* Noun & Gaëlle/MAP. **132** *(1)* A. Descat/MAP; *(2)* Garden World Images; *(3)* RD; *(4)* V. Klecka/ Rustica. **133** *tl* John Glover; *tr, cr & br* Lorna Rose; *cl* RD; *bl* Garden World Images. **134** *t* A. Descat - Jardin privé à St Helier (Jersey)/ MAP; *bl* A. Descat/ MAP; *br (1)* J. Creuse/Rustica; *br (2)* C. Hochet/ Rustica; *br (3)* A. Descat/MAP; *br (4)* N. & P. Mioulane/MAP. **135** *t* M. & J.C. Lamontagne; *br (above)* Y. Monel/ MAP; *br (below)* N. & P. Mioulane/MAP; *tr* Rob Walls/ Auscape; *cr* N. & P. Mioulane/MAP; *br* Ivy Hansen. **137** Ivy Hansen. **138** *t* Y. Monel/MAP; *tr, cr & br* N. & P. Mioulane/MAP; *br* Clive Nichols/Garden Picture Library. **139** *t* Andrew Lawson; Haseley Court, Oxford; *r* Clive Nichols/Garden Picture Library. **140** N. & P. Mioulane/MAP. **141** *t (1-6)* A. Schreiner/ Horizon; *b* C. Nichols - Sleightholme Dale Lodge, North Yorkshire/MAP. **142** Clive Nichols/Launa Slatter. **143** *tr* N. & P. Mioulane/ Horizon. **144** *lb* A. Guerrier/Horizon; *rt & rb* A. Schreiner/ Horizon; *rc* A. Descat/MAP.

145 (1) Lorna Rose - Garden: Lindfield Park, Mount Irvine, NSW; (2) Ivy Hansen; (3 & 4) Lorna Rose; (5) V. Vitis/Horizon; (6) M. & J.C. Lamontagne; (7 & 8) Y. Monel/MAP. 146 t V. Vitis/Horizon; b Ph. Asseray/Rustica. 147 (1-8) A. Schreiner/Horizon; rt M. & J.C. Lamontagne; rc A. Schreiner/Horizon; rb Ph. Asseray/Rustica. 148 t (1-2) N. & P. Mioulane/MAP; b (1-2) Noun & Gaëlle/MAP. 149 tl Lorna Rose - Garden: "Be Beah", Mount Wilson, NSW; tr Lorna Rose; br Chrysalis. 150 l Denis Crawford/Graphic Science; r N. & P. Mioulane/MAP. 151 tl & tr Denis Crawford/Graphic Science; tc Garden World Images; b N. & P. Mioulane/MAP. 152 t A. Breuil/MAP; cl Denis Crawford/Graphic Science; bl P. Aversenq/MAP. 153 t & b Denis Crawford/ Graphic Science; cl Noun/MAP. 154 Lorna Rose. 155 t M. & J.C. Lamontagne; c (above) M. & J.C. Lamontagne/Horizon; c (below) Noun/MAP; b F. Strauss/MAP. 156 Lorna Rose. 157 t C. Nichols - Ivy Cottage Dorset/MAP; c Lorna Rose - Romantic Cottage Gardens, Dromana, Vic. b M. & J.C. Lamontagne. 158 F. Marre - Le Bois Pinard - Styliste Marie Marcat/Rustica. 159 t Rustica - Le Potager de Grand Papa, Miromesnil; b Lorna Rose; Garden: J. Pickett, Vic. 160 t M. & J.C. Lamontagne; bl A. Descat/MAP; cl & br F. Didillon/MAP; cr M. & J.C. Lamontagne. 164 t M. & J.C. Lamontagne; bl Noun/MAP; br Ph. Asseray - Jardin du Feyel/Rustica. 165 (1-3) N. & P. Mioulane/MAP; (4) M. & J.C. Lamontagne. 166 t M. & J.C. Lamontagne; br O. Frimat/ BIOS. 167 t A. Descat/MAP; bl A. Schreiner/Horizon; bc C. Nichols/MAP; br M. & J.C. Lamontagne. 168 t C. Andrew Henley/ Auscape; b M. & J.C. Lamontagne. 169 tr (1-4) Noun & Gaëlle/MAP; bl M. & J.C. Lamontagne. 170 tl Eric Crichton Photos; tr M. & J.C. Lamontagne; b (1-3) Noun & Gaëlle/ MAP. 171 tl M. & J.C. Lamontagne; tr & b Noun & Gaëlle/MAP. 172 t M. & J.C. Lamontagne; b Jane Legate/Garden Picture Library. 173 tl b (1) A. Descat/MAP; bl (2) F. Didillon/MAP; bl (3) M. & J.C. Lamontagne; br (above) John McCammon/ Auscape; br (below) M. & J.C. Lamontagne. 174 both M. & J.C. Lamontagne. 175 t C. Andrew Henley/Auscape; b Ivy Hansen. 176 tl & bl M. & J.C. Lamontagne; br Ch. Hochet/Rustica. 177 tl Lorna Rose; tr RD; cl M. & J.C. Lamontagne/ Horizon; cr C. Andrew Henley/Auscape; bl G.R. 'Dick' Roberts/Natural Sciences Image Library; br Philippe Bonduel/Garden Picture Library. 178 tl John Glover/Garden Picture Library; tr A. Petzold - Les Jardins du Feyel/Rustica.

cr John McCammon/ Auscape; br Lorna Rose. 179 t C. Andrew Henley/Auscape; bl (1 & 2) RD; bl (3) M. & J.C. Lamontagne; br M. & J.C. Lamontagne. 180 all M. & J.C. Lamontagne. 181 t Thobois/ Rustica; b Colin Monteath/Auscape. 182 t F. Didillon/MAP; b Noun/MAP. 183 t Howard Rice/Garden Picture Library; cr Noun & Gaëlle/MAP; bl Howard Rice/Garden Picture Library. bc Noun/MAP; br M. & J.C. Lamontagne. 184 tr (1-3) Noun & Gaëlle/MAP; bl M. & J.C. Lamontagne; br Noun/MAP;. 185 tr Ph. Asseray/Rustica; c A. Descat/MAP; b (1-3) Garden World Images. 186 t (1 & 4) M. & J.C. Lamontagne; t (2 & 3) Noun/ MAP; b Garden World Images. 187 t Jerry Pavia/ Garden Picture Library; b both M. & J.C. Lamontagne. 188 t & c F. Didillon/MAP; b A. Descat/MAP. 189 l (1) M. & J.C. Lamontagne; l (2) N. & P. Mioulane/MAP; r both Noun/MAP. 190 tl V. Vitis/Horizon; tr A. Schreiner/Horizon; br N. & P. Mioulane/MAP. 191 t (1-4) N. & P. Mioulane/MAP; b all M. & J.C. Lamontagne. 192 lb Clay Perry/Garden Picture Library; rt Noun & Gaëlle/MAP; rb (1 & 3) N. & P. Mioulane/MAP; rb (2) Noun/MAP. 193 tr Michael & Lois Warren/ Photos Horticultural; bl Noun/MAP. 194 tl Eric Crichton Photos; tr (1-3) Noun/ MAP; br M. & J.C. Lamontagne. 195 tr G.R. 'Dick' Roberts/ Natural Sciences Image Library; b both RD. 196 M. & J.C. Lamontagne. 197 t & cr Lorna Rose; b (1-6) J.P. Delagarde/SRD. 198 tr RD; bl Noun/MAP. 199 tl Steven Wooster/ Garden Picture Library; tr V. Klecka - Les Jardins du Feyel/Rustica; cr M. Viard/Horizon; b M. & J.C. Lamontagne. 200 both M. & J.C. Lamontagne. 201 tl F. Strauss/ MAP; tr, cl & cr M. & J.C. Lamontagne; bl A. Descat/ MAP; br Noun/MAP. 202 tr (1-4) M. & J.C. Lamontagne; bc Noun/MAP. 203 F. Strauss/MAP. 204 tl C. Nichols/MAP; br (1-3) N. & P. Mioulane/MAP. 205 t & b Garden World Images; cl Denis Crawford/Graphic Science; cr S. Bonneau/ MAP. 206 t Garden World Images; b Denis Crawford/Graphic Science; bl D. Bernardin/MAP. 208 l Denis Crawford/Graphic Science; r G. Blondeau. 209 N. & P. Mioulane/ MAP. 210 Lorna Rose. 211 t Photos Horticultural; c (above) Jerry Harpur; c (below) Ivy Hansen; b Lorna Rose. 212 tl & br M. & J.C. Lamontagne; tr Noun & Gaëlle/MAP. 213 tr (1-4) Noun & Gaëlle/MAP; bc C. Andrew Henley/Auscape. 214 M. & J.C. Lamontagne. 215 tr M. & J.C. Lamontagne; cr J. Creuse/Rustica; bl (1) Garden World Images; b (2) J. Vurkulevicius/ courtesy of The Digger's Club; br (1-3) F. Didillon/ MAP. 216 bl Mayer & Le Scanff/Garden Picture Library; br Noun/MAP. 217 tl & br Garden World Images;

tr Photos Horticultural; cl, cr & bl A. Descat/ MAP. 218 tr (1-4) N. & P. Mioulane/MAP; bc M. & J.C. Lamontagne. 219 Lorna Rose. 220 t Ivy Hansen; br M. & J.C. Lamontagne. 221 M. & J.C. Lamontagne. 222 tl N. & P. Mioulane/ MAP; tr (1-4) N. & P. Mioulane/MAP; bl (1) Neil Holmes; bl (2) G.R. 'Dick' Roberts/Natural Sciences Image Library. 223 t Photos Horticultural; b (1) Ivy Hansen; b (2) Lorna Rose. 224 Steve Wooster/ Garden Picture Library. 225 all J.P. Delagarde/ SRD. 226 t M. Viard/Horizon; b both M. & J.C. Lamontagne. 227 (1-6) F. Didillon/ MAP. 228 t M. & J.C. Lamontagne; br M. & J.C. Lamontagne. 229 tl M. & J.C. Lamontagne; tc A. Descat/MAP; tr Rustica; br N. & P. Mioulane/MAP. 230 tl Andrew Lawson; tr Ph. Fauchere/MAP; br (1) F. Didillon/MAP; br (2) V. Maisons/Rustica; br (3) Garden World Images. 231 t Y. Monel/MAP; bl N. & P. Mioulane/MAP; br Rustica. 232 both Lorna Rose. 233 all Lorna Rose. 234 both Lorna Rose. 235 t Lorna Rose; cl & br Ivy Hansen. 236 t John Phipps; br Photos Horticultural. 237 tl Noun & Gaëlle/MAP; br Photos Horticultural. 238 Lorna Rose. 239 tl Jacqui Hurst/Garden Picture Library; tr & br Lorna Rose; cl Garden World Images; cr Jerry Harpur; bl Michael & Lois Warren/Photos Horticultural. 240 t A. Descat/MAP; tr Noun & Gaëlle/MAP; bl N. & P. Mioulane/MAP. 241 t M. & J.C. Lamontagne; b RD. 242 C. Andrew Henley/Auscape. 243 tl Lorna Rose; tr C. Andrew Henley/Auscape; cr M. Viard/Horizon; br C. Andrew Henley/Auscape. 244 t G.R. 'Dick' Roberts/Natural Sciences Image Library; bl Lorna Rose. 245 t & b Lorna Rose; bl Ivy Hansen. 246 t M. Viard/ Horizon; bl Mayer & Le Scanff/ Garden Picture Library. 247 tl Lorna Rose; tr (1-4) Noun & Gaëlle/MAP; bl Lorna Rose; br Ivy Hansen. 248 t N. & P. Mioulane/MAP; b M. & J.C. Lamontagne. 249 tl (1-6) A. Schreiner/ Horizon; br M. & J.C. Lamontagne. 250 Denis Crawford/ Graphic Science. 251 l M. & J.C. Lamontagne; c & r Denis Crawford/Graphic Science. 252 tl, tr & b Denis Crawford/Graphic Science. 254 l M. & J.C. Lamontagne; c P. Aversenq/ MAP; r Garden World Images. 255 Denis Crawford/Graphic Science. 256 L. Terestchenko/Inside. 257 t M. & J.C. Lamontagne; c (above) F. Strauss/MAP; c (below) Noun & Gaëlle/MAP; b Lorna Rose. 258 RD. 259 t (1-2) F. Strauss/MAP; b (1) Ph. Fauchere/MAP; b (2) N. & P. Mioulane/MAP; b (3) A. Descat/MAP. 260 t P. Glemas/Horizon; br M. & J.C. Lamontagne. 261 tl & br M. & J.C. Lamontagne; tr Ph. Asseray/Rustica. 262 t Lorna Rose - Garden: 'Karkalla', Sorrento, Vic;

cr Noun/MAP; bl both Noun & Gaëlle/MAP. 263 t Lorna Rose; b Boncourt/Rustica. 264 t F. Strauss/MAP; c M. & J.C. Lamontagne; b Noun & Gaëlle/MAP. 265 t (1-4) Noun & Gaëlle/MAP; b both N. & P. Mioulane/MAP. 266 M. & J.C. Lamontagne. 267 tl (1-8) Noun & Gaëlle/MAP; tr Noun/MAP; br N. & P. Mioulane/MAP. 268 l Noun/MAP; r Paul Hart/Garden Picture Library. 269 (1-4) Noun/MAP. 270 both M. & J.C. Lamontagne. 271 both M. & J.C. Lamontagne. 272 t & c both M. & J.C. Lamontagne; b (1-6) Noun & Gaëlle/MAP. 273 t & br RD; cr M. & J.C. Lamontagne. 274 F. Didillon/MAP. 275 tl Rob Walls/Auscape; tc Rustica; tr (1-4) Noun & Gaëlle /MAP. 276 t P. Glemas/Horizon; tr Garden World Images. 277 t F. Marre - Le Bois Pinard - Styliste Marie Marcat/Rustica; b both Lorna Rose. 278 Y. Monel/MAP. 279 t F. Strauss/MAP; b M. & J.C. Lamontagne. 280 tr (1-3) A. Schreiner/Horizon; bl M. & J.C. Lamontagne; br Noun/MAP. 281 tl Lorna Rose - Garden: "Bringalbit", Kyneton, Vic; br Paul Hart/Garden Picture Library. 282 both Lorna Rose. 283 both Lorna Rose. 284 Photos Horticultural. 285 l Ivy Hansen; cl Lorna Rose; cr M. & J.C. Lamontagne; r F. Strauss/MAP. 286 l Noun/MAP; cl Lorna Rose; r Anness Publishing. 287 l Noun & Gaëlle/MAP; cl C. Nichols/MAP; cr & r M. & J.C. Lamontagne. 288 l A. Schreiner/ Horizon; cl N. & P. Mioulane/MAP; cr A. Schreiner/Horizon; r Lorna Rose - Garden: "Bringalbit", Kyneton, Vic. 289 l M. & J.C. Lamontagne; cl RD; cr Boucourt - Jardin de Miromesnil/Rustica; r F. Strauss/MAP. 290 Michael & Lois Warren/Photos Horticultural. 291 l N. & P. Mioulane/MAP; cl N. & P. Mioulane/MAP; cr V. Klecka - Les Jardins du Feyel/Rustica; r A. Descat/MAP. 292 l F. Marre/ Rustica; cl V. Klecka - Latour-Marliac/ Rustica; cr Rustica; r Lorna Rose. 293 l Ph. Asseray/Rustica; cl A. Schreiner/Horizon; cr M. & J.C. Lamontagne; r F. Strauss/MAP. 294 Andrew Lawson. 295 l Garden World Images; cl Michael & Lois Warren/Photos Horticultural; cr M. & J.C. Lamontagne; r Lorna Rose. 296 l V. Vitis/Horizon; cl A. Schreiner/ Horizon; cr Noun & Gaëlle/MAP; r M. & J.C. Lamontagne. 297 l M. & J.C. Lamontagne; cl P. Glemas/ Horizon; cr F. Strauss/ MAP; r John Glover. 298 Ivy Hansen. 299 l N. & P. Mioulane/ MAP; cl A. Schreiner/Horizon; cr Thobois/Rustica; r A. Descat/MAP. 300 l Ph. Asseray/Rustica; cl Noun/ MAP; cr A. Schreiner/Horizon; r John Glover. 301 l A. Descat/MAP. cl M. & J.C. Lamontagne; cr Ivy Hansen; r N. & P. Mioulane/MAP.

SECRETS AND TIPS FROM YESTERDAY'S GARDENERS

Consultant for Australia and New Zealand
Jennifer Stackhouse

Writers
Vincent Gradwell, Katharine Gurney, Kay Maguire, Paul Patton, Barbara Segall, Jennifer Stackhouse, Jean Vernon, Tamsin Westhorpe

Project Editor Ariana Klepac
Art Director Sue Rawkins
Senior Designer Avril Makula
Design Manager Donna Heldon
Senior Editor Samantha Kent
Assistant Designer Claire Potter
Picture Researcher Annette Crueger
Proofreader Tim Learner
Indexer Max McMaster
Production Manager General Books Janelle Garside

READER'S DIGEST GENERAL BOOKS

Editorial Director Elaine Russell
Managing Editor Rosemary McDonald

Concept code FR/1577/IC
Product code 041 3128

Secrets and Tips from Yesterday's Gardeners is published by Reader's Digest (Australia) Pty Limited
80 Bay Street, Ultimo, NSW 2007
www.readersdigest.com.au, www.readersdigest.co.nz

First Australian and New Zealand edition 2005
Copyright © Reader's Digest (Australia) Pty Limited 2005
Copyright © Reader's Digest Association Far East Limited 2005
Philippines Copyright © Reader's Digest Association Far East Limited 2005

National Library of Australia Cataloguing-in-Publication data:
Secrets and tips from yesterday's gardeners: a practical guide.

Includes index.
ISBN 1 921077 27 1.

1. Gardening. 2. Gardens - History. I. Reader's Digest (Australia).

635

Prepress by Sinnott Bros, Sydney
Printed and bound in China by Everbest Printing Co Ltd.

We are interested in receiving your comments on the contents of this book.
Write to: The Editor, General Books Editorial, Reader's Digest (Australia) Pty Limited, GPO Box 4353, Sydney, NSW 2001
or email us at bookeditors.au@readersdigest.com

To order additional copies of *Secrets and Tips from Yesterday's Gardeners* call 1300 303 210 (Australia) or 0800 540 032 (New Zealand) or email us at customerservice@au.readersdigest.com

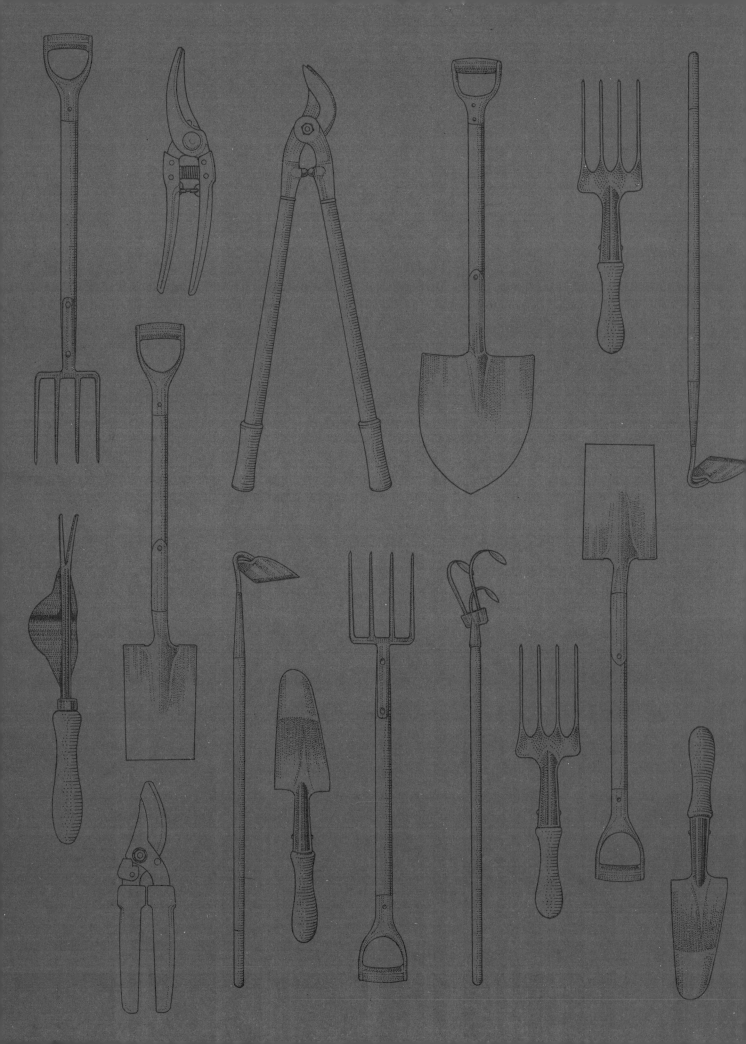